Landscape of Wisdom

A Guided Tour of Western Philosophy

CHRISTOPHER BIFFLE

Crafton Hills College

MAYFIELD PUBLISHING COMPANY

Mountain View, California

London • Toronto

Library of Congress Cataloging-in-Publication Data

Biffle, Christopher.
    Landscape of wisdom : a guided tour of western philosophy /
  Christopher Biffle.
      p. cm.
    Includes Index.
    ISBN-13: 978-1-55934-724-2
    ISBN-10: 1-55934-724-4
    1. Philosophy—Introductions.   I. Title.
  BD21.B44 1998
  190—dc21   98-39193
                                                CIP

Mayfield Publishing Company
1280 Villa Street
Mountain View, California 94041

Manufactured in the United States of America
13 12 11 10

Sponsoring editor, Ken King; *production editor,* Melissa Kreischer; *manuscript editor,* Joan Pendleton; *art director,* Jeanne M. Schreiber; *text and cover designer,* Joan Greenfield; *art editor,* Amy Folden; *illustrators,* Judith Ogus and Carto-Graphics, Alice and Will Thiede; *cover art,* © Diane Fenster; *manufacturing manager,* Randy Hurst. The text was set in 10/13 New Aster by G & S Typesetters, Inc., and printed on acid-free 45# Chromatone Matte, PMS color 3288, by Banta Book Group.

Credits

Art by M. C. Escher, pp. 18, 26, 52, 202, 268, 603, 649, 716, © 1998 Cordon Art-Baarn, Holland. All rights reserved. p. 210, From Plato, *The Last Days of Socrates,* translated by Hugh Trednick. Copyright © 1959 Hugh Trednick; pp. 230–234, 236–237, 241, From *The Republic of Plato,* translated by F. M. Cornford, 1941, Oxford University Press. Copyright © 1941 Oxford University Press. Reprinted by permission of Oxford University Press; pp. 248, 271, 275, 287, From *Aristotle* by Jonathan Barnes, Oxford University Press, 1982. Copyright © 1982 Oxford University Press. Reprinted by permission of Oxford University Press; pp. 318, 324, 325, 327, 330, From *Epicurus: The Extant Remains,* translated by Cyril Bailey, Oxford University Press, 1926. Copyright © 1926 by Oxford University Press. Reprinted by permission of Oxford University Press; pp. 342–357, Reprinted by permission of the publishers and the Loeb Classical Library from *Epictetus,* Vol. II translated by W. A. Oldfather, Cambridge, Mass: Harvard University Press, 1928.; pp. 365–368, 370, From *St. Anselm's Proslogion,* translated by M. J. Charlesworth, Oxford University Press, 1965. Copyright © 1965 Oxford University Press. Reprinted by permission of Oxford University Press; pp. 390–393, 397–401, 403, From St. Thomas Aquinas, *Summa Theologica,* "Treatise on God" Part I, Questions 1 & 2 translated by the Fathers of the English Dominican Province, 1947. Reprinted by permission of Benziger Books; pp. 426–427, 429–431, 434–439, 441, 445–449, 453–460, From Descartes, *Meditations,* translated by Ronald Rubin, Arete Press, 1986. Reprinted by permission of Arete Press and Ronald Rubin. pp. 714–717, 719–721, 723–732, From "Thus Spoke Zarathustra" by Friedrich Nietzsche, from *The Portable Nietzsche* by Walter Kaufmann, editor, translated by Walter Kaufmann. Translation copyright © 1954 by The Viking Press, renewed © 1982 by Viking Penguin Inc. Used by permission of Viking Penguin, a division of Penguin Putnam, Inc.

Preface

About 15 years ago, I cobbled together a photocopied version of the *Crito* with lots of notes describing what to underline. As a result, my students brought manuscripts to class that were satisfactorily messy. Then I began to have the fantasy that I could sit beside students as they read and ask them helpful questions. Exactly how to bring that off in a book was a difficult problem, though the solution looks simple enough now. In the six books that preceded this one, I've been delighted to explore the possibilities of a fill-in-the-blanks journey. It wasn't until *Landscape of Wisdom,* however, that I discovered how many ways there are to make a text interactive.

As far as I can tell, no other textbook addresses the three great problems of getting students involved in philosophy:

1. **Students have a difficult time reading philosophy.** Only *Landscape of Wisdom* gives students continuous help in analyzing primary sources. Annotation tasks in the margins, interactive dialogues, and countless exercises teach the art of deep reading.

2. **Students have a difficult time writing about philosophy.** On virtually every page of *Landscape of Wisdom,* students perform simple and sometimes complex writing tasks. It is impossible for anyone to complete the journey ahead and not, at minimum, strengthen their ability to paraphrase philosophical prose and analyze, criticize, and defend arguments.

3. **Students often don't find philosophy engaging.** There is a good deal of fun in *Landscape of Wisdom.* Chapters contain bizarre thought experiments, contests, riddles, and puzzles; the book is written in an informal, humorous style. I wanted the text to sound as if it were produced by a person, quirky as any, not a gray voice in the sky.

This book also directly involves students by drawing out and requiring them to defend their own metaphysical, epistemological, and ethical beliefs. At the beginning of chapters, students sketch out their philosophical self-portrait by deciding their position on key issues. The chapter explores the philosopher's views on these same topics. Thus, every thinker becomes relevant because each is continuously confronted as either a supporter or opponent of the student's own beliefs. Other textbooks treat students as spectators who watch philosophers battle over positions; *Landscape of Wisdom* thrusts students directly into the philosophical fray.

Here are some of the new features of *Landscape of Wisdom* that were not included or that were underutilized in earlier *Guided Tours:*

- *Numerous diagrams clarifying complex philosophical arguments.* I'm sure almost all philosophy teachers use blackboard diagrams. My experience can't be unique; when I can clearly illustrate a philosophical position, the majority of my students grasp it. At the beginning of most chapters I present a simple illustration and then add details as the chapter progresses. The diagrams function as a philosophical storyboard, providing a running visual aid to understanding an ever more detailed philosophical position.

- *Hundreds of critical-thinking exercises.* The exercises in *Landscape of Wisdom* were inspired by Moore and Parker's *Critical Thinking.* Now, instead of merely saying "read pages 23 to 44," you can supplement homework with tasks that focus on key aspects of the reading. Note especially two exercises that occur at the end of every chapter from Thales to Nietzsche: "Looking Back" and "Looking at the World Through the Eyes of . . ." The former provides a simple, but powerful, way for the student to summarize every section of a chapter; the latter is an extremely useful test that forces students to address issues from the perspective of the philosopher under examination. I am proud of this little exercise. I have always wanted students—and I imagine you have too—to let go of their own position and look directly out at the cosmos through the eyes of great thinkers. Classroom testing indicates that "Looking at the World Through the Eyes of . . ." is a good way to approach this goal.

- *Frequent opportunities for students to sketch their own philosophical position.* Though I alluded to this above, it is such an important new feature of *Landscape of Wisdom* that I want to mention it again. Students become involved in this text because, chapter by chapter, they are working out their own philosophies, borrowing arguments from allies, attacking arguments of opponents. Numerous exercises help students understand and elaborate their own place, the tradition they belong to, in the history of philosophy. Students don't passively observe the philosophical contest; they're down on the battlefield defending their own ramparts.

- *Lively chapter openings encouraging students to read further.* Every chapter begins with a thought experiment, puzzle, paradox, or some other attention-getting device. These chapter openings are designed to give students a concrete, dramatic reason for learning more about the philosopher under consideration.

- *Chapter heads stated as questions.* This simple device makes it easy for a teacher to evaluate students' progress. Pose the questions to your class. If their answers are foggy or uncertain, you know exactly where to focus your attention. Or use the questions for a large review. Go back to Chapter *X* to see if anyone remembers the answers to questions you're positive you covered masterfully.

- *Simple answers to blunt questions.* You know the situation. After you carefully explain Zeno's argument about motion, some bold soul asks, "Who would be so stupid as to believe that?" You'll find students' blunt questions throughout the text, usually near the end of a chapter, followed by my best answers.

- *Patient explication of complex philosophical arguments.* I move forward very slowly, often explaining the same point in several different ways. This pattern of explanation and reexplanation is a central feature of this text, because it seems to me to be a central feature of good teaching. As a sample of this approach, see the chapter on Anselm's ontological argument.

- *An appendix devoted to paraphrasing and argument analysis.* "Wisdom Skills" gives students an ample introduction to techniques that are fundamental to understanding philosophical prose.

- *A topical introduction to a historical survey of philosophy.* Other texts for introductory philosophy classes, which take a historical approach, jump right into the chronological sequence without first giving students some idea what philosophy is about. The second chapter, "The Planet Un-philosophos," surveys and clarifies key topics and fields in philosophy.

- *A jargon-free approach to philosophy.* I've deliberately kept philosophical vocabulary to a minimum. I'd prefer to use a few terms—such as metaphysics, epistemology, and ethics—frequently and be sure students learn them than use many terms infrequently.

If I summed up the virtues of *Landscape of Wisdom* in a phrase, I'd say that it teaches some of the fundamental arts of reflection. I believe no other text gets students so continuously involved in *doing* philosophy. From detecting and paraphrasing arguments, to assembling evidence to defend or attack a position, to looking out at the world through the eyes of great thinkers, *Landscape of Wisdom* gives students practice handling the tools that have for centuries torn down and erected philosophical monuments.

Following the usual practice, I am writing the introduction last. And so I am giddy. These words are the end of a quarter of a million . . . I sing out! *Thanks to everyone* from Bob Dylan and James Agee to Ben Thomerson, Bob Turley, and dear Janey Beitscher down the hall, to Jack Jackson, Sidney Allen, Roger Schmidt, Walt Douglas and Frank Bruno who used to be down the hall, to my wonderful students, especially John Ready and Zeke Stear, to my old school chums Bill Dickinson, Bill Greenwood, and my lifelong compañero Gary Love. Yeats once proclaimed that his glory would be that he had magnificent friends; Yeats's friends couldn't buckle my pals' shoes. If I have written anything helpful, it is due to Harry Berger, Jr., at the University of California, Santa Cruz, who, when I was an undergraduate, asked me great questions in the right order.

Intense thanks to my reviewers: David B. Annis, Ball State University; Ron Bombardi, Middle Tennessee State University; Lawrence J. Burke, De Anza Community College; Ronald Cox, San Antonio College; Dr. Anne M. Edwards, Austin Peay State University; Joram Graf Haber, Bergen Community College; Dasiea Cavers-Huff, Riverside Community College; Michael P. Koch, S.U.N.Y. College at Oneonta; Donald M. Nolan, Parkland College; Diane Percival, Wilbur Wright College; Dennis Ean Roby, Ohlone College; Robert Sessions, Kirkwood Community College; and Ron Wilburn, University of Nevada-Las Vegas. Very special thanks to my marvelous editors at Mayfield. Jim Bull started this project off, asking for something that looked like *Wired* magazine! How far I've drifted from that bizarre, lofty goal, you will see in the pages that follow. Ken King was the horse I changed to in midstream. He never bucked once, though I, doubtless, goaded him plenty. Copious thanks to all the superb hands at Mayfield, especially Amy Folden, Marty Granahan, Jeanne Schreiber, Susan Shook, Josh Tepfer, and dear Melissa Kreischer, all of whom suffered as I suffered, and then some. Finally, thanks to Judith Boss, who wrote the first draft of the philosophers' biographies, and sharp-eyed Joan Pendleton, who superbly edited the final draft of my manuscript.

My two daughters, Persephone and Saskia, loved me always as I rarely deserved to be loved. And to my wife Deidre. *Tu eres mi corazón, mi vida, mi alma.*

This book is dedicated to my four graces,
Deidre, Persephone, Saskia, Alea
and, once more, to
Harry

Contents

Preface   iii

CHAPTER 1   *Setting Forth*   1

CHAPTER 2   *Life on the Planet Unphilosophos*   7

CHAPTER 3   *Thales and the Beginning of Philosophy*   42

CHAPTER 4   *Heraclitus:* Breaking the Code of Reality   56

CHAPTER 5   *Parmenides:* What Is That Mysterious X Stuff?   73

CHAPTER 6   *Zeno and the Magical Illusion of Motion*   90

CHAPTER 7   *Socrates in the* Euthyphro: Grappling with Holiness   101

CHAPTER 8   *Socrates in the* Apology: The Philosopher on Trial   135

CHAPTER 9   *Socrates in the* Crito: The Philosopher in Prison   163

CHAPTER 10   *Plato's Metaphysics:* Divine Forms   180

CHAPTER 11   *Plato's Epistemology:* Remembering What You Didn't Know You Knew   206

CHAPTER 12   *Plato's Ethics:* The Riddle of the Loved Tyrant and the Hated Philosopher   224

CHAPTER 13   *Aristotle's Metaphysics and Epistemology:* The Mind of the Father of Science   246

CHAPTER 14   *Aristotle's Ethics:* Discovering Life's Purpose   281

CHAPTER 15   *Epicurus:* Life's Purpose Is Wise Pleasure   314

CHAPTER 16   *Epictetus:* Life's Purpose Is Virtuous Indifference   338

CHAPTER 17   *St. Anselm:* How to Refute Atheists   362

CHAPTER 18   *St. Thomas Aquinas:* Five Ways to Prove God's Existence   382

CHAPTER 19   *Descartes:* How to Destroy Skepticism   415

CHAPTER 20   *John Locke:* Prisoners in the Mind's Vault   468

CHAPTER 21   *George Berkeley:* Inside God's Mind   512

CHAPTER 22   *David Hume:* How to Destroy Certainty About the World, Self, and Mind   565

CHAPTER 23   *David Hume:* How to Destroy Certainty About Science, God, and Absolute Moral Values   591

CHAPTER 24   *Immanuel Kant:* A New Model of the Mind   634

CHAPTER 25   *Immanuel Kant Versus John Stuart Mill:* How to
Make Moral Choices   658

CHAPTER 26   *Friedrich Nietzsche:* The Prophet of God's Death   694

A MODERN READER   R-1

Jean-Paul Sartre: "Existentialism Is a Humanism"   R-2

Albert Camus: The Myth of Sisyphus   R-7

Simone de Beauvoir: The Second Sex   R-9

Bertrand Russell: "Do We Survive Death?"   R-11

Bryan Magee and John Searle: "A Dialogue on
Wittgenstein's Work"   R-14

A. J. Ayer: Language, Truth, and Logic   R-17

William James: What Is Pragmatism?   R-21

Mary Daly: "The Leap Beyond Patriarchal Religion"   R-23

APPENDIX   *Wisdom Skills*   A-1

INDEX   I-1

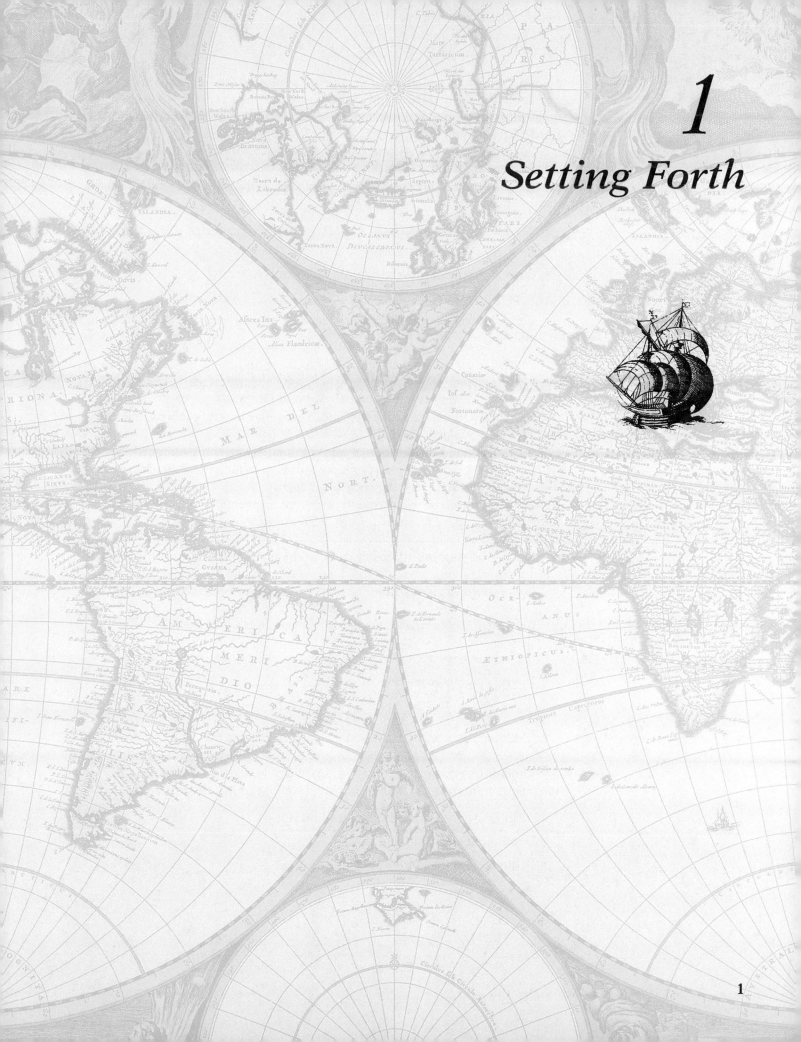

1
Setting Forth

On the journey ahead you will encounter sages and fools, geniuses and nincompoops. You'll pour over some of the greatest ideas ever created by the human brain and some of the wackiest. It will be up to you to sort golden truth from glittering falsehood.

On this tour, dawdling is encouraged. In the realms of philosophy, the slowest travelers are often the wisest. You will have plenty of opportunities to stop, ponder intellectual landmarks, and note your reflections. As you fill in the blanks ahead, you will create a journey unlike anyone else's.

- What is the nature of reality?
- How does your mind work?
- What is true happiness?
- What is the purpose of human life?
- What can you learn by looking out at the world through the eyes of famous philosophers?

You will discover your own answers to these and many other questions in the months ahead. When you are finished, you will have created a philosophical self-portrait. As you make a record of your mental travels, perhaps you will discover, as many others have, that the landscape of wisdom is best viewed through the telescope of a pen.

As your guide, I will introduce you to thinkers who claim enlightenment. I will not, however, do your philosophizing for you. In fact, I will do my very best to convince you that every philosopher is correct. It will be up to you and your classmates, the members of your tour group, to decide which positions have hidden flaws and which have hidden wisdom. Resourceful travelers compare notes.

Let this be your motto: Every error in the history of philosophy points toward truth.

If you could learn anything from the great philosophers, what would it be?

You respond thoughtfully, "More than anything else I would like to know _____

_____.

This is important to me because _____

_____

_____."

Though dawdling is encouraged, inactivity is not. On your travels during the next few months, you will frequently be engaged in one of three tasks:

- Acquiring core knowledge about philosophy
- Developing clear thinking skills
- Refining your own philosophy

How Will You Acquire Core
Knowledge About Philosophy?

At every turn on the tour, you will be involved in performing thought experiments, solving puzzles, and answering simple (and sometimes complex) quizzes to help you deepen your understanding of the fields, vocabulary, and problems of philosophical studies. Little by little, these exercises will build your core philosophical knowledge. When you have finished the tour, you will have a general understanding of many of the key themes in the history of philosophy, a working knowledge of fifteen to twenty important philosophical terms, and, most significantly, a fairly clear idea of the central beliefs of more than twenty major philosophers. To put this another way, though this tour will not make you a seasoned wisdom traveler, it will raise you high above the ranks of philosophical day trippers.

How Will You Develop
Clear Thinking Skills?

What is clear thinking? Many things. On this tour, clear thinking is defined as the paraphrasing, evaluation, and construction of philosophical arguments. If you can learn to put a philosophical argument into your own words, judge its strengths and weaknesses, and construct your own argument in response, then—so far as this tour is concerned—you will have significantly developed your clear thinking abilities.

Annotation tasks in the margins of selections from philosophical works will point you toward key ideas and help you read more deeply. Every blank that you fill in on your journey will give you practice in putting philosophical ideas into your own language. Numerous exercises ahead, including those that build your core knowledge of philosophy and refine your philosophical beliefs, will help you think and write more clearly about arguments. The appendix, "Wisdom Skills," provides help in detecting and analyzing philosophical arguments. Why this stress on arguments? As you will soon see, evidence and conclusion are the mortar and brick that thinkers use to construct their philosophical edifices.

Developing your clear thinking skills on this tour won't turn you overnight into a philosopher, but it will help you, even outside the realms of philosophical debate, to convince your family, friends, teachers, and employers that you have good reasons for your beliefs.

How Will You Refine
Your Own Philosophy?

On this tour, "your philosophy" is defined as not only what you believe is true, but also what you believe is false. Like any other philosopher, you will design your system out of what you borrow and also out of what you reject from the ideas of other thinkers. Reacting to philosophical positions that you think are wrong will force you to find evidence for what you think is right.

You will be creating your own philosophical arguments all through this text. For example, at the start of every chapter, you will complete a questionnaire, a philosophical self-portrait. Here is a sample from Chapter 5:

T or F: The universe had neither beginning nor end.

Evidence: _____

_____

_____.

To complete your philosophical self-portrait, first decide if the statement is true or false. Then add evidence that supports your view. The statement is the conclusion, the "therefore," of your argument. The evidence is the "because" of your argument. If your philosophical position is to have any value, you must be extremely careful with your evidence. *Evidence is everything. The strength of your evidence is the strength of your argument.* So take your time. At the beginning of each chapter and all through the chapter, there are numerous "becauses" to fill in. Think carefully. Stare at the ceiling. Find strong evidence. You are creating a philosophical portrait of who you are at this time in your life. Twenty years from now, there may be no more accurate image of your college days than the record you create of your journey through the lands of wisdom. This is a textbook, but you can turn it into an heirloom.

A Final Question

Before beginning your tour, what preconceptions do you have about philosophy?

You reply thoughtfully, "It seems to me that a philosopher is a person who

_____

_____.

In my opinion, what would make someone a great philosopher would be

_____

_____.

Philosophers try to answer questions like _____

_____

_____."

You'll soon learn more. (I'd enjoy hearing about your experiences on the tour, what confused and what enlightened you. My e-mail address is CBiffle@ AOL.com.)

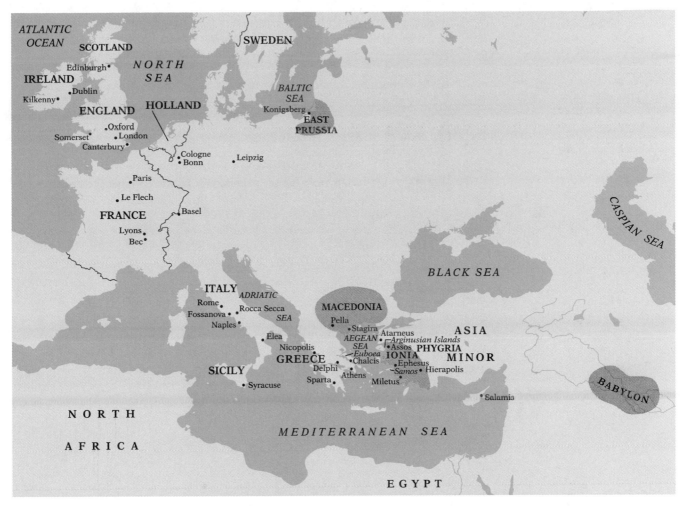

Important locations in the lives of the philosophers. (See the boxes with each philosopher's biography for more details.)

SUMMARY

Your tour guide will introduce you to more than twenty philosophers and try to convince you that each one is correct. It is up to you to sort wisdom from foolishness. You make this your own Guided Tour of Philosophy by filling in the blanks.

Completing the exercises will expand your core knowledge of philosophy; learning how to analyze arguments will sharpen your clear thinking skills; filling out the questionnaires and other tasks will clarify your philosophical self-portrait.

Note: By the end of this tour you will have completed hundreds of arguments that will chart the development of your philosophy—and will show how your views stack up with the beliefs of some of the Western world's greatest thinkers. By the final chapter, you will know much more about the core of your beliefs—

which philosophical tradition you belong to and which traditions you oppose. In other words, on this grand tour of 2,600 years of philosophy, you are the destination.

NEXT STOP

As an introduction to philosophy, you visit a world with no philosophers, the planet Unphilosophos.

Life on the Planet Unphilosophos

YOUR PHILOSOPHICAL SELF-PORTRAIT

As you will learn from the analysis at the end of this chapter, quite a bit about your general philosophical position can be determined by your answer to the following question. Think carefully and then add evidence that supports your answer.

1. Circle the statement that best expresses your view of all of reality.

   a. Reality is divided between the realm of God and the **physical universe.**

   b. The physical universe is the only reality, and everything else is an illusion.

   c. God is the only reality, and everything else is an illusion.

   d. It is not possible to know the nature of reality.

   e. None of the above. My answer is: _____

   _____.

   Evidence supporting my answer: _____

   _____

   _____.

Philosophy's importance can be seen in the large number of intellectual enterprises in the modern world that owe their birth to philosophers. Philosophy itself can be defined as the love of wisdom. Wisdom is the knowledge produced by answering universal questions. **Metaphysics** is a branch of philosophy that explores questions about reality; **epistemology** is the branch of philosophy that explores questions about the knowledge process; **ethics** is the branch of philosophy that explores questions about moral values. Philosophers engage in philosophy not merely by "thinking philosophically" but also by rigorously analyzing the works of other philosophers.

In order to understand the importance of philosophy, let's imagine a place where philosophy never existed.

THOUGHT EXPERIMENT

Imagine you visit a planet exactly like ours, except that, in the entire history of the planet, there has never been a philosopher or any philosophical thinking. Call the planet "Unphilosophos."

There would be no biology, botany, geology, meteorology, physics, or virtually any other science on Unphilosophos because the first scientists were philosophers and science developed as an offshoot of philosophy.

In the same way, there would be no psychology, political science, sociology, or anthropology. These disciplines were founded upon the works of philosophers.

The Unphilosophians, lacking the mathematical achievements of philosophers like René Descartes and Gottfried Leibniz, would have no calculus or higher mathematics.

People might tell each other stories on Unphilosophos but there would be no critical analysis of these stories. Literary criticism was first practiced by Aristotle, a philosopher.

There would be no universities on Unphilosophos because the first university was founded by a philosopher, Plato.

The goal of every generation of people on Unphilosophos would be to duplicate, as closely as possible, the beliefs of previous generations. Lacking habits of philosophical criticism and independence, the Old Way would be not only the Best Way but also the Only Way. Philosophy began, and continues to develop, by ceaselessly arguing that there are far better ways than the Old Way.

For better or worse, the two dominant forms of modern government, democracy and communism, would not exist on Unphilosophos because both of these are based, in important aspects, upon the ideas of philosophers.

Because philosophy was born when people began substituting reasoned arguments for mythological explanations, all disputes on Unphilosophos from legal to theological to moral would be settled by an appeal to ancient stories, not by an appeal to the principles of logic.

If philosophy begins, as Aristotle said, in wonder, then there would be no philosophical wonder on Unphilosophos. While Unphilosophians might wonder about their next meal or how to make more money or what to do tomorrow, there would be no wonder about:

- the size and origin of the universe
- the difference between illusion and reality
- the capacity and nature of the mind
- the essence of happiness
- the best form of government
- the characteristics of Justice
- the nature of virtue and vice
- the life of the soul
- the existence or nonexistence of God

There would be no wonder about these kinds of topics on Unphilosophos because the old stories would hold all the answers.

Now, despite what I've said, I don't want you to get the idea that philosophical thinking is simply "good thinking" and unphilosophical thinking, the kind done on Unphilosophos, is "bad thinking." Humans existed for millions of years without giving any evidence of philosophical thought. One could exist as a primitive hunter-gatherer or as a citizen of the great early civilizations of Sumeria, Babylonia, or Egypt and perform every activity of normal life without philosophical thinking. The first evidence of philosophical thought in Western culture, as you will see, did not occur until about the sixth century B.C., relatively late in the evolution of human culture.

Not only did philosophical thinking take a long time to appear in human culture, but it is also relatively rare in modern daily life. You and I spend almost all of our time thinking like the Unphilosophians. We think about breakfast, lunch, dinner; problems with the car; ways to entertain ourselves; people we should spend time with; figuring out how to program the VCR; and so forth. Unphilosophical thinking is "normal" thinking. Thus, the mind-set of Unphilosophos has been very satisfactory for much of human history and does very well to guide us through our daily lives.

However, when philosophy entered human culture, it produced enormous intellectual changes. As you have just learned, a very large number of courses in the university curriculum owe some debt to philosophy. In addition, in the 1 percent of our mental lives when we raise our eyes from the ordinary concerns of daily life to the extraordinary concerns of philosophy, we gain a vast new perspective on our existence. Instead of wondering if a chocolate shake will make us happy, we wonder about the nature of happiness. Instead of wondering if we should rent a video, we wonder about the purpose of life. Though we live much of our lives in the flatland, philosophy gives us a rare and extraordinary view from the peaks.

physical universe everything that can be known with the senses, all that is living and nonliving.

metaphysics The branch of philosophy that traditionally deals with two kinds of issues: the nature of reality as a whole and the nature of important parts of reality. A central task of metaphysics is to distinguish the "really real" from the illusory. Thus, a metaphysician might ask whether God is real or an illusion or whether the soul is real or an illusion.

epistemology (from the Greek *episteme*, for "knowledge"): The study of the knowledge process. Epistemologists try to determine, among other issues, the relationship between the mind and the senses. Is the mind simply filled by the senses (empiricism), or does it possess knowledge that goes beyond the senses (rationalism), or does it radically alter information provided by the senses (Kantian epistemology), or are the mind and senses incapable of reliable knowledge (skepticism)?

ethics (from the Greek *ethos*, for "character"): The study of, among other subjects, moral values. Typical ethical concerns include the investigation of the purpose of human life, the nature of happiness, the characteristics of virtue, and the rights and duties of the citizen of a state.

What Is Philosophy?

Philosophy comes from two Greek words, *philein* (love) and *sophos* (wisdom) and thus means, literally, the love of wisdom. **Wisdom** could be briefly defined as the knowledge produced by answering the largest questions. It is difficult to give you a vivid sense of the size of philosophy's questions. Put it this way: The difference between the questions of daily life and the questions of philosophy is something like the difference between a moment and eternity.

Here are two questions, one from daily life and one from philosophy:

Daily life: What should I do this weekend?

Philosophy: What is the purpose of human life?

The answer to the question from daily life would give you information that is relevant only to you and a small portion of your existence. The answer to the philosophical question would give you information about *all* people, at *all* times and *all* places. This is why philosophy's questions are called **universal questions.** They are, on a given topic, the absolutely largest questions that can be asked. Answers to universal questions would genuinely qualify as wisdom. If you knew what to do this weekend, you would merely know a little more than you do now. If you knew the purpose of human life, you would possess wisdom.

EXERCISE 2.1

Identifying Philosophical Questions

Philosophy asks universal questions, questions that are the largest that can be posed. Decide which of the following are philosophical (P) and which are non-philosophical (N).

_____ 1. Should I support a Democrat or a Republican?

_____ 2. What is Justice?

_____ 3. Can human minds know the nature of Justice?

_____ 4. Should we always tell the truth?

_____ 5. Should I tell John the truth?

_____ 6. Should Charles Manson be executed?

_____ 7. Is capital punishment just?

_____ 8. Are you sure that you are correct?

_____ 9. How can anyone be sure of anything?

_____ 10. What is the answer to this math problem?

_____ 11. Is God real?

_____ 12. Am I dreaming or awake?

_____ 13. How can dreaming be told from waking?

_____ 14. Can dreaming be told from waking?

_____ 15. Did Juanita get married of her own free choice?

_____ 16. Is "free choice" real or an illusion?

_____ 17. If I think positively, will I be able to jog farther?

_____ 18. Does the mind control the body or vice versa?

_____ 19. If the body controls the mind, can the mind know that?

Now look at the distinctions you have just made between philosophical and nonphilosophical questions. Can you see that you could be certain that your answer to the nonphilosophical question was correct only if you knew the answer to the related philosophical question? For example, you could be certain that your answer to the nonphilosophical question, "Should I tell John the truth?" was correct only if you knew the answer to the related philosophical question, "Should we always tell the truth?"

Your own example?

I could be certain that my answer to the nonphilosophical question,

"_____

_____?"

was correct only if I knew the answer to the related philosophical question,

"_____

_____?"

When we pass from topics that we deal with in daily life to philosophical topics, we are thinking *on the mind's largest scale.* The philosophical questions in Exercise 2.1 are the largest, on a given topic, that humans can grapple with. Philosophy is the kind of thinking that takes place at the mind's highest altitude.

Now, you might want to say, why would anyone ever want to deal with such big questions? What's the good of laboring all the way up to philosophy's peaks? The answer is quite simple. The higher you go, the more you can see. If you want to understand daily life *really well,* then you can do no better than climb out of the flatland.

Just look at the two questions I posed earlier:

Daily life: What should I do this weekend?

Philosophy: What is the purpose of human life?

If you knew the purpose of human life, you would not only know what to do this weekend, but also what to do every day for the rest of your life. The view from the peak is the best way to see which of life's roads lead to grassy meadows and which lead into swamps.

Of course, you may doubt that philosophers can answer universal questions. But this, in itself, is a philosophical position, a position on one of philosophy's peaks. You would hold that, for all times and places, no wisdom is possible. This is quite a big view. If you believe this, the tour will introduce you to philosophers who, among philosophy's pinnacles, have built a palace of doubts.

Thus, whether you believe universal questions can or can't be answered, you have a place on this tour. We're going to climb out of the lowlands together and contemplate the big view. And, of course, our climbing will be easier if we follow the wisest of those who have gone before.

We are going to investigate, in chronological order, more than twenty of the most influential philosophers in Western culture. All but the most modern will be men. Please don't take this as an indictment of your guide. Women began to make major contributions to philosophy only in the last 150 years as they began to escape the bondage of male-dominated culture.

wisdom The highest and most perfect knowledge. A wise gardener has the highest and most perfect knowledge about gardening; a wise teacher has the highest and most perfect knowledge about teaching. Insofar as our tour is concerned, a wise philosopher has the highest and most perfect knowledge about, at least, three topics: the nature of reality, the nature of the knowledge process, the nature of moral values.

universal questions The largest questions that can be asked on a topic. The questions, "What makes students happy?" or "What makes Americans happy?" are not universal questions because they are not the largest questions that can be asked about happiness. Universal questions apply to all possible cases. "What is the nature of happiness?" is a universal question because it asks what is happiness for everyone at all times and, thus, includes all possible cases.

The word "metaphysics" has an interesting origin. After Aristotle died (322 B.C.), an editor set out to give titles to Aristotle's works. The editor came upon a book of difficult material and, because he could not determine what to name it, simply called the word *ta meta ta physika* (the book after the physics book). Thus, the origin of the word "metaphysics" tells us only that it involves material that baffled an ancient editor.

Though philosophers ask numerous universal questions, we will confine our attention on the tour to only three areas: *metaphysics* deals with questions about the nature of reality; *epistemology* deals with questions about the nature of the knowledge process; *ethics* deals with questions about moral values. Other branches of philosophy, like logic, the study of the rules of reasoning; esthetics, the study of the nature of art; and political philosophy, the study of political systems, will be alluded to, but not dealt with in depth, on the tour.

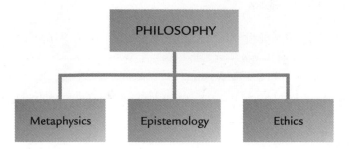

In this chapter, you'll learn more about metaphysics, epistemology, and ethics; in addition, I'll describe a few key features of the life of the philosopher.

Here are the questions ahead:

- What is metaphysics?
- What are two branches of metaphysics?
- What is epistemology?
- What are three branches of epistemology?
- What is ethics?
- What are two branches of ethics?
- What do philosophers do?
- How do philosophers acquire wisdom?

By the end of the chapter, you'll have a broad, though shallow, understanding of several key aspects of philosophy. At the conclusion of key sections of the tour, you'll encounter checkpoints like the following.

CHECKPOINT: Philosophy

Philosophy is the love of wisdom. Philosophy is distinguished from daily life because it seeks universal rather than specific knowledge. Philosophers pose the largest questions that can be asked about, among other topics, the nature of reality (metaphysics), the nature of the knowledge process (epistemology), and the nature of moral values (ethics).

What Is Metaphysics?

Metaphysics is the branch of philosophy that studies the nature of reality. Thus, in metaphysics we ask questions about what is real. For better or worse, Unphilosophians would never ponder any of the following:

- Does God exist?

- Is the soul real?

- Does the physical world exist, or is it just an illusion?

- Is the universe finite or infinite?

- Did the universe have a beginning? Will the universe have an end?

- Is there an afterworld?

- Is reincarnation fact or fiction?

- Is the mind nothing but the brain, or could the mind, for example, after death, exist independently of the brain?

- Does human life have a purpose?

- Are there many realities or only one?

- Does each person exist in his or her own reality?

- What, all in all, *is* reality?

By the word "reality," philosophers mean every single thing that genuinely exists, that has "being." In daily life we regard, among other objects, mountains, trees, houses, people, cars, and animals as having reality, as having "being." Reality is the sum totality of everything that has actual existence.

Metaphysics, like philosophy in general, involves a kind of thinking radically different from the mental activities of daily life. In daily life, we might wonder if someone's love is real, or if the amount of money we owe on a credit card bill is real, or if someone's statement is the real truth. In metaphysics, we wonder about reality *itself*.

But how do we wonder about reality itself? We have to leave behind the microscopic concerns of daily life and ponder the big picture. In metaphysics we try to draw a portrait of All.

In order to explore reality, philosophers have asked variations on two kinds of questions (all the questions above are versions of the following):

What is Everything?

What are the most important parts of Everything?

In answer to the question, "What is Everything?" philosophers have generally tried to describe all of reality in terms of only one or two key elements. For example, some philosophers have held that if you investigated Everything, the entire spectrum of reality, you would conclude that All is matter.

Reality

From this point of view, there is nothing to reality except the physical universe. For example, heaven, hell, soul, and God would be illusions.

Other philosophers have answered the question, "What is Everything?" by replying that Everything is divided into two very different regions. The lower region is the human realm, the higher region is God's realm. From this point of view, All is matter *and* spirit.

Reality

Of course, philosophers have described all of reality in other ways (but not as many as you might think). Practice making a few metaphysical statements. What are several other descriptions of all of reality that, you believe, philosophers may have proposed?

Perhaps philosophers have said All is _____

or All is _____ _____ or All is _____.

In my own view, All is _____.

In the next section, you'll learn the two most popular descriptions of all of reality.

In answer to the second large metaphysical question, "What are the most important parts of Everything?" philosophers have not looked at reality as a whole, but at some of its most significant features. Thus, philosophers have investigated, among other topics, the concepts of God, the soul, time, the mind, and reincarnation. Though each of these subjects hardly takes up the entire canvas, they are important features of the big picture.

EXERCISE 2.2

Identifying Metaphysical Statements

To begin to develop a feel for metaphysics, label statements from daily life D and metaphysical statements M. Metaphysical statements describe Everything or important aspects of Everything.

_____ 1. Last night I prayed to God.

_____ 2. God exists.

_____ 3. The cat is gray.

_____ 4. The color of anything is not part of its reality.

_____ 5. All is change.

_____ 6. Max is going through changes.

_____ 7. You are suffering from the illusion that I love you.

_____ 8. Love is illusory.

_____ 9. Spirit is the central characteristic of all that truly exists.

_____ 10. You act as if I don't exist.

_____ 11. Everything that can happen will happen over and over again forever.

_____ 12. I feel as if this has happened to me before.

_____ 13. The human will is manipulated by forces it cannot control.

_____ 14. The human mind is the type of thing that cannot know itself.

_____ 15. All is All.

_____ 16. All is not All.

_____ 17. There is way more to All than the All we think is All.

Now, we'll explore two opposing metaphysical portraits, two opposing views of all of reality. (We'll postpone other metaphysical considerations until later in the tour.)

What Are Two Branches of Metaphysics?

Philosophers have described all of reality in a variety of ways, but the two most popular have been monism and dualism. **Monism** is the view that all of reality is one kind of thing. **Dualism** is the view that all of reality is two kinds of things.

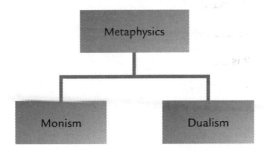

Though the definitions of monism and dualism sound bland, they are actually astonishing.

Think about everything in a set of encyclopedias from Aachen, Germany, all the way through to Vladimir Zworykin. Monism and dualism present the view that the pages of the encyclopedia don't contain a gazillion things, but _only one or, at the very most, two kinds of things._ Take every single cotton pickin' thing in the universe (and beyond!) that has reality. If you can throw it all into one pile, you're a monist. If you need two piles, you're a dualist.

When I said earlier that All is matter, I was taking a monistic position. When I said that All is divided between matter and spirit, I was taking a dualistic position.

Let's explore each view further.

Monism

If you are a monist, then you must hold that everything in reality shares one fundamental unifying characteristic. You could be a monist if you held any of the following (put a check mark beside views that intrigue you):

_____ All is matter.

_____ All is God.

_____ All is Spirit.

_____ All is atoms.

_____ All is change.

_____ All is unchanging.

monism (from _mono,_ "one"): The view that all of reality is unified by a single principle or substance. Philosophers who believe that everything that exists is fundamentally matter or God or change or any other single principle or substance are monists. Thales, Heraclitus, Parmenides, and Zeno, the first philosophers we will explore on our tour, were all monists because they believed that all of reality was basically one kind of thing (though they disagreed, as you will see, about the identity of this one thing).

dualism (from _duo,_ "two"): The view that all of reality is divided between two fundamentally different kinds of things. Philosophers who believe that all of reality is divided between God and the physical universe or between the unchanging and the changing, or between any other two mutually exclusive things are dualists.

Thus, you could be a monist if you held "All is X," where X was any one thing. But you could not be a monist if you held that "All is X *and* one or more other things."

Thales, the first philosopher on our tour, and Karl Marx, a nineteenth-century founder of communism, were both monists. Thales held that the essential element of reality was water. Trees, mountains, clouds, and humans all had water as their basic element. Marx believed there was nothing to reality except matter. He argued that God, heaven, hell, and the human soul were illusions generated by the upper class to make the lower class forget the pain of life in an unjust society. Religion, according to Marx, is the pain-numbing drug of the masses. Thus, both Thales and Marx, though they disagreed about the identity of the single unifying feature of reality, were monists because they held that All is One.

Monism

All is One

Reality

Monists play an important part on this tour. For future reference, sketch your initial reaction to monism.

I believe monism is the (correct, incorrect) view of reality because _____

_____

_____

_____.

Dualism

If you are a dualist you believe there is a chasm dividing reality into two opposite categories. Every single thing that exists falls on one side or the other of a very definite dividing line. You could be a dualist if you held any of the following (put a check mark beside views that intrigue you):

_____ All is divided between the realm of God and the physical universe.

_____ All is divided between the realm of Perfect, Eternal Truths and the changing realm of the senses.

_____ All is divided between things that are free (God and the human mind) and things that are not free (everything else).

_____ All is divided between the realm of Time and the realm of Eternity.

Thus, you could be a dualist if you held "All is X or Y" (where X and Y were two mutually exclusive categories of existence). But you could *not* be a dualist if you held "All is X or Y or Z." Interestingly enough, no major Western philosopher has been a tri-alist. There might be an opening for you!

Plato, a dualist whom we will expore on the first third of our tour, held that all of reality was divided between the realm of Perfect, Eternal Truths (which he called Forms—much more about these later) and the physical universe. According to Plato, the world we see around us is a mere shadow of the higher realm of Perfect, Eternal Truths. Today's apple is tomorrow's garbage, but the essence of Apple is unchanging, sweetly eternal. St. Augustine, a medieval dualist whom we will frequently mention on our tour, held that all of reality was divided between the realm of God and the human realm. We live in the dark human city, a metropolis of sin, confusion, and error. We aspire to the Eternal City where the divine sun never sets on God's goodness. Thus, both Plato and Augustine, though they disagreed about the identity of the two categories of reality, were dualists because they held All is Two.

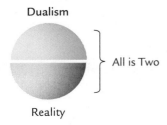

You will encounter many dualists on the tour. What is your initial reaction to dualism?

I believe dualism is the (correct, incorrect) view of reality because _____

_____.

EXERCISE 2.3
Identifying Monistic and Dualistic Statements

Some of the following statements are metaphysical; that is, they describe reality. For each statement that is metaphysical, label it either M for monistic or D for dualistic. If it is not metaphysical, label it N for nonmetaphysical.

_____ 1. All that exists is the physical universe.

_____ 2. "Workers of the world unite, you have nothing to lose but your chains."—Karl Marx

_____ 3. Reality is divided into two parts: the divine and the human.

_____ 4. God is All.

_____ 5. I know God is All.

_____ 6. There is nothing that is unchanging.

_____ 7. "Among the philosophic cranks of my acquaintance in the past was a lady all the tenets of whose system I have forgotten except one. Had she been born in the Ionian Archipelago some three thousand years ago, that one doctrine would probably have made her name sure of a place in every university curriculum and examination paper. The world, she said, is composed of only two elements, The Thick, namely, and The Thin. No one can deny the truth of this analysis, as far as it goes . . . and it is nowhere truer than in that part of the world called philosophy."—William James

_____ 8. Existence is twofold.

_____ 9. That which changes is **Becoming.** That which does not change is **Being.**

_____ 10. The **incorporeal** is greater than the **corporeal.**

_____ 11. I may not know much about art, but I know what I like.

_____ 12. Go with the flow.

_____ 13. All is flow.

_____ 14. "Whoever despises himself still respects himself as one who despises."—Friedrich Nietzsche

CHECKPOINT: Metaphysics

Metaphysics is the branch of philosophy that explores the nature of reality. The two most general metaphysical questions are "What is Everything?" and "What are the most important parts of Everything?" Monism is the subbranch of metaphysics which holds that Everything is one kind of thing. Dualism is the subbranch of metaphysics which holds that Everything is two kinds of things.

Now, let's pass from philosophical descriptions of *what* reality is to philosophical descriptions of *how* we know reality.

M. C. Escher, *Three Worlds*, lithograph, 1955.

ILLUSTRATION QUIZ

Thinking Metaphysically

Assume you have a friend who believes she knows something about philosophy. She shows you this etching and says, "This represents three different realities: the reality of the world below the water, the reality of the world above the water, and reality of the world reflected in the water's surface."

Based on your understanding of philosophy thus far, which of the following responses to her position would be correct? You may choose more than one.

1. "You are right. There are three different realities pictured here."

2. "You are wrong. There is only one reality pictured here, the reality of the material world."

3. "You are wrong. There are two different realities pictured here, the reality of the world below the water and the reality of the world above the water. The reflections on the water's surface are not a separate reality because they are produced by the world above the water."

4. "You are wrong. There are four realities pictured here—the three you mentioned and the additional one of the artist who created the etching."

5. "You are wrong. There are five realities pictured here—the three you mentioned, the additional one of the artist who created the etching, and the final one of the viewer of the etching."

6. "You are wrong. There are three *worlds* pictured here, but not three *realities*. All three worlds are part of the same reality."

What Is Epistemology?

Epistemology is the branch of philosophy that studies the knowledge process. Thus, in epistemology we ask questions about how and to what degree the mind can acquire truth. For better or worse, Unphilosophians would never ponder any of the following:

- What, if anything, can be known for certain?
- How much can the mind know?
- Are we born with truths in our minds?
- Can the senses be trusted to give us reliable information?
- Can the mind know truths independently of the senses?
- How does the mind process information?
- Can we know if God does or does not exist?
- Can the mind know ultimate reality?

Students often have difficulty distinguishing between metaphysics, the study of the nature of reality, and epistemology, the study of how the mind acquires knowledge about reality. Compare these questions:

1. Metaphysics: Does God exist?
2. Epistemology: Can the mind acquire knowledge about God's existence (or nonexistence)?

The metaphysical question is a question about what reality *is;* the epistemological question is a question about the process involved in *knowing* reality. Thus, in metaphysics we ask, "Is X real?" In epistemology, we ask, "Can the mind acquire knowledge about the reality or unreality of X?" In metaphysics we explore the nature of existence; in epistemology we explore how we acquire knowledge about the nature of existence.

Now, here is an interesting and very important philosophical question to help you understand the difference between metaphysics and epistemology. Which of the two questions above, 1 or 2, should a philosopher answer first?

The first question should be (1, 2) because _____

_____.

In general, ancient philosophers held that one could answer metaphysical questions before answering epistemological questions; many modern philosophers hold that one can never answer metaphysical questions unless one first has an answer to important epistemological questions.

Being and Becoming
Terms first developed by Greek philosophers for two different aspects of reality. Being, for the Greeks, was the unchangeable part of reality and Becoming was the changeable part of reality.

corporeal and incorporeal
A corporeal thing is a physical thing, like the human body; an incorporeal thing is a nonphysical thing, like the soul.

Epistemology, like metaphysics, involves thinking in a way that is very different from the thinking of daily life. In daily life we might ask if we know the answer to a science problem or if we know a particular person or if we know the location of the keys. In epistemology, because we are seeking information about the knowledge process itself, we ask how we know anything.

Now, what does it mean to ask how we know anything? Let me demonstrate two kinds of epistemological thinking.

I look out my window at my neighbor Jerry mowing his lawn. I ask, how do I know what I know about Jerry? I know he owns a rattletrap Chevy truck, loves hockey, and has two teenagers who go to the University of California at San Diego. As I wonder how I know all this, it seems obvious that all my knowledge about Jerry came to me through one of my five senses. In fact, going a step further, it seems that *everything* I know could be traced back to my senses. And, going a step still further, I could argue that everything anyone knows, from Aachen, Germany, all the way to Vladimir Zworykin must come through the senses. Thus, I end up with the epistemological view that all knowledge is sense-based.

Of course, I could come to a different epistemological conclusion. For example, let's say I think as follows. I look at Jerry and am convinced he is a being with a mind. Now, this knowledge *didn't* come to me through my senses. I can't see Jerry's mind. In addition, if it is true that Jerry has a mind, then certainly all humans have minds. But this is *more* knowledge that didn't come to me through my senses. I certainly have only encountered a small fraction of the human race; and yet I seem to have truths about all humans that go far beyond my senses. Thus, according to this epistemological view, the mind can know truths that go beyond the senses.

I have just sketched two epistemological positions, answers to the question, "How does the mind acquire knowledge?" According to the first view, the mind is limited to information that comes through the senses; according to the second view, the mind can gain information that goes far beyond the senses. I'll say more about both these positions (and a third one) in the next section. For now, develop a feel for epistemology in general by completing the following exercise.

EXERCISE 2.4

Distinguishing Between Metaphysics and Epistemology

Though you will eventually learn some interesting ways that metaphysics and epistemology shade into each other, for now, make a simple distinction between the two. Label the following statements M for metaphysics, E for epistemology, or N for neither.

_____ 1. Heaven has no reality.

_____ 2. The reality of Heaven can be known by the mind during prayer.

_____ 3. Humans should never lie.

_____ 4. It is impossible to understand the absolute Truth about anything.

_____ 5. The absolute Truth has no existence.

_____ 6. All the laws of science come to us through one of our five senses.

_____ 7. We cannot know the difference between dreaming and waking.

_____ 8. Abortion is immoral.

_____ 9. "Ask not what your country can do for you, but what you can do for your country."—John F. Kennedy

_____ 10. God is nothing but the psychological projection of our neurotic need for a father figure.

_____ 11. Time has no beginning or end.

_____ 12. Nothing can be known for certain.

_____ 13. "Motion being eternal, the first mover, if there is but one, will be eternal also."—Aristotle

_____ 14. "God is not the parent of evils. . . . Evils exist by the voluntary sin of the soul to which God gave free choice."—St. Augustine

_____ 15. There is nothing in the mind that was not first in the senses.

What Are Three Branches of Epistemology?

One of the largest epistemological questions is, as I said in the previous section, "How does the mind acquire knowledge?" Here are three answers with a rich philosophical heritage.

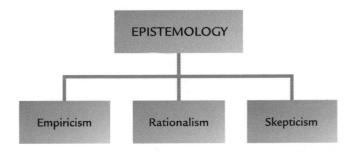

Empiricism

The epistemological view that all knowledge comes to the mind through the senses is called **empiricism.** Thus, when I said that everything I knew about my neighbor Jerry was sense-based, I was taking the empirical position.

If you are an empiricist, you must hold that every idea in your mind can be traced back to one of your senses. All that you know rests upon one of five kinds of data: eye data, ear data, skin data, nose data, tongue data. Though your senses may occasionally deceive you, you do not regard their errors as an important block to knowledge.

As an empiricist, you have a very high respect for the methods of science. Because much of science is based on the systematic interpretation of sense evidence, you probably cannot imagine a better way of acquiring knowledge than through the scientific method.

But could you, as an empiricist, believe in God? If all knowledge is limited to the world known by the senses, could you have any evidence that God existed?

empiricism The view that all knowledge originates with sense experience. Empiricism can be thought of as coming in two varieties, "soft" and "hard." Under the "soft" empirical view, even though all knowledge comes through the senses, the mind can deduce truths—for example, about the existence of God—that go beyond the sense world. Under the "hard" empirical view, the mind is strictly limited to information gained from the sense world. Thus, no knowledge about God's existence, or anything else that cannot be known directly by the senses, is possible. David Hume, one of the "hardest" of empiricists, held that the senses do not even provide evidence for the necessary relationship between cause and effect; because of this and other arguments, Hume believed that the laws of science have no reliable foundation (see Chapter 23).

Here is a sketch of how you might argue empirically for God's existence:

1. All knowledge comes to us through our senses.
2. Everything we know through our senses about the universe reveals that the universe could not exist unless God created it.
3. Therefore, God exists.

Thus, as an empiricist, you would attempt to argue from the visible realm, the universe, to the invisible realm, God. Though you had no direct, firsthand, information about God, you would argue that you had an enormous amount, an entire universe full, of secondhand information about God.

Aristotle, known as the Father of Science, was the first great empiricist. He used his senses to gather and organize information about the physical world and founded the sciences of biology, botany, and geology, among others. In Aristotle's view, every object in the physical universe could be fully explored by answering only four questions:

- What is the matter of the object?
- What is the essence of the object? (What does the object hold in common with all other objects of the same kind?)
- What is the origin of the object?
- What is the purpose of the object?

According to Aristotle, the answers to these questions could be entirely determined by sense evidence.

Here is a simple model of the knowledge process according to empiricism:

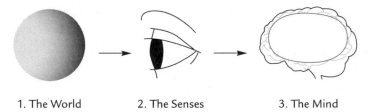

1. The World   2. The Senses   3. The Mind

You will learn in later sections of the tour that empiricism can be more complex than the three-step model above. For now, just note that a simple empirical process moves from the world (1), through the senses (2), to the mind (3).

We will say a lot more about empiricists on the tour. What is your initial reaction to empiricism?

I believe empiricism presents the (correct, incorrect) view of the knowledge

process because _____

_____.

Now, let's look at a second answer to the empirical question, "How does the mind acquire knowledge?"

Rationalism

The epistemological view that the mind knows at least some truths independently of the senses is called **rationalism.** Thus, when I looked out my window and believed that I knew that Jerry and all human beings had minds, I was taking a rationalistic view. I believed I had a truth, a truth about every human who had ever existed or could ever exist, that did not come to me through my senses.

As a rationalist, you must hold that your mind has some special power or capacity that allows you direct, non-sense-based access to truth. Instead of the empiricist's view that the senses are the sole source of certainty, you would have a tendency to argue that the senses are unreliable. Every time your senses report that the sun circles the earth or that a spoon is bent in a glass of water or there is a mirage in the desert or that you are awake when you are dreaming, your senses give evidence of their unreliability. Thus, as a rationalist, you would hold that insofar as science is based solely on sense evidence, partial truths are the best that can be hoped for through scientific investigation.

Following rationalism, you believe that you have one or more ideas in your mind that are not only fully true but are also impossible to trace to a sense origin. An example of such an idea would be the truth of God's existence.

As a rationalist, you could argue as follows:

1. Humans have an idea of God, a perfect, eternal, all-powerful being.

2. Human senses give no evidence for the existence of such a being.

3. Only God could have given humans the idea of God.

4. Therefore, God exists

As a rationalist, you would turn away from the deceptive realm of your senses and turn toward the truthful realm of your mind. But if the mind's truths don't come from the senses, what is their origin? Two rationalistic answers are

- We are born with truths that came from a source beyond our minds.

- God, during our life, puts truths directly into our minds.

Plato held the first view. The knowledge that we are born with is the knowledge of Perfect, Eternal Truths. We are born with this knowledge because our souls, prior to birth, existed in the realm of Perfect, Eternal Truths. St. Augustine held the second view. Whenever we know something for certain, it is because God is illuminating our mind. God is the sun that allows the eye of our mind to see. As we study a single triangle, God illuminates our mind to see truths about *all* triangles. Thus, both Plato and St. Augustine held that the mind gains information about reality not through the senses, but independently of the senses.

Here is a diagram of the rationalistic knowledge process according to St. Augustine (for Plato's view, substitute Perfect, Eternal Truths for God).

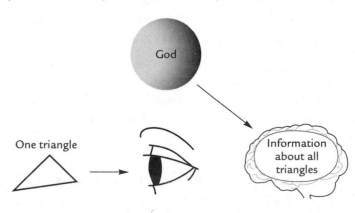

rationalism The view that the mind can know truths independently of the senses. In general, there are two kinds of rationalists: those who believe truths are present in the mind at birth that could not have come through the senses and those who believe the mind during life acquires truths that could not have come through the senses. A rationalist of the former kind could hold that knowledge of God's existence is present in the mind at birth; a rationalist of the latter kind could hold that the power of intuition provides the mind during life with truths that could not have come through the senses.

For future reference, sketch your initial reaction to rationalism.

I believe rationalism presents the (correct, incorrect) view of the knowledge

process because _____

_____.

Now, let's investigate a third answer to the question, "How does the mind acquire knowledge?"

Skepticism

The epistemological view that the mind has no reliable way of acquiring knowledge is called **skepticism.** If I looked out my window and took the skeptical position, then I would argue that I could know very little, if anything, for certain. For example, let me look skeptically at Jerry as he mows his lawn.

What do I *really* see? A pinkish shape moving along behind a greenish shape. I say that one is "a human" and one is "a machine." But where do I get this information? There is nothing I know through my senses that tells me Jerry is any different from the thing he pushes. They both move. They both occupy space. They both require liquids. Even if I went over and talked to Jerry, how could I know that he was "rational"? Nothing my senses tell me could give me any access to his "mind." Mind is said to be invisible; therefore, how could I ever distinguish between something *with* an invisible mind and something *without* an invisible mind? Taking the skeptical view, I see how little I can know for certain. I can't even tell if there is an essential difference between Jerry and his lawn mower!

As a skeptic, you would hold that rationalism and empiricism refute each other. You agree with the rationalists that the senses are unreliable, and you agree with the empiricists that the mind has no access to knowledge *except* through the senses. Thus, the mind's only source of truth, the senses, cannot be trusted. We are born empty-headed and fill our skulls with falsehoods we believe are true. The mind is an error bank.

David Hume is philosophy's most famous skeptic. In Hume's view, knowledge can enter the mind only through the senses, but this only means we know far less than we think we know. Hume, as you will eventually learn, argues that we have no knowledge, sense or otherwise, for any scientific truth or for the cause of any effect or for the existence of the self or for the existence of matter or for the existence (or nonexistence) of God.

Hume was an agnostic, one who believed that it is not possible to know whether God exists.

Here is an agnostic argument concerning God's existence:

1. All we know comes through our senses.
2. God is defined as a being that cannot be known through the senses.
3. Therefore, we cannot know whether God exists.

As a skeptic, you would criticize sense knowledge and also argue that the mind has no special power of its own to go beyond the senses. In your view, every alleged Truth can be overpowered by a more powerful Doubt.

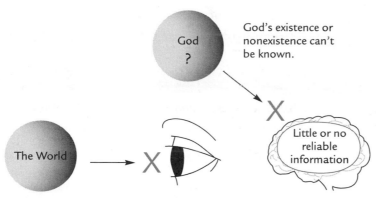

God's existence or nonexistence can't be known.

The senses are unreliable.

Little or no reliable information

You will encounter a number of powerful skeptics on our tour. Sketch your initial reaction to skepticism.

I believe skepticism presents the (correct, incorrect) view of the knowledge

process because _____

_____.

EXERCISE 2.5
Identifying Varieties of Epistemological Statements

Decide which of the following statements are epistemological—that is, which refer to the study of the nature of knowledge. If the statement is epistemological, label it either E for empiricism, R for rationalism, or S for skepticism. If the statement is not epistemological, label it N for nonepistemological.

_____ 1. God exists.

_____ 2. It is not possible to know whether or not God exists.

_____ 3. What the senses learn from the physical universe provides evidence that God exists.

_____ 4. God is good.

_____ 5. Seeing is believing.

_____ 6. ". . . the life of man is of no greater importance to the universe than that of an oyster."—David Hume

_____ 7. There is nothing in the mind that was not first in the senses.

_____ 8. The mind, independently of the senses, can have knowledge of God's existence.

_____ 9. "We must not pretend to do philosophy but really do it; for what we need is not the appearance of health but real health."—Epicurus

_____ 10. The senses cannot be trusted.

_____ 11. The mind recalls wisdom from its own previous existence.

_____ 12. "No man knows or ever will know, the truth about the gods and about everything I speak of: for even if one chanced to say the complete truth, nevertheless one would not know it."—Xenophanes

skepticism The view that the mind possesses little or no reliable knowledge. An extremely radical skeptic might hold that nothing is certain—including the view that nothing is certain.

_____ 13. "There is therefore but one categorical imperative, namely this: *act only on that maxim [principle] whereby thou canst at the same time will that it should become a universal law.*"—Immanuel Kant

_____ 14. The eye of the mind perceives eternal truths because it is illuminated by God's light.

_____ 15. All truths must be tested in the court of sense experience.

_____ 16. "I say quite deliberately that the Christian religion, as organized in its Churches, has been and still is the principal enemy of moral progress in the world."—Bertrand Russell

_____ 17. We don't even know for certain that we know nothing.

CHECKPOINT: Epistemology

Epistemology is the branch of philosophy that studies the knowledge process. Empiricism is the subbranch of epistemology which holds that all knowledge comes through the senses. Rationalism is the subbranch of epistemology which holds that the mind can know truths independently of the senses. Skepticism is the subbranch of epistemology which holds that we can know little, if anything, for certain.

M. C. Escher, *Hand with Reflecting Sphere*, lithograph, 1935.

ILLUSTRATION QUIZ

An Artist Looks (Philosophically) at Himself

This is a self-portrait of the artist M. C. Escher (1898–1972) holding a glass ball. To make your understanding of epistemology more vivid, circle the correct answers in the following simple test.

1. Assume Escher looks into the glass ball and believes that he has no way to tell sleeping from waking, and thus can know nothing for certain about his experience. In this case, Escher would be adopting the (empirical, rationalistic, skeptical) point of view.

2. Assume Escher looks into the glass ball and believes everything he knows about himself, the room, and its furniture is limited to the information that comes through his senses. In this case, Escher would be adopting the (empirical, rationalistic, skeptical) point of view.

3. Assume Escher looks into the glass ball and believes that God is illuminating his mind with the truth that all humans must seek self-knowledge. In this case, Escher would be adopting the (empirical, rationalistic, skeptical) point of view.

Now, let's turn from epistemology and descriptions of how we acquire knowledge to ethics and descriptions of how we ought to live.

What Is Ethics?

Ethics is the branch of philosophy that studies moral values. Thus, in ethics we ask questions about the nature and origin of virtue and vice.

Here are some ethical questions that Unphilosophians would never ponder:

- What are the characteristics of a good person?
- What is true happiness?
- As human beings, what are our duties?
- What is the best form of society?
- Is capital punishment (or abortion or euthanasia or war) moral?
- Is God (or society or nature or each individual) the source of moral values?
- Is lying always (or ever) wrong?
- When and on what basis is a law unjust?

Note the difference between epistemological, metaphysical, and ethical questions:

Metaphysics: Does God exist?

Epistemology: Can the mind acquire knowledge about God's existence (or nonexistence)?

Ethics: Given what can (or cannot) be known about God's existence, what is morally right?

Or, stated more generally:

Metaphysics: What is real?

Epistemology: How do we know the real? (Or, is knowledge of the real possible?)

Ethics: How should we act?

At this point you can see some important interrelationships between the three branches of philosophy. In metaphysics we explore the nature of reality; in epistemology we explore the process by which we know reality; in ethics, given *what* we know about reality and *how* we know reality, we explore the way we should act.

To give you a clearer sense of ethics, let me look out my window and think from two opposing ethical points of view.

I look at Jerry. He has stopped mowing and is now working in his vegetable garden. Every summer he donates almost everything he grows to a food program for the poor at the church. Now, giving to the poor is said to be a good action, an action that has goodness in it. But what is the *source* of the goodness involved in giving to the poor? Let us say I take the ethical position that any action is good that follows God's laws. According to this view, giving to the poor is good because it is in accordance with a higher, nonhuman standard. Thus, my ethical position would be that even if everyone in my city thought it was wrong to give food to the poor, Jerry would still be right, insofar as his action obeyed God's laws. The goodness of any action, from this point of view, finds its source in God's principles, not human opinions.

However, I could take a completely different ethical position. Perhaps the only thing that makes Jerry's action good is the values of the society he lives in. He has been taught since childhood that he should think about others "less fortunate" than he. If he had been raised in another kind of society, a Nazi society, for example, he might think that the very best thing that he could do for the poor, especially if they didn't belong to his race, would be to assist in their extermination. Thus, according to this ethical position, morality is nothing but the values of the culture we live in. There is no law in the sky that says one culture has more moral correctness than another. From this point of view, the goodness of any action comes from the shifting realm of cultural values and no other.

Of course, there is more to ethics than the two positions I just sketched. I'll say more about each view in the next section. For now, begin to develop a general understanding of ethical inquiry by completing the following exercise.

EXERCISE 2.6
Identifying Metaphysical, Epistemological, and Ethical Statements

Label each of the following either M for metaphysical, E for epistemological, Et for ethical, or N for not philosophical.

_____ 1. Each person should do what God commands.

_____ 2. All our information comes from the visible world.

_____ 3. The best people are those who serve others.

_____ 4. Humans should not be so foolish as to believe ghosts exist.

_____ 5. Ghosts don't exist.

_____ 6. Because ghosts are said to be invisible, it is not possible to know whether or not they exist.

_____ 7. Democracy is the best form of government.

_____ 8. The "welfare state" ought to be abolished.

_____ 9. Robert Jordan is the main character in *For Whom the Bell Tolls*.

_____ 10. We should all be as heroic as Robert Jordan.

_____ 11. "Better to die on your feet, than to live on your knees."—Emiliano Zapata

_____ 12. "I take as an illustration, a block of veined marble rather than a wholly uniform block or blank tablets, that is to say what is called tabula rasa. . . . If there were veins in the stone which marked out the figure of Hercules, this stone would be more determined thereto, and Hercules would be in some manner innate in it, although labor would be needed to uncover these veins. . . . It is in this way that ideas and truths are innate in us, like natural inclinations and dispositions, natural habits or potentialities."—Gottfried Leibniz

_____ 13. Charlemagne was crowned Holy Roman Emperor in A.D. 800.

_____ 14. "Simplify! Simplify!"—Henry David Thoreau

_____ 15. "Know thyself."—Inscription at Delphi, Greece

_____ 16. "'Tis not contrary to reason to prefer the destruction of the whole world to the scratching of my finger."—David Hume

_____ 17. "The hypothesis we embrace is plain. It maintains that morality is determined by sentiment [feeling]. It defines virtue to be whatever mental action or quality gives to a spectator the pleasing sentiment of approbation [approval]; and vice the contrary."—David Hume

_____ 18. ". . . that which produces effects within another reality must be termed a reality itself, so I feel as if we had philosophic excuse for calling the unseen or mystical world real."—William James

What Are Two Branches of Ethics?

One of the largest ethical questions is, "What is the source of moral values?" Here are two answers.

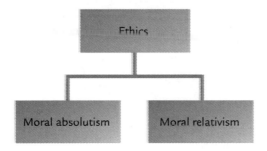

Moral Absolutism

The ethical view that moral values receive their authority from a realm independent of individual human choice is called **moral absolutism.** Thus, when I took the view that Jerry's giving to the poor was good because it obeyed God's laws, I was taking a morally absolutist position.

A philosopher who was a moral absolutist would hold that an absolute moral law is as independent of human choice as the law of gravity. An individual would be as foolish to create her own unique values as to create her own unique laws of physics. From the point of view of moral absolutism, even if everyone on earth decided that a wrong action should be right, they would have no more effect than if they decided an object should fall up.

Thus, as a moral absolutist, you must hold that what is Truly Right and Truly Wrong exists independently of anyone's point of view. Following moral absolutism, you could hold that God, Nature, or the realm of Perfect, Eternal Truths was the source of moral value; but you could not hold that one person's ethical opinion was just as good as another's. Some actions simply are morally right, and other actions simply are morally wrong. Humans can no more control morality than we can control the weather. Human opinions can no more change Wrong to Right than rain to sunshine.

Plato—like many other philosophers on this tour (including all Christian philosophers)—was an ethical absolutist. In Plato's view, what made any action

moral absolutism The view that there is a set of moral values that should serve as a standard for all individuals and all cultures. To say that a moral value is absolute is to say that it is unchanging, applies to everyone, and permits no exceptions. Absolute moral values are founded upon principles that cannot be altered by human actions. Two philosophically popular examples of these principles are God's law and the laws of nature.

just could be determined by how closely it approached Perfect Justice. A society could best approach Perfect Justice when its members performed the function they were best suited for. Thus, those suited to business should conduct business and must not go into government; those best suited to government should assist in ruling the state and must not be involved in business. Similarly, an individual could best approach Perfect Justice by having each part of her personality do what it was best suited for. Thus, the appetites should nourish the body and must not try to rule the personality. The reason should rule the personality and must not be the servant of the appetites.

Most Christians would consider themselves moral absolutists. What makes any action right or wrong is the degree to which it conforms to or departs from God's law. Humans may have differing interpretations of God's law, but these interpretations have no more effect upon the actual law itself than differing interpretations of a poem affect the actual words of the poem. Thus, a Christian moral absolutist would hold that a society was just to the degree that it embodied God's principles. Abortion, for example, might be legal or illegal, but its legal status would have no effect upon its moral status. Though earthly elections are determined by the majority, God counts no votes.

Here is a diagram of the Christian version of moral absolutism (for Plato's version, substitute Perfect, Eternal Truths for God).

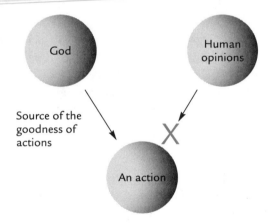

For future reference, how do you respond to moral absolutism?

I believe moral absolutism presents the (correct, incorrect) view of ethical values

because _____

_____.

Now let's look at a second answer to the ethical question, "What is the source of moral values?"

Moral Relativism

The ethical view that the individual or the individual's culture is the source of moral values is referred to as **moral relativism.** Thus, when I took the view that

Jerry's giving vegetables to the poor was a good action only because it upheld the values of his culture, I was taking a morally relativistic position.

A philosopher who is a moral relativist would hold that because moral values are produced by human choices, one value system is merely different from but not better than another. If you believe abortion is wrong and I believe abortion is right, there is no higher standard to determine who is "really right." Moral relativism is like playing baseball without an umpire. I think I was safe at first, you think I was out, and there is no independent third party to appeal to. Ethical absolutism, on the other hand, will use God or Nature (or some other source independent of human choice) as the impartial umpire of all moral disagreements.

As a moral relativist, you would reject every appeal to an absolute ethical standard. Moral systems based upon the "will of God" or "natural human rights" or "what is good for the planet" are, in your view, mere delusions. Morality is nothing but human opinion. One opinion has no more value than another. Following ethical relativism, you would hold that good and evil are just as much human creations as hairstyles. A right action has no more absolute superiority over a wrong action than short hair has superiority over long hair. It makes as much sense to force our morality on others as to force our haircuts on others.

David Hume based his moral relativism, to a large extent, upon his agnosticism, his view that it was not possible to know whether God existed. Hume argued that because we had no knowledge of any moral authority higher than our own desires, there was no way of criticizing *any* of our desires. Thus, as he put it, "it is not contrary to reason to prefer the destruction of the whole world to the scratching of my finger." If you'd rather have everyone die than suffer a pain in your finger, there is no moral standard that can prove you are wrong.

Here is a diagram of moral relativism (contrasting it with the view that moral values come from God).

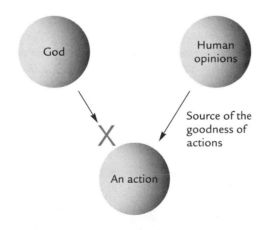

What is your initial reaction to moral relativism?

I believe moral relativism presents the (correct, incorrect) view of ethical values

because _____

_____.

moral relativism   The view that there is no set of moral values that should serve as a standard for all individuals and all cultures. A moral relativist holds that what makes any human action right or wrong is determined by the changing opinions of individuals and/or the shifting values of a culture.

EXERCISE 2.7

Identifying Varieties of Ethical Statements

Label the following either Ma for moral absolutism, Mr for moral relativism, or N for not an ethical statement.

_____ 1. Because he is the Son of God, we should follow Jesus' directive to "Seek the Kingdom of Heaven."

_____ 2. Because each person has his or her own system of values, no one can say anyone else is morally wrong.

_____ 3. Because the Bible is divinely inspired we must follow the precept: "Do unto others as you would have them do unto you."

_____ 4. We ought to "save the planet," because the earth is our Mother.

_____ 5. We must protect the Constitution because its authority is based upon universal human values.

_____ 6. We do not need to obey the Constitution because it merely reflects the upper-class social values of its designers.

_____ 7. Because tax laws are merely human inventions, the only thing really wrong with cheating on taxes is getting caught.

_____ 8. Because citizens have a natural obligation to support the state of which they are members, it is wrong to cheat on taxes.

_____ 9. Because God commanded us to "give unto Caesar what is Caesar's," we must not cheat on our taxes.

_____ 10. "Genius is 10 percent inspiration and 90 percent perspiration." —Albert Einstein

_____ 11. What is morally right for one person could be morally wrong for another.

_____ 12. Each society determines its own moral values.

_____ 13. "Being in company with a gentleman who thought fit to maintain Dr. Berkeley's ingenious philosophy, that nothing exists but as perceived by some mind; when the gentleman was going away, Johnson said to him, 'Pray, Sir, don't leave us; for we may perhaps forget to think of you, and then you will cease to exist.'"—James Boswell, _Boswell's Life of Johnson_

CHECKPOINT: Ethics

Ethics is the branch of philosophy that explores moral values. Moral absolutism is the subbranch of ethics which holds that moral values originate in a source independent of individual choice—for example, with God or Nature. Moral relativism is the branch of ethics which holds that moral values are determined by the individual or the individual's culture.

Now, having said all this about philosophy and some of its branches, what can be said about the life of a philosopher?

What Do Philosophers Do?

In today's world, most philosophers are employed by a college or university to teach philosophy; they also often publish articles and books on philosophical topics. The topics many modern philosophers write about are similar to the following:

"Plato's Theory of Justice in the *Republic*"

"An Analysis of Immanuel Kant's Categorical Imperative"

"Modern Alternatives to Descartes's Psychological Dualism"

As you can see, doing philosophy often means writing about what other philosophers have written about. There is an important lesson in this. Philosophers don't merely stare off into the sky and philosophize. Philosophers stare into the books of other philosophers and philosophize. *The art of deep, philosophical thinking is unshakably rooted in the art of deep, philosophical reading, and that is why large portions of this text are devoted to helping you read more deeply.*

How Do Philosophers Increase Their Wisdom?

Almost all philosophers use something like the following four-step method:

1. **Read and judge.** First, philosophers read (and reread) what others have said on the topic they are interested in. This step can take years. As part of this thorough reading, philosophers divide what they've read into three categories: that which is (more or less) correct, that which is (more or less) incorrect, and that which is irrelevant.

2. **Paraphrase and argue.** Next, philosophers begin to respond in writing to what they've read. They explain what is correct in the positions of others and why it seems correct and what is incorrect in the positions of others and why it seems incorrect. In step 2, philosophers engage in a great deal of paraphrasing and argument construction.

3. **Create a new position.** Next, philosophers try to go beyond what is correct in the positions of others to establish a "more correct" position. In other words, after laying extensive groundwork, the philosopher presents his or her own view.

4. **Wait for the flack.** Finally, philosophers wait for the onslaught of their critics. A philosopher's critics work over his or her writings just as rigorously as the philosopher worked over the writings of others. In philosophy, everybody does it to everybody else.

On this tour, to make you a more powerful thinker, you'll be taking the same four steps that professional philosophers follow.

1. **Read and judge.** You'll receive plenty of tips on how to read deeply and how to sort what you read into the correct, the incorrect, and the irrelevant.

2. **Paraphrase and argue.** All during the tour, you'll learn techniques to help you paraphrase the philosophy of others and construct arguments supporting and attacking philosophical positions.

3. **Create a new position.** Every chapter will give you interesting opportunities for doing original philosophical work and elaborating your philosophical system.

4. **Wait for the flack.** Your teacher and classmates will fill the role of your critics.

SUMMARY

The value of philosophy can be partly seen in the large number of intellectual disciplines that owe their birth to philosophical thinking. **Philosophy** is the study of the nature of wisdom. Wisdom is the knowledge produced by answering the largest possible questions.

In **metaphysics,** philosophers explore questions about reality: **Monism** is the branch of metaphysics which holds that all of reality is one kind of thing, and **dualism** is the branch of philosophy which holds that all of reality is two kinds of things.

In **epistemology,** philosophers explore questions about the knowledge process: **Empiricism** is the branch of epistemology which holds that all knowledge originates with the senses; **rationalism** is the branch of epistemology which holds that the mind can know some truths independently of the senses; **skepticism** is the branch of epistemology which holds that few, if any, truths can be known for certain.

In **ethics,** philosophers explore questions about moral values: **Moral absolutism** is the branch of ethics which holds that moral values originate in a source independent of individual choice; **moral relativism** is the branch of ethics which holds that moral values are determined by the individual or the individual's culture.

Philosophers develop their positions based upon a rigorous analysis of the works of other philosophers.

EXERCISE 2.8
Looking Back

Using your own paper, briefly answer the following questions explored in this chapter.

1. What is the importance of philosophy?

2. What is philosophy?

3. What is metaphysics?

4. What are two branches of metaphysics?

5. What is epistemology?

6. What are three branches of epistemology?

7. What is ethics?

8. What are two branches of ethics?

9. What do philosophers do?

10. How do philosophers acquire wisdom?

EXERCISE 2.9
Possible and Impossible Philosophical Positions (Relatively Simple)

Now, use your entire eleven-word philosophical vocabulary (philosophy, metaphysics, epistemology, ethics, monism, dualism, empiricism, rationalism, skepticism, moral absolutism, moral relativism) and label the following P for Possible or I for Impossible (or nonsensical).

_____ 1. A dualistic monist

_____ 2. A monistic dualist

_____ 3. An empirical monist

_____ 4. A monistic empiricist

_____ 5. A dualistic rationalist who holds that all knowledge comes through the senses

_____ 6. A monistic empiricist who believes that the higher realm of reality is knowable only through knowledge gained independently of the senses

_____ 7. A monistic, empirical, moral relativist

_____ 8. A moral absolutist who holds that God does not exist

_____ 9. A moral relativist with a strong strain of epistemological skepticism

_____ 10. A metaphysical dualist who is also an orthodox Christian

EXERCISE 2.10
Possible and Impossible Philosophical Positions (Complex)

Now add the four following terms, alluded to in this chapter, to your philosophical vocabulary. A **materialist** is a monist who believes all is matter. An **idealist** is a monist who believes all is immaterial (for example, all is God). A **Platonist** is a dualist who believes all is divided between the physical realm and the realm of Perfect, Eternal Truths. A **Christian,** from the philosophical point of view, is a dualist who believes that all is divided between the physical realm and the realm of God. These four terms add subbranches to monism and dualism.

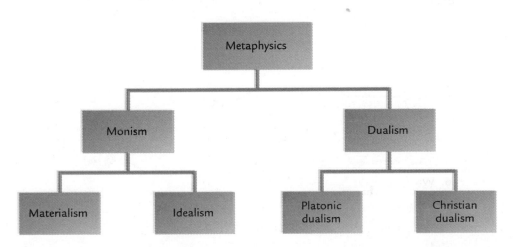

materialist One who holds that all that exists is made of matter. For example, a modern materialist might believe that ideas, though apparently nonphysical, can be entirely reduced to the chemistry of the brain.

idealist One who holds that all that exists is made of ideas or some other nonphysical principle. For example, a mystic might discover that the physical universe was an illusion and that All is Spirit. (Note: a philosophical *ideal*ist is different than an *ideal*ist; the former is concerned with ideas or other nonphysical entities; the latter is concerned with ideals.)

Platonist One who, agreeing with Plato, holds that all of reality is divided between a nonphysical realm of perfect truths and the physical universe (see Chapters 10 to 12).

Christian A follower of Jesus Christ. Christianity, like other world religions, embraces a wide variety of believers. For example, some who regard themselves as Christians believe the Bible is literally true; others who regard themselves as Christians believe the Bible is a mixture of fact and fiction.

Label the following P for Possible or I for Impossible (or nonsensical).

_____ 1. An empiricistic, morally absolutist, Christian monist

_____ 2. A rationalistic, dualistic, morally absolutist Platonic dualist

_____ 3. A monistic materialist who combines an epistemological skepticism with a strong belief in Platonic metaphysics

_____ 4. A metaphysical dualist of the Platonic variety who stoutly rejects empiricism and all varieties of materialism, believing that all knowledge comes only through the senses

_____ 5. A morally absolutist, metaphysical dualist of the Christian variety who stoutly rejects rationalism and all varieties of materialism, believing that all knowledge comes only through the senses

_____ 6. A metaphysical dualist of the Christian variety who stoutly rejects empiricism and all varieties of materialism, believing that all knowledge comes independently of the senses

_____ 7. A morally relativistic, monistic metaphysician who empirically holds that knowledge comes through the senses and believes that God does not exist and that all of reality is essentially matter

_____ 8. A morally absolutist, monistic metaphysician who empirically holds that knowledge comes through the senses and believes that God exists but that part of reality is essentially matter

_____ 9. A dualistic rationalist, strongly attached to disbelief in God's existence who holds that the higher realm of reality is actually the realm of perfect and eternal truths

_____ 10. A metaphysically dualistic Christian with a shallow epistemological skepticism who agrees with Karl Marx that all of reality is essentially physical

EXERCISE 2.11
Metaphysical, Epistemological, and Ethical Statements

The following statements briefly present a variety of philosophical positions, many of which you will study on our tour. First, decide if the statements are metaphysical, epistemological, or ethical. Then, if they are either metaphysical or epistemological, label them, if there is enough information, according to the subbranches of metaphysics or epistemology. (Include the four extra terms, materialism, idealism, Platonic dualism, and Christian dualism, defined in the previous exercise.)

Example:

Thales: All is water.

Metaphysics, monistic materialism

1. Parmenides: The physical world is an illusion. The only reality is the nonphysical One.

2. Socrates: I know that I know nothing.

3. Plato: All that one knows for certain is recalled from a time previous to birth.

4. Aristotle: There is nothing in the mind that was not first in the senses.

5. St. Augustine: The rule of life is "Love God and do as you wish."

6. Epicurus: Live the life of moderate pleasures.

7. Epictetus: Recognize that all you can control is your reaction to the world and not the world itself.

8. St. Anselm: Examining the idea of God proves that God exists.

9. St. Thomas Aquinas: Examining God's creations proves that God exists.

10. René Descartes: Reality is divided between things that have free will (God and humans) and things that do not (the rest of the universe).

11. John Locke: The senses add their own information to all that comes through the senses.

12. David Hume: No scientific principle can be known for certain.

13. Immanuel Kant: Treat people as ends not means.

14. Friedrich Nietzsche: All that can happen will happen over and over again.

EXERCISE 2.12

The Big View

Using all your philosophical vocabulary (philosophy, metaphysics, epistemology, ethics, monism, dualism, materialism, idealism, Christian dualism, Platonic dualism, empiricism, rationalism, skepticism, moral absolutism, and moral relativism), fill in the diagram below. Attach the names of the following philosophers to appropriate terms: Thales, Plato (three places), Aristotle, St. Augustine (two places), Karl Marx, David Hume (two places).

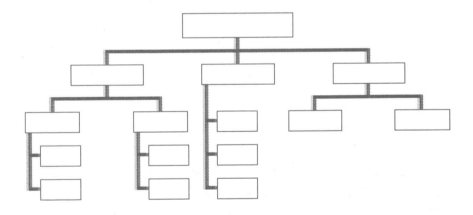

ANALYSIS OF YOUR PHILOSOPHICAL SELF-PORTRAIT

As you will be able to tell from the following analysis, a great deal about your metaphysics, epistemology, and ethics can be deduced from your answer to the single question below. Read the analysis carefully and then change your answer if you wish. Note how a position in one branch of philosophy influences positions in other branches of philosophy.

1. Circle the statement that best expresses your view of all of reality.

   a.   Reality is divided between the realm of God and the physical universe.

   Metaphysics. This choice makes you some variety of metaphysical dualist, one who holds that reality is divided into two mutually exclusive categories. This answer is consistent with the three major Western religious traditions—Jewish, Christian, and Islamic.

   Epistemology. Your metaphysical dualism does not commit you to either empiricism or rationalism, but you certainly can't be a skeptic. You could hold the empirical view that knowledge of the existence of a higher realm of reality can be deduced from sense evidence or the rationalistic view that knowledge of a higher realm can be known directly by the mind. Look at the empirical and rationalistic proofs of God's existence for samples of each approach. However, you could hardly be a skeptic if you believe that you have knowledge of the higher realm.

   Ethics. As a metaphysical dualist you almost have to be some variety of moral absolutist. Holding that all of reality is divided between the realm of God and the physical universe, you almost have to hold that God is the source of all moral values. If you've found a way to be a metaphysical dualist and a moral relativist, I'm sure your teacher will enjoy hearing from you.

   A problem to think about. If you are a Christian and believe God exists because His existence is testified to by the Bible and the Bible can be trusted because it is divinely inspired, why aren't you arguing in a circle? You can't use X (God's existence) to prove Y (the reliability of the Bible) *and* Y (the reliability of the Bible) to prove X (God's existence). To understand why this is true, assume you are an attorney interviewing two witnesses. Witness X says witness Y never lies; witness Y says you can totally trust witness X. Obviously nothing has been proved about the reliability of either witness.

   In order to break your circular argument, you need to show either:

   1. The absolute certainty of God's existence as testified to by evidence *other than* the Bible, or

   2. The absolute reliability of the Bible as evidence for God's existence as testified to by evidence *other than* God's existence.

   You would be in the strongest possible position, of course, if you had irrefutable evidence for both 1 and 2.

   b.   The physical universe is the only reality, and everything else is an illusion.

   Metaphysics. This choice makes you a monistic materialist, one who holds that all of reality is one kind of thing—and that one thing is matter. An important consequence of your view is the position you must take on what has come to be called the mind-brain controversy.

   Some philosophers hold that the mind is invisible and nonmaterial and thus a very different kind of thing from the brain. In this view, the brain is simply where the mind "resides" and is no more identical to its residence than an individual is identical to a house. Just as an individual is independent of and can control many operations of a house, so the brain is independent of and can control many operations of the brain and body.

On the other side of the controversy are philosophers who hold that the mind is *nothing but* the physical and chemical operations of the brain. In this view, the mind is identical to the brain. It seems impossible to philosophers of this persuasion that something nonphysical could have any effect upon something physical. A nonphysical mind could no more affect the physical brain and body than a nonphysical golf club could affect a physical golf ball. As a materialist, one who holds that all is matter, you side with those who hold that the mind is identical with the brain. In your view, the mind as an invisible, immaterial entity is just another illusion like God, the soul, and heaven and hell.

Epistemology. A materialistic metaphysics probably commits you to an empirical epistemology. Because there is no realm beyond the physical, all knowledge that is possible must come to you through your senses. Your materialism, therefore, probably makes you a strong supporter of the sciences. You worship at the altar of biology, physics, and other sciences insofar as these disciplines describe everything that exists in physical and mechanical terms. (You may draw back, at this point, from the view that everything is machinelike; but if you are a materialist, then you hold that there is nothing to reality but matter and thus must hold that humans operate on the same fundamental physical principles as, say, a lawn mower.)

Ethics. As a materialist, you are not necessarily committed to either moral absolutism or moral relativism. Though if you are a moral absolutist you would not, of course, hold that moral values came from God's realm or any realm other than the physical. You would be comfortable, however, with a moral absolutism grounded in Nature. Thus, you might hold that a right action is right because it was based upon "natural principles"; for example, you might cite survival of the fittest or, if you are a kinder, gentler materialist, you might hold that a right action is right because it "promotes life." Of course by "life" you would mean a process that was governed by the same physical principles as a machine.

A problem to think about. If "All is matter," then human actions appear to be as determined as the actions of any machine. Thus, humans are no more responsible for their actions than a machine is responsible for its actions. Just as we do not blame an assault rifle for committing mass murder, so we should not blame a mass murderer who uses the assault rifle. The murderer is just one machine using another machine. If "All is matter," then humans aren't free moral agents. And if humans aren't free moral agents, how can we say any human action is wrong?

c. God is the only reality, and everything else is an illusion.

Metaphysics. This choice indicates that you are a most unusual student in an introductory philosophy class. George Berkeley will be your strongest supporter on the tour. Parmenides will support you with some powerful arguments against the reality of the physical world. You may even accept some aid from Plato, who was deeply suspicious of the world we know with our senses.

Epistemology. Surprise! Even if you hold that the physical world is an illusion, you can still be an empiricist, one who holds that all knowledge comes through your senses. To understand how this trick is possible, you'll have to read about George Berkeley in Chapter 21. Odds are, however, that your idealistic monism gives you a deep attraction for rationalism. When the mind operates independently of the senses, you believe it can have the purest knowledge that All is

God. You are probably deeply interested in mysticism; and if you aren't, you should be. For an intoxicating, multicultural introduction to the great mystics, start with Aldous Huxley's *The Perennial Philosophy*.

Ethics. Again, just as any believer in God, you almost have to be a moral absolutist. God's values, in your view, are the only real values.

A problem to think about. If "All is God," how can you say there is any evil? Murder and genocide, to take only two examples, would be just as full of God's spirit as giving money to the poor.

d.   It is not possible to know the nature of reality.

Metaphysics. This choice indicates that you take the radical view that all metaphysical talk is nonsense. Nothing of value can be known about the nature of reality.

Epistemology. You are certainly a skeptic. But odds are that you have more impatience with rationalism than empiricism. The rationalist claim that the mind has some special power that gives it access to Truth seems ludicrous to you. You probably base your skepticism upon the view that while knowledge does come through the senses, no knowledge about ultimate reality comes through the senses. You have a limited appreciation for science insofar as science makes modest knowledge claims and does not try to describe the "really real."

Ethics. Given your skepticism, it is hard to see how you could be anything but a moral relativist. Because you hold that we can know nothing about ultimate reality, you probably believe that we can know nothing about the source of absolute moral values.

A problem to think about (read this one slowly). As a skeptic, you believe you know enough to know that very little can be known for certain. For you to know even this much for certain, you must believe that your reason can freely choose between truth and falsehood. If your reason can freely choose between truth and falsehood, then you have chosen a metaphysic that affirms human freedom and rejected a metaphysic that denies human freedom. This is a very grand metaphysical position, indeed. Thus, having some type of metaphysic, a view of reality, you can hardly call yourself a skeptic.

If you try to escape this problem by saying you are skeptical of your own skepticism, then you still hold that you can tell the difference between truth and falsehood. It is more true to be skeptical of skepticism than not to be skeptical of skepticism. Which means you still believe in human freedom; hence, you still have a grand metaphysical belief. Get it? If you don't, look at these last two paragraphs after you finish the tour. Then take two aspirin and send me some e-mail.

e.   None of the above.

This choice indicates that you've taken a design-your-own position. So, go ahead.

Fill in your metaphysical position, your view of reality: _____

_____

_____

_____

_____

_____.

Fill in your epistemological position, your view of the knowledge process:

_____
_____
_____
_____
_____.

Fill in your ethical position, your view of moral values: _____
_____
_____
_____
_____
_____.

GOOD BOOKS

Angeles, Peter A. *Dictionary of Philosophy*. New York: Barnes & Noble, 1981. A handy, clear guide.

Collinson, Diane. *Fifty Major Philosophers*. London: Routledge, 1988. An outstanding *short* guide to the history of philosophy.

Copleston, Frederick, S.J. *A History of Philosophy*. New York: Doubleday, 1985. After Jones (see below), an excellent place to go for a second opinion on a philosopher.

Edwards, Paul, editor. *The Encyclopedia of Philosophy*. New York: Macmillan & Free Press, 1967. A massive, eight-volume work. Extremely useful.

Gaarder, Jostein. *Sophie's World*. New York: Berkley, 1997. A delightful, brilliant introduction to philosophy written in the form of a novel. I can't recommend this one too highly.

Jones, W. T. *A History of Western Philosophy*, 2nd ed. New York: Harcourt Brace Jovanovich, 1970. There are many histories of philosophy, but none better than Jones's. He is especially strong on giving the cultural and literary background for philosophers.

NEXT STOP

You meet Western culture's first philosopher.

3

Thales and the Beginning of Philosophy

YOUR PHILOSOPHICAL SELF-PORTRAIT

Based on what you know thus far about philosophy and your own best guess, circle what you think is the answer to each of the following:

1. T F   The earliest philosophical statements were metaphysical, rather than ethical or epistemological.

2. T F   There is no way to say for certain that any person was the *first* philosopher.

3. T F   Because religion came before philosophy, the first recorded philosophical explanation of the universe was religious.

4. T F   The earliest philosophers probably rejected rather than supported the views of their society.

On this section of the tour, you meet the first philosopher, Thales, and explore the cosmic problem that he tried to solve (and that we're still trying to solve), the problem of the One and the Many.

What would it be like to look out at the world through the eyes of the first philosophers, men who lived 2,600 years ago? Is there any way we could cross the enormous span of centuries and view the world as they did? Nothing remains of their cities—Miletus, Ephesus, Elea—but a few ruins on the shores of the Mediterranean; very little remains of their actual words. How did their minds work?

It is fairly easy to reexperience the problem the first philosophers confronted, the problem of the One and the Many, but somewhat harder to get a feel for their various solutions to this problem.

In this chapter, I'll answer two questions:

- What was the first philosophical problem?
- What was Thales' solution to the problem of the One and the Many?

What Was the First Philosophical Problem?

When I look out my window, I see many different things: a boy across the street playing basketball, four houses in the cul de sac, the San Bernardino Mountains, a horse-shaped cloud above the mountains. The variety of things I know through my senses are what the first philosophers called the Many.

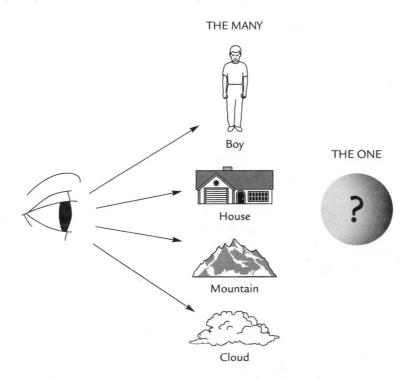

THE MANY

Boy

House

Mountain

Cloud

THE ONE

?

The problem of the One and the Many is central to this chapter and to the next three chapters.

The problem the first philosophers tried to solve was, "What is the One behind the Many?" What is the one thing, substance, or process that unifies the many different aspects of existence? As you can see, philosophy began with the most ambitious of all tasks. The first philosophers wanted to know the ultimate nature of reality. In other words, the first philosophical problem was metaphysical. Metaphysics, as you learned in the previous chapter, explores the nature of the real.

I look out my window at the living—the boy, his dog, the trees in my neighbor's yard—and the non-living—the cement street, the mountains, the gauzy clouds. Is there any One which unifies this Many?

Well?

I believe _____

because _____

_____.

Let's begin, as the first philosophers must have, by excluding the easy answers.

Thus, we could not say that the One which unifies the Many is matter. This would merely raise a new problem. What is matter? Is cloud matter the same as mountain matter or boy matter? To reply, as some of my students have, that matter is "what fills up space" isn't as helpful as it appears. You could just as well define water as what fills up buckets. The ingredients of water are two molecules of hydrogen and one molecule of oxygen. Thus, water is more than bucket filler. But what are the ingredients of matter? And if matter does have ingredients, is there one ingredient that is the most basic of all?

A second too-easy answer to the problem of the One and the Many is that the Many are just the Many. There is no One. Probably no philosopher or scientist has ever held this. It seems like a good answer but it really leads nowhere. If you say the Many is the Many, then you mean one of the following:

1. Every single thing in the universe is unlike every other single thing in the universe.

2. Every single thing in the universe has common properties with some other things in the universe.

But position 1 is surely not the case. One cloud has something in common with another cloud; one boy has something in common with another boy. Thus, every single thing in the universe is not different from every other single thing in the universe. But if you hold position 2, you have not helped yourself either. If the Many has common properties, then the Many falls into groups. But what are the groups? And is there one substance, process, or state that some or maybe all of the groups hold in common? Sorting the Many into groups and looking for the basic elements among these groups just brings you back to the original problem. Is there a One that unifies the Many?

And so, look out my window with me. The boy plays basketball in front of his house. The clouds float above Cherokee Peak. What is the hidden One behind the Many? What is the nature of reality? This is the ancient question.

And now let's consider the first surprising answer.

Thales (c. 634 – c. 546 B.C.)

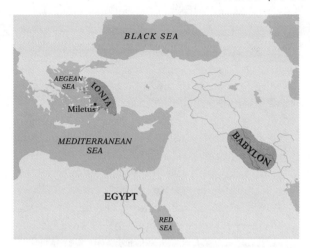

Honored by posterity as "the father of philosophy" and revered by his Greco-Roman contemporaries as one of the "Seven Sages" of Greece, Thales is the first known philosopher in Western culture.

Most of the events of Thales' life are lost to us. None of his writings, if he wrote at all, survive. What we know of Thales' teachings was transmitted orally to Greek scholars who wrote down the stories and doctrines that we know today.

Although it is not known where Thales was born or if his parents were Greek or Phoenician, we do know that he was born around 634 B.C. and that he lived most of his life in Miletus, a thriving and sprawling city-state and Greek colony in Ionia (on the west coast of present-day Turkey). It is not surprising that Miletus was the birthplace of Western philosophy. Prior to its conquest at the hands of the Persians, the city was one of the most powerful and prosperous commercial centers in the ancient world, a melting pot where radical ideas could be openly discussed. The wealth acquired from trade gave the citizens of Miletus the leisure time to engage in speculation and the study of the arts and science.

One can easily imagine Thales as a boy listening attentively to the wisdom of travelers from faraway Babylon, Egypt, and the Orient.

According to legend, Thales received part of his early education in Egypt, where he impressed the pharaoh and his court by calculating the heights of the great pyramids (see Box 3.1). An accomplished astronomer, Thales was the first Westerner to determine the sun's course from solstice to solstice and to accurately estimate the size of the sun and moon. His greatest accomplishment, however, if we are to believe the stories about him, was his prediction of a total eclipse of the sun that occurred during a battle between the Medes and Lydians on May 28 in the year 585 B.C. This remarkable achievement cemented his reputation as a great astronomer.

Thales' accomplishments, however, went beyond the study of the heavens. Aristotle identified him as the first *phusikos*—that is, the first thinker to make philosophical inquiries into the fundamental nature of things. Unlike Socrates and later Greek philosophers, Thales was more interested in the nature of the physical universe than in the human world. For countless generations before Thales, poets had explained the universe as the creation of gods. Thales, however, rejected the past and established an account of the cosmos based on reason, not ancient stories. His quest was to discover the first principle underlying all of reality. Thales concluded that everything can be reduced to one fundamental substance—water. According to later sources, Thales also taught that the earth is a large disk floating on water, that the magnet has a soul, and that all things are full of the gods or alive.

While Thales' theories on the nature of the universe have since been discarded, his quest for a single ultimate principle or substance continues to intrigue scientists and philosophers.

Match Wits With Legendary Thales

All we know about Thales' life consists of brief tales told about him several hundred years after his death. Plato relates the following: "A witty and attractive Thracian servant girl is said to have mocked Thales for falling in a well while he was observing the stars and gazing upwards. She declared that he was eager to know the things in the sky, but that what was behind him and just by his feet escaped his notice."

According to Aristotle, "When they reproached him [Thales] because of his poverty, as though philosophy were no use, it is said that, having observed through his study of the heavenly bodies that there would be a large olive crop, he raised a little money while it was still winter and paid deposits on all the olive presses in Miletus and Chios, hiring them cheaply because no one bid against him. When the appropriate time came there was a sudden rush of requests for the presses. He then hired them out on his own terms and so made a large profit, thus demonstrating that it is easy for philosophers to be rich, if they wish, but that it is not in this that they are interested."

Odds are these are simply the kind of stories that grow up around famous figures, interesting to hear but unreliable as biographical information. How likely is it, for example, that an olive harvest could be predicted by stargazing? The stories are useful, nonetheless, because they give us small portraits of the ancient "media image" of philosophers. Think of the second story as countering the bad publicity of the first story.

Of all the tales told about Thales, one of the most intriguing is associated with the Pyramids. Called to Egypt by the Pharaoh, so the story goes, Thales is set the apparently simple task that had, nonetheless, confounded all the wise men of the court. How high is the Great Pyramid? Thales thrusts aside stacks of complex mathematical computations that the wise men have used and boldly declares, "Give me a stick that is precisely my height and I will tell you the height of the Great Pyramid *before the sun goes down.*" Using the stick, in a simple but brilliant fashion, and without climbing the Pyramid, Thales produces a solution that not only astounds but also convinces everyone. How did he do it? Match wits with the legendary Thales. How could Thales use a stick whose length equaled his height to exactly measure the height of the Great Pyramid? (The answer is somewhere in this book.)

What Was Thales' Solution to the Problem of the One and the Many?

We don't know why philosophy began at the end of the seventh century B.C. in Miletus, a busy Greek trade city in a region called Ionia on the western coast of Asia Minor. We know very little, in fact, about Thales, the first philosopher (see Box 3.1). None of his works have survived. If other philosophers hadn't quoted Thales, we would never have been aware of his existence.

Only three statements are directly attributed to Thales:

- The earth floats on water.
- All things are full of gods. The magnet is alive, for it has the power to move iron.
- All is water.

That's it! Memorize these claims, and you can tell your friends that you can recite the entire works of an ancient Greek philosopher.

But how are any of these statements a solution to the metaphysical problem of the One and the Many?

If Thales had said only "the earth floats on water," he would simply have been repeating a view found in ancient Greek and Egyptian religion. If Thales had said only that "all things are full of gods; the magnet is alive, for it has the power to move iron," he would have simply been repeating a view we now call "animism." Animism holds that the world is populated by spirits. Many primitive tribes believe that there is a spirit associated with each kind of tree, with each important location in their region, with animals, and with other important features of their environment.

The ancient patterns of animism, or what might be called mythic thinking, not only served primitive cultures for hundreds of thousands of years but also were the only mode of cosmic explanation in early civilizations. Mythic thinking explains the formation of the world and the human situation through tales of gods, goddesses, legendary heroes, animals, and even insects. Several short examples:

- According to the San bushmen of the Kalahari Desert, all life was created by Cagn, a supreme being, symbolized by a praying mantis. Cagn created all animals and gave them colors and names. His spirit is said to live with the antelopes, following wherever they graze.

- In the view of the Mbuti Pygmies of Zaire, the chief god, referred to as the Father or Grandfather, created the world and humans and lived with them peacefully until humans disobeyed him. Thereupon, plants and animals turned against the humans. Father returned to the sky.

- In the Babylonian epic *Enuma Elish,* the world is the result of a battle between Marduk, king of the gods, and Tiamat, the sea goddess. Marduk, a two-headed, fire-breathing giant, defeats Tiamat and forms the world from her body. He then creates humans to serve as slaves of the gods and establishes the city of Babylon, where he will be worshiped.

EXERCISE 3.1

Mythic Thinking

Here is a longer sample of mythic thinking that the earliest philosophers like Thales were probably familiar with, a description of the first four races of men from the Greek poet Hesiod.

> In the beginning the Olympians under Kronos created the race of the Men of Gold. In those days men lived like gods in unalloyed happiness. They did not toil with their hands, for earth brought forth her fruits without their aid. They did not know the sorrows of old age, and death to them was like passing away in a calm sleep. After they had gone hence, their spirits were appointed to dwell above the earth, guarding and helping the living.

> The gods next created the Men of Silver, but they could not be compared in virtue and happiness with the men of "the elder age of golden peace." For many years they remained mere children and as soon as they came to the full strength and stature of manhood they refused to do homage to the gods and fell to slaying one another. After death they became the good spirits who live within the earth.

Hesiod

Hesiod was a Greek poet of the eighth century B.C. Along with Homer, he established the mythic background for ancient Greek life. Hesiod was from Boeotia, in central Greece. According to legend, he was a shepherd until the Muses commanded him to write about the gods. In *Works and Days,* Hesiod tells the story of Prometheus, a human hero who steals fire from the gods. This work also gives some details of Hesiod's own life and relates important features of agricultural life. In *The Theogeny,* a more purely religious work, Hesiod relates stories of the creation of the world and describes relations between humans and the gods.

The Men of Bronze followed, springing from ash trees and having hearts which were hard and jealous, so that with them "lust and strife began to gnaw the world." All the works of their hands were wrought in bronze. Through their own inventions they fell from their high estate and from the light they passed away to the dark realm of King Hades [god of the underworld] unhonored and unremembered.

Zeus then placed upon earth the race of the Heroes who fought at Thebes and Troy, and when they came to the end of life the Olympian [Zeus] sent them to happy abodes at the very limits of the earth.

After the Heroes came the Men of Iron—the race of these wild days. Our lot is labor and vexation of spirit by day and night, nor will this cease until the race ends, which will be when the order of nature has been reversed and human affection turned to hatred.[1]

1. Myths are, at least partly, dramatized explanations of important features of the world. Place a check beside each of the following aspects of the world which Hesiod attempts to explain:

   a. The origin of the human race

   b. The beginning of the universe

   c. The origin of spirits who live in the earth

   d. The origin of spirits who help the living

   e. The end of the human race

   f. The development of ancient cities

   g. The discovery of fire

   h. The source of the unhappiness of contemporary life

   i. The changing of the seasons

   j. The origin of an important metal

---

[1] Hesiod, *Theogeny,* trans. Norman O. Brown (New York: Liberal Arts Press, 1953) p. 50.

2. Now, pick any subject from the list above and write an explanation of its origin that most modern people would accept. Include a description of the differences between the mythic explanation and the modern explanation.

Thales became the Father of Philosophy by rejecting mythic thinking and asserting that "All is Water." In other words, water is the One that, somehow, lies behind, unites, the Many.

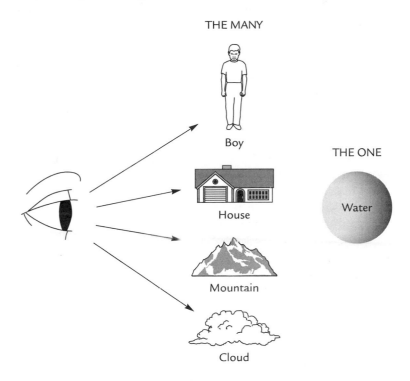

THE MANY

Boy

House

Mountain

Cloud

THE ONE

Water

But how could Water "lie behind" the Many? How could water be the One? What does that mean?

Historians of philosophy have tried to piece together Thales' reasoning. We know that the Greeks believed that there were four basic elements: fire, air, earth, and water. Of these four, water is a good choice for the "most basic." Water occurs in three forms: solid (ice), gas (steam), and liquid. In addition, observation of the processes of the world might have given Thales more evidence that water was the most basic element. A spring might have seemed to Thales like evidence for earth turning into water; water boiling might have seemed like evidence of water turning into air; rain might have seemed like evidence of air turning into water; rain soaking into the ground might have seemed like evidence of water turning into earth. Add to all these reasons the necessity of water to life, and one might begin to see the sources of the first philosopher's reasoning.

If I look out my window and imagine I am Thales, the first philosopher, what would I see? I would see the solution to the problem of the One and the Many.

The Many change: the boy across the street grows older, the clouds shift above Cherokee Peak, the trees lose their leaves. But behind all this change, there is something, a basic substance that doesn't change. As Thales, I would believe that all solids, traced far enough back, must have come from water. Behind the changing Many is the unchanging One, water.

But what is truly important about saying this? Why do we begin our study of philosophy, of metaphysics, with Thales?

The following exercise will give you the answer.

EXERCISE 3.2
Friedrich Nietzsche on Thales

Friedrich Nietzsche, a philosopher we will meet near the end of our tour, presents the following insightful analysis of Thales' importance:

> Greek philosophy seems to begin with an absurd notion, with the proposition that water is the primal origin and the womb of all things. Is it really necessary for us to take serious notice of this proposition? It is, and for three reasons. First, because it [1] tells something about the primal origin of all things; second, because it does so in language devoid of image or fable, and finally, because contained in it, if only embryonically, is the thought, "all things are one." The first reason still leaves Thales in the company of the religious and the superstitious; the second takes him out of such company and shows him as a natural scientist, but the third makes him the first Greek philosopher. Had he said, "water turns into earth" we should have but a scientific hypothesis, a wrong one but difficult to disprove. But he went beyond scientific considerations. By presenting his unity-concept in the form of his water-hypothesis, Thales did not, it is true, overcome the low level of empiric insight prevalent in his time. What he did was to pass over its horizon. The sparse and un-ordered observations of an empirical nature which he made regarding the occurrence and the transformations of water (more specifically, of moisture) would have allowed, much less made advisable, no such gigantic generalization. What drove him to it was a metaphysical conviction which had its origin in a mystic intuition. We meet it in every philosophy, together with the ever-renewed attempts at a more suitable expression, this proposition that "all things are one."[2]

1. " . . . because it [1]" refers to _____?

2. Which of the following are consistent with Nietzsche's analysis of Thales? (You may choose more than one.)

   a. Thales' significance is that his philosophy confirmed the religious view of the "primal origin of all things."

   b. Thales' significance is that he was a natural scientist.

   c. Thales' significance is that he was the first Greek philosopher.

   d. From Thales' view that "All is water," one can deduce that he also held that "All things are one," and that the latter is far more philosophically important than the former.

   e. If Thales had said "water turns into earth," he would not be regarded as the first philosopher.

   f. If Thales had said "water turns into earth," he would not be regarded as the first philosopher because this is a scientific, not a philosophical, statement.

---

[2] Nietzche, Friedrich, *Philosophy In the Tragic Age of the Greeks,* (New York: Regenery Publishing, 1996) p. 75.

g. Thales went beyond science.

h. "All is water" is a "gigantic generalization" that Nietzsche finds foolish.

i. Thales' quest for the source of the unity of all things is the embodiment of what every philosopher tries to do.

3. On your own paper, practice your paraphrasing skills by putting Nietzsche's account of Thales in your own words.

Occasionally in the course of this tour, I'll imagine that you ask me a blunt question. Here is your first.

Question: How could anyone be so stupid as to think that water was the basic substance of the universe? How can a rock be water? How can dust be water?

Answer: It would probably be stupid for anyone in the twentieth century to think water was the basic substance of the universe. But we know enormously more about the universe than Thales did. And just as it would hardly rate a headline if someone today managed to fly an airplane 80 feet off a windy hill, it was a pretty big deal when the Wright Brothers achieved this at Kitty Hawk. The point was not even the distance they flew, but that they got off the ground at all; the Wright Brothers did a kind of thing that had never been done before. The point is not so much what Thales said, but that he said a kind of thing that had never been said before.

As wrong as Thales was, he knew infinitely more than anyone before him. All previous explanations of the universe were story-based (see Box 3.2). Thales' explanation was reason-based. Using your reasoning about the universe to show that Thales' reason-based explanation of the universe was wrong shows how indebted you are to his genius! The kind of reasoning you are using was invented by Thales. Think of that. Thales invented reasoning about the universe. Not even Einstein could make such a claim.

BOX 3.2

Before Philosophy: Stories About the Cosmos

The Babylonian epic *Gilgamesh* and, among other books of the Bible, *Genesis* are two examples of prephilosophical, story-based descriptions of the universe. Two hundred years earlier than Thales, Homer's *Iliad* and *Odyssey* are the prime Greek examples of stories that provide accounts of the universe. In the *Iliad*, Homer describes Zeus, the leader of the gods, as often but not always powerless before Fate, a force that attempts to guide human lives. On the occasions when Zeus is able to control Fate, we have a less philosophical, more mythic portrait of the cosmos; on the occasions when Fate is seen as superior to the will of Zeus, we begin to see a description of the cosmos in impersonal and therefore more philosophical terms. To hold the equivalent of "Fate rules all," as Homer occasionally does, is a step in the direction of Thales' impersonal description of reality, "All is water."

M. C. Escher, *Day and Night*, woodcut, 1938.

SUMMARY

The first philosophical problem, the problem of the One and the Many, was a metaphysical problem because it posed a question about the nature of reality. The first philosophers tried to pierce through the changing aspects of experience to discover what One thing gave the Many unity. Thales, the first philosopher, concluded that the One was water. His observations of natural processes may have given him evidence for his conclusion. Thales is important for the new kind of explanation of the universe he offered, an explanation based on reason, rather than mythology.

EXERCISE 3.3
Looking Back

On your own paper, summarize the important points made about the following questions used as subheads in this chapter.

1. What was the first philosophical problem?

2. What was Thales' solution to the problem of the One and the Many?

EXERCISE 3.4
Looking at the World Through Thales' Eyes

Here is the first of many opportunities on the tour to look out at the world through the eyes of a famous philosopher.

Decide if Thales would answer each of the following True or False and then offer evidence that supports your answer. (Because we know so little of Thales' philosophy, you could offer similar evidence for several of your answers.)

1. T F All of reality is one kind of thing.

    Evidence: _____

    _____

    _____.

2. T F Materialism, the view that all of reality is essentially matter, is
           correct.

    Evidence: _____

    _____

    _____.

3. T F The most accurate view of the cosmos is the oldest view of the
           cosmos.

    Evidence: _____

    _____

    _____.

4. T F Dualism presents a more accurate view of reality than does monism.

    Evidence: _____

    _____

    _____.

5. T F Reality is not what it appears to be.

    Evidence: _____

    _____

    _____.

ANALYSIS OF YOUR PHILOSOPHICAL SELF-PORTRAIT

I've underlined the correct answer to each of the following.

1. <u>T</u> F *The first philosophical statements were metaphysical, rather than ethical
           or epistemological.*

    As you now know, "All is water" is a metaphysical statement—that is, a statement describing the nature of reality. In general, the first philosophers concentrated far more heavily upon metaphysics than any other area of philosophy.

Ethical questions did not come to the fore until Socrates, who lived several generations after Thales. Plato, Socrates' student, was the first philosopher to make an attempt to link metaphysics, ethics, and epistemology into a single coherent account of existence. (It is for this reason, among others, that Plato is considered the first great philosopher.)

2. <u>T</u> F *There is no way to say for certain that any person was the* first *philosopher.*

When historians say Thales was the first philosopher, they mean, naturally enough, that he is the first philosopher we have information about. Nonetheless, cultural historians and anthropologists have studied countless societies at earlier stages of development than Thales' Miletus and found no evidence for blunt statements like his that reject all inherited tradition and give a nonreligious, non-story-based explanation of the cosmos. Thus, even though Thales may not have been absolutely the first philosopher, he was a very rare bird.

3. T <u>F</u> *Because religion came before philosophy, the first recorded philosophical explanation of the universe was religious.*

Not only did Thales offer a new explanation of the universe, but, and this is what is startling about him, he also offered a new *kind* of explanation, an explanation based upon observation and reason rather than mythology. Imagine that someone today announces, "Instead of using human reason to explain the universe, I will use human mumphla to explain the universe." And then it turns out that human mumphla, whatever that is, produces far superior explanations of the universe than do accounts based on human reason. Thales, in other words, mumphled mythology.

4. <u>T</u> F *The earliest philosophers probably rejected rather than supported the views of their society.*

Thales, along with the other early philosophers, presented a view that strongly challenged the beliefs of the masses. Not until we meet Aristotle will we find a philosopher, for better or worse, who makes some attempt to support the views of society and "common sense."

Evaluation: Number of points in agreement with Thales = _____ of 4 possible.

A position of Thales' that you strongly (support, oppose) is

_____

because _____ .

GOOD BOOKS

Barnes, Jonathan. *The Presocratic Philosophers.* Rev. ed. London: Routledge & Kegan Paul, 1982. A good introduction to the early philosophers by a respected scholar.

Burnet, John. *Early Greek Philosophy.* 4th ed. London: Macmillan, 1930. A classic treatment of the first philosophers.

Cornford, F. M. *From Religion to Philosophy.* New York: Harper & Row, 1957. A classic, superbly written account of the development from what this chapter terms "mythic thinking" to early philosophy.

Kirk, G. S., Raven, J. E., and Schofield, M. *The Pre-Socratic Philosophers: A Critical History with a Selection of Texts.* 2nd ed. Cambridge: Cambridge University Press, 1983. An indispensable overview.

NEXT STOP

You meet Heraclitus, who is, for most students, the most mysterious and also the most convincing of the early philosophers.

Solution to Match Wits with Thales, p. 46: To find the height of the Great Pyramid, Thales waits until a time of day when his shadow is equal to his height. He measures the shadow with the stick, and then uses the stick to measure the length of the Great Pyramid's shadow. The pyramid's shadow, if Thales hurries, will be equal to its height.

4

Heraclitus
Breaking the Code of Reality

YOUR PHILOSOPHICAL SELF-PORTRAIT

Heraclitus had a very strong opinion on each of the following statements, but you won't know what his opinion was until you complete this chapter. To compare your thinking with Heraclitus's, decide which of the following are true and which are false. After each answer, offer evidence that supports your position. (Incidentally, simply understanding some of the statements may be as difficult as deciding if they are true or false.)

1. T F You can't step into the same river twice.
    Evidence: _____
    _____.

2. T F All is Change.
    Evidence: _____
    _____.

3. T F The way up and the way down are the same.
    Evidence: _____
    _____.

4. T F Day and night are one.
    Evidence: _____
    _____.

5. T F Almost everyone is a fool.
    Evidence: _____
    _____.

6. T F The universe had neither beginning nor end.
    Evidence: _____
    _____.

7. T F There is no One that unifies the Many.
    Evidence: _____
    _____.

Examining a simple universe of numbers helps us understand the problem and goal of the first philosophers.

Heraclitus opposes Thales' solution to the problem of the One and the Many by emphasizing ceaseless change and the power of the Logos, the deep, ordering pattern of reality. According to Heraclitus, the mass of people, even including the "wise," take a partial view of reality and do not understand that opposites are identities and that "strife" on both a human and cosmic scale is a necessary feature of existence.

Look at this series of numbers:

2, 4, 6, 8, 10, . . .

What is the next number?

"It is _____."

In order to predict the next number in the series, you had to identify the hidden principle that produced the numbers. The hidden principle in the series could be stated as "to get the next number, add two to the preceding number" or "count by twos."

Think of the number series as a little universe. The series of numbers is like the Many; the hidden principle is like the One that produces the Many. In our number universe, nothing happens except counting by twos.

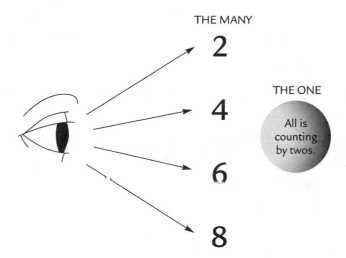

What you had to do to solve the problem of the number series was to look through the Many and find the hidden One. In other words, you had to think like the first philosophers.

Once you understood the One, the hidden principle, you knew all about the number universe. You could predict not only the next event, but also the next

Heraclitus (c. 540–470 B.C.)

Little is known about Heraclitus's life. We do know that he was born in Ephesus in Ionia on the shores of what is now Turkey. Ephesus at the time was a major Greek seaport and home to the temple of Artemis—one of the seven wonders of the ancient world. It was also in Ephesus that the apostle Paul, several centuries later, established one of the first churches.

According to legend, Heraclitus was a descendent of the earlier kings of Ephesus. Although he was of noble birth, Heraclitus chose instead to live the life of a recluse, giving up his family wealth to his younger brother.

Despite his preference for the simple life, Heraclitus believed in the rule of the aristocracy and had acid contempt for democracy as well as for other philosophers, politicians, and poets. In his estimation, very few of the other Greek philosophers had wisdom, including such notables as Xenophanes and Pythagoras, whose philosophical inquiries he referred to as "an art of mischief." [2] The feeling of dislike was appar-

A group of citizens once encountered Heraclitus playing dice with children. When they asked why he spent his time playing games, Heraclitus snapped, "Why are you surprised, you wretches? Isn't it better to do this than playing politics with you?" [1] Apparently a man of haughty temperament, Heraclitus was aloof and contemptuous of the masses. His disgust with what he saw as the stupidity of his fellow citizens gave rise to the fable of Heraclitus as the "weeping philosopher."

[1] Story from Diogenes Laertius, *Lives of Eminent Philosophers*, IX.3.

[2] Quotes from "Fragments" of Heraclitus in Dagobert D. Runes, *Treasury of Philosophy* (New York: Philosophical Library, 1955), pp. 495–502.

thousand events. Your knowledge was complete, entire, perfect—godlike. The first philosophers, like most philosophers after them, sought the same kind of knowledge.

In this chapter, we'll explore the views of Heraclitus, which are, for many introduction to philosophy students, both mysterious and fascinating. I'll answer the following questions:

- How did Heraclitus view reality?
- What is (and isn't) the Logos?
- How can "the way up and the way down" be the same?
- How can day and night be "one"?
- What does Heraclitus mean by "strife"?
- What are two views of the Many?

Heraclitus (continued)

ently mutual; his reputation among his fellow philosophers seems to have been strongly unfavorable.

Hermodorus, one of Heraclitus's teachers, was one of the few philosophers who was not a target of his constant barbs. When Heraclitus's fellow Ephesians put Hermodorus on trial for corrupting the youth and raising questions about the gods, Heraclitus declared, "The Ephesians would do well to hang themselves, every adult man, and bequeath their city-state to adolescents."

Heraclitus was one of the first to question the validity of the senses, arguing that we can be deceived by appearance. "Eyes and ears," he wrote, "are bad witnesses to men." Heraclitus instead emphasized the unity that underlies the physical world of change. "The one wise thing," Heraclitus wrote, "is to know the plan which steers all things through all things." This "plan" is the universal reason, or *Logos*. Though Heraclitus believed that the Logos was universally accessible, he was also an elitist who believed that the vast majority of people live in ignorance and are unaware of the Logos.

Heraclitus also noted that the world is constantly changing. One of his most famous aphorisms, rephrased by Plato, is "You can't step into the same river twice." As you will soon learn, Heraclitus was making a point not only about rivers, but also about the universe.

Heraclitus also held that "strife" is a necessary feature of existence. "It should be understood that war is the common condition, that strife is justice, and that all things come to pass through the compulsion of strife. . . . The thunderbolt pilots all things."

Heraclitus wrote at least one book, *On Nature*, fragments of which have survived mainly in the form of quotations by Plato, Aristotle, and other ancient philosophers. He wrote in an enigmatic, cryptic style that earned him the nicknames "the Obscure" and "the Riddler." The concept of a logos was later adopted in Christian philosophy to mean the word of God. Heraclitus's view that "All is Change" was strongly rejected by Plato and vastly elaborated upon by Aristotle. The nature and riddle of change, which Heraclitus was the first philosopher to emphasize, puzzles thinkers to this day.

How Did Heraclitus View Reality?

Just like Thales, Heraclitus of Ephesus tried to solve the problem of the One and the Many. But, as you might expect, when Heraclitus looked through the Many, he did not find water.

Plato paraphrased Heraclitus and provides us with the most famous summary of Heraclitus's philosophy:

You cannot step into the same river twice.

Heraclitus is telling us something about rivers in order to tell us something about reality. But first, what is he telling us about rivers?

What does it mean to say you cannot step into the same river twice? I step into the Mississippi today; tomorrow I step into the Mississippi again. Heraclitus's original version of this saying provides a clue:

You cannot step twice into the same river, for other waters are continually flowing on.

Thus, from Heraclitus's point of view, today's Mississippi is not tomorrow's Mississippi, or even the next instant's Mississippi. Every instant "other waters are continually flowing on." The Mississippi at noon is a completely different river from the Mississippi at one second past noon.

Do you agree?

I believe Heraclitus is (right, wrong) because _____

_____.

If you think about it, you will see that Heraclitus was not just talking about rivers. We could expand his saying:

- You can't write twice on the same desk.
- You can't pet the same dog twice.
- You can't look in the mirror at the same face twice.
- You can't walk twice under the same starry sky.

Or?

Or _____.

Or _____.

Or _____.

Whereas according to Heraclitus, the One is change, according to Thales, the One

is _____.

According to Heraclitus, All is Change. Change is the One which lies behind and unifies the Many.

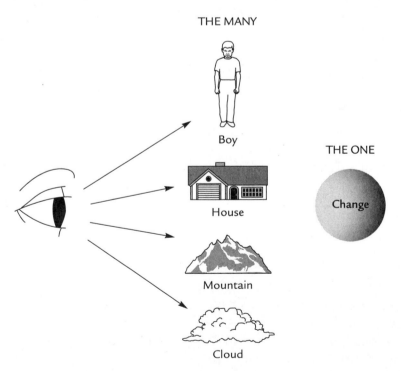

THE MANY

Boy

House

Mountain

Cloud

THE ONE

Change

Looking out my window through Heraclitus's eyes, I see double.

First, I see the boy across the street as part of the Many. But, following Heraclitus, when I look at the boy more deeply, I pierce through his visual appearance and understand that he is in the process of changing. I see he is a river of boyness, changing so fast that every glance contemplates a new individual. Or rather, I don't actually see this, but I understand this.

Heraclitus urges us to go beyond our seeing. We visually see the Mississippi or any other apparently stable part of the Many; but thinking more deeply about what we see, we understand that there is no stability and that every instant a new river is born inside the old river. I look at the boy and, despite what I see, understand that every instant he is a different person.

So, try out Heraclitus's way of interpreting the world.

I look at _____ and visually see _____

_____

_____.

But when I think more deeply about what I see, I understand _____

_____

_____

_____.

I look out my window again. I understand that every moment the boy's house makes itself into a different house. Cherokee Peak is not Cherokee Peak; it is Cherokee Peaks. The lamppost is one lamppost after another. The stable is the unstable. Only the slowly changing clouds give me any visual clue to their real nature. Unlike the boy, his house, or Cherokee Peak, I can actually observe the clouds constantly changing. The slow changes I see in the clouds point me toward the rapid changes everywhere else that I cannot see.

Looking at one cloud in the eastern sky, I watch it shift from a parrot to a locomotive. The cloud is really more like a verb than a noun, more an activity than an object. From Heraclitus's point of view, the cloud is not a cloud, but cloud-ing. Across the street is boy-ing, house-ing, and on the horizon, Cherokee Peak-ing. Everything in the universe is constantly shifting, changing shape. I look out my window and, seeing through Heraclitus's eyes, I see All All-ing.

Heraclitus believed that he had cracked the code of the universe. Just as "counting by twos" was the hidden principle that produced our number universe, Heraclitus held that Change was the hidden principle that produced the Many.

What Is (and Isn't) the Logos?

Heraclitus had a good deal more to say about the One than that it was Change. Here is what many scholars believe is the opening of his only book:

> Although this Logos is eternally valid, yet men are unable to understand it— not only before hearing it, but even after they have heard it for the first time. That is to say, although all things come to pass in accordance with this Logos, men seem to be quite without any experience of it—at least if they are judged in the light of such words and deeds as I am here setting forth.

What Is Logos?

Logos is an important word for philosophers other than Heraclitus, but unfortunately its meaning varies. For Plato, *logos* refers to the rational element in the human soul; for Stoic philosophers *logos spermatikos* was the source of cosmic order; for Christian thinkers *Logos* refers generally to the word of God and specifically in the New Testament to Christ. As the suffix "logy," *logos* survives in many modern words with the meaning "the study of." Thus, geology is the study of the earth (geos: earth); psychology is the study of the human mind (psyche: mind); embryology is the study of embryos. You are now engaged in Heraclitusology.

The key word here is *Logos;* but, unfortunately, scholars cannot decide exactly what Heraclitus meant (see Box 4.1). *Logos* is Greek for "word," but it has connotations, among others, of "pattern," "order," and "principle." For the purposes of our tour, we will take "ordering pattern" as a synonym for Heraclitus's Logos.

First, let's try to say what Heraclitus's Logos, his ordering pattern, is not.

A blueprint is the pattern of a building, but it is not an ordering pattern. The blueprint does not control the actual construction and functioning of the building. In the same sense, one could say that the U.S. Constitution was the pattern of our government but not the ordering pattern. The Constitution provides the underlying design for how the government *ought* to function, but the Constitution has no power over the *actual* functioning of the government. The Constitution is just paper, a set of powerless, printed concepts. Thus, the Logos is not like a blueprint or a set of principles such as the Constitution, because though these things provide a pattern, they have no power over what they provide a pattern for. And there is no doubt that one feature of the Logos is its power; as Heraclitus says, "all things come to pass in accordance with this Logos."

A better example than a blueprint or the Constitution of an ordering pattern is a computer program. Take the word processor that I write with. The word processor's computer code not only sets forth the features of the program but also guides its functioning. The word processor can do nothing but follow the ordering pattern, the Logos, of its program. In fact, if the computer hardware is in good working order, it is impossible for me, while typing on the keyboard, to violate the ordering pattern of the word processor. The word processor controls all the possibilities of what appears on the screen; its Logos is a powerful and complete ordering pattern.

Our genetic code is another good example of Logos. At birth, everything from the color of our hair to the size of our toes is a product of our genetic code. To be a human baby is to be a product of the ordering pattern of the human genetic Logos.

Thus, Heraclitus's Logos is something like the computer program of the universe, the genetic code of the universe, an ordering pattern that underlies the Many and absolutely controls all that exists.

Putting this together with what we learned about Heraclitus's views by analyzing his river epigram, we have a somewhat more detailed picture of his metaphysics, his portrait of reality. Heraclitus is not simply saying that all things change, but also that there is a hidden principle, an ordering pattern, that absolutely controls the way all things change. Change is not random, but deeply structured. Beneath the chaos of the Many is a deep ordering principle that controls change in a powerful way. According to Heraclitus, the universe has a Logos, a hidden program, which orchestrates all its transformations. The river epigram draws our attention to the fact of ceaseless change; the concept of Logos points us toward the ordering principle that guides ceaseless change.

What do you understand about Heraclitus thus far?

The most important points are _____

_____.

We can now improve our earlier portrait of Heraclitus's metaphysics. The One is not just Change but the Logos of Change. The Many, according to Heraclitus's epigram about the river, has the appearance of stability but is actually unstable.

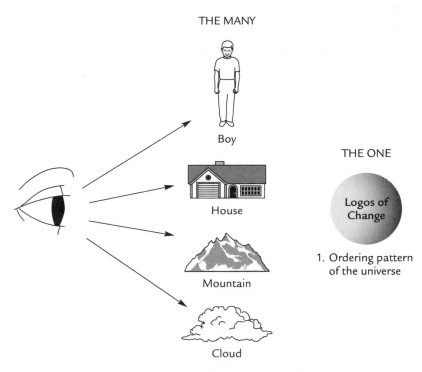

THE MANY

Boy

House

Mountain

Cloud

apparent stability—actual instability

THE ONE

Logos of Change

1. Ordering pattern of the universe

How Can "the Way Up and the Way Down" Be the Same?

To add more details to Heraclitus's view of reality, look again at the opening statement of Heraclitus's book (emphasis added):

Although this Logos is eternally valid, yet men are unable to understand it—not only before hearing it, but even after they have heard it for the first time. That is to say, although all things come to pass in accordance with this Logos, *men seem to be quite without any experience of it—at least if they are judged in the light of such words and deeds as I am here setting forth.*

Heraclitus is talking not only about the Logos, but also about humanity's ignorance of the Logos. If Heraclitus were saying only that all things change, then why does he believe such a concept is hard to grasp? What is so mysterious about change that Heraclitus believed that "men are unable to understand it"? The mystery must be involved with the way things change, with the way the Logos operates. Certainly, the way a computer program controls the changes we see on the screen or, more so, the way human genetic code controls the changes in our body is quite mysterious.

Here are three more sayings that may help us understand the mysterious ways of the Logos of Change:

1. The way up and the way down are one and the same.
2. Hesiod, whom so many accept as their wise teacher, did not even understand the nature of day and night; for they are one.
3. It should be understood that war is the common condition, that strife is justice, and that all things come to pass through the compulsion of strife.

Let's take these individually. Each of these statements will tell us something about the universe and its Logos, the Many and the One.

First, what does it mean to say that "the way up and the way down are one and the same"? It means that things are not the way we think they are. We believe that "the way up" and "the way down" are opposites. But Heraclitus claims they are identical. To get a clearer idea of what he is saying, let's expand the saying:

- The way in and the way out are the same.
- The way East and the way West are the same.
- The way left and the way right are the same.

Or, in a similar spirit:

- The hot and the cold are the same.
- The weak and the strong are the same.

Or?

Heraclitus is claiming that, from his point of view, opposites are identical. How can this be?

There is a sense in which opposites are the same. If I go from Los Angeles "up" to San Francisco, I travel on highway 5. If I go "down" from San Francisco to Los Angeles, I travel the same highway. The way up and the way down, on any road, travel the same route. If I go in the front door, or if I go out of the front door, I travel the same path.

Heraclitus's point seems to be that from one frame of reference, our normal point of view, we see opposing things, we see differences, "up" and "down" as opposites. But from a truer point of view, we would see the unification, the identification of opposites, "up" and "down" as the same. From "our side," the Many seems to be made up of opposing pairs; from the side of the One, opposing pairs vanish, are identical. If all I do is travel highway 5 from Los Angeles to San Francisco and back again, I will think of "up" and "down" as opposites. However, if I take a more objective, godlike view and look down at highway 5 on a map, then I see that opposite directions, in fact, are nothing but journeys on the same route. Heraclitus is providing us with a map of reality. When we look, through his eyes, at the opposing Many, we see they are the unified One.

How Can Day and Night Be "One"?

Our interpretation seems to be reinforced by the second epigram.

> Hesiod, whom so many accept as their wise teacher, did not even understand the nature of day and night; for they are one.

Hesiod, according to Heraclitus, does not understand the identity of opposites. Hesiod takes the point of view of daily life; day is one thing, and night is another. Day is bright and night is dark; day is one time period and night is another time period. But, Heraclitus might say, though day and night are two different time periods, they are still part of the same time, still part of ceaseless change, the ordering pattern of the Logos. Day and night are halves of the same circle. In a similar vein he points out,

> In the circle the beginning and end are common.

What Does Heraclitus Mean by "Strife"?

Now, let's look at the third epigram:

> It should be understood that war is the common condition, that strife is justice, and that all things come to pass through the compulsion of strife.

This will be a bit clearer if we combine it with a statement Heraclitus made about Homer.

> Homer was wrong in saying, "Would that strife might perish from amongst gods and men." For if that were to occur, then all things would cease to exist.

VANTAGE POINT

Homer

Homer was a Greek of the eighth-century B.C., and one of the world's great poets. In the *Iliad*, Homer describes the conclusion of a long war between the Greeks and the Trojans. In the *Odyssey*, Homer narrates the adventures of Odysseus on his return home from the war. Achilles' unjust wrath against his fellow Greeks is a central element of the *Iliad*; Odysseus's cunning and foolish pride are central elements of the *Odyssey*. In both tales, Homer describes heroic virtues and failings, the life of the gods, and the relations between gods and men, all in the context of the norms and values of his own warrior culture.

Once more, Heraclitus is criticizing our commonsense point of view (which, according to him, is shared even by a great poet like Homer). From "our side" of the Many, strife is the opposite of justice; strife is something that should not happen; strife is evil. But Heraclitus claims a more enlightened view. He says that strife is the same as justice; strife *is* justice; strife is good, so good that without it "all things would cease to exist." What can this mean?

If all things, and not just all men and gods, would cease to exist without strife, then Heraclitus must be talking about some kind of strife other than war and human violence. Strife must be part of some kind of universal process, a process that sustains all that exists. Strife, therefore, must be part of the "ordering pattern" of the Logos.

In other sayings, Heraclitus adds details to his picture of cosmic strife:

> Fire lives in the death of earth, air in the death of fire, water in the death of air, and earth in the death of water.
>
> The thunderbolt pilots all things.
>
> It throws apart and then brings together again; it advances and retires.

The ordering pattern of the Logos is not only necessary to all existence but also full of violence. Heraclitus's universe is not a peaceful world ruled by a benevolent God or one where, like a great clock, mechanical events plod after each other. "Thunderbolt pilots all." The universe is a violent, strife-filled crashing together of extremes. But isn't that something like the view we began with? The Mississippi constantly unmakes itself. Every instant the entire universe is torn down and rebuilt.

M. C. Escher, *Print Gallery*, lithograph, 1956.

ILLUSTRATION QUIZ

Thinking Like the First Philosophers

Thales, Heraclitus, and the other early philosophers, as you now know, sought the One that unifies the Many. They were trying to detect a hidden principle, a hidden design, that both ordered and controlled the apparent confusion of the world. The problem of finding this hidden design can be clarified by examining Escher's "The Print Gallery." Look closely at this strange work. Note that the boy on the left side is *inside* the work of art he stares at! The frame of a picture in the print gallery swirls open to include everything in the world outside the frame. Escher based the entire work upon a hidden geometric design. To detect this design, try to see how the swirling curves in the etching are related. Find the repeated curves and trace them with your pencil. Note that as you attempt to do this, you must look past the many different figures to find a deeper unity. You must, like the first philosophers, find the hidden One that orders and controls the Many.

If you have a difficult time finding the design that orders the etching—and you probably will—then contemplate the difficulty of the task faced by the first philosophers (and most after them) of finding the hidden design that orders the universe. (The design that Escher used is on page 72.)

What Are Two Views of the Many?

Heraclitus is pointing out the difference between a partial and an inclusive perspective of reality. From his point of view, the masses of people take the partial perspective. The Many appear to be stable; today's Mississippi is tomorrow's Mississippi; up is one direction, and down is another; opposites are opposites; night and day are polarities. However, there is another perspective, very rare from Heraclitus's point of view. Even the wisest, like Hesiod and Homer, don't understand reality. The inclusive perspective sees the big picture, sees beyond the Many to the One. From the inclusive perspective, which understands the nature of the Logos, the Mississippi is destroyed and re-created every instant; up and down are welded into identities; opposite things are the same things; All is, paradoxically, well-ordered strife.

But how can we cling to this inclusive perspective, so different from our ordinary view? Heraclitus provides a simple but powerful metaphor to sum up the essence of the reality:

> There is exchange of all things for fire and of fire for all things; as there is gold for wares and wares for gold.
>
> This universe, which is the same for all, has not been made by any god or man, but it always has been, is, and will be—an ever-living fire, kindling itself by regular measures and going out by regular measures.
>
> All is Fire.

In fire we can see the orderly rage that characterizes Heraclitus's reality. Fire changes all things into itself and all things can change into fire. An eternal fire, one that "always has been, is, and will be," continuously lives in the destruction and re-creation of all things. Looking through Heraclitus's eyes, we see the cosmic blaze that kindles itself in the constant, strife-filled remaking of the universe.

Putting all this together, we can now add several more details to our model of Heraclitus's view of reality. (Remember that by the Many, we don't just mean boys, houses, mountains, and clouds, but everything in the universe—everything from aardvarks to xylophones.) Heraclitus presents us with two views of the Many. The mass of people (including even the "wise" like Hesiod and Homer) take the partial view of the Many and see a world of stability, opposites as opposites, and strife as "unjust." However, the true view of the Many, presented by Heraclitus, is inclusive: The Many are ceaselessly changing and, hence, unstable; opposites are identities; and strife, the ceaseless clashing together of extremes, is "just"—that is, necessary to the continued existence of the universe. The Logos of Change, the hidden ordering pattern of the universe, can be understood as an eternal, self-kindling fire.

Note that we can even add a time line to our model; Heraclitus holds that the cosmic Fire had no beginning and will never go out.

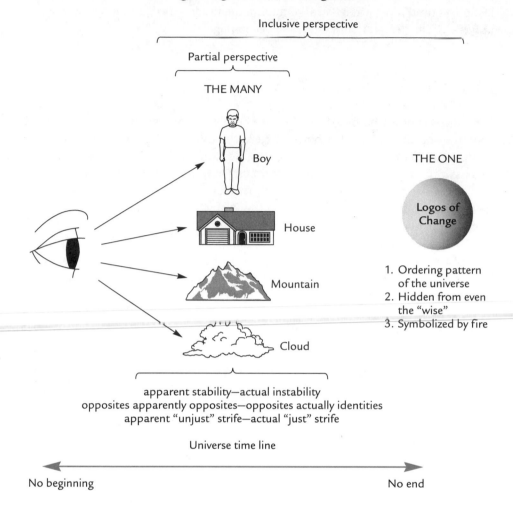

SUMMARY

Numbers in an ordered series are like the Many; the principle that produces the numbers is like the One. When we perceive the One behind the Many in an ordered series of numbers, we are mimicking the kind of thinking the first philosophers did (on a far larger scale) when they tried to perceive the One behind the many parts of reality. Heraclitus held that the One was the Logos of ceaseless change; opposites are identities; strife is necessary to the continued existence of the cosmos. Fire is Heraclitus's symbol for the violent (though orderly) transformations of the universe.

EXERCISE 4.1
Looking Back

On your own paper, practice your paraphrasing skills by answering each of the following questions:

1. How did Heraclitus view reality?

2. What is (and isn't) the Logos?

3. How can "the way up and the way down" be the same?

4. How can day and night be "one"?

5. What are two views of the Many? (Include a description of the difference between a partial and an inclusive view of reality.)

EXERCISE 4.2
Looking at the World Through Heraclitus's Eyes

How would Heraclitus answer each of the following? Include evidence from this chapter to support your answer.

1. T   F   Reality is not what it appears to be.

Evidence: _____

_____

_____.

2. T   F   We should abide by the beliefs of the majority.

Evidence: _____

_____

_____.

3. T   F   One opinion is just as good as another.

Evidence: _____

_____

_____.

4. T   F   The only unchanging thing is Change.

Evidence: _____

_____

_____.

5. T   F   The truly wise are enemies of society.

Evidence: _____

_____

_____.

6. T   F   The Many are the Many.

Evidence: _____

_____

_____.

EXERCISE 4.3
The Heraclitus Riddle

Here is a very challenging puzzle that will give you experience in thinking like a historian of philosophy. All that we know of Heraclitus comes from fragments of his philosophy quoted by others, sometimes centuries after his death. Everyone who tries to understand Heraclitus faces the same puzzle—how to put together the bits and pieces into a sensible whole. Philip Wheelwright, one of the foremost Heraclitus's scholars, divided the fragments below into the following groups. (The numbers in parentheses identify how many fragments fit in a group.)

A. The Way of Inquiry (5 fragments) [An "inquiry" is a close, careful examination.]

B. Universal Flux (3 fragments) [A synonym for "flux" is "change."]

C. The Processes of Nature (2 fragments)

D. In Religious Perspective (2 fragments)

E. Man Among Men (4 fragments)

F. **Relativity** and **Paradox** (4 fragments)

G. The Hidden Harmony (3 fragments)

Of course, I have scrambled their order. Label each of the following A, B, C, D, E, F, G. One good strategy is to begin by picking a large group, like A, which has five fragments, and find a few fragments that seem to share a common topic (in the case of A, The Way of Inquiry). Work from the obvious to the less obvious.

1. War is both father and king of all; some he has shown forth as gods and others as men, some he has made slaves and others free.

2. The Ephesians had better go hang themselves, every man of them, and leave their city to be governed by youngsters, for they have banished Hermadorus, the finest man among them, declaring: "Let us not have anyone amongst us who excels the rest; if there should be such a one, let him go and live elsewhere."

3. The sun is new each day.

4. Much learning does not teach understanding.

5. Although intimately connected with the Logos, men keep setting themselves against it.

6. Nature loves to hide.

7. Cool things become warm, the warm grows cool; the moist dries, the parched becomes moist.

8. The hidden harmony is better than the obvious.

9. Into the same rivers we step and we do not step.

10. Every beast is driven to pasture by a blow.

11. Seekers after gold dig up much earth and find little.

12. To me one man is worth ten thousand if he is first-rate.

13. They pray to images, much as if they should talk to houses; for they do not know the nature of gods and heroes.

14. To God all things are beautiful, good, and right; men, on the other hand, deem some things right and others wrong.

15. Wisdom is one—to know the intelligence by which all things are steered through all things.

16. The best of men choose one thing in preference to all else, immortal glory in preference to mortal goods; whereas the masses simply glut themselves like cattle.

17. Listening not to me but to the Logos, it is wise to acknowledge that all things are one.

18. What mental grasp have they, what sense have they? They believe the tales of the poets and follow the crowd as their teachers, ignoring the adage that the many are bad, the good are few.

19. To be temperate is the greatest virtue; Wisdom consists in speaking and acting the truth, giving heed to the nature of things.

20. Opposition brings concord. Out of discord comes the fairest harmony.

21. It is in changing that things find repose.

22. Donkeys would prefer straw to gold.

23. The things of which there can be sight, hearing, and learning—these are what I especially prize.

EXERCISE 4.4
Writing About Heraclitus

Explain and offer an example for the following fragments in exercise 4.3: 4, 5, 6, 8, 9, 10, 11, 12, 13, 14, 20, 21, 22. For example, for fragment 3, "The sun is new each day," you might write the following:

Explanation: According to a partial perspective of reality, every day the sun is the same sun. But according to a more inclusive perspective of reality, the sun is "new each day" because the sun, like everything else, is constantly changing.

Example: One could also say, "the earth is new each day" or "I am new each day."

ANALYSIS OF YOUR PHILOSOPHICAL SELF-PORTRAIT

I've underlined Heraclitus's answers; circle the answers that you believe are correct.

1. T F *You can't step into the same river twice.*

   As you now know, answering this question true puts you, at least to some degree, in the same camp as Heraclitus (especially if, when you answered this question, you realized that it was not merely describing rivers).

2. T F *All is Change.*

   If you answer both 1 and 2 true or both 1 and 2 false, give yourself a point for philosophical consistency. Question 2 is simply a more general version of question 1. Of course, answering both 1 and 2 true means that, at the start of this section, you had a strong disposition to see reality from Heraclitus's point of view. I hope that my description of his position did nothing to blunt your enthusiasm.

3. T F *The way up and the way down are the same.*

   If you answered this true, you're as bizarre as Heraclitus. You might consider starting a Heraclitus fan club. It's possible you'll be the only member, which is perfectly consistent with Heraclitus's view of the foolish masses.

relativity If X is "relative" to Y, then X is closely related to Y. Thus, one could say that your weight is relative to the amount you eat, because body weight is closely related to food consumption.

paradox An apparently contradictory statement that is, nonetheless, presented as a truth. For example, when Socrates claims that he "knows that he knows nothing" this is a paradox, because Socrates is presenting as a truth the contradictory statement that his knowledge involves the absence of knowledge.

4. <u>T</u> F *Day and night are one.*

Again, holding that this is true makes you a Heraclitean. From your point of view, you are you and not you.

5. <u>T</u> F *Almost everyone is a fool.*

There is no doubt that Heraclitus had a low opinion of the wisdom of almost everyone, including "the wise." If you answered this true, you could agree with Heraclitus's opinion of humanity and also hold a dim view of Heraclitus's intelligence because he was merely "wise."

6. <u>T</u> F *The universe had neither beginning nor end.*

Heraclitus is not the only philosopher to believe this, but the first to state it.

7. T <u>F</u> *There is no One that unifies the Many.*

Answering true to this statement puts you at odds with Heraclitus and most of the other philosophers before Socrates (which is all right—Plato and Aristotle, to name only two of many philosophical giants, would agree with you). Answering true also makes you either a dualist (all of reality is divided into two parts), a pluralist (all of reality is divided into many parts), or a (confused) skeptic (no knowledge is possible about reality). Holding the latter skeptical position means you, in effect, believe no knowledge about reality is possible except the knowledge that there is no One that unifies the Many—which is quite a lot of knowledge about reality. Clean up your skeptical act!

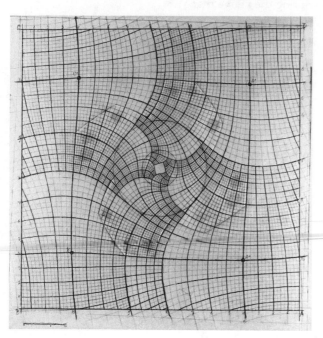

M. C. Escher, Grid for *Print Gallery*.

Evaluation: Number of points in agreement with Heraclitus = _____ of 7 possible.

A position of Heraclitus's that you strongly (support, oppose) is

_____

because _____.

GOOD BOOKS

Edwards, Paul, editor. *The Encyclopedia of Philosophy.* New York: Macmillan & Free Press, 1967. Look up the entry on Heraclitus.

Wheelwright, Philip. *Heraclitus.* Princeton, N.J.: Princeton University Press, 1959. The standard work on Heraclitus, brief and superbly written. Contains an analysis of all the known fragments of Heraclitus.

NEXT STOP

Get ready for Parmenides, Heraclitus's polar opposite.

5

Parmenides
What Is That Mysterious X Stuff?

YOUR PHILOSOPHICAL SELF-PORTRAIT

Circle what you believe is the correct answer to the questions below and offer evidence supporting your view.

1. T   F   If there is a One that unifies the Many, then it must have characteristics very unlike those of the Many.

    Evidence: _____

    _____.

2. T   F   Our senses deceive us about the nature of reality far more often than they tell us the truth.

    Evidence: _____

    _____.

3. T   F: All that is real changes.

    Evidence: _____

    _____.

4. T   F   For an object to change into another object, the first object must cease to exist.

    Evidence: _____

    _____.

5. T   F   All that is real is eternal.

    Evidence: _____

    _____.

Parmenides' solution to the problem of the One and the Many is that the One is unchanging and hidden behind the illusion of the changing Many.

Parmenides argues that change is an illusion because any change, from any X to any Y, involves the impossibility of X passing into the state of nonexistence. Parmenides also argues that since the One isn't changing, it must be eternal. Finally, since there is "no nothing" to divide the One, the One must be undivided.

Parmenides of Elea made one of the most astonishing claims in the history of philosophy: All change is an illusion.

A boy grows into a man; a house slowly ages; a cloud changes shape; a mountain erodes away into a hill. All of these are examples of change; and, according to Parmenides, they are all illusions!

Parmenides is obviously on the opposite side of the fence from Heraclitus. The One, for Heraclitus, is constant flux, constant change. There is no stability, no permanence. According to Heraclitus, every time you step into the Mississippi, it's a new river. Parmenides, however, disagrees completely. Not only isn't the Mississippi constantly changing, but it isn't even there!

You might be surprised to learn that most scientists also believe that all we see is an illusion. Physicists, for reasons other than those of Parmenides, tell us that matter only appears to be solid but is actually mostly empty space. This apparently solid book that you are holding in your hand, from the standpoint of modern physics, is mostly the nonsolid space between its molecules. You may ask then, if this book is mostly empty space, why can't you poke your finger through it? If you tried to drive a bulldozer through a forest, you might not notice all the empty space between the trees. If you try to poke a big thing like your finger through your book, you wouldn't notice all the empty space between the molecules.

Thus, you should not be completely shocked when Parmenides argues that all you see with your senses is an illusion. But unlike modern physics, the reality Parmenides sees behind the illusion of the sense world is not swirling molecules. Reality is not the buzzing activity of atomic particles but, interestingly enough, almost the exact opposite, a motionless, undivided, unchanging entity that Parmenides simply refers to as "What Is."

Students almost always look baffled when I say reality for Parmenides is "What Is." Parmenides also calls it Being. When I mention that, not a single face lights up. Neither "What Is" nor "Being" helps beginners in philosophy understand what on earth Parmenides is talking about. Until further notice, we'll just call reality as Parmenides sees it "The Mysterious X Stuff."

Thus, Parmenides' solution to the problem of the One and the Many is that the changing, divided, impermanent Many are an illusion; reality is really The Mysterious X Stuff.

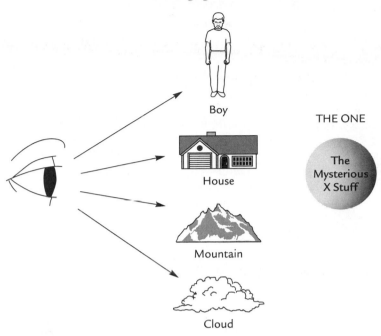

The Changing MANY = Illusion!

Boy

House

Mountain

Cloud

THE ONE

The Mysterious X Stuff

To explore Parmenides, I'll answer the following questions:

- What is an illusion?
- What is Parmenides' argument that change is an illusion?
- What is that Mysterious X Stuff?

What Is an Illusion?

Before investigating Parmenides' intriguing argument that the Many are an illusion, we need to first understand what it means to say that *anything* is an illusion.

An illusion is something that appears to be real but isn't. Here are several examples:

- A lake appears to shimmer in the desert but is only a mirage.
- A magician appears to saw a lady in half, but the saw never passes through her body.
- Railroad tracks appear to come to a point on the horizon but actually never touch.
- A straight spoon appears bent in a glass of water.
- A painting like the *Last Supper* appears to have depth but is only paint on flat canvas.
- The sun appears to move across the sky.
- In the movie *Jurassic Park,* computer-generated colored shapes appear to be dinosaurs.

Parmenides (c. 515–456 B.C.)

Very little is known about the life of Parmenides except that he was a native of Elea in southern Italy. According to ancient tradition, he was born into a life of wealth and luxury and enjoyed an early life of sensual pleasure.

Parmenides may have lived part of his adult life in Athens, a hub of philosophical activity. After joining a Pythagorean brotherhood, Parmenides came to see the futility of wealth and his feverish pursuit of revelry.

Parmenides eventually settled in his native town of Elea, where he founded what has come to be known as the Eleatic school of philosophy. Zeno of Elea (see Chapter 6) was one of his noteworthy students. One of the leading citizens of Elea, Parmenides is reputed to have drawn up laws for his native city. He also continued to travel and share ideas with other great thinkers of the time. In his dialogue *Parmenides,* Plato tells of a meeting between the elderly Parmenides and Socrates, who was described as "very young." Parmenides presents complex and finally devastating arguments against key elements in Plato's metaphysics. The dialogue, though probably imaginary, is a significant tribute to Parmenides.

The encounter is the only occasion in Plato's works where Socrates loses an argument. More intriguing is that Plato puts into Parmenides' mouth an attack on his (Plato's) own central doctrines. This marks perhaps the only occasion in the history of philosophy where a philosopher presents an unanswered refutation of his own position. Whatever Plato's purpose (thought experiment? self-criticism?), the dialogue indicates his high esteem for Parmenides.

At the core of Parmenides' philosophy is a twin conception that Plato must have found very attractive: The world of the senses is an illusion; reality, which cannot be known by the senses, is unchanging and divine. Unlike Plato, however, Parmenides held that the unseen reality was a single unified whole that he termed "Being" or "What Is." You'll discover the odd, even startling, ramifications of Parmenides' view in this and the next chapter.

All that remain of Parmenides' writings are 160 lines of a poem he wrote in honor of his student Zeno. The poem describes a journey through darkness to light in which the Goddess of Wisdom appears to him. She tells him of "both the unshakable heart of well-rounded Truth, and the beliefs of mortals, in which there is no true reliability"—and instructs him in how to discover the Truth about reality.[1] It has been suggested that in writing this poem Parmenides was a mystic or was claiming to have received a divine revelation. However, it is more likely that Parmenides wrote the poem simply to give his philosophy greater authority by putting it into the mouth of a goddess.

---

[1] Quoted from Parmenides' poem in Paul Edwards, editor, *The Encyclopedia of Philosophy* (New York: Macmillan, 1967), p. 49.

Now add a few examples of your own.

_____

_____

_____

_____ .

As you can probably see, all illusions have two common characteristics: appearance and actuality. The lake appears to be in the desert but is actually shimmering sand. The dinosaurs in *Jurassic Park* appear real, but they're actually computer-generated fictions.

In all cases of illusion, appearance hides actuality. Appearance is what we see first; actuality is what is covered up. Appearance takes us in and deceives our senses. Actuality lies behind and is masked by appearance. The apparent shimmering lake keeps us from seeing the actual desert sand.

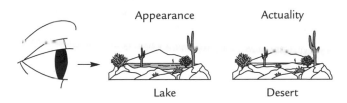

All change, from Parmenides' point of view, is the case of appearance hiding actuality. Things appear to change from A to B, but actually don't. All change is a mirage!

According to Parmenides, snow melting into water is a mirage, an illusion. A puppy growing into a dog is a mirage, an illusion. A pencil making a mark on paper is a mirage, an illusion. Day changing into night is a mirage, an illusion. Every kind of change is merely a deceptive mirage—an appearance covering up a hidden actuality.

Using your own example, explain the point I just made about Parmenides.

My example is _____

_____. You are saying Parmenides believes

_____

_____

_____ .

Parmenides asks you to make a great leap. The changing world you see with your senses is exactly like the false lake in the desert.

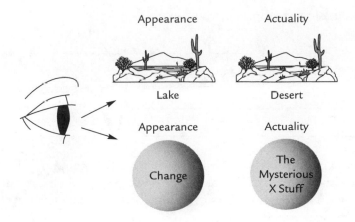

Look at this diagram for a few moments to get a feel for Parmenides' view of reality.

Note that just as the lake mirage blocks your eye from seeing the actuality of the desert, the change mirage blocks your eye from seeing the actuality of The Mysterious X Stuff. Thus, just as you could not prove the desert existed behind the lake mirage simply by looking at the lake mirage, you cannot prove that The Mysterious X Stuff exists behind illusory change simply by looking at illusory change. In both cases, you must use your mind and a process of reasoning to leap over appearance and discover actuality.

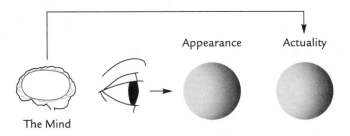

The process of reasoning you would use to leap over the appearance of the lake mirage to get at the actuality of the desert would be very simple.

1. This is the desert.
2. There are no lakes in the desert.
3. Therefore, the lake that I see is a mirage that hides desert sand.

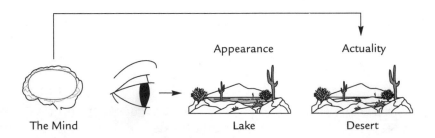

The process of reasoning that Parmenides uses to leap over the appearance of change to get at the actuality of The Mysterious X Stuff is more complex.

What Is Parmenides' Argument
That Change Is an Illusion?

Parmenides, like most philosophers, didn't simply make claims about reality; he also backed up his claims with arguments. What argument could he possibly use to show that change was an illusion? How could anyone try to prove that what so obviously takes place isn't taking place? You move your hand across the page, the sun moves across the sky, a seed grows into a plant, change is everywhere! How could it be an illusion? How will Parmenides use his mind to leap over the illusion encountered by his senses?

Parmenides' process of reasoning starts with two apparently innocent claims.

1. What is cannot be what is not.

2. What is not cannot be what is.

What could be simpler than that? Existence cannot be nonexistence. Nonexistence cannot be existence. Existence and nonexistence are mutually exclusive categories.

Take these two cases:

A three-sided triangle that has existence.

A four-sided triangle that has no existence.

The three-sided triangle that has existence cannot have nonexistence. And the impossible four-sided triangle that has no existence cannot have existence.

From the mutual exclusiveness of existence and nonexistence, Parmenides produces a philosophical whammy.

If *X* exists, then it cannot pass into nonexistence. All change is the case of some *X* appearing to pass into nonexistence. Therefore, all change is an illusion!

I am absolutely, totally positive I have lost you. I have had twenty-eight years' experience in losing students at precisely this point. I never fail! Usually going over Parmenides' argument a few more times and using a simple example helps.

Let's say you are standing at the border between California and Arizona.

With one step you could go from California into Arizona and back again. Standing in one state you could go to another, because both states exist.

And, just as you obviously can step from California to Arizona because the two states exist, you *cannot* step from California into the state of Zembulon because the state of Zembulon does not exist.

Thus, as a general principle, you can go from *A* to *B* if both *A* and *B* exist. But you cannot go from *A* to *B* if *B* doesn't exist.

My students usually follow me to this point. Now, pay close attention.

In order to understand Parmenides, let us replace the states of California and Arizona with different kinds of states: the state of existence and the state of nonexistence.

Right now, you are in the state of existence.

Is it possible for you ever to pass into the state of nonexistence?

Remember, you can go from A to B if B exists, but not if B doesn't exist.

Well then, does the state of nonexistence exist? Just mull over that question for a moment. Does the state of nonexistence exist?

Is the state of nonexistence like the state of Arizona or like the state of Zembulon?

What do you think?

Could the state of nonexistence exist in the way Arizona exists?

Wouldn't that be impossible?

How could the state of nonexistence exist?

How could nonexistence, that which has no existence, have existence?

My answer is _____

_____

From Parmenides' point of view, existence, obviously, exists; nonexistence, equally obviously, doesn't exist. There is no nothing. Therefore, you can never pass into the state of nonexistence because the state of nonexistence doesn't exist for you to pass into!

I am fairly positive you still don't quite get it, so let's go over this one more time. Very slowly! We'll do philosophy together.

EXERCISE 5.1
A Review of Parmenides' Argument

Check off each point below as you understand it.

1. At the border between California and Arizona, you can go from California to Arizona and back again because both states exist.

2. You can go from any state (or situation, condition) to any other state (situation, condition) only if both exist.

3. You are presently in the state of existing (you have existence).

4. You can pass into the state of nonexistence only if nonexistence exists.

5. Nonexistence cannot have existence.

6. Therefore, you cannot pass into the state of nonexistence.

7. If you, something that has existence, cannot pass into the state of nonexistence, then nothing that has existence can pass into the state of nonexistence.

8. Everything that appears to change appears to pass into the state of nonexistence.

9. All change is an illusion.

EXERCISE 5.2
Attacking and Defending Parmenides

1. Reread Exercise 5.1. At which statement, according to you, does Parmenides go wrong? In other words, what is the first false statement? Give reasons to support your argument. Fill in the following blanks:

    Statement _____ is false because _____

    _____

    _____

    and because _____

    _____

    _____

    and because _____

    _____

    _____.

2. Now use your own paper to attack your own attack on Parmenides. What reasons would he give to show that your reasons are wrong?

Before we go further and to help you get still clearer on Parmenides, compare his solution to the problem of the One and the Many with those of Thales and Heraclitus.

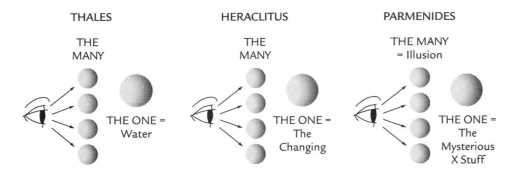

The Many for all three philosophers is essentially the same. The Many represents the changing world we perceive with our senses. The Many is the world outside the window. But note that each philosopher describes the One differently. The One, for Thales, is a substance, water. The One, for Heraclitus, is the process of change. The One for Parmenides is The Mysterious X Stuff.

What Is That Mysterious X Stuff?

Parmenides deduces everything he knows about The Mysterious X Stuff from what we've established thus far. Change involves the impossible—the proposition that something that exists passes into the state of nonexistence. There is no state of nonexistence. Therefore, reality, the real, that Mysterious X Stuff, must be unchanging.

Think through that reasoning again.

Assume you know I am writing this book in one of two states, Arizona or California. Assume you then prove that I can't be writing this in Arizona. You have then also proved that I am writing this book in California. Parmenides uses a similar argument. Reality is either changing or unchanging. He believes he has proved that reality is not changing. Therefore, reality is unchanging.

We now know one thing about that Mysterious X Stuff!

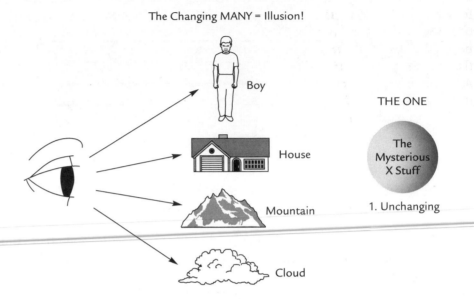

By establishing that the One is unchanging, Parmenides can add another characteristic. If something is unchanging, then it must last forever. If your car was unchanging, then it couldn't rust, fade, or in any other way decay. The One, according to Parmenides, can never change. Reality, so to speak, can never rust, fade, or in any other way decay. Because the One is unchanging, therefore the One is eternal.

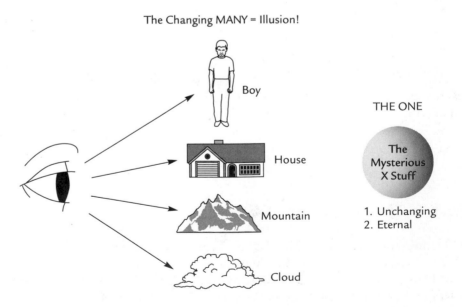

The third characteristic of The Mysterious X Stuff is the strangest of all.

Remember, I said that, according to Parmenides, there is no nothing? Well, if there is no nothing, then empty space, like change, is not real. And if empty space is not real, then The Mysterious X Stuff is one single undivided whole.

Try that one more time.

There is no nothing. According to Parmenides, nothing is merely a concept, an impossible concept like a four-sided triangle. When we try to think about a four-sided triangle existing, we can't. We can't even conceive of the existence of a three-sided figure that has four sides. In the same way, we cannot think of nothing, that which has no existence, as having existence. And if this is true, then empty space, just like change, is an illusion. Empty space doesn't exist. And if empty space doesn't exist, then the One, The Mysterious X Stuff, can't be divided into parts. There is no nothing to separate the Mysterious X Stuff. Thus, we've discovered the final characteristic of the One according to Parmenides.

The Changing MANY = Illusion!

Boy

House

Mountain

Cloud

THE ONE

The Mysterious X Stuff

1. Unchanging
2. Eternal
3. Undivided

What does all this mean?

The separate things you see around you are an illusion. The change you see every day is an illusion. Every cotton pickin' thing you see with your senses is an illusion! Behind the illusion of change is a single, unchanging, eternal, undivided One.

Look out my window with me.

The elm tree (illusion) waves (illusion) in the wind (illusion). A boy walks his dog. An illusion illusions his illusion.

And what is behind all this? The Mysterious X Stuff. What is. Being.

SUMMARY

Parmenides holds that all change is an illusion. The One (The Mysterious X Stuff) that unites the Many is unchanging, eternal, and undivided.

Parmenides attempts to prove that the changing Many has no reality because all change involves the impossibility of something that exists passing into nonexistence. Because nonexistence does not exist, all change is an illusion. Thus, if the One is not changing, it must be unchanging; and if the One is unchanging, it must be eternal. In addition, since there is "no nothing" to divide the One, the One must also be undivided. Parmenides' name for the unchanging, eternal, undivided One is Being or What is.

EXERCISE 5.3
Looking Back

Practice your paraphrasing skills by answering the following questions on your own paper.

1. What is an illusion? (Illustrate your answer with an original example.)

2. What is Parmenides' argument that change is an illusion? (See if you can reduce the argument to only three or four statements.)

3. What is that Mysterious X Stuff?

EXERCISE 5.4
Looking at the World Through Parmenides' Eyes

How would Parmenides answer the following questions? After each answer, provide an explanation that is consistent with Parmenides' point of view. For example:

T <u>F</u> The actuality of the Many is hidden behind the illusion of the One.

Explanation: Parmenides held that the actuality of the One is hidden behind the illusion of the Many.

1. T   F   Empty space has no genuine reality.
   Explanation: _____
   _____
   _____.

2. T   F   The mind can know truths independently of the senses.
   Explanation: _____
   _____
   _____.

3. T   F   All of reality is divided into two equally real parts.
   Explanation: _____
   _____
   _____.

4. T   F   It is not possible to know the nature of reality.
   Explanation: _____
   _____
   _____.

5. T   F   The changing has more reality than the unchanging.

    Explanation: _____

    _____

    _____

    _____.

6. T   F   Change is impossible because it involves "what is not" becoming
              "what is."

    Explanation: _____

    _____

    _____

    _____.

7. T   F   Change is impossible because it involves "what is" becoming "what
              is not."

    Explanation: _____

    _____

    _____

    _____.

8. T   F   The One is to the Many as Illusion is to Actuality.

    Explanation: _____

    _____

    _____

    _____.

9. T   F   The One is to the Many as "What Is" is to "Being."

    Explanation: _____

    _____

    _____

    _____.

10. T   F   Parmenides does not genuinely exist.

    Explanation: _____

    _____

    _____

    _____.

EXERCISE 5.5
Mind Wars

Write a short debate between Heraclitus and Parmenides. Use some of Heraclitus's fragments as illustrations of his position.

ANALYSIS OF YOUR PHILOSOPHICAL SELF-PORTRAIT

I've underlined Parmenides' answers; circle the answers you believe are correct.

1. <u>T</u> F *If there is a One that unifies the Many, then it must have characteristics very unlike those of the Many.*

   True puts you in the camp of the three pre-Socratic philosophers we have examined on our tour. Despite the differences among Thales, Heraclitus, and Parmenides, they all agree that our senses give us a poor version of the really real. Parmenides' view sounds strange to us precisely because it is exactly the opposite of what our senses report; but simply because a view of reality is the opposite of what our senses report is no reason to reject it. But modern physicists would also agree that the underlying basis of reality is not what our senses tell us. Parmenides' description of reality is surely no odder than that of the physicists who tell us that all substance is made up of substanceless particles like quarks—in other words, every something is made up of billions of nothings. Is this truly any odder than saying that an undivided One lies behind the divided Many?

   Your response?

   I believe _____

   _____.

2. <u>T</u> F *Our senses deceive us about the nature of reality far more often than they tell us the truth.*

   True puts you in the camp of all the rationalists on the tour: Parmenides, Plato, Anselm, and Descartes and against all the empiricists: Aristotle, Aquinas, Locke, Berkeley, and Hume. Parmenides is a rationalist because he holds that the mind attains a picture of reality only when it rejects what the senses report. In case you are fond of relying on your senses, you might note that your senses tell you the earth is flat, the sun circles the earth, and the earth is the center of the starry universe.

3. T <u>F</u> *All that is real changes.*

   True makes you an ally of Heraclitus and an enemy of Parmenides—and also an enemy of most monotheists, those who believe God exists. Just as Parmenides held that a fundamental feature of reality is that it is unchanging, so most monotheists hold that God is unchanging. As Aristotle will point out, God is perfect and therefore can't change. For God to change, he would have to become less perfect.

4. <u>T</u> F *For an object to change into another object, the first object must cease to exist.*

   If you answered True, be careful! You're thinking like Parmenides.

   Parmenides held, as you just learned, that any change, any *X* changing into any *Y*, involves *X* ceasing to exist (and *Y* suddenly coming into existence). And this change, Parmenides believed, was impossible because it was impossible for anything in existence to pass into the state of nonexistence, nothingness. You can go to Arizona because there is an Arizona, but you can't go nowhere because there's no nowhere to go too.

Change is a mysterious puzzle that troubled the early philosophers. And it should have. Without an accurate description of change, there can be no accurate description of the world we live in. Students, however, often have a hard time seeing what is so puzzling about change. Ice melts. Eggs produce chicks. Day becomes night. Where is the puzzle?

To understand the puzzle of change, consider the impossibility of a ray gun vaporizing a rock and causing it to cease to exist.

Wouldn't you agree that there is no force, no ray gun, that could turn a rock into absolute nothingness? Not even a hydrogen bomb could turn something into nothing (hydrogen bombs turn something into smaller somethings). When you think about the impossibility of a ray gun absolutely vaporizing a rock, perhaps there is even some obscure phrase in the back of your head from high school physics, "the law of the conservation of mass/energy." This "law" reminds you that matter can become energy and vice versa but that it is absolutely impossible for matter to simply cease to exist. *But this is exactly the impossibility that seems to occur when any* X *changes into any* Y. Take ice appearing to melt into a liquid. Ice absolutely and completely ceases to exist. When ice apparently "melts," it vaporizes, passes into absolute nothingness—just as if it were zapped by a ray gun. And since this is impossible, it is impossible that change is real.

Your response?

I believe _____

_____

_____

But perhaps you want to say that when ice melts into a liquid, the matter does not vanish. The *matter* of ice becomes the *matter* of water. Matter is conserved; it doesn't vanish. This, as you will see, is Aristotle's attempted solution to the problem of change. But you are still left with the problem of what happened to the *ice* part of the matter. Vaporized? Vanished? Zapped? Day changes into night. A twig burns in a flame. Rock turns into lava. Zap. Zap. Zap. Day, twig, and rock become nothingness. And then we are left with Parmenides' problem: How can anything become nothing, pass into a state that has no existence? It seems to make as much sense to say that when ice melts it passes into the state of nonexistence as it would to say that when ice melts it passes into the state of Zembulon.

5. T F *All that is real is eternal.*

True gives you at least one foot in Parmenides' camp. Parmenides held that the One is the only reality and is eternal, unchanging, and undivided.

If you are a Christian who holds that God will reign at the "end of time," then you would probably answer this question False. You believe we live in a real world that will not last forever. In other words, reality, which is currently divided into two parts, will eventually have only one part.

VOCABULARY MAP

Parmenides

Parmenides' **metaphysics** is usually described as **monistic idealism.** This means that his view of reality (his **metaphysics**) is that all of reality is one kind of thing (**monism**). We explored two kinds of **monists** in the second chapter: **materialists** (those who hold that the essential element of reality is matter) and **idealists** (those who hold that the essential element of reality is akin to ideas—that is, it is nonphysical). Parmenides is an **idealist** because Being, What Is, is nonphysical.

Parmenides' **epistemology** is usually described as **rationalistic.** This means that his theory of knowledge (his **epistemology**) is that the mind can know truths independently of the senses. This view of the mind's ability to go beyond the senses, as you learned in the second chapter, is **rationalism.**

Parmenides did not develop an **ethics,** a position on moral values.

Thus, on our diagram of the fields of philosophy, we can locate Parmenides in two places.

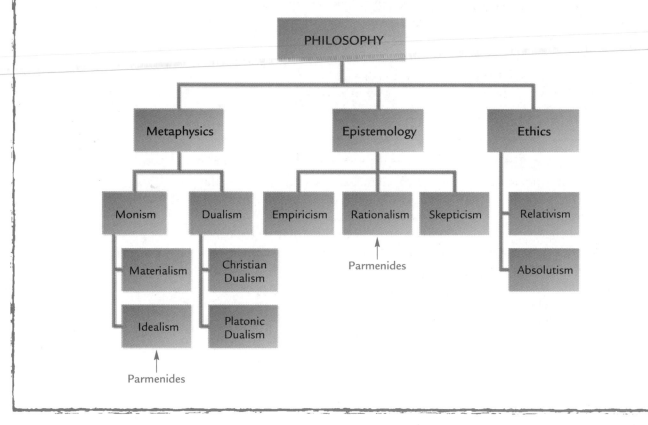

Evaluation: Number of points in agreement with Parmenides = _____ of 5 possible.

A position of Parmenides' that you strongly (support, oppose) is

_____

because _____.

GOOD BOOKS

Grant, Michael. *The Classical Greeks.* New York: Scribner's, 1989. Of countless books on the
subject, this a good place to start for an overview of Greek society.

Ring, Merrill. *Beginning with the Pre-Socratics.* Mountain View, Calif.: Mayfield, 1987. A
clearly written guide for the student of introductory philosophy.

NEXT STOP

**Get ready for Parmenides' star pupil, Zeno—who has
baffled generations of philosophy students.**

6

Zeno and the Magical Illusion of Motion

YOUR PHILOSOPHICAL SELF-PORTRAIT

Add more details to your philosophical self-portrait by answering the questions below and providing evidence for your answer.

1. T   F   It is not possible to arrive at the end of an infinite number of units of anything.

    Evidence: _____
    _____
    _____.

2. T   F   The distance from you to the nearest wall contains an infinite number of units of space.

    Evidence: _____
    _____
    _____.

3. T   F   If you moved from your current location to the nearest wall, you would have to go through an infinite number of units of space.

    Evidence: _____
    _____
    _____.

4. T   F   If it is not possible to go through an infinite number of units of space and if there are an infinite number of units of space between your current location and the nearest wall, then when you move from your current location to the nearest wall, your movement is an illusion.

    Evidence: _____
    _____
    _____.

5. T   F   All motion is an illusion.

    Evidence: _____
    _____
    _____.

Zeno, a student of Parmenides, uses an imaginary race between the Greek hero Achilles and a turtle to argue that motion is an illusion. For Achilles to pass the turtle, Achilles must first travel half the distance between himself and the turtle. But half the distance between himself and the turtle can be divided in half again—and the resulting halves can be divided again and so on for infinity. Thus, Zeno argues, since any space contains an infinite number of units of space, not only isn't it possible for Achilles to pass the turtle, but it is not even possible for Achilles to move; no motion is possible. Zeno concludes that because all motion involves the impossibility of coming to the end of an infinite number of units of space, all motion is an illusion.

Zeno, Parmenides' most famous follower, drives students crazy.

Zeno supported his teacher with several famous paradoxes which argue that motion has no reality—is an illusion. The mind-warping argument you are about to encounter will, at first reading, seem ridiculously easy to defeat—like popping a balloon with a pin. But then, as you ponder Zeno's argument further, you'll feel as if you are in a mad dream; your pin turns to rubber and the balloon turns to steel. Take comfort in the fact that Zeno's views have stood the test of time; weighty books have been written in this century arguing that he is right!

Following, I present one of Zeno's paradoxes by restating it in the form of a story. We'll explore the following questions in the story:

- According to Zeno, what problem does Achilles encounter in a race with a turtle?

- What is Zeno claiming with his description of Achilles and the turtle?

According to Zeno, What Problem Does Achilles Encounter in a Race with a Turtle?

Imagine that one sunny day, Achilles, the fastest of all mortals, is challenged to a race by an uppity turtle. Achilles, being a sport and needing a little exercise, gives the turtle a lengthy head start. As Achilles looks down the course, he sees that to win he must first travel half the distance between himself and his foolish opponent. Achilles must pass through M1, the midway point.

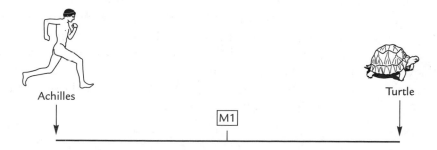

Achilles, never having lost a race in his life, feels confident. But, as he stares at the racecourse, he sees that in order to reach M1, he must first go halfway and reach M2.

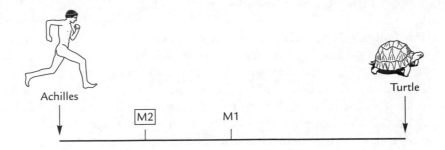

It's a sunny day. Perhaps too sunny. The heat seems to be affecting Achilles' mind. He realizes that in order to get to M2, he must first reach M3.

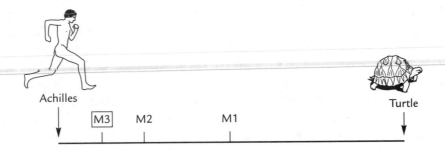

Our hero feels slightly woozy. Standing at the start, looking up the course at his little green opponent, Achilles understands that to complete any distance, he must first go halfway. Thus, in order to get to M3 he must get to M4.

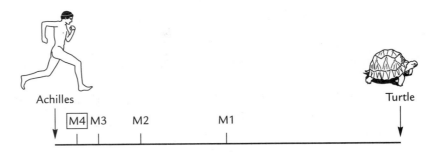

Achilles wonders if he had too much to drink the night before. Or perhaps reading philosophy fogged his mind. He thinks back over his reasoning. "To win the race, I first have to go halfway and arrive at the midpoint M1. But to get to M1, I have to get to a second midpoint, M2. But M2 has a midpoint at M3 and so forth. Every distance I have to travel in this race will always have a midpoint. I can never go all the way until I go half the way."

The distance from Achilles to M4 is a mere step. He stares at the dusty earth, sweating. "What do I have to do to take that step?"

Achilles trembles. He sees that in order to go all the way to M4, to take that whole step, he first has to take half a step and arrive at M5. (The distance between Achilles and M4 is enlarged so that you can see it more clearly.)

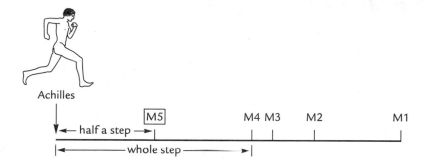

Achilles hangs his head in humiliation. He understands that any space that he tries to cross in the race can be divided in half. Over and over and over again. Any space contains an infinite number of units of space. He thinks dejectedly, "M5 is certainly not the last division. There could be an M6, an M100, an M1,000,000. Just as there is no end to the number series, there is no end to M points. I'll never get anywhere."

Achilles walks away but realizes he doesn't—really. He tells himself sadly, "All motion involves going through an infinite number of units of space. Walking away is just as much an illusion as trying to beat that *#@!% turtle. I can't even cook him for dinner. In order to get the spoon to my mouth, the spoon would have to go through an infinite series of midpoints."

What Is Zeno Claiming with His Description of Achilles and the Turtle?

Zeno's argument can be simply stated:

1. Any unit of space contains an infinite number of units of space.

2. It is not possible to go through an infinite number of units of space.

3. Achilles' motion—and, therefore, all motion—is not possible.

Zeno always startles and usually aggravates students.

But think about what he is saying.

Begin with the concept of infinity. Let's say you have an infinite number of socks on the floor of your room, and you decide it's time to pick them up. Will you ever get to the last sock? If you use a shovel? If you have all the neighbors come in with shovels? How many dump trucks of socks will you fill before you pick up the last one?

Those trucks would be hauling socks forever.

Just as you could never finish picking up an infinite number of socks, so Achilles could never go through an infinite number of units of space. Infinite means "that which has no end."

Zeno (c. 490–430 B.C.)

An astonishing story is told of Zeno. According to ancient tradition, in his later years, Zeno conspired to overthrow the Sicilian tyrant Nearchus. When the tyrant publicly tortured him in an attempt to make him betray his political associates, Zeno responded by naming all the members of the tyrant's court—a possibility that was not so far-fetched, given the times. The tyrant, confused and terrified, was dumbstruck. Zeno, turning to the crowd, exclaimed, "If you can consent to be slaves from fear of what you see me now suffer, I can only wonder at your cowardice." He then bit off his tongue with his teeth and threw it in the face of his tormentor. The crowd of bystanders were so moved by Zeno's act of courage that they rushed the tyrant and killed him.[1] Although this story is hearsay, it graphically illustrates some of Zeno's most outstanding qualities: his courage, his quick intellect, and his single-minded loyalty to his state and friends.

Born in Elea, a Greek colony in southern Italy, around 490 B.C., Zeno lived during a politically charged period in Greek history. Greece was experimenting with democracy and struggling to liberate itself from Persian rule and political

tyranny. During the first part of Zeno's life, he was the student of Parmenides. So devoted were the two to each other that, according to some sources, Parmenides even adopted Zeno as his own son. Like Parmenides, Zeno lived in Athens for a number of years. In his dialogue *Parmenides*, Plato describes Zeno as having been "close to forty" when Zeno and Parmenides came to Athens for a festival where they met with the young philosopher Socrates.

According to Aristotle, Zeno learned the art of the dialectic, a question-and-answer method of seeking truth, from Socrates (see Plato's *Euthyphro, Apology,* and *Crito* later in the tour for samples). In the hands of Socrates and Plato, the dialectic became a powerful tool for seeking the truth. Zeno, it is said, also instructed the Athenian general and statesman Pericles, one of the leading advocates of democracy.

Despite these notable achievements, Zeno is best known for his paradoxes. The paradox of Achilles and the turtle is perhaps the most famous. Zeno points out that if the turtle were given a head start in a race, Achilles would never be able to overtake it, since at every point Achilles would have to travel half the distance between himself and the turtle, ad infinitum (see this chapter for more details). While some people dismiss Zeno as a clever riddler who delighted in creating paradoxes to confuse those of lesser wit, in fact the real intention of his paradoxes was quite serious—to defend Parmenides' twin thesis that reality is One and all change is an illusion.

Zeno never developed a philosophy of his own; instead, he devoted his intellectual energy to responding to criticisms of Parmenides' philosophy. Plato attributes only one work to Zeno, a book of forty paradoxes. Although later sources claim that he wrote more, there is no evidence of any other works by Zeno. Of his forty paradoxes, only eight have survived.

---

[1] This story is retold in G. H. Lewes, *A Biographical History of Philosophy*, vol. I. (London: Charles Knight & Co., 1845), p. 96.

In order for Achilles to move his foot even one-fourth of an inch forward, he would have to go to the halfway point at one-eighth inch, which would involve another halfway point at one-sixteenth inch, and so on infinitely. Achilles can't move. Motion isn't possible.

At this point, students have asked one or more of the following blunt questions.

According to Zeno and Parmenides, the One is unchanging; according to Thales, the one is

_____;

according to Heraclitus, the

One is _____ _____.

Question: Is Zeno saying that if I punch you in the nose, you won't feel it?

Answer: Zeno is saying that for your fist to reach my nose, it would first have to travel half the distance between where your fist started and where my precious nose is. And, in order to travel that half distance, your fist would have to travel another half distance and another and another in an infinite series of subdivisions. Since it is not possible for your fist to go through the infinite series of subdivisions that any motion would involve, your fist not only doesn't actually hit my nose, but, in addition, it can't even get started. Zeno has nothing to say about the illusion of my pain.

Your most thoughtful reply?

I believe your answer is (right, wrong) because _____

_____.

Question: But I see motion take place. Motion is everywhere. How can Zeno deny what I see?

Answer: *Zeno is not saying that you don't see motion.* He is saying that what you see is *an illusion.*

To make this clearer, think of a magician sawing a lady in half. No one would argue that you don't see the lady cut in half, only that what you see has no reality, is an illusion. Thus, Zeno is not arguing that you don't see motion, only that what you see has no reality. All motion is reality's magic trick.

Your most thoughtful reply?

I believe your answer is (right, wrong) because _____

_____.

Question: You say that any space could be infinitely divided. But wouldn't you eventually get to a space so small that it could not be cut in half?

Answer: Any space, no matter how small, has a beginning and an end. Anything with a beginning and an end can be divided. Thus, every unit of space, no matter what its infinitesimal size, can be divided infinitely. Consider the bizarre problem we would face if this were not true. Imagine you divided and redivided a unit of space until you arrived at almost the smallest possible unit; call it the Teensy unit.

On dividing the Teensy unit, you arrive at two of the smallest possible units; call them the Tiniest units. Tiniest units are so small they cannot be further divided. But the only way the Tiniest units could not be further divided would be if they had no size. And this is not possible. How could you take two of the Tiniest units *of no size* and put them back together to form the Teensy unit *with a size*? In fact, a million billion Tiniests would not add up to one micro-measly Teensy.

Your most thoughtful reply?

I believe your answer is (right, wrong) because _____

_____.

Question: If you look at a ruler, you can see that any space has a finite number of units of space. For example, from the 1-inch mark to the 2-inch mark there are only sixteen smaller marks. Thus, isn't Zeno wrong when he says any space contains an infinite number of units of space?

Answer: There are at least three kinds of infinities; call them both-ends-open, one-end-open, and both-ends-closed. The number series from negative infinity to positive infinity is a both-ends-open infinity. The number series from 1 to positive infinity is a one-end-open infinity. However, there is also an infinity between any two numbers. One-sixteenth of an inch contains two one-thirty-seconds of an inch and so forth. The infinity between any two numbers is a both-ends-closed infinity and *is just as infinite as the other two kinds.* Any motion from *X* to *Y* involves coming to the end of a both-ends-closed infinity; and since any infinity is unending, this is impossible.

As a matter of fact, if you think about it, there is not just one both-ends-closed infinity between *X* and *Y*, but there is another both-ends-closed infinity between *X* and halfway to *Y* and another both-ends-closed infinity from halfway to *Y* and *Y* and so on and on infinitely. *Thus, any motion from* X *to* Y *actually involves coming to the end of an infinite number of infinities!*

Your most thoughtful reply?

I believe your answer is (right, wrong) because _____

_____.

SUMMARY

Zeno supports Parmenides by arguing that motion, an important kind of change, is an illusion. Zeno is not arguing that we don't see motion, only that what we see could not actually take place. Achilles appears to pass the turtle but actually doesn't, because passing the turtle involves going through an infinite number of units of space. Since it is not possible to go through an infinite number of units of anything, Achilles' motion is only apparent, not actual. If this is true for Achilles, it is true for all motion.

EXERCISE 6.1
Looking Back

Use your own paper to answer the following:

1. According to Zeno, what problem does Achilles encounter in a race with a turtle?

2. What is Zeno claiming with his description of Achilles and the turtle?

3. What is the difference between logical and physical impossibility? (See Box 6.1.)

BOX 6.1
Logical Impossibility Versus Physical Impossibility

Zeno's paradoxes explore a special kind of impossibility—logical impossibility. He argues that it is logically impossible to come to the end of an infinite series; therefore, motion is impossible. Students often claim that just because something is a logical impossibility, that doesn't mean it can't happen. This probably involves a confusion between logical impossibilities and physical impossibilities.

Compare the two:

Logical impossibilities: a four-sided triangle, a married bachelor, coming to the end of infinity

Physical impossibilities: going back in time, traveling at a speed faster than light, living forever

One could say that while something is physically impossible now—for example, going back in time—that doesn't mean that it will always be physically impossible. It was once physically impossible to travel to the moon, but science made great advances and accomplished that impossi-

bility. Perhaps at some time in the future, we will be able to go back in time. A current physical impossibility is merely impossible at the present time. Thus, it would be accurate to say that just because something is a physical impossibility (now), that doesn't mean it can't happen.

But logical impossibilities last forever and thus are truly impossible. No advance in science will ever create a four-sided triangle. A triangle is a geometrical figure that has three sides; if it doesn't have three sides, it isn't a triangle. If someone claimed, "Ah, I have invented a four-sided triangle!" we could reply, "That's not true. All you have done is falsely change the meaning of the word triangle to include four-sided objects. You are free to make words mean whatever you want, but you will never create a three-sided object that has four sides. That is logically impossible. Now. And Forever." Coming to the end of an infinite series is a similar logical impossibility. An infinite series has no end. You can't arrive at the end of that which has no end. You can't get to Zembulon if there ain't no Zembulon.

EXERCISE 6.2
Looking at the World Through Zeno's Eyes

How would Zeno answer each of the following? Explain the reasoning behind your answer.

1. T   F   The world is not the kind of place it appears to be.

    Explanation: _____

    _____.

2. T   F   Our senses deceive us.

    Explanation: _____

    _____.

3. T   F   The mind, independently of the senses, can know reality.

    Explanation: _____

    _____.

4. T F You *can* step into the same river twice.

Explanation: _____

_____.

5. T F All is One.

Explanation: _____

_____.

ANALYSIS OF YOUR PHILOSOPHICAL SELF-PORTRAIT

I've underlined Zeno's answers.

1. <u>T</u> F *It is not possible to arrive at the end of an infinite number of units of anything.*

True means you are thinking like Zeno. And, so far as I can tell, Zeno is right. Infinite means unending. (Incidentally, there is, according to mathematics, no such thing as a larger and smaller infinity. There are just as many units between 1 and 2 as there are between 1 and positive infinity. Think about that, take two aspirin, and don't call me.)

2. <u>T</u> F *The distance from you to the nearest wall contains an infinite number of units of space.*

Some students will, on reflection, argue that this is True; and then suddenly find they are Zenoites. If there is a weak point in Zeno's argument, it is probably here; but I've had fewer than twenty students in my twenty-eight-year career who have been able to clearly state the weakness. Once you admit that there is such a thing as an infinity with both ends closed—and it seems hard to argue that there isn't such an infinity—then it is very difficult to argue that there isn't an infinite number of units of space between you and the nearest wall.

Well, can you find the weakness in Zeno's argument?

Perhaps the weakness is: _____

_____.

3. <u>T</u> F *If you moved from your current location to the nearest wall, you would have to go through an infinite number of units of space.*

Answering the previous question True forces you to answer this question as True. Answering this question False involves thinking through the problem of a both-ends-closed infinity, which is just as large as any other kind of infinity.

4. <u>T</u> F *If it is not possible to go through an infinite number of units of space and if there are an infinite number of units of space between your current location and the nearest wall, then when you move from your current location to the nearest wall, your movement is an illusion.*

"If" is the crucial word here; thus, I think the only sensible answer to this question is True. If you give Zeno the first two "ifs," then the conclusion appears inevitable.

5. <u>T</u> F *All motion is an illusion.*

A True, of course, is your ticket to Zenoland.

VOCABULARY MAP
Zeno

Zeno's **metaphysics** is **monistic.** This means his view of reality (his **metaphysics**) is that all of reality is one kind of thing (**monism**). Zeno's brand of **monism** is probably **idealism.** In other words, the one kind of thing that he thinks reality is, is probably something nonphysical, such as ideas. (I say "probably" because Zeno's paradoxes are mainly concerned with showing that motion is an illusion, not with describing the kind of reality that lies behind motion.)

Zeno's **epistemology** is **rationalistic:** His view of knowledge (his **epistemology**) is that the mind can know truths independently of the senses (**rationalism**).

Zeno's paradoxes present no **ethics,** no view of moral behavior.

All in all, Zeno's position, so far as this tour is concerned, is identical to Parmenides'.

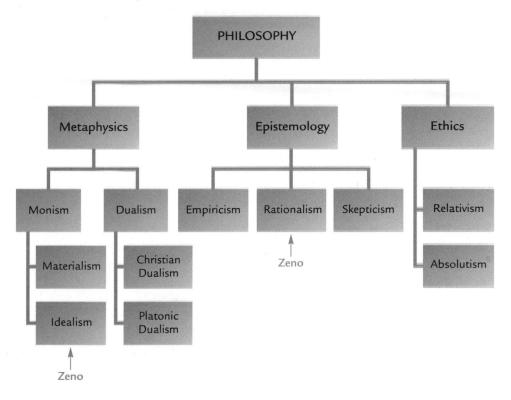

Evaluation: Number of points in agreement with Zeno = _____ of 5 possible.

A position of Zeno's that you strongly (support, oppose) is

_____

because _____.

GOOD BOOKS

Edwards, Paul, editor. *The Encyclopedia of Philosophy.* New York: Macmillan & The Free Press, 1967. Try the Zeno article.

Kirk, G. S., Raven, J. E., and Schofield, M. *The PreSocratic Philosophers: A Critical History with a Selection of Texts.* 2nd ed. Cambridge: Cambridge University Press, 1983. If Zeno has you hooked, look up his other paradoxes in this text.

NEXT STOP

If every philosopher in the world voted on the single most remarkable personality in the history of philosophy, odds are the next thinker on the tour would win hands down. You're about to meet the man who made all the pre-Socratics, *pre*-Socratics. Introducing, "philosophy's saint," Socrates.

Socrates in the Euthyphro
Grappling with Holiness

YOUR PHILOSOPHICAL SELF-PORTRAIT

Circle what you believe is the correct answer to the questions below and offer evidence supporting your view.

1. T F What is holy to one person could be unholy to another; the holiness of an action is entirely determined by individual opinion.

    Evidence: _____
    _____
    _____ .

2. T F It is not possible to know the essence of holiness.

    Evidence: _____
    _____
    _____ .

3. T F The true philosopher is a critic of the values of the masses.

    Evidence: _____
    _____
    _____ .

Socrates lived in ancient Athens during its democratic period and was both teacher and gadfly. Whereas the pre-Socratics were concerned with metaphysical questions, Socrates was concerned with ethical questions. In the *Euthyphro*, a dialogue written by Plato that presents Socrates' encounter with Euthyphro, a pompous prophet, Socrates attempts to find a definition of the holy.

Athens, the city of Socrates' birth in the fourth century B.C., was a *polis*, a state that was a small city. Other ancient Greek cities, such as Sparta, Thebes, and Corinth, were city-states as well. Each was a legal and political system unto itself. Imagine New York ruled by a king, Philadelphia by a democratic government, and Boston by a curious mixture of the two, and you have an idea of the nature of the Greek city-states.

Athens, of course, was the democracy. Democracy grew slowly in the two centuries before Socrates' birth. The movement began when Draco published the laws of the state in 621 B.C. This act was significant because written laws were less subject to the whim of judge or ruler than were a flexible body of traditional practices. Solon and Cleisthenes in the sixth century B.C. gave larger groups of citizens direct access to Athenian political processes. By the middle of the fifth century B.C., the Golden Age of Pericles, a democratic system, more radical than our own in some ways, was fully established. Although women,

VANTAGE POINT

Athenian Leaders

Athens was known as much for its political leaders as for its philosophers, playwrights, and artists.

Draco, who lived in the last half of the seventh century B.C., developed a code of laws. Although it was a significant advance over traditional practices, his recommendation of death for even trivial crimes has made "draconian" a synonym for harsh legislation.

Solon (c. 639–559 B.C.) canceled all debts during an economic crisis. He established four classes based upon wealth, with important political rights for the top three classes. He may also have established the Athenian Senate, a body made up of the representatives of the wealthiest Athenians.

Cleisthenes (570–508 B.C.) reorganized Athe-

nian clans into demes, political organizations based on locale rather than family ties. In addition, he extended Athenian citizenship to large numbers of resident aliens.

Pericles (495–429 B.C.) was the greatest of the Athenian leaders. He ruled from 460 to 429. In addition to being a force for democratic reform, he fostered a remarkable growth of literature, architecture, and other arts. Pericles also led Athens in its war against Sparta, established numerous Athenian colonies in the Aegean, and increased the treasuries of Athens through an efficient collection of tributes from its dependent cities. During a war with Sparta, which would eventually prove disastrous for the Athenians, Pericles died of the plague.

slaves, and foreigners had no vote, the 40,000 free men had amazing power. In the United States our representatives make decisions for us. If we ourselves could vote to go to war, to make peace, to ratify a treaty, to raise or lower taxes, or to enact any other major policy decision, then we would be as democratic as was Athens.

Besides the growth of democracy, the other major event in the early life of Athens was the repulsion of the armies of Persia, an iron-based civilization of enormous size. In two wars, Athens, united with other Greek city-states, defeated the Persian Goliath through cunning, bravery, and what the Athenians held to be a superior political system. The Greeks were free and fought by choice. According to the Greek historian Herodotus, the Persians had to drive their soldiers into battle with whips.

It is simple to state the chronology of events that led to the rise of democracy and the fall of the Persians. It is more difficult to convey the incredible constellation of brilliant individuals who lived in Athens in the fifth and fourth centuries B.C. Let us imagine a single fabulous city, fill it with some of the greatest geniuses of all time, and then compare this impossible dream city with Socrates' Athens.

THOUGHT EXPERIMENT

Walking through the marketplace of the finest city we can imagine, we find Isaac Newton discussing the nature of God with Tolstoy. Along the narrow streets we look into the studios of Picasso, Leonardo da Vinci, and Vincent van Gogh. A young Charles Dickens sits in a coffee shop with Galileo. The Wright brothers, with bicycle parts in a wheelbarrow, wave their greeting from the crowded street. In a grove of glistening green alders, Julius Caesar addresses a crowd, and in the noisy crowd Michelangelo and Richard the Lionhearted exchange views on the speaker's merits. Isadora Duncan leads a group of her students, like a cloud of bright butterflies, among the latest black-bronze statues of the city's most famous sculptor, Auguste Rodin. Her group argues among themselves about the virtues of his latest work, *The Thinker*. In a theater outside the city we see a world-premiere presentation of a play by an interesting new talent, William Shakespeare. On a hill at the center of our wondrous city, Frank Lloyd Wright guides the completion of a cluster of white marble temples. Within a small courtyard crowded with stunned onlookers, a bespectacled German mathematician, Albert Einstein, discusses the curvature of space. And the popular leader of this menagerie of genius? Let us imagine it is Teddy Roosevelt.

Now, if you were born in such a city, believed its laws were the most just on earth, owed your entire education and upbringing to it, and had fought to defend it in a long war, you might prefer to die, as Socrates did, rather than leave.

Socrates' Athens was probably even more astonishing than our imaginary city. We had to ransack the ages and three continents to fill our dream. Athens, 2,500 years ago, never had a population larger than 250,000.

Socrates (c. 469–399 B.C.)

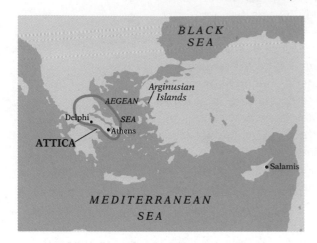

Socrates never recorded his philosophy. What we know of his life and views comes mainly from the early writings of his student Plato.

According to Plato, Socrates claimed that his philosophical career began with an incident at the temple in Delphi, which was considered to be the center of the world by the ancient Greeks. One of Socrates' friends went to the official oracle, the priestess at the temple of Delphi, and asked who was the wisest of mortals. She replied, "There is no one wiser than Socrates."

When Socrates heard of the pronouncement, he was disturbed, since he believed or claimed to believe that he was ignorant. He set out to prove the oracle wrong by going to those who claimed to be authorities in their fields. To his dismay, he discovered that though authorities believed they had knowledge, in fact they had none. Socrates concluded, ironically, that he was the wisest of mortals because he alone knew that he knew nothing. (You will discover much more about the irony, or hidden meaning, of Socrates' ignorance in this and the next two chapters.)

Socrates was born in Attica into a middle-class family; his father, Sophroniscus, was most likely a stonemason, and his mother, Phaenarete, a midwife. Socrates performed his military service as an infantryman in the Peloponnesian War, where he distinguished himself for his courage.

Socrates lived his adult life in Athens, the center of Greek culture and power. At some point in his life Socrates married Xanthippe. According to legend, she was a shrewish, quarrelsome woman and their marriage an unhappy one. They had at least three sons, one of whom was still an infant when Socrates died at age 70.

Of course, Xanthippe may have had good reason to nag her husband. Money and social status meant nothing to him. There is no evidence that Socrates held a regular job. He also showed little concern for his appearance, wearing the same shabby cloak winter and summer. A strikingly unattractive man with his snub nose, bulging eyes, prominent stomach, and peculiar

During the fifth and fourth centuries B.C., fifteen of the world's most influential geniuses could be found in Athens. Aeschylus, Sophocles, Aristophanes, and Euripides are still among the world's most influential playwrights. Countless buildings have been modeled after the Parthenon and its sister temples on the Acropolis, which were designed by the Athenians Ictinus and Callicrates. Although Phidias's Athena, a 40-foot miracle of gold and ivory has not survived, there are 10,000 copies of the statues of Praxiteles. Pericles ranks among the greatest of the world's leaders; historians are indebted to Thucydides and Herodotus, as are doctors to Hippocrates; and, of course, there are Plato, Aristotle, and philosophy's saint, Socrates.

On this section of our tour, I'll answer the following questions:

- Who was Socrates?
- What is the difference between Socrates and the pre-Socratics?
- What are some key features of the *Euthyphro*?

walk, he was easy to recognize as he shambled through the streets of Athens barefoot in search of wisdom.

Despite his lack of concern with wealth and status, Socrates was friends with some of Athens' most influential citizens. Several wealthy young men of Athens accompanied the philosopher, delighting in the way he cleverly refuted the views of those who thought themselves wise. One of these young men was Plato.

In his youth Socrates started hearing a mysterious "voice" that gave him warnings as well as useful instructions. This voice has been interpreted by later thinkers as being caused by anything from religious ecstasy to simple mental concentration. In any case, Socrates' claim to divine inspiration did not sit well with the authorities.

Apparently Socrates already had a notorious reputation as a gadfly by the time he was in his mid-forties, when the comic dramatist Aristophanes wrote *Clouds*. The "Socrates" in Aristophanes' *Clouds* is portrayed as the vain and amoral operator of a "think-shop" who struts around like a peacock in front of gullible students who pay to listen to his ridiculous quibbling.

The Greek historian Xenophon, who studied under Socrates, gives us a much different picture of Socrates. In his *Symposium,* Xenophon portrays Socrates as a rather bland teacher, spouting obvious truths.

This description, however, is at odds with Plato's Socrates, which is the one generally accepted by scholars as the most accurate. While immortalizing Socrates' wit and charisma, Plato also mentions at least two instances where Socrates showed great courage. The first happened when the public demanded that the ten generals who led the Athenian victory at the Arginusian islands be tried for desertion. Socrates refused to take part in the trial, arguing that it was illegal. In a later incident, Socrates refused to participate in what he thought was the wrongful arrest by the Thirty Tyrants of Leon of Salamis. On both occasions, his refusal to obey the political authorities could have cost Socrates his life.

Socrates' habit of challenging those in power finally caught up with him. At the age of seventy, he was arrested and charged with blasphemy, making the weaker argument defeat the stronger, and corrupting the youth of Athens. He was tried by a jury of about 500 (a typical Athenian jury) and found guilty. Socrates refused exile and was sentenced to death by drinking hemlock, a poison. His last words were that he owed the sacrifice of a rooster to Asclepius, the god of health. Socrates' fine ironic point was that dying was a cure for the illness of life.

Who Was Socrates?

According to Plato, his student and biographer, Socrates had a pug nose, ample belly, and bulging eyes; he went about barefoot summer and winter. In addition, he scorned money; was a great botherer of the pompous, a fearsome soldier, and an adorer of handsome youths; was able to drink all night with no ill effect in the morning; was advised by an inner spirit; and occasionally passed into mysterious trances. Plato also tells us that Socrates was husband to Xanthippe, father of three children, and happy to do nothing with his days but talk philosophy in the marketplace.

When we analyzed the pre-Socratics, we tried to piece together a jigsaw puzzle of ideas; we now have to piece together a lively, complex personality. Socrates gives philosophy its first and probably most engaging human face.

Xenophon, c. 430–c. 354 B.C., was an Athenian soldier and historian. He appears to have known Socrates for about a year and left a portrait of him in his *Memorabilia* and other writings.

Aristophanes, c. 445– c. 385 B.C., was an Athenian comic playwright. Aristophanes, author of some of the greatest comedies every written, humorously attacked, besides Socrates, other popular figures of his day including Cleon, a political leader, and Euripides, the great Athenian dramatist.

The oracle at Delphi was a famous source of prophetic knowledge who often spoke in riddles.

Born about 470 B.C., Socrates never recorded his own views. Virtually all we know about him comes from three sources: Plato, Xenophon, and the playwright Aristophanes. Moreover, these three sources offer different accounts. For example, Aristophanes' Socrates in *The Clouds* is a fool. Plato's account, however, is by far the most historically influential.

Plato tells us that Socrates had been named by the oracle at Delphi, "the wisest of all mortals." Socrates, holding that he "knew nothing," set out to prove the oracle wrong by finding someone wiser:

> Accordingly I went to one who had the reputation of wisdom and observed him—his name I need not mention; he was a politician whom I selected for examination. When I began to talk with him I could not help thinking he was not really wise, although he was thought wise by many and wiser still by himself. I tried to explain to him that he thought himself wise but was not really wise. The result was he hated me, and his hatred was shared by several who were present and heard me. So I left him, saying to myself, as I went away: "Well, although I do not suppose either of us knows anything really beautiful and good, I am better off than he is—for he knows nothing and thinks that he knows. I neither know nor think that I know. In this latter, then, I seem to have an advantage over him." Then I went to another who had still higher philosophical pretensions, and my conclusion was exactly the same. I made another enemy of him and of many others besides him.

Socrates' first encounters established what became a pattern. All whom he talked to who claimed to have wisdom had none, and they became Socrates' enemy when he pointed out their deficiency.

Socrates' quest for someone wiser than he, pursued for years, eventually got him into serious difficulties. In the politically chaotic atmosphere after Sparta's victory over Athens, Socrates was brought to trial before the Athenian Assembly. He was charged with corrupting the youth, believing in new gods, and making the weaker argument defeat the stronger. In other words, Socrates was a considerable troublemaker. Found guilty of the charges, he was allowed, as was the Athenian custom, to propose his own punishment. With fine humor, Socrates suggested that an excellent punishment would be for the state to support him for the rest of his life. In response, his jury sentenced him to death. A few days later, surrounded by his followers, Socrates drank hemlock, a poison. Socrates' last words instructed his friend Crito to sacrifice a rooster to Asclepius, the god of health. Socrates' point was apparently that in dying, he had escaped the illness of life.

What Is the Difference Between Socrates and the Pre-Socratics?

A good way to understand Socrates' uniqueness is to contrast his concerns with those of the pre-Socratics.

If I look out my window from the point of view of Thales, Heraclitus, Parmenides, or Zeno, then I am confronting the metaphysical problem of the One and the Many.

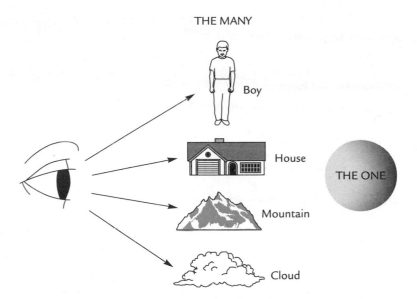

Thinking like a pre-Socratic, I want to understand the single element that unifies all of reality. I wonder if the unifying element is water, as Thales held, or the Logos of Change as Heraclitus held, or unchanging Being as Parmenides and Zeno held.

Socrates, however, takes a radically different approach to philosophy. He reduces the Many to a single fascinating element, human nature. Thus, if I look out my window and think like Socrates, I would focus only upon the person across the street. *Every other aspect of the pre-Socratic problem becomes irrelevant.*

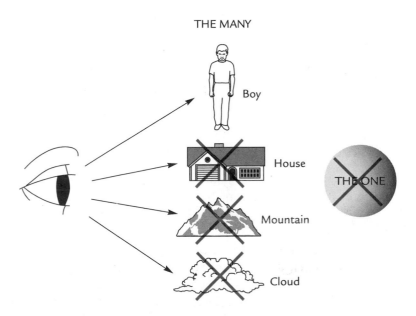

Thinking like the pre-Socratics, I would ask questions like

Is the One changing or unchanging?

Are the Many real or an illusion?

Can reality be known only through the senses or independently of the senses?

Thinking like Socrates, who focused intensely upon the human situation, I would ask myself questions like

What is virtue?

What is self-knowledge?

What kinds of actions harm the soul?

What is wisdom?

What is courage?

What is the individual's obligation to the state?

Simply to get a feel for the large difference between Socrates' questions and the pre-Socratic questions, answer one of each.

If I ask myself, Are the Many real or an illusion? my answer is

_____

because _____

_____

_____.

However, if I ask myself, What kinds of actions harm the soul? my answer is

_____

because _____

_____

_____.

Socrates was not concerned with the cosmos but with human nature. He drove philosophy inward, urging his fellow Athenians to ponder their souls. And thus Socrates introduced ethics, the study of moral action, as a new area of philosophical concern.

This new turn in philosophy may have been Socrates' response to the sophists, a group of teachers who offered to show anyone with money how to be influential in the Assembly. Their concern was not with truth or spiritual values but with reputation. Protagoras, one of the chief sophists, held that every individual's opinion is equally correct. Therefore, if truth is unreachable, the individual can do no better than seek acclaim. In the first dialogues Plato wrote, including *Euthyphro, Apology,* and *Crito,* Socrates held that if the majority hold a belief, that belief is likely to be wrong. Or, to put it another way, acclaim is philosophical death. As represented by Plato's portrait of Socrates, the real philosopher is the outsider, the outlaw. The more a person is honored and considered wise by society, the less that person is in contact with Truth. The genuine philosopher persistently delivers an unpopular message, often at his own peril.

The *Euthyphro,* the first dialogue we will investigate, is an excellent example of the kinds of concerns that put Socrates at odds with the Athenian majority.

What Are Some Key Features of the *Euthyphro*?

In the last weeks of his life, Socrates meets an acquaintance, Euthyphro, outside the court. Socrates is there to defend himself against charges of impiety and corrupting the youth of Athens. Euthyphro has come to bring a charge of murder against his father. Euthyphro explains the somewhat complex circumstances of his case:

> The man who is dead was a servant of mine who worked for us as a field laborer at Naxos. One day in a fit of drunken passion he got into a quarrel with one of our domestic servants and killed him. My father tied him hand and foot and threw him into a ditch and then sent to Athens to ask of a priest what he should do with him. Meantime, my father had no thought of him, being under the impression the man was a murderer and that even if he did die there would be no great harm. This was just what happened. For such was the effect of cold, hunger, and chains upon the laborer, he was dead before the messenger returned from the seer. My father and family are angry with me for taking the side of the murderer and prosecuting my father. They say he did not kill him, and if he did, the dead man was nothing but a murderer, and I should not take any notice, for a son is unholy who prosecutes a father. That shows, Socrates, how little they know of the opinions of the gods about the holy and the unholy.

Socrates immediately leaps upon Euthyphro's claim to have knowledge about the holy and the unholy. The dialogue is a record of Socrates' struggle to get Euthyphro to give a satisfactory definition of holiness.

To give you a running start at the *Euthyphro*, let's review key features of the first two definitions of the holy. Here is Euthyphro's first definition:

> Holiness is doing as I am doing: prosecuting anyone who is guilty of murder, sacrilege, or any other similar crime—whether he be your father or mother or some other person, that makes no difference—and not prosecuting them is unholy.

Now, let's think this through.

Euthyphro has improperly defined holiness by giving an *example* of holiness. In the same way, one might improperly define ice cream as Rocky Road or a personal computer as a Macintosh. A few more samples of this kind of mistaken definition would be . . . ?

One might improperly define _____ as

_____ , or one might improperly define

_____ as _____ .

Obviously, an example does not serve as a definition. A definition states the general characteristics of a class of objects. An example is simply one member of the class. Thus, we could not define ice cream as Rocky Road simply because there are other kinds of ice cream besides Rocky Road. A more satisfactory definition of ice cream might be something like "a frozen dessert made from milk and sugar." This is the type of response Socrates is looking for, a description of the general nature of holiness, not an example of one kind of holiness.

Socrates makes this point in the following interchange:

> SOCRATES: . . . Right now I would rather hear from you a more precise answer, which you have not as yet given, my friend, to the question, "What is the holy?" In reply, you only say that holiness is doing as you do, charging your father with murder.
>
> EUTHYPHRO: And that is true, Socrates.
>
> SOC: I am sure, Euthyphro, but there are many other holy acts.
>
> EUTH: There are.
>
> SOC: Remember, I did not ask you to give me two or three examples of holiness, but to explain the essential characteristic or form which makes all holy actions to be holy. Do you not recollect that there was one essential characteristic or form which made the unholy unholy, and the holy holy?
>
> EUTH: I remember.
>
> SOC: Tell me what this is and then I shall have a standard which I may look at and by which I may measure the nature of actions, whether yours or anyone's, and say this action is holy, and that unholy.

Euthyphro tries to satisfy Socrates with an improved definition of holiness: "Holiness . . . is what the gods love, and unholiness is what the gods hate."

Socrates grants that this is an improvement. Euthyphro's new definition at least attempts to describe the entire class of holiness. However, under Socrates' analysis, this definition also proves unsatisfactory. Socrates gets Euthyphro to admit to the following points:

1. The gods have disagreements about moral issues.

2. Thus, the same human action could be loved by some gods and hated by other gods.

3. Thus, according to Euthyphro's definition, the same action could be both holy and unholy.

Euthyphro obviously has a problem. His definition produces the impossible circumstance that a single action could be simultaneously holy and unholy. This would be as ridiculous as a definition that defined ice cream as the same thing as what is not ice cream. Whatever holiness is, it can't be the opposite of itself!

When the second definition collapses, Euthyphro is ready to quit. Socrates, however, manages to coax him into several more attempts. Annotation Tasks in the margins of the *Euthyphro* will point you toward key features of these arguments.

You're now ready to contemplate the first complete work of philosophy on the tour. Travel far by reading slowly.

READING:
PLATO'S *EUTHYPHRO*

Thus far you have responded thoughtfully to my questions. This chapter includes your first extended reading on this tour. For this reading and those that follow, you will be underlining and making notes in the book's margins. These Annotation Tasks will help you understand the general concepts of each dialogue. Then, after each selection, we will have a dialogue of our own to help you more clearly comprehend the philosophy you read.

In the *Euthyphro* the Annotation Tasks involve finding background information and understanding the main theme of the dialogue.

Every piece of literature introduces characters and provides information about their world. Important pieces of this information usually appear in the first few pages. In the *Euthyphro* you will have no trouble finding Euthyphro's and Socrates' reasons for coming to court. You will have to read slowly, however, to find information about the differences in their personalities. Search for examples of Socrates' use of irony. Start by underlining anything he says that sounds mocking or not entirely serious. Underline Euthyphro's profession and anything he says that gives you clues about his character.

Once you are past the opening pages of the dialogue, the Annotation Tasks will help you find each definition of holiness and the main points Socrates makes to improve and/or refute each definition.

Euthyphro

EUTHYPHRO: Why have you left the Lyceum, Socrates, and what are you doing by the court of the king archon? Surely you cannot be engaged in an action before the king, as I am.

SOCRATES: Not in an action, Euthyphro. Indictment is the word the Athenians use.

EUTH: What! I suppose someone is prosecuting you; I cannot believe you are prosecuting someone else.

SOC: Certainly not.

EUTH: Then someone else is prosecuting you?

SOC: Yes.

EUTH: Who is he?

The Lyceum was a popular area of Athens where Aristotle would later establish his school. The king archon was a judge who presided over trials involving religious issues.

Underline in the following:
1. Socrates' reason for being at court.
2. Meletus's charge against Socrates.
3. Examples of Socrates' irony.

Socrates' ironic opinion of

Meletus is _____

_____

_____

_____

_____.

Underline:
1. Two indications of Euthyphro's profession.
2. Euthyphro's purpose in court.
3. Examples of Socratic irony.

Soc: A young man who is little known, Euthyphro, and whom I hardly know. His name is Meletus of the township of Pitthis. Perhaps you know his appearance. He has a beaklike nose, long straight hair, and straggly beard.

Euth: No, I do not remember him, Socrates. What is the charge he brings against you?

Soc: What is the charge? Well, a very serious charge, which shows a good deal of character in the young man, and for which he is certainly to be respected. He says he knows how the youth are corrupted and who are their corruptors. I believe he must be a wise man, and seeing I am anything but a wise man, he has discovered me and is going to accuse me of corrupting his young friends. Of this our mother the State is to be the judge. Of all our political men he is the only one who seems to me to begin in the right way, with the cultivation of virtue in the youth. He is a good farmer who takes care of the young shoots first and clears away us who are their destroyers. That is the first step; he will afterwards attend to the elder branches, and if he goes on as he has begun, he will be a very great public benefactor.

Euth: I hope he may, but I fear, Socrates, the reverse will turn out to be the truth. My opinion is in attacking you he is simply aiming a blow at the very heart of the city. But in what way does he say you corrupt the young?

Soc: He brings a strange charge against me, which at first hearing is surprising. He says I am an inventor of new gods and deny the existence of old ones. This is the basis of his indictment.

Euth: I understand, Socrates. He intends to attack you about the spiritual sign which occasionally, as you say, comes to you. He thinks you have unorthodox beliefs and is going to bring you before the court for this. He knows such a charge is readily received, for the world is always jealous of novelties in religion. I know when I speak in the Assembly about divine things, and foretell the future to them, they laugh at me as if I was a madman. Yet every word I say is true. But they are jealous of all of us; I suppose we must be brave and not mind them.

Soc: Their laughter, friend Euthyphro, is not important. A man may be thought wise, but the Athenians, I suspect, do not care much about this, until he begins to make other men wise. Then for some reason, perhaps, as you say from jealousy, they are angry.

Euth: I have no wish to discover their attitude toward me about this.

Soc: Perhaps you don't mingle with the masses and are not likely to impart your wisdom. But I have a benevolent habit of pouring myself out to everybody and would even pay for a listener, and I am afraid that the Athenians know this. Therefore, as I was saying, if the Athenians would only laugh at me as you say they laugh at you, the time might pass pleasantly enough in the court. But perhaps they are serious, and then what the end will be only you prophets can predict.

Euth: I believe the affair will end in nothing, Socrates, and you will win your case. And I think I shall win mine.

Soc: And what is your case? Are you the prosecutor or defendant, Euthyphro?

Euth: I am the prosecutor.

Soc: Of whom?

EUTH: You will think me mad when I tell you whom I am prosecuting.

SOC: Why, will the criminal fly off?

EUTH: No, he is not very lively at his time of life.

SOC: Who is he?

EUTH: My father.

SOC: Your father! Good heavens, you don't mean that?

EUTH: Yes.

SOC: Of what is he accused?

EUTH: Murder, Socrates.

SOC: By the powers, Euthyphro! How little does the common herd know about what is right in such a case. A man must be an extraordinary man and have made great strides in wisdom before he could have been able to bring this charge.

Socrates' general attitude toward Euthyphro is _____ _____ _____ _____.

EUTH: Indeed, Socrates, he must have made great strides.

SOC: I suppose the man whom your father murdered was one of your relatives. If he had been a stranger you would never think of prosecuting him.

EUTH: I am amused, Socrates, at your distinction between one who is a relation and one who is not a relation. For surely the pollution is the same in either case if you knowingly associate with the murderer when you ought to cleanse yourself and him by bringing him to court.

The real question is whether the murdered man has been justly slain. If justly, then your duty is to let the matter alone; but if unjustly, then even if the murderer lives under the same roof with you and eats at the same table, prosecute him. The man who is dead was a servant of mine who worked for us as a field laborer at Naxos. One day in a fit of drunken passion he got into a quarrel with one of our domestic servants and killed him. My father tied him hand and foot and threw him into a ditch, and then sent to Athens to ask of a priest what he should do with him. Meantime, my father had no thought of him, being under the impression the man was a murderer and that even if he did die there would be no great harm. This was just what happened. For such was the effect of cold, hunger, and chains upon the laborer, he was dead before the messenger returned from the seer. My father and family are angry with me for taking the side of the murderer and prosecuting my father. They say he did not kill him, and if he did, the dead man was nothing but a murderer, and I should not take any notice, for a son is unholy who prosecutes a father. That shows, Socrates, how little they know of the opinions of the gods about the holy and the unholy.

In essence, Euthyphro is arguing that _____ _____ _____ _____ _____ _____.

SOC: Good heavens, Euthyphro! Have you such precise knowledge of the holy and the unholy, and of divine things in general, that you are not afraid you too may be doing an unholy thing bringing a case against your father?

EUTH: The best of Euthyphro, and that which distinguishes him, Socrates, from other men, is his exact knowledge of all these matters. What should I be good for without that?

SOC: Rare friend! I think I cannot do better than be your disciple, before the trial with Meletus begins. Then I shall challenge him, and say I have always had a great interest in religious questions, and now, as he charges me with innovations in religion, I am your disciple.

Socrates wants Euthyphro to

think _____

_____,

but, in fact, Socrates means

_____

_____.

Therefore, this is another example of Socrates' irony.

Underline:
1. Euthyphro's first attempt at
   defining the holy.
2. Socrates' reaction to this
   attempt.

Zeus was the ruler of the
Greek gods; Cronos was
Zeus's father, who was killed
by Zeus; and Uranus was
Zeus's grandfather and first
ruler of the Universe, killed by
Cronos. The "nameless manner" of his death involved
castration.

Euthyphro argues his action is

holy because _____

_____

_____

_____

_____.

The Panathenaea is an Athenian religious festival held
once every four years.

Thus far, the main differences
between Socrates and

Euthyphro are: _____

_____

_____

_____

_____

_____

_____.

"Now you, Meletus," as I shall say to him, "acknowledge Euthyphro to be a great theologian and sound in his opinions. If you think that of him, you should think the same of me and not have me into court. You should begin by indicting my teacher who is the real corruptor, not of the young, but of the old; that is to say, of myself whom he instructs, and of his old father whom he admonishes and chastises." And if Meletus refuses to listen to me, but will go on, and will not shift the indictment from me to you, I cannot do better than say in court that I challenged him in this way.

EUTH: Yes, Socrates, and if he attempts to indict me I will find his weak point. The court shall have a great deal more to say to him than to me.

SOC: I know that, dear friend, and that is the reason I desire to be your disciple. I observe no one, not even Meletus, appears to notice you. His sharp eyes have found me out immediately and he has indicted me for impiety. And therefore I beg you to tell me the nature of the holy and the unholy, which you said you knew so well. Is not holiness in every action always the same? And is not unholiness always the opposite of holiness and always the same in every case?

EUTH: Of course, Socrates.

SOC: Then what is holiness and what is unholiness?

EUTH: Holiness is doing as I am doing; prosecuting anyone who is guilty of murder, sacrilege, or of any other similar crime—whether he be your father or mother, or some other person, that makes no difference—and not prosecuting them is unholy. Please consider, Socrates, what a clear proof I will give you of the truth of what I am saying, which I have already given to others. For do not men regard Zeus as the best and most righteous of the gods?—and even they admit he bound his father (Cronos) because he wickedly devoured his sons, and he too had punished his own father (Uranus) for a similar reason, in a nameless manner. And yet when I bring a case against my father, they are angry with me. This is their inconsistent way of talking when the gods are concerned and when I am concerned.

SOC: Is this the reason, Euthyphro, why I am charged with impiety—that I cannot get away with these stories about the gods? And therefore I suppose people think me wrong. But, as you who are well informed about the gods believe in them, I cannot do better than assent to your superior wisdom. For what else can I say, confessing as I do, that I know nothing of them. I wish you would tell me whether you really believe such stories are true.

EUTH: Yes, Socrates, and things more wonderful still, of which the world is in ignorance.

SOC: Do you really believe the gods fought with one another, had quarrels, battles, and the like, as the poets say, and as you may see represented in the works of great artists? The temples are full of them, especially the robe of Athena, embroidered with them, which is carried up to the Acropolis at the great Panathenaea. Are all these tales of the gods true, Euthyphro?

EUTH: Yes, Socrates, and, as I was saying, I can tell you, if you would like to hear them, many other things about the gods which would amaze you.

SOC: I believe you. You shall tell me them at some other time when I have leisure. Right now I would rather hear from you a more precise answer, which you have not as yet given, my friend, to the question, "What is the holy?" In reply, you only say that holiness is doing as you do, charging your father with murder.

EUTH: And that is true, Socrates.

SOC: I am sure, Euthyphro, but there are many other holy acts.

EUTH: There are.

SOC: Remember I did not ask you to give me two or three examples of holiness, but to explain the essential characteristic or form which makes all holy actions to be holy. Do you not recollect that there was one essential characteristic or form which made the unholy unholy, and the holy holy?

EUTH: I remember.

SOC: Tell me what this is and then I shall have a standard which I may look at and by which I may measure the nature of actions, whether yours or anyone's, and say this action is holy, and that unholy.

EUTH: I will tell you, if you like.

SOC: I would like it very much.

EUTH: Holiness, then, is what the gods love, and unholiness is what the gods hate.

SOC: Very good, Euthyphro. You have now given me just the sort of answer I wanted. Whether it is true or not I cannot tell, although I believe you will show me the truth of your words.

EUTH: Of course.

SOC: Come, then, let us examine what we are saying. That thing or person which the gods love is holy and the thing or person which the gods hate is unholy. Was that what you said?

EUTH: Yes, I said that.

SOC: And that seems to have been very well said too?

EUTH: Yes, Socrates, I think so.

SOC: And further, Euthyphro, the gods were admitted to have enmities and hatreds and differences—that was also said?

EUTH: Yes, that was said.

SOC: And what sort of difference creates hatred and anger? Suppose for example you and I, my good friend, disagree about a number. Do differences of this sort make us enemies and set us against one another, or do we at once calculate and end them by a sum?

EUTH: We do.

SOC: Or, suppose we differ about the size of something, do we not quickly put that difference to an end by measuring?

EUTH: That is true.

SOC: And we end a controversy about heavy and light by using a scale?

EUTH: Of course.

SOC: But what are the disagreements which, because they cannot be thus decided, make us angry and set us against one another? I believe the answer does not occur to you at the moment and therefore I will suggest this

Underline:
1. The main points Socrates makes against the first definition of the holy.
2. Euthyphro's second definition of the holy.

Socrates' point about disagreements about numbers, size, and

weight is _____

_____

_____

_____ .

The differences between these disagreements and the previous

is _____

_____

_____

_____ .

Underline this. It is an important point in Socrates' argument against Euthyphro

because _____

_____

_____ .

Hephaestus is a Greek god and the deformed son of Hera, a Greek goddess.

Euthyphro's second definition of the holy is not satisfactory

because _____

_____

_____

_____ .

happens when the disagreements are about the just and unjust, good and evil, honorable and dishonorable. Are not these the issues about which, when disagreeing, and unable satisfactorily to decide our disagreement, we quarrel?

EUTH: Yes, Socrates, that is the nature of the disagreements about which we quarrel.

SOC: And the quarrels of the gods, noble Euthyphro, when they occur, are they similar?

EUTH: They are.

SOC: They have differences of opinion, as you say, about good and evil, just and unjust, honorable and dishonorable. There would have been no quarrels among them, if there had been no such differences—would there?

EUTH: You are quite right.

SOC: Does not every man love what he believes noble and just and good and hate the opposite?

EUTH: Very true.

SOC: But then, as you say, people regard the same things differently, some as just and others as unjust; they argue about this and there arise wars and fights among them.

EUTH: Yes, that is true.

SOC: The same things are hated by some gods and loved by other gods and are both hateful and dear to them?

EUTH: True.

SOC: Then the same things, Euthyphro, will be holy and also unholy?

EUTH: That, I suppose, is true.

SOC: Then, my friend, I am surprised you have not answered what I asked. For I certainly did not ask what was both holy and unholy: And what is loved by the gods appears also to be hated by them. Therefore, Euthyphro, in bringing your father to trial you may very likely be doing what is agreeable to Zeus but disagreeable to Cronos or Uranus and what is acceptable to Hephaestus but unacceptable to Hera, and there may be other gods who have similar differences of opinion.

EUTH: But I believe, Socrates, that all the gods would be agreed about the correctness of punishing a murderer. There would be no difference of opinion about that.

SOC: Well, but speaking of men, Euthyphro, did you ever hear anyone arguing that a murderer or any sort of evildoer should be let off?

EUTH: They are always arguing this, especially in courts of law. They commit all sorts of crimes and there is nothing they will not do or say to escape punishment.

SOC: But do they admit their guilt, Euthyphro, and yet say they ought not to be punished?

EUTH: No, they do not.

SOC: Then there are some things which they do not try to say and do. They do not try to argue the guilty are to be unpunished, but they deny their guilt, do they not?

EUTH: True.

SOC: And the gods are in the same situation if, as you say, they quarrel about the just and unjust, and some say they wrong one another, and others deny this. For surely neither the gods nor man will ever try to say the doer of evil is not to be punished—you don't mean to tell me that?

EUTH: That is true, Socrates, in general.

SOC: But they disagree about particulars and this applies not only to men but also to the gods. If they disagree at all they disagree about some act which is called in question, and which some affirm to be just, others to be unjust. Is that true?

EUTH: Quite true.

SOC: Well then, my dear friend Euthyphro, do tell me, for my instruction, what proof do you have that in the opinion of all the gods a servant who is guilty of murder, and is put in chains by the master of the dead man, and dies because he is put in chains before his corrector can learn from the authorities what he ought to do with him, dies unjustly; and that on behalf of him a son should proceed against his father and accuse his father of murder? How would you show that all the gods absolutely agree in approving of his act? Prove that to me and I will applaud your wisdom as long as you live.

Socrates' general point is

_____

_____

_____

_____.

EUTH: That would not be an easy task, although I could make the matter very clear to you.

SOC: I understand. You mean I am not so quick as the jury, for to them you will be sure to prove the act is unjust, and hateful to the gods.

EUTH: Yes indeed, Socrates, at least if they will listen to me.

SOC: They will be sure to listen if they find you are a good speaker. There was a notion that came into my mind while you were speaking. I said to myself: "Well, and what if Euthyphro does prove to me that all the gods regarded the death of the laborer as unjust, how do I know anything more of the nature of holy and unholy? Granting this action may be hateful to the gods, still these distinctions have no bearing on the definition of holy and unholy, for that which is hateful to some of the gods has been shown to be also pleasing and dear to others." And therefore, Euthyphro, I don't ask you to prove this. I suppose, if you like, all the gods hate such an action. But I will change the definition to say that what *all* the gods hate is unholy, and what they *all* love is holy and what some of them love and others hate is both or neither. Shall this be our definition of holiness and unholiness?

Find and underline the third definition of the holy.

EUTH: Why not, Socrates?

SOC: No reason as far as I am concerned, Euthyphro. But whether this admission will greatly assist you in instructing me as you promised is what you should consider.

EUTH: Yes, I would say what all the gods love is holy and the opposite, which they all hate, unholy.

SOC: Should we investigate into the truth of this, Euthyphro, or simply accept the mere statement on our own authority and that of others?

EUTH: We should investigate, and I believe the statement will stand the test of our investigation.

The next two pages are the most challenging in the *Euthyphro*. Read them several times and underline important points.

Soc: That, my good friend, we shall know better in a little while. The point which I want first to understand is whether the holy is loved by the gods because it is holy, or holy because it is loved by the gods.

Euth: I don't understand your meaning, Socrates.

Soc: I will try to explain. We speak of carrying and we speak of something being carried, of leading and something being led, seeing and something being seen. And there is a difference which you understand.

Euth: I think I understand.

Soc: And is something that is loved different from the one who does the loving?

Euth: Certainly.

Soc: Well tell me, is what is carried in this condition of being carried because someone carries, or for some other reason?

Euth: No, that is the reason.

Soc: And the same is true of what is led and of what is seen?

Euth: True.

The major idea Socrates establishes is _____ _____ _____ _____ _____ .

Soc: And someone does not see an object because it is a seen object, it is a seen object because someone sees it. Someone does not lead an object because it is a led object, it is a led object because someone leads it. Something is a carried object because someone carries it, someone does not carry the object because it is a carried object. And now I think, Euthyphro, my meaning will be clear and my meaning is that any effect [like being carried] implies a previous cause [like someone carrying]. It is not an effect because it is an effect, but it is an effect because of a previous cause. It does not occur because it is in a state of occurring, but it is in a state of occurring because something caused it to occur. Do you admit that?

Euth: Yes.

Socrates is saying _____ _____ _____ _____ _____ .

Soc: Is that which is loved either the cause or the effect of something else?

Euth: Yes.

Soc: And the same holds as in the previous instances; the effect of something being loved follows the cause of someone loving it. The effect does not come before the cause.

Euth: That is certain.

A good example would be _____ _____ _____ _____ .

Soc: And what do you say of the holy, Euthyphro: Is the holy, according to your definition, loved by all the gods?

Euth: Yes.

Soc: Because it is holy, or for some other reason?

Euth: No, that is the reason.

Soc: It is loved because it is holy, not holy because it is loved?

Euth: Yes.

Soc: And that which is loved by the gods is in a state of being loved by them because they love it.

Euth: Certainly.

Soc: Then what is loved by the gods, Euthyphro, is not the same as the holy, nor is what is holy the same as what is loved by the gods, as you say. They are two different things.

EUTH: What do you mean, Socrates?

SOC: I mean the holy has been defined by us as loved by the gods because it is holy, not holy because it is loved.

EUTH: Yes.

SOC: But that which is defined as loved by the gods has that definition because the gods love it. They do not love something because they love it.

EUTH: True.

SOC: But, friend Euthyphro, if that which is holy is the same as that which is loved by the gods and that which is holy is loved because it is holy, then that which is loved by the gods would have been loved because it is loved by the gods; but if what is loved by the gods is loved by them because it is loved by them, then that which is holy would have been holy because it is loved by them. But now you see that the reverse is the case, and that they are quite different from one another. The one is loved because it is initially worthy of love, the other is worthy of love because it is initially loved. Thus you appear to me, Euthyphro, when I ask you what is the essence of holiness, to offer a characteristic only, and not the essence—the characteristic of being loved by all the gods. But you still refuse to explain to me the essence of the holy. And therefore, if you please, I will ask you not to hide your treasure but tell me once more what holiness really is, whether loved by the gods or not, for that is a matter about which we will not quarrel. And what is unholiness?

EUTH: I really do not know, Socrates, how to say what I mean. Somehow or other our arguments, on whatever ground we rest them, seem to walk away.

SOC: Your words, Euthyphro, are like the sculptures of my ancestor Daedalus. If I were the creator of them, you might say this comes from my being his relation and this is the reason why my arguments walk away and won't remain fixed where they are placed. But now, as the words are your own, you must find some other complaint, for they certainly, as you yourself say, show an inclination to be on the move.

EUTH: No, Socrates, I still say you are the Daedalus who sets arguments in motion. I do not make them move for they would never have stirred, as far as I am concerned.

SOC: Then I must be greater than Daedalus. He only made his own inventions move, I move those of other people as well. And the wonder of it is, I would rather they did not. I would give the wisdom of Daedalus and the wealth of Tantalus to be able to hold them and keep them still. But enough of this. As I see you are lazy, I will try to show you how you might teach me the nature of piety; and I hope that you will work harder. Tell me, then, is not that which is holy also morally right?

EUTH: Yes.

SOC: And is, then, all that is morally right also holy? Or, is that which is holy all morally right, but that which is morally right only in part, and not all, holy?

EUTH: I don't understand you, Socrates.

SOC: And yet I know you are as much wiser than I as you are younger. But, as I was saying, dear friend, the abundance of your wisdom makes you lazy.

Stop. There is nothing more difficult on our tour than this paragraph. Be *very* patient. You will understand slightly more with each rereading. For extra help, complete pages 125–127.

The basic idea of this paragraph seems to be _____

_____

_____

_____

_____

_____ .

Daedalus was a legendary master craftsman.

Since the beginning of the dialogue, Euthyphro's mood has changed from _____

_____

to _____

_____ .

Tantalus was sentenced to dwell in Hades by Zeus for his crimes. In Hades, he stood knee-deep in water that receded when he tried to drink, beneath branches of fruit too high for him to reach.

An example of the relationship between the holy and the morally right would be the relationship between

_____

and _____ .

Stasinus is a poet about whom nothing is known except this quotation.

Please exert yourself, for there is no real difficulty in understanding me. What I mean I will explain by an illustration of what I do not mean. The poet (Stasinus) sings "Of Zeus, the author and creator of all these things, You will not tell: for where there is fear there is also reverence."

I disagree with this poet. Shall I tell you why I disagree?

EUTH: Please do.

SOC: I would not say where there is fear there is also reverence. I am sure many persons fear poverty and disease, and similar evils, but I do not see they reverence what they fear.

EUTH: Very true.

SOC: But where reverence is, there is fear. He who has a feeling of reverence about any action also fears a bad reputation.

EUTH: No doubt.

From here until the end of the *Euthyphro,* underline each new definition of the holy and any other important points.

SOC: Then are we wrong in saying where there is fear there is also reverence? No, there is not always reverence where there is fear; for fear is a more extended concept, and reverence is a part of fear, just as the odd is a part of number, and number is a more extended concept than the odd. I suppose you follow me now?

EUTH: Quite well.

SOC: That was the sort of question I meant to raise when asking whether the morally right is the holy, or the holy the morally right; and whether there may be moral rightness where there is no holiness; for moral rightness is the larger concept of which the holy is only a part. Do you agree in that?

EUTH: Yes, that, I think, is correct.

SOC: Then if holiness is a part of moral rightness, I suppose we should inquire what part? If you had asked me what is an even number, and what part of number the even is, I should have had no difficulty in replying, a number which can be divided into two equal whole numbers. Do you agree?

EUTH: Yes.

SOC: In the same way, I want you to tell me what part of the morally right is the holy. Thus, will I be able to tell Meletus not to do me injustice, or indict me for impiety, as I am now adequately instructed by you in the nature of holiness and its opposites.

EUTH: The holy, Socrates, appears to me to be part of moral rightness which attends to the gods, as there is the other part of moral rightness which attends to men.

SOC: That is good, Euthyphro; yet still there is a little point about which I would like to have further information. What is the meaning of "attention"? For attention can hardly be used in the same sense when applied to the gods as when applied to other things. For instance, horses are said to require attention, and not every person is able to attend to them, but only a person skilled in horsemanship. Is that true?

EUTH: Quite true.

SOC: I suppose that the art of horsemanship is the art of attending to horses?

EUTH: Yes.

SOC: Nor is everyone qualified to attend to dogs, but only the huntsman.

EUTH: True.

SOC: And I would also think the art of the huntsman is the art of attending to dogs?

EUTH: Yes.

SOC: As the art of the oxherd is the art of attending to oxen?

EUTH: Very true.

SOC: And holiness is the art of attending to the gods—that would be your meaning, Euthyphro?

EUTH: Yes.

SOC: And is not attention always designed for the good or benefit of that to which the attention is given? As in the case of horses, you may observe that when attended to by the horseman's art they are benefited and improved, are they not?

EUTH: True.

SOC: As dogs are benefited by the huntsman's art, and oxen by the art of the oxherd, and all other things are tended or attended for their good and not for their harm?

EUTH: Certainly, not for their harm.

SOC: But for their good?

EUTH: Of course.

SOC: And does holiness, which was defined as the art of attending to the gods, benefit or improve them? Would you say when you do a holy act you make any of the gods better?

EUTH: No, no, that is certainly not my meaning.

SOC: Indeed, Euthyphro, I did not suppose this was your meaning. That was the reason I asked you the nature of this attention, because I thought this was not your meaning.

EUTH: Thank you, Socrates, for that is not what I meant.

SOC: Good, but I must still ask what is this attention to the gods which is called holiness?

EUTH: It is the same, Socrates, as servants give to their masters.

SOC: I understand—a sort of service to the gods.

EUTH: Exactly.

SOC: Medicine is also a kind of service to attain some goal. Would you not say the goal was health?

EUTH: Yes.

SOC: Again, there is an art of the shipbuilder with a specific goal?

EUTH: Yes, Socrates, the goal of building a ship.

SOC: As there is an art of the house-builder with the goal of building a house?

EUTH: Yes.

SOC: And now tell me, my good friend, about this art which serves the gods: What work does that help to accomplish? For you must surely know if, as you say, you are of all men living the one who is best instructed in religion.

EUTH: And that is true, Socrates.

By this point in the dialogue, the reader understands Euthyphro is the kind of person who

_____

_____

_____

_____

_____

_____

SOC: Tell me then, oh tell me—what is the good work which the gods do by the help of us as their servants?

EUTH: Many, Socrates, are the works which they do.

SOC: Why, my friend, and so are those of a general. But the main one is easily described. Would you not say that victory in war is the main one?

EUTH: Certainly.

SOC: Many, too, are the works of the farmer, if I am not wrong; but his chief work is growing food.

EUTH: Exactly.

SOC: And of the many things which the gods do, which is the main one?

EUTH: I have told you already, Socrates, that to learn all these things accurately will be very tiresome. Let me simply say that holiness is learning how to please the gods in word and deed, by prayers and sacrifices. That is holiness, which is the salvation of families and states, just as unholiness, which is unpleasing to the gods, is their ruin and destruction.

SOC: I think you could have answered in many fewer words the main question I asked, Euthyphro, if you had chosen. But I see plainly you do not want to instruct me: Otherwise why, when we had reached the present point, did you turn aside? If you had only answered me, I would have learned from you by this time the nature of holiness. Now, as the asker of a question is necessarily dependent on the answerer, where you lead I must follow. I can only ask again, what is the holy, and what is holiness? Do you mean they are a sort of science of praying and sacrificing?

EUTH: Yes, I do.

SOC: And sacrificing is giving to the gods, and prayer is asking of the gods?

EUTH: Yes, Socrates.

SOC: According to this, then holiness is a science of asking and giving?

EUTH: You understand me perfectly, Socrates.

SOC: Yes, my friend, the reason is I am a follower of your science, and give my mind to it, and therefore nothing which you say will be thrown away. Please then tell me, what is the nature of this service to the gods? Do you mean that we make requests and give gifts to them?

EUTH: Yes, I do.

SOC: Is not the right way of asking to ask of them what we want?

EUTH: Certainly.

SOC: And the right way of giving is to give to them in return what they want from us. There would be no meaning in an art which gives to any one what he does not want.

EUTH: Very true, Socrates.

SOC: Then holiness, Euthyphro, is an art which gods and men have of doing business with one another?

EUTH: That is an expression which you may use, if you like.

SOC: But I have no particular liking for anything but the truth. I wish, however, you would tell me what benefit comes to the gods from our gifts. That they are the givers of every good to us is clear; but how we can give any

Socrates is the kind of person who _____

_____

_____

_____

_____ .

good thing to them in return is far from being equally clear. If they give everything and we give nothing, that must be an affair of business in which we have a great advantage over them.

EUTH: And do you imagine, Socrates, that any benefit comes to the gods from what they receive from us?

SOC: But if not, Euthyphro, what sort of gifts do we give the gods?

EUTH: What should we give them, but tributes of honor and, as I was just now saying, what is pleasing to them?

SOC: Holiness, then, is pleasing to the gods, but not beneficial or dear to them?

EUTH: I should say that nothing could be dearer.

SOC: Then once more the assertion is repeated that holiness is dear to the gods?

EUTH: No doubt.

SOC: And when you say this, can you wonder at your words not standing firm, but walking away? Will you accuse me of being the Daedalus who makes them walk away, not seeing there is another and far greater artist than Daedalus who makes them go round in a circle and that is yourself. For, the argument, as you will see, comes round to the same point. I think you must remember our saying the holy was not the same as that which is loved by the gods. Do you remember that?

EUTH: I do.

SOC: And do you not see what is loved of the gods is the holy and this is the same as what is dear to them?

EUTH: True.

SOC: Then either we were wrong before, or, if we were right then, we are wrong now.

EUTH: I suppose that is the case.

SOC: Then we must begin again and ask, what is holiness? That is an inquiry which I shall never be tired of pursuing as far as I can. I beg you not to reject me, but to apply your mind to the utmost and tell me the truth. For, if any man knows, you are the one and therefore I shall hold you, like Proteus, until you tell me. For if you had not known the nature of holiness and unholiness, I am confident you would never have, on behalf of a laborer, charged your aged father with murder. You would not have run such a risk of doing wrong in the sight of the gods and you would have had too much respect for the opinions of men. I am sure, therefore, you know the nature of holiness and unholiness. Speak out then, my dear Euthyphro, and do not hide your knowledge.

EUTH: Another time, Socrates, for I am in a hurry and must go now.

SOC: Alas! My companion, will you leave me in despair? I was hoping you would instruct me in the nature of holiness and unholiness, so I might have cleared myself of Meletus and his indictment. Then I might have proved to him I had been converted by Euthyphro and had given up rash innovations and speculations, in which I had indulged through ignorance, and was about to lead a better life.

What has happened to

Euthyphro is _____

_____

_____

_____

_____

_____.

EXERCISE 7.1

Thinking About the *Euthyphro*

Respond to the following questions in the spaces provided.

1. Perhaps this is the first piece of philosophy you have ever read. Why do you think Plato wrote it?

Perhaps because _____

_____

_____

_____

_____ or because _____

_____

_____

_____. My main reaction was _____

_____

_____

_____

_____.

   a. What kind of person is Socrates?

If I had to pick three characteristics, I would say he is _____

_____

_____ because _____

_____

_____ and he is _____

_____

_____ because _____

_____

_____. He also is _____

_____

_____ because _____

_____

_____.

   b. How about Euthyphro?

Euthyphro's three main characteristics and one good example of each are _____

_____

_____

_____

_____

_____

_____

_____.

2. How many different definitions of holiness did you find?

I think there are _____. The first one, of course, is _____

_____

_____

_____. The others, in order, are _____

_____

_____

_____

_____

_____

_____

_____

_____

_____

_____

_____.

3. Now, let us consider two of Socrates' refutations in more detail. Euthyphro's first definition of the holy is that holiness is the act of prosecuting his father for murder. How does Socrates show Euthyphro this is wrong?

Socrates argues this is not a definition of holiness because _____

_____

_____

_____

_____

_____.

If you were asked to define a car, you would be duplicating Euthyphro's kind of error if you said that a car is _____

_____

_____

_____. In fact, a real definition of a car would involve _____

_____

_____

_____

_____.

4. In the refutation of the third definition of the holy, Socrates states, "Someone does not see an object because it is a seen object, it is a seen object because someone sees it. Someone does not lead an object because it is a led object, it is a led object because someone leads it." This may not be simple to understand. Think of your own example and try to explain his point.

One example of what Socrates is saying would be _____
_____
_____
_____
_____. The point he is trying to make is _____
_____
_____
_____
_____
_____
_____.

5. Later in this refutation, Socrates asks Euthyphro if (a) the gods love something because it is holy or (b) something is holy because the gods love it. Let
   us say you make a holy prayer to get a good grade in philosophy. In the case
   of (a), which comes first—the holiness of your prayer or the gods loving it?

I would say _____ comes first in the case of (a), because
_____
_____
_____
_____.

6. Let's try that one more time. In the case of (a), is your prayer holy and then
   the gods love it, or does the prayer become holy because the gods love it?

I would say _____
_____
_____
_____ because _____
_____
_____
_____.

7. Now, from the point of view of statement (b), which comes first—the holiness of the prayer or the gods' love of it?

I would say _____
_____
_____
_____ because _____
_____
_____
_____
_____.

8. Which comes first, cause or effect?
_____ always comes before _____.

9. What is the cause and effect in statement (a)? In statement (b)?

In (a) the cause is _____

_____ and the effect is _____

_____. In (b) the cause is

_____ and the effect is _____

_____.

10. Which of the two does Euthyphro choose, (a) or (b)?

Looking back in the text, I see Euthyphro chooses _____

as a definition of holiness. This cannot be a definition of the holy because _____

_____

_____

_____

_____

_____

_____.

11. Of all the definitions of the holy, which do you think is closest to the truth?

The best definition is probably _____

_____

_____

_____

_____

_____.

12. Now, try your own hand at thinking about the holy. Let us say we both agree that Mother Teresa of India was holy. She lived in poverty, helped the poorest of the poor, and had no concern for herself. And let us assume that God loved her. Did God's love make her holy, or was she holy and God loved her as a result?

I would say _____

_____

_____ because _____

_____

_____

_____.

13. Take this another step. Let us say you perform the good action of sending money to Mother Teresa's mission. Is this a good action because God loves such actions, or is it good all by itself? Does the goodness come from the action or from God's approval? If you take the coward's way out and say "both," then tell me the difference between the goodness that comes from sending money and the goodness that comes from God.

I would say that the act of sending money _____

_____

_____

_____

_____

_____

_____

_____.

14. See if you can do better than Euthyphro in defining the holy. Here are three actions, which we will assume are holy: giving money to the poor, going to church regularly, and loving your enemies. A definition of the holy would show what all these actions have in common. What do you say holiness is?

Several possible definitions occur to me. One thing these actions have in common is _____

_____

_____. Thus, holiness might be _____

_____

_____

_____

_____

_____ . Another thing these actions

have in common is _____

_____

_____

_____. Therefore, holiness would be

_____

_____

_____

_____

_____. Finally, my own view is that

the holy is _____

_____

_____

_____

_____

_____. However, a possible

criticism of this might be that _____

_____

_____

_____

_____.

EXERCISE 7.2
Euthyphro Quiz

The following quiz is, obviously, open book. I've mixed up easy with challenging questions.

1. Euthyphro's first definition of the holy is (exact quote): "_____
   _____
   _____."

In his first definition, Euthyphro confuses a definition with an example. Review pages 114–115 and then answer the following.

2. T F From Socrates' point of view, examples are more general than definitions.

3. T F It would be consistent with Socrates' point of view to say that a mammal is an example of a dog.

4. T F Defining a flower as a rose would be an example of Euthyphro's kind of error.

5. T F Defining freedom as the rights given to Americans in the Bill of Rights would be an example of Euthyphro's kind of error.

6. The second definition of the holy is (exact quote): "_____
   _____
   _____."

Socrates' refutation of Euthyphro's second definition involves a distinction between two kinds of disagreements. Carefully review what Socrates says on pages 115–117 about the kinds of issues the gods can and cannot agree upon. Which of the following statements are generally consistent (C) or generally inconsistent (I) with Socrates' position?

7. C I Zeus and Hera will never be able to agree about the distance between Athens and Sparta.

8. C I Apollo and Dionysus will be able to agree on the number of steps leading to the Parthenon.

9. C I If Aphrodite and Demeter disagree about the nature of love, they may not be able to resolve their disagreements.

10. C I If Athena loves Euthyphro and finds him righteous and Zeus hates Euthyphro and finds him unrighteous, then it is correct to say that Euthyphro is both righteous and unrighteous.

11. C I Because the gods may disagree on moral issues, there is no absolute right and wrong.

12. The third definition of the holy is (exact quote): "_____
   _____
   _____."

After the third definition of the holy, Socrates makes a distinction between (a) something being holy because the gods love it and (b) the gods loving something because it is holy.

13. T F In the case of (a), the gods' love is the effect of something being holy.

14. T F In the case of (b), the gods' love is the cause of something being holy.

15. T F In the case of (a), the gods' love is the essence of the holy.

16. T F In the case of (b), the gods' love is a nonessential characteristic of the holy.

17. T F In the case of (a), the gods are so powerful that whatever they love becomes holy.

18. T F In the case of (b), the gods are so weak that even if they hate something, it does not become unholy.

19. T F In the case of (a), the gods' love is to the holy as circularity is to circle. (In other words, you can't have the holy without the gods' love, just as you can't have a circle without circularity.)

20. T F In the case of (b), the gods' love is to the holy as "presidentialness" is to Bill Clinton.

21. T F In the case of (a), the gods' love is to the holy as "presidentialness" is to the president.

Socrates presents a complex refutation of the third definition. Which of the following statements are generally consistent (C) or generally inconsistent (I) with Socrates' refutation?

22. C I A seen object is to the one who sees it as cause is to effect.

23. C I To say that the gods' love is the result of something's holiness is to describe the holy in terms of what is nonessential rather than what is essential.

24. C I To say the gods' love is the cause of an action's holiness is more like a definition than to say the gods' love is the effect of an action's holiness.

25. C I The gods will never agree on what is holy.

26. C I The holy is a kind of trading skill between the gods and men.

27. The fourth definition of the holy is (exact quote): "_____
_____
_____."

Socrates makes a point about the relationship between the holy and the morally right. Decide which of the following analogies are True (accurate analogies) or False (inaccurate analogies).

28. T F The holy is to the morally right as cat is to dog.

29. T F The holy is to the morally right as orange is to fruit.

30. T F The holy is to the morally right as the United States is to Missouri.

31. T F The holy is to the morally right as 1 is to the set of all numbers.

32. T F The holy is to the morally right as cow is to mammal.

33. T F The holy is to the morally right as Bob Dylan is to singers.

34. T F The holy is to the morally right as world capitals are to Athens.

35. T F The holy is to the morally right as high is to low.

36. T F The holy is to the morally right as the morally right is to the holy.

EXERCISE 7.3
Vote and Debate

Your teacher may decide to use the following to prompt a class discussion. Cast you vote, Agree or Disagree, on each of the following assertions and then write down evidence to back up your position.

1. Socrates plays mind games.

Agree _____ Disagree _____ Evidence: _____

_____

_____

_____.

2. Holiness has no universal essence. What is holy for one person would be unholy to another.

Agree _____ Disagree _____ Evidence: _____

_____

_____

_____.

3. Euthyphro is a bad person.

Agree _____ Disagree _____ Evidence: _____

_____

_____

_____.

4. Because the dialogue does not define the holy, Plato accomplished nothing in writing the *Euthyphro*.

Agree _____ Disagree _____ Evidence: _____

_____

_____

_____.

5. Euthyphro would make a better roommate than Socrates.

Agree _____ Disagree _____ Evidence: _____

_____

_____

_____.

SUMMARY

Athens, Socrates' birthplace, was a center of remarkable cultural activity. Socrates' ironic attempt to find someone wiser than he set him at odds with the Athenian majority. He substituted ethical concerns for the pre-Socratics' metaphysical concerns. The first two definitions of the holy that Socrates investigates in the *Euthyphro* are (1) the holy is prosecuting your father for manslaughter, and (2) the holy is what the gods love. Socrates argues that the problem with the first definition is that it is an example, not a definition; the problem with the second definition is that, because the gods disagree, the same action could be loved my some gods and thus be holy and be hated by other gods and thus be unholy.

EXERCISE 7.4
Looking Back

Use your own paper to answer the following:

1. Who was Socrates?

2. What is the difference between Socrates and the pre-Socratics?

3. What are some key features of the *Euthyphro*?

EXERCISE 7.5
Looking at the World Through Socrates' Eyes

Based on what you learned in this chapter, how would Socrates answer each of the following? Explain your reasoning.

1. T   F   No one is wiser than Socrates.

   Explanation: _____

   _____

   _____

   _____.

2. T   F   There are more important things to fear than death.

   Explanation: _____

   _____

   _____

   _____.

3. T   F   It is impossible to define holiness.

   Explanation: _____

   _____

   _____

   _____.

ANALYSIS OF YOUR PHILOSOPHICAL SELF-PORTRAIT

I've underlined Socrates's answers; circle the answers you believe are correct.

1. T **F** *What is holy to one person could be unholy to another; the holiness of an action is entirely determined by individual opinion.*

   By now, you can probably recognize that True commits you to moral relativism. The morality of an action is "relative" to the one judging the action. Socrates and Plato would disagree with this position. If Socrates, or even Euthyphro, had held that holiness was simply a matter to be determined by individual opinion, then the dialogue could have come to a quick end with Euthyphro simply declaring something like "Socrates, I feel my action is holy, and, while you may not, that doesn't show that I am wrong. Holiness is nothing but what each person believes it to be." This view often sounds attractive to my students. Moral relativism is especially appealing when we are accused of doing something wrong. We can simply reply, "What is wrong from your point of view is not wrong from my point of view." However, moral relativism is less attractive when we feel the wrong action has been done to us. Then we want to say, "There is a clear difference between right and wrong—and you're wrong if you think you're right!"

2. T **F** *It is not possible to know the essence of holiness.*

   Socrates, Plato, and even Euthyphro would hold that this is False. In their view, just as there are defining characteristics that all chairs hold in common, so there are defining characteristics that all holy actions hold in common.

3. **T** F *Seeking wealth and physical comfort will corrupt one's spirit.*

   As you will learn in the *Apology,* Socrates holds this is True. His position would make him something of an ascetic. Asceticism is the view that physical pleasure is wrong because it corrupts the human spirit. Hedonism, the opposite of asceticism, is the view that physical pleasure is good and does not harm the spirit. If hedonism appeals to you, then you will be intrigued by the arguments of Epicurus, who will try to guide you toward the joys of wise pleasure.

4. **T** F *The true philosopher is a critic of the values of the masses.*

   Both Socrates and Plato would hold that this is True. Your own position is probably determined by how low an opinion you have of "common sense" and "normal everyday life." Socrates held that the masses were wrong to value material things over the health of the soul and should have recognized that they didn't know what they thought they knew. Plato would have agreed and gave, as you will see, a detailed description of the truths the masses ignored. Plato, going further than Socrates, was a strong critic of democracy. He had such a low opinion of the values and intelligence of the masses that he believed letting the majority rule was a disastrous idea. Of course, Plato had seen the majority put Socrates to death.

   If you hold that the masses are fools, then you must have a difficult time supporting democracy, the rule of the masses. But what other form of government could you favor? Plato, you will learn, has an answer for you.

Evaluation: Number of points in agreement with Socrates = _____ of 3 possible.

A position of Socrates' that you strongly (support, oppose) is

_____

_____

because _____

_____

_____.

NEXT STOP

Listen as Socrates, on trial, defends himself against his critics.

Socrates in the Apology
The Philosopher on Trial

YOUR PHILOSOPHICAL SELF-PORTRAIT

Circle what you believe is the correct answer to the questions below, and offer evidence supporting your view.

1.   T   F   Seeking wealth and physical comfort will corrupt the spirit.

     Evidence: _____
     _____
     _____.

2.   T   F   Wisdom is knowing that you know nothing.

     Evidence: _____
     _____
     _____.

3.   T   F   Socrates makes the weaker argument defeat the stronger.

     Evidence: _____
     _____
     _____.

You will listen to Socrates defending himself against the charges brought by the Athenians. The *Apology* has six parts.

What Are Some Key Features of the *Apology*?

The *Apology,* Plato's account of the trial of Socrates, can be divided into six parts. The word "apology" here means "a formal justification," not an expression of regret.

In the first part, Socrates introduces himself and describes his two groups of accusers. One group has angrily circulated rumors about him for many years. These people have been continually offended by Socrates' philosophical activities. Except for Aristophanes, the comic playwright, Socrates is uncertain of the members of this shadowy group. The second group of accusers are the ones who have brought Socrates to trial. They are Meletus, representing the poets, Anytus, representing the craftsmen, and Lycon, representing the orators. Socrates says the first group of accusers will be harder to defend himself against because they have had many years to influence the minds of his jury.

In the second part of the *Apology,* Socrates constructs his defense against the first group of accusers. He imagines they would say

> Socrates is an evildoer and a curious person, who searches into things under the earth and in the heavens. He makes the weaker argument defeat the stronger, and he teaches these doctrines to others.

Socrates explains that trouble began long ago with this group of individuals. According to his friend Chaerephon, the oracle at Delphi declared there was no mortal wiser than Socrates. Socrates believed he could easily prove the oracle wrong by finding someone wiser than he. Socrates had no trouble finding many who thought they were wise, but their wisdom vanished under his questioning. Numerous rich young men, after watching Socrates deflate these pretenders to knowledge, imitated his activities:

> They [the rich young men] often imitate me and examine others themselves. There are plenty of persons, as they soon enough discover, who think they know something, but really know little or nothing. Then those who are examined by the young men, instead of being angry with themselves, are angry with me. "This confounded Socrates," they say, "this villainous misleader of youth!"

Thus, Socrates explains that his bad reputation with his first group of accusers is merely the result of his questioning those claiming wisdom and having his method of questioning imitated by young men. Socrates' victims have covered their embarrassment at knowing nothing by attacking Socrates as a "corrupter of youth."

In the third part of the *Apology,* Socrates turns his attention to his more recent group of accusers. He says their charges against him are that

Socrates is a doer of evil and corrupter of the youth, and he does not believe in the gods of the state. He has other new divinities of his own.

In a lively exchange, Socrates cross-examines the poets' representative, Meletus. Socrates traps Meletus into making the remarkable claim that "every Athenian improves and elevates" the youth and only Socrates is their "corrupter." Socrates quickly points out that Meletus must be wrong. Using the example of horse training, Socrates argues that it is not the masses who know the proper care of horses, but only a few experts. According to his reasoning, it must be the same with the youth. Only a few people will be wise enough to be "improvers of the youth" and not the masses—certainly not every Athenian. Socrates argues that Meletus's ignorance of this fact not only demonstrates Meletus's lack of concern for the youth, but also his carelessness in the charges he brings to court. Socrates continues his attack upon Meletus and forces him into several more contradictions. These flaws in Meletus's thinking, from Socrates' point of view, demonstrate that Meletus has not thought very deeply about the case he presents to the Assembly.

In the fourth part of the *Apology*, Socrates continues his speech to the jury by making several points about his life:

- He says he has been like a gadfly (horsefly) whose irritation of the state, "a great and noble steed," was an attempt to guide it in the right direction.

- All his life he has been advised by a spiritual voice that never has told him what to do, only what *not* to do. This voice has kept him from entering politics, where, he believes, his commitment to right action would have ended his life long ago.

- Socrates cites several examples of occasions when his values set him at odds with the Athenian government.

The fifth section of the *Apology* opens with the jury's return of a guilty verdict and Meletus proposing the death penalty. Socrates responds by humorously proposing an alternate punishment: He has been so useful to Athens that the state should pay for his food and lodging for the rest of his life! If this punishment does not strike his jury as satisfactory, Socrates, bowing to the urgings of his friends, is willing to pay a small fine.

The sixth section of the *Apology* contains Socrates' fatalistic response to the jury's decision to sentence him to death:

And now I depart hence condemned by you to suffer the penalty of death, and they [his accusers] too go their ways condemned by the truth to suffer the penalty of wickedness. I must abide by my award—let them abide by theirs. I suppose these things may be regarded as fated—and I think things are as they should be.

In addition, Socrates argues that death is not to be feared:

Either death is a state of nothingness and utter unconsciousness, or, as men say, there is a change and migration of the soul from this world to another. Now if you suppose there is no consciousness, but a sleep like the sleep of him who is undisturbed even by the sight of dreams, death will be an unspeakable gain. . . . But if death is the journey to another place, and there, as men say, all the dead are, what good, O my friends and judges can be greater than this? . . . Nay, if this is true, let me die again and again. I, too, shall have a wonderful interest in a place where I can converse with Palamedes, and

Ajax, the son of Telamon, and other heroes of old who have suffered death through an unjust judgment.

Now, after reading the *Euthyphro* and this brief introduction to the *Apology*, what is your estimation of Socrates?

Socrates is a man who _____

_____.

He values _____

_____.

His strengths seem to be _____

_____.

His weaknesses seem to be _____

_____.

READING:
PLATO'S *APOLOGY*

In this dialogue Socrates is in court and offers not an "apology," but a defense. The Athenian jury in this case consists of 501 citizens. It was the custom for each side to present its case and then, if the defendant was found guilty, each side would propose a punishment. The jury would then choose between the proposed punishments.

The *Apology* contains a considerable amount of information about Socrates' life. Confine your attention in the first few pages to finding the two groups of accusers and the charges against him.

The theme is simply Socrates' defense. First, look for the main points he makes against his accusers, and then look for the points he makes after hearing the jury's verdict.

Apology

According to Socrates, the difference between him and his

accusers is _____

_____

_____

_____

_____

_____.

SOCRATES: How you have felt, O men of Athens, hearing the speeches of my accusers, I cannot tell. I know their persuasive words almost made me forget who I was, such was their effect. Yet they hardly spoke a word of truth. But many as their falsehoods were, there was one of them which quite amazed me—I mean when they told you to be on your guard and not let yourselves be deceived by the force of my eloquence. They ought to have been ashamed of saying this, because they were sure to be detected as soon as I opened my lips and displayed my deficiency. They certainly did appear to be most shameless in saying this, unless by the force of eloquence they mean the force of truth; for then I do indeed admit that I am eloquent. But in how different a way from theirs!

Well, as I was saying, they have hardly uttered a word, or not more than a word, of truth. You shall hear from me the whole truth: not, however, delivered in their manner, in an oration ornamented with words and phrases. No, indeed! I shall use the words and arguments which occur to me at the moment. I am certain this is right, and at my time of life I should not appear before you, O men of Athens, in the character of a juvenile orator — let no one expect this of me. And I must beg you to grant me one favor, which is this—if you hear me using the same words in my defense which I have been in the habit of using, and which most of you may have heard in the agora, and at the tables of the money-changers, or anywhere else, I ask you not to be surprised at this, and not to interrupt me. I am more than seventy years of age and this is the first time I have ever appeared in a court of law, and I am a stranger to the ways of this place. Therefore, I would have you regard me as if I were really a stranger whom you would excuse if he spoke in his native tongue and after the fashion of his country. That, I think, is not an unfair request. Never mind the way I speak, which may or may not be good, but think only of the justice of my cause, and give heed to that. Let the judge decide justly and the speaker speak truly.

First, I have to reply to the older charges and to my first accusers, and then I will go on to the later ones. I have had many accusers who accused me in the past, and their false charges have continued during many years. I am more afraid of them than of Anytus and his associates, who are dangerous, too, in their own way. But far more dangerous are these, who began when you were children and took possession of your minds with their falsehoods, telling of Socrates, a wise man, who speculated about the heavens above, and searched into the earth beneath, and made the worse argument defeat the better. These are the accusers whom I fear because they are the circulators of this rumor and their listeners are too likely to believe that speculators of this sort do not believe in the gods. My accusers are many and their charges against me are of ancient date. They made them in days when you were impressionable—in childhood, or perhaps in youth—and the charges went by unanswered for there was none to answer. Hardest of all, their names I do not know and cannot tell, unless in the chance case of a comic poet. But the main body of these slanderers who from envy and malice have convinced you—and there are some of them who are convinced themselves, and impart their convictions to others— all these, I say, are most difficult to deal with. I cannot have them up here and examine them. Therefore, I must simply fight with shadows in my own defense and examine when there is no one who answers. I will ask you then to assume with me that my opponents are of two kinds: one more recent, the other from the past. I will answer the latter first, for these accusations you heard long before the others, and much more often.

Well, then, I will make my defense, and I will try in the short time allowed to do away with this evil opinion of me which you have held for such a long time. I hope I may succeed, if this be well for you and me, and that my words may find favor with you. But I know to accomplish this is not easy—I see the nature of the task. Let the event be as the gods will; in obedience to the law I make my defense.

I will begin at the beginning and ask what the accusation is which has given rise to this slander of me and which has encouraged Meletus to

The most difficult group of accusers to refute is _____

_____

because _____

_____

_____

_____

_____.

The comic poet is Aristophanes.

Underline these charges and
note how Socrates refers to
them later.

Gorgias, a skeptic; Prodicus, a
sophist; and Hippias, a general
know-it-all, are contemporaries of Socrates.

Evenus the Parian is a poet
and specialist in rhetoric
whose fee is about $1000.

Socrates' ironic point about

Evenus is _____

_____

_____

_____

_____ .

proceed against me. What do the slanderers say? They shall be my prosecu-
tors and I will sum up their words in an affidavit. "Socrates is an evildoer
and a curious person, who searches into things under the earth and in
the heavens. He makes the weaker argument defeat the stronger, and he
teaches these doctrines to others." That is the nature of the accusation and
that is what you have seen in the comedy of Aristophanes. He introduced a
man whom he calls Socrates, going about and saying he can walk in the air
and talking a lot of nonsense concerning matters which I do not pretend to
know anything about—however, I mean to say nothing disparaging of anyone who is a student of such knowledge. I should be very sorry if Meletus
could add that to my charge. But the simple truth is, O Athenians, I have
nothing to do with these studies. Very many of those here are witnesses to
the truth of this and to them I appeal. Speak then, you who have heard me,
and tell your neighbors whether any of you ever heard me hold forth in few
words or in many upon matters of this sort. . . . You hear their answer. And
from what they say you will be able to judge the truth of the rest.

There is the same foundation for the report I am a teacher and take
money; that is no more true than the other. Although, if a man is able to
teach, I honor him for being paid. There are Gorgias of Leontium, Prodicus of Ceos, and Hippias of Elis, who go round the cities and are able to
persuade young men to leave their own citizens, by whom they might be
taught for nothing, and come to them, whom they not only pay but are
also thankful if they may be allowed to pay them.

There is actually a Parian philosopher residing in Athens who charges
fees. I came to hear of him in this way: I met a man who spent a world of
money on the sophists, Callias, the son of Hipponicus, and knowing he
had sons, I asked him: "Callias," I said, "if your two sons were foals or
calves, there would be no difficulty in finding someone to raise them. We
would hire a trainer of horses, or a farmer probably, who would improve
and perfect them in their own proper virtue and excellence. But, as they
are human beings, whom are you thinking of placing over them? Is there
anyone who understands human and political virtue? You must have
thought about this because you have sons. Is there anyone?"

"There is," he said.

"Who is he?" said I. "And of what country? And what does he charge?"

"Evenus the Parian," he replied. "He is the man and his charge is five
minae."

Happy is Evenus, I said to myself, if he really has this wisdom and
teaches at such a modest charge. Had I the same, I would have been very
proud and conceited; but the truth is I have no knowledge like this, O
Athenians.

I am sure someone will ask the question, "Why is this, Socrates, and
what is the origin of these accusations of you; for there must have been
something strange which you have been doing? All this great fame and talk
about you would never have come up if you had been like other men. Tell
us then, why this is, as we should be sorry to judge you too quickly."

I regard this as a fair challenge, and I will try to explain to you the origin of this name of "wise" and of this evil fame. Please attend then and
although some of you may think I am joking, I declare I will tell you the
entire truth. Men of Athens, this reputation of mine has come from a cer-

tain kind of wisdom which I possess. If you ask me what kind of wisdom, I reply, such wisdom as is attainable by man, for to that extent I am inclined to believe I am wise. Whereas the persons of whom I was speaking have a superhuman wisdom which I may fail to describe, because I do not have it. He who says I have, speaks false and slanders me.

O men of Athens, I must beg you not to interrupt me, even if I seem to say something extravagant. For the word which I will speak is not mine. I will refer you to a wisdom which is worthy of credit and will tell you about my wisdom—whether I have any and of what sort—and that witness shall be the god of Delphi. You must have known Chaerephon. He was a friend of mine and also a friend of yours, for he shared in the exile of the people and returned with you. Well, Chaerephon, as you know, was very impetuous in all his doings, and he went to Delphi and boldly asked the oracle to tell him whether—as I said, I must beg you not to interrupt—he asked the oracle to tell him whether there was anyone wiser than I was. The Pythian prophetess answered, there was no man wiser. Chaerephon is dead himself but his brother, who is in court, will confirm the truth of this story.

Why do I mention this? Because I am going to explain to you why I have such an evil name. When I heard the answer, I said to myself, "What can the god mean and what is the interpretation of this riddle? I know I have no wisdom, great or small. What can he mean when he says I am the wisest of men? And yet he is a god and cannot lie; that would be against his nature." After long consideration, I at last thought of a method of answering the question.

I reflected if I could only find a man wiser than myself, then I might go to the god with a refutation in my hand. I would say to him, "Here is a man who is wiser than I am, but you said I was the wisest." Accordingly I went to one who had the reputation of wisdom and observed him—his name I need not mention; he was a politician whom I selected for examination. When I began to talk with him I could not help thinking he was not really wise, although he was thought wise by many and wiser still by himself. I tried to explain to him that he thought himself wise but was not really wise. The result was he hated me, and his hatred was shared by several who were present and heard me. So I left him, saying to myself, as I went away: "Well, although I do not suppose either of us knows anything really beautiful and good, I am better off than he is—for he knows nothing and thinks that he knows. I neither know nor think that I know. In this latter, then, I seem to have an advantage over him." Then I went to another who had still higher philosophical pretensions, and my conclusion was exactly the same. I made another enemy of him and of many others besides him.

After this I went to one man after another, being aware of the anger that I provoked; and I lamented and feared this, but necessity was laid upon me. The word of the god, I thought, ought to be considered first. And I said to myself, "I must go to all who appear to know and find out the meaning of the oracle." And I swear to you Athenians, by the dog, I swear, the result of my mission was this: I found the men with the highest reputations were all nearly the most foolish and some inferior men were really wiser and better.

I will tell you the tale of my wanderings and of the Herculean labors, as I may call them, which I endured only to find at last the oracle was right. When I left the politicians, I went to the poets: tragic, dithyrambic, and

Underline on this and on the next two pages the main points Socrates makes about his experience with the oracle at Delphi. The god of Delphi spoke through a female oracle who passed into a trance after sitting above a fissure in the earth from which gases escape. The messages were frequently paradoxical.

Socrates' plan is to _____ _____ _____ because _____ _____ _____ _____.

"By the dog" is a favorite comic oath of Socrates.

"Herculean labors" refer to the legendary hero Hercules, who was sentenced to twelve great labors for killing his wife and children.

all sorts. There, I said to myself, you will be detected. Now you will find out you are more ignorant than they are. Accordingly, I took them some of the most elaborate passages in their own writings and asked what was the meaning of them—thinking the poets would teach me something. Will you believe me? I am almost ashamed to say this, but I must say there is hardly a person present who would not have talked better about their poetry than the poets did themselves. That quickly showed me poets do not write poetry by wisdom, but by a sort of inspiration. They are like soothsayers who also say many fine things, but do not understand the meaning of what they say. The poets appeared to me to be much the same, and I further observed that upon the strength of their poetry they believed themselves to be the wisest of men in other things in which they were not wise. So I departed, conceiving myself to be superior to them for the same reason I was superior to the politicians.

At last I went to the artisans, because I was conscious I knew nothing at all, and I was sure they knew many fine things. In this I was not mistaken, for they did know many things of which I was ignorant, and in this they certainly were wiser than I was. But I observed even the good artisans fell into the same error as the poets. Because they were good workmen, they thought they also knew all sorts of high matters, and this defect in them overshadowed their wisdom. Therefore, I asked myself on behalf of the oracle whether I would like to be as I was, having neither their knowledge nor their ignorance, or like them in both. I answered myself and the oracle that I was better off as I was.

This investigation led to my having many enemies of the worst and most dangerous kind and has given rise also to many falsehoods. I am called wise because my listeners always imagine I possess the wisdom which I do not find in others. The truth is, O men of Athens, the gods only are wise and in this oracle they mean to say wisdom of men is little or nothing. They are not speaking of Socrates, only using my name as an illustration, as if they said, "He, O men, is the wisest who, like Socrates, knows his wisdom is in truth worth nothing." And so I go my way, obedient to the gods, and seek wisdom of anyone, whether citizen or stranger, who appears to be wise. If he is not wise, then in support of the oracle I show him he is not wise. This occupation quite absorbs me, and I have no time to give either to any public matter of interest or to any concern of my own, but I am in utter poverty by reason of my devotion to the gods.

There is another thing. Young men of the richer classes, who have little to do, gather around me of their own accord. They like to hear the pretenders examined. They often imitate me and examine others themselves. There are plenty of persons, as they soon enough discover, who think they know something, but really know little or nothing. Then those who are examined by the young men, instead of being angry with themselves, are angry with me. "This confounded Socrates," they say, "this villainous misleader of youth!" Then if somebody asks them, "Why, what evil does he practice or teach?" they do not know and cannot tell. But so they may not appear ignorant, they repeat the ready-made charges which are used against all philosophers about teaching things up in the clouds and under the earth, and having no gods, and making the worse argument defeat the stronger. They do not like to confess their pretense to knowledge has been detected, which it has. They are numerous, ambitious, energetic and are all in battle array and have persuasive tongues. They have filled your ears with their loud and determined slanders. This is the reason why my three accusers, Meletus and Anytus and Lycon, have set upon me. Meletus has a quarrel with me on behalf of the poets, Anytus, on behalf of the craftsmen, Lycon, on behalf of the orators. As I said at the beginning, I cannot expect to get rid of this mass of slander all in a moment.

This, O men of Athens, is the truth and the whole truth. I have concealed nothing. And yet I know this plainness of speech makes my accusers hate me, and what is their hatred but a proof that I am speaking the truth? This is the reason for their slander of me, as you will find out either in this or in any future inquiry.

I have said enough in my defense against the first class of my accusers. I turn to the second class who are headed by Meletus, that good and patriotic man, as he calls himself. Now I will try to defend myself against them: These new accusers must also have their affidavit read. What do they say? Something of this sort: "Socrates is a doer of evil and corrupter of the youth, and he does not believe in the gods of the state. He has other new divinities of his own." That is their charge and now let us examine the particular counts. He says I am a doer of evil who corrupts the youth, but I say, O men of Athens, Meletus is a doer of evil, and the evil is that he makes a joke of a serious matter. He is too ready to bring other men to trial from a pretended zeal and interest about matters in which he really never had the smallest interest. And the truth of this I will try to prove to you.

Come here, Meletus, and let me ask a question of you. You think a great deal about the improvement of youth?

MELETUS: Yes I do.

SOCRATES: Tell the judges, then, who is their improver. You must know, as you have taken the pains to discover their corruptor and are accusing me before them. Speak then, and tell the judges who their improver is. Observe, Meletus, that you are silent and have nothing to say. But is this not rather disgraceful and a very great proof of what I was saying, that you have no interest in the matter? Speak up, friend, and tell us who their improver is.

MEL: The laws.

SOC: But that, my good sir, is not my meaning. I want to know who the person is, who, in the first place, knows the laws.

MEL: The jury, Socrates, who are present in court.

SOC: Do you mean to say Meletus, they are able to instruct and improve youth?

MEL: Certainly they are.

SOC: All of them, or only some and not others?

MEL: All of them.

SOC: By the goddess Hera, that is good news! There are plenty of improvers, then. And what do you say of the audience—do they improve them?

MEL: Yes, they do.

SOC: And the senators?

MEL: Yes, the senators improve them.

Socrates' main defense against his first class of accusers is

_____

_____

_____

_____

_____.

Underline on this and the next three pages Socrates' main points in his examination of Meletus.

SOC: But perhaps the members of the Assembly corrupt them? Or do they too improve them?

MEL: They improve them.

SOC: Then every Athenian improves and elevates them, all with the exception of myself. I alone am their corruptor? Is that what you say?

MEL: Most definitely.

SOC: I am very unfortunate if that is true. But suppose I ask you a question. Would you say that this also holds true in the case of horses? Does one man do them harm and everyone else good? Is not the exact opposite of this true? One man is able to do them good and not the many. The trainer of horses, that is to say, does them good, and others who deal with horses injure them? Is that not true, Meletus, of horses or any other animals? Yes, certainly. Whether you and Anytus say yes or no, that is no matter. Fortunate indeed would be the condition of youth if they had one corruptor only and all the rest of the world were their improvers. You, Meletus, have sufficiently shown you never had a thought about the young. Your carelessness is seen in your not caring about the matters spoken of in this very indictment.

And now, Meletus, I must ask you another question: Which is better, to live among bad citizens or among good ones? Answer, friend, I say, for that is a question which may be easily answered. Do not the good do their neighbors good and the bad do them evil?

MEL: Certainly.

SOC: And is there anyone who would rather be injured than benefited by those who associate with him? Answer, my good friend, the law requires you to answer—does anyone like to be injured?

MEL: Certainly not.

SOC: And when you accuse me of corrupting the youth, do you charge I corrupt them intentionally or unintentionally?

MEL: Intentionally, I say.

SOC: But you just admitted that the good do their neighbors good, and the evil do them evil. Now, is that a truth which your superior wisdom has recognized thus early in life, and am I, at my age, in such ignorance as not to know if a man with whom I associate is corrupted by me, I am very likely to be harmed by him? Yet you say I corrupt him and intentionally too; of that you will never persuade me or any other human being. But either I do not corrupt them, or I corrupt them unintentionally, so that on either view of the case you lie. If my offense is unintentional, the law does not mention unintentional offenses. You ought to have taken me aside and warned me, because if I had been better advised, I should have stopped doing what I only did unintentionally—no doubt I should. Instead, you hated to talk with me or teach me and you indicted me in this court, which is a place not of instruction, but of punishment.

I have shown, Athenians, as I was saying, Meletus has no care at all, great or small, about the matter. But still I should like to know, Meletus, in what way do I corrupt the young? I suppose you mean, as I infer from your indictment, I teach them not to acknowledge the gods which the state acknowledges, but some other new divinities or spiritual agencies instead. These are the lessons which corrupt the youth, as you say.

The horse trainer is to horses as

_____

_____ is

to _____

_____.

Thus, Socrates is arguing that

_____

_____

_____

_____.

The key ideas in this paragraph

are _____

_____

_____

_____

_____

_____.

MEL: Yes, I say that emphatically.

SOC: Then, by the gods, Meletus, of whom we are speaking, tell me and the court, in somewhat plainer terms, what you mean! I do not understand whether you charge I teach others to acknowledge some gods, and therefore do believe in gods, and am not an entire atheist—but only that they are not the same gods which the city recognizes—or, do you mean to say that I am an atheist simply, and a teacher of atheism?

MEL: I mean the latter—that you are a complete atheist.

SOC: That is an extraordinary statement, Meletus. Why do you say that? Do you mean that I do not believe the sun or moon are gods, which is the common belief of all men?

MEL: I assure you, jurymen, he does not believe in them. He says the sun is stone and the moon, earth.

SOC: Friend Meletus, you think you are accusing Anaxagoras and you have a bad opinion of the jury, if you believe they do not know these doctrines are found in the books of Anaxagoras the Clazomenian. These are the doctrines which the youth are said to learn from Socrates, when these doctrines can be bought in the marketplace. The youth might cheaply purchase them and laugh at Socrates if he pretends to father such eccentricities. And so, Meletus, you really think that I do not believe in any god?

> Anaxagoras was an eminent philosopher who was also tried for impiety.

MEL: I swear by Zeus that you absolutely believe in none at all.

SOC: You are a liar, Meletus, not believed even by yourself. I cannot help thinking, O men of Athens, Meletus is reckless and impudent and has written this indictment in a spirit of wantonness and youthful bravado. He has made a riddle, thinking to fool me. He said to himself: "I shall see whether this wise Socrates will discover my ingenious contradiction, or whether I shall be able to deceive him and the rest of them." For he certainly does appear to me to contradict himself in the indictment as much as if he said that Socrates is guilty of not believing in the gods, and yet of believing in them—but this surely is a piece of nonsense.

I should like you, O men of Athens, to join me in examining what I conceive to be his inconsistency and you, Meletus, answer. And I must remind you not to interrupt me if I speak in my accustomed manner.

Did any man, Meletus, ever believe in the existence of human things and not human beings? . . . I wish, men of Athens, that he would answer and not be always trying to create an interruption. Did ever any man believe in horsemanship and not in horses? Or in flute playing and not in flute players? No, my friend, I will answer for you and to the court, as you refuse to answer for yourself. There is no man who ever did. But now, please answer the next question. Can a man believe in spiritual and divine activities and not in divine beings?

MEL: He cannot.

SOC: I am glad I have extracted that answer, by the assistance of the court. Nevertheless you swear in the indictment that I teach and believe in divine activities (new or old, no matter for that). At any rate, I believe in divine activities, as you swear in the affidavit, but if I believe in divine activities, I must believe in divine beings. Is that not true? Yes, that is true, for I may assume that your silence gives assent to that. Now what are divine beings? Are they not either gods or the sons of gods? Is that true?

Meletus's contradiction is

_____

_____

_____

_____

_____ .

Stop for a moment and think about what you have read. There have been three major sections in the *Apology* thus far: an introduction, an answer to the first group of accusers, and an answer to the second group. The most important points

were (1) _____

_____

_____

(2) _____

_____

_____

(3) _____

_____

_____

_____ .

In the rest of the *Apology*, draw a line across the page wherever you think a new section begins.

MEL: Yes, that is true.

SOC: But this is just the ingenious riddle of which I was speaking. The divine beings are gods and you say first that I don't believe in gods, and then again that I do believe in gods; that is, if I believe in divine beings. For if the divine beings are the illegitimate sons of gods, whether by the nymphs or by any other mothers, as is thought, that, as all men will agree, necessarily implies the existence of their parents. You might as well affirm the existence of mules, and deny the existence of horses and donkeys. Such nonsense, Meletus, could only have been intended by you as a test of me. You have put this into the indictment because you had no real charge against me. But no one who has a particle of understanding will ever be convinced by you that the same men can believe in divine and superhuman activities and yet not believe that there are gods and demigods.

I have said enough in answer to the charge of Meletus. Any elaborate defense is unnecessary but, as I was saying before, I certainly have many enemies and this will be my destruction if I am destroyed; of that I am certain—not Meletus, nor Anytus, but the envy and slander of the world, which has been the death of many good men and will probably be the death of many more. I will not be the last of them.

Someone will say: Are you not ashamed, Socrates, of a way of life which is likely to bring you to an untimely end? To him I answer: There you are mistaken. A man who is good for anything should not calculate the chance of living or dying. He should only consider whether in doing anything he is doing right or wrong and acting the part of a good man or of a bad. Whereas, according to your view, the heroes who fell at Troy were not good for much, and the son of Thetis [Achilles] above all, who altogether despised danger in comparison with disgrace. His goddess mother said to him, in his eagerness to slay Hector, that if he avenged his companion Patroclus, and slew Hector, he would die himself.

"Fate," as she said, "waits upon you next after Hector."

He, hearing this, utterly despised danger and death, and instead of fearing them, feared rather to live in dishonor and not to avenge his friend.

"Let me die next," he replied, "and be avenged of my enemy, rather than stay here by the beaked ships to be mocked and a burden on the earth."

Had Achilles any thought of death and danger? For wherever a man's place is, whether the place which he has chosen or that in which he has been placed by a commander, there he should remain in the hour of danger. He should not consider death or anything else but only disgrace. And this, O men of Athens, is a true saying.

My conduct would be strange, O men Athens, if I, who was ordered by the generals you chose to command me at Potidaea, Amphipolis, and Delium, remained where they placed me, like any other man facing death, should now when, as I believe, God orders me to fulfill the philosopher's mission of searching into myself and other men, desert my post through fear of death or any other fear. That would indeed be strange, and I might be justly arraigned in court for denying the existence of the gods, if I disobeyed the oracle because I was afraid of death. Then I should be supposing I was wise when I was not wise.

This fear of death is indeed the imitation of wisdom, and not real wisdom, being the appearance of knowing the unknown. No one knows whether death, which they in their fear believe to be the greatest evil, may not be the greatest good. Is there not here the pretense of knowledge, which is a disgraceful sort of ignorance? This is the point in which, as I think, I am superior to men in general and in which I might believe myself wiser than other men. Whereas I know little of the other world, I do not suppose that I know. But I do know that injustice and disobedience to a better, whether god or man, is evil and dishonorable, and I will never fear or avoid a possible good rather than a certain evil. Therefore if you let me go now, reject the advice of Anytus, who said if I were not put to death I should not have been prosecuted, and that if I escape now, your sons will all be utterly ruined by listening to my words. If you say to me, Socrates, this time we will not listen to Anytus and will let you off, but upon one condition, you are not to inquire and speculate in this way any more and if you are caught doing this again you shall die—if this was the condition on which you let me go, I would reply: Men of Athens, I honor and love you but I shall obey the god rather than you. While I have life and strength I shall never cease from practicing and teaching philosophy, exhorting anyone whom I meet in my usual way and convincing him, saying: O my friend, why do you, who are a citizen of the great and wise city of Athens, care so much about laying up the greatest amount of money, honor, and reputation, and so little about wisdom, truth, and the greatest improvement of the soul, which you never regard or heed at all? Are you not ashamed of this? If the person with whom I am arguing says: Yes, but I do care; I do not depart or let him go at once. I question, examine and cross-examine him, and if I think he has no virtue, but only says he has, I reproach him with undervaluing the greater, and overvaluing the lesser. This I would say to everyone I meet, young and old, citizen and alien, but especially to the citizens, inasmuch as they are my brethren. This is the command of the god, as I would have you know and I believe that to this day no greater good has ever happened in the state than my service to the god.

I do nothing but go about persuading you all, old and young alike, not to take thought of yourself or your properties, but to care about the improvement of your soul. I tell you virtue is not acquired with money, but that from virtue come money and every other good of man, public as well as private. This is my teaching, and if this is the doctrine which corrupts the young, my influence is certainly ruinous. If anyone says this is not my teaching, he is speaking a lie. Therefore, O men of Athens, I say to you, do as Anytus bids or not as Anytus bids, and either acquit me or not; but whatever you do, know that I shall never change my ways, not even if I have to die many times.

Men of Athens, do not interrupt, but hear me. There was an agreement between us that you should hear me out. I think what I am going to say will do you good: For I have something more to say, which you may be inclined to interrupt but I ask you not to do this.

I want you to know if you kill someone like me, you will injure yourselves more than you will injure me. Meletus and Anytus will not injure me. They cannot because it is not possible that a bad man should injure someone better than himself. I do not deny he may, perhaps, kill him, or drive him into exile, or deprive him of civil rights. He may imagine, and others may imagine, he is doing him a great injury but I do not agree with

Socrates sees his mission as

_____

_____

_____

_____

_____

_____.

Underline Socrates' analogy between himself and a gadfly (horsefly).

him. The evil of doing as Anytus is doing—of unjustly taking away another man's life—is far greater.

Now, Athenians, I am not going to argue for my own sake, as you may think, but for yours, that you may not sin against the gods or lightly reject their favor by condemning me. If you kill me you will not easily find another like me, who, if I may use such a ludicrous figure of speech, am a sort of gadfly, given to the state by the gods. The state is like a great and noble steed who is slow in his motions owing to his very size and needs to be stirred into life. I am that gadfly which the gods have given the state and all day long and in all places am always fastening upon you, arousing, persuading, and reproaching you. As you will not easily find another like me, I would advise you to spare me. I believe you may feel irritated at being suddenly awakened when you are caught napping. You may think if you were to strike me dead, as Anytus advises, which you easily might, then you would sleep on for the remainder of your lives, unless the god in his care of you gives you another gadfly. That I am given to you by the god is proved by this: If I had been like other men, I should not have neglected my own concerns all these years, and been occupied with yours, coming to you individually like a father or elder brother, exhorting you to think about virtue. This, I say, would not be like human nature. If I had gained anything, or if my exhortations had been paid, there would be some sense in that; but now, as you see, not even my accusers dare to say I have ever sought pay from anyone. They have no witnesses for that. I have a witness of the truth of what I say; my poverty is my witness.

Someone may wonder why I go about in private giving advice and busying myself with the concerns of others, but do not come forward in public and advise the state. I will tell you the reason for this. You have often heard me speak of a spiritual sign which comes to me and is the divinity which Meletus ridicules in the indictment. This sign I have had ever since I was a child. The sign is a spiritual voice which comes to me and always forbids me to do something which I am going to do, but never commands me to do anything. This is what stands in the way of my being a politician. And correctly I think. For I am certain, O men of Athens, if I had engaged in politics, I would have perished long ago, and done no good either to you or to myself. Do not be offended at my telling you the truth. The truth is no man who goes to war with you or any other multitude, honestly struggling against acts of unrighteousness in the state, will save his life. He who will really fight for the right, if he would live even for a little while, must have a private station and not a public one.

I can give you proofs of this, not words only, but deeds, which you value more than words. Let me tell you a part of my own life which will prove to you I would never have yielded to injustice from any fear of death, and that in not yielding I should have died at once. I will tell you a story—tasteless perhaps and commonplace, but nevertheless true. . . .

The only office of state which I ever held, O men of Athens, was when I served on the council. The clan Antiochis, which is my clan, had the presidency at the trial of the generals who had not taken up the bodies of the slain after the battle of Arginusae. You proposed to try them all together, which was illegal, as you all thought afterward, but at the time I was the only one of the committee who was opposed to the illegality. I gave my

Socrates' service to the state is

_____

_____

_____

_____ .

Socrates did not become a politician because _____

_____

_____

_____

_____ .

vote against you. When the orators threatened to impeach and arrest me and have me taken away, and you called and shouted, I made up my mind I would run the risk, having law and justice with me, rather than take part in your injustice because I feared imprisonment and death. This happened in the days of the democracy. But when the oligarchy of the Thirty was in power, they brought me and four others into the rotunda, and told us to bring in Leon from Salamis because they wanted to execute him. This was an example of the sort of commands which they were always giving in order to implicate as many as possible in their crimes. Then I showed, not in word only but in deed, if I may be allowed to use such an expression, I cared not a straw for death, and my only fear was the fear of doing the unrighteous or unholy thing. The strong arm of that oppressive power did not frighten me into doing wrong. When we came out of the rotunda the other four went to Salamis and fetched Leon, but I went quietly home. For this I might have lost my life, had not the power of the Thirty shortly afterward come to an end. And to this many will witness.

The point of this story about the Thirty is _____ _____ _____ _____.

Now do you really imagine I could have survived all these years if I had led a public life, supposing that like a good man I always supported the right and made justice, as I should, the first thing? No indeed, men of Athens, neither I nor any other. I have been always the same in all my actions, public as well as private, and never have yielded to any base agreement with those who are slanderously termed my disciples, or to any other. The truth is I have no regular disciples, but if anyone likes to come and hear me while I am pursuing my mission, whether he be young or old, he may freely come. Nor do I converse with those who pay only, and not with those who do not pay; but anyone, whether he be rich or poor, may question and answer me and listen to my words. If he turns out to be a bad man or a good one, I am not responsible, as I never taught him anything. If anyone says he has ever learned or heard anything from me in private which all the world has not heard, I would like you to know that he is lying.

I will be asked, why do people delight in continually conversing with you? I have told you already, Athenians, the whole truth about this. They like to hear the cross-examination of the pretenders to wisdom; there is amusement in this. This is a duty which the gods have imposed upon me, as I am assured by oracles, visions, and in every sort of way which the will of divine power was ever made plain to anyone. This is true, O Athenians or, if not true, would be soon refuted. If I am really corrupting the youth and have corrupted some of them already, those who have grown up and are aware I gave them bad advice in the days of their youth should come forward as accusers and take their revenge. If they do not like to come themselves, some of their relatives, fathers, brothers, or other kinsmen should say what evil their families suffered at my hands. Now is their time. I see many of them in the court.

Underline the major point Socrates makes in this paragraph.

There is Crito, who is of the same age and of the same township as myself, and there is Critobulus, his son, whom I also see. There is Lysanias of Sphettus, who is the father of Aeschines—he is present; and also there is Antiphon of Cephisus, who is the father of Epigenes; and there are the brothers of several who have associated with me. There is Nicostratus the son of Theosdotides, and the brother of Theodotus (not Theodotus himself—he is dead, and therefore, he will not seek to stop him). There is

Paralus, the son of Demodocus, who had a brother Theages; and Adeimantus, the son of Ariston, whose brother Plato is present; and Aeantodorus, who is the brother of Apollodorus, whom I also see. I might mention a great many others, any of whom Meletus could have produced as witnesses in the course of his speech. Let him still produce them, if he has forgotten—I will make way for him. Let him speak, if he has any testimony of this sort which he can produce. Nay, Athenians, the very opposite is the truth. For all these are ready to witness on behalf of the corruptor, of the destroyer of their kindred, as Meletus and Anytus call me; not the corrupted youth only—there might have been a motive for that—but their uncorrupted elder relatives. Why should they too support me with their testimony? Why indeed, except for the reason of truth and justice, and because they know I am speaking the truth and Meletus is lying.

Well, Athenians, this and similar to this is nearly all the defense I have to offer. Yet a word more. Perhaps there may be someone who is offended by me, when he calls to mind how he himself on a similar, or even a less serious occasion, had recourse to prayers and supplications with many tears, and how he produced his children in court, which was a moving spectacle, together with a group of his relations and friends. I, who am probably in danger of my life, will do none of these things. Perhaps this may come into his mind and he may be set against me and vote in anger because he is displeased at this. Now if there is such a person among you I reply to him: My friend, I am a man, and like other men, a creature of flesh and blood and not of wood or stone, as Homer says. I have a family, yes, and sons, O Athenians, three in number, one of whom is growing up and two others who are still young. Yet I will not bring any of them here in order to beg you for an acquittal. And why not? Not from any self-will or disregard of you. Whether I am, or am not, afraid of death is another question, of which I will not now speak. My reason is that I feel such conduct to be discreditable to myself, you, and the whole state. One who has reached my years and who has a name for wisdom, whether deserved or not, should not lower himself. The world has decided that Socrates is in some way superior to other men. And if those among you who are said to be superior in wisdom, courage, and any other virtue lower themselves in this way, how shameful is their conduct!

I have seen men of reputation, when they have been condemned, behaving in the strangest manner. They seemed to believe they were going to suffer something dreadful if they died, and they could be immortal if you only allowed them to live. I think they were a dishonor to the state, and any stranger coming in would say the most eminent men of Athens, to whom the Athenians themselves give honor and command, are no better than women. I say these things ought not to be done by those of us who are of reputation; and if they are done, you ought not to permit them. You ought to show you are more inclined to condemn, not the man who is quiet, but the man who gets up a doleful scene and makes the city ridiculous.

Setting aside the question of dishonor, there seems to be something wrong in begging a judge and thus procuring an acquittal instead of informing and convincing him. For his duty is not to make a present of justice, but to give judgment. He has sworn he will judge according to the laws and not according to his own good pleasure. Neither he nor we

"As Homer says" refers to a quotation from his *Odyssey*, the story of Odysseus's return from the Trojan War.

should get into the habit of perjuring ourselves—there can be no piety in that. Do not require me to do what I consider dishonorable, impious, and wrong, especially now, when I am being tried for impiety on the indictment of Meletus. For if, O men of Athens, by force of persuasion and entreaty, I could overpower your oaths, then I should be teaching you to believe there are no gods and convict myself in my own defense of not believing in them. But that is not the case. I do believe there are gods and in a far higher sense than any of my accusers believe in them. To you and to the gods I commit my cause, to be determined by you as is best for you and me.

(The jury returns a guilty verdict and Meletus proposes death as punishment.)

There are many reasons why I am not grieved, O men of Athens, at the vote of condemnation. I expected this and am only surprised the votes are so nearly equal. I thought the majority against me would have been far larger, but now, had thirty votes gone over to the other side, I would have been acquitted. And I may say I have escaped Meletus's charges. And I may say more; without the assistance of Anytus and Lycon, he would not have had a fifth part of the votes, as the law requires, in which case he would have incurred a fine of a thousand drachmae.

He proposes death as the penalty. What shall I propose on my part, O men of Athens? Clearly what is my due. What is that which I ought to pay or to receive? What shall be done to the man who has never been idle during his whole life, but has been careless of what the many care about— wealth, family interests, military offices and speaking in the Assembly, and courts, plots, and parties. Believing I was really too honest a man to follow in this way and live, I did not go where I could do no good to you or to myself. I went where I could do the greatest good privately to every one of you. I sought to persuade every man among you that he must look to himself and seek virtue and wisdom before he looks to his private interests, and look to the welfare of the state before he looks to the wealth of the state. This should be the order which he observes in all his actions. What shall be done to someone like me? Doubtless some good thing, O men of Athens, if he has his reward and the good should be suitable to him. What would be a reward suitable to a poor man who is your benefactor, who desires to instruct you? There can be no more fitting reward than maintenance in the Prytaneum, O men of Athens, a reward which he deserves far more than the citizen who wins the prize at Olympia in the horse or chariot race, whether the chariots were drawn by two horses or many. For I am in need and he has enough. He only gives you the appearance of happiness and I give you the reality. Thus, if I am to estimate the penalty justly, I say maintenance in the Prytaneum is just.

Perhaps you think I am mocking you in saying this, as in what I said before about the tears and prayers. But that is not the case. I speak because I am convinced I never intentionally wronged anyone, although I cannot convince you of that—for we have had a short conversation only. If there were a law at Athens, such as there is in other cities, that a case involving the death penalty should not be decided in one day, then I believe I would have convinced you. Now the time is too short. I cannot quickly refute great slanders and, as I am convinced that I never wronged another, I will

Stop again and think about what you read. The major points established since page 146 were

_____

_____

_____

_____

_____

_____

_____

_____.

The number of lines you drew

across the page is _____.

Continue to divide the *Apology* into logical units and underline important points. Practice adding your own notes in the margin.

The Prytaneum was a building maintained by Athens to provide lodging and food for important visitors and particularly deserving citizens.

Socrates' point in the "penalty" he proposes seems to be

_____

_____

_____

_____.

Number the alternative penalties Socrates rejects.

assuredly not wrong myself. I will not say of myself that I deserve any evil, nor propose any penalty. Why should I? Because I am afraid of the penalty of death which Meletus proposes? When I do not know whether death is a good or an evil, why should I propose a penalty which would certainly be an evil? Shall I say imprisonment? And why should I live in prison, and be the slave of the judges of the year—of the Eleven? Or shall the penalty be a fine, and imprisonment until the fine is paid? There is the same objection. I should have to stay in prison for I have no money and cannot pay. And if I say exile, and this may be the penalty which you will affix, I must indeed be blinded by love of life, if I do not realize that if you, who are my own citizens, cannot endure my words and have found them so hateful you want to silence them, others are not likely to endure me. No indeed, men of Athens, that is not very likely. And what a life should I lead, at my age, wandering from city to city, living in ever-changing exile and always being driven out! For I am quite sure that whatever place I go, the young men will come to me. If I drive them away, their elders will drive me out. And, if I let them come, their fathers and friends will drive me out for their sakes.

Someone will say: Yes, Socrates, but can you not hold your tongue and then go into a foreign city, and no one will interfere with you? Now I have great difficulty in making you understand my answer to this. If I tell you this would be a disobedience to a divine command, and therefore I cannot hold my tongue, you will not believe I am serious. If I say again that greatest good is daily to converse about virtue and all that concerning which you hear me examining myself and others, and that the life which is unexamined is not worth living—that you are still less likely to believe. And yet what I say is true, although it is hard for me to persuade you. Moreover, I am not accustomed to thinking I deserve any punishment. Had I money I might have proposed to give you what I had and would have been none the worse. But you see I have none and can only ask you to proportion the fine to my means. However, I think I could afford a mina, and therefore I propose that penalty. Plato, Crito, Critobulus, and Apollodorus, my friends here, bid me say 30 minae and they will pay the fine. Well, then, say 30 minae, let that be the penalty for that they will be ample security to you.

(The jury votes again to decide between Socrates' proposal of a fine and Meletus's proposal of the death penalty. The verdict is death.)

Not much time will be gained, O Athenians, in return for the evil name you will get from the enemies of the city, who will say you killed Socrates, a wise man. They will call me wise even though I am not wise when they want to reproach you. If you waited a little while, your desire would have been fulfilled in the course of nature. I am far advanced in years, as you may perceive, and not far from death. I am speaking now only to those of you who have condemned me to death. And I have another thing to say to them: You think I was convicted through deficiency of words—I mean, if I had thought fit to leave nothing undone, nothing unsaid, I might have gained an acquittal. Not so, the deficiency which led to my conviction was not of words—certainly not. I did not have the boldness or impudence or inclination to address you as you would have liked me to address you, weeping, wailing, and lamenting, and saying and doing many things which you have been accustomed to hear from others, and which, as I say, are un-

Socrates' mood is _____

_____

_____

because _____

_____

_____

_____ .

worthy of me. I believed I should not do anything common or cowardly in the hour of danger. I do not now repent the manner of my defense. I would rather die having spoken after my manner than speak in your manner and live. Neither in war nor yet at law ought any man to use every way of escaping death. Often in battle there is no doubt if a man will throw away his arms and fall on his knees before his pursuers, he may escape death. In other dangers there are other ways of escaping death, if a man is willing to say and do anything.

The difficulty, my friends, is not in avoiding death, but in avoiding evil; for evil runs faster than death. I am old and move slowly, and the slower runner has overtaken me, and my accusers are keen and quick, and the faster runner, who is evil, has overtaken them. And now I depart hence condemned by you to suffer the penalty of death, and they too go their ways condemned by the truth to suffer the penalty of wickedness. I must abide by my award—let them abide by theirs. I suppose these things may be regarded as fated—and I think things are as they should be.

Note the comparison Socrates makes here.

And now, O men who have condemned me, I would prophesy to you. I am about to die and that is the hour in which men are gifted with prophetic power. I prophesy to you who are my murderers that, immediately after my death, punishment far heavier than you have inflicted on me will await you. You have killed me because you wanted to escape the accuser, and not to give an account of your lives. That will not be as you suppose. I say there will be more accusers of you than there are now, accusers I have restrained: And as they are younger they will be more severe with you and you will be more offended at them. For if you think that by killing men you can avoid the accuser censuring your lives, you are mistaken; that is not a way of escape which is either possible or honorable. The easiest, noblest way is not to be crushing others but to be improving yourselves. This is the prophecy which I utter before my departure to the members of the jury who have condemned me.

Socrates' prophecy is that

Friends who have acquitted me, I would like also to talk with you about this thing which has happened, while the judges are busy, and before I go to the place where I must die. Stay awhile, for we may as well talk with one another while there is time. You are my friends and I would like to show you the meaning of this event which has happened to me. O my judges—for you I may truly call judges—I should like to tell you of a wonderful occurrence. Before this, the spiritual voice within me has constantly been in the habit of opposing me even about trifles, if I was going to make a slip or error about anything. Now, as you see there has come upon me what may be thought, and is generally believed to be, the last and worst evil. But the spiritual voice made no sign of opposition, either as I was leaving my house and going out in the morning, or when I was going up into this court, or while I was speaking at anything I was going to say. I have often been stopped in the middle of a speech, but now in nothing I either said or did has the spiritual voice opposed me. Why is this? I will tell you. I regard this as a proof that what has happened to me is a good, and that those of us who think that death is an evil are in error. This is a great proof to me of what I am saying, for the customary sign would surely have opposed me had I been going to evil and not to good.

Socrates believes that death might be a good because

Let us reflect in another way, and we shall see there is great reason to hope that death is a good. Either death is a state of nothingness and utter

Socrates' points about death

are _____

_____

_____

_____

_____.

Minos, Rhadamanthus, Aeacus are the mortal sons of Zeus; they lived so justly that they were given the honor of being judges in Hades. Orpheus and Masaeus were legendary poets. Hesiod, author of *Works and Days*, was a close contemporary of Homer. Palamedes and Ajax are heroes of the Trojan War. Sisyphus, the king of Corinth, was sentenced for his disrespect by Zeus to eternally push a boulder up a hill only to have it roll down again.

Socrates might be happy to die "again and again" because

_____

_____

_____

_____

_____.

unconsciousness, or, as men say, there is a change and migration of the soul from this world to another. Now if you suppose there is no consciousness, but a sleep like the sleep of him who is undisturbed even by dreams, death will be an unspeakable gain. If a person were to select the night in which his sleep was undisturbed even by dreams and were to compare this with the other days and nights of his life, and then were to tell us how many days and nights he passed in the course of his life better and more pleasantly than this one, I think any man, even a great king, will not find many such days or nights, when compared with the others. Now if death is like this, I say to die is to gain, for eternity is then only a single night. But if death is the journey to another place, and there, as men say, all the dead are, what good, O my friends and judges, can be greater than this? If indeed when the traveler arrives in the other world, he is delivered from the false judges in this world and finds the true judges who are said to give judgment there, Minos, Rhadamanthus, Aeacus, and Triptolemus, and other sons of the gods who were righteous in their own life, that journey will be worth making. What would a man give if he might converse with Orpheus and Masaeus and Hesiod and Homer? Nay, if this is true, let me die again and again. I, too, shall have a wonderful interest in a place where I can converse with Palamedes, and Ajax, the son of Telamon, and other heroes of old who have suffered death through an unjust judgment. I think there will be pleasure in comparing my own suffering with theirs. Above all, I shall be able to continue my search into true and false knowledge. As in this world, so also in that; I shall find out who is wise and who pretends to be wise but is not. What would a man give, O judges, to be able to examine the leader of the great Trojan expedition, or Odysseus or Sisyphus, or numberless others, men and women too! What infinite delight would there be in conversing with them and asking them questions! For in that world they do not put a man to death for such investigations, certainly not. For besides being happier in that world than in this, they will be immortal, if what is said is true.

Wherefore, O judges, be of good cheer about death, and know this truth—no evil can happen to a good man, either in life or after death. He and his are not neglected by the gods nor has my own approaching end happened by mere chance. I see clearly that to die and be released was better for me and therefore my spiritual voice gave no sign. Because of this also, I am not angry with my accuser or condemners. They have done me no harm, although neither of them meant to do me any good; and for this I gently blame them.

Still I have a favor to ask of them. When my sons are grown up, I would ask you, O my friends, to punish them. I would have you trouble them, as I trouble you, if they seem to care about riches, or anything, more than virtue. Or, if they pretend to be something when they are really nothing, then chastise them, as I chastised you, for not caring about what they ought to care, and thinking they are something when they are really nothing. And if you do this, I and my sons will have received justice at your hands.

The hour of departure has arrived, and we go on our different ways—I to die, and you to live. Which is better only the god knows.

EXERCISE 8.1

Thinking About the *Apology*

1. The *Apology* is the best source on our tour for discovering Plato's view of his teacher, Socrates. What did you learn about Socrates' life?

A great deal. He believes he has two groups of accusers. The first group is

_____

_____

_____ and the second is _____

_____

_____. He tells a story about the oracle of Delphi partly to explain his bad reputation. The main points in the story are

_____

_____

_____

_____

_____

_____

_____. Other things I learned about Socrates' life were _____

_____

_____

_____

_____.

2. Now, think about Socrates' conversation with Meletus. Why does Socrates mention horse trainers?

This is an important part of his refutation of Meletus. Looking back at the dialogue, I see the point he makes specifically about horses and horse trainers is

_____

_____

_____. The way this applies to Meletus is that _____

_____

_____

_____. Socrates is trying to show the members of the jury that Meletus is _____

_____

_____

_____

_____.

3. Shortly after this, Socrates says to Meletus, "you have just admitted that the good do their neighbors good, and the evil do them evil. Now, is that a truth which your superior wisdom has recognized thus early in life, and am I, at my age, in such a darkness and ignorance as not to know if a man with whom I have to associate is corrupted by me, I am very likely to be harmed by him? Yet you say I corrupt him and intentionally, too; of that you will never persuade me or any other human being. But either I do not corrupt them, or I corrupt them unintentionally, so that on either view of the case you lie. If my offense is unintentional, the laws do not mention unintentional offenses. You ought to have taken me aside and warned me, because if I had been better advised, I should have stopped doing what I only did unintentionally—no doubt I should."

What points does Socrates make here?

Socrates makes several interesting points. He says he either corrupts the youth intentionally or unintentionally. The reason he says he could not be corrupting them intentionally is _____

_____

_____

_____

_____. And if he has been

corrupting them unintentionally, then _____

_____

_____

_____

_____

_____. In either

case bringing Socrates to court is wrong. It is wrong in the first case because

_____

_____

_____

_____

_____. And it is obviously wrong in the

second case because _____

_____

_____

_____

_____.

4. At one point Socrates compares himself to a gadfly (a horsefly) and Athens to a "great and noble steed." Why?

Socrates believes he is like a gadfly because _____

_____

_____

_____. Perhaps an example of

this from *Euthyphro* is _____

_____

_____

_____ .

5. Still later Socrates says, "I say again the greatest good of man is daily to converse about virtue and all that concerning which you hear me examining myself and others, and that the life which is unexamined is not worth living. . . ."

   The pre-Socratic philosophers like Thales were all interested in one thing. Contrast their interest with Socrates' in this statement.

As you saw earlier in the tour, the pre-Socratics were all trying to answer the

same question. That question was _____

_____

_____

_____ . A major change, occurring with

Socrates, as illustrated by this quotation, is _____

_____

_____

_____

_____

_____ . The relationship between this

concern and his story about the oracle at Delphi is _____

_____

_____

_____

_____

_____ .

6. One thing Plato attempts in this dialogue is to draw a large contrast between Socrates and the majority of the people in Athens. How would you sum up the difference between them?

Socrates is _____

_____

_____

_____

_____ . The people of Athens are _____

_____

_____

_____

_____

_____ .

7. Now it is time for your verdict. Weigh your judgment carefully, but to simplify matters, perhaps you should stick to the single charge of "corrupting the youth."

From Meletus's point of view, Socrates is guilty of corrupting the youth because

_____

_____

_____

_____

_____

_____. Meletus would probably define

corruption as _____

_____

_____

_____

_____. According to Meletus, someone

who did not corrupt the youth but taught them correctly would be someone who

_____

_____

_____

_____

_____. From Socrates' point of view,

he is not a corruptor of the youth because _____

_____

_____

_____

_____

_____. Someone who would truly corrupt the

youth from his point of view would be _____

_____

_____

_____. In Socrates' opinion the best education

youth could have would involve _____

_____

_____

_____

_____. Choosing between Meletus and

Socrates, I would say _____

_____

_____

_____

_____

_____

_____

_____. An example of the truth of

my view is ___ _____

_____

_____. In conclusion, _____

_____

_____

_____

_____

_____.

Thinking back on the tour thus far, the five most important things I've learned about Socrates are:

a. _____

_____

b. _____

_____

c. _____

_____

d. _____

_____

e. _____

_____

EXERCISE 8.2
Apology Quiz

In order to get an overview of the general structure of the *Apology,* arrange the following in the order, 1–9, that they occur in the dialogue: Socrates' service as a soldier, the story about the oracle at Delphi, Socrates proposes his punishment, the refutation of the older accusers, the refutation of the newer accusers, Socrates confronts Meletus, the death verdict, the guilty verdict, Socrates tells about resisting the Thirty.

1. _____

2. _____

3. _____

4. _____

5. _____

6. _____

7. _____

8. _____

9. _____

10. At the time of his trial, Socrates was _____ years old.

11. According to Socrates, he is charged with (direct quote): "_____

_____

_____

_____."

Socrates is famous for irony, that is, saying one thing and meaning another. Decide if the following are Ironic (I) or Nonironic (N).

12. I N Socrates claims that the "persuasive words" of his accusers "almost made me forget who I was, such was their effect."

13. I N " . . . this is the first time I've appeared in a court of law."

14. I N "I have had many accusers who accused me in the past and their false charges have continued during many years."

15. I N Socrates claims he has no wisdom and is only wise in knowing that he is not wise.

16. I N Socrates says he questioned others in order to support the view of the oracle at Delphi that he is the wisest of mortals. "And so I go my way, obedient to the gods, and seek wisdom of anyone, whether citizen or stranger who appears to be wise. If he is not wise, then in support of the oracle I show him he is not wise."

17. I N After being condemned to death, Socrates says, "I am about to die and that is the hour in which men are gifted with prophetic power. I prophesy to you who are my murderers that, immediately after my death, punishment far heavier than you have inflicted on me will await you."

Near the end of the *Apology*, Socrates says, "The difficulty, my friends, is not in avoiding death, but in avoiding evil; for evil runs faster than death. I am old and move slowly, and the slower runner has overtaken me, and my accusers are keen and quick, and the faster runner, who is evil, has overtaken them."

18. The slower runner who has overtaken Socrates is _____.

19. The four participants in the "race" are: _____

_____

20. T F Socrates points out the paradox that even though he is slower, he has beaten his fast accusers by arriving at death before they have.

21. T F Socrates points out the paradox that even though he is slow, he has not been overtaken yet by death, the fast runner who overtakes everyone.

22. T F Socrates points out the paradox that even though he is old and slow, he has not been overtaken by evil, which is fast.

23. T F Socrates sees evil as fast because it is more likely to catch an individual before death.

EXERCISE 8.3
Vote and Debate

1. Socrates was guilty of believing in new gods.

Agree _____ Disagree _____ Evidence: _____

_____

_____

_____.

2. Socrates was guilty of making the weaker argument defeat the stronger.

Agree _____ Disagree _____ Evidence: _____

_____

_____

_____.

3. Socrates wanted to die and thus did not defend himself as strongly as he might have.

Agree _____ Disagree _____ Evidence: _____

_____

_____

_____.

SUMMARY

The *Apology* can be divided into six parts. In the first part, Socrates introduces himself and describes his two groups of accusers. One group has been angry at him for many years; the other group is represented by three men who are bringing him to trial. In the second part, Socrates defends himself against the first group by describing his response to the declaration by the oracle at Delphi that he, Socrates, was the wisest of mortals. In the third part, Socrates defends himself against his newer accusers, chiefly by cross-examining Meletus. In the fourth part, Socrates concludes his defense by making several points about his life. In the fifth part, after learning that he has been found guilty, Socrates proposes modest punishments. In the sixth part, Socrates accepts the verdict of death and argues that death is not to be feared.

EXERCISE 8.4
Looking Back

Use your own paper to answer the following.

1. What are some key features of the *Apology*? (Briefly summarize important aspects of each of the six parts.)

ANALYSIS OF YOUR PHILOSOPHICAL SELF-PORTRAIT

I've underlined Socrates' answers; circle the answers that you believe are correct.

1. <u>T</u> F *Seeking wealth and physical comfort will corrupt one's spirit.*

    Socrates, of course, would answer True. In his view, considerably expanded by Plato, human nature is divided into two normally warring parts, body and soul. The body's desire for physical pleasure is opposed by the soul's desire for wisdom. The more diligently we seek to satisfy one, the more we have to abandon the other. Seeking wealth and physical comfort, according to both Socrates and Plato, would satisfy our body but starve our soul.

2. T <u>F</u>(!) *Wisdom is knowing that you know nothing.*

    Socrates' view that he "knows nothing" is certainly ironic. He says one thing and means another. It is clear, even in the *Apology,* that Socrates knows a great deal. He knows that his questioning is a service to the state, that the masses are foolish and the few are wise, that the gods exist, that a commitment to right action and the political life are mutually inconsistent, that death should not be feared, and so forth. Why, then, does Socrates claim to know nothing? The *Euthyphro* provides a strong clue. If Socrates had simply accused Euthyphro of foolishness, Euthyphro would never have questioned his own beliefs. By posing as someone who was ignorant, Socrates drew Euthyphro forward, at least to the degree of understanding the great difficulty in defining holiness. In the same way, Socrates' lifelong claim to know nothing was a strategic ploy to draw others, as his "teacher," into contact with their own ignorance.

3. T <u>F</u> *Socrates makes the weaker argument defeat the stronger.*

    Socrates, of course, would not have agreed with this. The ability to win arguments through cunning rather than a commitment to truth was a skill taught by the sophists, a group whom Socrates scorned.

    If you would like to see Socrates defeated in an argument, read Plato's *Parmenides,* a confrontation between the youthful Socrates and the elderly Parmenides. In the *Parmenides,* Socrates attempts to defend many of Plato's central beliefs and is defeated by Parmenides at every turn. Why on earth would Plato present a refutation of his own views? More about this strange dialogue later on the tour.

    Evaluation: Number of points in agreement with Socrates = _____ of 3 possible.

    A position of Socrates' that you strongly (support, oppose) is

    _____

    because _____.

NEXT STOP
How will Socrates respond when offered a chance to escape from prison?

Socrates in the Crito
The Philosopher in Prison

YOUR PHILOSOPHICAL SELF-PORTRAIT

Circle what you believe is the correct answer to the questions below and offer evidence supporting your view.

1   T   F   Because Socrates was unjustly convicted, he had no obligation to remain in prison.

Evidence: _____

_____.

2.   T   F   Socrates' obligation to the state to keep his just agreements (even if it leads to his death) is higher than his obligation to remain alive and raise his children.

Evidence: _____

_____.

In prison, Socrates refutes the arguments that he should escape to save his life. The *Crito* is about virtue and justice in relation to the laws and the state.

What Are Some Key Features of the *Crito*?

The *Crito*, an encounter in prison between Socrates and his old friend Crito, is elegantly structured. The dialogue opens with Crito waking Socrates at dawn. A brief interchange sketches the emotional differences between the calm Socrates and his perturbed friend. Crito then pours out a string of arguments, trying to convince Socrates that he should escape from jail. Socrates responds with two extended arguments. In the first, Socrates reviews the belief he and Crito have shared that wrong actions are harmful to the soul. In the second, Socrates answers Crito's arguments by proposing that the state is like a caring parent who must be obeyed. Thus, the dialogue falls into four brief acts. In the first act, we meet the emotionally opposed main characters. In the second act, Crito, obsessed with the problem of his friend's imprisonment, steps forward to pour out a cascade of arguments urging Socrates to escape. In the next two acts, Socrates takes over the drama. Socrates first turns Crito's attention away from the present by reestablishing the truth of their belief that the health of the soul is preserved through right action. In the concluding act of the little drama, Socrates focuses this belief upon the present situation to demonstrate that escape would be inconsistent with virtue.

READING:
PLATO'S *CRITO*

In the first few pages, underline the time of day, the personality differences between Socrates and Crito, and Socrates' prophetic dream.

Look for Crito's reasons in favor of Socrates' escape and the main points in Socrates' argument in favor of remaining in jail.

Crito

SOCRATES: Why have you come at this hour, Crito? It must be quite early?

CRITO: Yes, it certainly is.

SOC: What time is it?

CR: The dawn is breaking.

SOC: I am surprised the keeper of the prison let you in.

CR: He knows me because I come often, Socrates, and he owes me a favor.

SOC: Did you just get here?

CR: No, I came some time ago.

SOC: Then why did you sit and say nothing, instead of waking me at once?

CR: Why, indeed, Socrates. I myself would rather not have all this sleeplessness and sorrow. I have been wondering at your peaceful slumber and that was the reason why I did not [wake] you. I wanted you to be out of pain. I always thought you fortunate in your calm temperament, but I never saw anything like the easy, cheerful way you bear this calamity.

SOC: Crito, when a man reaches my age he should not fear approaching death.

CR: Other men of your age in similar situations fear death.

SOC: That may be. But you have not told me why you come at this early hour.

CR: I bring you a sad and painful message; not sad, as I believe, for you, but to all of us who are your friends, and saddest of all to me.

SOC: Has the ship come from Delos, on the arrival of which I am to die?

CR: No, the ship has not actually arrived, but it will probably be here today because people who came from Sunium tell me they left it there. Therefore, tomorrow, Socrates, will be the last day of your life.

SOC: Very well, Crito. If it is the will of the gods, I am willing, but I believe there will be a delay of a day.

CR: Why do you say that?

SOC: I will tell you. I am to die on the day after the arrival of the ship?

CR: Yes, that is what the authorities say.

SOC: I do not think the ship will be here until tomorrow. I had a dream last night, or rather only just now, when you fortunately allowed me to sleep.

CR: What was your dream?

SOC: I saw the image of a wondrously beautiful woman, clothed in white robes, who called to me and said: "O Socrates, the third day hence to fertile Phthia shalt thou go."

CR: What a strange dream, Socrates!

SOC: I think there can be no doubt about the meaning, Crito.

CR: Perhaps the meaning is clear to you. But, oh my beloved Socrates, let me beg you once more to take my advice and escape! If you die I shall not only lose a friend who can never be replaced, but there is also another evil: People who do not know you and me will believe I might have saved you if I had been willing to spend money, but I did not care to do so. Now, can there be a worse disgrace than this—that I should be thought to value money more than the life of a friend? The many will not be persuaded I wanted you to escape and you refused.

SOC: But why, my dear Crito, should we care about the opinion of the many? Good men, and they are the only persons worth considering, will think of these things as they happened.

CR: But do you see, Socrates, the opinion of the many must be regarded, as is clear in your own case, because they can do the very greatest evil to anyone who has lost their good opinion.

SOC: I only wish, Crito, they could. Then they could also do the greatest good and that would be excellent. The truth is, they can do neither good nor

A major difference already established between Socrates and Crito is _____

_____

_____

_____.

In general, the relationship between the two men is _____

_____

_____

_____.

Phthia was the home of Achilles. The dream probably symbolized to Socrates that dying meant returning home.

Here and on the next two pages, number each reason Crito gives Socrates to escape. There are at least eight.

evil. They cannot make a man wise or make him foolish, and whatever they do is the result of chance.

CR: Well, I will not argue about that. But please tell me, Socrates, if you are acting out of concern for me and your other friends. Are you afraid if you escape we may get into trouble with the informers for having stolen you away and lose either the whole or a great part of our property, or an even worse evil may happen to us? Now, if this is your fear, be at ease. In order to save you we should surely run this, or even a greater, risk. Be persuaded, then, and do as I say.

SOC: Yes, Crito, that is one fear which you mention, but by no means the only one.

CR: Do not be afraid. There are persons who at no great cost are willing to save you and bring you out of prison. As for the informers, they are reasonable in their demands, a little money will satisfy them. My resources, which are ample, are at your service and if you are troubled about spending all mine, there are strangers who will give you theirs. One of them, Simmias the Theban, brought a sum of money for this very purpose. Cebes and many others are willing to spend their money, too. I say, therefore, do not hesitate about making your escape and do not say, as you did in the court, you will have difficulty in knowing what to do with yourself if you escape. Men will love you in other places you may go and not only in Athens. There are friends of mine in Thessaly, if you wish to go to them, who will value and protect you; and no Thessalian will give you any trouble. Nor can I think you are justified, Socrates, in betraying your own life when you might be saved. This is playing into the hands of your enemies and destroyers. Besides, I say you are betraying your children. You should bring them up and educate them; instead you go away and leave them, and they will have to grow up on their own. If they do not meet with the usual fate of orphans, there will be small thanks to you. No man should bring children into the world who is unwilling to continue their nurture and education. You are choosing the easier part, as I think, not the better and manlier, which you should as one who professes virtue in all his actions. Indeed, I am ashamed not only of you, but also of us, your friends, when I think this entire business of yours will be attributed to our lack of courage. The trial need never have started or might have been brought to another conclusion. The end of it all, which is the crowning absurdity, will seem to have been permitted by us, through cowardice and baseness, who might have saved you. You might have saved yourself, if we had been good for anything, for there was no difficulty in escaping, and we did not see how disgraceful, Socrates, and also miserable all this will be to us as well as to you. Make up your mind then. Or rather, have your mind already made up, for the time of deliberation is over. There is only one thing to be done, which must be done if at all this very night, and which any delay will render all but impossible. I plead with you therefore, Socrates, to be persuaded by me, and do as I say.

SOC: Dear Crito, your zeal is invaluable if right. If wrong, the greater the zeal the greater the evil. Therefore, we must consider whether these things should be done or not. I am, and always have been, someone who must be guided by reason, whatever the reason may be which, upon reflection, ap-

Now, go back and put a star by the best reasons, according to you, for escaping.

pears to me to be the best. Now that this misfortune has come upon me, I cannot put away my old beliefs. The principles I honored and revered I still honor; and unless we can find other and better principles, I will not agree with you. I would not even if the power of the multitude could inflict many more imprisonments, confiscations, and deaths, frightening us like children with foolish terrors.

What will be the best way of considering the question? Shall I return to your old argument about the opinions of men, some of which should be considered, and others, as we were saying, are not to be considered. Now were we right in maintaining this before I was condemned? And has the argument, which was once good, now proved to be talk for the sake of talking—in fact an amusement only and altogether foolish? That is what I want to consider with your help, Crito: whether, under my present circumstances, the argument appears to be in any way different or not and is to be followed by me or abandoned. That argument, I believe, held by many who claim to be authorities, was to the effect that the opinions of some men are to be considered and of other men not to be considered. Now you, Crito, are not going to die tomorrow—at least, there is no probability of this. You are therefore not likely to be deceived by the circumstances in which you are placed. Tell me, then, whether I am right in saying that some opinions are to be valued and other opinions are not to be valued. I ask you whether I was right in believing this?

Cr: Certainly.

Soc: The good opinions are to be believed and not the bad?

Cr: Yes.

Soc: And the opinions of the wise are good and the opinions of the foolish are evil?

Cr: Certainly.

Soc: And what was said about another matter? Is the gymnastics student supposed to attend to the praise and blame and opinion of every man, or of one man only—his physician or trainer, whoever that is?

Cr: Of one man only.

Soc: And he should fear the blame and welcome praise of that one only, and not of the many?

Cr: That is clear.

Soc: He should live and train, eat and drink in the way which seems good to his single teacher who has understanding, rather than according to the opinion of all men put together?

Cr: True.

Soc: And if he disobeys and rejects the opinion and approval of the one, and accepts the opinion of the many who have no understanding, will he not suffer evil?

Cr: Certainly he will.

Soc: And how will the evil affect the disobedient student?

Cr: Clearly, it will affect his body; that is what is destroyed by the evil.

Soc: Very good. Is this not true, Crito, of other things which we need not

On the following pages, underline each of the main points in Socrates' answer to Crito.

separately consider? In the matter of the just and unjust, the fair and foul, the good and evil, which are the subjects of our present discussion, should we follow the opinion of the many and fear them, or the opinion of the one man who has understanding? Is he the one we ought to fear and honor more than all the rest of the world? If we leave him, we shall destroy and injure that principle in us which may be assumed to be improved by justice and deteriorated by injustice? Is there not such a principle?

CR: Certainly there is, Socrates.

SOC: Take a similar case. If, acting under the advice of men who have no understanding, we ruined what is improved by health and destroyed by disease—would life be worth having? You understand I mean the body?

CR: Yes.

SOC: Could we live having an evil and corrupted body?

CR: Certainly not.

SOC: And will life be worth having, if the soul is crippled, which is improved by justice and harmed by injustice? Do we suppose the soul to be inferior to the body?

CR: Certainly not.

SOC: More important, then?

CR: Far more important.

SOC: Then, my friend, we must not consider what the many say of us, but what he, the one man who has understanding of the just and unjust will say, and what the truth will say. Therefore, you begin in error when you suggest we should consider the opinion of the many about the just and unjust, the good and evil, the honorable and dishonorable. For what if someone says, "But the many can kill us"?

CR: Yes, Socrates, that will clearly be the answer.

SOC: Still I believe our old argument is unshaken. I would like to know whether I may say the same of another proposition—that not life, but a good life, is to be chiefly valued?

CR: Yes, that is also true.

SOC: And a good life is equivalent to a just and honorable one—that is also true?

CR: Yes, that is true.

SOC: From these beliefs I am ready to consider whether I should or should not try to escape without the consent of the Athenians. If I am clearly right in escaping, then I will make the attempt, but if not, I will remain here. The other considerations which you mention, of money and loss of reputation and the duty of educating children, are, I fear, only the beliefs of the many, who would be as ready to bring people to life, if they were able, as they are to put them to death. The only question remaining to be considered is whether we shall do right escaping or allowing others to aid our escape and paying them money and thanks or whether we shall not do right. If the latter, then neither death nor any other calamity which may result from my remaining here must be allowed to influence us.

CR: I think you are right, Socrates. But, how shall we proceed?

Crito has been wrong because

_____

_____

_____

_____

_____

_____ .

Several of Crito's arguments are dismissed here because _____

_____

_____

_____ .

SOC: Let us consider the matter together and either refute me if you can and I will be convinced; or else cease, my dear friend, from repeating to me that I ought to escape against the wishes of the Athenians. I am extremely eager to be persuaded by you, but not against my own better judgment. And now please consider my first position and do your best to answer me.

CR: I will do my best.

SOC: Are we to say we are never intentionally to do wrong, or that in one way we should and in another way we should not do wrong? Or is doing wrong always evil and dishonorable, as I was just now saying? Are all our former admissions to be thrown away because of these last few days? Have we, at our age, been earnestly discoursing with one another all our life long only to discover we are no better than children? Or, are we convinced in spite of the opinion of the many and in spite of consequences of the truth of what we said, that injustice is always an evil and dishonor to him who acts unjustly? Shall we agree to that?

CR: Yes.

SOC: Then we must do no wrong?

CR: Certainly not.

SOC: Nor when injured should we injure in return, as the many imagine. We must injure no one at all?

CR: Clearly not.

SOC: Again, Crito, can we do evil?

CR: Surely not, Socrates.

SOC: And what of doing evil in return for evil, which is the morality of the many—is that just or not?

CR: Not just.

SOC: For doing evil to another is the same as injuring him.

CR: Very true.

SOC: Then we ought not to retaliate or render evil for evil to any one, whatever evil we may have suffered from him. But I would have you consider, Crito, whether you really mean what you are saying. For this opinion has never been held, and never will be held, by many people. Those who are agreed and those who are not agreed upon this point have no common ground, and can only despise one another when they see how widely they differ. Tell me, then, whether you agree with my first principle, that neither injury nor retaliation nor returning evil for evil is ever right. Shall that be the premise of our argument? Or do you disagree? For this has been and still is my opinion; but, if you are of another opinion, let me hear what you have to say. If, however, you remain of the same mind as formerly, I will go to the next step.

CR: You may proceed, for I have not changed my mind.

SOC: The next step may be put in the form of a question: Ought a man to do what he admits to be right, or ought he to betray the right?

CR: He ought to do what he thinks right.

A similar Christian belief is

_____

_____

_____

_____

_____.

At this point, Socrates ends his review of his past beliefs and begins a long internal dialogue. The major points established

thus far are _____

_____

_____

_____

_____

_____ .

From here until the end, number and underline each new reason Socrates gives Crito for not escaping.

SOC: But if this is true, what is the application? In leaving the prison against the will of the Athenians, do I wrong anyone? Or do I wrong those whom I ought least to wrong? Do I abandon the principles which were acknowledged by us to be just? What do you say?

CR: I cannot tell, Socrates, because I do not know.

SOC: Then consider the matter in this way—imagine I am about to escape, and the laws and the state come and interrogate me: "Tell us, Socrates," they say, "what are you doing? Are you going to overturn us—the laws and the state, as far as you are able? Do you imagine that a state can continue and not be overthrown, in which the decisions of law have no power, but are set aside and overthrown by individuals?"

What will be our answer, Crito, to these and similar words? Anyone, and especially a clever orator, will have a good deal to say about the evil of setting aside the law which requires a sentence to be carried out. We might reply, "Yes, but the state has injured us and given an unjust sentence." Suppose I say that?

CR: Very good, Socrates.

SOC: "And was that our agreement with you?" the law would say, "Or were you to abide by the sentence of the state?" And if I were surprised at their saying this, the law would probably add: "Answer, Socrates, instead of opening your eyes: you are in the habit of asking and answering questions. Tell us what complaint you have against us which justifies you in attempting to destroy us and the state? In the first place did we not bring you into existence? Your father married your mother by our aid and conceived you. Say whether you have any objection against those of us who regulate marriage?" None, I should reply. "Or against those of us who regulate the system of care and education of children in which you were trained? Were not the laws, who have the charge of this, right in commanding your father to train you in the arts and exercise?" Yes, I should reply.

"Well then, since you were brought into the world, nurtured and educated by us, can you deny in the first place that you are our child and slave, as your fathers were before you? And if this is true you are not on equal terms with us. Nor can you think you have a right to do to us what we are doing to you. Would you have any right to strike or do any other evil to a father or to your master, if you had one, when you have been struck or received some other evil at his hands? And because we think it is right to destroy you, do you think that you have any right to destroy us in return, and your country so far as you are able? And will you, O expounder of virtue, say you are justified in this? Has a philosopher like you failed to discover your country is more to be valued and higher and holier by far than mother and father or any ancestor, and more regarded in the eyes of the gods and of men of understanding? It should be soothed and gently and reverently entreated when angry, even more than a father, and if not persuaded, it should be obeyed. And when we are punished by the state, whether with imprisonment or whipping, the punishment is to be endured in silence. If the state leads us to wounds or death in battle, we follow as is right; no one can yield or leave his rank, but whether in battle or in a court of law, or in any other place, he must do what his city and his country order him. Or, he must change his view of what is just. If he may do no violence

The comparison Socrates makes

is between _____

_____

and _____

_____ .

His point is _____

_____

_____

_____

_____

_____

_____ .

to his father or mother, much less may he do violence to his country." What answer shall we make to this, Crito? Do the laws speak truly, or do they not?

CR: I think that they do.

SOC: Then the laws will say: "Consider, Socrates, if this is true, that in your present attempt you are going to do us wrong. For, after having brought you into the world, nurtured and educated you, and given you and every other citizen a share in every good we had to give, we further give the right to every Athenian, if he does not like us when he has come of age and has seen the ways of the city, he may go wherever else he pleases and take his goods with him. None of us laws will forbid or interfere with him. Any of you who does not like us and the city, and who wants to go to a colony or to any other city, may go where he likes, and take his possessions with him. But he who has experience of the way we order justice and administer the state, and still remains, has entered into an implied contract to do as we command him. He who disobeys us is, as we maintain, triply wrong; first, because in disobeying us he is disobeying his parents; second, because we are the authors of his education; third, because he has made an agreement with us that he will duly obey our commands. He neither obeys them nor convinces us our commands are wrong. We do not rudely impose our commands but give each person the alternative of obeying or convincing us. That is what we offer and he does neither. These are the sort of accusations to which, as we were saying, Socrates, you will be exposed if you do as you were intending; you, above all other Athenians." *Find and underline the sentence with three reasons for not escaping.*

Suppose I ask, why is this? They will justly answer that I above all other men have acknowledged the agreement.

"There is clear proof," they will say, "Socrates, that we and the city were not displeasing to you. Of all Athenians you have been the most constant resident in the city, which, as you never leave, you appear to love. You never went out of the city either to see the games, except once when you went to the Isthmus, or to any other place unless you were on military service; nor did you travel as other men do. Nor had you any curiosity to know other states or their laws: Your affections did not go beyond us and our state; we were your special favorites and you agreed in our government of you. This is the state in which you conceived your children, which is a proof of your satisfaction. Moreover, you might, if you wished, have fixed the penalty at banishment in the course of the trial—the state which refuses to let you go now would have let you go then. You pretended you preferred death to exile and that you were not grieved at death. And now you have forgotten these fine sentiments and pay no respect to us, the laws, whom you destroy. You are doing what only a miserable slave would do, running away and turning your back upon the agreements which you made as a citizen. First of all, answer this very question: Are we right in saying you agreed to be governed according to us in deed, and not in word only? Is that true or not?"

How shall we answer that, Crito? Must we not agree?

CR: We must, Socrates.

SOC: Then will the laws say: "You, Socrates, are breaking the agreements which you made with us at your leisure, not in any haste or under any compulsion or deception, but having had seventy years to think of them, during which time you were at liberty to leave the city, if we were not to your lik- *Continue underlining each new reason for not escaping.*

ing or if our covenants appeared to you to be unfair. You might have gone either to Lacedaemon or Crete, which you often praise for their good government, or to some other Hellenic or foreign state. You, above all other Athenians, seemed to be so fond of the state and of us, her laws, that you never left her. The lame, the blind, the maimed were not more stationary in the state than you were. Now you run away and forsake your agreements. Not, Socrates, if you will take our advice; do not make yourself ridiculous by escaping out of the city.

"Just consider, if you do evil in this way, what good will you do either yourself or your friends? That your friends will be driven into exile and lose their citizenship, or will lose their property, is reasonably certain. You yourself, if you fly to one of the neighboring cities, like Thebes or Megara, both of which are well-governed cities, will come to them as an enemy, Socrates. Their government will be against you and all patriotic citizens will cast suspicious eye upon you as a destroyer of the laws. You will confirm in the minds of the judges the justice of their own condemnation of you. For he who is a corruptor of the laws is more than likely to be corruptor of the young. Will you then flee from well-ordered cities and virtuous men? Is existence worth having on these terms? Or will you go to these cities without shame and talk to them, Socrates? And what will you say to them? Will you say what you say here about virtue, justice, institutions, and laws being the best things among men. Would that be decent of you? Surely not.

"If you go away from well-governed states to Crito's friends in Thessaly, where there is a great disorder and immorality, they will be charmed to have the tale of your escape from prison, set off with ludicrous particulars of the manner in which you were wrapped in a goatskin or some other disguise and metamorphosed as the fashion of runaways is—that is very likely. But will there be no one to remind you in your old age you violated the most sacred laws from a miserable desire of a little more life? Perhaps not, if you keep them in a good temper. But if they are angry you will hear many degrading things; you will live, but how? As the flatterer of all men and the servant of all men. And doing what? Eating and drinking in Thessaly, having gone abroad in order that you may get a dinner. Where will your fine sentiments about justice and virtue be then? Say that you wish to live for the sake of your children, that you may bring them up and educate them—will you take them into Thessaly and deprive them of Athenian citizenship? Is that the benefit which you would confer upon them? Or are you under the impression that they will be better cared for and educated here if you are still alive, although absent from them because your friends will take care of them? Do you think if you are an inhabitant of Thessaly they will take care of them, and if you are an inhabitant of the other world they will not take care of them? No, if they who call themselves friends are truly friends, they surely will.

"Listen, then, Socrates, to us who have brought you up. Think not of life and children first, and of justice afterwards, but of justice first, that you may be justified before the rulers of the other world. For neither will you nor your children be happier or holier in this life, or happier in another, if you do as Crito bids. Now you depart in innocence, a sufferer and not a doer of evil; a victim, not of the laws, but of men. But if you escape, returning evil for evil and injury for injury, breaking the agreements which you have made with us, and wronging those whom you ought least to wrong, that is to say, yourself, your friends, your country, and us, we shall be angry with you while you live. Our brethren, the laws in the other world, will receive you as an enemy because they will know you have done your best to destroy us. Listen, then, to us and not to Crito."

This is the voice which I seem to hear murmuring in my ears, like the sound of a divine flute in the ears of the mystic. That voice, I say, is humming in my ears and prevents me from hearing any other. I know anything more which you may say will be useless. Yet speak, if you have anything to say.

CR: I have nothing to say, Socrates.

SOC: Then let me follow what seems to be the will of the god.

Socrates' most convincing arguments for not escaping were

_____

_____

_____

_____

_____

_____

_____

_____ .

EXERCISE 9.1
Thinking About the *Crito*

1. Think of the *Crito* as falling into three large parts. The first part introduces the two main characters and states Crito's arguments for escaping. The second part reviews some of Socrates' past philosophical principles. The last part applies these principles to his present situation and presents arguments for not escaping.

Looking back at the notes in the margin, I see the first part ends on about page _____ .

What we learn about the differences between Socrates and Crito is _____

_____

_____

_____

_____

_____

_____. Crito's main arguments for

escaping are _____

_____

_____

_____. What many of these arguments have

in common is _____

_____

_____

_____

_____. Thus, we see Crito is

a person who _____

_____

_____

_____. The principles Socrates

states in the second part of the dialogue are his beliefs that _____

_____

_____

_____

_____. In the third section he

speaks to himself in the voice of the laws. The points he makes against escaping

are _____

_____

_____

_____

_____.

2. Socrates asks, "When injured should we injure in return . . . ?" To what two injuries does he refer?

The injury that has already occurred is _____

_____

_____. The other injury will be _____

_____

_____

_____.

3. Assume you are Crito. Offer your best single argument to Socrates for escaping. Remember, you will not be successful if you try to get him to violate his principles.

I would say that there is at least one more argument in favor of your escape. I will

state it briefly and then expand it. In essence, my argument is _____

_____

_____

_____. My reasons for saying this

are _____

_____

_____

_____

_____. What you have not realized is _____

_____

_____

_____. If you escape, you would not be

returning an injury for an injury because _____

_____

_____

_____

_____. Nor would you be harming

your soul as you fear because _____

_____

_____

_____

_____. Even though
the laws are, in some sense, your guardians and parents, what you should have
replied to them is _____

_____

_____

_____

_____. I can even find evidence
for my view from your own life. When I look at what you said in the *Apology* I see

_____

_____

_____

_____

_____

_____.

   4. Now try your hand at composing a question on *Crito.*

A good question to ask about the *Crito,* which would help a careful reader see
the dialogue more clearly, would be _____

_____

_____

_____

_____. And if you had asked me that fine
question, my answer would have been _____

_____

_____

_____

_____.

EXERCISE 9.2

Crito Quiz

Which of the following statements are consistent (C) or inconsistent (I) with
Crito's reasons for Socrates to escape?

   1. C   I   We should worry about what others think of us.

   2. C   I   Living justly is more important than living.

   3. C   I   Obey the will of the gods.

   4. C   I   Athens is an unjust state.

5. C I   By staying in jail, Socrates is contradicting his former ethical beliefs.

6. C I   By staying in jail, Socrates is avoiding his responsibility as a parent.

7. C I   Because he is old, Socrates should cling to his last few years.

8. C I   Socrates' death will make his enemies happy.

9. C I   Socrates has an obligation to his wife to escape.

10. C I   There is no afterlife; therefore, Socrates should enjoy this life while he can.

11. C I   Socrates conducted a weak defense at his trial.

Which of the following statements are consistent (C) or inconsistent (I) with Socrates' reasons for not escaping?

12. C I   The laws are like our parents.

13. C I   The laws are like gods.

14. C I   We should keep our just agreements unless we violate the will of the gods in doing so.

15. C I   It is not right to return a wrong for a wrong.

16. C I   The soul and the body are of relatively equal value.

17. C I   Immoral actions harm the soul.

18. C I   Immoral actions will cause the gods to punish us.

19. C I   Children should be free to look after their own education.

20. C I   Socrates' friends will be punished if he escapes.

21. C I   The members of the jury are wise; therefore, their verdict should be obeyed.

22. C I   We should not listen to the opinions of the many.

23. C I   The noblest death is dying for one's beliefs.

24. C I   Choosing to spend one's life in a state constitutes an implicit agreement that the state's laws are just.

25. C I   The gods punish cowardly actions.

EXERCISE 9.3
Vote and Debate

1. Socrates should have taken Crito's offer and escaped from jail.

Agree _____ Disagree _____ Evidence: _____

_____

_____

_____.

2. Socrates did not believe in civil disobedience.

Agree _____ Disagree _____ Evidence: _____

_____

_____

_____.

3. Crito did not understand Socrates.

Agree _____ Disagree _____ Evidence: _____

_____

_____

_____ .

4. Socrates did not understand Crito.

Agree _____ Disagree _____ Evidence: _____

_____

_____

_____ .

EXERCISE 9.4
Looking Back

1. What are some key features of the *Crito*?

EXERCISE 9.5
Looking at the World Through Socrates' Eyes

How would Socrates answer each of the following? Offer one example from any of the three chapters on Socrates that supports your answer.

1. T   F   Because each person has an equally valid point of view, there is no such thing as an absolutely wrong action or an absolutely right action.

Example: _____

_____ .

2. T   F   The gods exist.

Example: _____

_____ .

3. T   F   It is impossible to know the essence of a term like "holiness."

Example: _____

_____ .

4. T   F   Civil disobedience, the deliberate, public violation of a government's law, is an immoral act.

Example: _____

_____ .

5. T   F   The masses are foolish.

Example: _____

_____ .

6. T   F   Democracy is a poor form of government.

Example: _____

_____ .

7. T F The soul is immortal.

Example: _____

_____.

8. T F The mind can know truths that did not come through the senses.

Example: _____

_____.

ANALYSIS OF YOUR PHILOSOPHICAL SELF-PORTRAIT

To see how your views stack up against Socrates', read my analysis below, re-think your position, and then circle what you believe is the correct answer. I've underlined Socrates' answers.

1. T _F_ *Because Socrates was unjustly convicted, he had no obligation to remain in prison.*

Socrates, of course, would answer this False. Essentially, Socrates argues as follows:

1. One must perform right actions, because wrong actions harm the soul, the most valuable part of the self.

2. Keeping one's implicit agreement with the state not to violate its laws is a right action that comes before all other agreements (for example, the implicit agreement to raise one's children).

3. Therefore, one must not escape from jail, because this would be a wrong action, violating one's implicit agreement with the state.

What is the strongest argument you could make against Socrates' position? Attack arguments 1 and 2, or attempt to show that even if arguments 1 and 2 are correct, they do not establish the truth of argument 3.

_____

_____

_____

_____

_____

2. _T_ F *Socrates' obligation to the state to keep his just agreements (even if it leads to his death) is higher than his obligation to remain alive and raise his children.*

Naturally, Socrates would answer this True. Of all of Crito's arguments for escaping, Socrates' obligation to remain alive and care for his children often strikes students as the strongest. But what if Socrates argued, as he well might, as follows? "If I escape from jail, then I will provide my children with the example of a coward, who, through fear of death, abandoned his values. However, by going to my death I leave my children with the memory of a father they could truly love and respect, a man who died preserving his values."

Your response?

_____

_____

_____

_____

_____

Evaluation: Number of points in agreement with Socrates = _____ of 2 possible.

A position of Socrates' that you strongly (support, oppose) is _____

_____

because _____.

GOOD BOOKS

Guthrie, W. K. C. *Socrates.* Cambridge: Cambridge University Press, 1971. A good, though rather technical, overview.

Plato. *The Collected Dialogues.* Edited by Edith Hamilton and Huntington Cairns. New York: Pantheon, Bollingen Series LXXI, 1966. A wonderful book to put under your own Christmas tree. Plato is the most readable of all the great philosophers. The *Theatetus,* a description of Socrates' actions the day *before* he encounters Euthyphro, is a good dialogue to investigate next. Then go on to *Gorgias, Protagoras,* and *Symposium.*

Renault, Mary. *The Last of the Wine.* New York: Vintage, 1956. A novelistic re-creation of the world of Socrates; a masterpiece by one of this century's greatest historical novelists.

Stone, I. F. *The Trial of Socrates.* Toronto: Little, Brown, 1988. An intriguing reinvestigation of Socrates by a nonacademic.

NEXT STOP

You meet Plato, the first of the great philosophers.

10
Plato's Metaphysics
Divine Forms

YOUR PHILOSOPHICAL SELF-PORTRAIT

Add details to your philosophical self-portrait by answering the questions below and explaining your answers.

1. T F Everything that is real has a height, width, and depth; that is, it occupies a measurable physical space.

    Evidence _____

    _____

    _____.

2. T F All holy actions are poor copies of perfect Holiness.

    Evidence _____

    _____

    _____.

3. T F Even if there were no holy actions, perfect Holiness would still exist.

    Evidence _____

    _____

    _____.

4. T F All of reality is divided between the physical realm and the divine realm.

    Evidence _____

    _____

    _____.

We'll undertake a thought experiment to briefly summarize the views of Thales, Heraclitus, Parmenides, and Socrates and then introduce Plato. By considering the difference between physical triangles and the Form of Triangle, you'll be able to develop a simplified portrait of Plato's view of reality. Physical triangles are changing, imperfect copies of the unchanging, eternal, perfect Form of Triangle. By considering other physical objects and their corresponding Forms, you will gain an increasingly complex sense of Plato's portrait of reality. An analysis of Plato's "Allegory of the Cave" will complete your introduction to Platonic metaphysics.

THOUGHT EXPERIMENT

I look out my window at Jerry mowing his lawn and think, one after the other, like Thales, Heraclitus, Parmenides, Socrates, and Plato!

Thinking like Thales, I understand that Jerry, his lawn mower, his lawn, and every other thing I see is simply the Many unified by the One, which is water.

Thinking like Heraclitus, I see the same Many but believe it is unified by a different One, the Logos of Change.

Thinking like Parmenides, I believe the Many is an illusion, hiding the One, which is unchanging, undivided Being.

Thinking like Socrates, I forget the problem of the One and the Many and want to go talk to Jerry and ask him about the nature of holiness.

Thinking like Plato, I think most strangely. I see the same Many as the pre-Socratics, but believe all I see is a poor copy of a higher, unseen realm of reality. In addition, when I imagine Socrates questioning Jerry, I imagine Socrates coming up with answers!

Plato presents us with two portraits of Socrates. In Plato's early dialogues, like the ones you've just read, Socrates is full of questions but few answers. In Plato's middle and late dialogues, like the *Symposium, Republic,* and *Phaedo,* Socrates makes repeated sketches of elaborate philosophical answers. Thus, the "later Socrates" attempts to answer questions posed by the "earlier Socrates." Scholars believe that starting in the middle of his career, Plato began testing his own positions by putting them into Socrates' mouth. This device allowed Plato to demonstrate that his own views were continuations of the concerns of his beloved teacher.

Had Plato only been the author of the early dialogues, then he would be remembered as a remarkable biographer of Socrates. It is from the positions developed in the middle and late dialogues, positions which we will consider in this and the following two chapters, that Plato is remembered as the first great

Plato (428–348 B.C.)

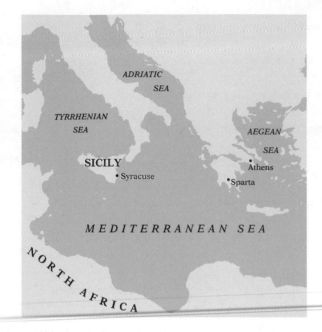

The modern philosopher Alfred North White-head once claimed that the entire history of Western philosophy has been little more than "a series of footnotes to Plato." Born in Athens to a prominent aristocratic family that was actively involved in politics, Plato was an exceptionally bright and athletic youth, excelling in poetry, music, and wrestling. According to some ac-

counts, he was originally named Aristocles and was given the name Plato (the term "platys" in Greek meaning "broad") because of his powerful physique.

Plato grew up during the twenty-seven-year Peloponnesian war between the rival Greek city-states Athens and Sparta. The surrender of Athens to Sparta brought an end to Athenian dominance and democracy and marked the beginning of the end of the splendor of ancient Greek civilization. Two members of the Thirty Tyrants, an antidemocratic group who took control of Athens after its surrender to Sparta in 404 B.C., were Plato's relatives. Disillusioned by the surrender of Athens as well as his family's role in the destruction of the Athenian government, Plato rejected the political life and took up the career of a philosopher.

Plato suffered another tragedy when his beloved teacher Socrates was put to death by the state five years later. The trial and death of Socrates by a vote of 501 representatives of the Athenian populace further contributed to Plato's distrust of democracy. Following his teacher's death, Plato traveled through southern Italy, Sicily, and northern Africa, where he came into contact with the ideas of other philosophers. It

philosopher and one of the greatest philosophers of all time. But what are these positions? How does Plato answer the questions that fascinated Socrates?

Plato holds that reality is divided into two parts: a realm of physical things and a realm of what he calls Forms (sometimes translated as Ideas). If you are like most students, you will have no trouble understanding what Plato means by the realm of physical things, but understanding the realm of Forms will take a bit longer.

The realm of physical things is simply what the pre-Socratics called the Many: clouds, houses, people, mountains, and so forth. The realm of physical things is the world you and I sit in right now. For Plato, key features of our physical world are that it is constantly changing and known by the senses. The realm of Forms, however, is unchanging and known by the mind. Every class of physical things—clouds, apples, triangles—has a corresponding Form, the Form of Cloud, the Form of Apple, the Form of Triangle.

was during these travels that Plato began writing his first dialogues.

While Plato rejected the political life, he was still deeply involved in political theorizing, believing that philosophers were the best suited to be leaders of states. After returning to Athens in 387 B.C., Plato founded a school dedicated to the study of philosophical problems and the training of future political leaders. His Academy was located on and named after the sacred site of the hero Academus on the outskirts of Athens. Plato's best-known student was Aristotle, who joined the Academy as a teenager, staying for twenty years until Plato's death at the age of eighty-one.

The Academy lasted over nine hundred years and could be termed Europe's first university. Plato's famous school was not like universities today, with organized classes, degrees, and specialized faculty. Instead it was more of a fellowship of intellectuals interested in Athenian culture and the opportunity to exchange ideas with the great philosopher Plato. On at least one occasion Plato gave a public lecture on the "Good as One," which apparently left many in the audience baffled and disappointed.

In 367 B.C., following the death of Dionysus—

the tyrant of Syracuse and one of Plato's devoted friends—Plato was persuaded to return to Sicily to undertake the education of the tyrant's son, also named Dionysus, the city's new ruler. Plato's experiment in training the younger Dionysus to be a philosopher-king was disastrous. (According to some tales, the young man had his teacher sold into slavery!) In 361 B.C., Plato returned to Athens, where he remained until his death.

A prolific writer, Plato wrote more than twenty dialogues covering numerous philosophical topics. His dialogues can be divided into roughly three periods. While his early works seem to be based primarily on Socrates' philosophy, in his later dialogues he develops his own views.

The following is a list of Plato's writings:

- Early works: *Apology, Charmides, Crito, Euthydemus, Euthyphro, Gorgias, Hippias Minor, Hippias Major, Ion, Laches, Lysis, Menexenus, Protagoras.*

- Middle works: *Cratylus, Meno, Phaedo, Phaedrus, Republic, Symposium, Theatetus.*

- Later works: *Parmenides, Critias, Law, Philebus, Politicus, Timaeus, Sophist.*

To sum up Platonic metaphysics in a sentence: Physical things are changing, **temporal,** imperfect copies of unchanging, eternal, perfect Forms. Thus, Plato asks us to see reality this way:

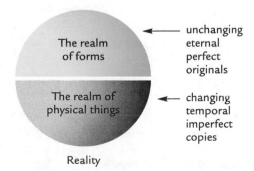

Reality

temporal Of, or related to, time. A tree is thought of as a temporal thing because it exists in time; God is not (usually) thought of as a temporal thing because God does not exist in time.

As you will learn in the "Allegory of the Cave," Plato describes the relationship between the two realms in a striking manner. Everything in the physical world can be thought of as a mere *shadow* of the realm of Forms. Individual trees are like shadows cast by the Form of Treeness; physical mountains are like shadows cast by the Form of Mountainness; you and I are like shadows cast by the Form of Humanness. While we believe the physical world is the only reality, we are entirely wrong. We live among a collection of flickering shadows of the far higher and infinitely perfect realm of Forms.

Now why would anyone believe such a strange view of reality?

I'm not only going to answer that question, but I'm also going to do my best to convince you that Plato's view is correct. By the end of this chapter, if you're not careful, Plato's strange metaphysics will seem perfectly sensible.

Here is my strategy. I will convince you of almost all the features of Plato's view of reality simply by describing the difference between one class of physical things, physical triangles, and one Form, the Form of Triangle. Next, I'm going to add other Forms to my argument. Finally, I'll guide you through Plato's "Allegory of the Cave." By chapter's end, you may be ready to join countless others in the Plato Fan Club.

I'll answer the following questions:

- What is evidence that the Form of Triangle exists?

- What is evidence that the Form of Triangle is unchanging?

- What is evidence that the Form of Triangle is eternal?

- What is evidence that the Form of Triangle is nonmaterial?

- What is evidence that the Form of Triangle is perfect?

- What is evidence that individual triangles are imperfect copies of the Form of Triangle?

- What is evidence for the existence of other Forms?

- What are the main features of Plato's "Allegory of the Cave"?

- What can be learned about Plato's metaphysics from the "Divided Line"?

- Why would anyone believe Plato's strange view of reality?

What Is Evidence That the Form of Triangle Exists?

Surprisingly enough, quite a bit can be understood about Plato's view of reality simply by thinking about the difference between individual triangles and the Form of Triangle.

And so, let's start with a few triangles:

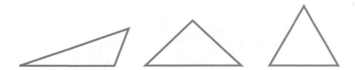

The first triangle has no equal sides or equal angles; the second triangle has two equal sides opposite two equal angles; the third triangle has three equal sides opposite three equal angles. So, insofar as these three triangles are concerned, we could say that equal angles are opposite equal sides (and unequal angles are opposite unequal sides). To represent this, I've labeled one of the triangles; you label the other two.

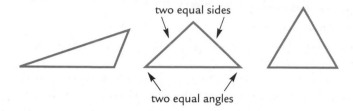

Now let us say you wonder if this might be true of other triangles. So, in order to see if equal angles will be opposite equal sides, sketch a few triangles below:

The more carefully you draw your triangles, the more clearly you will be able to see the idea we've been investigating. At this point you know something about a small collection of triangles. And so, in the triangles you have looked at, would you agree with the generalization that equal angles are opposite equal sides?

I (agree, disagree) because _____

_____.

Now sketch a few more triangles.

You are probably beginning to see that it is a general truth that equal angles will always be opposite equal sides. You can prove this to yourself simply by realizing that what "makes" any two sides of a triangle equal are its equal angles. And the reverse. What "makes" any two sides of a triangle unequal are its unequal angles.

And so, won't you now agree that in any triangle, equal angles will *always* be opposite equal sides and unequal angles will *always* be opposite unequal sides?

I (agree, disagree) because _____

_____ .

If you are like almost all of my students, you have agreed and, in so doing, *perceived a truth about Triangleness.*

Now pay close attention.

What are you thinking about when you perceive a truth about Triangleness? You are certainly *not* thinking about the few triangles in this chapter. *You are thinking about the universal features of every triangle that ever existed, exists now, or could ever exist in the future.* In every possible, conceivable triangle, equal sides will make equal angles and unequal sides will make unequal angles. This is a truth about Triangleness—or, as Plato would put it, *the Form of Triangle.*

I'll go over that again. When you understand that equal sides make equal angles and unequal sides make unequal angles, you are not thinking about a few triangles. You are contemplating a truth about all triangles. When you contemplate a truth about all triangles, you are contemplating Triangleness. Plato's term for Triangleness is the Form of Triangle.

Here are a few more truths that will help you contemplate the Form of Triangle.

1. All triangles have three sides.
2. The area of all triangles is equal to half the base of the triangle multiplied by the height of the triangle.
3. The internal angles of all triangles are equal to two right angles.
4. All triangles are two-dimensional figures.

Note that when you think of these truths you are thinking not merely about the triangles in this book or the triangles you have seen in your life. You are thinking about concepts that apply to every conceivable triangle. Contemplating concepts that apply to every conceivable triangle, you are contemplating Triangleness, the Form of Triangle.

Now, thus far, all I've presented is some evidence that the Form of Triangle exists and is described by truths about all individual triangles. Thus, we have a clear but very incomplete portrait of existence.

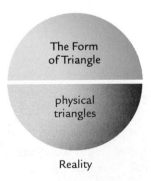

Reality

Let's go on to our next question and add another detail to this portrait.

What Is Evidence That the Form of Triangle is Unchanging?

One obvious difference between individual triangles and the Form of Triangle is that the former change, while the latter is unchanging.

For example, I'll make some changes in the first triangles I drew.

I have certainly changed the triangles, *but I have not changed the Form of Triangle in the slightest.* The Form of Triangle still consists of the truths we've mentioned. It is still true that equal sides make equal angles, unequal sides make unequal angles, that all triangles have three sides, and so forth. Even though I've destroyed a few triangles, I have not damaged, in any way, the Form of Triangle.

Will you agree that by erasing parts of individual triangles, we make no change in the Form of Triangle?

I (agree, disagree) because _____

_____

_____.

Imagine that someone finds this book a hundred years from now. The individual triangles have faded. The particles of ink have flaked off the paper or done whatever particles of ink do after a hundred years. But even though the individual triangles have become fainter, Triangleness itself has not changed. A million years from now when this book has turned to dust and its drawings of triangles have blown to the four winds, *Triangleness itself will not have changed in the slightest.*

Do you agree that Triangleness will never change?

I (agree, disagree) that Triangleness will never change because _____

_____

_____.

If you agree that Triangleness, the Form of Triangle, will never change, then you see our simple portrait of Platonic reality this way:

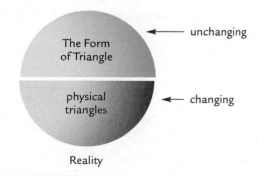

Reality

What Is Evidence That the Form of Triangle Is Eternal?

Let us say your body never changed. Your body would then last forever, would be eternal. Or, let us say you had an apple that never changed; therefore, the apple would last forever, would be eternal. If something never changes, there is no way for it to pass out of existence. Thus, something unchanging must be eternal.

Will you agree that if something is unchanging, then it is eternal?

I (agree, disagree) because _____

_____

_____.

If you agree, then you've added another important distinction to our picture of reality. The higher realm containing the Form of Triangle is not only unchanging, but also eternal. The lower realm containing physical triangles is changing and temporal.

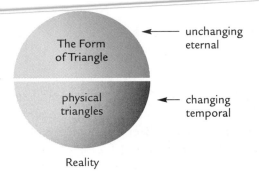

Reality

Now let's add another feature to this portrait of reality.

What Is Evidence That the Form of Triangle Is Nonmaterial?

I don't think I'll have any trouble convincing you that individual triangles are material things and the Form of Triangle is a nonmaterial thing. Just think for a moment. The triangles in this book are made of the materials ink and paper. Individual triangles could also be made of wood, stone, metal, or any other matter. But the Form of Triangle is not made of ink and paper—or wood, stone, metal, or any other matter. The Form of Triangle is simply a collection of truths. Truths are not made of matter. Truths are nonmaterial.

You can completely convince yourself that this is correct simply by realizing that while you *could* measure the height and width of any physical triangle, you *could not* measure the height and width of the Form of Triangle. Individual triangles have height and width because they are material things; the Form of Triangle has no height or width because it is a nonmaterial thing.

Is the height of the Form of Triangle three inches, three feet, three miles? The Form of Triangle has no height because it is not made of matter.

And so, will you agree that individual triangles are material things and that the Form of Triangle is a nonmaterial thing?

I (agree, disagree) because _____

_____

_____ .

If you agree, then this is your portrait of reality:

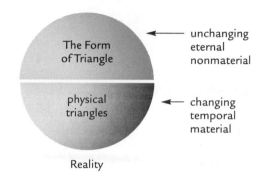

Reality

What Is Evidence That the Form of Triangle Is Perfect?

Now let's add another very important distinction. The Form of Triangle is perfect; individual triangles are imperfect.

You can see that this is the case simply by understanding that it is impossible for any physical thing to consist of perfectly straight lines. The lines on the sides of the triangles in this book are only as straight as current printing machinery can make them. A microscopic analysis of any physical line would show that it contains countless irregularities and bumps. Thus, all physical triangles are made not of straight lines but of bumpy, irregular shapes that approximate straight lines. The Form of Triangle, however, is made of perfectly straight lines. The Form of Triangle contains, in fact, the Form of a Straight Line. The Form of a Straight Line is perfectly straight. The physical lines that make up physical triangles are simply imperfect copies of Perfectly Straight Lineness. (We'll develop this point in the next section.)

Another way of seeing that individual triangles are imperfect and the Form of Triangle is perfect is to see that the former are destructible and the latter is indestructible. Remember that we said that individual triangles are temporal and the Form of Triangle is eternal. This means that all individual triangles will eventually cease to exist. The Form of Triangle, however, will last forever. Isn't it true that something that is temporal and destructible is clearly less perfect than something that is eternal and indestructible?

And so, would you agree that individual triangles are imperfect and that the Form of Triangle is perfect?

I (agree, disagree) because _____

_____

_____.

If you agree, then we can add another important feature to our growing portrait of reality according to Plato.

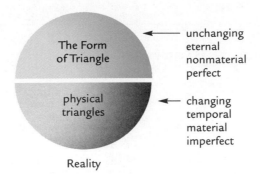

Now let's build on what we've just established and add still another distinction between physical triangles and the Form of Triangle.

What Is Evidence That Physical Triangles Are Imperfect Copies of the Form of Triangle?

Look back at the triangles I've drawn in this chapter. All of them, if you think about it, are imperfect copies of the Form of Triangle.

If I carefully measured the area of each of the triangles, I'd find that the area *approximately* equals one half the base multiplied by the height. If I carefully measured the internal angles of each of the triangles I'd find that the sum of these angles *approximately* equals the sum of two right triangles. If I carefully measured the sides and angles of the triangles, I'd find that there are *approximately* equal sides opposite *approximately* equal angles.

But in the Form of Triangle, area is *exactly* equal to half the base multiplied by half the height; the sum of internal angles *exactly* equals the sum of two right angles; and equal sides, *exactly* equal sides, are opposite *exactly* equal angles.

My physical triangles are only approximations, poor copies, of the truths contained in the Form of Triangle. The Form is the original; every physical triangle is a knockoff.

Don't you have to agree? Physical triangles are imperfect copies of the Form of Triangle.

I (agree, disagree) because _____

_____

_____.

Here is our picture of reality:

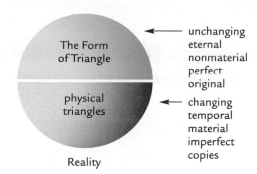

Reality

What Is Evidence for the Existence of Other Forms?

Now I'm going to add two large categories to our Platonic model of reality: all geometric figures and all numbers.

Geometric Figures

Obviously, what we have said about the Form of Triangle and triangles is also true about the Form of Square and physical squares, the Form of Circle and physical circles, the Form of Cube and individual cubes, and all other two- and three-dimensional shapes. If you have agreed that the Form of Triangle is the unchanging, eternal, nonmaterial, perfect original that all changing, temporal, material, imperfect triangles are copies of, then it seems you must agree to the same kind of description about the Forms of all geometric figures and individual geometric figures. For example:

1. Just as the Form of Triangle consists of truths about Triangleness, so the Form of Square consists of truths about Squareness and the Form of Sphere consists of truths about Sphereness.

2. Just as the Form of Triangle is unchanging, while physical triangles are changing, so the Form of Square is unchanging, while physical squares are changing, and the Form of Sphere is unchanging, while physical spheres are changing.

3. Just as the Form of Triangle is eternal because it is unchanging, so the Form of Square is eternal because it is unchanging and the Form of Sphere is eternal because it is unchanging.

And so forth.

Will you agree that all physical, two- and three-dimensional geometric shapes have a corresponding Form?

I (agree, disagree) because _____

_____

_____.

Thus, if you agree, we have enormously increased the number of items in our portrait of reality.

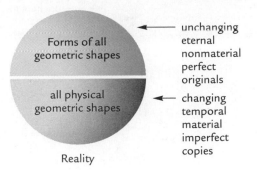

Reality

Numbers

The relationship between physical numeric symbols and their corresponding Forms is exactly like the relationship between physical triangles and the Form of Triangle.

As an example, let's use symbols for three and the Form of Three.

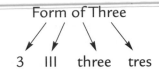

The Form of Three, Threeness, is one thing, and symbols for the Form are another. The first symbol comes from Arabic culture, the second from Roman culture, the third from English culture, and the last from Spanish culture. While each culture uses different symbols, *they all point to the identical Form of Three. Threeness is Threeness no matter what symbol you use to represent it.* And, as you might suspect, everything we said about the Form of Triangle could be said about the Form of Three.

1. *The Form of Three is unchanging.* In a thousand years, when this book has turned to dust and all the symbols in it have vanished, the Form of Three, just like the Form of Triangle, will not have changed in the slightest. Physical triangles and physical symbols will come and go, but Triangleness and Threeness will be completely unaffected.

2. *The Form of Three is eternal.* Just as the Form of Triangle was eternal because it was unchanging, so the Form of Three is eternal because it is unchanging.

3. *The Form of Three is nonmaterial.* Just as the Form of Triangle is not made of ink and paper, or stone, metal, or any other material, so the Form of Three is not made of ink and paper, or stone, metal, or any other material. Just as you could not measure the height of the Form of Triangle, so you could not measure the height of the Form of Three. The Form of Three, just like the Form of Triangle, is nonmaterial.

4. *The Form of Three is the original that physical threes imperfectly copy.* Just as the Form of Triangle was imperfectly copied by physical triangles, so

the Form of Three is imperfectly copied by physical threes. The Arabic three is made of two curves; the Roman three is made of three straight lines; the English word is made of five letters; and the Spanish word is made of four letters. All of these symbols imperfectly copy the Form of Three *because the Form of Three is not made of curves, straight lines, five letters, or four letters.* The Form of Three is perfect, nonmaterial Threeness, which all symbolic threes point toward but, because they are material, imperfectly copy.

Now, will you agree to statements 1 through 4 above?

I (agree, disagree) with statement 1 because _____

_____

_____.

I (agree, disagree) with statement 2 because _____

_____

_____.

I (agree, disagree) with statement 3 because _____

_____

_____.

I (agree, disagree) with statement 4 because _____

_____

_____.

Everything we said about the Form of Three could apply to the Form of Ten, the Form of One Thousand, the Form of One Million, and every other number.

Thus, if you agreed to the preceding points, we have enormously expanded our portrait of reality to include all numbers.

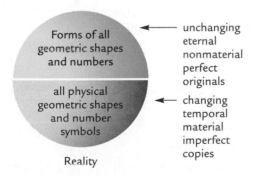

Plato would add two more large categories to this portrait of reality: the categories of all physical things and all moral values. Thus, just as there is the Form of Triangle and physical triangles, Plato would add the Form of Cloud and physical clouds, the Form of Mountain and physical mountains, the Form of Human and physical humans, the Form of Courage and courageous acts, the Form of Holiness and holy acts, and so forth.

But, as I promised at the beginning, I will let Plato speak for himself. Now that you've had a bit of practice in thinking Platonically, you're ready to read his "Allegory of the Cave."

READING:
PLATO'S "ALLEGORY OF THE CAVE"

What Are the Main Features?

"The Allegory of the Cave" is a short section from the *Republic*, a dialogue written during the middle of Plato's career. The *Republic* attempts to define the principle of justice, but in doing so presents Plato's view of the ideal state. In the following section, Plato not only describes his view of the nature of reality but also the relationship between the philosopher and society, the stages of enlightenment, and some important features of the philosophical personality.

Underline the major symbols and Plato's explanation of them.

Allegory of the Cave (from the Republic)

SOCRATES: And now let me show you in a story to what degree we are enlightened or unenlightened. Can you see human beings living in a cave, which has a mouth open toward the light? Here they have been from their childhood and have their legs and necks chained so they cannot move. They can only see in front of them, being prevented by the chains from turning their heads around. Above and behind them a fire is blazing at a distance, and between the fire and the prisoners there is a raised walkway. You will see, if you look, a low wall built above the walkway like the screen which puppet players have in front of them, over which they show the puppets.

GLAUCON: I see.

SOC: And do you see men passing along the wall carrying all sorts of vessels and statues and figures of animals made of wood, stone, and various materials, which appear over the wall? Some of the men are talking, others silent.

GLAU: You show me a strange image, and they are strange prisoners.

SOC: Like ourselves, and they see only their own shadows, or the shadows of one another, which the fire throws on the opposite wall of the cave.

GLAU: True, how could they see anything but the shadows if they were never allowed to move their heads?

SOC: And of the objects which are being carried, in the same manner they would see only the shadows?

GLAU: Yes.

SOC: And if they were able to talk to each other, would they suppose they were naming what was actually before them?

GLAU: They would.

Soc: And suppose further the prison had an echo that came from the cave wall. Would they be sure to believe when one of the passers-by behind them spoke that the voice which they heard came from the passing shadow?

Glau: Yes.

Soc: To them the truth would be literally nothing but the shadows of the images.

Glau: That is certain.

Soc: And now look again and see what will naturally follow if the prisoners are released and their error is corrected. At first, when any of them is liberated and suddenly compelled to stand up and turn his neck around and walk and look toward the light, he will suffer sharp pains. The glare will hurt him and he will be unable to see the realities of which, in his former state, he has only seen the shadows. Then imagine someone says to him that what he saw before was an illusion; but now, when he is approaching nearer to reality and his eye is turned toward more real existence, he has a clearer vision. What will be his reply? You may further imagine his instructor is pointing to the objects as they pass and requiring him to name them—will he not be confused? Will he not believe the shadows he formerly saw are truer than the objects which are now shown to him?

Glau: Far truer.

Soc: And if he is compelled to look straight at the fire, will he not have pain in his eyes which will make him turn away and take refuge in the shadows which he can see, and which he will believe to be clearer than the things which are now being shown to him?

Glau: True.

Soc: And suppose once more he is reluctantly dragged up the steep and rugged ascent and held until he is forced into the presence of the sun, is he not likely to be pained and irritated? When he approaches the sunlight his eyes will be dazzled, and he will not be able to see anything at all of what are now called realities.

Glau: Not all at once.

Soc: He will need to grow accustomed to the sight of the upper world. And first he will see the shadows best, next the reflections of men and other objects in the water, and then the objects themselves. Then he will gaze upon the light of the moon and the stars and the spangled heaven. He will see the sky and the stars by night better than the sun or the light of the sun by day?

Glau: Certainly.

Soc: Last of all he will be able to see the sun and not mere reflections of it in the water, but he will see the sun in its own proper place, and not in another. And he will contemplate the sun as it is.

Glau: Certainly.

Soc: He will then proceed to argue that this is what controls the seasons and the years, and is the guardian of all that is in the visible world, and in a certain way the cause of all things which he and his fellows were accustomed to behold?

Glau: Clearly, he would first see the sun and then its nature.

The major symbols Socrates has established are _____

_____

_____

_____.

In essence, he seems to be saying _____

_____

_____

_____

_____

_____.

Soc: And when he remembered his old dwelling and the wisdom of the cave and his fellow prisoners, do you suppose he would be happy about his change and pity the prisoners?

Glau: Certainly, he would.

Soc: And if the prisoners were in the habit of conferring honors among themselves on those who were quickest to observe the passing shadows and to discuss which of them went before, and which followed after, and which were together, and who were therefore best able to draw conclusions as to the future, do you think he would care for such honors and glories or envy the possessors of them? Would he not say with Homer, "Better to be the slave of a slave," and to endure anything, rather than think as they do and live in their way?

Glau: Yes, I think he would rather suffer anything than entertain those false notions and live in that miserable manner.

Soc: Imagine once more, such a one coming suddenly out of the sun and returning to his old situation. Would he not be certain to have his eyes full of darkness?

Glau: Certainly.

Soc: And if there was a contest and he had to compete in measuring the shadows with the prisoners who had never moved out of the den, while his sight was still weak and before his eyes had become steady, would he not seem ridiculous? Men would say of him that he left and returned without his eyes and that it was better not even to think of leaving. If anyone tried to free another and lead him up to the light, let them only catch the offender, and they would put him to death.

Glau: No question.

Now Socrates begins to interpret the Allegory. Underline each symbol he explains.

Soc: This entire allegory you may add, dear Glaucon, to the previous argument. The cave is the world of sight, the light of the fire is the sun, and you will not misunderstand me if you interpret the journey upwards to be the ascent of the soul into the world of Forms, which according to my poor belief, at your desire, I have described—whether rightly or wrongly the god knows. But, whether true or false, my opinion is that in the higher world the Form of the Good appears last of all and is seen only with an effort. When seen, it is also inferred to be the universal author of all things beautiful and right, parent of light and the sun in this visible world, and the immediate source of reason and truth in the higher world. This is the power upon which he who would act rationally either in public or private life must have his eye fixed.

Glau: I agree as far as I am able to understand you.

Soc: Moreover, you must not wonder that those who achieve this wonderful vision are unwilling to descend to human affairs. Their souls are always hastening into the upper world where they desire to dwell. This desire of theirs is very natural, if our allegory can be trusted.

Glau: Yes, very natural.

Soc: And is there anything surprising in one who passes from divine contemplations to the evil state of man, appearing in a ridiculous manner if, while his eyes are blinking and before he has become accustomed to the surrounding darkness, he is compelled to fight in courts of law or in other places about the shadows of images of justice and is trying to answer the ideas of those who have never yet seen the Form of Justice?

GLAU: Anything but surprising.

SOC: Anyone who has common sense will remember there are two kinds and two causes of confused eyesight. These occur either when coming out of the light or when going into the light, which is true of the mind's eye just as much as of the bodily eye. He who remembers this, when he sees anyone whose vision is confused and weak, will not be too ready to laugh. He will first ask whether the soul of that man has come out of the brighter light and is unable to see because unaccustomed to the dark or, having turned from darkness to the day, is dazzled by excess of light. And he will believe the one happy in his condition, and he will pity the other. Or if he wants to laugh at the one who comes from below into the light, there will be more reason in this than in laughing at one who returns from the light into the cave.

GLAU: That is a very just distinction.

SOC: But then, if I am right, certain teachers must be wrong when they say they can put knowledge into the soul which was not there before, like sight into blind eyes.

GLAU: They undoubtedly say this.

SOC: Whereas, our argument shows the power and capacity of learning exists in the soul already. Just as the eye was unable to turn from darkness to light without the whole body, so too the mind can only by the movement of the whole soul be turned from the world of change into that unchanging reality, and learn by degrees to endure the sight of reality, and of the brightest and best of reality, or in other words, of the Good.

EXERCISE 10.1
Illustrating Plato

In order to see Plato's "Allegory" more clearly, make a stick-figure drawing of the prisoners, the cave, the fire, the one who escapes, and important parts of the world outside. Label each feature.

"Allegory of the Cave" by _____

As you can tell, two realms exist in the "Allegory": inside the cave and outside the cave. These symbolize the two parts of reality for Plato: what we've called the realm of physical things and the realm of Forms.

The most interesting aspects of this allegory are _____

_____

_____

_____

_____

_____

_____ .

Here are two exercises to help you see Plato's allegory more clearly.

EXERCISE 10.2
Decoding Plato

An allegory is a symbolical story. Each part of Plato's "Allegory of the Cave" represents a different aspect of his philosophy. For example, the sun represents the highest Form, the Form of the Good. What do each of the following represent?

1. The shadows in the cave
2. The prisoners
3. The prisoner's chains
4. The fire
5. The one who releases the prisoner
6. The prisoner who gets released
7. The journey out of the cave
8. The released prisoner's confusion on emerging from the cave
9. The shadows and reflections the released prisoner first sees on emerging from the cave
10. The return to the cave
11. The rejection of the other prisoners when the released prisoner returns

EXERCISE 10.3
Thinking Like Plato

Look at the following list and decide which items Plato would classify as part of the physical world (the Cave of Shadows) and which as part of the realm of Forms (outside the Cave). Use an L to indicate lower-world items, an H for higher-world items.

_____ 1. A wood desk
_____ 2. This book
_____ 3. The essence of holiness
_____ 4. Perfect circularity
_____ 5. A beautiful sunset
_____ 6. Beauty itself
_____ 7. Sunset itself
_____ 8. The works of Einstein
_____ 9. The truth of the works of Einstein
_____ 10. A newspaper
_____ 11. Perfect justice
_____ 12. The Mona Lisa
_____ 13. The ideal woman
_____ 14. Socrates
_____ 15. These words

_____ 16. A courageous action

_____ 17. The essence of courage

_____ 18. The U.S. Constitution

_____ 19. The gods

_____ 20. The words in the dictionary that define wisdom

_____ 21. What the words in the dictionary refer to when they define wisdom

I hope you find some of these obvious and some debatable.

What Can Be Learned About Plato's Metaphysics from the "Divided Line"?

In another section of the *Republic*, Plato uses a divided line to add additional details to his portrait of reality.

Realm of Forms	Form of the Good
	Forms of the Wisdom, Courage, Temperance, Justice
	Forms of geometry and math
Physical World	Physical objects
	Images

THE DIVIDED LINE

In Plato's view, both the Realm of Forms and the physical world have two divisions.

Images (shadows, reflections, pictures) occupy the lowest level of reality because, according to Plato, they are dependent for their existence upon physical objects. For example, the shadow of the chair I am sitting in would not exist without the chair itself.

And just as images depend for their existence upon physical objects, so physical objects depend for their existence upon their corresponding Forms. Thus, for example, if the Form of Chair didn't exist, my chair, and all other chairs, would not exist.

Above the Forms of physical objects are the Forms of Wisdom, Courage, Temperance, and Justice. These moral Forms cannot be learned through the sciences of geometry and mathematics as can the Forms of physical objects, but must be studied by dialectic, the philosophical question-and-answer process. We will have more to say about the moral Forms and dialectic in the next chapter.

For now, let's add what we have learned from the "Allegory of the Cave" and the "Divided Line" to our portrait of Plato's view of existence.

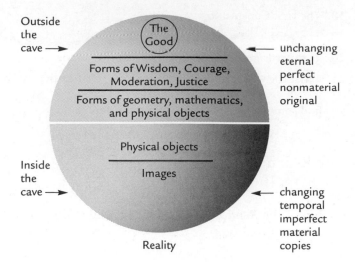

At about this point, if not earlier, some students are usually ready to raise the following objection to Plato's metaphysics. (I've followed it with my best answer.)

Objection

Everything you are calling a Form is just an idea in our minds. We have an idea of triangleness, an idea of threeness, and so forth, but these are only *human* ideas; to say that these ideas are eternal and possess all the other characteristics attributed to Forms is ridiculous. Before there were human minds, there was no Form of Triangle because the Form of Triangle is nothing but a collection of ideas, and ideas need human minds to exist.

Answer

The question is, do Forms exist independently of human minds? If all humans perished, would Plato's Forms continue to exist?

Let's go back to triangles. Perhaps you recall something like the following diagram and formula from high school.

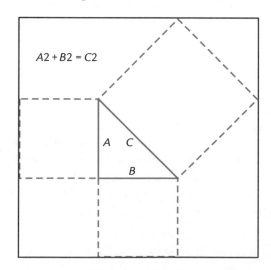

The diagram and formula assert that if you take a right triangle with sides A, B, and C and make squares from those sides, something quite unexpected results. The sum of the areas of the squares made from the two smaller sides, A and B, is exactly equal to the area of the square made from the larger side, C. This, as you may remember, is called the Pythagorean Theorem. Pythagoras was a Greek philosopher before Plato.

Now, which of the following statements is most likely to be correct?

1. Pythagoras *invented* the truth of $A^2 + B^2 = C^2$; and if there were no human minds, this truth about right triangles would not exist. The Pythagorean theorem is a *mind-dependent* truth.

2. Pythagoras *discovered* the truth of $A^2 + B^2 = C^2$; and even if there were no human minds, this truth about right triangles would continue to exist. The Pythagorean theorem is a *mind-independent* truth.

Plato, of course, would argue for statement 2. Truths about triangles and all other truths are "out there" independent of the minds that perceive them. These truths are eternal, unchanging, and unaffected by the minds that contemplate them. If you don't believe this is the case, then ponder this:

If all humans on earth decided that $A^2 + B^2$ did not equal C^2, would that make it true? Would all right triangles suddenly change so that the sum of the areas of the two smaller squares would suddenly *not* equal the area of the larger square? If you argue that truths are mind-dependent, then you'll need some evidence to show that if humans changed their minds about truths describing right triangles, then right triangles themselves would also change.

I believe _____

_____

_____.

Now, let's go on to our last question.

Why Would Anyone Believe Plato's Strange View of Reality?

There are at least five large groups of individuals who believe some or all of Plato's metaphysics.

Platonically Inclined Mathematicians

Some mathematicians take the view that the truths of mathematics are not only independent of the minds that contemplate them but also completely independent of the physical universe. For these mathematicians, naturally enough, Plato's eternal, perfect realm of Forms, which exists independently of the physical world, is a strongly appealing metaphysics.

Platonically Inclined Artists

Artists who have a strong drive toward "the perfect" are often attracted to Plato. The potter who strives to create the perfect, or ideal, pot and the painter who strives to paint the perfect, or ideal, tree often feel as if their works are poor copies, shadows, of something higher and more perfect.

Christians

Many Christians are strongly attracted to Plato's dualistic view of reality. For example, Augustine, a Christian philosopher occasionally mentioned on our tour, substitutes God for the Form of the Good and interprets the Forms as the originals that God used as models to create the physical universe. Augustine and many others since him have held that Plato presented a remarkable anticipation of the Christian cosmos.

Moral Absolutists

Plato's view that the Form of Justice, the Form of Courage, the Form of Temperance, and other ethical Forms are eternal, perfect models that humans should attempt to embody has, historically, appealed to moral absolutists, those who believe that moral values are independent of all cultures and human opinions. Plato's arguments, in fact, were the first philosophical attempt to prove that moral values *were* absolute.

Visionaries of Various Kinds

Many people simply have a deep feeling that this world is imperfect and that there is something "beyond," something "higher." The Platonic vision as embodied in the "Allegory of the Cave" and elsewhere in his writings, with its dramatic contrast between the lower world of daily life and the higher world of perfect truths, is strongly appealing to those who dream of a better world.

M. C. Escher, *Sky and Water I,* woodcut, 1938.

ILLUSTRATION QUIZ

Escher and Plato

Assume that M. C. Escher created this print after studying Plato's metaphysics. In what ways is Escher's print like Plato's dualism?

Escher's print is like Plato's dualism because _____
_____
_____
_____
_____.

In what ways is Escher's print unlike Plato's dualism?

Escher's print is unlike Plato's dualism because _____
_____
_____
_____
_____.

SUMMARY

Plato holds a dualistic metaphysics. The lower realm is the physical world, the world we know with our senses. This world is changing, imperfect, material, and a copy of the higher realm. The higher realm is the realm of Forms. Forms are eternal, perfect, and nonmaterial. The "Allegory of the Cave" symbolizes this dualism by distinguishing between the Cave of Shadows and the outer world.

EXERCISE 10.4
Looking Back

Use your own paper to practice your paraphrasing skills. Answer each of the following:

1. What is evidence that the Form of Triangle exists?
2. What is evidence that the Form of Triangle is unchanging?
3. What is evidence that the Form of Triangle is eternal?
4. What is evidence that the Form of Triangle is nonmaterial?
5. What is evidence that the Form of Triangle is perfect?
6. What is evidence that individual triangles are imperfect copies of the Form of Triangle?
7. What is evidence for the existence of other Forms?
8. What are the main features of Plato's "Allegory of the Cave"?
9. What can be learned about Plato's metaphysics from the "Divided Line"?
10. Why would anyone believe Plato's strange view of reality?

EXERCISE 10.5
Thinking Against Plato

Offer your best argument against each of the answers to 1–10 above.

EXERCISE 10.6
Platonist Test

What do you and Plato agree on? Plato believed some of the following statements were true. Decide what your position is and then read the evaluation on pages 243–245 to see how much of a Platonist you are.

1. T F The soul is immortal.
2. T F Rule by the wise, not democracy, is the best form of government.
3. T F Might makes right.
4. T F The physical universe is the only reality.
5. T F The mind can know truths independently of information from the senses.
6. T F Our reason exists to effectively serve our desires.
7. T F The majority of people are foolish.

8. T F In a just society, all people would share equally.

9. T F We should have faith that God exists.

10. T F We never truly learn anything new. All wisdom is recollected from a time before our birth.

11. T F If the realm of Forms didn't exist, the physical universe wouldn't exist.

12. T F All knowledge in our minds came through our senses.

13. T F All of reality is constantly changing.

14. T F There are two levels to reality: the lower, physical level is a copy of the higher, nonphysical level.

15. T F The ideal society would be ruled by a philosopher-king.

16. T F The ideal society would be ruled by a philosopher-queen.

17. T F Perfect Beauty exists.

18. T F Perfect Courage exists.

19. T F Perfect Justice exists.

20. T F The highest principle in reality is the essence of Goodness.

21. T F Nothing for certain can be known about anything that changes.

22. T F The body is the prison of the soul.

23. T F Virtuous people are rare.

24. T F If triangles didn't exist, then the Form of Triangle wouldn't exist.

25. T F A true philosopher is regarded as a fool by the majority of people.

ANALYSIS OF YOUR PHILOSOPHICAL SELF-PORTRAIT

To see how your views about reality stack up against Plato's, read my analysis below, rethink your position, and then circle what you believe is the correct answer. I've underlined Plato's answers.

1. T _F_ *Everything that is real has a height, width, and depth; that is, it occupies a measurable physical space.*

   Plato, of course, would answer this False. The Forms do not occupy physical space. Thus, for example, the Form of Triangle has no height, width, or depth. What is the height represented by the *truth* of the statement, "All triangles have three sides"? Individual triangles have a height, but truths about all triangles have no height because they do not exist in physical space. If it is hard to think of anything existing that doesn't exist in physical space, think of God. God is not said to be 6 feet tall nor 6 miles tall nor anywhere in between.

2. _T_ F *All holy actions are poor copies of perfect Holiness.*

   If you answered this and the next question True, then Plato must have made a great deal of sense to you.

3. _T_ F *Even if there were no holy actions, perfect Holiness would still exist.*

   Obviously, it would be philosophically inconsistent to answer this or the previous question True and also answer the first question True.

4.   <u>T</u>   F   *All of reality is divided between the physical realm and the divine realm.*

Plato holds that the realm of Forms is divine, simply because he holds that anything that is perfect, eternal, and nonmaterial has the same characteristics as the divine. If you answered this question True because you are a Christian or any other kind of theist, then odds are you regard Platonic metaphysics as presenting a congenial portrait of reality.

Evaluation: Number of points in agreement with Plato = _____ of 4 possible.

A position of Plato's that you strongly (support, oppose) is _____

_____

because _____.

GOOD BOOKS

Grube, G. M. A. *Plato's Thought.* London: Methuen, 1935. Contains a good discussion of the theory of the Forms.

Taylor, A. E. *Plato: The Man and His Work.* London: Methuen, 1926. A standard work, good overview of the dialogues.

Vlastos, Gregory, editor. *Plato: A Collection of Critical Essays.* Garden City, N.Y.: Anchor, 1971. A good, occasionally difficult sampler of recent studies of aspects of Plato's thought.

NEXT STOP

What is Plato's epistemology, and where was your soul before your birth?

11

Plato's Epistemology
Remembering What You Didn't Know You Knew

PREVIEW

Epistemology is distinguished from metaphysics. Plato argues that knowledge of the Forms is made possible by the soul's recollection of its existence in the realm of Forms prior to the birth of the physical body. Plato's epistemology describes the way we know the various aspects of the physical world and the realm of Forms.

Happily for you, there are only two genuinely complex terms you have to wrestle with on this tour: "metaphysics" and "epistemology." You've already encountered metaphysics, the study of the nature of reality. A great deal of what we've talked about in the pre-Socratics involved metaphysics. When Thales says, "All is Water," or Heraclitus says, "All is Change," or Parmenides says, "All is Unchanging," they are making metaphysical statements, statements about the nature of reality. In addition, you've just investigated Plato's metaphysics. According to Plato, all of reality is divided into two parts. Thus, at this point, you probably have a rough feel for some kinds of metaphysical investigations. However, except for some discussion in the second chapter, you haven't dealt with the other complex term, "epistemology," the study of the nature of knowledge.

It is sometimes unclear to students what it means to "study knowledge." A contrast between metaphysics and epistemology often helps.

Metaphysics studies *what* we know about reality; epistemology studies *how* we know reality. For example, Plato's metaphysics describes *what* we know, the realm of Forms; Plato's epistemology will describe *how* we know the Forms, the process by which knowledge of the Forms comes to us.

To take another example, if I look out my window and describe the reality of *what* I see, then I am engaged in metaphysics; if I describe *how* I acquire knowledge about what I see, then I am engaged in epistemology. In short, metaphysics deals with the known; epistemology deals with the knower.

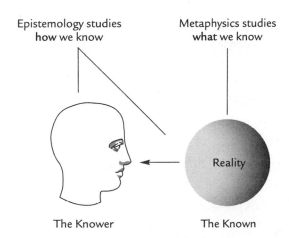

Here is an exercise, similar to the ones you completed in Chapter 2, to help you distinguish between metaphysical and epistemological statements.

EXERCISE 11.1
Distinguishing Between Metaphysical and Epistemological Statements

Label each of the following statements M for metaphysics, E for epistemology, or N for neither. Metaphysical statements describe all (or an important part of) reality. Epistemological statements describe how we know (or do not know) reality.

_____ 1. God is a Great Spirit who protects all living things.

_____ 2. The physical world is constantly changing.

_____ 3. Information about the physical world comes to humans through their senses.

_____ 4. In all activities, seek moderation.

_____ 5. By reasoning from the seen to the unseen, we can gain evidence that God is the cause of all motion.

_____ 6. God is the cause of all motion.

_____ 7. Nothing can be known for certain.

_____ 8. The mind acquires all its truths directly from God.

_____ 9. Live for pleasure.

_____ 10. All knowledge is recollected from the soul's existence, previous to birth, in the realm of Forms.

In this chapter, we'll explore Plato's epistemology, his description of how we have knowledge of reality.

I'll answer the following questions:

- What is Plato's epistemological problem?

- What is Plato's solution to his epistemological problem?

- What is the life of the soul (and how does this illustrate the relationship between Plato's metaphysics and epistemology)?

- What additional details about Plato's epistemology can be learned from the "Divided Line"?

What Is Plato's Epistemological Problem?

THOUGHT EXPERIMENT

Imagine you are eight-year-old Plato. You are attending a geometry lesson, and your teacher draws a triangle on a piece of slate.

Your teacher shows you that you can calculate the area of the triangle by multiplying the height of the triangle by one half its base, $A = \frac{1}{2}B \cdot H$. Your teacher then draws a few more triangles on the slate and shows you that their areas can be computed in exactly the same way.

It suddenly dawns on you that you now know how to calculate the area of *all* triangles, every single triangle that ever existed, does exist, or could exist. And you are stunned. You've looked at only a few triangles and suddenly have universal knowledge. The formula, $A = \frac{1}{2}B \cdot H$, applies to every triangle, everywhere. It's as if you looked at the patch of ground you stand on and suddenly understood the nature of the cosmos. You wonder, as you gaze at the triangles on the slate, how could you get so much knowledge from so little information?

And so, as a child genius, you begin to do philosophy. (The following blanks are a chance to match wits with Plato; the more thoughtfully you complete them, the more you'll appreciate Plato's remarkable answer, revealed in the next section.) "Perhaps," you think, "I got universal knowledge about the area of all triangles

from the few triangles by _____

_____.

Or, perhaps I acquired this knowledge by _____

_____."

With this thought experiment, you've experienced what was probably Plato's central epistemological problem. How do minds acquire knowledge of the Forms? When our senses show us only a few triangles, a few acts of holiness, a few clouds, how do we gain knowledge of Triangleness (the Form of Triangle), Holiness (the Form of Holiness), and Cloudness (the Form of Cloud)? How do we get universal, godlike knowledge when all that our senses show us are a few trifling particulars?

In terms of the tour thus far, no other philosopher has squarely faced this problem. Thales, Heraclitus, Parmenides, and Zeno had *assumed* that they had universal, godlike knowledge about reality, but had never systematically investigated how this knowledge came to them. In other words, they had constructed metaphysical positions, positions about the nature of reality, without considering the related epistemological problem, the problem of how they acquired *knowledge* of these positions. Socrates, when questioning Euthyphro and others, seems to have assumed that something like the Forms existed, but his central concerns were ethical (how we should live) rather than epistemological (how we know what we know).

Here is another exercise that will help you develop a feel for the relationship between metaphysics and epistemology.

EXERCISE 11.2

Linking Epistemology to Metaphysics

Assume you are 100 percent certain of each of the following metaphysical positions. Supply a brief epistemology, a statement about *how* you know what you know.

1A. Metaphysical position: God exists.

1B. Epistemological position: The way I gain knowledge of God's existence is

_____.

I believe this is true because _____

_____

_____.

2A. Metaphysical position: All that is real is constantly changing.

2B. Epistemological position: The way I gain knowledge of the fact that reality is

constantly changing is _____.

I believe this is true because _____

_____

_____.

3A. Metaphysical position: All humans have free will.

3B. Epistemological position: The way I gain knowledge of the fact that all

humans have free will is _____.

I believe this is true because _____

_____

_____.

Now, let's see how Plato solves his epistemological problem. By what process, if our senses know only objects in the physical world, do we gain knowledge of the universal truths in the realm of Forms?

READING:
EXCERPT FROM THE *PHAEDO*

What Is Plato's Solution to His Epistemological Problem?

In the *Phaedo,* Plato presents one of his clearest accounts of his epistemology. Socrates, awaiting his execution, talks to his friend Simmias about the nature of perfect equality and, in the process, presents a general theory of how we acquire knowledge of the Forms.

Underline important points and make notes in the margin.

"Here is a further step," said Socrates. "We admit, I suppose, that there is such a thing as equality—not the equality of stick to stick and stone to stone, and so on, but something beyond all that and distinct from it—absolute equality. Are we to admit this or not?"

"Yes indeed," said Simmias, "most emphatically."

"And do we know what it is?"

"Certainly."

"Where did we get our knowledge? Was it not from the particular examples that we mentioned just now? Was it not from seeing equal sticks or stones or other equal objects that we got the notion of equality, although it is something quite distinct from them? Look at it in this way. Is it not true that equal stones and sticks sometimes, without changing in themselves, appear equal to one person and unequal to another?"

"Certainly."

"Well, now, have you ever thought that things which were absolutely equal were unequal, or that equality was inequality?"

"No, never, Socrates."

"Then these equal things are not the same as absolute equality."

"Not in the least, as I see it, Socrates."

"And yet it is these equal things that have suggested and conveyed to you your knowledge of absolute equality, although they are distinct from it?"

"Perfectly true."

"Whether it is similar to them or dissimilar?"

"Certainly."

"It makes no difference," said Socrates. "So long as the sight of one thing suggests another to you, it must be a cause of recollection, whether the two things are alike or not."

"Quite so."

"Well, now," he said, "what do we find in the case of the equal sticks and other things of which we were speaking just now: do they seem to us to be equal in the sense of absolute equality, or do they fall short of it in so far as they only approximate to equality? Or don't they fall short at all?"

"They do," said Simmias, "a long way."

"Suppose that when you see something you say to yourself, 'This thing which I can see has a tendency to be like something else, but it falls short and cannot be really like it, only a poor imitation'; don't you agree with me that anyone who receives that impression must in fact have previous knowledge of that thing which he says that the other resembles, but inadequately?"

"Certainly he must."

"Very well, then; is that our position with regard to equal things and absolute equality?"

"Exactly."

"Then we must have had some previous knowledge of equality before the time when we first saw equal things and realized that they were striving after equality, but fell short of it."

"That is so."

"And at the same time we are agreed also upon this point, that we have not and could not have acquired this notion of equality except by sight or touch or one of the other senses. I am treating them as being all the same."

"They are the same, Socrates, for the purpose of our argument."

"So it must be through the senses that we obtained the notion that all sensible equals are striving after absolute equality but falling short of it. Is that correct?"

"Yes, it is."

"So before we began to see and hear and use our other senses we must somewhere have acquired the knowledge that there is such a thing as absolute equality; otherwise, we could never have realized, by using it as a standard for comparison, that all equal objects of sense are desirous of being like it, but are only imperfect copies."

"That is the logical conclusion, Socrates."

"Did we not begin to see and hear and possess our other senses from the moment of birth?"

"Certainly."

"But we admitted that we must have obtained our knowledge of equality before we obtained them."

"Yes."

"So we must have obtained it before birth."

"So it seems."

"Then if we obtained it before our birth, and possessed it when we were born, we had knowledge, both before and at the moment of birth, not only of equality and relative magnitudes, but of all absolute standards. Our present argument applies no more to equality than it does to absolute beauty, goodness, uprightness, holiness, and, as I maintain, all those characteristics which we designate in our discussions by the term 'absolute.' So we must have obtained knowledge of all these characteristics before our birth."

"That is so."

"And unless we invariably forget it after obtaining it, we must always be born *knowing* and continue to *know* all through our lives; because 'to know' means simply to retain the knowledge which one has acquired, and not to lose it. Is not what we call 'forgetting' simply the loss of knowledge, Simmias?"

"Most certainly, Socrates."

"And if it is true that we acquired our knowledge before our birth, and lost it at the moment of birth, but afterwards by the exercise of our senses upon sensible objects, recover the knowledge which we had once before, I suppose that what we call learning will be the recovery of our own knowledge; and surely we should be right in calling this recollection."

"Quite so."

Now, make an attempt at briefly stating Plato's solution to his epistemological problem. How do we gain knowledge of the Forms, and what is his evidence?

According to Plato, we gain knowledge of the Forms _____

_____

_____

_____

_____.

His evidence for this is _____

_____

_____.

Here is a restatement of Plato's major points. Decide if you agree or disagree with statements 2–6.

1. When we look at two approximately equal things—for example, the two shapes below—we see they are equal in one way (for example, height) but not equal another way (for example, width).

2. Thus, we know these two things are very unlike perfect equality, because perfect equality is not equal in one way and unequal in another. Perfect equality is perfectly equal.

I (agree, disagree) because _____

_____

_____.

3. The two approximately equal things, therefore, helped us to *recall*, to remember, perfect equality.

I (agree, disagree) because _____

_____

_____.

4. Everything we've ever known with our senses falls short of perfect equality; therefore, we never learned about perfect equality at any time during our lives.

I (agree, disagree) because _____

_____

_____.

5. Therefore, we must have learned about perfect equality before our birth.

I (agree, disagree) because _____

_____

_____.

For the Greeks, "soul" is identical to "mind." The Greek word for both is "psyche."

6. Therefore, something about us (Plato calls it our soul) existed before our birth and gained knowledge of the Forms.

I (agree, disagree) because _____

_____

_____.

7. We forgot this knowledge at birth and recall it during our lives. Thus, all knowledge is recollection of our soul's existence in the realm of Forms.

I (agree, disagree) because _____

_____

_____.

The majority of my students aren't convinced by this argument, and many don't even see its force. So, imagine that a teacher and a student re-created the key ideas in Plato's epistemology. If you don't agree with one or more of the student's answers, write better ones in the margin.

(The teacher begins by drawing two lines of unequal length on the blackboard and then asks the student to come forward.)

TEACHER: Are these two lines equal in length?
STUDENT: No.
TEACHER: Could you make them somewhat more equal?
STUDENT: Yes.
TEACHER: Please do so.

(The student uses an eraser to shorten the longer line.)

TEACHER: Are the two lines now perfectly equal?
STUDENT: No.
TEACHER: But you *do* know what I mean by perfectly equal?
STUDENT: Yes.
TEACHER: You could not have made the lines somewhat more equal unless you knew what I meant by perfectly equal, correct?
STUDENT: That's correct.
TEACHER: So you have the idea of the perfectly equal in your mind?

STUDENT: Yes.

TEACHER: Well, have you ever seen perfect equality?

STUDENT: I'm not sure.

TEACHER: I am not asking if you have ever seen two apples you thought were perfectly equal or two oranges you thought were perfectly equal. I am asking if you have ever seen perfect equality itself. Have you?

STUDENT: No.

TEACHER: So, you have seen only *representations* of perfect equality; you've never seen perfect equality itself?

STUDENT: That's correct.

TEACHER: And, therefore, you have an idea in your mind, the idea of perfect equality itself, that never came through your senses.

STUDENT: Apparently not.

TEACHER: Well, if this idea never came to you at any time you used your senses, then it never came to you from your birth until now. Is this correct?

STUDENT: Yes.

TEACHER: If this idea never came to you through your senses from your birth until now, at what time must it have come to you?

STUDENT: I'm not sure.

TEACHER: Well, let's think this through. Here is a time line representing your entire life from the moment of your birth until the present.

birth   present

And you have agreed that the idea of perfectly equality never came to you through your senses during this entire period of time. Is that correct?

STUDENT: Yes.

TEACHER: And so, if it never came to you during the period of time *after* your birth, what is the only other period of time available to you?

STUDENT: The period before my birth?

TEACHER (with her best impersonation of a Socratic grin): Precisely! And what must have happened in that period before your birth?

STUDENT: I must have somehow gained knowledge of perfect equality.

TEACHER: Do you remember that experience before your birth?

STUDENT: No.

TEACHER: Thus, you must have forgotten that experience at birth?

STUDENT: Apparently so.

TEACHER: Therefore, some part of you, we'll call it your soul, existed prior to birth and gained knowledge of perfect equality, and then forgot that experience at birth. And all we have said about these unequal lines helps you to recall it now.

STUDENT: Well, . . .

What should the student's last response be?

The student should say _____

_____

_____.

And so now we can answer Plato's epistemological problem.

Problem: How do we gain knowledge of the Forms—for example, the Form of Equality, when our senses show us only a few physical objects, such as a few approximately equal things?

Solution: Looking at physical objects helps us recall their corresponding Forms. And, since we never gained this knowledge of the Forms through our senses, we must have gained this knowledge prior to using our senses—that is, prior to our birth. Thus, our souls existed prior to birth in the realm of Forms and forgot that existence at birth, but our souls occasionally recall the wisdom gained in that existence during life. Thus, *all wisdom is recollection.*

Plato is saying something beautiful and amazing. He claims that we are born with knowledge of the Forms and *never acquire any new knowledge during life.* When you understood the truths of geometry in high school, had some conception of holiness while reading the *Euthyphro,* or had some idea of perfect equality while thinking through the passage from *Phaedo* above, you were not learning anything new, but only remembering the wisdom your soul gained in the realm of Forms and forgot at birth.

Your reaction?

I believe Plato is (right, wrong) because _____

_____

_____.

Now, let's stop for a moment at this point on our tour, and allow me to make a few personal remarks. In general, philosophy teachers try to be as objective as possible and present each philosophical position, even those they disagree with, in its strongest possible light. But occasionally, when we are talking about an idea or philosopher that is a particular favorite, we have to and probably should let the mask of impartiality slip.

Personally, I find the idea that all wisdom is recollection powerfully appealing. Ordinarily, we think of wisdom as something external to us, something "out there." But Plato takes the opposite view. *All we need to know is already inside us.* We don't acquire wisdom, we re-member it, literally put it back together. As a teacher, I usually assume that I have knowledge and my students don't. And so, what I'm trying to do is get my own knowledge into students' heads. However, Plato counsels me to take a different approach. If all we need to know is already inside us, then I shouldn't be trying to get knowledge into my students; I should be trying to *draw it out of them.* As a Platonically inspired teacher, I should help my students learn what they already know and thus discover their forgotten knowledge. But how is this possible? Socrates, naturally enough, provides the best model for wisdom extraction. Inner wisdom is unlocked by asking the right questions in the right order. In this book, I try to follow Socrates' model by putting the right blanks in the right places. Thus, my goal on the tour is partly Platonic. I want to help you learn what you didn't know you knew.

What Is the Life of the Soul (and How Does This Illustrate the Relationship Between Plato's Metaphysics and Epistemology)?

We can now make a diagram of the life of the soul that will also show the relationship between Plato's epistemology and metaphysics.

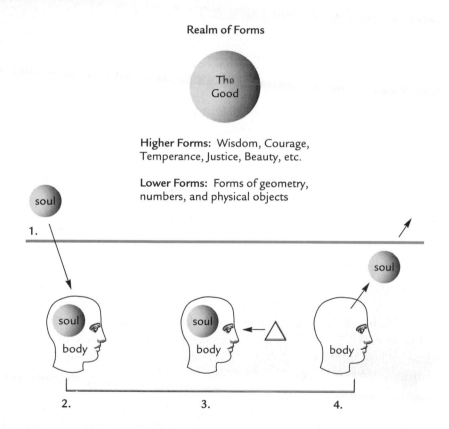

The soul begins in the higher world (1), where it gains knowledge of the Forms. At birth (2), the soul joins a body and forgets its previous existence. During life (3) when the soul receives sense knowledge of an object, such as a triangle, the soul recollects the related Form, the Form of Triangle, from its experience in the realm of Forms. At death (4), the soul leaves the body and returns to the realm of Forms. This process repeats itself forever. Therefore, Plato believes in reincarnation.

You can see in the diagram the strong relationship between Plato's metaphysics and his epistemology. He holds that reality is divided between the realm of Forms and the physical world. That is his metaphysics, his description of *what* we know. He also holds that all knowledge we have is acquired by the soul's recollection of its experience in the realm of Forms prior to birth. That is his epistemology, his description of *how* we know.

As you may recall from Chapter 2, three branches of epistemology are empiricism, skepticism, and rationalism. Without reading my analysis after the exercise, try this little test.

EXERCISE 11.3
An Epistemological Test

Here are the definitions of three branches of epistemology. Plato supports one view and rejects the others.

1. Empiricism: the view that the mind knows truths only through the senses.

Plato (supports, does not support) this position because _____

_____

_____.

2. Skepticism: the view that the mind knows few, if any, truths.

Plato (supports, does not support) this position because _____

_____

_____.

3. Rationalism: the view that the mind can know truths independently of the senses.

Plato (supports, does not support) this position because _____

_____

_____.

Plato isn't an empiricist, one who believes that knowledge comes entirely through the senses. In his view, the world we know with our senses is merely the Cave of Shadows, where we contemplate flickering images of truth, not Truth itself. The senses tell us only about imperfect triangles, approximately equal lines, somewhat holy actions. Genuine knowledge is produced by contemplating eternal, unchanging entities, the Form of Triangle, the Form of Equality, the Form of Holiness.

Plato also isn't a skeptic, one who believes the mind knows few, if any, truths. He clearly believes, as you can tell from this and the previous chapter, that knowledge is possible, that there is a way out of the cave.

Plato is a rationalist, one who believes that the mind gains knowledge independently of the senses. In his view, our knowledge of the Form of Triangle and all other Forms is recollected by the soul from its existence before birth in the realm of the Forms. Thus, the soul is born with knowledge that it acquired before it had senses.

Now, let's complete our portrait of Plato's epistemology by returning to the divided line.

What Additional Details About Plato's Epistemology Can Be Learned from the "Divided Line"?

As you recall, Plato used the divided line to describe the four levels of existence. Corresponding to each level is a kind of thinking.

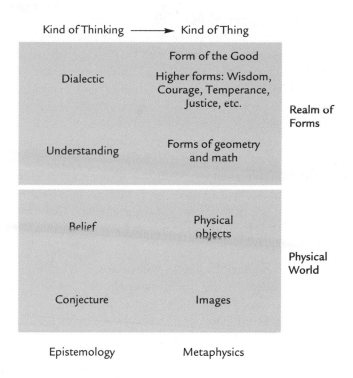

The left side of the diagram, the epistemological side, represents the kind of thinking that Plato believes is possible in regard to the right side of the diagram, the metaphysical side. Using a simple example, a wood triangle, let's begin at the bottom and climb upward.

1. If I am looking at an image (or shadow, or reflection) of a wood triangle, then I cannot know very much about the wood triangle itself. This lowest level of thinking Plato calls conjecture. At the level of conjecture, I am, in effect, dealing with copies of copies. An image is a copy of a physical object, and a physical object is a copy of a Form. Thus, when I contemplate the wood triangle's image, I am very far from the "really real" Form of Triangle; I am looking at an inferior version of an inferior version of Triangleness. The best I can do is "make guesses," conjecture. If, for example, all anyone knew about you was your shadow, they could make only the wildest conjectures about who you are.

2. Now, let us say I look at the wood triangle itself. At this point, I am, at least, above the level of images. I can see that without the wood triangle, its images, shadows, and reflections would not exist. I have passed beyond conjecture and risen to the level that Plato calls belief. But beliefs hardly qualify as knowledge. As you recall, Plato holds that the physical

world is changing and imperfect. Thus, any information that I have about the wood triangle will only be information about a changing, imperfect object. And so, just as the shadow gives me a very imperfect understanding of the wood triangle, so the wood triangle gives me a very imperfect understanding of the Form of Triangle. As long as all I contemplate is an object in the physical world, I can't leave the darkness of the cave.

3. But now let us say I am able to think about the Form of Triangle.

I have finally emerged into the light!

My understanding extends far beyond the wood triangle to all triangles that ever existed, exist now, or will exist in the future. I have climbed out of the cave of particulars and emerged into the sunlight of universal knowledge. Thinking about the Form of Triangle, I contemplate the unchanging, eternal, perfect original that all triangles, wood and otherwise, imperfectly copy. This level of understanding Plato terms knowledge. Thus, I don't have knowledge, information that is truly reliable, until I pass beyond the conjectures and beliefs that my senses produce in contemplating the physical world. But how do I climb to the level of genuine knowledge? According to Plato, I must turn to geometry and other mathematical sciences. These disciplines teach the mind to think abstractly—that is, to think about the nonmaterial realm of universal truths.

4. Now, how shall I go higher? In Plato's view, there is a realm of reality above the Forms studied by the mathematical sciences. And so, I must leave the Form of Triangle behind. No matter how long I study geometry, I will learn nothing about Courage. The highest Forms are reached by dialectic. Early modern philosophers like G. W. F. Hegel and Karl Marx use this term to describe complex historical processes; in Plato's hands, "dialectic" simply means philosophical question and answer. For example, Socrates and Euthyphro engaged in an unsuccessful dialectic as they sought the definition of holiness; Socrates and Simmias, as you learned in this chapter, engaged in a successful dialectic as they gained knowledge about perfect equality. Dialectic is thus a conversation whose goal is philosophical enlightenment. But this raises a very important and, for this chapter, concluding point. In Plato's view, philosophy is not conducted in private. The search for wisdom takes two: one who is willing to endure the long ascent and one who knows the way.

SUMMARY

Metaphysics involves descriptions of *what* we know about reality; epistemology involves descriptions of *how* we know reality. Plato's epistemological problem was to determine how we acquire universal knowledge, knowledge of the Forms, when our senses show us only particular things. Plato's solution was to argue that sense knowledge helps us to recollect what our soul learned in the realm of Forms prior to our birth. The life of the soul involves three stages: existence in the realm of Forms, existence with a body, return to the realm of Forms. This process repeats itself forever; thus, Plato believes in reincarnation.

Plato is a rationalist because he holds that the soul gains knowledge independently of the senses during its sojourn in the realm of Forms. The four levels of existence have four corresponding levels of understanding; we conjecture about images, hold beliefs about physical objects, have understanding about the mathematical Forms, and must use dialectic to gain knowledge of the higher Forms.

EXERCISE 11.4
Looking Back

Use your own paper to answer the following questions.

1. What is Plato's epistemological problem?

2. What is Plato's solution to his epistemological problem?

3. What is the life of the soul (and how does this illustrate the relationship between Plato's metaphysics and epistemology)?

4. What additional details about Plato's epistemology can be learned from the "Divided Line"?

EXERCISE 11.5
Looking at the World Through Plato's Eyes

How would Plato answer each of the following? In your explanation, indicate some aspect of Plato's philosophy that supports your answer.

1. T   F   If there were no realm of Forms, nothing could be known for certain.
   Explanation: _____
   _____
   _____.

2. T   F   Learning is remembering.
   Explanation: _____
   _____
   _____.

3. T   F   Everything the mind knows can be traced back to information that came through the senses.
   Explanation: _____
   _____
   _____.

4. T   F   Perfect equality does not exist in the physical world.
   Explanation: _____
   _____
   _____.

5. T   F   Any infant possesses as much wisdom as Einstein.
   Explanation: _____
   _____
   _____.

ANALYSIS OF YOUR PHILOSOPHICAL SELF-PORTRAIT

To see how your epistemology and metaphysics stack up against Plato's, read my analysis below, rethink your position, and then circle what you believe is the correct answer. I've underlined Plato's answers.

1. <u>T</u> F *The realm of Forms exists.*

    Not too much doubt about how Plato would answer this one.

2. T <u>F</u> *All that we learn comes through our senses.*

    I'll ask you to ponder this and other key epistemological statements a number of times on the tour because I want to give you a chance to change your mind or, if you don't change your mind, to refine your evidence. Answering this question True would make you an empiricist. Plato, as you now know, holds that we do not gain knowledge through the senses; according to his analysis, symbolized by the divided line, the best the senses can do is supply us with conjectures and beliefs.

3. <u>T</u> F *It is possible to have knowledge of features of reality that cannot be known by the senses.*

    You might think answering the previous question True would mean you would have to answer this question False. In other words, holding that all we learn comes through our senses would imply that we can have no knowledge of any realm of reality that lies beyond our senses. Specifically, you might believe that being an empiricist means you couldn't believe in God. But you would be wrong. Aristotle and Aquinas are staunch empiricists and believe they have knowledge that God exists. But how on earth could Aristotle, Aquinas, and other empiricists hold that all knowledge comes through the senses and also believe they could be certain of the existence of a being that the senses can't perceive? Wait and see.

    Plato, as you now know, does not share the empiricist problem. He says that knowledge of the realm of the Forms is gained by the mind prior to its residence in the body.

4. <u>T</u> F *The doctrine of reincarnation, the view that after death the soul is reborn in a new body, is correct.*

    Plato holds that the soul endlessly inhabits one body after another. Thus, he does not take the Hindu view that the soul can escape the cycle of birth and rebirth. Nor does Plato believe that the soul can recall previous lives. Our recollection never goes back before our existence in the realm of Forms. In addition, Plato also has some quirky views about the reincarnation process that often intrigue students. But before I briefly present these views, understand that Plato distinguishes between arguments and "stories." He is often, as in this case, very careful to distinguish between what he can and can't prove. The following falls into the latter category.

    According to Plato, it is possible that human souls could be reborn in a non-human form—for example, as a donkey or even a wasp. How so? Assume you live a pleasure-loving, reason-hating, soul-polluting life. All that you do nourishes the desires of your body and starves the desires of your soul. Upon death, your corrupted soul passes into the realm of Forms. In the realm of Forms, you eventually have an opportunity to choose a new life. (Plato doesn't say how long you'll wait.) If your soul has been intoxicated with bodily pleasures during your previous life, you may choose a life that has nothing at all to do with reason—for example, the life of a donkey or an insect. So be careful with that flyswatter! You may be smashing some poor soul who was too corrupted by physical pleasure to choose human existence.

Evaluation: Number of points in agreement with Plato = _____ of 4 possible.

A position of Plato's that you strongly (support, oppose) is _____

_____

because _____.

NEXT STOP

Plato solves a mind-bending ethical problem and describes the purpose of human life.

12

Plato's Ethics
The Riddle of the Loved Tyrant and the Hated Philosopher

YOUR PHILOSOPHICAL SELF-PORTRAIT

Add more details to your philosophical self-portrait by answering the questions below and offering evidence for your answers.

1. T F The life of physical pleasure is the highest happiness.

   Evidence: _____

   _____

   _____.

2. T F If everyone hates you, it is impossible to be truly happy.

   Evidence: _____

   _____

   _____.

3. T F We should be ruled by the wisest philosopher, not by the most popular politician.

   Evidence: _____

   _____

   _____.

4. T F The best leaders will want the fewest possessions.

   Evidence: _____

   _____

   _____.

5. T F The wise are the only ones who are truly happy.

   Evidence: _____

   _____

   _____.

The subject of Plato's ethics is introduced by considering which of two individuals lives a happier life:

- A man who is genuinely wicked, but who has a reputation for perfect goodness
- A man who is genuinely good, but who has a reputation for perfect wickedness

Plato is asking, "Is happiness something that is dependent upon or independent of external rewards?" In order to answer this question, the three parts of the soul—reason, spirited element, and irrational desires—must be described. In the good soul, Wisdom is the virtue of reason; Courage is the virtue of the spirited element; Temperance is the virtue that assures a harmonious relationship between the parts of the soul; Justice is the virtue that assures that each part of the soul fulfills its proper function. Plato argues that the good man, no matter what terrible things happen to him, is infinitely happier than the wicked man, no matter what wonderful things happen to him. The chapter concludes with a brief discussion of the relationship between Plato's metaphysics, epistemology, and ethics.

Well, here's the payoff.

You've learned Plato's metaphysics, the view that all of reality is divided between the realm of Forms and the physical world, and his epistemology, the view that knowledge is recollection of the soul's experience prior to birth. But the most important question remains unanswered: What should we *do*? Given the nature of reality and knowledge, how should we live our lives? By chapter's end, you'll understand Plato's portrait of true happiness.

In this section of the tour, we investigate Platonic ethics. Ethics, as you remember, is the study of moral actions. What is virtue? What is vice? What is the purpose of life? These are ethical questions. You can probably dream up a few more. What other questions about morality—right and wrong behavior—could one investigate?

Perhaps questions like _____ _____

_____

_____ .

EXERCISE 12.1

Identifying Ethical Statements

Ethics investigates morality, what we should and should not do. Place an (E) beside each ethical statement; place an (N) beside each nonethical statement.

_____ 1. A bird in the hand is worth two in the bush.

_____ 2. Obey God.

_____ 3. Be all you can be.

_____ 4. I think; therefore, I am.

_____ 5. The mind, at birth, is a blank slate.

_____ 6. God is dead.

_____ 7. Treat others the way you wish to be treated.

_____ 8. Don't return a wrong for a wrong.

_____ 9. The road of excess leads to the palace of wisdom.

_____ 10. It is impossible to know anything for certain.

_____ 11. All is Change.

_____ 12. Smoking is hazardous to your health.

_____ 13. Don't drink and drive.

_____ 14. The good die young.

_____ 15. Follow your bliss.

In the _Republic_, Plato ponders a fascinating ethical problem that will lead him to a description of happiness (see Box 12.1).

Here is Plato's problem:

Assume there are two men, one who is genuinely wicked, but who has a reputation for perfect goodness, and one who is genuinely good, but who has a reputation for perfect wickedness. We'll call the first, the Loved Tyrant, and the second, the Hated Philosopher. The Loved Tyrant has a reputation for being noble and generous but is actually ruthless and greedy. He secretly lives a life of thievery, rape, and murder, while everyone believes him to be the finest man in the community. The Hated Philosopher, on the other hand, is despised by all. Though the philosopher's soul is genuinely good, the worst crimes are attributed to him. Even though he has never harmed anyone, the Hated Philosopher has a reputation as the most evil of mortals.

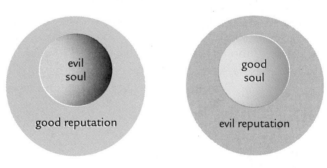

The Loved Tyrant   The Hated Philosopher

Now, what would the lives of these two people be like? Which one would be the happier?

I believe the (Loved Tyrant, Hated Philosopher) would have the happier life

because _____

_____

_____.

Think a little more about these two. The Loved Tyrant would receive awards from his community for all his (supposedly) noble acts, be easily elected to any office, be adored everywhere he went, have all the finest material possessions. In addition, the Loved Tyrant would be able to gratify all his wicked desires and get off scot-free. Thus, he would appear to have the best of both worlds. The Loved Tyrant would have all the good things that come from a noble reputation *and* all the good things that come from being able to satisfy every wish. The Hated Philosopher, on the other hand, would seem to have the most miserable of lives. According to Plato, he "will be thrown into prison, scourged and racked, will have his eyes burnt out, and, after every kind of torment, will be impaled." Detested by everyone, tortured to death, the Hated Philosopher's life would seem to be entirely miserable.

But Plato doesn't think so!

By chapter's end, you'll understand why Plato argues that the life of the Loved Tyrant will be miserable and the life of the Hated Philosopher will be happy. Does that sound ridiculous? How on earth will Plato be able to argue for such a strange position?

One good way to appreciate a philosopher's ability is to try to solve the same problems he or she solves. And so, match wits with Plato. Create your strongest argument for his apparently odd position.

I believe the life of the Hated Philosopher will be happier than the life of the Loved

Tyrant because _____

_____

_____.

By contrasting the lives of the Hated Philosopher and the Loved Tyrant, Plato is asking the ethical question, "What is a happy person?" Is happiness something that is determined by or entirely independent of external rewards?

To describe Plato's position, I'll answer the following questions.

- What is a person?
- What is a good person?
- What is a bad person?
- Why is the Hated Philosopher happier than the Loved Tyrant?
- What is the connection between Plato's metaphysics, epistemology, and ethics?

What Is a Person?

Obviously, in order to answer the question, "What is a happy person?" we would first have to answer the question, "What is a person?"

As you remember from the previous chapter, Plato defines a person as being composed of two very different parts, a mortal body and an immortal soul. In this section, we will expand Plato's definition of a person by seeing how he analyzes the soul.

BOX 12.1

Plato's Ideal Society

Plato's *Republic* is regarded by many as his masterwork. To give you a sense of its remarkable scope, the following is a summary of some of its major features.

The dialogue opens in the house of Cephalus, a retired businessman living near Athens. The most important of those present are Socrates; Plato's older brothers, Glaucon and Adeimantus; Cephalus's son, Polemarchus; and Thrasymachus, an abrasive teacher of public speaking.

The conversation soon turns to the nature of justice, a term which will take the entire *Republic* to define. Cephalus defines justice as telling the truth and "paying back anything we have received."

Socrates quickly refutes this definition by pointing out it would not be just to return a weapon to a friend if the friend had gone mad.

Cephalus's son, Polemarchus, makes the next attempt at defining justice. He says justice is "giving each man his due." Using this definition, he can counter Socrates' argument. It would *not* be just to return a weapon to a mad friend, because that would not be what the friend is "due."

Under questioning by Socrates, Polemarchus expands his definition to describe justice as "helping friends and harming enemies." This had been an accepted moral principle in Greece. Socrates objects by pointing out that harming anyone means making them less perfect. And making someone less perfect means making them "less just." Therefore, it would be wrong to define justice as something that produced the "less just." Given the warlike character of Greek culture, Socrates' position is remarkable: "So it was not a wise saying that justice is giving every man his due, if that means that harm is due from the just man to his enemies. . . . That is not true; because we have found that it is never right to harm anyone."

After Socrates refutes Polemarchus, Thrasymachus furiously intervenes. He says Socrates and the others have been behaving in an "imbecile way." According to Thrasymachus, justice is nothing but what is the interest of the stronger. Might makes right. Therefore, the "just" society will simply be the one in which the strong ruler is able to use his power to satisfy all his desires. The strong ruler's "justice" exists in his ability to terrorize others into serving him. Justice is whatever the strongest individual commands.

Socrates argues that "no ruler, in so far, as he is acting as a ruler" can act "for his own interest." Thus, for example, a good shepherd is not one who butchers his flock, but one who cares for them. Socrates offers several other arguments which quiet but do not convince Thrasymachus.

At the next stage of the dialogue, Glaucon challenges Socrates to clearly define justice. Glaucon is afraid that the only reason we act justly is because we fear punishment, and he uses the example of a magical ring (see the Gyges' Ring exercise at the end of this chapter) to support his argument. Glaucon wants Socrates to prove that a wicked man who is adored by his community will be unhappy and that a good man who is hated by his community will be happy. (I have termed these two individuals, the Loved Tyrant and the Hated Philosopher.) In other words, Glaucon wants evidence that the life of justice is good in itself and not good because of any external rewards it brings.

This challenge launches Socrates into an extended discussion of justice. He proposes to describe the just state, before describing the just individual, because it seems easier to first see justice on a large scale. His listeners assent, and so Socrates describes the main features of an imaginary just society, the "Republic."

Some of the main features of this society are

1. The ideal society would be divided into three classes that correspond to the three kinds of individuals. The lowest part of society would be made up of traders, farmers, crafts workers, those who work for material gain. The middle element of society would be made up of those who have no interest in money—Guardians, or "warrior athletes" who are trained from birth to guard the state against its enemies and value nothing but the "gold and silver" in their souls. The highest position in society would be held by the philosopher-king (or philosopher-queen; Plato took the un-Greek view that women could hold any office), the noblest, most skilled of all the Guardians. The philosopher-king's task would be to selflessly rule the state, based on knowledge of the Good, in a way that was best for all sectors of society.

2. Rank in the state would be determined by merit, not by wealth or family background. Thus, members of the lowest class could advance, if they proved themselves during a rigorous education, to the highest levels.

3. Wealth would be unequally distributed—in a novel way. The lowest class of society would be allowed to amass as many possessions as they wished. The Guardians, and the philosopher-king, however, would live in Spartan simplicity and would be allowed no private property, thus ensuring that they could not be bribed.

4. The virtue of Wisdom would be demonstrated in the philosopher-king's rule; Courage would be demonstrated in the Guardians' defending the state against internal and external enemies; Temperance would be present in the state as the harmonious agreement of the lower classes to be ruled by the philosopher-king; Justice (defined at last!) would be present when each element in the state fulfilled its proper function. Thus, the state would be just when the ruler ruled, the Guardians acted as a proper military body defending the state, and the lower classes produced the state's wealth, but did not try to gain political power for themselves.

5. After describing the three parts of the ideal society, Socrates can then go on to describe the three parts of the soul and its attendant virtues (the subjects of this section of the tour). The soul is seen as a miniature version of the state. Reason is analogous to the philosopher-king; the spirited element is like the Guardians; the irrational desires are similar to the lower class that seeks material wealth.

6. In order to describe the knowledge of the philosopher-king, Plato presents the "Allegory of the Cave" and the "Divided Line."

7. Near the end of the *Republic,* Plato argues, as described in this chapter of the tour, that the life of the wicked man, even though he is loved and rewarded by his community, will be miserable and that the life of the good man, even though he is hated and punished by his community, will be happy.

All in all, the *Republic* brings together a remarkable number of philosophical concerns. Plato's political theory is embodied in his description of the ideal state; his educational philosophy is presented in his description of the schooling of the Guardians; his metaphysics is sketched out in his account of the cave and the divided line; and his ethics is set forth in his analysis of the difference between the wicked man and the good man.

Think about the problem of trying to analyze the soul. You can't see the soul, turn it over in your hands, examine its parts. How would you define soul?

I would say soul is _____ _____ _____

_____ .

How will Plato go about describing something that he can't see? By reasoning from the seen, our behavior, to the unseen, the nature of the soul that controls our behavior.

In the *Republic,* by considering, oddly enough, what can happen when we are thirsty, Plato cleverly dissects our soul. Socrates is questioning Glaucon, one of Plato's older brothers:

> SOCRATES: Now is it sometimes true that people are thirsty and yet unwilling to drink?
>
> GLAUCON: Yes, often.
>
> SOC: What, then, can one say of them, if not that their soul contains something which urges them to drink and something which holds them back, and that this latter is a distinct thing and overpowers the other?
>
> GLAU: I agree.
>
> SOC: And is it not true that the intervention of this inhibiting principle in such cases always has its origin in reflection; whereas the impulses driving and dragging the soul are engendered [produced] by external influences and abnormal conditions?
>
> GLAU: Evidently.
>
> SOC: We shall have good reason, then, to assert that they are two distinct principles. We may call that part of the soul whereby it reflects, rational; and the other, with which it feels hunger and thirst and is distracted by sexual passion and all the other desires, we will call irrational appetite.[1]

EXERCISE 12.2

Paraphrasing Plato

On your own paper, paraphrase the main points in the preceding passage.

Thus, by examining internal conflict, Plato deduces that the soul has at least two parts, one rational and the other irrational. It is easy to support Plato's reasoning; life seems to be full of occasions when the soul is divided between two opposing forces. Our irrational desires are constantly checked by our reason. It should be fairly simple to think of your own examples:

After Thanksgiving dinner, the irrational element of your soul looks at the pie and thinks, "It would be wonderful to eat it all."

The rational element of your soul replies, "_____

_____. "

---

[1] *The Republic of Plato,* trans. F. M. Cornford (Oxford University Press, 1941) pp. 136–137.

Or some weekday morning the irrational element of your soul suggests, "It would be great to stay in bed until noon."

The rational element of your soul replies, "_____

_____."

Or, seeing an unattended Ferrari, with keys in the ignition, the irrational element of your soul says, "Let's go!"

The rational element of your soul replies, "_____

_____."

According to Plato, the chief irrational desires include the desires for food, sex, physical comfort, and possessions. Our irrational desires, unchecked by reason, would do *anything* to achieve their ends. As we will see in a moment, these desires are forcefully displayed in the lustful, murderous life we live in dreams.

Plato summarizes the opposition between rational and the irrational elements with a simple analogy:

> It is like an archer drawing the bow; it is not accurate to say that his hands are at the same time both pushing and pulling it. One hand does the pushing, the other the pulling.[2]

And so the opposing parts of our soul push us one way and pull us another.

But is there anything more to the soul than the rational and irrational elements?

I believe _____

_____

_____.

In Plato's view, there is a third part, the "passionate element which makes us feel angry and indignant." Let us say that after Thanksgiving dinner you are thinking about eating a second piece of pie. And then you become angry at yourself for thinking something so foolish. The irrational element of your soul says "eat"; the rational element says "don't eat"; and then what Plato calls the "spirited element" sides with your reason and angrily chastises your irrational desire.

To illustrate the three parts of the soul, Plato tells the story of a man who

> noticed the bodies of some criminals lying on the ground, with the executioner standing by them. He wanted to go and look at them, but at the same time he was disgusted and tried to turn away. He struggled for some time and covered his eyes, but at last the desire was too much for him. Opening his

---

[2] *The Republic of Plato,* p. 136.

eyes wide, he ran up to the bodies and cried, "There you are, curse you; feast yourselves on this lovely sight."[3]

The irrational element wanted to see the corpses; the rational element was disgusted with this desire; the spirited element angrily sided with reason. Thus, whenever you are angry or indignant at your irrational desires, you are displaying, according to Plato, the third element of your soul.

Putting reason, the spirited element, and the irrational desires into a diagram, we can sum up Plato's answer to the question, "What is a person?"

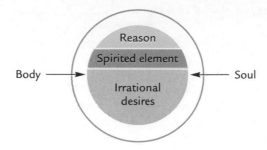

Now, understanding the nature of the soul, let's go on to consider how it should function correctly.

What Is a Good Person?

If we could investigate the soul of a good person, what would we discover? How does a good soul "operate"?

According to Plato, the rational and spirited element in a good soul work together to control the irrational desires. Like a wise ruler leading a state, reason issues commands that are carried out by the spirited element. The purpose of these commands is, in many cases, to ensure that the irrational desires do not take over the soul.

For example, assume that a student, on the night before a calculus midterm, is invited to go drinking with her friends. The irrational element of her soul fills with desires to party. The rational element wisely opposes these desires by recalling the importance of passing the midterm; and, to enforce its position, the rational element enlists the anger of the spirited element. According to Plato, if the student's reason has been nourished by the correct education (see Box 12.2) and if the spirited element is obedient to reason, then the irrational desires will be controlled.

Here is Plato's description of how the good soul functions:

SOCRATES: And it will be the business of reason to rule with wisdom and forethought on behalf of the entire soul; while the spirited element ought to act as its subordinate and ally. The two will be brought into accord, as we said earlier, by that combination of mental and bodily training which

---

[3] *The Republic of Plato*, p. 137.

Education in the Ideal State

Let's say you were a citizen in the Republic: What would your schooling be like?

From childhood until seventeen or eighteen, you would be educated in reading, writing, memorizing and reciting famous poems, harp playing, singing, athletic exercises, and the basics of arithmetic and geometry. This education, with an important exception, would closely follow the schooling of Athenian upper-class youths in Plato's time. The exception is that the literature you would read would be heavily censored. Plato believed that the stories Homer and other poets told about the immoral gods would have a corrupting influence upon young minds.

From seventeen to twenty, you would have a strenuous course in physical and military training.

From twenty to thirty, if you had distinguished yourself in your education thus far, you would receive training in mathematics designed to teach your mind to contemplate aspects of the realm of the Forms.

From thirty to thirty-five, your education would turn to dialectic, the special method of philosophical question and answer practiced by Socrates. This training would lead you to investigation of the higher Forms (like Wisdom, Courage, Temperance, and Justice).

From thirty-five to fifty, if you had continued to distinguish yourself, you would receive practical training in the affairs of the state by serving in low-ranking governmental offices.

By age fifty, if you were one of the very best, you would finally achieve a vision of the Form of the Good. Henceforward, you would spend the rest of your days divided between ruling the state and studying philosophy.

---

will tune up one string of the instrument and relax the other, nourishing the reasoning part on the study of noble literature and allaying the other's wildness by harmony and rhythm. When both have been thus nurtured and trained to know their own true functions, they must be set in command over the appetites, which form the greater part of each man's soul and are by nature insatiably covetous. They must keep watch lest this part, by battening on the pleasures that are called bodily, should grow so great and powerful that it will no longer keep to its own work, but will try to enslave the others and usurp a dominion to which it has no right, thus turning the whole of life upside down. At the same time, those two together will be the best of guardians for the entire soul and for the body against all enemies from without: the one will take counsel, while the other will do battle, following its ruler's commands and by its own bravery giving effect to the ruler's commands and by its own bravery giving effect to the ruler's designs.

GLAUCON: Yes, that is all true.

SOC: And so we call an individual brave in virtue of this spirited part of his nature, when, in spite of pain or pleasure, it holds fast to the injunctions of reason about what he ought or ought not to be afraid of.

GLAU: True.

SOC: And wise in virtue of that small part which rules and issues these injunctions, possessing as it does the knowledge of what is good for each of the three elements and for all of them in common.

GLAU: Certainly.

SOC: And, again, temperate by reason of the unanimity and concord of all three, when there is no internal conflict between the ruling element and its two subjects, but all are agreed that reason should be ruler.

GLAU: Yes, that is an exact account of temperance, whether in the state or in the individual,

SOC: Finally, a man will be just by observing the principle we have so often stated . . . [not allowing] the several elements in his soul to usurp one another's function.[4]

EXERCISE 12.3
Paraphrasing Plato

On your own paper, paraphrase the main points in the preceding passage.

The soul of a truly good person possesses four virtues: Courage, Wisdom, Temperance, and Justice.

Courage is the unique virtue of the spirited element and is present when "in spite of pain or pleasure" this element follows the directions of reason about what should or should not be feared. Thus, the soul has Courage when it fears what should be feared—dishonesty, for example—but does not fear what should not be feared—the opinions of the masses, for example.

Wisdom is the unique virtue of the rational element and is present when reason uses its "knowledge of what is good for each of the three elements and for all of them in common." Thus, the soul has Wisdom when it is properly ruled by its highest element.

Temperance is present in a virtuous soul when "there is no internal conflict between the ruling element and its two subjects, but all are agreed that reason should be the ruler." Thus, the soul has Temperance when its lower parts, the spirited element and the irrational desires, subordinate themselves to its higher part, reason.

Justice, an extremely important word for Plato (see Box 12.1), is present in a virtuous soul when each part of the soul performs the function for which it is best suited. Thus, a soul will have Justice when the reason rules, the spirited element serves the reason, and the irrational desires seek nothing but serving the necessary needs of the person.

Because both Temperance and Justice deal with the entire soul, a few more words need to be said about each. Temperance is the virtue that determines how the parts of the soul *work together*. Thus, you are temperate when you have the internal harmony produced by the lower elements following the guide of the higher element. Justice is the virtue that determines how each part of the soul should *work on its own*. Thus, your soul has justice when reason does what it does best, rule, and the spirited element does what it does best, support reason, and the irrational desires do what they do best, properly nourish the body's appetites. The key element in the virtue of Justice is that the irrational desires *not* assume a role they are unfitted for, the rule of the soul.

---

[4]*The Republic of Plato*, p. 140–141.

The soul of a good person

Let us return to our student and imagine that her soul possesses the four virtues. Her spirited element will exhibit Courage because, fearing what should be feared, losing the knowledge gained by study, and not fearing what should not be feared, the ridicule of her friends, she carries out the orders of her reason; her reason will exhibit Wisdom in issuing the commands that will be best for the entire soul; she will have the internal harmony of Temperance because the two lower parts of the soul, the spirited element and the irrational desires, agree to follow the commands of reason; and she will have inner Justice because each part of her soul performs its proper function.

What Is a Bad Person?

The short answer to this question is that a bad person is one whose irrational desires govern the soul. In such a situation, all the virtues flee. Since it is ruled by desire, reason loses its wisdom; with reason toppled, the spirited element lacks courage because it cannot tell the difference between what should and should not be feared; the soul, as a whole, is no longer temperate because the lowest element rules the higher elements; finally, the soul is no longer just because the irrational desires are doing what they are least fit to do, rule the entire individual. In effect, the soul of a bad person is "upside down."

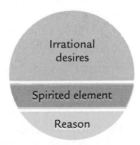

The soul of a bad person

Near the end of the *Republic,* Plato gives several forceful descriptions of the nature of irrational desires. We see these desires clearly in our most criminal dreams.

GLAUCON: What kind of desires do you mean?

SOCRATES: Those which bestir themselves in dreams, when the gentler part of the soul slumbers and the control of reason is withdrawn; then the wild beast in us, full-fed with meat or drink, becomes rampant and shakes off sleep to go in quest of what will gratify its own instincts. As you know, it will cast away all shame and prudence at such moments and stick at nothing. In phantasy, it will not shrink from intercourse with a mother or anyone else, man, god or brute, or from forbidden food or any deed of blood. In a word, it will go to any length of shamelessness and folly.[5]

In dreams, all is permitted, every passion indulged. We do as we please, murder whom we want, participate in every criminal, foolish, and shameful activity our irrational desires can create. When we sleep, we encounter "the wild beast in us" unrestrained by reason. Thus, a bad person is one who allows the murderous, lust-filled, animalistic side of personality to escape from dreams and rule waking life.

Can you think of a few examples, perhaps from history or the newspaper, of individuals who, in waking life, engaged in the nightmarish activities that others experience only in dreams?

Some examples might be: _____

_____

Shortly after the preceding quotation, Plato presents another strong description of the soul of the individual ruled by irrational desires.

Like a swarm buzzing round this creature [the ruling passion of a wicked person], the other desires come laden with incense and perfumes, garlands and wines, feeding its growth to the full on the pleasures of a dissolute life, until they have implanted the sting of a longing that cannot be satisfied. Then at last this passion, as leader of the soul, takes madness for the captain of its guard and breaks out in a frenzy; if it can lay hold upon any thoughts or desires that are of good report and still capable of shame, it kills them or drives them forth, until it has purged the soul of all sobriety and called in the partisans of madness to fill the vacant place. . . . A drunken man, too, has something of this tyrannical spirit; and so has the lunatic who dreams that he can lord it over all mankind and heaven besides. Thus, when nature or habit or both have combined the traits of drunkenness, lust, and lunacy, then you have the perfect specimen of the despotic [wicked] man.[6]

Now we have a fuller portrait of the inner life of a bad person. If we surrender to our lowest appetites, we become the monsters of our dreams. When the soul is ruled by irrational desires, it is a hellish place of "drunkenness, lust, and lunacy" where madness murders reason. Think of a drug addict, in the full insanity of her addiction, feeling the desperate "sting of a longing that cannot be satisfied." Her irrational desires rule all her choices. And all her choices result in self-torture. To surrender our minds to the tyranny of desire is to endlessly butcher ourselves.

---

[5] *The Republic of Plato*, pp. 296–297.
[6] *The Republic of Plato*, p. 298.

At this point, you may be able to wisely guess how Plato will answer the riddle of the Loved Tyrant and the Hated Philosopher.

I believe Plato will say the life of the Hated Philosopher is far happier than the

Loved Tyrant because _____   _____   _____

_____

_____.

Now, let's see how right you are.

Why Is the Hated Philosopher Happier Than the Loved Tyrant?

To drive home his argument that the life governed by reason is far happier than the life governed by irrational desires, Plato creates a marvelous image of the three parts of the soul.

> Imagine, to begin with, the figure of a multifarious and many-headed beast, girt round with heads of animals, tame and wild, which it can grow out of itself and transform at will. . . . Now add two other forms, a lion and a man. The many-headed beast is to be the largest by far, and the lion next to it in size. Then join them in such a way that the three somehow grow together into one. Lastly, mould the outside into the likeness of one of them, the man, so that, to eyes which cannot see inside the outward sheath, the whole may look like a single creature, a human being.[7]

As you might guess, the irrational desires are symbolized by the many-headed beast, the spirited element is symbolized by the lion, and reason is symbolized by the inner man. With this in mind, you should be able to see why Plato would strongly argue against the life of the Loved Tyrant and for the life of the Hated Philosopher.

> We can now reply to anyone who says that for this human creature wrongdoing pays and there is nothing to be gained by doing right. This simply means, we shall tell him, that it pays to feed up and strengthen the composite beast and all that belongs to the lion, and to starve the man till he is so enfeebled that the other two can drag him whither they will, and he cannot bring them to live together in peace, but must leave them to bite and struggle and devour one another. On the other hand, to declare that justice pays is to assert that all our words and actions should tend towards giving the man within us complete mastery over the whole human creature, and letting him take the many-headed beast under his care and tame its wildness, like the gardener who trains his cherished plants while he checks the growth of weeds. He should enlist the lion as his ally, and, caring for all alike, should foster their growth by first reconciling them to one another and to himself.[8]

---

[7] *The Republic of Plato*, p. 316.
[8] *The Republic of Plato*, pp. 316–317.

Plato is saying that when our souls are in moral chaos, when we are ruled by the insane desires of the many-headed beast, *it doesn't matter what good things happen to us*. The Loved Tyrant could have all the material blessings in the world and would still be miserable because he is enslaved by his own horde of deranged appetites. In fact, Plato says, the *worst* thing that could happen to the Loved Tyrant would be for him to be never discovered in his crimes. So long as he is undetected, so long as he is loved and not recognized for his wickedness, the Loved Tyrant will have no help in combating the many-headed beast. The secrecy that apparently crowned his triumph ensures the Loved Tyrant's continuous inner torture.

But what of the Hated Philosopher? How could anyone be happy who "will be thrown into prison, scourged and racked, will have his eyes burnt out, and, after every kind of torment, will be impaled"? Is it really possible for someone to be indifferent to terrible physical pain? Martyrs who placidly die horrible deaths provide us with examples. To protest the Vietnam War, Buddhist monks doused themselves with gasoline and sat *motionless* while they burned to death. The flames never touched their spirits. It seems to be this kind of self-control that Plato held up as an ethical ideal centuries ago. When we have true inner harmony, when the virtues of Wisdom, Courage, Temperance, and Justice produce spiritual health, *it doesn't matter what bad things happen to us*. In Plato's view, the temple of the philosopher's soul can never be disturbed by the tortures of the world.

What Is the Connection Between Plato's Metaphysics, Epistemology, and Ethics?

We can look back to the "Allegory of the Cave" to see the way important elements of Plato's philosophy link together.

Plato's dualistic metaphysics is represented by the two realms described in the allegory; the cave symbolizes the physical world and the region outside the cave symbolizes the realm of Forms.

According to Plato's epistemology, the soul of each person in the cave existed, prior to birth, in the higher world but forgot that existence at birth. Those who seek knowledge only through their senses stare at shadows, the illusory region of physical objects.

Plato's ethics can be seen in the one who escapes from the cave. The long ascent symbolizes the arduous study necessary to establish the four virtues in the soul. According to Plato, the journey out of the cave, for even the most dedicated, can take fifty years. Fifty years to hammer the virtues into the soul! But once out of the cave, the reward is not only the divine delight of contemplating eternal Truths, but also a soul perfectly forged with indestructible happiness.

SUMMARY

The loved, wicked man is contrasted with the hated, good man. The question is, "What is a happy person?" A person consists of body and soul; soul is divided between reason, spirited element, and irrational desires. In a good person, Wisdom is the virtue of reason; Courage is the virtue of the spirited element; Temperance is the virtue which harmoniously links the parts of the soul together;

VOCABULARY MAP

Plato

Plato's **metaphysics,** his view of reality, is **dualistic.** This means that he holds that all of reality is divided into two parts: specifically, the realm of Forms and the physical universe.

Plato's **epistemology,** his view of the knowledge process, is **rationalistic.** In other words, he holds that the mind can know at least some truths independently of the senses. According to Plato, the mind (soul) exists previous to birth in the realm of Forms and can recall the truths learned during this existence during life. The truths learned in the realm of Forms obviously did not come through the senses because, prior to birth, the soul had no body.

Plato's **ethics,** his view of moral values, is **absolutistic.** In other words, he holds that moral values are independent of and superior to the human world. The Form of Courage, for example, is not determined by any human opinion or culture. A **relativistic** view of courage, on the other hand, might hold that the essence of courage is determined by public opinion, what members of a particular society value. Courage is Courage, according to Plato, no matter what any society or individual believes.

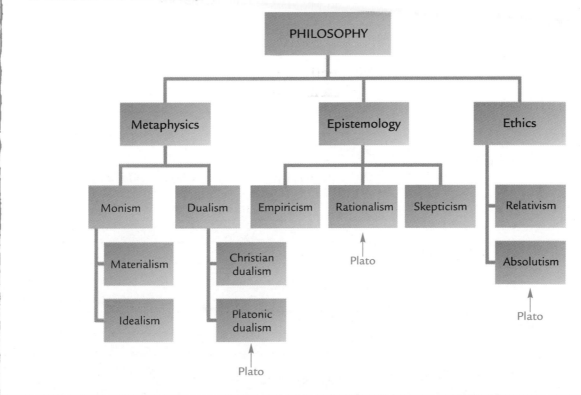

Justice is the virtue which ensures that each part of the soul performs its own function. The soul of a bad person is "upside down," with the irrational desires ruling the spirited element and the reason. The loved, wicked man will be miserable because he is ruled by the many-headed beast of his desires; the hated, good man will be happy because his soul is so well-ordered that no calamity can harm him.

EXERCISE 12.4
Looking Back

Summarize important points in the chapter by answering the following on your own paper.

1. What is a person?
2. What is a good person?
3. What is a bad person?
4. Why is the Hated Philosopher happier than the Loved Tyrant?
5. What is the connection between Plato's metaphysics, epistemology, and ethics?

EXERCISE 12.5
Looking at the World Through Plato's Eyes

How would Plato answer each of the following? Use evidence from this chapter to support your view.

1. T   F   All desires exist to be satisfied.

   Evidence: _____
   _____
   _____.

2. T   F   What is a moral action for one person might be an immoral action for another.

   Evidence: _____
   _____
   _____.

3. T   F   Our happiness is determined by who we are, not by what happens to us.

   Evidence: _____
   _____
   _____.

4. T   F   Might makes right.

   Evidence: _____
   _____
   _____.

5. T   F   If it feels good, do it.

   Evidence: _____
   _____
   _____.

EXERCISE 12.6

Gyges' Ring

Near the beginning of the *Republic*, Plato uses a story told by Glaucon to pose a fascinating ethical question: Do we obey laws simply because we are afraid of being caught? For example, assume you had a ring that made you invisible, and so you could commit any crime you wished and be confident you would never be caught. Would you continue to be a law-abiding citizen?

I believe _____

_____

_____.

Here is Glaucon's story:

"The story tells how he [Gyges] was a shepherd in the King's service. One day there was a great storm, and the ground where his flock was feeding was rent by an earthquake. Astonished at the sight, he went down into the chasm and saw, among other wonders of which the story tells, a brazen horse, hollow, with windows in its sides. Peering in, he saw a dead body, which seemed to be of more than human size. It was naked save for a gold ring, which he took from the finger and made his way out. When the shepherds met, as they did every month, to send an account to the King of the state of his flocks, Gyges came wearing the ring. As he was sitting with the others, he happened to turn the bezel of the ring inside his hand. At once he became invisible, and his companions, to his surprise, began to speak of him as if he had left them. Then, as he was fingering the ring, he turned the bezel outwards and became visible again. With that, he set about testing the ring to see if it really had this power, and always with the same result: according as he turned the bezel inside or out he vanished and reappeared. After this discovery he contrived to be one of the messengers sent to the court. There he seduced the Queen, and with her help murdered the King and seized the throne.

"Now suppose there were two such magic rings, and one were given to the just man, the other to the unjust. No one, it is commonly believed, would have such iron strength of mind as to stand fast in doing right or keep his hands off other men's goods, when he could go the market-place and fearlessly help himself to anything he wanted, enter houses and sleep with any woman he chose, set prisoners free and kill men at his pleasure, and in a word, go about among men with the powers of a god. He would behave no better than the other; both would take the same course. Surely this would be strong proof that men do right only under compulsion; no individual thinks of it as good for him personally, since he does wrong whenever he finds he has the power. Every man believes that wrong-doing pays him personally much better, and, according to this theory, that is the truth. Granted full license to do as he liked, people would think him a miserable fool if they found him refusing to wrong his neighbors or to touch their belongings, though in public they would keep up a pretense of praising his conduct, for fear of being wronged themselves."[9]

---

[9]*The Republic of Plato*, p. 44.

It takes Socrates the entire *Republic* to refute the conclusions of the tale of Gyges.

1. Summarize the story.

_____

_____

_____

_____

_____

_____

_____ .

According to Glaucon's story:

2. T   F   If a just and an unjust man each had an invisible ring, they would act the same.

3. T   F   We obey laws simply because we are afraid of being caught.

4. T   F   Virtue is not its own reward.

5. T   F   Our highest happiness is the satisfaction of our desires.

6. Assume you knew someone who had Gyges' ring and was going to use its powers to live a life of unpunished crime. What are the strongest arguments you could offer that such a life would be miserable?

_____

_____

_____

_____

_____

_____

_____

_____ .

ANALYSIS OF YOUR PHILOSOPHICAL SELF-PORTRAIT

To see how some of your ethical beliefs stack up against Plato's, read my analysis below, rethink your position, and then circle what you believe is the correct answer. I've underlined Plato's answers.

1. T   <u>F</u>   *The life of physical pleasure is the highest happiness.*

   Plato doesn't think very highly of physical pleasure. The Guardians, the highest class in the ideal society described in the *Republic,* lead austere lives in which physical pleasure is severely limited. In the *Phaedo,* an account of Socrates' last days, the body and its pleasures are seen as the enemy of the soul.

2. T   <u>F</u>   *If everyone hates you, it is impossible to be truly happy.*

   Plato, of course, would answer this False. He believes a person with a well-ordered soul will be impervious not only to the attitudes of others, but also to the mental distress produced by physical pain.

Aristotle, interestingly enough, does not agree with Plato. As you will see in Chapter 14, Aristotle argues for the importance of friends and the physical comforts of life. In fact, Aristotle even holds that it would be difficult to be happy if you were ugly! Poor Socrates!

3. T F *We should be ruled by the wisest philosopher, not the most popular politician.*

Socrates' death at the hands of the Athenian majority probably went a long way in convincing Plato that democracy was not the best form of government. In fact, in the *Republic,* democracy is seen as little better than mob rule. Plato held that the only hope for a well-ordered society was the incorruptible rule of the wisest, who rejected all values of the cave. It is interesting to ponder whether Plato's politics led him to his ethics or vice versa. Did the three levels of the just state lead Plato to describe the soul with its three elements, or was it the other way around? My own guess is that Socrates' example of a wise, fearless life led Plato to embody Socrates' virtues in the ideal society.

4. T F *The best leaders will want the fewest possessions.*

It is interesting to note that, centuries ago, Plato was concerned about the way wealth could corrupt rulers. His novel solution was to allow rulers no material possessions. All the goods of the Guardians and the philosopher-king would be "held in common."

5. T F *The wise are the only ones who are truly happy.*

Imagine you conducted a survey in which you asked people to make three wishes. Odds are most people would wish for things like wealth, fame, health, some variety of material blessing. In Plato's view, happiness is an internal, not an external, phenomenon. The happiness of the wise is not the happiness brought on by birthday parties, Christmas, or lottery wins. The wise are the truly happy because their souls are perfectly ordered. Thus "happiness" is not, for Plato, jolliness or even contentment so much as the steady bliss produced by a well-ordered spirit.

Evaluation: Number of points in agreement with Plato = _____ of 5 possible.

A position of Plato's that you strongly (support, oppose) is _____

_____

because _____.

Answers to Platonist Test (page 203)

I've underlined what I believe Plato's answers would be.

1. T F The soul is immortal.
2. T F Rule by the wise, not democracy, is the best form of government. (This is Plato's position in the *Republic.*)
3. T F Might makes right. (Thrasymachus holds this view in the *Republic,* and Socrates refutes it.)

4. T <u>F</u> The physical universe is the only reality. (The "Allegory of the Cave" argues that the physical world is only the lower and less real part of reality.)

5. <u>T</u> F The mind can know truths independently of any information from the senses. (Many of Plato's dialogues hold this.)

6. T <u>F</u> Our reason exists to effectively serve our desires. (The philosopher David Hume held this view, but Plato certainly didn't.)

7. <u>T</u> F The majority of people are foolish. (This could be supported by the "Allegory of the Cave.")

8. T <u>F</u> In a just society, all people would share equally. (Plato takes the view in the *Republic* that the lower classes should have the wealth. The upper classes would be content with the gold and silver in their souls.)

9. T <u>F</u> We should have faith that God exists. (Plato says nothing about faith and very little about anything we would understand as "God.")

10. <u>T</u> F We never truly learn anything new. All wisdom is recollected from a time before our birth. (Plato elaborates this view in many dialogues.)

11. <u>T</u> F If the realm of Forms didn't exist, the physical universe wouldn't exist

12. T <u>F</u> All knowledge in our minds came through our senses. (According to Plato, sense knowledge is only knowledge of "shadows.")

13. T <u>F</u> All of reality is constantly changing. (Heraclitus held this, but not Plato.)

14. <u>T</u> F There are two levels to reality: The lower physical level is a copy of the higher nonphysical level. (Plato is a dualist.)

15. <u>T</u> F The ideal society would be ruled by a philosopher-king. (According to the *Republic*)

16. <u>T</u> F The ideal society would be ruled by a philosopher-queen. (Plato, taking an advanced view for a Greek, says in the *Republic* that women could rule his ideal state.)

17. <u>T</u> F Perfect Beauty exists.

18. <u>T</u> F Perfect Courage exists.

19. <u>T</u> F Perfect Justice exists.

20. <u>T</u> F The highest principle in reality is the essence of Goodness. ("Allegory of the Cave")

21. <u>T</u> F Nothing for certain can be known about anything that changes. (This is one of Plato's fundamental principles.)

22. <u>T</u> F The body is the prison of the soul. (Plato's *Phaedo* contains eloquent arguments for this view.)

23. <u>T</u> F Virtuous people are rare. (Few people want to be led out of the cave or are capable of the difficult ascent.)

24. T <u>F</u> If triangles didn't exist, then the Form of Triangle wouldn't exist. (This is the exact opposite of the theory of Forms.)

25. <u>T</u> F A true philosopher is regarded as a fool by the majority of people. (The "Allegory of the Cave" supports this view.)

For each question that you and Plato agree on, give yourself 1 point. Score as follows: 23–25: Plato would be happy to have you teach in his Academy. 20–22: Plato would hold that you are on the right track but probably need work in abstract reasoning. Take a refresher course in geometry. 12–20: You're in danger of corrupting your soul with foolishness. 10–14: Welcome to the cave. 5–9: Welcome to the cave basement. 1–4: Form a Euthyphro fan club. 0: In your next life, you'll be reborn as a slug.

GOOD BOOKS

Plato, *The* Republic. Translated by F. M. Cornford. New York: Oxford University Press, 1966. A good argument could be made that this is the greatest work of philosophy ever written. Plato not only answers all the big questions here, about the nature of reality, the mind, virtue, and government, but also stitches them together in a lively dramatic format. The Cornford translation is superb; excellent notes throughout.

White, Nicholas. *A Companion to Plato's* Republic. Indianapolis: Hackett, 1979. A helpful guide.

NEXT STOP

Aristotle, the most influential philosopher who ever lived.

13
Aristotle's Metaphysics and Epistemology
The Mind of the Father of Science

YOUR PHILOSOPHICAL SELF-PORTRAIT

Add more details to your philosophical self-portrait by answering the questions below and offering evidence for your answers.

1. T   F   The world we know with our senses is real.
    Evidence: _____
    _____
    _____.

2. T   F   Plato's realm of Forms does not exist.
    Evidence: _____
    _____
    _____.

3. T   F   A brick's color is just as real as a brick's matter.
    Evidence: _____
    _____
    _____.

4. T   F   Everything that exists has its own unique purpose.
    Evidence: _____
    _____
    _____.

5. T   F   God is the cause of all motion.
    Evidence: _____
    _____
    _____.

6. T   F   All we know comes through our senses.
    Evidence: _____
    _____
    _____.

7. T   F   Love makes the world go 'round.
    Evidence: _____
    _____
    _____.

Aristotle introduces a very important new perspective in the history of philosophy: a close attention to the world we know with our senses. He rejects Plato's theory of Forms and holds that the form of an object is the sense characteristics that the object shares with all other similar objects. Everything we know with our senses exists in the ten categories of being and has four causes. Using the ten categories and the four causes, Aristotle is able to describe change in far more detail than any previous philosopher. His portrait of reality contains six levels, culminating in God, the Unmoved Mover.

Aristotle's empirical epistemology holds that the mind gains knowledge by constructing universal truths from experiences built up from sense perceptions stored in memory.

You are standing at one of the most important crossroads on the tour.

In one direction lies Plato's path, the route taken by those who believe that the mind can know truths independently of the senses. This is the way of rationalism (Parmenides and Zeno were also rationalists). Along the rationalistic path ahead, you will encounter St. Anselm and René Descartes. Travelers of this path believe that the senses are seriously flawed. Rationalists hold that wisdom is acquired by training the mind to perceive unchanging reality beyond the changing physical world.

In the other direction lies Aristotle's path, the route taken by those who hold that the mind is limited to what can be known directly by or deduced from the senses. This is the way of empiricism. On the empirical path ahead you will encounter St. Thomas Aquinas, John Locke, George Berkeley, and David Hume. Travelers of this path hold that the senses are the *only* window the mind has on reality. Empiricists believe wisdom is acquired by carefully analyzing sense information and rejecting, as airy falsehood, any knowledge that is not sense-based.

The empiricist painstakingly sifts through sense data that the rationalist believes is, at very best, second-rate information.

And so, standing at this crossroads, consider what the nineteenth-century English Romantic poet Samuel Taylor Coleridge said: "Everyone is born either a follower of Plato or Aristotle." According to Coleridge, everyone travels one of the two paths before you.

In the last three chapters, I did my best to convince you to be a Platonist. In this and the next chapter, I will do my best to convince you to be an Aristotelian.

Aristotle is often called the Father of Science. In our day, scientists achieve fame by making contributions to a *branch* of science. Stephen Hawking, for example, is esteemed for his work on black holes and the big bang theory. James Watson's renown is based upon his discovery of the molecular structure of DNA. These two men are certainly geniuses, but Aristotle's genius was not only in making important discoveries, but also in laying the foundation for science itself. Aristotle built the ground floor of the temple inhabited by Hawking, Watson, and every other scientist.

Aristotle was obsessively curious about nature. He laid the foundation of science by very carefully examining, dissecting, and categorizing everything he could get his hands on.

Here is Aristotle on the egg:

> Generation from the egg proceeds in an identical manner with all birds, but the full periods from conception to birth differ. . . . With the common hen after three days and three nights there is the first indication of the embryo; with larger birds the interval being longer, with smaller birds shorter. Meanwhile the yolk comes into being, rising towards the sharp end, where the primal element of the egg is situated, and where the egg gets hatched; and the heart appears, like a speck of blood, in the white of the egg. This point beats and moves as though endowed with life, and from it two vein-ducts with blood in them trend in a convoluted course . . . ; and a membrane carrying bloody fires now envelops the yolk leading off from the vein-ducts. A little afterwards the body is differentiated, at first very small and white. The head is clearly distinguished, and in it the eyes, swollen out to a great extent.[1]

This description, with the same degree of loving detail, continues for many pages.

Here is the beginning of Aristotle's description of the octopus:

> The octopus uses its tentacles both as feet and as hands; it draws in food with the two that are placed over its mouth; and the last of its tentacles, which is very pointed and the only one of them which is whitish and bifurcated at the tip (it uncoils towards the *rhachis*—the *rhachis* is the smooth surface on the other side from the suckers)—this it uses for copulation. In front of the sac and above the tentacles it has a hollow tube by which it discharges the seawater which gets into the sac whenever it takes anything in with its mouth. It moves this tube to right and to left; and it discharges milt through it. It swims obliquely in the direction of the so-called head, stretching out its feet.[2]

Aristotle's passion for the natural world produced equally detailed accounts of spiders, bees, sheep, cuttlefish, elephants, crocodiles, goats, deer, pigs, lions, hyenas, camels, mice, mules, swallows, dolphins, pigeons, quails, woodpeckers, eagles, crows, blackbirds, cuckoos, tortoises, lizards, oxen, vipers, whales, flies, oysters, bison, horses, cheese mites, and other creatures.

Aristotle's obsessive curiosity also produced the first detailed descriptions of plants, the earth, and the weather. In addition, he wrote the first book on logic, the first history of philosophy, and the first literary criticism. Aristotle wanted to know everything about everything. Odds are, no one ever possessed a more encyclopedic knowledge. Aristotle's primary tool was an amazingly careful use of his senses. So began the empiricist's path.

Some students arrive at this crossroads on the tour dazzled and confused. They took philosophy because, in one way or another, they wanted wisdom; and thus far they have encountered only the very odd beliefs of Thales, Heraclitus, Parmenides, and Zeno; the exasperating personality of Socrates; and the high-sounding strangeness of Plato. Such students long for a philosopher who describes the world as it appears, a philosopher who is straightforward and immediately believable. Aristotle, the Father of Science, is their man.

---

[1] *Historia Animalium,* trans. D. W. Thompson, in *Works,* Vol. IV.
[2] Jonathan Barnes, *Aristotle,* (New York: Oxford University Press, 1982) p. 10.

To describe Aristotle's view of reality, I'll answer the following questions:

- What is new in Aristotle's metaphysics?
- How does Aristotle attack Plato's theory of Forms?
- What is Aristotle's conception of substance?
- What are Aristotle's ten categories of being?
- What are the four causes?
- How do things change?
- What is Aristotle's portrait of reality?

Finally, I'll show how Aristotle's empiricism makes his metaphysics possible:

- What is Aristotle's epistemology?

Let's begin by investigating the major innovation Aristotle makes in describing reality.

What Is New in Aristotle's Metaphysics?

I've carried a brick in from outdoors. Because there are few physical things simpler, I'll use it to summarize how the philosophers we've examined thus far and then Aristotle describe the physical world.

According to Thales, this brick is part of the Many, unified by the One, water; according to Heraclitus, this brick is part of the Many and its constant change is controlled by the One, the hidden Logos; according to Parmenides and Zeno, this brick is part of the Many, and thus it is an illusion hiding the undivided, unchanging One; according to Plato, this brick is a shadow, a poor copy, of the Form of Brick.

Thus, every metaphysical position we've studied so far holds that this brick is *not* what it appears to be. The brick is water or Logos or illusion or shadow. But so far on the tour, *it isn't a brick!*

Think about that.

Thales, Heraclitus, Parmenides, Zeno, and Plato say bricks aren't bricks. *What we see is not reality.* Our senses don't give us a copy of the really real.

What's your reaction? Your senses tell you this book is a book—not water, Logos, illusion, or shadow. Are your senses right or wrong?

I believe that when my senses tell me this book is a book and nothing else but a

book, they are (right, wrong) because _____

_____

_____.

Many students find Aristotle refreshing. Unlike the philosophers we've examined, he steps forward and boldly declares that the physical world, just as it appears to us, is really real. According to Aristotle, this brick is a brick! It doesn't hide anything else, nor is it a poor version of anything else. It's as real as real can be.

Aristotle (384–322 B.C.)

Born in Stagira, a Greek colony about 200 miles north of Athens, Aristotle spent most of his childhood at Pella, the capital of Macedonia in northern Greece. His father, Nicomachus, was a court physician and scholar. Aristotle was a scientist, philosopher, logician, poet, and psychologist who enjoyed the company of the rich and powerful. Unlike his forerunners, Socrates and Plato, Aristotle had a fondness for luxury, even owning several slaves. A handsome man, Aristotle dressed in rich robes and adorned his fingers with expensive rings.

At about the age of seventeen, Aristotle journeyed to Athens to study at Plato's Academy, where he remained until Plato's death twenty years later. While the mature Aristotle disagreed with Plato on many crucial issues (as you'll see in this and the next chapter), there is no evidence that, as long as Plato lived, Aristotle ever had an open break with his teacher.

After the death of Plato, Aristotle traveled throughout Asia Minor collecting biological specimens. He also founded a branch of the Academy at Assos. Here Aristotle formed a close and lifelong friendship with Hermias, ruler of the city of Atarneus. Hermias was a eunuch who had risen from slavery to become a wealthy banker and owner of mining property. Aristotle obtained a share of the family fortune when he married Pythias, Hermias's niece and adopted daughter. It is said that Hermias gave his new son-in-law 800 talents (the equivalent of $4,000,000 in today's economy) to buy equipment for scientific research.[1] Their marriage was happy; Aristotle spoke fondly of Pythias in his will.

In 342 B.C., King Philip of Macedonia asked Aristotle to tutor his young son, Alexander, giving Aristotle the opportunity to try to achieve Plato's ideal of educating a "philosopher-king" by taking this twelve-year-old lad under his tutelage. However, there is conflicting evidence concerning the relationship between Aristotle and his young pupil. Some say Alexander's education did not shape his life as it could have. Alexander's vision of an empire is certainly different from Aristotle's vision of society, which seems never to have expanded beyond the city-state. Yet there are stories of an older Alexander ordering his troops to send back to his former mentor biological specimens found during the conquest of new lands. After a few years with this special pupil, Aristotle moved back to Stagira, his original home. In 336 B.C. Alexander took over as king of Macedonia and soon embarked on what has been dubbed the first "world war" in history, an attempt to conquer the Western world.

The next year Aristotle returned to Athens, where he founded a school, the Lyceum. Aris-

---

[1] Will Durant, *The Story of Philosophy* (New York: Simon and Schuster, 1926), p. 63.

Aristotle (continued)

tolle's reputation as a great philosopher, scholar, and scientist attracted many distinguished pupils. As many as 2,000 students may have attended the Lyceum during the twenty years Aristotle was in charge.[2] The pupils themselves came up with the rules for the school, electing a new student leader every ten days. Most of the instruction was informal. The students ate their meals in common with the teacher. The school seemed to emphasize descriptive analysis over the dialectic of question and answer that was Plato's lasting contribution to philosophy. Aristotle spent the mornings walking with students and discussing philosophy. Because of this practice, philosophy at the Lyceum was called *peripatetic*, the Greek word for "walking around."

When Alexander died in 323 B.C., there was a resurgence of anti-Macedonian sentiment in Athens. Aristotle was charged with impiety. Plato's teacher, Socrates, had been accused of impiety and sentenced to death for the charge. Aristotle decided not to give Athens, as he said, "the opportunity to sin twice against philosophy" and fled to the city of Chalcis. He died the next year, still observing the world around him. In his final days he was at work on a study of the tides in the Gulf of Euripus.

The era in which Aristotle lived has been called the first "axial age." At that time, human culture seemed to make a gigantic intellectual leap in various places around the globe—especially India, Greece, and China. Aristotle lived in one of those hot spots of radical cultural and intellectual change. Surely the constellation of

Socrates, his pupil Plato, and Plato's pupil Aristotle constitutes a crucial pivot, or axis, in Western thought. Since then most of the dominant philosophical trends in every age in the West have contained either a response to or a continuation of Aristotle's concerns.

Aristotle's interests in philosophy ranged even wider than Plato's. Aristotle had a passion for the concrete, the physical, all that can be known by the senses. One critic argues that the central distinction between Aristotle and Plato is that the latter took mathematics as his ideal and the former took biology. Plato thus prefers truths about the aspects of reality that are unchanging, perfect, and lifeless; Aristotle prefers truths about the aspects of reality that are imperfect, changing, and living. One of Aristotle's great achievements was to begin to categorize and describe the physical universe. He made such important contributions to biology, meteorology, geology, and botany that he is called the Father of Science. Aristotle can also be called one of the inventors of logic. To a large degree, he advanced and systematized the rules for rational thinking. Rhetoric, poetics, and theory of knowledge were other areas of interest to Aristotle. His ethical reflections and analysis of daily life make his investigation of human behavior classic. Aristotle's philosophical concerns have been transmitted through Arab scholars and Thomas Aquinas, among others, to form a dominant philosophical foundation of modern thought.

Aristotle's philosophical writings include *Metaphysics*, *Nicomachean Ethics*, *Eudemian Ethics*, *Magna Moralia*, *Politics*, *Rhetoric*, and *Poetics*.

---

[2] D. W. Hamlyn, *Being a Philosopher* (London: Routledge, 1992), p. 26.

You can clearly see what is new in Aristotle's metaphysics by examining the pictures below.

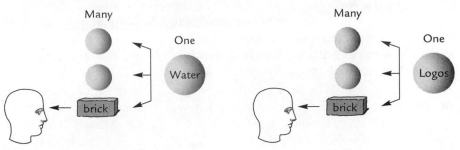

Thales: The brick we know with our senses is part of the Many, which conceals the One, Water.

Heraclitus: The brick we know with our senses is part of the Many, which conceals the One, the Logos of Change.

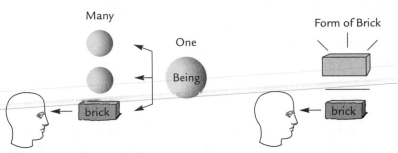

Parmenides: The brick we know with our senses is part of the Many, which conceals the One undivided Being.

Plato: The brick we know with our senses is part of the changing realm, which is a poor copy of the realm of Forms.

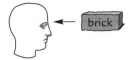

Aristotle: The brick we know with our senses is a brick!

As you can see, what is new in Aristotle's metaphysics is his belief that the world we know with our senses does not keep us from reality, but *is* reality. My brick, like every other sense object, is entirely real. Laying the foundation for all the natural and physical sciences, this is an exceedingly powerful point of view.

Aristotle's new position obviously rejects the metaphysics of his teacher, Plato. Let's examine a few of Aristotle's arguments attacking the theory of Forms.

How Does Aristotle Attack Plato's Theory of Forms?

For twenty years, Aristotle was a student, probably the star student, at Plato's Academy. He doubtless heard the theory of Forms described many times by the master himself. Nonetheless, in Aristotle's maturity, he rejected Plato's theory.

Here is one of his objections:

In seeking to find the causes of things that are around us, they [Plato and his followers] have introduced another lot of objects equal in number to them. It is as if someone who wanted to count, thought that he would not be able to do so while the objects in question were relatively few, and then proceeded to do so when he had made them more numerous.[3]

In other words, instead of explaining the world, the Platonists have compounded the problem by adding an entirely new world, which also needs explaining. Plato's attempt to explain my brick explains nothing. It simply adds another object, the Form of Brick, to the problem. If your task was to count all the things in the world, then adding an entirely new realm of Higher Things would only make your task more difficult.

Aristotle also criticizes the theory of Forms because the Forms provide no description of a very important phenomenon—change. Everything in the physical world changes. Even my brick will eventually fall to pieces. How can the unchanging realm of Forms explain the changing physical world? Aristotle believes the Platonists have no answer for this question. And without a description of change, Platonists have missed a fundamental feature of the universe. Given Aristotle's passionate curiosity about nature, any metaphysics that couldn't account for the way nature changed would have to be rejected.

Aristotle makes a third criticism of Plato's metaphysics: that it is founded upon an intellectual error. When I look at my brick, I can think about its redness, but that doesn't mean that a divine Form of Red actually exists. I can think about brickness, but that doesn't mean that a divine Form of Brick actually exists. In Aristotle's view, Plato confuses intellectual abstraction, what we can think about, with independent existence, what is out there on its own.

EXERCISE 13.1
Aristotle's Attack on Plato's Metaphysics

Plato would describe this book as the changing, imperfect copy of the Form of Book. Using each of Aristotle's three criticisms of the theory of Forms, what is wrong with this description?

First, _____

_____

_____.

Second, _____

_____

_____.

Third, _____

_____

_____.

---

[3] *Metaphysics* in *The Philosophy of Aristotle*, ed. Renford Bambrough (New York: New American Library, 1963) p. 9.

Understanding what Aristotle thinks is the wrong view of reality, Plato's metaphysics, let's now return to my brick and begin to develop a model of what Aristotle thinks is the right view of reality.

What Is Aristotle's Conception of Substance?

The most fundamental characteristic of my brick, according to Aristotle, is that it is a **substance.** All substances have two components: matter and form. Let's start by dealing with matter, the simpler of these two terms.

The matter of my brick is quite easy to describe. It is hard-baked clay, the physical stuff that occupies space. The matter of the brick is what would cause pain if dropped on a foot. Thus, the matter of anything is the "stuff" that it is made out of. Here are three simple examples:

- The matter of a silver spoon is silver.
- The matter of a plastic cup is plastic.
- The matter of a glass marble is glass.

You try it.

The matter of a _____ is _____.

The matter of a _____ is _____.

The matter of a _____ is _____.

In regard to Aristotle's concept of matter, there is only one small complication. Matter can be either physical or nonphysical. For example, the matter, "stuff," of the U.S. Constitution is law because law is what the U.S. Constitution is made out of. The matter of a play is characters because characters are what plays are made out of. The matter of speech is sound because sound is what speech is made out of.

To sum up, matter is the "stuff," physical or nonphysical, that any entity consists of.

Now, let's go on to form the more complex component of substance. Aristotle inherits the term "form" from Plato but uses it in an important new way. To distinguish between the two, it is traditional to use Form when referring to Plato and form when referring to Aristotle.

Let's begin with the *similarity* between Form and form. Form for Plato and form for Aristotle identify an object's **essence.** The essence of an object is simply what it holds in common with all other similar objects. The essence of a brick is what all bricks hold in common. The essence of a spoon is what all spoons hold in common. In regard to anything that exists, both Platonic Form and Aristotelian form refer to the essence that a thing shares with similar things.

Students usually have no problem understanding the similarity between Platonic Form and Aristotelian form. But understanding the difference can be

Plato held that the essence of an object, its fundamental, necessary features, exists in the realm of Forms and is not part of its matter. Aristotle takes the more common-sensical view that an object's essence is always linked to its matter.

more difficult. *For Plato, Form is separate from matter; for Aristotle form is united with matter.*

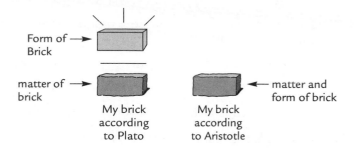

Form of → Brick

matter of → brick

My brick according to Plato

My brick according to Aristotle

matter and form of brick ←

The two philosophers disagree on the *location* of essence.

In Plato's view, the Form, the essence of an object, is perfect and invisible. Thus, the Form could never be part of the material world, because the material world is imperfect and visible.

Aristotle conceives of form in a different way. He supports the view of common sense, which turns out to be a superb way to begin the sciences. Actually, the confusing thing about Aristotle's approach is that it is so simple. Here's the key: *When your senses tell you which unique characteristic(s) an object shares with all similar objects, you know the object's form.* That's it. That's all there is to Aristotelian form.

Let me give you a few examples.

My senses tell me that the unique characteristic that my brick shares with other bricks is brick shape. So brick shape is my brick's form, its essence.

My senses tell me that the unique characteristic that a silver spoon shares with all other spoons is spoon shape. So spoon shape is a silver spoon's form, its essence.

You try it.

My senses tell me that the unique characteristic that a glass marble shares with all

other marbles is _____. So _____ is a glass marble's form, its essence.

The most common mistake students make is to confuse matter with form. The matter of my brick is hard-baked clay. The form of my brick is brick shape. Hard-baked clay could not be the *unique* characteristic that my brick shares with all other bricks because many things, such as cups and statuettes, could be made of hard-baked clay.

Distinguish between the matter and form of a glass marble.

The matter of a glass marble is _____. The form of a glass

marble is _____. _____ could not be the unique characteristic

that a glass marble shares with all other marbles because many things, such as

_____, could be made of _____.

substance For Aristotle, the primary feature of anything that is real. A substance has two facets, matter and form. Every individual apple, rose, dog, or donkey is an individual substance. Aristotle distinguishes substances from their attributes. An apple is a substance that has the attributes, among others, of color and shine. A substance has an independent existence; an attribute has a dependent existence.

essence The central, defining characteristics of a thing. Take the case of a red square. The essence of the square is that it is a two-dimensional geometric figure with four equal sides and four internal right angles. Redness is not part of the square's essence.

For Aristotle, in general, the form of a physical object must pass three simple tests (there are some special cases, but we won't be concerned with them).

Test 1: The form of an object must have the unique characteristic(s) that the object shares with all similar objects.

Test 2: The form of an object must be linked to the matter of the object.

Test 3: The form of an object must be known by the senses.

Note how what I said about my brick and a silver spoon pass these tests:

Test 1: Brick shape is the unique characteristic my brick shares with all other bricks. Spoon shape is the unique characteristic that a silver spoon shares with all other spoons.

Test 2: Brick shape is linked to hard-baked clay matter. Silver spoon shape is linked to silver matter.

Test 3: Brick shape and silver spoon shape are known by the senses.

EXERCISE 13.2
Matter and Form

Describe, from Aristotle's point of view, the matter and form of each of the items listed below. Remember that the matter is the "stuff," physical or non-physical, that composes an object. Form is the unique characteristic(s) known by the senses that the object shares with all similar objects. In the case of bricks, spoons, and marbles, form is identical to shape. But this is not always the case—more on this point soon.

Use these steps:

a. Determine if matter is something that is physical or nonphysical.

b. Determine if form is closely related to or independent of shape.

c. Describe the form, the characteristics known by the senses that the object shares with all similar objects.

Example: racquetball

a. Matter is physical, rubber.

b. Form is closely related to shape; a racquetball's round shape is an essential characteristic of a racquetball.

c. A round, very bouncy, hollow rubber ball, approximately 3 inches in diameter

1. A pencil
2. Steel scissors
3. An ice cube
4. Ice
5. A glass dog
6. A robin's song
7. A rose
8. Socrates

9. Mt. Everest

10. A telephone

11. A quarter

12. The characters in a play

You can now see that, from Aristotle's point of view, when you think about an object's form, its essence, you are *not* thinking about a perfect, invisible, immaterial something that exists in a higher realm. You are simply thinking about the object's defining features, linked to its matter, that are known by your senses. The enormous power of this approach is that by very carefully describing these defining features, one can develop a systematic account of anything in the natural world. Science begins, in Aristotle's hands, by meticulously describing the forms of objects in nature: eggs, octopuses, and cheese mites.

Now, let's add three additional points about Aristotle's description of the form of a thing.

1. While we can logically think of form and matter as two separate things, as I have done above, in reality they are inseparable. At every place where I point to a part of my brick's matter, I also point to a part of my brick's form. The matter and form of my brick are as united as the concave and convex parts of a curve.

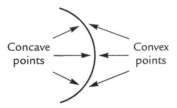

Every concave point on the curve is also a convex point.

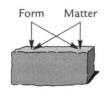

Each part of the brick's shape, its form, is also part of the brick's matter.

According to Aristotle, matter and form are absolutely united. You can no more have the form of an object apart from its matter than you can have the concave section of a curve apart from the convex section.

2. In traditional Aristotelian terminology, my brick's matter is the feature that gives my brick "thisness." My brick's form is the feature that gives it "whatness." Don't let these terms throw you.

The matter, stuff, of my brick makes it *this* particular brick; the form, essence, of my brick makes it *what* it is, the brick shape that it holds in common with all other bricks. Matter separates; form unites.

Each brick has separate matter. Matter is thisness, the characteristic that makes each brick, *this* brick.

Each brick has the same form. Form is whatness, the characteristic that makes each brick *what* it is.

3. The form of an object is sometimes identical with its shape *but not always*. For example, the form of my brick is brick shape because hard-baked clay with a brick shape *is* a brick. If the hard-baked clay in front of me had a different shape—a cup shape, for example—then it would be not a brick but a cup. In the case of hard-baked-clay bricks and cups, shape is form.

On the other hand, shape has nothing to do with the form of water or any other liquid. Water is water no matter whether it has the shape given to it by a glass, bucket, or swimming pool. To take another example, shape has nothing to do with form in the case of humans. The absence of arms and legs does not make an individual less human than the possession of arms and legs.

Name three things in which shape is identical to or a very important part of form.

Shape is closely related to form in _____

_____.

Name three things in which shape has nothing to do with form.

Shape has no relationship to form in _____

_____.

Now that we have explored Aristotle's concept of substance, the unity of matter and form, let's see what more he has to say about reality.

What Are Aristotle's Ten Categories of Being?

Odds are that the above question makes as much sense to you as if I had asked, "What are Aristotle's ten categories of mumphla?" The philosophical use of "being" often confuses beginning philosophy students. If I talk about being, I am talking about what exists. Thus, the being of an object refers to its existence. And so, if I describe the ten categories of my brick's being, I am simply describing ten aspects of my brick's existence.

We've already explored one of the categories of my brick's being, its substance, its unity of matter and form. But when I have described my brick's substance, have I entirely described every aspect of its being? Contrast these two descriptions:

1. My brick's substance consists of matter, hard-baked clay, and form, brick shape.

2. My brick's substance consists of matter, hard-baked clay, and form, brick shape—*and* it is red, rough, and sits long side up on my desk to the left of my computer at seven o'clock in the morning.

Obviously, the second sentence is a much more complete description of my brick's being. I *do* know something important about my brick when I know its substance. But knowledge of its qualities (red and rough), place (on my desk), spatial relationship to other objects (to the left of my computer), and its temporal location (seven o'clock in the morning) add important information about its being.

As a description of my brick, here are Aristotle's ten categories of being:

Substance: my brick's matter and form

Location: on my desk (or in the kitchen or any other location)

Time: seven o'clock in the morning (or 10 o'clock yesterday or any other time)

Quantity: one brick

Quality: red (or rough or any other quality)

Relationship: to the left of my computer (or half of two bricks or any other numerical or spatial relationship)

Posture: long side up (Aristotle's examples, describing humans, are "reclining at table, sitting down")

State: being clean (Aristotle's examples, describing humans, are "having shoes on, being in armor")

Doing something: sitting (as opposed to, say, falling through the air; Aristotle's examples are "cutting, burning")

Undergoing something: being examined (Aristotle's examples are "being cut, being burnt")

As compared with Plato's metaphysics, note what a rich description of my brick is made possible by Aristotle's ten categories of being.

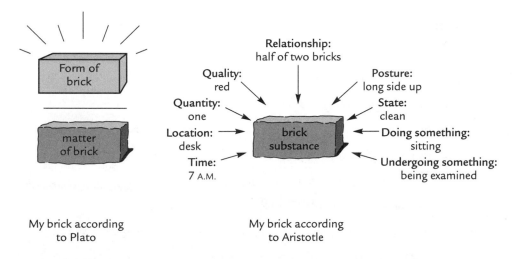

My brick according to Plato

My brick according to Aristotle

According to Aristotle, substance is the *primary* category that makes the existence of the other categories possible. Thus, the category of the brick's substance makes possible the existence of the category of the brick's location. The brick could not exist at a place unless it first existed as a brick. The nine categories (location, time, quantity, quality, relationship, posture, state, doing something, undergoing something) depend upon, are "attached to," the tenth category, substance.

Without the brick's substance, its surrounding categories, pictured above, could not exist. Prove this to yourself.

Without the brick's substance, its quality "red" could not exist because _____ ___

_____

_____.

Without the brick's substance, its state "sitting" could not exist because _____

_____

_____.

Without the brick's substance, its posture "long side up" could not exist because

_____

_____.

What makes my brick the brick that it is, is its substance, its matter and form, not the time that it exists or its location, or any of the other nine categories.

EXERCISE 13.3
Aristotle's Ten Categories of Being

The ten Aristotelian categories that describe the way a thing exists are, once more: Substance (S), Time (T), Location (L), Quantity (Q), Quality (QL), Relationship (R), Posture (P), State (ST), Doing something (DS), and Undergoing something (US).

Label each underlined term in the following sentences with one of Aristotle's categories.

1. The train arrived at 10 P.M.

2. The meat was being chopped.

3. The bird is black with ruffled feathers and sits on the roof of the house.

4. The big pig is eating at noon.

5. The little pig is being eaten at midnight.

6. The woman wearing a hat and leaning on the fence yesterday was happy.

7. The two dogs, one twice as big as the other, were sniffing the white ball.

8. A bird in the hand is worth two in the bush.

9. At the end of the day, the six-foot-tall boy in a black jacket slouched in his seat in the classroom while eating a bagel and having his hair combed by the strange girl behind him.

EXERCISE 13.4
Using the Ten Categories

Write five sentences, each one containing at least eight of the ten categories.

EXERCISE 13.5

Applying the Ten Categories to Yourself

Describe yourself at the current moment in terms of each of the ten categories.

Before we go on to the next question, let's pause here for a moment. Note what Aristotle is doing. He is providing a very detailed and powerfully general description of *anything* that exists in the sense world. Anything from a brick to a silver spoon to a cheese mite is composed of matter and form and exists in the ten categories of being. These concepts are, for Aristotle, like a set of magic goggles that reveal features of nature that had never been systematically examined before.

Now try to match wits with the Father of Science. What is missing from his general description of nature? When you look out at the world through Aristotle's goggles, as they have been constructed thus far, what *don't* you see?

Aristotle has not yet described _____

_____.

Now, compare your answer to Aristotle's in the next two sections.

What Are the Four Causes?

Let's consider my brick from a different angle. If I asked you, "What causes my brick to be a brick?" what would you reply?

I would say _____.

According to Aristotle, everything that exists has four causes. Aristotle's word for cause, *aitia*, translates as "the reason for something happening." Here are the four causes, the four reasons for the "happening" of my brick. (Conveniently enough, you already know two of four.)

1. **Efficient cause:** my brick's origin (a brick maker)
2. **Material cause:** my brick's matter (hard-baked clay)
3. **Formal cause:** my brick's essence (brick shape)
4. **Final cause:** my brick's purpose (to be part of a wall)

Odds are, when you answered the question above, you described some aspect of my brick's origin as its cause. In the modern world, we define cause as something like "that which initiates a thing." Thus, a brick maker would be considered what "initiates," what causes, my brick. Aristotle, terming this the efficient cause, agrees but adds three other causes.

In an earlier section, we discussed my brick's matter and form. A moment's reflection should be enough to see Aristotle's reasoning for identifying these two aspects of substance as causes. If we say that in order for my brick to exist, it must have an origin, it also makes sense to say that in order for my brick to exist, it must be made of something (matter) and it must have some essential characteristics (form). Thus, the material and formal causes contribute to my brick's being just as does its efficient cause.

According to Aristotle, everything that exists has an inherent purpose. This purpose he identifies as a thing's final cause. My brick's purpose is to be part of a wall. That is what bricks are for. Because this is the most difficult cause for students to understand, let's examine the final cause of a few simple objects: a knife, a shovel, and a screwdriver.

The inherent purpose of a knife is to cut; the inherent purpose of a shovel is to dig; the inherent purpose of a screwdriver is to turn screws. Now, you *could* use a knife to dig or a screwdriver to try to cut or, if you wanted to alarm your neighbors, you could use a shovel to try to turn screws; but each of these uses is not the tool's inherent purpose, the purpose it was designed for. This inherent purpose Aristotle terms a thing's final cause, because this cause of the thing is what it is "finally for."

Now this is clear when we consider objects designed by humans. Tools, desks, houses, can openers, and other human artifacts all have an inherent purpose. Everything we make is *for* something and thus has a special use, a final cause. But how would Aristotle describe the final cause of a stone, a bee, or an apple?

As I said, the final cause of anything is its inherent purpose. The inherent purpose of a stone is very simple, because a stone is a very simple thing. A stone's final cause is simply to fall. When a stone rolls down a hill, it is completely fulfilling the function of its stony nature. In the same way, when a bee pollinates a flower, it is fulfilling its nature, realizing its inherent purpose. When an apple rots and its matter provides nutrient for its seeds, and an apple tree is eventually produced, the apple is realizing its nature, realizing its inherent purpose.

In Aristotle's view everything crafted by humans and everything in nature has its own special future, some goal that it is intended for. This is often termed Aristotle's **teleological** view of the world. The Greek word *telos* means "end," or "purpose." Thus, to take the teleological perspective is to believe that everything has its own end, or purpose.

If you think of my brick's efficient cause as describing its past, "where it came from," and the material and formal causes as describing its present, "what it is now," then the final cause can be seen as describing my brick's future, "what it's for." Thus, we can add the four causes to our expanding portrait of my brick.

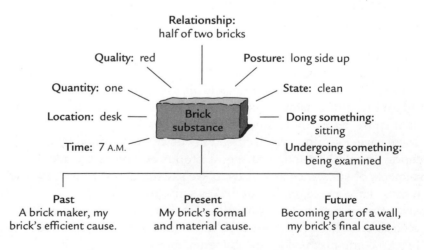

Here are some examples of the four causes of various objects. Note that I can often determine the form of an object by stating its definition. A definition describes an object's unique characteristics, those that it shares with all similar objects.

	An apple	A pen	A novel	A chicken
Efficient cause (origin)	apple tree	pen factory	the author	a chicken egg
Material cause (stuff)	apple matter	plastic and metal	characters and plots	chicken matter
Formal cause (form, essence)	"a firm, edible fruit, high in sugar…"	"an instrument for writing or drawing… with ink"	the story itself	"the common domestic fowl, *Gallus domesticus*"
Final cause (purpose, goal)	to produce an apple tree	to write or draw	to entertain and/or instruct	to produce eggs

EXERCISE 13.6
Aristotle's Four Causes

Make a grid, similar to the one above, and identify the four causes of each of the following:

1. A passenger airplane
2. A toy airplane
3. A news story about an airplane crash
4. An airplane pilot
5. Peanut butter
6. A Las Vegas casino
7. The Pacific Ocean
8. The Mona Lisa
9. The Empire State Building
10. A boulder

Now that we understand Aristotle's description of substance, the ten categories of being, and the four causes, let's examine his solution to the troubling problem which he believed his predecessors had failed to solve, the problem of change.

teleology (from the Greek *telos*, "goal," and *logos*, "theory") The view that the universe has a purpose. On a smaller scale, an individual might hold that everything that occurs in life happens for a purpose; on the cosmic scale, the teleological view holds that everything that occurs in the universe happens for a purpose.

How Do Things Change?

First, let me try to show you why the problem of change *is* troubling.

Getting more mileage out of bricks, let's take a very simple sequence of change. A lump of clay becomes a brick, and then the brick becomes part of a wall.

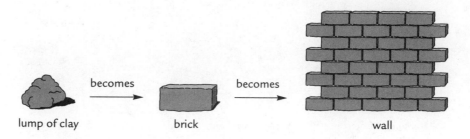

lump of clay   becomes   brick   becomes   wall

What could possibly be troubling about this sequence of change?

The trouble is that the clay *appears to remain the same* in this sequence and the clay also *appears to change*. So the clay does something impossible. It changes while it doesn't change. That's troubling.

Here is a simple, obvious reason for saying that *the clay changes.* First the clay is a lump, then it is a brick, and then it is part of a wall. The clay changes because it goes through three different states.

Here is an equally simple, and equally obvious, reason for saying that *the clay doesn't change:* First it is a lump of *clay,* then it is a *clay* brick, and then it is a *clay* brick in a wall. It's always clay. It never changes.

Because both of these accounts are equally correct, we seem to have to say something like *the clay is changing while it doesn't change.*

How can this be?

How can something change while it doesn't change? Do you see the trouble?

I see _____

_____ .

Here's another example of the problem with change:

I put a quantity of ice in a pot and before long it becomes a quantity of water. Then I turn on the fire and soon it is a quantity of steam.

The H_2O changes. First, it's solid, then it's liquid, then it's gas. Big changes.

The H_2O doesn't change. It's always H_2O. No change.

Here is a second chance to match wits with Aristotle (see Box 13.1). What is your best answer to the question, "How can something change while it doesn't change?" Use the lump of clay to brick to wall sequence as an example.

My answer is _____

_____ .

Obviously, a solution to this paradox is enormously important. Understanding change unlocks the secret of all transformations in the universe. Clay changes to bricks. Water changes to ice. Seeds change to plants. The living change to the dead. How can change be explained?

Let's start simply by considering the lump of clay.

BOX 13.1

Aristotle Versus His Predecessors on the Problem of Change

Using the sequence of the lump of clay to brick to wall, let's examine how Aristotle's predecessors dealt with the problem of change.

Given Thales' metaphysics, his account of change would simply be that the lump of clay, which is essentially water, becomes a brick, which is essentially water, and the brick becomes a wall, which is essentially water. And that would be that. In other words, Thales had no clear description of change. To say that water is the One that unifies the Many is to say nothing about how the Many change.

Heraclitus would say something more complex about change, but it would be no more helpful. In his view, at every instant the lump of clay, the brick, and the wall are a new lump of clay, a new brick, and a new wall. In addition, when the clay changes into the brick and the brick changes into the wall, this "violent" change is controlled by the hidden Logos. But Heraclitus tells us nothing about *how* things change, only that change is always occurring and that it is "violent." In answer to the question, "*How* does a lump of clay change into a brick?" he replies, in effect, "it certainly does . . . and very violently."

Parmenides and Zeno would simply deny that any real change ever takes place. In order for the lump of clay to become a brick, the lump would have to pass out of existence, which is impossible, and the brick would have to spring into existence, which is impossible. Thus, if we turn to these two pre-Socratics for an account of what change *really is,* we, unhelpfully, learn that change *really isn't.*

Socrates, given his ethical orientation, would not be interested in our metaphysical problem. If we asked him how a lump of clay changes into a brick, he would want to know what good that knowledge would be for our souls.

Plato, as you recall, held a low opinion of change. In his view, wondering about how lumps of clay turn into bricks is cave wonder. Better to get out into the sunlight and contemplate the eternal, unchanging Form of Clay and Form of Brick.

Aristotle, as you will see, uses the concepts of matter and form and the four causes to give a much richer and more satisfying account of change than do any of his predecessors.

Remember that, in Aristotle's view, the lump of clay is a substance—form and matter. Its form is its essence, what it uniquely holds in common with other lumps of clay; its matter is its physical stuff, what divides it from other lumps of clay. As I said previously, form unites; matter separates.

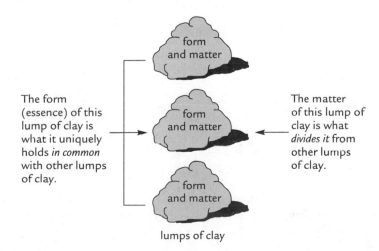

The form (essence) of this lump of clay is what it uniquely holds *in common* with other lumps of clay.

form and matter

form and matter

form and matter

The matter of this lump of clay is what *divides it* from other lumps of clay.

lumps of clay

Let's say I shape the middle lump of clay into a brick. What I pat in my hands *is not its form (essence) but its matter. It is not the form but the matter of the lump of clay that changes into a new thing, a brick.*

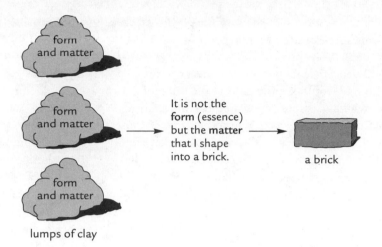

lumps of clay

Now let's add another detail. When I pat the matter of the lump of clay into a brick, I give the matter *a new form.* The matter leaves the old form behind and inherits a new form.

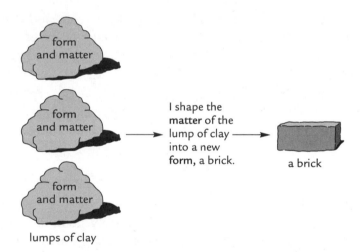

lumps of clay

All change is matter leaving behind old forms and taking on new forms. Doesn't that make perfect sense? Look at the whole sequence.

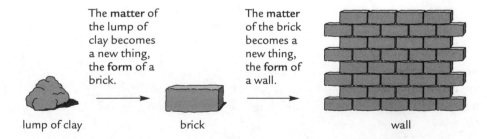

To clarify the process of change, Aristotle adds two very helpful terms, **potentiality** and **actuality.** Matter contains potentiality; form contains actuality.

The matter of the lump of clay contains the *potential* to become something else, a brick; the form of the lump of clay is what the lump of clay *actually is,* a lump of clay.

Let's add potentiality and actuality to our Aristotelian description of change: The *matter* of the lump of clay has the *potentiality* to become the *actuality* of the new *form* of a brick. And the *matter* of the brick has the *potentiality* to become the *actuality* of the new *form* of a wall. Here's the diagram:

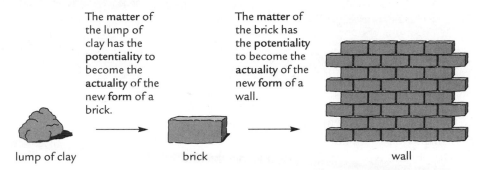

The **matter** of the lump of clay has the **potentiality** to become the **actuality** of the new **form** of a brick.

The **matter** of the brick has the **potentiality** to become the **actuality** of the new **form** of a wall.

lump of clay   brick   wall

You try it. Let's say the wall becomes part of a house, and then the house is eventually destroyed and becomes part of a landfill. Think like Aristotle.

The (matter, form) of the wall contains the (potentiality, actuality) to become the (potentiality, actuality) of the new (matter, form) of a house. And the (matter, form) of the house contains the (potentiality, actuality) to become the (potentiality, actuality) of the new (matter, form) of a landfill.

EXERCISE 13.7
Matter and Form: Potentiality and Actuality

Answer each of the following from Aristotle's point of view:

1. The (matter, form) of blank paper (has the potentiality to become, is the actuality of) a letter to a friend.
2. The (potentiality, actuality) of the (matter, form) of an apple seed is to become the (matter, form) of a tree.
3. (Matter, form) is actualized potential.
4. (Actuality, potentiality) can become (actuality, potentiality), but (actuality, potentiality) cannot become (actuality, potentiality).
5. When we swallow the (matter, form) of a hamburger, we transform its (actuality, potentiality) to the (actuality, potentiality) of human nourishment.

We can now see how Aristotle would elegantly answer the paradoxical question about change, "How can something change while it doesn't change?" His answer would be that what changes is form; what doesn't change is matter. The clay changes its form from lump to brick to wall; the matter of the clay doesn't change.

Now let's complete Aristotle's portrait of change by adding the efficient and final cause. I'll take the role of the efficient causes of brick maker and bricklayer. Note how much more richly detailed Aristotle's description of change is than

potentiality/actuality Potentiality is what a thing can become; actuality is a thing's current identity. A tree's potentiality is what it can become—lumber. A tree's actuality is its current identity—a tree. Potentiality is linked to a thing's matter; actuality is linked to a thing's form. All change, according to Aristotle, is from potentiality to actuality.

are those of his predecessors (refer back to Box 13.1). Aristotle describes *how* things change.

As a brick maker, I am the **efficient cause** that works upon the **potentiality** of the **matter** of the lump of clay to realize the **actuality** of its **final cause**, the new form of a brick.

As a bricklayer, I am the **efficient cause** that works upon the **potentiality** of the **matter** of the brick to realize the **actuality** of its **final cause**, the new form of a wall.

lump of clay   brick   wall

Granted, this description is a mouthful, but it is a historically important mouthful. Just think about what Aristotle has accomplished. He has described not simply the way clay changes into bricks and bricks change into walls but also *the central features in every kind of change in the universe*. In every stone, plant, insect, and animal, change marches forward from potentiality to actuality; matter takes on ever new forms, shaped by its efficient cause in the direction of its final cause. Lumps of clay become walls, apple seeds become apple trees, fawns become deer, infants become adults. By turning his powerful analysis to groups of similar things, Aristotle creates new sciences; by showing what all sciences hold in common, he creates a new portrait of Being.

M. C. Escher, *Reptiles*, lithograph, 1943.

ILLUSTRATION QUIZ

Summing up Aristotle

Assume you are Aristotle attempting to understand the strange world Escher created in this lithograph. You focus upon the reptile snorting smoke through its nose.

Use your own paper to answer the following questions:

1. How could the reptile be described in terms of the four causes? (Make your best guesses as to the reptile's matter, form, and final and efficient cause.)

2. How could the reptile be described in terms of the ten categories of being? (See page 259 for a list of the ten categories.)

3. What process of change is the reptile part of? (Use the terms matter, form, actuality, and potentiality in your answer.)

Parts of reality seem to change, and parts of reality seem unchanging. We have followed this theme almost from the beginning of our tour. Heraclitus emphasizes the changing and says the unchanging is an illusion; Parmenides and Zeno emphasize the unchanging and say the changing is an illusion. Plato and Aristotle combine these views in different ways.

According to Plato, the lower world we know with our senses is the changing Heraclitean realm; the higher realm of Forms we recollect with our minds is the unchanging Parmenidean realm.

According to Aristotle, the changing forms that we know with our senses are Heraclitean; the unchanging matter that we also know with our senses is Parmenidean.

Of all these accounts of the changing and the unchanging, which is correct?

I believe _____

_____

because _____

_____

_____ .

Your answers to these questions will give you a compact summary of many key features of Aristotle's metaphysics—and also, perhaps, a good deal of fun.

Now we can at last complete our sketch of Aristotle's metaphysics.

What Is Aristotle's Portrait of Reality?

Keeping in mind that existence is characterized by the ten categories, the four causes, and the change from potentiality to actuality, let's build a simple model of Aristotle's reality from bottom to top. At the end of this discussion, I'll make some qualifying remarks about our model.

We begin with the inorganic level—stones, earth, all that is nonliving. Our lump of clay, brick, and wall would fit in this category, all of whose members share the fundamental characteristic of occupying space.

Inorganic	Occupies space

Level

The next higher level is occupied by plants, which not only occupy space but also are capable of reproduction.

Plant	Occupies space, reproduces
Inorganic	Occupies space

Level

The next higher level is occupied by animals, which not only occupy space and are capable of reproduction, but also are self-moving.

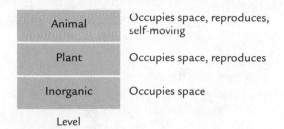

The next higher level is occupied by humans, who share all the characteristics of the lower levels and, in addition, can reason. (We'll have much more to say about humans in Chapter 14 when we explore Aristotle's ethics.)

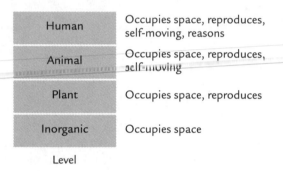

Now let's pause for a moment. We have described everything that exists on earth, the center of the universe according to Aristotle. Each level on earth has all the capacities of the levels below it and a unique capacity of its own. In addition, according to Aristotle, all that is living and nonliving is composed of some combination of the four basic elements: fire, air, earth, and water.

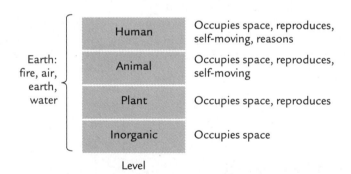

At the next higher level we leave the earth behind and enter the heavens: the moon, sun, planets, and fixed stars. These heavenly bodies, according to Aristotle, are made of a special fifth element, "quintessence," because "[their] nature is more honorable in that it is further removed from the world below." The heavenly bodies are not only composed of quintessence but are also living, thinking beings!

> It is the function of what is most divine to think and to use its intellect . . . we tend to think of them [heavenly bodies] as though they were simply bodies— units exhibiting order but quite without life—[but] we must suppose that they partake in action and in life. . . . We must think that the actions of the stars are just like those of animals and plants.[4]

Thus, we have an important new "unearthly" level of reality.

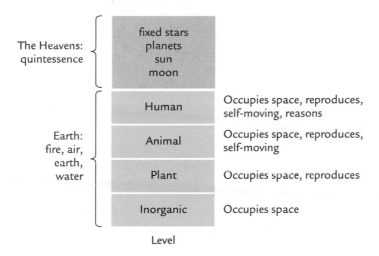

Level

But what about the universe as a whole? Is space finite or infinite? Did the universe have a beginning, or is it eternal? Does God exist? If so, what is his purpose? Aristotle has a very definite answer to each of these questions.

First, Aristotle holds that the universe is spatially finite, shaped like a vast sphere. Time, however, is infinite. Thus, the universe is an enormous ball that is eternal. In addition, change in the universe is also eternal. There never was a time when the universe wasn't changing. Aristotle's proof of this last point is intriguing.

I'll explain his argument with an analogy: Assume your finger is compressing a spring. Your finger is keeping the spring from changing. When you remove your finger, the spring changes, enlarges. Thus, obviously, before the first change of the spring, there must be some prior change—the change of your finger's position.

Now, instead of a spring and your finger, let's say we are considering the first thing that changes and whatever blocking force is keeping it from changing. When the blocking force is removed, then the first thing changes. Thus, obviously, before the change of the first thing, there must be some prior change— the change, removal, of the blocking force. Thus, the first change *cannot be the first change* . . . because there was a change preceding it.

---

[4] Quoted in *Aristotle*, Jonathan Barnes, p. 64.

This diagram walks you through the argument. For simplicity, we'll assume the first change involved something smaller becoming something larger (like matter expanding during the big bang).

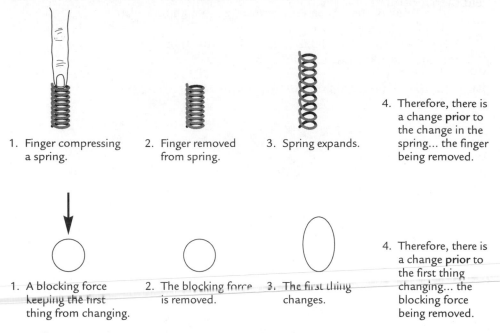

1. Finger compressing a spring.
2. Finger removed from spring.
3. Spring expands.
4. Therefore, there is a change **prior** to the change in the spring... the finger being removed.

1. A blocking force keeping the first thing from changing.
2. The blocking force is removed.
3. The first thing changes.
4. Therefore, there is a change **prior** to the first thing changing... the blocking force being removed.

Thus, according to Aristotle, whenever we try to think about the first change, we realize there must have been a prior change that made this first change possible. Therefore, there could be no *first* change. Change in the universe could have no beginning and is thus eternal.

Do you agree or disagree with this argument?

I (agree, disagree) because _____

_____

_____.

Now the next question is, What could possibly cause eternal change in the universe? Aristotle believed there had to be a cause of all the motion we see; otherwise, the motion wouldn't exist. The only possible cause, in his view, of the eternal motion of the universe is God. Thus, God is the cause of all motion. And since there could be nothing causing God to move, he must be the Unmoved Mover.

We have seen that God could not be somewhere back at the beginning of the changing universe, because the changing universe had no beginning. Thus, God does not cause motion by initiating it, starting it off. God causes motion by *continuously keeping it going.* But how?

God is perfect and the supreme object of love in the universe. Therefore, he causes motion in the same way that a loved object causes motion.

The final cause [God] then moves things because it is loved, whereas all other things move because they are themselves moved.[5]

---

[5] *Metaphysics* in *The Philosophy of Aristotle,* ed. Renford Bambrough (New York: New American Library, 1963) p. 12.

God moves things without being moved in the same way that an object of love moves things without itself being moved. Take the example of Mt. Fuji in Japan. Mt. Fuji has been the subject of countless paintings and poems and is held sacred by many Japanese. Every summer thousands of tourists climb to a shrine on its peak. Mt. Fuji, as an object of love, causes an extraordinary amount of activity without, of course, itself being moved. Thus, it is the unmoved mover of all those who love it. In the same way, God is the Unmoved Mover of those entities in the universe who adore God. And who are those entities? The living stars who move in circles in emulation of God's perfection and thereby transfer motion to all things on earth.

But if God is not directly involved in causing motion, what does God do? God, logically enough, does what is most perfect. The most perfect action, in Aristotle's view, is thinking. Thus, God is a thinker. And what does God think about? Obviously, God would think only about the most perfect things. And what is that? His own thought. Thus, God spends eternity thinking about his own thinking!

Aristotle's God provides a powerful contrast to Jewish, Christian, and Islamic monotheistic traditions. Aristotle's God is not the creator of the universe, only the object of the universe's love. He does not listen to or answer prayers—or even have the slightest concern for things on earth. He is the perfect philosophical God, pondering his own pondering.

Here is Aristotle's description of God's life:

> Its [God's] life is like the best that we can enjoy—and we can enjoy it for only a short time. It is always in this state (which we cannot be). . . . If, then, God is always in the good state which we are sometimes in, that is something to wonder at; and if he is in a better state than we are ever in, that is to be wondered at even more. This is in fact the case, however. Life belongs to him too; for life is the actuality of mind, and God is that actuality; and his independent actuality is the best life and eternal life. We assert, then, that God is an eternal and most excellent living being, so that continuous and eternal life and duration belong to him. For that is what God is.[6]

Now let me add a few qualifying remarks about our model of Aristotle's metaphysics.

First, there is no single place in Aristotle's work where he lays out his portrait of reality, as I have done, from top to bottom. The details of this portrait are pieced together from his *Metaphysics, On the Soul, History of Animals, Generation of Animals, Parts of Animals.* To get the real flavor of Aristotle's view of reality, imagine our model filled with detailed descriptions, as densely packed as his account of the egg and the octopus. Our model is the bare outline of Aristotle's encyclopedia.

Second, Aristotle mentions that it is occasionally difficult to distinguish between the living and the nonliving and between plants and animals. For example, coral are animals, but they are not self-moving; therefore, they share a characteristic with plants. Thus, from Aristotle's point of view, the dividing lines between categories can be fuzzy.

---

[6]*Metaphysics* in *The Philosophy of Aristotle,* ed. Renford Bambrough (New York: New American Library, 1963) p. 7.

VOCABULARY MAP

Aristotle's Metaphysics

Aristotle provides an excellent example of the way in which philosophers do not always fit neatly within the "fields of philosophy." On the one hand, it is probably correct to say that Aristotle's **metaphysics,** his view of reality, is **dualistic.** He distinguishes between God and the physical universe. God is one sort of thing, unmoving and independent of matter; the universe is another sort of thing, moving and rooted in matter. Thus reality, for Aristotle, has two faces, is dual. However, unlike other dualists—for example, Plato and Christian philosophers—Aristotle does not place much emphasis upon the higher world. The material world of nature

fascinates him; and so, if he is a dualist, he is weakly so. The "lower" part of reality seems far more important to him than the "higher" part.

Looked at in still another way, some historians of philosophy would argue that Aristotle's **metaphysics** *is* obviously **dualistic.** Aristotle holds that form and matter are the two features of existence. Form is one thing; matter is another. Therefore, reality has two faces, is dual. What this short discussion demonstrates is that philosophers produce their views and then historians (and textbook writers) come along afterwards and try, not always neatly, to summarize these views with preexisting terminology.

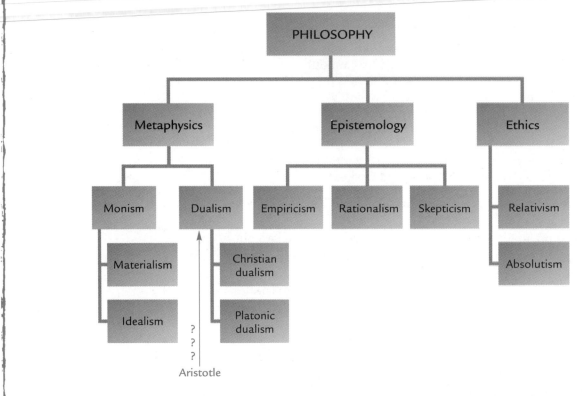

Third, the four causes and actuality and potentiality apply to *almost* everything in the universe. God, lacking matter, has no material cause. Without matter, he therefore has no potentiality. God cannot be anything more than God. Thus, God is pure form, pure actuality. In addition, Aristotle also held that some things don't have a final cause, a purpose. For example:

> The bile in the liver is a residue, and is not for sake of anything—like the sediment in the stomach and in the intestines. Now nature sometimes uses even residues for some advantageous purpose; but that is no reason for seeking a final cause in all cases.[7]

Fourth, even though God, at the top of the scale is pure form, it would be wrong to think there would be pure matter at the bottom of the scale. Matter in and of itself cannot exist. Everything that exists must be some kind of thing, must have essential characteristics, some form; pure matter would be no kind of thing and thus it is no-thing.

Now that we have sketched out Aristotle's metaphysics, only one question remains. How does the mind gain knowledge of reality?

What Is Aristotle's Epistemology?

Here is one of Aristotle's descriptions of the knowledge process.

> All animals . . . have an innate capacity to make discriminations, which is called perception; and if perception is present in them, in some animals the percept is retained and in others it is not. Now for those in which it is not retained . . . there is no knowledge outside perception. But for some perceivers it is possible to hold the percept in their minds; and when many such things have come about, there is a further difference, and some, from the retention of such things, come to have a general account, while others do not. Thus from perception there comes memory, as we call it; and from memory (when it occurs often in connection with the same thing) experience—for memories that are many in number form a single experience. And from experience, or from the whole universal that has come to rest in the mind . . . there comes a principle of skill and of knowledge.[8]

Aristotle distinguishes between animals who can remember their perceptions and animals who cannot. Humans are animals who can remember their perceptions. When we have enough perceptions in our memory, we can be said to have an experience. And from an experience, we can come to a general understanding, the knowledge of a universal truth.

Let me give you two examples.

I have a number of perceptions of apples growing on apple trees. I store these perceptions in my memory, and when I have had a sufficient quantity, I then can say that I have had an experience of apples growing on apple trees. From this experience, I can form a universal truth, "All apples grow on apple trees."

Or I have a number of perceptions of rain falling from clouds. I store these

---

[7] Quoted in *Aristotle,* Jonathan Barnes, p. 75.
[8] Quoted in *Aristotle,* Jonathan Barnes, p. 58.

VOCABULARY MAP

Aristotle's Epistemology

Unlike the problem with neatly labeling Aristotle's **metaphysics** (see page 254), there is no difficulty in identifying Aristotle's **epistemology,** his view of the knowledge process. Aristotle holds that all that we know comes through or is deduced from sense knowledge. Thus, he is an **empiricist.**

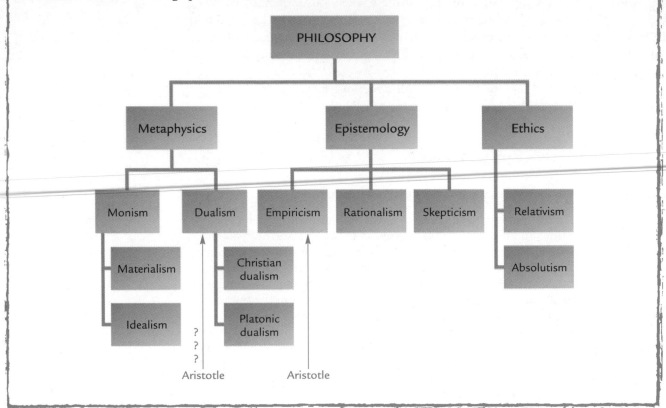

perceptions in memory, and when I have had a sufficient quantity, I then can say that I have had an experience of rain falling from clouds. From this experience, I can form a universal truth, "All rain falls from clouds."

Briefly put, "Knowledge . . . is bred by generalization out of perception." And so, at this point, what is your overall reaction to Aristotle? Have I convinced you to be an Aristotelian?

Of all the philosophers we've examined thus far, I believe Aristotle is _____

because _____

_____

_____

SUMMARY

One of Aristotle's greatest metaphysical innovations is his description of the sense world. Though he agrees with Plato that the form of an object is its essence, he holds that form is always united to matter. Form and matter are an object's substance. Substance is one of the ten categories of being (the other nine are location, time, quantity, quality, relationship, posture, state, doing something, undergoing something). Aristotle's account of cause includes an object's origin (efficient cause), form (formal cause), matter (material cause), and purpose (final cause). Matter is linked to potentiality; form is linked to actuality. The problem of change is solved by seeing that matter itself is unchanging while it goes through various forms. Aristotle labels the levels of reality as inorganic, plants, animals, humans, heavenly bodies, God. God is the Unmoved Mover who causes all motion.

Aristotle's epistemology describes how the mind, by building experiences from perceptions stored in memory, can form universal truths and thus gain knowledge.

EXERCISE 13.8
Looking Back

On your own paper, answer the following questions. Where possible, use original examples.

1. What is new in Aristotle's metaphysics?
2. How does Aristotle attack Plato's theory of Forms?
3. What is a substance?
4. What are the ten categories of being?
5. What are the four causes?
6. How do things change?
7. What is Aristotle's view of the universe?
8. What is Aristotle's epistemology?

EXERCISE 13.9
Looking at the World Through Aristotle's Eyes

How would Aristotle answer each of the following? Offer evidence from the chapter to support your answer.

1. T   F   What a thing will become is an important part of what a thing is.

   Evidence: _____

   _____.

2. T   F   All that is really real is unchanging.

   Evidence: _____

   _____.

3. T   F   Everything that is real is constantly changing.

   Evidence: _____

   _____.

4. T F Without the category of this book's location, the category of this book's substance would not exist.

   Evidence: _____

   _____.

5. T F When you write in this book, you will have actualized its potential.

   Evidence: _____

   _____.

6. T F If a teacher says you have "enormous potential," you should be insulted.

   Evidence: _____

   _____.

7. T F We can prove God's existence by reasoning from what we don't see to what we do see.

   Evidence: _____

   _____.

ANALYSIS OF YOUR PHILOSOPHICAL SELF-PORTRAIT

To see how your views stack up against Aristotle's, read my analysis below, rethink your position, and then circle what you believe is the correct answer. I've underlined Aristotle's answers.

1. T F *The world we know with our senses is real.*

    As you now know, according to Aristotle, everything we encounter with our five senses is real. However, he would not hold that the *only* real things are things we know with our senses. God, for Aristotle, is certainly real but only the effects of his reality, the motion of the universe, is known by the senses, not his reality itself.

2. T F *Plato's realm of Forms does not exist.*

    Though Aristotle denies that Plato's realm of Forms exists, he holds that forms are unchanging. The form of brick never changes. A brick always had and always will have the same definition. And thus, since the universe is eternal, Aristotle, because he had no idea of evolution, would have held that the form of brick would be eternal. Unlike Plato, of course, he would hold that the brick's form is always linked to its matter.

3. T F *A brick's color is just as real as a brick's matter.*

    In Aristotle's view, there are two ways a thing can exist, dependently or independently. The brick's color exists dependently; in other words, the color depends upon the brick's substance to exist. The brick's substance, however, exists independently; the substance doesn't depend upon the brick's color to exist. Thus, of the two, the brick's color could be said to be less real because it could not exist without the brick's substance. In the same way, of the ten categories, the category of substance is the most real, because the other categories depend for their existence upon substance.

4. <u>T</u> F *Everything that exists has its own unique purpose.*

According to Aristotle, purpose is one of the four causes, the final cause. In the next chapter, you'll discover Aristotle's description of the purpose of human life!

5. <u>T</u> F *God is the cause of all motion.*

Aristotle, obviously, agrees. But remember, because the motion of the universe is eternal, God didn't start the universe. He only keeps the universe going. And he keeps it going indirectly by being the object of love of the fixed stars.

6. <u>T</u> F *All we know comes through our senses.*

Aristotle begins the empiricist's path. Though others before him certainly used their senses to examine the world, no philosopher until Aristotle was so painstakingly systematic. His reliance upon the senses will be supported by other empiricists and attacked by rationalists on the tour for the next 2,000 years. And then something odd happens. In the seventeenth century, the British empiricists endorse Aristotle in such a strange way that almost nothing is left of his position! After witnessing Aristotle's treatment in the hands of his "supporters," Locke, Berkeley, and Hume, you may believe he was better off in the hands of his enemies.

7. <u>T</u> F *Love makes the world go 'round.*

We can add a few more details here about Aristotle's view of how the universe operates. Think of the earth at the center of a set of crystal spheres. The moon, the sun, and then the planets are set each in its own sphere, each one touching the other. The fixed stars are at the outermost physical boundary of the universe and are set in their own sphere.

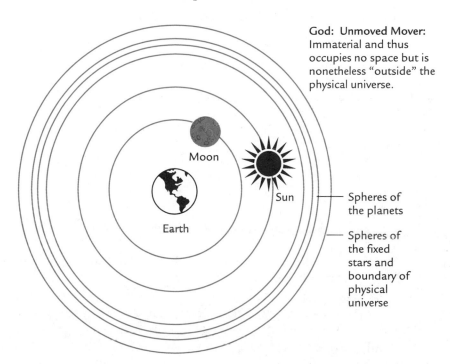

God: Unmoved Mover: Immaterial and thus occupies no space but is nonetheless "outside" the physical universe.

Spheres of the planets

Spheres of the fixed stars and boundary of physical universe

(Note: For clarity, the spheres of the moon, sun, planets and fixed stars have been separated, but according to Aristotle they are touching.)

The sphere of the fixed stars rotates. Its motion is caused, inspired, by the fixed stars' love of God's perfection. This movement is physically transferred to each of the inner spheres because the spheres are touching. In addition, because each of the heavenly bodies is a living intelligence, it has its own motion. Thus, the movement of any particular planet or star—let's say the moon—has two sources. The moon, as a living being, has its own motion and a motion transmitted down through the spheres outside it from the fixed stars.

This is a fairly simple description of what, in Aristotle's hands, turns out to be very complex. In order to account for all the motion of the planets and stars, he says there must be a large number of lesser unmoved movers (fifty-five!) among the spheres to keep everything going. So, in his view, love *really* makes the world go 'round.

Evaluation: Number of points in agreement with Aristotle = _____of 7 possible.

A position of Aristotle's that you strongly (support, oppose) is _____

_____

because _____

_____.

GOOD BOOKS

Adler, Mortimer J. *Aristotle for Everybody.* New York: Macmillan, 1978. A breezy, but useful guide written for the general public.

Barnes, Jonathan. *Aristotle.* New York: Oxford University Press, 1983. A superb, short introduction to Aristotle's work, highly recommended.

Grene, Marjorie. *A Portrait of Aristotle.* Chicago: University of Chicago Press, 1963. A very readable overview of Aristotle's work, especially good on the differences between Aristotle and Plato.

Ross, David. *Aristotle.* 5th ed. London: Methuen, 1949. A standard work by a respected Aristotle scholar.

NEXT STOP

You discover Aristotle's view of the purpose of life— and your own.

14
Aristotle's Ethics
Discovering Life's Purpose

YOUR PHILOSOPHICAL SELF-PORTRAIT

Add more details to your philosophical self-portrait by answering the questions below and offering evidence for your answers.

1. T F A good person obeys God's commandments.

   Evidence: _____

   _____

   _____.

2. T F Human life has no purpose.

   Evidence: _____

   _____

   _____.

3. T F It is possible to live irrationally and be happy.

   Evidence: _____

   _____

   _____.

4. T F Virtue lies in choosing the middle path between
         extremes.

   Evidence: _____

   _____

   _____.

To prepare for an analysis of selections from Aristotle's *Nicomachean Ethics*, we examine an important ethical question: What is the purpose of human life? Three answers are briefly considered: The purpose of human life lies beyond this world; the purpose of human life lies within this world; human life has no purpose. To understand Aristotle's own position, we explore his analysis of human nature. Whereas Plato argues that humans are a duality of soul and body, Aristotle argues that humans are a unity of soul and body. In Aristotle's view, the purpose of human life is to achieve *eudaimonia*. We'll explore the meaning of this intriguing Greek word.

THOUGHT EXPERIMENT

You've tuned in to K-ARI, a cable television station devoted to the philosophy of Aristotle. You watch *All About the Cheese Mite!* and *The Young and the Empirical* and then a sitcom, *The Adventures of Joe Doofus.*

Joe Doofus takes his life savings to Las Vegas. He plays blackjack but doesn't know the rules. At first Joe thinks the purpose of the game is to get as many cards as possible, and so he keeps asking for cards from the dealer. And he loses. Next, Joe thinks the purpose of blackjack is to get as few cards as possible and so, he never takes cards from the dealer. And he loses. Next, Joe tries playing blackjack according to the rules of poker, bridge, and finally Old Maid. And he loses everything. In the final scene, you see Joe Doofus trying to use a banana for a car key.

After watching a few more episodes you realize that Joe Doofus must be Aristotle's version of a fool. Joe doesn't know the purpose of blackjack, car keys, bananas, anything. Because Joe lacks knowledge of purpose, everything he does turns out disastrously.

After many days' viewing, you stop laughing at Joe. It no longer seems funny watching him use shovels for screwdrivers and cupcakes for hammers. The deep point of the program dawns on you.

Everything we do has a purpose. Those who lack knowledge of purpose live disastrously. Knowledge of the purpose of anything from card games to cupcakes is all-important knowledge.

Joe Doofus is a small-time fool. He doesn't know the purpose of any of life's activities. *A big-time fool, however, wouldn't know the purpose of life.* Lacking knowledge of blackjack's purpose, Joe merely risks his life savings. Lacking knowledge of life's purpose, we risk all our days.

Ponder that. If you don't know the purpose, goal, object, of blackjack, you will never be successful at blackjack; if you don't know the purpose, goal, object, of life, you will never be successful at life.

Every decision you make is a gamble that you know what living is all about. And so, what is the purpose of life? What view have you bet your existence on?

I believe the purpose of life is _____ _____

_____ .

Of course, if you're wrong, then you've lost everything. Joe Doofus is your life story.

Aristotle is convinced that he knows the purpose of human life—and how to achieve it. But before we examine his answer, one of the most influential in the history of ethics, let me help you clarify your position. You could support one of three views: you could believe the purpose of human life lies beyond this world or that the purpose of human life lies within this world or that human life has no purpose. Let's consider each in turn.

Position 1: The purpose of human life lies beyond this world. Plato and most Jews, Christians, Muslims, and Buddhists would agree that the purpose of human life lies beyond this world. If you hold, for example, that the soul is immortal, then you probably believe that what gives your existence its ultimate goal lies beyond your life on earth. If you believe God exists, then you believe that just as a game designer determines the rules and object of a game, so God, as the designer of human life, has determined the rules and object of the game of human life. Any of the following might state a life purpose that lies beyond this world (underline any you support):

- Obeying Allah
- Doing God's will
- Reaching heaven
- Achieving Nirvana

Any of these life purposes lies beyond our experience in this world. Humans are engaged in a game they didn't design, for a goal they didn't establish. Our only decision in the cosmic casino is how to play our cards, not what the game is about.

Position 2: The purpose of human life lies within this world. If you are an atheist or an agnostic *and* you believe life has a purpose, then you almost certainly believe that its purpose is achieved entirely in this world. The rules and object of the game of life are determined solely by its human players. Thus, any of the following might state a life purpose that lies within this world (underline any you support):

- Being a financial success
- Having as much pleasure as possible
- Raising a good family
- Fully developing personal skills
- Making the world a better place

Any of these life purposes lies within our experience on earth. Humans are playing a game for entirely human goals according to rules that arise out of human nature. What we should do with our cards is determined by the most important features of our humanity and the world we live in.

Position 3: Human life has no purpose. Some atheists and agnostics believe that life has no purpose in or beyond this world. Therefore, the best thing to do in the game of life is to realize that it has no point. Humans should do whatever they want with their cards, except try to follow nonexistent rules or believe there is a way of "winning."

A former student once asked me, "What difference does it make what I do? In a few million years, the earth will fall into the sun." For this student and others of his persuasion, life has neither an internal nor an external goal.

To sum up these three positions, think of our purpose as life's target. The question then becomes, Is life's target set up beyond this world, is it set up within this world, or does life have no target?

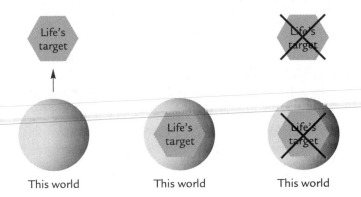

This may be the most important philosophical question you ever consider. Your answer will determine whether or not you lose everything. Which of the three positions above are you betting your life on?

I believe _____

because _____

_____.

EXERCISE 14.1
Human Purpose

To help you to continue to clarify your understanding of the purpose of human life, identify on your own paper the purpose of each of the following activities and then answer questions 14–17.

For you, what is the purpose of:

1. Mowing the lawn

2. Going to the movies

3. Praying

4. Getting a good job

5. Getting married

6. Having children

7. Using a word processor

8. Going to church

9. Gaining wisdom

10. Washing the car

11. Taking an introductory philosophy class

12. Getting an education

13. Getting exercise

14. Which two activities above have the least to do with helping you achieve the purpose of human life? Why?

15. What other activities do you engage in that have little to do with helping you achieve the purpose of human life?

16. Which two activities above have the most to do with helping you achieve the purpose of human life? Why?

17. What other activities do you engage in that have a great deal to do with helping you achieve the purpose of human life?

Aristotle is convinced he knows the purpose of human life *and* the activities we should engage in to achieve it. To explain his position, one that convinces many of my students, I'll present Aristotle's answer to the following questions:

- What is a human being?
- What is the purpose of human life?

We'll conclude with selections from Aristotle's ethical masterwork, the *Nicomachean Ethics,* which expands his analysis of human purpose.

What Is a Human Being?

Often, students can't see the difficulty of this question. Humans are humans. And that's that. But a moment's reflection will show that human nature is deeply mysterious:

How do humans relate to other humans?

How do individual humans and human culture interact?

What is the nature of the human mind?

How have humans governed themselves?

These are, respectively, central questions of sociology, anthropology, psychology, and political science. In a lifetime, no one could read, much less evaluate, a fraction of the works written on one of these questions. The riddle of human nature fills libraries. For several thousand years, thinkers have generated mountains of paper trying to solve the mystery of the kind of being you are. You baffle the ages.

On this tour we'll investigate some of the most brilliant and influential answers to the riddle of human nature. Consider each answer a portrait of your essential qualities.

In an earlier chapter, I described Plato's portrait of you. Remember that he believed you are a mortal body inhabited by an immortal soul. Your soul is divided into three parts: reason, spirited element, and irrational desires. Aristotle, as you might imagine, disagrees.

According to Plato, you are a *duality* of body and soul; according to Aristotle, you are a *unity* of body and soul.

You according to Plato

You according to Aristotle

The word Aristotle uses that is customarily translated as soul is psyche (pronounced with a long e). However, a translation of *psyche* that would give modern readers a clearer idea of what Aristotle is describing would be "animating principle" or "life force." Thus, your soul, in Aristotle's view, is what animates you, what makes you alive. Your little toe is just as alive, has just as much soul, as your brain.

Because soul is life force, your soul is *all through* your body, indivisible from your body, just as the essence of an apple is all through, indivisible from, the matter of an apple. Every bit of apple matter is a bit of apple essence; every bit of your body is a bit of your soul.

This view of soul gives Aristotle an understanding of death very different from Plato's. According to Plato, as you remember, when you die, your soul, because it is a completely separate thing from your body, survives to go on to the realm of Forms. According to Aristotle, when you die, your soul because it is absolutely connected to your body ceases to exist. In Aristotle's view, soul could no more exist without the body than walking could exist without feet or a heartbeat without a heart.

Here is a short argument that sums up Aristotle's view of death:

In the *Generation of Animals*, Aristotle seems to indicate that thought somehow might exist without a body, but exactly how this could be or what he intends by this position perplexes his commentators. It is generally accepted, however, that Aristotle denies personal immortality, the survival of the individual soul.

1. Your soul is your body's life force.

2. Death is the extinction of your body's life force.

3. Therefore, death is the extinction of your soul.

Is Aristotle right? What do you think will happen when your body dies?

I believe Aristotle is (right, wrong) because _____

_____

_____

Because soul is life force, everything that is alive has a soul. Plants, insects, animals, and humans have souls, life forces, that possess various powers:

> Some things possess all the powers of the soul, others some of them, others one only. The powers we mentioned were those of nutrition, of perception, of appetition, of change in place, of thought. Plants possess only the nutritive power. Other things possess both that and the power of perception. . . . Some things possess in addition to these the power of locomotion; and others also possess the power of thought and intelligence.[1]

Your human soul, your life force, is a hierarchy of powers. With all plants, your soul shares the power of nutrition; with all animals, your soul shares the powers of perception and locomotion; finally, with all humans, your soul shares the power of thought, of reasoning. And so, in an ascending scale, let's add these characteristics to Aristotle's portrait of you.

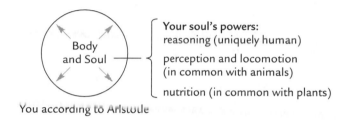

You according to Aristotle

If you think about it, this portrait is wonderful. Within your animating principle, you possess the characteristics of all things that live. Your soul embodies the universe of life.

But do you agree with Aristotle thus far? Do you possess a life force that vanishes at death and that, besides the uniquely human power of reasoning, also shares powers in common with animals and plants?

I believe Aristotle is (completely right, partially right, entirely wrong) because

_____

_____

_____ .

What Is the Purpose of Human Life?

Keeping in mind what we've said about the nature of the soul and the body, let's now use Aristotle's four causes to describe human beings and the purpose of human life.

Remember that the *material cause* of anything is the matter, the stuff, of the thing. Thus, the material cause of a brick is its clay. Your material cause as a human being is your flesh and bones, your physical body.

---

[1] Quoted in *Aristotle*, Jonathan Barnes, p. 66.

The *efficient cause* of anything is its origin, the forces that produce it. Thus, the efficient cause of a brick is a brick maker. Your efficient cause as a human being is your biological parents.

The *formal cause* of anything is its essence, its defining characteristics. Thus, the formal cause of a brick is its shape. Your formal cause as a human being is your soul, specifically the uniquely human power of reasoning in your soul.

The *final cause* of anything is its goal, its purpose. Because this is the central theme of this chapter, let's pause here. The final cause of a brick, its purpose, is to be part of a brick wall. The final cause of a hammer is to pound nails. The final cause of a knife is to cut. In Aristotle's view, as you recall from the last chapter, everything that exists has a final cause, a purpose. And so, what is your purpose as a human being?

The purpose of human life, according to Aristotle, is to achieve eudaimonia. But what's that?

Eudaimonia is an intriguing Greek word that is usually translated as "happiness." Unfortunately, we have no single word that best expresses its meaning. Synonyms for eudaimonia might be "life success" or "human flourishing." Birthday parties and funny movies make us happy, but they don't make us a success at life or a flourishing human being. According to Aristotle, instead of trying to have a good time, we should be trying to have a good life. Instead of seeking the shallow pleasures of ordinary experience, we should be seeking the deep pleasure of self-perfection.

To understand Aristotle's point, imagine a dancer named Saskia, who experiences the happiness of daily life and then the happiness of dancing well and, finally, the happiness of eudaimonia.

When Saskia receives birthday presents or eats a delicious meal at a restaurant or watches a funny movie, she experiences the happiness of daily life. This happiness is temporary and shallow. Today's good meal can be tonight's indigestion. Tonight's funny movie is tomorrow's bill at the video store. The best that daily life can offer is an intense, brief gladness. We can smile only so long, and then our face hurts.

A stronger, more long-lasting happiness comes to Saskia when she dances excellently. This happiness is stronger because it satisfies a deeper, more important part of her personality. She certainly doesn't think of herself as a restaurant patron or a movie watcher; Saskia thinks of herself as a dancer. Dancing is her destiny. And so, when she dances excellently, she is deeply happy. Saskia is doing what she believes she was meant to do. Performing her craft superbly, she is completely fulfilling her purpose as an artist.

But let us say Saskia reads Aristotle. She begins to see that there is something far deeper, far broader, than her artistic self that needs fulfillment. She begins to see that dancing is the destiny of only a small part of her being. Saskia has experienced the shallow fulfillments of daily life, the happiness of a restaurant patron, the happiness of a movie watcher, and she has experienced the deeper fulfillment of her career, the happiness of dancing well; but she wonders what it would be like to be fulfilled as *an entire human being*. Saskia sees that this would involve a large change of perspective. Human fulfillment would involve not mastering the art of dancing, but mastering the art of living. The stage extends everywhere Saskia goes. The dance is everything she does.

Reading Aristotle, Saskia learns that eudaimonia, human flourishing, is her real, her complete destiny. She understands that life *as a whole* promises far more than moving expressively to music. As a great dancer, she would only dance excellently; as a great person, she would live excellently.

Now, let us say Saskia dedicates herself to seeking eudaimonia, human flourishing. What does Aristotle teach her? Here are five important lessons from the *Nicomachean Ethics:*

Aristotle's first lesson is that human flourishing is achieved only by the excellent use of our unique human gift, our reason. Just as great dancers use their bodies excellently, great humans use their reason excellently.

We would not call Saskia an excellent human being just because she superbly nourished herself. This is an excellence she would share with plants. Nor would we call her an excellent human being just because she was superb at perception or reproduction. This is an excellence she would share with animals. *Saskia is an excellent human being when she is superb at reasoning, because reasoning is the unique human excellence.* Thus, just as she must carefully train her body to be a great dancer, Saskia must even more carefully train her reason to be a great human being.

Aristotle's second lesson is that human flourishing, which we now understand involves reasoning excellently, is concerned with choosing the mean between excess and deficiency. Thus, "being a great human being" does not involve being famous; it involves making wise choices. In every activity in her life, Saskia has three choices: doing too much, doing too little, or doing just the right amount. According to Aristotle, it does not matter whether we are eating, exercising, being angry, making jokes, feeling pride, or participating in any other human activity, the middle path between too much and too little leads to life success, human flourishing. And doesn't this make sense? Saskia could hardly be called an excellent human being if, for example, she lived a life that oscillated between excess and deficiency. She would not have mastered the art of living if today she is excessively angry and excessively proud and tomorrow she is deficiently self-controlled and deficiently generous. Human excellence, in Aristotle's view, consistently steers the middle course between extremes. In regard to this lesson, Aristotle adds two important qualifications. The middle course between excess and deficiency cannot be determined mathematically. If six pounds of food is too much for Saskia and two pounds of food is too little for her, it does not follow that four pounds, the mathematical mean, is just the right amount. Aristotle's second qualification is that the mean is not the same for everyone. If, say, three pounds of food was the right amount for Saskia, that does not mean it would be right for everyone. These are two key points. They indicate that the middle course is not easy to determine and that it can vary for each individual.

Aristotle's third lesson for achieving human flourishing is that a certain amount of external good fortune is required. Unlike Plato, who argued that perfect happiness would be possible even if one were imprisoned and tortured, Aristotle believes that the physical and familial blessings of life are vital. Having

eudaimonia Greek word usually and inadequately translated as "happiness" but better translated as "human flourishing." To flourish is to thrive, to be vigorously alive. In Aristotle's view, eudaimonia involves well-balanced and lifelong development of one's powers, especially reason.

close friends, good children, noble birth, even good looks, makes human flourishing far easier to achieve.

> A man is not likely to be happy if he is very ugly, or of low birth, or alone in the world, or childless, and perhaps still less if he has worthless children or friends.

Thus, if Saskia is extremely ugly or poor, or if she lacks good friends and good children, her path to eudaimonia will be very difficult. Don't you have to admit Aristotle is right? Isn't he simply being realistic? Friendship, family, a certain amount of wealth, and, at least, a nonhideous appearance are important aids to life happiness.

Aristotle's fourth lesson for achieving human flourishing is that being a success at life takes, naturally enough, an entire life. Thus, Saskia could not claim she was a successful human being until she neared the end of her days. As Aristotle puts it, "one swallow or one fine day does not make a spring." Using her reason excellently a few times would not make Saskia an excellent human being. She, along with the rest of us, runs the long course. And we must run it all well to be considered a success at living.

Aristotle's fifth lesson for achieving human flourishing is that the philosopher leads the best of all possible lives. Aristotle distinguishes between three possible goals for life: physical pleasure, fame, and wisdom. He dismisses physical pleasure as life's goal because this would make us no better than animals. Certainly the goal of human life has to be something nobler than a cow contentedly chewing its cud or a dog happily scratching its fleas. In addition, Aristotle dismisses fame as life's goal because fame depends upon others. If Saskia is an excellent human and has achieved life's goal, it certainly won't be because she has a fan club or frequently has her name in the paper. If fame makes Saskia an excellent human, then her excellence depends upon others and is not uniquely her own. This leaves us with wisdom, philosophical contemplation, as life's highest goal. And doesn't this follow from what Aristotle has said about human nature? If our uniquely human excellence is to use our reason, then we use our reason best when we are seeking wisdom, when we are contemplating the largest questions that the human mind can pose. Aristotle supports his position by arguing that the philosophical life is deeply pleasurable and self-sufficient.

> We think too that pleasure ought to be one of the ingredients of eudaimonia; but of all virtuous activities it is agreed that the pleasantest is the exercise of wisdom. Philosophy is said to have pleasures that are admirable in purity and steadfastness . . . the wise man . . . is able to contemplate truth even by himself, and the wiser he is the more he is able to do this . . . he is more self-sufficient than anybody else.[2]

To be an excellent human being, Saskia must make full use of her reason. Seeking wisdom, contemplating eternal truths, is the activity that makes the most full use of reason. Thus, to achieve eudaimonia, Saskia must live the life of the philosopher.

---

[2] Christopher Biffle, *A Guided Tour of Selections from Aristotle's Nichomachean Ethics*, (Mountain View, Calif.: 1991) p. 30.

To sum up, what is your position on these five important lessons?

1. Human flourishing is achieved only by the excellent use of our unique human gift, our reason.

This is (right, wrong) because _____

_____

_____.

2. Human flourishing involves choosing the mean between excess and deficiency.

This is (right, wrong) because _____

_____

_____.

3. For someone to flourish as a human, external good fortune (good friends, good children, moderate wealth, not being ugly) is very helpful.

This is (right, partly right, wrong) because _____

_____

_____.

4. Human flourishing, being a success at life, takes an entire life.

This is (right, partly right, wrong) because _____

_____

_____.

5. Human flourishing is best achieved by the life of philosophical contemplation.

This is (right, partly right, wrong) because _____

_____

_____.

Of the three options we examined at the beginning of this chapter, Aristotle would take the view that the purpose of human life lies within this world. Just as a hammer has no purpose beyond its physical existence as a hammer and just as a knife has no purpose beyond its physical existence as a knife, so humans have no purpose beyond their physical existence as humans. A good hammer hammers well, a good knife cuts well, a good human reasons well.

Now that you have an initial understanding of Aristotle's view of human nature, the purpose of human life, and how that purpose is achieved, you are ready for an examination of selections from Aristotle's masterwork in ethics, the *Nicomachean Ethics*.

READING:
SELECTIONS FROM ARISTOTLE'S
NICOMACHEAN ETHICS

What Are Some Key Features?

Aristotle's *Nicomachean Ethics* begins and ends with references to political science. To Aristotle, human beings are political and social beings. Moral action is possible only within society and community. Isolated individual activity is not the realm of ethics or, for that matter, of human existence. Modern **existentialism** takes isolation, alienation, and "forlornness" as central characteristics of the human situation, but these concepts are alien to Aristotle. (See the selections by Jean-Paul Sartre and Albert Camus in "A Modern Reader" at the end of this book. At the end of Jean-Paul Sartre's *No Exit*, a character announces, "Hell is other people."). Toward the end of the *Nicomachean Ethics*, Aristotle considers the question of how many friends we should have. He considers many alternatives, but he never wonders if we should have no friends. For Aristotle, to be human is to be with others.

Before you read the *Nicomachean Ethics* you should realize that it was not intended for publication in any modern sense of that term. Most critics agree that what we have is something like a set of lecture notes collected and edited at a later time (perhaps by Aristotle's son Nicomachus, to whom the work is dedicated). This is important because it explains several obvious characteristics of the *Ethics*. The analysis is often abrupt, occasionally circular, sometimes dense, and at other times simply poorly organized. In fact, the notes appear to have been accumulated over a period of years and occasionally contain two or more approaches to the same topic.

Here are the opening sentences of the *Nicomachean Ethics*. Underline and then ponder the key words. If you find yourself staring off into space, you are on the right track. As you now know, philosophical reading is slow, thoughtful reading.

Try to think of examples of what Aristotle means.

Every art and every kind of scientific inquiry and also every action and choice seem to aim at some good. Thus, it has been well said that the good is that at which everything aims.

A synonym for *good* as Aristotle uses the term is *goal*. Thus, the goal of the art of religious sculpture might be to produce an image of a god. The good or goal of a craft like shoemaking would be to produce shoes. What good or goal does an exercise like jogging aim at?

The good of jogging might be _____, or, looked at

in another way, it might be _____.

Think of examples of an art and an action and the good each aims at.

An example of an art is _____ and the good at which it

aims is _____. An example of an action is

_____ and the good at which it aims is

_____.

Now we are ready to go on to the second paragraph of the *Nicomachean Ethics*. Underline, write your own notes in the column, and think of examples.

> There is a difference, however, among these aims [goals]. What is aimed at is sometimes an activity and sometimes a result or product of an activity. In this latter case where the goal is some product of an activity, the product is naturally superior to the activity itself.

What do you think this means?

I think he means _____

_____.

The phrase I understood the most clearly was, "_____

_____."

This means that _____

_____.

An example would be _____

_____.

According to Aristotle, some activities, such as the pursuit of pure scientific knowledge, are ends in themselves. In other words, an astronomer studies the stars not for any other end than to know more about the stars. In fact, Aristotle might argue that if an astronomer studied the stars for some other reason, like achieving fame or getting away from her husband or making a living, then she wouldn't really be an astronomer. She would be a fame seeker, an unhappy spouse, or a college employee.

Now look again at the third sentence: "In this latter case where the goal is some product of an activity, the product is naturally superior to the activity itself." Think of an activity that creates a product and explain in what sense the product might be said to be superior to the activity.

The activity I am thinking of is _____. The

product it produces is _____. The reason the

product might be said to be superior to the activity is _____

_____.

existentialism At the core of existentialism is Jean-Paul Sartre's statement that "existence precedes essence." Human existence determines human nature. We are nothing but the sum total of the choices we make in our existence and can freely change our nature with new choices.

Think of the activity of chopping wood. The products that are created are logs for the fireplace. Unless we are at a dude ranch, chopping wood is not an end in itself. The logs are "superior" to the chopping because the hard work of chopping serves no purpose in itself; we chop wood to produce the logs that keep us warm on winter nights. What we really want are logs, not sweat. Once again think of an example of an activity and the product it produces, and then try to apply my explanation to your example.

Take the activity _____. Its

product is _____. The product is superior to the

activity because _____.

The way the example of chopping wood applies to this is _____

_____.

To understand Aristotle or any other philosopher, you must practice your slow reading skills. At frequent intervals, stop reading and simply think about what Aristotle is saying, find your own examples, underline, write notes in the margin, and reread. It is better to read one sentence five times and understand it than to read five sentences once and be lost. Slow reading saves time.

Each book of the *Nicomachean Ethics* is divided into chapters. I have given each of these chapters a title in the form of a question. The question is often (but not always) answered in the opening paragraph. Use the title to guide your underlinings. For example, the title of the first chapter is "What do all human actions aim at?" You will be underlining Aristotle's answer to this question and a few of the key statements he uses to expand his answer. Don't underline everything! Use underlining to create an outline of the most important sentences and phrases. This will simplify rereading.

Book I

1. *What Do All Human Actions Aim At?*

Every art and every kind of scientific inquiry and also every action and choice seem to aim at some good. Thus, it has been well said that the good is that at which everything aims.

There is a difference, however, among these aims [goals]. What is aimed at is sometimes an activity and sometimes a result or product of an activity. In this latter case where the goal is some product of an activity, the product is naturally superior to the activity itself.

Since there are many kinds of actions and many arts and sciences, it follows that there are also many goals. Health is the goal of medicine, ships are the goal of shipbuilding, victory is the goal of the art of war, and wealth is the goal of economy.

When several of these activities are subordinated to a particular art— as the making of bridles and other trappings is subordinated to the art of horsemanship, and this in turn, along with all else that the soldier does, is

Another example would be

_____

_____

is the end of _____

_____.

subordinated to the art of war, and so on—the goal of the master art is always more desired than the goals of the subordinate arts. The reason for this is that the subordinate arts are pursued for the sake of the master art. This is equally true whether the goal is the activity or, as in cases just mentioned, in something beyond the activity.

Health, ships, victory, and wealth are all examples of _____s.

Review your underlinings. According to Aristotle, the master art is _____

_____,

and it is preferred to subordinate arts like _____

because _____

_____

_____.

In the next short section underline the key statements Aristotle makes in answer to the question posed in the chapter title.

2. What Science Studies the Supreme Good?

If in what we do there is some goal that we wish for its own sake, choosing all other goals as a means to this one most desirable goal, but each goal is not desired as a goal leading to something else and so on forever, because then our desire would be futile and pointless, this most desirable goal will be the good or [better] the supreme good.

The chief good is what we desire for _____

_____

_____.

Surely from a practical point of view it is important for us to know this supreme good because then, like archers shooting at a definite target, we shall be more likely to attain what we want. If this is true, we must try to indicate roughly what the supreme good is, and first of all, to which of the arts or sciences it belongs. The supreme good seems to belong to the art or science that most of all deserves the name of master art or master science.

Politics seems to answer to this description. Politics prescribes which of the sciences a state needs, and which each man shall study, and up to what point; and to politics we see subordinated even the highest arts, such as economy, oratory, and the art of war.

Since politics makes use of the other practical sciences, and since it further ordains what men are to do and from what to refrain, its goal must include the goals of the others, and must be the proper good of man.

For though this good is the same for the individual and the state, yet the good of the state seems a more perfect thing both to attain and to safeguard; though it is good to attain the goal for one man, it is far better to attain it for a people and nobler and more divine still to attain it for a nation.

This then is the aim of the present inquiry, which is a type of political inquiry.

Aristotle says politics is the science of the supreme good, or the goal of all goals,

because _____

_____

_____.

In this passage Aristotle divides a large topic into a number of subtopics, or a whole into its parts. What is an example of a whole and its parts in this section?

The first whole is _____

and the parts he mentions are _____

_____.

Aristotle says:

For though this good [the good of man] is the same for the individual and the state, yet the good of the state seems a more perfect thing both to attain and to safeguard; though it is good to attain the end for one man, it is far better to attain it for a people and nobler and more divine still to attain it for a nation.

In this paragraph Aristotle is saying _____

_____

_____.

My reaction to Aristotle thus far is

_____

_____.

To get more out of my reading I could _____

_____.

Try your advice in the next section.

3. Why Can't the Investigation of Politics Be Exact?

We must be content if we can attain as much precision in our investigation as the subject before us allows, because the same degree of precision is no more to be expected in all kinds of reasoning than in all kinds of manufactured articles. Now what is noble and just, which is what politics deals with, is so various and so uncertain that some people think morality exists merely by custom and not as part of the nature of things.

There is also a similar uncertainty about what is good, because good things often do people harm: Men have before now been ruined by wealth and have lost their lives through courage.

Because our subject and our data are of this kind, we must be content if we can indicate the truth roughly and in outline. Dealing with matters that are not amenable to unchanging laws and reasoning from premises that are only probable, we can only arrive at broad, general conclusions.

The reader, on his part, should take each of my statements in the same spirit because it is the mark of an educated man to require in each kind of inquiry only as much exactness as the subject allows: It is equally absurd to accept probable reasoning from a mathematician as to demand rigid scientific proof from an orator.

Each man can form a judgment about what he knows, and he is called a good judge of a particular field when he has received education in that particular field. He is called a good judge in general when he has received a broad and well-rounded education. Thus a young man is not qualified to be a student of politics because he lacks broad experience of the affairs of life, which form the data and the subject matter of politics. Further, since a young man is apt to be swayed by his feelings, he will derive no benefit from a study whose aim is not knowledge but action.

In this respect immaturity in character is the same as immaturity in years because the young man's disqualification is a matter not of time but of the fact that feeling rules his life and directs all his desires. Men of this character turn the knowledge they get to no use in practice, as we see with those we call morally unstable; but those who direct their desires and actions by reason will gain much profit from the knowledge of these matters.

So much, then, by way of preface to the student, the spirit in which he must accept what we say, and the object that we propose to ourselves.

The words "this kind" refer back to _____ .

The two kinds of absurdity are

_____

and _____

_____ .

Aristotle's reasons why this investigation cannot be exact are (1) _____

_____ and

(2) _____

_____ .

Three main topics are summarized in this paragraph.

The student of politics needs to be _____ .

The spirit he or she should approach the subject with should be _____

_____

_____ .

And the object is, of course, _____

_____ .

4. What Is the Supreme Good, and What Are Some of the Views About It?

Since all knowledge and all purpose aim at some good, what is this that we say is the aim of politics; or, in other words, what is the highest of all realizable goods?

As to its name, I suppose nearly all men are agreed, because the masses and men of culture alike declare that it is happiness [eudaimonia] and hold that to "live well" or to "do well" is the same as to be "happy."

But they differ as to what this happiness [eudaimonia] is, and the masses do not give the same account of it as the philosophers. The former take it to be something clear and obvious such as pleasure, wealth, or fame. One man holds it to be this, and another that. Often the same man is of different minds at different times: After sickness it is health, and in poverty it is wealth. When they are impressed with the consciousness of their own ignorance, they admire most those who say grand things that are above their comprehension.

On the other hand, some philosophers have thought that, besides these particular good things, there is an "absolute" good [such as Plato's Form of the Good], which is the cause of whatever good there is in these particular good things.

As it would hardly be worthwhile to review all the opinions that have been held, we will confine ourselves to those that are most popular or seem to have some foundation in reason.

The "former" are the _____
_____.

Aristotle says the supreme good is _____ and his

only reason thus far is _____

_____.

What does Aristotle mean when he says, "after sickness it is health, and in poverty it is wealth. When they are impressed with the consciousness of their ignorance, they admire most those who say grand things that are above their comprehension"?

The "it" he is referring to is _____.

The general point he is making about the masses is _____

_____

_____.

Underline the various incorrect views of happiness in this chapter.

5. What Are Other Incorrect Views of the Supreme Good, Happiness [Eudaimonia]?

As to men's notions of the good or happiness [eudaimonia], it seems that the masses, to judge from their lives, hold it to be pleasure and so accept the life of pleasure as their ideal.

The three most well known kinds of life are the life of pleasure, the life of the statesman, and the contemplative life.

The mass of men are completely slavish in their preference for the life of brute beasts, but their views must be considered because many of those in high places have the tastes of Sardanapalus.

Cultivated and active men prefer honor because I suppose we may say that honor is the aim of the statesman's life. But this seems too superficial to be the good we are seeking, for honor appears to depend on those who give rather than those who receive it, while we have the feeling that the good is something that is uniquely a man's own and cannot easily be taken away from him.

The difference between honor and the good is that honor is

_____

_____

_____

while the good is _____

_____

_____

Moreover, these same men seem to pursue honor so that they can be assured of their own virtue. At least they wish to be honored by intelligent men and those who know them on the basis of their virtue. It is plain, then, that in their view virtue is better than honor; and perhaps we should take this to be the end of the statesman's life, rather than honor.

But virtue also cannot be the goal we want, because it seems that a man might have virtue and yet be asleep or inactive all his life and might, moreover, meet with the greatest disasters and misfortunes. No one would maintain that such a man is happy [possesses eudaimonia], except for argument's sake. We will not dwell on those matters now, for they are sufficiently discussed in [my] popular treatises.

The third kind of life is the life of contemplation: We will discuss it further on.

As for the money-making life, it lacks freedom and wealth. It is evidently not the good we search for because it is merely useful as a means to something else. Thus we might take pleasure, virtue, or excellence to be ends rather than wealth, for they are chosen on their own account. But it seems that not even they are the end, though much breath has been wasted in attempts to show that they are.

Think about ends and means. You pull weeds, not as an end in itself, but to produce a weedless lawn. A weedless lawn might be a means to the end of selling your house; selling your house might be a means to the end of retiring by the seashore; you might retire by the seashore to pursue some hobby; and so forth. Each end was *a* good but not *the* good, not the supreme good that your whole life and every action are ultimately aimed at. But is there any end that is not a means to something else? Is there an end of all ends? Aristotle would say, as I pointed out earlier, that happiness (eudaimonia) is the end that we all strive for. We do not achieve happiness (eudaimonia) so that we can go on to something further. Happiness (eudaimonia) is the genuine end, the supreme good.

Before Aristotle explains his definition of happiness, he refutes Plato's doctrine of the Form of the Good. Aristotle agrees that the good is the end or goal of life but does not agree that this good is the Form of the Good. This chapter is the most difficult in Book I. Read slowly.

6. What Are the Arguments Against Plato's Doctrine of the Form of the Good?

Dismissing those views, then, we must now consider the Form of the Good, and state the difficulties it presents; though such an inquiry is not a pleasant task because of our friendship with the author of the Doctrine of Ideas. But we believe that this is the right course, and that in the interests of truth we ought to sacrifice even what is nearest to us, especially as we call ourselves philosophers. Both are dear to us, but it is a sacred duty to give the preference to truth. . . .

[The first and second refutations are omitted.]

Thirdly, since there is but one science of all the things that come under one idea, there would be but one science of all good things; but as it is, there are many sciences of good things; there are many sciences even of the goods that come under one category; for example, the science that deals with the correct or good timing in war is strategy, but the science that deals with the correct or good timing in curing disease is medicine. The science of the correct or good amount in regard to food is medicine, but the science that deals with the correct or good amount in regard to exercise is the science of gymnastics.

Fourth, one might ask what those who hold the Theory of Forms mean by the absolute. In *absolute man* and *man* the word *man* has one and the same sense because in regard to manhood there will be no difference between them. Thus, there will be no difference in regard to goodness between absolute good and good.

Fifthly, they do not make the good any more good by making it eternal. A white thing that lasts a long time is no whiter than what lasts but a day. . . .

Good, then, is not a term that is applied to all these things alike in the same sense or with reference to one common Idea or Form. . . .

We can dismiss the further consideration of the Idea because even granting that this term *good*, which is applied to all these different things, has one and the same meaning throughout, or that there is an absolute good apart from these particulars, it is evident that this good will not be anything that man can realize or attain. But it is a good of this kind [that can be attained] that we are now seeking.

It might perhaps be thought that it would nevertheless be well to acquaint ourselves with this Form of the Good, with a view to the goods that are attainable and realizable. With this for a pattern, it may be said, we shall more readily know our own good and, knowing, achieve it.

There certainly is some plausibility in this argument, but it seems to be at variance with the existing sciences, because though they are all aiming at some good and striving to fill up their gaps [of knowledge], they neglect to inquire about this form of the good. It is unlikely that the practitioners of the arts and sciences should not know or even look for what would help them so much.

I also wonder how the weaver or the carpenter would be aided in his craft by a knowledge of the Form of the Good, or how a man would be more able to heal the sick or command an army by contemplation of the pure form or idea. It seems to me that the physician does not seek for health in this abstract way but for the health of man—or rather of some particular man, for it is individuals that he has to heal.

The "author" Aristotle refers to is _____.

Underline Aristotles's key points in each of the following arguments.

The words "this argument" refer to _____
_____
_____
_____.

Aristotle's point in this argument is _____
_____
_____
_____.

Let me guide you through one of Aristotle's refutations of Plato's doctrine of the Form of the Good.

Aristotle says in his third refutation, "Thirdly, since there is but one science of all the things that come under one concept, there would be but one science of all good things."

Aristotle is saying that just as biology is the study of all kinds of life, we could reason that there would be a study of all kinds of goods (good food, good luck, good people) if there really were a Form of the Good. Since life has common characteristics, we can study it under one science, biology. Because there is no "science of the good," there cannot be any common characteristics that all good things share; therefore, there is no Form of the Good. Try putting this argument in your own words, but use a science other than biology.

Aristotle seems to be saying _____

_____

_____

_____

_____.

Then Aristotle says:

but as it is, there are many sciences of good things; there are many sciences even of the goods that come under one category. For example, the science that deals with the correct or good timing in war is strategy, but the science that deals with the correct or good timing in curing disease is medicine. The science of the correct or good amount in regard to food is medicine, but the science that deals with the correct or good amount in regard to exercise is the science of gymnastics.

Aristotle describes the good or right opportunity (different things in war and medicine) and the good or right amount (different things in medicine and gymnastics). How does this observation refute Plato?

I would have to say _____

_____

_____.

Summing up some of Aristotle's main points in this selection, _____

_____

_____

_____

_____.

This chapter is divided into two parts. Note that Aristotle now returns to the description of happiness.

7A. *What Is the Supreme Good for Mankind, and What Arguments Support This View?*

Leaving these matters let us return once more to the question, What is the nature of the good we are seeking?

This good seems to be different in different kinds of action and in different arts—one thing in medicine, another in war, and so on. What then is the good in each of these cases? Surely it is that for the sake of which all else is done. In medicine the end is health, in war it is victory, in building it is a house—a different thing in each different case—but there is always, in whatever we do and in whatever we choose, an end or goal. For it is always for the sake of the end that all else is done.

If then there be one end of all that man does, this end—or these ends, if there be more than one—will be the good attainable by action.

Our argument has thus come round by a different path to the same point as before. [Chapter 2] This point we must try to explain more clearly.

We see that there are many ends. But some of these are chosen only as means, as wealth, flutes, and the whole class of instruments. So it is plain that not all ends are final. But the supreme good must be something final. If there is only one final end, this will be what we are seeking—or if there are more than one, the most final of them.

Whatever is pursued as an end in itself is more final than whatever is pursued as means to something else. And whatever is never chosen as a means is more final than whatever is chosen both as an end in itself and as a means to another end. The strictly final end is the one that is always chosen as an end in itself and never as a means.

Happiness [eudaimonia] seems more than anything else to answer to this description, for we always choose happiness for itself and never for the sake of something else. On the other hand, we choose honor, pleasure, reason, and all virtue or excellence partly for themselves but partly also for the sake of happiness [eudaimonia], because we believe that they will help make us happy. But no one chooses happiness [eudaimonia] for the sake of these things or as a means to anything else at all.

We seem to be led to the same conclusion when we start from the notion of self-sufficiency.

The final good is thought to be self-sufficient. An example of the way we are using this term [self-sufficient] is that we do not regard a man as a solitary self, but we also take account of parents, children, wife, and, in short, friends and fellow citizens generally, since man is by nature a political being. Some limit must indeed be set to this, because if you go on to parents and descendants and friends of friends, you will never come to a stop. But this we will consider further on. For the present we will take self-sufficient to mean what by itself makes life desirable and lacking in nothing. Happiness [eudaimonia] is believed to answer this description.

Furthermore, happiness [eudaimonia] is believed to be the most desirable thing in the world and not merely one among other good things. If it were merely one among other good things (so that other things could be added to it), it is plain that the addition of the least of other goods must make it more

The reason no one chooses happiness as a means to another

end is _____

_____

_____.

The "conclusion" Aristotle refers to is _____

_____

_____.

desirable. The reason for this is that the addition would produce an extra amount of good, and of two goods the greater is always more desirable.

   Thus it seems that happiness [eudaimonia] is something final and self-sufficient and is the end of all that man does.

Label two of the main points you underlined in this chapter as A and B; put them in your own words and give an original example of each.

I underlined "_____

_____

_____."

What Aristotle means in A is _____

_____

_____

_____

_____.

An example of this would be _____

_____

_____.

I also underlined "_____

_____

_____."

What Aristotle means in B is _____

_____

_____

_____

_____.

An example of this would be _____

_____

_____.

Put this passage into your own words:

Whatever is pursued as an end in itself is more final than whatever is pursued as means to something else. And whatever is never chosen as a means is more final than whatever is chosen both as an end in itself and as a means to another end. The strictly final end is the one that is always chosen as an end in itself and never as a means.

In the first sentence Aristotle is saying _____

_____.

For example, _____.

In the second sentence his point is _____

_____.

For example, _____.

In the third sentence _____

_____

Aristotle's example of this is _____.

Note how Aristotle expands his description of eudaimonia in this section by linking it to human purpose.

Underline Aristotle's answer to the question posed in the title to 7B.

7B. *What Is Happiness* [*Eudaimonia*], *and How Does It Relate to the Purpose of Man?*

But perhaps the reader thinks that though no one will dispute the statement that happiness [eudaimonia] is the best thing in the world; nonetheless, a still more precise definition of it is needed.

This will be achieved, I think, by asking: "What is the purpose of man?" Just as the goodness and the excellence of a flute player, or a sculptor, or any craftsman—and generally of those who have any special job or profession—lies in that purpose, so man's good seems to lie in his purpose, if he has one.

But can we suppose that, while a carpenter and a cobbler have purposes and specialized activities of their own, man has no specialized activities and no purpose assigned him by nature? Surely as each part of his body—eye, hand, and foot—obviously has its own purpose, so we must suppose that man also has some purpose above all these.

What is it?

Man evidently has life in common even with the plants, but we want a characteristic that is peculiar to him. Therefore we must exclude the life of mere nutrition and growth.

Next to this comes the life of sense perception; but this too man plainly shares with horses and cattle and all kinds of animals.

There remains then the life whereby he acts—the life of his rational soul, with its two sides or divisions, one rational in that it obeys the rule of reason, the other rational as it actually possesses and exercises the power of reasoning. . . .

The purpose of man, then, is an activity of the soul in conformity with reason, or at least not divided from reason. . . .

Man's purpose being, as we say, a kind of life—that is to say, exercise of

What man shares with plants is

_____.

What is unique about man is

_____

_____.

his soul in conformity with reason—the good man's purpose is to do this well and beautifully or nobly. And the purpose of anything is done well when it is done in accordance with the excellence or virtue of that thing. Putting all this together, then, we find that the good of man is an activity of his soul in accordance with virtue, or, if there be more than one, in accordance with the best and most complete virtue.

But there must also be a complete life span for this activity; for one swallow or one fine day does not make a spring, nor does one day or any small space of time make a blessed or happy man.

This may be taken as a rough outline of the good, because this, I think, is the proper method: first to sketch the outline and then to fill in the details. It seems that, once the outline is well done, anyone can carry on the work and fill in the items that time reveals to us or helps us to find. And indeed this is the way in which the arts and sciences have grown, because it requires no extraordinary genius to fill up the gaps.

However, we must bear in mind what was said above and not demand the same degree of accuracy in all branches of study, but in each case only as much as the subject matter allows and as is proper to that kind of inquiry. The carpenter and the geometer both look for the right angle, but in different ways. The former wants only the kind of approximation that his work requires, but the latter wants to know what constitutes a right angle, or what is its special quality. His aim is to find out the truth. And so in other cases we must follow the same course lest we spend more time on smaller points than the major task.

Aristotle's definition of happiness (eudaimonia) is "_____
_____
_____."

Now think about the concept of purpose. The purpose of a hammer is obviously

to _____.

The purpose of a pen is obviously to _____.

Aristotle says the purpose of a man is _____

_____

_____.

From Aristotle's point of view, everything that exists has a special purpose, something that it is suited for better than any other thing. Just as the parts of humans have a purpose (the eye to see, the ear to hear, and so forth) humans as a whole must have some special purpose. Fulfilling this purpose, which humans alone can do, would result in fulfillment or happiness (eudaimonia). The human purpose, as Aristotle pointed out, is "an activity of the soul in accordance with virtue." To live in accordance with virtue is to fulfill the unique potential of the human soul; nothing else in the universe has this potential. Remember that Aristotelian virtue involves avoiding excess and deficiency by choosing the middle path.

In the following section Aristotle shows how well-known views of eudaimonia support his definition. This is an important test of the truth of ethical statements for Aristotle. While Plato and Aristotle take the aristocratic position that the masses are generally foolish, Aristotle takes the paradoxical view that even though the masses live foolishly, somehow the norms and popular opinions of society hold wisdom. Often in the *Nicomachean Ethics* Aristotle tests his conclusions to see how well they accord with what is generally believed to be true.

Underline answers to the title question and information about Aristotle's view of possessions.

8. *What Other Current Views Support This Account of Happiness* [*Eudaimonia*]?

We must not be satisfied, then, with examining this starting point or principle of ours as a conclusion from our data but must also view it in its relation to current opinions on the subject. All facts harmonize with a true principle, but a false one is soon found to be incompatible with the facts.

Our account [of happiness], again, is in harmony with the common saying that the happy man lives well and does well because we may say that happiness [eudaimonia], according to us, is living well and doing well.

And, indeed, all the characteristics that men expect to find in happiness [eudaimonia] seem to belong to happiness as we define it.

Some hold it to be virtue or excellence, some prudence, others a kind of wisdom; others, again, hold it to be all or some of these, with the addition of pleasure, either as an ingredient or as a necessary accompaniment; and some even include external prosperity in their account of it.

Now some of these views have the support of many voices and of traditional authorities; others have few voices, but those are held in high prestige. It is probable that neither one side nor the other is entirely wrong but that in some one point at least, if not in most, they are both right.

First, then, the view that happiness [eudaimonia] is virtue or a kind of virtue harmonizes with our account because "actions of the soul in conformity with virtue" belong to virtue.

But I think we may say that it makes no small difference whether the good is conceived as the mere possession of something or as its use—as a disposition, or as the exercise of that disposition. For the disposition may be present and yet produce no good result, as when a man is asleep or in any other way hindered from his function; but with its exercise this is not possible for it must show itself in acts and in good acts. Just as at the Olympic games it is not the fairest and strongest who receive the crown but those who contend, for among these are the victors, in life the winners are those who not only have all the virtues but also act on them.

Furthermore, the life of these men is in itself pleasant because pleasure belongs to the soul, and each man takes pleasure in what he is said to love— he who loves horses in horses, he who loves theater in plays. In the same way he who loves justice takes pleasure in acts of justice, and generally the lover of excellence or virtue takes pleasure in virtuous acts. . . .

And while with most men there is a perpetual conflict among the many things in which they find pleasure, since these are not naturally pleasant, those who love what is noble take pleasure in that which is naturally pleasant. . . .

What Aristotle is going to do in this chapter is _____

_____

_____

because _____

_____

The comparison Aristotle makes between successful Olympic athletes and virtuous individuals is that both _____

_____

_____

_____

_____

Their life [those who do virtuous acts], then, does not need pleasure to be added to it as an appendage but contains pleasure in itself.

Indeed, in addition to what we have said, a man is not good at all unless he takes pleasure in noble deeds. No one would call a man just who did not take pleasure in doing justice nor generous who took no pleasure in acts of generosity, and so on.

If this be so, the actions performed in conformity with virtue will be pleasant in themselves. But they are also both good and noble in the highest degree, at least if the man of good character's judgment about them is right. . . .

Happiness [eudaimonia], then, is the best and noblest and pleasantest thing in the world, and these are not separated, as the Delian inscription would have them be:

What is most just is noblest, health is best,
Pleasantest is to get your heart's desire.

For all these characteristics are united in the best activities of our soul, and these, or some one of them that is better than all the others, we identify with happiness [eudaimonia].

Nevertheless, happiness [eudaimonia] plainly requires external goods because it is impossible, or at least not easy, to act nobly without some material goods. There are many things that can only be done through instruments, so to speak, such as friends, and wealth, and political influence. There are some things whose absence takes the bloom from our happiness [eudaimonia], as good birth, the blessing of children, personal beauty. A man is not likely to be happy if he is very ugly, or of low birth, or alone in the world, or childless, and perhaps still less if he has worthless children or friends or has lost good ones that he had.

As we said, then, happiness seems to stand in need of this kind of prosperity, and so some identify it with good fortune, just as others identify it with virtue.

Aristotle's point in this paragraph is _____

_____

_____

_____

_____

_____.

Here is an interesting problem to try to solve before you begin reading the next chapter. Aristotle's definition of eudaimonia is "an activity of the soul in conformity with virtue." Under this definition, could an animal be called happy? Could a child?

Thinking about whether or not an animal could be happy, I personally would say

_____

_____ because _____

_____

_____.

Aristotle, according to his definition, would probably say _____

_____

_____.

About a child he would say _____

_____ because _____

_____

_____. My own view is _____

_____

_____. Two pieces of evidence to support my view

are first _____

_____ and second _____

_____ .

Now see what Aristotle says.

9. *Is Happiness [Eudaimonia] Acquired or a Gift of the Gods or of Chance?*

This has led people to ask whether happiness [eudaimonia] is acquired by learning, the formation of habits, or any other kind of training or comes by some divine gift or even by chance.

Well, if the gods do give gifts to men, happiness [eudaimonia] is likely to be among these gifts, more likely than anything else, in proportion as it is better than all other human things.

This belongs more properly to another branch of inquiry, but we may say that even if happiness is not a gift of the gods, but comes as a consequence of virtue or some kind of learning or training, it still seems to be one of the most divine things in the world because the crown and end of virtue appears to be better than anything else and something divine and blessed.

Again, if it is thus acquired, it will be widely accessible because it will then be in the power of all, except those who have lost the capacity for virtue, to acquire it by study and diligence.

The words "this way" refer to

_____

_____ .

And if it is better that men should attain happiness [eudaimonia] in this way rather than by chance, it is reasonable to suppose that it is so, since in the realm of nature all things are arranged in the best possible way. This is also true in the realm of art, and of any kind of causation, and most of all in the realm of the highest kind of causation. Indeed it would be too absurd to leave what is highest and fairest to the mercy of chance.

But our definition itself clears up the difficulty because happiness [eudaimonia] was defined as a certain kind of activity of the soul in accordance with virtue. Of the remaining goods, other than happiness [eudaimonia] itself, some must be present as necessary prerequisites, while others are aids and useful instruments to happiness [eudaimonia]. This agrees with what we said at the beginning. We then established that the end of the science of politics is the best of all ends, but the chief purpose of that science is to make citizens of a certain character, that is, good and disposed to perform virtuous actions. It is not without reason, then, that we do not call an ox, or a horse, or any brute happy because none of them is able to share in this kind of activity.

For the same reason also a child is not happy; he is as yet, because of his age, unable to perform such things [that is, activities of the soul in conformity with virtue]. If we ever call a child happy, it is because we hope he has promise of doing them in the future. For, as we said, happiness [eudaimonia] requires not only perfect excellence or virtue but also a full term of years for its exercise. Our life is liable to many changes and to all sorts of chances, and it is possible that he who is most prosperous now will in his old age meet with great disasters, as is told of Priam in the tales of the heroes. A man who thus encounters such blows of fate and comes to a miserable end cannot be called happy.

In regard to the happiness [eudaimonia] of animals and children, Aristotle says

"_____

_____

_____ _____." His point is

_____

_____

_____.

EXERCISE 14.2
Review of *Nichomachean Ethics*

Review your notes and then, using your own paper, answer each of these chapter title questions.

1. What do all human actions aim at?

2. What science studies the supreme good?

3. Why can't the investigation of politics be exact?

4. What is the supreme good, and what are some of the views about it?

5. What are other incorrect views of the supreme good, happiness (eudaimonia)?

6. What are the arguments against Plato's doctrine of the Form of the Good? (Try to state the one we went through together.)

7A. What is the supreme good for mankind, and what arguments support this view?

7B. What is happiness (eudaimonia), and how does it relate to the function of man?

8. What other current views support this account of happiness (eudaimonia)?

9. Is happiness (eudaimonia) acquired or a gift of the gods or of chance?

SUMMARY

The purpose of human life may lie beyond this world or within this world, or human life may have no purpose. Aristotle holds that the purpose of human life lies within this world and is achieved by reasoning excellently.

Unlike Plato, who believes that body and soul are separable, Aristotle believes that body and soul are intimately united. Because the human soul is the human life force and is indivisible from the body, the soul cannot survive death. Our soul contains a hierarchy of powers. With all plants we share the capacity for nutrition; with all animals we share the capacity for perception and reproduction; with all humans we share the capacity for reason.

The purpose of human life is to achieve eudaimonia, human flourishing. Eudaimonia requires that we reason excellently, choose the middle path between extremes, and have a reasonable amount of external good fortune. In addition, achieving eudaimonia requires that we dedicate ourselves to philosophical contemplation over an entire life.

EXERCISE 14.3
Looking Back

Use your own paper to answer the following questions. I've added a few not stated in chapter subheads.

1. What are three views of life's purpose?

2. What is a human being?

3. What are some differences between Plato's and Aristotle's view of a human being?

4. What is the purpose of human life?

5. What are five lessons Aristotle teaches about the purpose of human life?

EXERCISE 14.4
Looking at the World Through Aristotle's Eyes

How would Aristotle answer each of the following? Provide evidence from this chapter that supports your answer.

1. T   F   No soul survives death.

    Evidence: _____

    _____.

2. T   F   Body and soul are in a constant struggle.

    Evidence: _____

    _____.

3. T   F   Understanding the Form of the Good is the goal of human life.

    Evidence: _____

    _____.

4. T F It is possible to reason excellently and be a bad person.

Evidence: _____

_____ .

5. T F "The road of excess leads to the palace of wisdom." (William Blake, English Romantic poet)

Evidence: _____

_____ .

6. T F The best life is the life of the fewest possessions.

Evidence: _____

_____ .

EXERCISE 14.5
Finding the Middle Path

According to Aristotle, we should avoid excess and deficiency by choosing the middle path in all our actions. In addition, this middle path can vary from individual to individual. For you, what is too much, too little, the right amount, and the *actual* amount of each of the following activities? Record the time measured in hours per week.

	Too much	Too little	Right amount	Actual amount
Studying				
Watching television				
Spending time with friends				
Exercising				
House (or apartment room) cleaning				
Daydreaming				
Earning money				
Praying (or any other spiritual activity)				
Reading (non-school) materials				
Engaging in a hobby (or any other leisure activity)				
Partying				

How close are you to Aristotle's portrait of the virtuous life? Score as follows: Give yourself 1 point for each activity that is excessive or deficient. The lower your score, the closer you are to human excellence and your weekly share of eudaimonia.

ANALYSIS OF YOUR PHILOSOPHICAL SELF-PORTRAIT

To see how some of your ethical beliefs stack up against Aristotle's, read my analysis below, rethink your position, and then circle what you believe is the correct answer. I've underlined Aristotle's answers.

1. T <u>F</u> *A good person obeys God's commandments.*

   If you believe a good person obeys God's commandments, then you also believe that life's purpose lies beyond this world. According to Aristotle, God has no involvement in human affairs. God is the philosopher in the sky thinking about his own thinking. Our purpose is to perfect our human nature, which means to reason excellently by avoiding excess and deficiency and contemplating philosophical truths.

2. T <u>F</u> *Human life has no purpose.*

   In Aristotle's view, the purpose of human life is continuously before us. Our goal is not somewhere out in the future; it is not, for example, to get a great job or live in a great place. If we reason excellently, then we are achieving our purpose every moment of our life.

   If you're like many students, you find this refreshing. Too often we live as if our purpose is out of our grasp, a carrot on a stick. Every day that you reason excellently is a day you have achieved that day's entire goal. We live superbly when we reason superbly; we live terribly when we reason terribly. According to Aristotle, this is because our reason is what is divine in us. He even terms reason our "inner god." Every day that we listen to the inner god of our reason, we are flourishing human beings.

3. T <u>F</u> *It is possible to live irrationally and be happy.*

   Almost no philosopher, and especially no Greek philosopher, would agree with this. As you can tell by now, the Greeks placed a great emphasis upon the connection between reasoning well and being happy. According to Plato, when you reason well and control your desires, you can be happy, even serene, in prison. According to Aristotle, it is not that reasoning well brings the deepest happiness, but it is that reasoning well *is* the deepest happiness. Christian philosophers, on the other hand, take a different view of human faculties. St. Augustine, for example, stresses the primacy of will. A good person is not so much a person who reasons well, but one whose will submits to God.

4. <u>T</u> F *Virtue lies in choosing the middle path between extremes.*

   Aristotle certainly disagrees with some versions of Christian ethics. According to some Christians, it is impossible to have too much humility or self-denial. In Aristotle's view, to think too little of ourselves is just as much a vice as to think too much of ourselves. We should steer the middle course, aiming at proper self-regard, avoiding the deficiency of self-denial and the excess of self-love.

   Evaluation: Number of points in agreement with Aristotle = _____ of 4 possible.

   A position of Aristotle's that you strongly (support, oppose) is _____

   _____

because _____

_____

_____

GOOD BOOKS

Biffle, Christopher, *A Guided Tour of Selections from Aristotle's* Nicomachean Ethics. Mountain View, Calif.: Mayfield, 1991. An introduction for philosophy students by a likable author.

Hardie, W. F. R. *Aristotle's Ethical Theory.* Oxford: Clarendon Press, 1968. A good companion to the *Nicomachean Ethics.*

Taylor, A. E. *Aristotle.* New York: Dover, 1955. A nontechnical introduction to Aristotle.

NEXT STOP

Epicurus, the apostle of pleasure. If it feels just right, do it repeatedly.

15

Epicurus
Life's Purpose Is Wise Pleasure

YOUR PHILOSOPHICAL SELF-PORTRAIT

Add more details to your philosophical self-portrait by answering the questions below and offering evidence for your answers.

1. T F The soul survives death.

    Evidence: _____
    _____.

2. T F Thinking about the certainty of death will make us enjoy our life more fully.

    Evidence: _____
    _____.

3. T F All pleasurable actions are moral.

    Evidence: _____
    _____.

4. T F All moral actions produce pleasure.

    Evidence: _____
    _____.

5. T F A life with a few possessions produces more pleasure than a life with many possessions.

    Evidence: _____
    _____.

6. T F Humans should seek pleasure and avoid pain.

    Evidence: _____
    _____.

7. T F All that humans do is seek pleasure and avoid pain.

    Evidence: _____
    _____.

8. T F God has no control over our life.

    Evidence: _____
    _____.

After briefly investigating Democritus's atomism, which provides a key idea for Epicurus's metaphysics, we examine Epicurus's "Letter to Menoeceus." Epicurus argues that philosophy can be profitably studied by both the young and the old, that the gods exist but have no concern for the human realm, that we should not fear death, and that the life of simple pleasures is the highest good.

You are a mass of worries, have two great fears, and don't know what life's all about.

You worry about your grades, your current job, your future career, your current bills, your future bills, your health, your car, your clothes, your peace of mind (and lack of it), and your choices (and how to tell a good one from a bad one); in other words, you worry about . . . everything.

And you have a deep fear of death.

And you are afraid that God will punish you.

And, despite what you've read thus far on the tour, you still don't know the purpose of life.

Epicurus has the answer to all your problems.

In 306 B.C., approximately a century after Socrates' death, Epicurus established his own school of philosophy, the Garden, in Athens. Of almost saintlike disposition, he was deeply admired by his followers. Epicurus preached and lived the simple life, wrote an enormous amount of material, of which only three "open letters" remain, and founded his philosophy upon the wise pursuit of pleasure. Epicureanism, as a united body of teaching handed down from generation to generation, survived for more than 500 years.

In Epicurus's view, all your worries stem from either unnatural or unnecessary desires. Unnatural desires are desires that you are not born with and are thus not a genuine part of your human nature; unnecessary desires are simply desires that you do not need to fulfill. By satisfying only your *necessary, natural* desires, you will eliminate all your worries!

Following Epicurus's advice will not only eliminate your worries but also remove your fear of death and God's punishment. In addition, Epicurus will teach you, despite what you've learned from Socrates, Plato, and Aristotle, the *true* purpose of life.

No more worries? No more fears? And life's true purpose? Epicurus, in one of the shortest documents on the tour, reveals All.

To present his main views, I need to answer only two questions:

- How did Democritus influence Epicurus's metaphysics?

- What is the message of Epicurus's "Letter to Menoeceus"?

Let's begin with Epicurus's philosophical background.

Epicurus (341–270 B.C.)

Catholic philosopher George Santayana wrote that the philosophy of Epicurus, with its emphasis on serenity and escape from pain, is "perhaps the greatest thought that mankind has ever hit upon."[1] Epicurus was born to Athenian parents on Samos, a prosperous and picturesque island of vineyards and olive orchards, located in the Aegean Sea off the southeast coast of Greece.

Epicurus grew up toward the end of the Golden Age of ancient Greek philosophy. Though Aristotle's school was founded in Athens when Epicurus was a boy and Plato's Academy still

---

[1] Quoted in Henry Thomas, *Understanding the Great Philosophers* (Garden City, N.Y.: Doubleday, 1962), p. 140.

flourished, no Greek thinkers after Plato and Aristotle would come close to their genius.

During the reign of Macedonian king Alexander the Great from 336 to 323 B.C., Greek ideas and culture spread rapidly through the civilized world to the East. The untimely death of Alexander in 323 B.C. was followed by a period of insecurity and skepticism. The Hellenistic Age—the period running from the death of Alexander to the annexation of the last Greek state, Egypt, by the Romans in 31 B.C.—was ushered in with constant warring between Alexander's generals, each greedy for his piece of their dead leader's empire.

When Epicurus was about thirty-five, he settled in Athens, where he established his own school and community. Epicurus wanted his community to be a haven in a world of uncertainty as well as a model of the good life. The Garden, as it was known, gained notoriety for including women, at least one slave, and even philosophically inclined prostitutes.

A gentle and generous man, Epicurus spent much of his time writing to friends and their children. Friendship was extremely important to Epicurus and he had a genius for it:

> Cultivate this [friendship] greatest of all our blessings. Make a religion of it. Worship it.
>
> For friendship is a sweet and beautiful and holy thing. The sympathy of true friendship is the only certain gift we possess in this world of doubtful values.

How Did Democritus Influence Epicurus's Metaphysics?

It may surprise you to know that the belief that all things are made of atoms was first presented by an ancient Greek philosopher. Democritus (460–370 B.C.) developed the theory of atomism originally proposed by his teacher, Leucippus. Democritus described reality as

> atoms and empty space; everything else is merely thought to exist. The worlds are unlimited; they come into being and perish. Nothing can come into being

Epicurus (continued)

If the sufferings can reconcile us to death, the joys of friendship can reconcile us to life.[2]

A man of great charisma and wisdom, Epicurus was revered by many of his followers as almost a demigod. Unlike Aristotle, Epicurus taught that happiness was *ataraxia,* freedom from inner turmoil, not *eudaimonia,* human flourishing. Although Epicurus has sometimes been accused of promoting a life of self-indulgence, this is a gross misinterpretation of his philosophy. Instead, Epicurus taught that we need to learn how to control our desires and engage in honest self-examination if we are to achieve happiness. Epicurus himself led a simple life. A meal of barley bread shared with a friend was sufficient for him.

Epicurus wanted to make his teachings available to everyone, regardless of education, social status, or gender. For those who wanted a short course in philosophy, there were maxims that could be memorized. More detailed writings were available for those who wanted to delve more deeply into philosophy.

The community's focus on happiness and friendship, instead of on abstract philosophical ideas, led to its ridicule by opponents. Despite its detractors, the Garden thrived.

Toward the end of his life, Epicurus was beset by a painful obstruction of the bladder. He wrote in a letter to a friend, "I am now passing through the last day of my life. . . . I am wracked with torments which the body can no longer endure. But over against all this, I set my joy in the recollection of our thoughts and words in the past."[3] Surrounded by his friends, he died a peaceful death with no fear for the future.

After the death of Epicurus, his followers took over the school, which continued to flourish for the next five centuries. Other highly successful Epicurean communities, which were as much communes as colleges, were also established. Epicureanism not only enjoyed great popularity throughout the Greek-speaking world, but also influenced the teachings of modern philosophers such as Voltaire, Rousseau, Jeremy Bentham, and John Stuart Mill.

Although Epicurus wrote many books, only a few of his writings have been preserved. These include three letters. The first, the "Letter to Herodotus," includes a summary of his physics. His "Letter to Menoeceus" (see this chapter) summarizes his ethics, and the "Letter to Pythocles" summarizes his meteorology and astronomy.

---

[2] Quoted in Henry Thomas, *Understanding the Great Philosophers*, p. 139.

[3] Quoted in Henry Thomas, *Understanding the Great Philosophers*, p. 140.

---

from that which is not nor pass away into that which is not. Further the atoms are unlimited in size and number, and they are borne along in the whole universe in a **vortex,** and thereby generate all composite things—fire, water, air, earth; for even these are conglomerations of given atoms. And it is because of their solidity that these atoms are impassive and unalterable. The sun and the moon have been composed of such smooth and spherical masses [atoms] and so also the soul, which is identical with reason.[1]

vortex A swirling movement of air or water which draws particles to its center. For example, a tornado and water pouring down a drain are examples of a vortex.

---

[1] From *Early Greek Philosophy,* trans. J. Burnet (London: C. Black, 1920) p. 316.

The English word "atom" comes from the Greek *atom*, meaning, literally, "not cut." Thus, Democritus's atoms are the smallest possible (not cuttable) units of matter. In addition to being infinitely small and indivisible, Democritus also holds that atoms are eternal and indestructible. Our world was generated from a vortex of atoms and, because space, "the void" in Democritus's terms, is infinite, is only one of many possible worlds. Thus, the universe we live in has neither design nor purpose and is simply the result of the mechanistic conglomeration of infinitely small particles. Our souls, also composed of atoms, simply "come apart" at death.

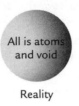

All is atoms and void

Reality

There is no freedom in Democritus's universe. Just as the movement of a sand dune is completely determined by the movement of sand grains, so the motion of everything in the universe is completely determined by the motion of atoms. In Democritus's view, we have no more choice in our actions than a sand dune has a choice in its shape.

Epicurus built his metaphysics, with one crucial modification, upon Democritus's atoms. Epicurus agrees that all is atoms but holds that as atoms fall through infinite space, their motion is not purely mechanical. Atoms can, as Epicurus put it, "swerve." In other words, the motion of atoms is not entirely determined by the sum total of the mechanical forces operating upon them. Epicurus never described what made swerving possible, but this unpredictability in the universe allowed him to argue that humans are free. Without human freedom, the ability to choose right from wrong—ethical action—is not possible.

Now with this in mind, let's turn to Epicurus's ethics.

What Is the Message of Epicurus's "Letter to Menoeceus"?

Here is the first paragraph of Epicurus's "Letter to Menoeceus."

> Let no one when young delay to study philosophy, nor when he is old grow weary of his study. For no one can come too early or too late to secure the health of his soul. And the man who says that the age for philosophy has either not yet come or has gone by is like the man who says that the age for happiness is not yet come to him, or has passed away. Wherefore both when young and old a man must study philosophy, that as he grows old he may be young in blessings through the grateful recollection of what has been, and that in youth he may be old as well, since he will know no fear or what is to come. We must then meditate on the things that make our happiness, seeing that when that is with us we have all, but when it is absent we do all to win it.[2]

If humans are not free, then it makes no sense to describe what they ought and ought not to do. For example, just as a robot programmed by its designer to take various actions could not be criticized for making wrong choices, so humans, programmed by God or nature or some other power, could not be criticized for making wrong choices. Whenever in daily life we criticize someone for choosing a wrong action or praise someone for choosing a right action, we implicitly assume they were free to do otherwise. Thus, at least so far as daily life is concerned, we are all "free willists." Epicurus was the first philosopher to explicitly defend the concept of free will.

---

[2] From *Epicurus: The Extent Remains*, trans. Cyril Bailey (New York: Oxford University Press, 1926).

This paragraph can be thought of as evidence for the conclusion stated in the first sentence, "Let no one when young delay to study philosophy, nor when he is old grow weary of his study."

Paraphrase Epicurus's evidence for this conclusion.

_____

_____

_____

_____ .

Part of Epicurus's argument is an argument by analogy. An analogy is a comparison. Thus, if I say life is like a seven-course meal, I am making a comparison, an analogy, between life and a seven-course meal. If I *argue* by analogy, then I would be using this comparison to support a conclusion. Thus, I could argue that because life is like a seven-course meal, you should enjoy every moment. Of course, the strength of an argument by analogy rests upon the strength of the comparison. *If* life is truly like a seven-course meal, then it would make sense to conclude that one should enjoy every moment of life.

Here are several more arguments by analogy:

- Because the body is like a garment worn by the soul, the decay of the body has no effect upon the soul.

- Because God is like a king, he has complete power over us.

- Because the world of the senses is like a cave, we should train our minds to see a higher reality that can't be perceived by the senses.

Now, make several arguments by analogy of your own.

First, because _____ ,

_____ .

Second, because _____ ,

_____ .

Third, because _____ ,

_____ .

Epicurus presents the following analogy: "And the man who says that the age for philosophy has either not yet come or has gone by is like the man who says that the age for happiness is not yet come to him, or has passed away."

Unlike my arguments by analogies, Epicurus leaves his conclusion unstated. What point is he making?

He is drawing a comparison between _____ and

_____ . His point is _____

_____

_____ .

Now read the next paragraph of Epicurus's letter. Fill in each [_____] with the word or phrase referred to. I filled in the first for you.

The things which I used unceasingly to commend to you, these do and practice, considering them to be the first principles of the good life. First of all believe that god is a being immortal and blessed, even as the common idea of a god is engraved on men's minds, and do not assign to him [__god__] anything alien to his immortality or ill-suited to his blessedness; but believe about him everything that can uphold his blessedness and immortality. For gods there are, since the knowledge of them is by clear vision. But they [_____] are not such as the masses believe them to be; for indeed they [_____] do not consistently represent them [_____] as they [_____] believe them to be. And the impious [lacking reverence or respect] man is not he who denies the gods of the masses, but he who attaches to the gods the beliefs of the masses. For the statements of the masses about the gods are not conceptions derived from sensation, but false suppositions, according to which the greatest misfortunes befall the wicked and the greatest blessings the good by the gift of the gods. For men being accustomed always to their own virtues welcome those like themselves, but regard all that is not of their nature as alien.

"Derived from sensation" (produced by the senses)

In order to test your understanding of this passage, complete the following exercise.

EXERCISE 15.1
Understanding Epicurus

Some of the following statements are paraphrases of ideas in the selection above. Mark the accurate paraphrases A (Accurate) and the inaccurate paraphrases I (Inaccurate).

_____ 1. We should reject the beliefs of the masses.

_____ 2. Because the foolish masses believe god exists, we can be confident that god doesn't exist.

_____ 3. The masses have the wrong idea about the gods.

_____ 4. It is obvious that the gods exist.

_____ 5. The beliefs of the masses about the gods are not based on sound evidence.

_____ 6. The masses are wrong in believing that the gods punish the wicked and reward the good.

_____ 7. The gods occasionally act immorally.

_____ 8. True impiety is disbelief in the gods.

In a series of short arguments in the next paragraph of his letter, Epicurus turns his attention to death. Place a number at the beginning of each argument and fill in each [_____].

Become accustomed to the belief that death is nothing to us. For all good and evil consists in sensation, but death is deprivation of sensation. And therefore a right understanding that death is nothing to us makes the mortality of life enjoyable, not because it [_____] adds to it [_____] an infinite span of time, but because it [_____] takes away the craving for immortality. For there is nothing terrible in life for the man who has truly comprehended that there is nothing terrible in not living. So that the man speaks but idly who says that he fears death not because it will be painful when it comes but because it is painful in anticipation. For that which gives no trouble when it comes, is but an empty pain in anticipation. So death, the most terrifying of ills is nothing to us, since so long as we exist, death is not with us; but when death comes, then we do not exist. It [_____] does not then concern either the living or the dead, since for the former it is not, and the latter are no more.

Epicurus argues that we should not fear death. What is his evidence?

_____

_____

_____

Practice thinking like Epicurus. Assume you have a friend who is troubled by death. Fill in the following short dialogue with ideas consistent with Epicurus's views.

YOUR FRIEND: Death is terrible.

YOU: _____

_____

YOUR FRIEND: It's not only death, but also the fear of its approach that is terrible.

YOU: _____

_____

YOUR FRIEND: After I die, I am afraid to think of what might happen to me. Maybe I'll go to hell!

YOU: _____

_____

Underline the argument by analogy in the next paragraph.

But the masses at one moment shun death as the greatest of evils, at another yearn for it as a respite from the evils in life. But the wise man neither seeks to escape life nor fears the cessation of life, for neither does life offend him nor does the absence of life seem to be any evil. And just as with food he does not seek simply the larger share and nothing else, but rather the most pleasant, so he seeks to enjoy not the longest period of time, but the most pleasant.

According to Epicurus, what is the difference between the way the many view death and the way the wise man views death?

Sometimes the masses shun death because _____

_____.

Other times the masses look forward to death because _____

_____.

The wise man is not so contradictory because _____

_____.

Now, paraphrase Epicurus's argument by analogy.

Epicurus compares _____ to _____.

The point he is making is _____

_____

_____.

Underline important points in the next paragraph of Epicurus's letter.

And he who counsels the young man to live well but the old man to make a good end, is foolish, not merely because of the desirability of life, but also because it is the same training which teaches to live well and to die well. Yet much worse still is the man who says it is good not to be born, but "once born make haste to pass the gates of Death" [Theognis]. For if he says this from conviction why does he not pass away out of life? For it is open to him to do so, if he had firmly made up his mind to this. But if he speaks in jest, his words are idle among men who cannot receive them.

Epicurus considers two kinds of errors. What are the errors and how does he attack them?

The first error is _____.

His answer to this error is _____

_____.

The second error is _____.

In the next short paragraph Epicurus sums up his view of the future.

We must then bear in mind that the future is neither ours, nor yet wholly not ours, so that we may not altogether expect it as sure to come, nor abandon hope of it, as if it will certainly not come.

Look at some important event in your future in the way Epicurus recommends.

According to Epicurus, when I look to the future and think about _____

I should not "expect it as sure to come" because _____

_____.

But, also, I should not "abandon hope of it" because _____

_____.

Let's now summarize some of Epicurus's arguments together. I'll present his conclusions and you present at least one of his pieces of evidence.

This is a good test of your understanding of Epicurus's position. Work through it slowly.

1. Because _____

_____

_____,

philosophy is useful to the old.

2. Because _____

_____

_____,

philosophy is useful to the young.

3. Because the many believe the gods _____

_____

_____,

the many are wrong about the gods.

4. Because _____

_____

_____,

death should be no concern for the living.

5. Because _____

_____

_____,

death is no concern for the dead.

6. Because _____

_____

_____,

we should not be sure about what the future will bring.

7. Because _____

_____

_____,

we should not abandon hope about the future.

EXERCISE 15.2

Answering Epicurus

On your own paper, write Epicurus a note that summarizes what you think are the strongest and weakest points among 1–7 above. Use short arguments, similar to his, to back up your views. Try at least one argument by analogy.

In the next paragraph of his letter, Epicurus turns his attention from death to the nature of desires and the importance of pleasure. The first sentence presents a somewhat complex hierarchy.

Examples of natural desires are

_____

_____

_____ .

Examples of unnatural desires

are _____

_____

_____ .

We must consider that of desires some are natural, others vain [unnatural], and of the natural some are necessary and others merely natural [unnecessary]; and of the necessary some are necessary for happiness, others for the repose [ease] of the body, and others for life itself. The right understanding of these facts enables us to refer all choice and avoidance to the health of the body and the soul's freedom from disturbance, since this is the aim of the life of Blessedness. For it is to obtain this end that we always act, namely, to avoid pain and fear. And when this [_____] is once secured for us, all the tempest of the soul is dispersed, since the living creature has not to wander as though in search of something that is missing, and to look for some other thing by which he can fulfill the good of the soul and the good of the body. For it is then that we have need of pleasure, when we feel pain owing to the absence of pleasure; but when we do not feel pain, we no longer need pleasure. And for this cause we call pleasure the beginning and end of the blessed life. For we recognize pleasure as the first good innate in us, and from pleasure we begin every act of choice and avoidance, and to pleasure we return again, using the feeling as the standard by which we judge every good.

Let's begin our analysis of this important paragraph by looking closely at the hierarchy in the first sentence.

We must consider that of desires some are natural, others vain, and of the natural some are necessary and others merely natural; and of the necessary some are necessary for happiness, others for the repose of the body, and others for very life.

In essence, Epicurus is providing an outline of desires. Here is his outline, with examples that are consistent with Epicurus's philosophy.

I. Desires
  A. Vain [unnatural] desires (for example, concerns about appearance or social status, desire for costly possessions, exotic foods or alcohol)
  B. Natural desires
    1. Necessary desires
      a. Necessary for happiness (for example, friendship, the life of reason)
      b. Necessary for repose of the body (for example, clothing, shelter, sleep)
      c. Necessary for life itself (for example, food and drink)
    2. Merely natural [unnecessary] desires (sexual desire)

Thus, here is Epicurus's portrait of your desires.

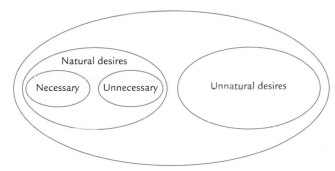

Epicurus's portrait of your desires

According to Epicurus, eliminating unnatural desires and unnecessary desires will make your life far simpler and happier. All that you *really* require is the satisfaction of the necessary, natural needs for clothing, shelter, sleep, food and drink, friends, and the guidance of reason. To feel the strength of Epicurus's argument, simply think of the misery, worry, and heartache you cause yourself by going beyond your simplest needs.

At this point, I believe Epicurus is (wrong, right, partly right) because _____

_____

_____.

After presenting the varieties of desire, Epicurus says, "The right understanding of these facts enables us to refer all choice and avoidance to the health of the body and the soul's freedom from disturbance, since this is the aim of the life of Blessedness." In other words, by understanding that some desires are unnatural, others are necessary, and still others are unnecessary, we can make correct choices that will lead to healthy bodies and peaceful souls. To determine if Epicurus is correct, look at the list of desires above and decide which desires, in your view, could lead to healthy or unhealthy bodies and which could lead to peaceful or "disturbed" souls.

The desires that could lead to a healthy body would be _____

_____

because _____

_____ .

The desires that could lead to an unhealthy body would be _____

_____

because _____

_____ .

The desires that would lead to a peaceful soul would be _____

_____ .

The desires that would lead to inner "disturbance" would be _____

_____

because _____

_____ .

According to Epicurus, pleasure is "the standard by which we judge every good." What exactly is Epicurus claiming?

Let's begin by exploring what it means to judge anything by a standard, and then we will be able to clarify what it means to judge every good by the standard of pleasure. Here are some examples of judging things by a standard:

- If the Lexus is the standard for a luxury car, then we can determine the excellence of any luxury car by comparing it to a Lexus.

- If Baskin and Robbins is the standard for ice cream, then we can determine the excellence of any ice cream by comparing it to Baskin and Robbins ice cream.

- If Gandhi is the standard for political leadership, then we can determine the excellence of political leaders by comparing them to Gandhi.

When we judge things by a standard, we establish the standard as a yardstick (the best luxury car, the best ice cream, the greatest leadership) and measure everything else by comparison.

Now, make two statements of your own, similar to mine, that are examples of judging things by a standard.

First, if _____ , then

_____

_____ .

Second, if _____ , then

_____

_____ .

Epicurus presents pleasure as the standard for every good. In other words, pleasure is the yardstick used to determine the good of every human action. The more pleasure the action brings, the more good it contains.

Now, how would this work in practice? Let us say I am thinking of buying a vacation cabin and am trying to measure how much pleasure it will bring—and how much pain. I might think as follows:

> To buy the cabin I will have to endure the pain of working and saving a considerable amount of money . . . but then when I have my cabin I will have the pleasure of having a pleasant place to stay for the summer . . . but then during the school year I will have the great worry about any damage that might come to my cabin . . . but I can look forward to the pleasure of perhaps being able to sell it for a profit some day. All in all, I'd say that the pain significantly exceeds the pleasure, so I'll give up my vacation cabin dream.

Following Epicurus's thinking, I must use pleasure as my only standard for the morality of buying a vacation cabin *or performing any other action*. Instead of other possible standards, such as to what degree I would be doing God's will or to what degree I would be serving my family, my own pleasure is the yardstick of all morality. The more pleasure an act brings, the more moral the act. The philosophical term for this position is **hedonism.** Hedonism is the view that only pleasurable actions are morally right.

EXERCISE 15.3
Thinking Like Epicurus

On your own paper, practice thinking like Epicurus. Using my example of a vacation cabin as a model, consider a major choice and then evaluate its potential for pleasure and pain.

In the next paragraph of the "Letter to Menoeceus," Epicurus argues that some pleasures are better than others. To prepare for his argument, imagine that you and a friend both find Epicurus convincing and vow to live his version of the life of Blessedness. In other words, you will both seek pleasure and avoid pain. Your friend, however, is foolish; you, of course, are wise. Thus, your friend seeks pleasure and avoids pain in a foolish way; you seek pleasure and avoid pain wisely. Describe some of your friend's foolish actions and some of your wise actions.

Examples of my friend foolishly seeking pleasure would be _____

_____ .

These are foolish because _____

_____

_____ .

Examples of my friend foolishly avoiding pain would be _____

_____ .

hedonism The view that pleasure is the goal of life. Hedonism comes in many varieties. In modern usage, a hedonist is often someone who madly pursues physical pleasure. Epicurean hedonism, however, emphasizes the pleasures produced by a life of moderation and self-control, guided by reason.

These are foolish because _____

_____

_____.

Examples of my own wise seeking of pleasure would be _____

_____.

These are wise because _____

_____

_____.

Examples of my wise avoidance of pain would be _____

_____.

These are wise because _____

_____.

Now, keep in mind your own view of wise and foolish pleasure seeking and compare it with Epicurus's view.

And since pleasure is the first good and natural to us, for this very reason we do, and choose, every pleasure but sometimes we pass over many pleasures, when greater discomfort comes to us as the result of them: and similarly we think many pains better than pleasures, since a greater pleasure comes to us when we have endured pains for a long time. Every pleasure then because of its natural kinship to us is good, yet not every pleasure is to be chosen: even as every pain also is an evil, yet not all are always of a nature to be avoided. Yet by a scale of comparison and by the consideration of advantages and disadvantages we must form our judgment on all these matters. For the good on certain occasions we treat as bad, and conversely the bad as good.

Name some pleasures that you think Epicurus would avoid because they lead to

pain. _____

_____.

Name some pains that you think Epicurus would not avoid because they lead to

pleasure. _____

_____.

Epicurus distinguished between two kinds of pleasures: katastematic and kinematic. Katastematic pleasures are long-lasting pleasures. For example, the company of good friends is katastematic, because its pleasure is long-lasting. Kinematic pleasures are more intense but short-lasting. For example, sexual pleasure is kinematic because its pleasure is short-lived.

Katastematic pleasures are often pleasures of rest; kinematic pleasures are often pleasures of motion.

EXERCISE 15.4
Two Kinds of Pleasure

Label each of the following pleasures (Ka) katastematic or (Ki) kinematic.

_____ 1. Rubbing velvet on your skin

_____ 2. Sitting in a sauna

_____ 3. Reading philosophy

_____ 4. Sitting in a garden

_____ 5. Talking to your best friend

_____ 6. Shopping

_____ 7. Traveling to foreign countries

_____ 8. A diet of vegetables

_____ 9. A diet of meat and processed foods

_____ 10. Water as your only drink

_____ 11. Soda as your only drink

_____ 12. Watching TV

_____ 13. Praying

_____ 14. Walking

_____ 15. Daydreaming

Because the Epicurean goal is ***ataraxia,*** freedom from inner disturbance, katastematic pleasures are seen as far superior to kinematic pleasures. Epicurus argues that the life of a simple diet, a few possessions, and the company of good friends consistently produces enduring pleasures and thus is far superior to any life of intense, but brief pleasures—which can often be followed by pain.

> And again independence of desire we think a great good—not that we may at all times enjoy but a few things, but that, if we do not possess many, we may enjoy the few in the genuine persuasion that those have the sweetest pleasure in luxury who least need it and that all that is natural is easy to be obtained, but that which is superfluous is hard. And so plain tastes bring us a pleasure equal to a luxurious diet, when all the pain due to want is removed; and bread and water produce the highest pleasure when one who needs them puts them to his lips. To grow accustomed therefore to simple and not luxurious diet gives us health to the full, and makes a man alert for the needful employments of life, and when after long intervals we approach luxuries, disposes us better toward them, and fits us to be fearless of fortune.

Put the last sentence in your own words and then offer an example that illustrates Epicurus's point.

Epicurus is saying: _____

_____

_____.

ataraxia Freedom from inner disturbance. *Ataraxia* is the inner peace produced by living a life of simple pleasures, free of fear of the gods and death. In the Epicurean view, the gods should not be feared because their lives are so pleasurably divine that they have no reason to trouble humans; death should not be feared because death is nonexistence. The thought of the nonexistence that follows our death should be no more fearful than the thought of the nonexistence that preceded our birth.

For example, _____

_____

Now, carefully read the closing three paragraphs of Epicurus's letter. Underline key points.

When, therefore, we maintain that pleasure is the goal, we do not mean the pleasures of profligates [those whose lives are filled with sensual indulgence] and those that consist in sensuality, as is supposed by some who are either ignorant or disagree with us or do not understand, but freedom from pain in the body and from trouble in the mind. For it is not continuous drinkings and revelings, nor the satisfaction of lusts, nor the enjoyment of fish and other luxuries of the wealthy table, which produce a pleasant life, but sober reasoning, searching out the motives for all choice and avoidance, and banishing mere opinions, to which are due the greatest disturbance of the spirit.

Of all this the beginning and the greatest good is prudence. Wherefore prudence [wise caution] is a more precious thing even than philosophy: for from prudence are sprung all the other virtues, and it teaches us that it is not possible to live pleasantly without living prudently and honorably and justly, nor, again, to live a life of prudence, honor, and justice without living pleasantly. For the virtues are by nature bound up with the pleasant life, and the pleasant life is inseparable from them. For indeed who, think you, is a better man than he who holds reverent opinions concerning the gods, and is at all times free from fear of death, and has reasoned out the end ordained by nature? He understands that the limit of good things is easy to fulfill and easy to attain, whereas the course of ills is either short in time or slight in pain: he laughs at destiny, whom some have introduced as the mistress of all things. He thinks that with us lies the chief power in determining events, some of which happen by necessity cannot be called to account, he sees that chance is inconstant, but that which is in our control is subject to no master, and to it are naturally attached praise and blame. For, indeed, it were better to follow the myths about the gods than to become a slave to the destiny of the natural philosophers: for the former suggests a hope of placating the gods by worship, whereas the latter involves a necessity which knows no placation. As to chance, he does not regard it as a god as most men do (for in a god's acts there is no disorder), nor as an uncertain cause of all things: for he does not believe that good and evil are given by chance to man for the framing of a blessed life, but that opportunities for great good and great evil are afforded by it [_____]. He therefore thinks it better to be unfortunate in reasonable action than to prosper in unreason. For it is better in a man's actions that what is well chosen should fail, rather than that what is ill chosen should be successful owing to chance.

Meditate therefore on these things and things akin to them night and day by yourself, and with a companion like yourself, and you shall never be disturbed waking or sleeping, but you shall live like a god among men. For a man who lives among immortal blessings is not like a mortal being.

In this selection, Epicurus lists many characteristics of a wise person. Here are two:

- A wise person is prudent because all virtues are linked to prudence.

- A wise person understands that life's pains are either short-lasting or easily bearable.

In Epicurus's view a "natural philosopher" is a philosopher of nature (that is, of all that exists) who holds that there is no freedom. All actions, including human actions, are controlled by preceding natural forces.

What are some other characteristics of a wise person? _____

_____

_____.

Now look back at your notes in this chapter. What has Epicurus said that is sensible? What is foolish? What could you apply to your life? Especially consider the wisdom and foolishness of using pleasure as your moral standard.

The most sensible points Epicurus makes are _____

_____

_____.

In general, these seem sensible because _____

_____

_____.

The most foolish points he makes are _____

_____

_____.

In general, these seem foolish because _____

_____

_____.

If I followed Epicurus's wisest advice I would stop _____

_____

because _____

_____

_____.

And I would start _____

_____

because _____

_____

_____.

When I consider using pleasure as my sole moral standard, I think _____

_____

_____

_____.

SUMMARY

Epicurus based part of his metaphysics upon Democritus's view that all is atoms—except that Epicurus held that the universe is not completely mechanistic because atoms can "swerve." Thus, humans, composed of nothing but atoms, are capable of free choice. Epicurus argues that we should exercise our free choice by enjoying philosophy from youth to old age, by wisely understanding that death should not be feared, and by choosing enduring (katastematic) pleasures over short-lived (kinematic) pleasures. The life of wisdom is seen as a life of simplicity whose goal is freedom from inner disturbance.

EXERCISE 15.5
Looking Back

Answer the following on your own paper.

1. How did Democritus influence Epicurus's metaphysics?
2. What is the message of Epicurus's "Letter to Menoeceus"?

EXERCISE 15.6
Looking at the World Through Epicurus's Eyes

How would Epicurus respond to the following? After each answer, offer evidence consistent with Epicurus's philosophy.

1. T   F   The one who dies with the most toys wins.
   Evidence: _____
   _____
   _____.

2. T   F   The goal of life is to eat, drink, and be merry.
   Evidence: _____
   _____
   _____.

3. T   F   A virtuous person obeys God.
   Evidence: _____
   _____
   _____.

4. T   F   If it feels good, do it.
   Evidence: _____
   _____
   _____.

5. T   F   "Simplify! Simplify!"—Henry David Thoreau

Evidence: _____

_____

_____.

6. T   F   All is matter.

Evidence: _____

_____

_____.

7. T   F   The pleasures of this world are the greatest pleasures we will ever know.

Evidence: _____

_____

_____.

EXERCISE 15.7
Thinking Like a Modern Epicurean

Assume you are a modern follower of Epicurus trying to use his system to evaluate several contemporary desires. Use your own paper, and label each of the following desires NH (necessary for happiness), NE (necessary for ease), NL (necessary for life), VD (vain desire), or NC (no category mentioned by Epicurus). After you label each desire, explain your answer.

_____ 1. Irene feels left out at work and has an intense desire to be accepted by her colleagues.

_____ 2. Manuel can't get along with his parents and desires independence.

_____ 3. Lucille hates to lose an argument because she desires to win.

_____ 4. John intensely wants good grades.

_____ 5. Mary intensely wants to go out with John.

_____ 6. Isabella wants a good job.

_____ 7. Tim wants a more positive self-image.

_____ 8. Yang wants equal pay for equal work.

_____ 9. Sarah wants to be president.

_____ 10. Eileen wants to be more assertive.

_____ 11. Tanya wants to have a personal relationship with Jesus.

_____ 12. Adelina wants to know Placido Domingo.

_____ 13. Allen wants to lose weight.

_____ 14. Sam has been poor all his life and wants to live in a big house.

_____ 15. Sanji wants to know more about herself.

EXERCISE 15.8
Pleasure as a Moral Standard

Epicurus argues that pleasure should be the standard for moral action. The more pleasure an action brings, as long as that pleasure does not lead to pain, the more virtuous the action. Assume that the people in Exercise 15.7 come to you to help them evaluate the morality of their desires. Using Epicurus's standard of pleasure as moral action, make up a "possible pain/possible pleasure" balance sheet.

Example: Irene wants to gain acceptance by her colleagues at work.

Possible pains: Having to work to get acceptance, having to be nice to unpleasant people, having to get involved in office politics.

Possible pleasures: Feeling part of a group, working in a friendly environment, developing friendships that extend beyond work hours.

Make a similar balance sheet for each of the other individuals in Exercise 15.7.

EXERCISE 15.9
Obeying God's Will as a Moral Standard

Of course, there are other standards of moral action besides the amount of pleasure an action produces. Instead of taking the position that moral action is pleasure and immoral action is pain, take the position that obeying God is moral action and disobeying God is immoral action. Using your own conception of God, reevaluate each of the cases in Exercise 15.7.

Example: Irene wants to gain acceptance by her colleagues at work.

Obeying God: God would want us to love our neighbors; therefore, if gaining acceptance by her colleagues was a result of loving them, then Irene would be committing a moral act.

Disobeying God: God does not want us to violate His rules; therefore, if gaining acceptance by her colleagues involved violating any of God's rules, then Irene would be committing an immoral act.

Make a similar analysis for the other fourteen people in Exercise 15.7.

EXERCISE 15.10
Personal Growth as a Moral Standard

Fostering personal growth is a popular modern standard of moral action. Under this view, an action is good if it makes us develop as a person, if it fosters inner growth; and an action is immoral if it keeps us from developing as a person, if it stunts our inner growth.

For example: Irene wants to gain acceptance by her colleagues at work.

Fosters growth: If Irene is a shy person and wants to overcome this part of her personality, then being outgoing and working to be part of the crowd at work would be a moral action.

Inhibits growth: If Irene has low self-esteem and simply wants to be validated by others, then working to gain acceptance by people at work would make her more dependent on others and would be an immoral action.

Make a similar analysis for the other fourteen people in Exercise 15.7.

EXERCISE 15.11
Developing Your Own Classification of Desires

1. Assume you want to develop your own classification of desires and will begin by sorting all desires into two groups, the moral and immoral. Use your own paper to answer the following:

   a. What are some examples of moral desires?

   b. What are some characteristics moral desires hold in common?

   c. What are some examples of immoral desires?

   d. What are some characteristics immoral desires hold in common?

   e. Are there any situations in which a moral desire can become immoral? (Explain your answer with examples.)

   f. Are there any situations in which an immoral desire can become moral? (Explain your answer with examples.)

2. Using your system of classification, label each desire in Exercise 15.7 moral or immoral and explain your reasoning.

ANALYSIS OF YOUR PHILOSOPHICAL SELF-PORTRAIT

To see how your views stack up against Epicurus's, read my analysis below, rethink your position, and then circle what you believe is the correct answer. I've underlined Epicurus's answers.

1. T <u>F</u> *The soul survives death.*

   Because he agreed with Democritus, Epicurus held that the soul was composed of atoms and, like the body, decomposed at death. For Epicurus, this was far from being a distressing thought, for he held that the recognition of the soul's mortality would save us the "disturbance" of craving immortality and fear of an unknown afterlife.

   If you answered this True, then you are supported by Plato and all Christian philosophers on the tour.

2. T <u>F</u> *Thinking about the certainty of death will make us enjoy our life more fully.*

   Epicurus would have answered this False. He held that because death was the absence of sensation, death was simply "nothing." Thus, to the degree that thinking about the certainty of death involved fear of death or regret at the shortness of life, such thoughts were immoral (because they produced pain, not pleasure).

   If you answered this True, then you can test the soundness of your view by performing the following experiment. Set aside a short period of time each day for a week. Think about the certainty of death and then see if you enjoy your life on that day more fully.

3. <u>T</u> <u>F</u> *All pleasurable actions are moral.*

On the one hand, Epicurus would answer this True, simply because he held that pleasure was the standard of moral actions. However, Epicurus would have answered this False when considering actions whose short-term pleasure might lead to long-term pain (like getting drunk). However, to be entirely consistent with his own views, Epicurus would have had to say that getting drunk would be pleasurable if the hours and intensity of the pleasure of drunkenness exceeded the hours and intensity of the pain of a hangover.

4. <u>T</u> F *All moral actions produce pleasure.*

Epicurus would certainly have answered this True because he held that pleasure was the only standard of morality. If, for example, you gave money to the poor and felt no pleasure, Epicurus would have to say that your giving money was an immoral act.

If you answered this False, then you probably strongly disagree with Epicurus's ethic. In your view, there is another standard for morality, perhaps a standard established by God or human nature, and thus some actions would be moral even if they produced extreme, long-lasting pain. For example, you might hold that it is moral to rescue a child from a burning building because, even though you might suffer extreme pain, this action would be pleasing to God or in accord with the natural human desire to help others.

5. <u>T</u> F *A life with a few possessions produces more pleasure than a life with many possessions.*

Epicurus would certainly hold that this is true. A life with many possessions is a life of vain desires. In addition, the pain required to get possessions, according to Epicurus, would far outweigh the pleasure the possessions could bring.

6. <u>T</u> F *Humans should seek pleasure and avoid pain.*

For Epicurus, the only, but important, modification to this statement would be that humans should *wisely* seek pleasure and avoid pain. Milder, longer lasting pleasure is to be preferred to intense, brief pleasure.

7. <u>T</u> F *All that humans do is seek pleasure and avoid pain.*

Epicurus seems to hold that the desire for pleasure is an inborn part of our human nature. But if what all humans *actually* do is seek pleasure and avoid pain, how can Epicurus urge that this is also what we *ought* to do? If, for example, every human went to church, it would not seem to make sense to say that going to church was also what every human ought to do. Epicurus would probably point out that while all humans seek pleasure and avoid pain, not all humans seek pleasure and avoid pain wisely.

8. <u>T</u> F *God has no control over our life.*

Epicurus holds that the gods have no control over our life, because they are too divine to trouble themselves with us. His view is somewhat reminiscent of Aristotle's, who holds that God is not concerned with humans because he is doing what is most perfect, thinking about his own thinking.

Evaluation: Number of points in agreement with Epicurus = _____ of 8 possible.

A position of Epicurus's that you strongly (support, oppose) is

_____

_____

because _____

_____

_____

GOOD BOOKS

Dewitt, Norman Wentworth. *Epicurus and His Philosophy.* Minneapolis: University of Minnesota Press, 1954. If Epicurus intrigues you, this text will fill in many details not explored in this chapter.

Ewing, A. C. *Ethics.* New York: Free Press, 1953. An interesting overview of ethical theory.

NEXT STOP

You discover Sylvester Stallone's Roman ancestors.

16
Epictetus
Life's Purpose Is Virtuous Indifference

YOUR PHILOSOPHICAL SELF-PORTRAIT

Add more details to your philosophical self-portrait by answering the questions below and providing evidence for your answers.

1. T F All we can control is our attitude toward the world.
    Evidence: _____
    _____.

2. T F There is nothing more important than peace of mind.
    Evidence: _____
    _____.

3. T F Because our free choices shape our destiny, Fate is an illusion.
    Evidence: _____
    _____.

4. T F Death is a worse calamity than fear of death.
    Evidence: _____
    _____.

5. T F Love is the highest virtue.
    Evidence: _____
    _____.

6. T F The wisest person has the fewest possessions.
    Evidence: _____
    _____.

7. T F Nothing can harm a wise person.
    Evidence: _____
    _____.

After reviewing several important aspects of stoicism, we'll examine Epictetus's *Encheiridion*. Epictetus distinguishes between what we can control (our response to external events) and what we cannot control (external events themselves). Thus, in the stoic view, wisdom is controlling the controllable and being indifferent to the rest. Using this concept of wisdom, Epictetus analyzes, among other topics, the proper attitude toward loved ones, possessions, accidents, illness, and death.

Hollywood tough guys are stoic wannabes.

In the first Rambo movie, *First Blood*, Sylvester Stallone, with a bloody arm wound, finds himself holed up in a cave. He unscrews the hollow handle of his survival knife, pours out a needle and thread. The camera goes in for a tight shot as Sly calmly stitches up his bloody gash. Tough guys don't even wince. In the old Westerns, the only anesthetic a wounded cowpoke needed was a chunk of rawhide to bite on. The Romans, who spread stoic philosophy from one end of their empire to the other, were far tougher, or, as they would have preferred to put it, far more indifferent. A favorite stoic tale describes the reaction of a Roman senator imprisoned by Nero:

> On the first day of the senator's imprisonment, Nero, attempting to crush his spirit, sent a servant to announce, "The emperor is going to seize all your lands, burn your mansions, and destroy your olive groves. You will be poorer than the poorest slave."
>
> The stoic senator responded, "Send the emperor my good wishes."
>
> The servant returned the second day and said, "The emperor was so furious at your reaction that he tortured to death your wife and children."
>
> The stoic senator responded, "Tell the emperor it was pleasantly cool here today."
>
> The servant returned the third day and said, "You have gone too far! The emperor has ordered that in the morning you will be tied to four horses and pulled limb from limb!"
>
> The stoic senator asked, "Will that be before or after breakfast?"

Your reaction?

I believe the stoic senator was _____   _____

_____.

Many students find the senator absurd, if not insane. Nonetheless, I believe I can convince you, by the end of this section of the tour, that the senator's behavior, and stoicism in general, contain hidden wisdom.

Founded in Athens about 300 B.C. by Zeno of Citium (not to be confused with Zeno, the follower of Parmenides), stoicism took its name from the painted

Epictetus (c. A.D. 55–130)

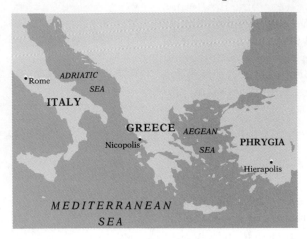

Born to a slave woman in Hierapolis, a city in Phrygia in what is now central Turkey, Epictetus grew up as a slave in the Roman emperor Nero's household. When Epictetus was nine years old, he watched as Rome, the heart of the Roman empire, burned to the ground. Nero promptly accused the Christians of setting the fire and began what was to be almost three centuries of persecution of the Christians in Rome. The Christians were not the only ones mistreated by the cruel and emotionally unstable emperor. Shortly after the rebuilding of Rome, the people rose up in revolt against their cruel, unstable emperor. Aban-doned even by his own guards, Nero committed suicide.

Following the death of Nero in A.D. 68, Epictetus entered the service of Epaphroditus, a free-man who had been administrative secretary to Nero. Impressed by the quick wit and brilliant mind of the slave boy, Epaphroditus gave Epictetus his freedom and sent him to study under Caius Musonius Rufus—a stoic philosopher whom Epictetus greatly admired.

Upon completion of his studies, Epictetus taught philosophy in Rome until about A.D. 90, when he and all other philosophers were banished by the emperor Domitian. Like the Athenian jury who had sentenced Socrates to death, Domitian did not take well to having his ideas challenged.

Undeterred, Epictetus moved across the Adriatic Sea to Nicopolis in Greece, where he established a school for young men interested in studying logic, physics, and the ethics of stoicism. Here the ex-slave taught young men how to lead happy lives. Unlike Aristotle, who defined happiness as eudaimonia, and Epicurus, who defined happiness as freedom from inner turmoil, Epictetus took the stoic position that happiness was indifference, *apathia*, toward all

porch of columns (*Stoa Poikile*) in Athens where Zeno lectured. During its 500-year history, stoicism had an energetic influence in the late Greek world and became one of the dominant philosophies of the Roman Empire. The range of its influence can be judged from the fact that one of its leading Roman exponents, Marcus Aurelius, was Roman emperor (from A.D. 161 to 180) and the other, Epictetus, the subject of this section of the tour, was an ex-slave. Marcus Aurelius's *Meditations* is a stoic masterpiece.

The stoics held that the human mind was a fragment of a Divine Reason that guided the universe. Because all things that happened come from God, we should accept, rather than resist, external events. In other words, since the flow is divine, we should go with the flow—even when it threatens to drown us. In

Epictetus (continued)

harsh, external circumstances. His teachings attracted a large following, including the Roman emperor and philosopher Marcus Aurelius.

Described by one biographer as a "moral activist," Epictetus was primarily concerned with practical ethics. His early life as a slave no doubt contributed to the recurring theme of freedom in his teachings. According to Epictetus, we need to distinguish between that which is within our power and that which is not. The only thing in our power is our reason and mental disposition. All externals, including family, physical circumstances, and even our own bodies, are outside our control. We cannot use our outer circumstances, no matter how oppressive, as an excuse for failing to seek the highest good. Only by focusing on what we can control, our mental attitude, can we achieve happiness.

Like that of most stoics, Epictetus's message was intended not just for the aristocracy but for everyone. Epictetus insisted that we improve ourselves morally by engaging in daily self-examination. Epictetus compared moral improvement to medical treatment. The process of healing involves pain. The pain we suffer, he taught, strengthens our souls.

Epictetus was said to be one of the happiest of men. He lived a simple life in a house that had only a rush mat, a pallet for sleeping, and an earthenware lamp. A sweet and compassionate person, he had a special place in his heart for children. When Epictetus was older, he married in order to take in a boy whose parents were going to abandon him.

Epictetus taught that God is all-powerful, all-wise, and all-good. The remarkable similarity between some of his teachings and those of the early Christians has not escaped the notice of commentators. However, Epictetus was not a Christian, nor is there any evidence that he sympathized with the plight of the early Christians in Rome. At the time, the Christians were considered the primary enemy of the Roman Empire, a belief held also by Epictetus's devoted follower Marcus Aurelius.

Like Socrates, whom he greatly admired, Epictetus did not leave any writings. Instead his ideas were recorded by his student Flavius Arrianus and published posthumously. His most popular work, the *Encheiridion,* or "Handbook," is a collection of practical instructions on seeking moral progress.

---

the stoic view, there is little room for human freedom because everything is controlled by Divine Reason. In a favorite analogy of the stoics, we are like dogs tied behind the wagon of Fate. Our only choice is whether we want to trot or be dragged.

As strange as it may sound, the highest stoic virtue was apathy (*apathia*). Interpreted as a calm indifference to calamity, stoic apathy was a twofold wisdom. First, if we cannot control threatening external events, then it is wise to be indifferent to their consequences. Second, if the universe is guided by Divine Reason, then it is wise to remain undisturbed even during the greatest troubles.

To explain the core of Epictetus's philosophy, I'll give a many-part answer to one question.

- What is the message of Epictetus's *Encheiridion*?

apathia "Freedom from passion." To be apathetic, in the modern sense, is to be unhappy, listless, uncaring. To achieve stoic *apathia* is to be wisely indifferent to the pains that can be produced by external events. *Apathia* is not so much apathy as serenity.

READING:
EPICTETUS'S *ENCHEIRIDION*

What Is the Message?

The following selection is from the *Encheiridion*, a summary of Epictetus's philosophy composed by his student Arrian. To simplify analysis, I've divided the important first paragraph into four units.

> [1] (1A) Some things are under our control, while others are not under our control.
>
> (1B) Under our control are conception, choice, desire, aversion, and in a word, everything that is our own doing; not under our control are our body, our property, reputation, office and, in a word, everything that is not our own doing.
>
> (1C) Furthermore, the things under our control are by nature free, unhindered, and unimpeded; while the things not under our control are weak, servile [slavish], subject to hindrance, and not our own.
>
> (1D) Remember, therefore, that if what is naturally slavish you think to be free, and what is not your own to be your own, you will be hampered, will grieve, will be in turmoil, and will blame both gods and men; while if you think only what is your own to be your own, and what is not your own to be, as it really is, not your own, then no one will ever be able to exert compulsion upon you, no one will hinder you, you will blame no one, will find fault with no one, will do absolutely nothing against your will, you will have no personal enemy, no one will harm you, for neither is there any harm that can touch you.[1]

In (1A) Epictetus distinguishes between things "under our control" and things "not under our control" and then gives examples of each in (1B).

Right now I am looking out my window at an early spring snowstorm. If I think, "the snow is going to kill my Blue Girl roses," this conception is under my control; wishing that my roses might not die in the snow is a desire that is under my control; feeling a strong dislike for the sight of my unprotected roses is an aversion under my control; going outside to cover my roses is a choice that is under my control. But whether my Blue Girl roses actually die, no matter what I think, wish, feel, or choose is *not* under my control.

Reread (1A) and (1B) and then construct your own example of what is and is not under your control.

A conception under my control is _____.

A desire under my control is _____.

An aversion under my control is _____.

---

[1] From Epictetus, *Encheiridian*, trans. W. A. Oldfather (Cambridge: Harvard University Press).

A choice under my control is _____.

Some things not under my control are _____

_____

Epictetus divides reality into a small region where we are absolutely supreme and an enormous region where we are absolutely powerless. We are captains of our tiny ships upon uncontrollable seas. The mistake we make is thinking we have as much control of the seas as we do of the running of our vessels. Everything in regard to our mind, our emotions, and our choices is under our control; everything the external world does to us is out of our control. Wisdom, for Epictetus, is controlling what we can control and being indifferent to the rest.

Assume you come home and find someone has broken in and stolen all your valuables: What is under your control and what is not under your control?

Under my control are conceptions like _____,

desires like _____, aversions like _____

_____, and choices like _____.

Not under my control is _____.

Epictetus says you must distinguish between what is and is not your own. How does this apply to the burglary incident?

My own is _____.

Not my own is _____.

Make your situation even more difficult. Imagine you are in the situation of Charles Bronson in the first of the "Death Wish" movies. You come home and find your family slaughtered.

According to Epictetus, what would be the foolish, and what would be the wise, reaction?

The foolish reaction to the death of my family would be _____

_____.

This would be foolish because _____.

The wise reaction would be _____.

This would be wise because _____.

Though the stoic attitude is obviously very difficult, the reward is substantial. In (1D) above Epictetus says, if we only try to control what we can control,

then no one will ever be able to exert compulsion upon you, no one will hinder you, you will blame no one, will find fault with no one, will do absolutely nothing against your will, you will have no personal enemy, no one will harm you, for neither is there any harm that can touch you.

How can it be that with the stoic attitude no one could compel or hinder us and we would blame no one, find fault with no one, have no personal enemies, and, most amazingly, never be harmed?

The stoic attitude would give us these results because _____

_____ .

Key points that Epictetus has established thus far are

_____

_____

_____

_____ .

With such high aims [the high aims of stoicism], therefore, remember that you must bestir yourself with no slight effort to lay hold of them [_____], but you will have to give up some things, entirely, and defer others for the time being. But if you wish for these things [_____] also, and at the same time for both office and wealth, it may be that you will not get even these latter [_____], because you aim also at the former [_____], and certainly you will fail to get the former, which alone bring freedom and happiness.

Make it, therefore, your study at the very outset to say to every harsh external impression, "You are an external impression and not at all what you appear to be." After that examine it and test it by these rules which you have, the first and most important of which is this: Whether the impression has to do with the things which are under our control, or with those which are not under our control; and, if it has to do with some one of the things not under our control, have ready to hand the answer. "It is nothing to me."

Practice the stoic point of view in the next exercise.

EXERCISE 16.1
Understanding Epictetus

When confronted by a "harsh external impression," Epictetus recommends a three-step process.

A. Realize that the impression *is* external, not attached to you, and therefore not what it appears to be.

B. Determine if the impression "has to do with the things which are under our control, or with those which are not under our control."

C. If the impression is one of the things "not under our control," then understand "it is nothing to me."

For example, assume that because of a recession, I am laid off work. Thinking through the three-step process, I would end up with the following:

A. Losing my job feels as if it is something happening inside me, but really it is only something happening outside me. Though it feels as if I *am* my job, this is not true. My job is not part of me. The loss of my job is merely a "harsh *external* impression."

B. How I perform my job is something that is under my control. Whether or not I have a job is not something under my control.

C. Since losing my job is not something I can control and is not something that I "own," not something that is truly a part of me, I realize that the loss of work need not affect me. I should worry only about what I can control, and I can't control my school district that cost me my job.

Using your own paper, follow the three-step process for each of the following problems:

1. You are sitting in class and suddenly feel sick to your stomach.
2. You go home and discover that your dog destroyed your collection of Johnny Cash tapes.
3. Your Great American Novel is rejected by the thirty-fifth publisher you have submitted it to.
4. You refuse to look over the edge of the Empire State Building because you are afraid of heights.
5. Your doctor informs you that you have cancer.

Now, read the second section of the *Encheiridion*. You may have to go through it several times to understand Epictetus's point.

[2] Remember that the promise of desire is the attainment of what you desire, that of aversion is not to fall into what is avoided, and that he who fails in his desire is unfortunate, while he who falls into what he would avoid experiences misfortune. If, then, you avoid only what is unnatural among those things which are under your control, you will fall into none of the things which you avoid; but if you try to avoid disease, or death, or poverty, you will experience misfortune. Withdraw, therefore your aversion from all the matters that are not under our control, and transfer it [_____] to what is unnatural among those which are under our control. But for the time being remove utterly your desire; for if you desire some one of the things that are not under our control you are bound to be unfortunate; and at the same time, not one of the things that are under our control, which it would be excellent for you to desire, is within your grasp. But employ only choice and refusal, and these too but lightly, and with reservations, and without straining.

Epictetus argues that if we try to avoid what we have no control over—for example, catching a disease—then we will "experience a misfortune." In other words, we will be trapped.

What shocking point does Epictetus make in the following section?

[3] With everything which entertains you, is useful, or of which you are fond, remember to say to yourself, beginning with the very least things, "What is its nature?" If you are fond of a jug, say, "I am fond of a jug"; for when it is broken you will not be disturbed. If you kiss your own child or wife, say to yourself that you are kissing a human being; for when it dies you will not be disturbed.

Epictetus argues that we should not be disturbed when a jug that we love is

broken because _____

_____

_____.

We should not be disturbed when our beloved spouse or child dies because

_____

_____

_____.

I think what Epictetus has to say about possessions we love is _____

_____

because _____

_____

_____.

I think what Epictetus has to say about people we love is _____

_____

because _____

_____

_____.

[4] When you are on the point of putting your hand to some undertaking, remind yourself what the nature of that undertaking is. If you are going out of the house to bathe, put before your mind what happens at a public bath—those who splash you with water, those who jostle against you, those who vilify you and rob you. And thus you will set about your undertaking more securely if at the outset you say to yourself, "I want to take a bath, and, at the same time, to keep my moral purpose in harmony with nature." And so do in every undertaking. For thus, if anything happens to hinder you in your bathing, you will be ready to say, "Oh, well this was not the only thing that I wanted, but I wanted also to keep your moral purpose in harmony with nature; and I shall not so keep it if I am vexed at what is going on."

You are about to drive home through rush hour traffic. What does Epictetus recommend your thoughts should be?

I should recognize that _____

_____

_____. If something out

of my control like _____ happened, I

would tell myself _____

_____ .

Or, let's say you decide to have some friends come over for a wild party.

I should recognize that _____

_____ . If something out

of my control like _____ happened, I

would tell myself _____

_____ .

Is Epictetus wise or foolish?

I would say Epictetus is (wise, foolish) because _____

_____

_____ .

[5] It is not the things themselves that disturb men, but their judgments about these things. For example, death is nothing dreadful, or else Socrates too would have thought so, but the judgment that death is dreadful, this is the dreadful thing. When, therefore, we are hindered, or disturbed, or grieved, let us never blame anyone but ourselves, that means, our own judgments. It is the part of an uneducated person to blame others where he himself fares ill; to blame himself is the part of one whose education has begun; to blame neither another nor his own self is the part of one whose education is already complete.

Make a distinction between "things themselves" and "judgments about these things."

Assume that I lose my wallet. The thing itself would be _____ .

The judgment about the thing would be _____

_____ .

Regarding death, the thing itself would be _____ .

The judgment would be _____

_____ . What is

dreadful is _____ . What is not dreadful is

_____ .

What distinction is Epictetus making between the uneducated person, the "one whose education has begun," and the "one whose education is already complete"?

Assume I am in a car wreck. According to Epictetus, as an uneducated person, I

would think _____

_____.

As "one whose education had begun," I would think _____

_____.

As "one whose education was already complete," I would think _____

_____.

In general, you believe Epictetus's position is (correct, incorrect) because

_____

_____

_____

_____.

[6] Be not elated at any excellence which is not your own. If the horse in his elation were to say, "I am beautiful," it could be endured; but when you say in your elation, "I have a beautiful horse," rest assured that you are elated at something good which belongs to a horse. What then, is your own? The use of external impressions. Therefore, when you are harmony with nature in the use of external impressions, then be elated; for then it will be some good of your own at which you will be elated.

Imagine you just bought your dream car and you're sitting behind the wheel.

"Ah, how wonderful the world looks over the hood of a _____

_____!"

Deepen the fantasy.

My dream car is the perfect shade of _____.

I look around at the interior and see _____.

I rub my hand across the passenger's seat. It is _____.

I put my hands on the steering wheel and feel _____. This

vehicle makes my car dreams come true because _____.

Now, experience your dream car from the stoic perspective that Epictetus recommends.

Everything wonderful about my dream car belongs to _____;

therefore, what I should feel is _____.

Now, someone sideswipes your car. What is your most natural reaction? How, following Epictetus's advice, could you feel "elation"?

Bad dream! I watch an idiot smash into my car door and immediately feel

_____. But I remember that

Epictetus said I only own the use of my "external impressions." Adopting this attitude, I tell myself _____

_____.

And I feel _____.

Is Epictetus wise or foolish?

I believe Epictetus is (wise, foolish) because _____

_____.

[7] Just as on a voyage, when your ship has anchored, if you should go on shore to get fresh water, you may pick up a small shell-fish or little bulb on the way, but you have to keep your attention fixed on the ship, and turn about frequently for fear lest the captain should call; and if he calls, you must give up all these things, if you would escape being thrown on board all tied up like the sheep. So it is also in life: If there be given you, instead of a little bulb and a small shell-fish, a little wife and child, there will be no objection to that; only, if the Captain calls, give up all these things and run to the Ship, without even turning around to look back. And if you are an old man, never even get very far away from the ship, for fear that when He calls you may be missing.

Explain and evaluate Epictetus' symbolism:

The shore is _____. The ship is _____.

The Captain is _____. Being "called" by the Captain is

_____. The attitude toward life which

Epictetus recommends is to _____

_____.

This is different from our normal attitude because _____

_____.

Epictetus is (wise, foolish) because _____

_____

_____.

[8] Do not seek to have everything that happens happen as you wish, but wish for everything to happen as it actually does happen, and your life will be serene.

Translate.

An example of wanting something to happen as I wish would be _____

_____. This might not lead to serenity

because _____. An

example of wishing for something to happen as it actually does happen would be

_____
.

This would lead to serenity because _____.

[9] Disease is an impediment to the body, but not to the moral purpose, unless that [_____] consents. Lameness is an impediment to the leg, but not to the moral purpose. And say this to yourself at each thing that befalls you; for you will find the thing to be an impediment to something else, but not to yourself.

By "moral purpose" Epictetus means _____.

A disease like AIDS would harm my body but not necessarily my moral purpose

because _____

_____.

Having AIDS would harm my moral purpose only if _____

_____.

If something terrible happened to me like having AIDS, Epictetus would say I

should see it as an "impediment" to _____

not to myself because _____.

[10] In the case of everything that befalls you, remember to turn to yourself and see what faculty you have to deal with it. If you see a handsome lad or woman, you will see what faculty you have to deal with it. If you see a handsome lad or woman, you will find continence [self-restraint] the faculty to employ here; if hard labor is laid upon you, you will find endurance; in this fashion, your external impressions will not run away with you.

According to Epictetus, we are equipped with all the virtues we need to deal with every hardship. If we are tempted by lust, then we should employ the virtue of continence. If we are given a difficult physical task, then we should employ the virtue of endurance. But if we let our "external impressions" run away with us, then we will be overcome by the challenges the world flings at us. Try to apply this to your own life.

If I get a bad grade, I should employ the virtue of _____.

If I'm broke and find a wallet full of cash, I should employ the virtue of

_____. If I get very sick, I should employ

the virtue of _____. If I

didn't employ these virtues, then _____

_____.

[11] Never say about anything, "I have lost it," but only "I have given it back." Is your child dead? It has been given back. Is your wife dead? She has been given back. "I have had my farm taken away." Very well, this too has been given back. "Yet it was a rascal who took it away." But what concern is it of yours by whose instrumentality the Giver called for its return? So long as He gives it to you, take care of it as of a thing that is not your own, as travelers treat their inn.

At every turn stoicism challenges our natural reactions to painful experiences. Being a stoic means doing what is wisely unnatural. The more trivial the pain, the wiser and more possible the stoic reaction seems. The more intense the pain, the "less human" and more impossible the stoic reaction seems. Is Epictetus's advice correct, no matter how intense the pain that our external impressions bring us?

EXERCISE 16.2
Practicing Stoicism

Try this experiment. Imagine you lose four things, each one slightly more painful to lose than the last. Try taking the stoic attitude at each imaginary loss and then evaluate stoicism, based strictly on whether or not it is wiser than your "normal" reaction.

All right. I'll imagine I lose _____, something that wouldn't cause me much pain. I say to myself, "I have not lost it. I have given it back." I feel _____ because _____

_____

_____. This is (better, worse) than

my normal reaction because _____

_____

_____ .

Now, I imagine I lose __ _____ , something
that causes me genuine pain. I say to myself, "I have not lost it. I have given it
back." I feel _____ because _____

_____

_____ . This is (better, worse) than
my normal reaction because _____

_____

_____ .

Now, I imagine I lose _____ , something that
causes me a large amount of pain. I say to myself, "I have not lost it. I have given
it back." I feel _____ because _____

_____

_____ . This is (better, worse) than
my normal reaction because _____

_____

_____ .

Now, I imagine I lose _____ , something that
causes me an extremely large amount of pain. I say to myself, "I have not lost it. I
have given it back." I feel _____ because _____

_____

_____ . This is (better, worse) than
my normal reaction because _____

_____

_____ .

Now, imagine the worst kind of pain, one that is not only extremely painful but
also that is caused by something entirely unjust. Epictetus uses the example of
having a farm stolen by "a rascal." Imagine something even more painful and
more unjust—and then try the stoic response.

Now, I imagine I lose _____ , something that
causes me almost unbearable pain. In addition, the absolutely unjust cause of
this loss is _____ . I say to
myself, "I have not lost it. I have given it back." I feel _____

_____

because _____ .
This is (better, worse) than my natural reaction because _____

_____

_____ .

[12] If you wish to make progress, dismiss all reasoning of this sort: "If I neglect my affairs, I shall have nothing to live on." "If I do not punish my slave-boy he will turn out bad." For it is better to die of hunger, but in a state of freedom from grief and fear, than to live in plenty, but troubled in mind. And it is better for your slave-boy to be bad than for you to be unhappy. Begin, therefore, with the little things. Your paltry oil gets spilled, your miserable wine stolen; say to yourself, "This is the price paid for a calm spirit, this the price for peace of mind." Nothing is got without a price. And when you call your slave-boy, bear in mind that it is possible he may not heed you, and again, that even if he does heed, he may not do what you want done. But he is not in so happy a condition that your peace of mind depends upon him.

Epictetus recommends a workout program for the spirit. Start with easy "weights," or problems, and build up to larger ones. The goal is to make your spirit so strong that no matter what happens, you remain sturdily calm. According to Epictetus, nothing that happens to you is worth the destruction of your peace of mind. What, in fact, is gained by letting terrible "impressions" make you miserable? You get a bad grade. Is it wise to make things worse, by sacrificing your peace of mind to something you don't "own"—the black mark on your transcript? What good does your inner misery do for you?

You might answer, "When something awful happens it is very difficult to maintain peace of mind." If you wanted to be a body builder, would you start by lifting the heaviest weights? This is why Epictetus recommends his spiritual training course; start with small problems and build your strength to endure large problems.

One of my most frequent, small worries is _____

_____. This upsets my peace of mind because

_____

_____. If I looked at this stoically, I would tell

myself _____

_____

_____   _____

_____.

One of my most frequent, large worries is _____

_____. This upsets my peace of mind because

_____   _____

_____. If I looked at this stoically, I would tell

myself _____

_____

_____

_____.

[13] If you wish to make progress, then be content to appear senseless and foolish in externals, do not make it your wish to give the appearance of knowing anything; and if some people think you to be an important personage, distrust yourself. For be assured that it is no easy matter to keep your moral purpose in a state of conformity with nature, and, at the same time, to keep externals; but the man who devotes his attention to one of these two things must inevitably neglect the other.

Translate key ideas in this passage.

By "progress" Epictetus means _____. By

"externals" Epictetus means _____. By

"moral purpose" Epictetus means _____. By

keeping "moral purpose in a state of conformity with nature" Epictetus means

_____

_____.

Explain the last phrase, "but the man who devotes his attention to one of these two things must inevitably neglect the other."

The "two things" are _____ and _____.

If we devote our attention to the former, then we must neglect the latter because

_____

_____. If

we devote our attention to the latter, then we must neglect the former because

_____

_____.

[14] (A) If you make it your will that your children and your wife and your friends should live forever, you are silly; for you are making it your will that things not under your control should be under your control, and that what is not your own should be your own. (B) In the same way, too, if you make it

your will that your slave-boy be free from faults, you are a fool; for you are making it your will that vice be not vice, but something else. (C) If, however, it is your will not to fail in what you desire, this is in your power. (D) Wherefore, exercise yourself in that which is in your power. (E) Each man's master is the person who has the authority over what the man wishes or does not wish, so as to secure it, or take it away. (F) Whoever, therefore, wants to be free, let him neither wish for anything, nor avoid anything, that is under the control of others; or else he is necessarily a slave.

Explain Epictetus's point in each of the six sentences.

(A) _____

_____.

(B) _____

_____.

(C) _____

_____.

(D) _____

_____.

(E) _____

_____.

[15] Remember that you ought to behave in life as you would at a banquet. As something is being passed around it comes to you; stretch out your hand and take a portion of it politely. It passes on; do not detain it. Or it has not come to you yet; do not project your desire to meet it, but wait until it comes in front of you. So act toward children, so toward a wife, so toward office, so toward wealth; and then some day you will be worthy of the banquets of the gods. But if you do not take these things even when they are set before you, but despise them, then you will not only share the banquet of the gods, but share also their rule. For it was by so doing that Diogenes and Heraclitus, and men like them, were deservedly divine and deservedly so called.

Epictetus describes four ways of behaving at the banquet of life. We can try to detain dishes that are passed to us, or wait impatiently for dishes to arrive, or take our proper portion, or refuse to take any portion. Thus, for example, I could try to hold onto my possessions, look forward impatiently toward having more possessions, have possessions but not be possessed by them, or reject, as far as possible, all possessions.

Diogenes of Sinope, who died in 320 B.C., was a Greek philosopher who protested the falsity of his society by living in a tub and going about in daylight with a lantern "looking for an honest man." An intriguing figure, Diogenes also mocked the customs of his day by doing everything in public that dogs do. Imagine that.

Now, using the example of a spouse, explain Epictetus's reasoning.

_____

_____

_____

_____

_____

_____.

[16] When you see someone weeping in sorrow, either because a child has gone on a journey, or because he has lost his property, beware that you be not carried away by the impression that the man is in the midst of external ills, but straightway keep before you this thought: "It is not what has happened that distresses this man (for it does not distress another), but his judgment about it." Do not, however, hesitate to sympathize with him so far as words go, and, if occasion offers, even to groan with him; but be careful not to groan also in the center of your being.

Assume you are a stoic comforting a neighbor whose mother has died.

I would say to myself, it is not _____ that

distresses you but _____.

What is the difference between a groan that does, and does not, come from the center of your being?

A groan for my neighbor that does not come from the center of my being would

be _____

_____.

A groan that does come from the center of my being would be _____

_____.

Is Epictetus recommending you be insincere when you comfort your neighbor?

I believe Epictetus (is, isn't) recommending insincerity when I comfort my neighbor

because _____

_____

_____

_____.

[17] Remember that you are an actor in a play, the character of which is determined by the Playwright; if He wishes the play to be short, it is short; if long, it is long; if he wishes you to play the part of a beggar, remember to act even this role adroitly; and so if your role be that of a cripple, an official, or a layman. For this is your business, to play admirably the role assigned you; but the selection of that role is Another's.

In the stoic's view of the human situation, we have no more control over our destiny than does a character in a play has over hers. Unlike the character, however, we should recognize that we are in a play. The best we can do is act our part well. Thus, if one asked Epictetus whether humans are free or not free, he would probably answer "both." Our station in society and the length of our life are out of our hands, assigned to us by the Divine Playwright. However, the way we interpret our role, whether we act it nobly or poorly, is our free choice.

I would say this view is (right, wrong) because _____

_____.

Here are a few last selections from the *Encheiridion*.

[28] If someone handed over your body to any person who met you, you would be vexed [annoyed]; but that you hand over your mind to any person that comes along, so that, if he reviles [attacks with abusive language] you, it is disturbed and troubled: are you not ashamed of that?

[38] Just as you are careful, in walking about, not to step on a nail or to sprain your ankle, so be careful also not to hurt your governing principle. And if we observe this rule in every action, we shall be more secure in setting about it [_____].

[53] Upon every occasion we ought to have the following thoughts at our command:

Lead thou me on, O Zeus, and Destiny,
To that goal long ago to me assigned,
I'll follow and not falter; if my will
Prove weak and craven [cowardly], still I'll follow on.
—Cleanthes

"Whoso has rightly with necessity complied, We count him wise, and skilled in things divine."
—Euripides

"Well, O Crito, if so it is pleasing to the gods, so let it be."
—Socrates [*Crito*]

"Anytus and Meletus can kill me, but they cannot hurt me."
—Socrates [*Apology*]

Cleanthes (331–232 B.C.) was a Greek stoic philosopher and pantheist. Consistent with pantheism (pan = all; theos = god), he held a view attractive to some students that God and the physical universe are identical.

EXERCISE 16.3
Summing Up

Sum up the most important aspects of Epictetus's philosophy and then evaluate its wisdom.

1. The main points Epictetus makes in *Encheiridion* are _____ _____ _____ _____ _____.

2. The wisest point he makes is _____ because _____.

3. The most foolish point he makes is _____ _____.

After reading Epictetus, a number of my students find stoicism inhuman. Here is a version of a blunt question that is frequently asked, and my best answer.

Question: How can stoic virtue be considered "good"? Stoics are inhuman; they don't care about anything! How, for example, can it be good to be as indifferent to the death of your spouse as to the breaking of a jug?

Answer: My answer is that in defense of the stoics, one might investigate what it is that allows us to endure the death of someone we love. Grief at the death of the beloved often goes through well-defined stages that begin with denial and end, finally, with acceptance. When we are in the stage of denial, we cannot accept that someone we love has died. Our lives come to a standstill because we cannot face the truth of mortality. When we finally reach the stage of acceptance, we understand that our beloved is gone. We can then get on with our lives because we recognize that all humans are mortal. Stoics understand the truth of mortality *while* they love and not simply after the death of the beloved. Thus, it is not the case that stoics don't care, only that they do not blindly care.

And so, have I convinced you that stoicism contains hidden Wisdom?

I believe stoicism (does, does not) contain hidden Wisdom because

_____

_____

_____

_____.

SUMMARY

By recognizing the difference between what we "own," our mental attitude, and what we don't "own," everything else that happens to us, the stoic can remain unmoved by all calamities. To maintain peace of mind, the stoic recognizes that all possessions are temporary and perishable, accepts the inevitability of death, realizes it is impossible to escape unpleasant experiences, serenely accepts the role Fate has assigned, and plays this role to the best of his or her ability.

EXERCISE 16.4
Looking Back

On your own paper, write a short essay answering the following question: What is the message of Epictetus's *Echeiridion*? Use original examples to illustrate Epictetus's position.

EXERCISE 16.5
Looking at the World Through Epictetus's Eyes

Answer each of the following as Epictetus would and then add evidence from this chapter to support your answer.

1. T F A good person feels no emotional pain.

   Evidence: _____

   _____

   _____.

2. T F A good person has no emotions.

   Evidence: _____

   _____

   _____.

3. T F Self-control is one of the highest virtues.

   Evidence: _____

   _____

   _____.

4. T F Obedience to God is the highest virtue.

   Evidence: _____

   _____

   _____.

5. T F Our lives should be guided by love, not reason.

   Evidence: _____

   _____

   _____.

6. T F What will be, will be.

   Evidence: _____

   _____

   _____.

ANALYSIS OF YOUR PHILOSOPHICAL SELF-PORTRAIT

To see how your views stack up against Epictetus's, read my analysis below, rethink your position, and then circle what you believe is the correct answer. I've underlined Epictetus's answers.

1. <u>T</u> F *All we can control is our attitude toward the world.*

   Epictetus makes this point at the beginning of the *Encheiridion*. When you think how often in daily life we become upset over what we have no control over, Epictetus makes sense. If stoicism has any appeal to you, try the experience of maintaining a stoic attitude for a week and keeping a journal of your reactions. As a true stoic, don't simply react unfeelingly to the world, but analyze each upsetting event in one of the creative ways Epictetus recommends in this chapter. Try "giving it back," "staying close to your Ship," and so forth.

2. <u>T</u> F *There is nothing more important than peace of mind.*

   Peace of mind is a pleasing description of the stoic virtue of *apathia* (apathy). But stoic apathy would not have to mean listless inactivity, as it usually does in the modern world; the stoically apathetic could be *energetically* indifferent.

3. T <u>F</u> *Because our free choices shape our destiny, Fate is an illusion.*

   Recognizing the power of Fate, and the forces of Nature is taken by the stoic as a mental tonic.

4. T <u>F</u> *Death is a worse calamity than fear of death.*

   Epictetus distinguishes between events and attitudes toward events. All of the pain of the sting of death is in our attitude toward death, not death itself.

5. T <u>F</u> *Love is the highest virtue.*

   If you are supposed to regard your child or spouse with the same indifference as a lovely but breakable jug, then love is hardly the highest stoic virtue. This, of course, does not mean that stoics are loveless but that they believe wisdom (which understands the perishability of everything in the world) is a higher virtue than love.

6. <u>T</u> F *The wisest person has the fewest possessions.*

   Stoics often looked to Socrates as an ideal. Socrates did not tour the Athenian marketplace in a gilded chariot.

7. <u>T</u> F *Nothing can harm a wise person.*

   Again, Socrates is an excellent model of the stoic ideal: "Anytus and Meletus can kill me, but they cannot hurt me."

   One story about Epictetus relates that he was being tortured by his owner. While his owner was twisting Epictetus's leg, Epictetus calmly said, "If you keep twisting my leg, you will break it."

   The owner, undeterred by his slave's calm reaction, or perhaps *because* of his slave's calm reaction, kept twisting the leg until it broke. Epictetus responded, "I told you so."

Evaluation: Number of points in agreement with Epictetus = _____ of 7 possible.

A position of Epictetus's that you strongly (support, oppose) is _____

_____

because _____.

GOOD BOOKS

Aurelius, Marcus. *The Meditations.* Translated by G. M. A. Grube. Indianapolis: Hackett, 1983. The philosophical diary of a brilliant Roman emperor, a stoic masterpiece. Highly recommended.

Burns, David. *Feeling Good: The New Mood Therapy.* New York: Avon, 1992. Despite the pop-psych title, this is a serious presentation of key elements of cognitive therapy, a psychological approach to self-analysis that traces its roots back to Epictetus and Marcus Aurelius. One of the most useful books that I've ever read.

NEXT STOP

Anselm, the first Christian philosopher on our tour, presents an intriguing proof of God's existence.

17

St. Anselm
How to Refute Atheists

YOUR PHILOSOPHICAL SELF-PORTRAIT

Add more details to your philosophical self-portrait by answering the questions below and providing evidence for your answers.

1. T F It is possible to prove that God exists. (Note that this is different from stating: "T or F: God exists." One can believe on faith that God exists without believing that God's existence can be proven.)

Evidence: _____

_____.

2. T F God can be defined.

Evidence: _____

_____.

3. T F Nothing that exists is perfect.

Evidence: _____

_____.

4. T F It is possible to think of God as not existing.

Evidence: _____

_____.

5. T F It is possible to imagine a being superior to God.

Evidence: _____

_____.

6. T F The mind can know truths independently of the senses.

Evidence: _____

_____.

7. T F It is greater for a thing to exist in the mind *and* in external reality than for it to exist only in the mind.

Evidence: _____

_____.

Anselm tries to prove that God exists by showing that atheists are wrong in denying God's existence. To refute atheism, Anselm argues that an investigation of the definition of God will prove God's existence. In other words, just as the investigation of the concept of triangle will prove that a triangle must have three sides, an investigation of the concept of God will prove that God must have existence.

Anselm begins with a definition of God as a being of which none greater can be thought—that is, as a being whom our conceptions cannot exceed. He then points out that when an atheist denies God's existence, the idea of God must exist at least in the atheist's mind. Anselm's next step is to argue that the atheist is self-refuting because to say God exists only as an idea is to say, in effect, that an unlimited being is a limited being. (This difficult point will be explored.)

Anselm concludes that because atheists are wrong in saying God does not exist, it is true to say God does exist.

I look out my window. A red foam of blossoms pours down my neighbor's rose trellis. The morning light turns all the leaves in the trees to leaves of light. A red-tailed hawk glides above Cherokee Peak. I wonder if there is any evidence out there that God exists.

And then I wonder how I could prove anything.

If I add two leaves to three leaves, couldn't I prove that the result is five leaves? Everyone but a skeptic would agree that this and similar mathematical statements are provable.

If a red-tailed hawk is a bird and all birds are animals, then it certainly seems obvious that a red-tailed hawk is an animal. This and similar linguistic relationships seem obviously provable.

But what is it that *makes* the truths of mathematics and relationships between words provable?

A successful proof requires obviously true evidence combined in a way that makes the conclusion undeniable. If it is obviously true that I have three leaves and two leaves, then, when combined, this evidence makes undeniable the conclusion that I have five leaves. If it is obviously true that a red-tailed hawk is a bird and that all birds are animals, then, when combined, this evidence makes undeniable the conclusion that a red-tailed hawk is an animal.

But where could anyone find obviously true evidence that, when properly combined, makes undeniable the conclusion that God exists?

Give it your best shot.

My obviously true evidence is _____

_____

_____

_____.

Therefore, God exists.

Anselm (1033–1109)

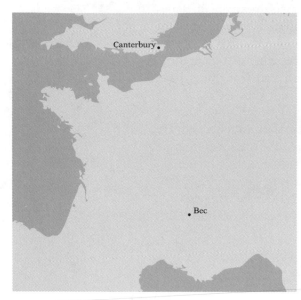

Anselm shaped his life, in great measure, by resisting the will of his father and two kings of England.

Born in northwestern Italy to a noble family, Anselm rejected his father's urging that he enter politics. Instead he entered the monastic life, where he received an excellent education through the study of ancient Roman writers as well as the Bible. In 1057, Anselm left Italy to join the monastery of Bec, in southern France. He took his final monastic vows there in 1060 at the age of 27, and, because of his remarkable intelligence and piety, was elected prior of the monastery three years later.

In 1077 Anselm wrote the first of his three great works. In the *Monologium* ("Monologue"), he presented an argument for God's existence based upon the different degrees of goodness, justice, and power in the world. Such various degrees, he argued, indicated an absolute standard. This standard is God; thus God exists.

Shortly after writing the *Monologium*, Anselm became abbot of Bec. Under his leadership, the monastery became a well-known center of learning. While abbot, Anselm composed the *Proslogium* ("Address"), which contains his famous ontological (so-called by Kant) argument for God's existence. Anselm argues that the existence of God can be proved by a careful examination of the idea of God.

While visiting England, Anselm was convinced by William II to become archbishop of Canterbury. Anselm's hesitancy was based upon his well-founded fear that the king would, as his father William I had, heavily tax the Church and maintain political control over its leaders. During his tenure as archbishop, Anselm became deeply involved in what has become known as the investiture controversy. The superficial issue involved whether or not the king had the right to bestow upon, or invest, a bishop with the symbols of his office. The deeper issue involved a contest between pope and king as to who would have ultimate authority, including financial control, over religious institutions. Anselm took the side of the clergy against both William II and his successor, Henry I. Though it cost him a three-year exile from England, Anselm's side of the debate proved victorious when Henry I at the Synod of Westminster agreed to renounce his claims to investiture rights in exchange for bishops and abbots swearing allegiance to him prior to their consecration.

During this political turmoil, Anselm wrote *Cur Deus homo?* ("Why Did God Become Man?") He presented the satisfaction theory of redemption, which became a classic Medieval description of the relationship between humans and God. Accepting the standard view of the Middle Ages, that the higher the rank of the individual one committed a crime against, the greater the penalty, satisfaction, one would have to pay, Anselm argued that our crimes, sins, against God, the supreme ruler, demanded the supreme penalty, eternal death. Only by God's intervention, in the person of Christ, are we spared this just penalty.

After spending a considerable portion of his life in a struggle with the English kingship, Anselm lived his last two years in peace, dying on April 21, 1109. Fifty years later, at the urging of another archbishop of Canterbury who would have great troubles with an English king, Thomas Beckett, Anselm was canonized as a saint.

Surprisingly enough, St. Anselm and other great philosophers have held that God's existence can be proven as certainly, even more certainly, than the truth of $2 + 3 = 5$. How can this be?

Anselm's proof of God's existence is called the **ontological** argument.

The ontological argument is both amazing and difficult. Anselm's proof is amazing because he tries to demonstrate God's existence by analyzing our *definition* of God. In other words, he tries to show that the clearest way to prove the existence of the author of the **cosmos** is to turn inward and examine our idea of God. Anselm's difficulty lies in three areas: his unusual-sounding definition of God, his analysis of what it means to think of this definition, and his indirect method of proving God's existence by attacking atheism.

One of the easiest ways to understand Anselm's argument for God's existence is to think of his proof as answering the following questions. The questions are

- What is a definition of God?

- What must even an atheist admit about God?

- What is wrong with an atheist's understanding of the idea of God?

- Why are atheists self-contradictory?

- How can a refutation of atheism prove that God exists?

- What are some objections that can be offered to the ontological argument?

First, we'll examine Anselm's ontological argument and explore, in detail, his answers to the first five questions. Then we'll evaluate some of the most common objections to Anselm's proof.

What Is a Definition of God?

Here are the first two sentences of Anselm's proof:

[1] Well then, Lord, You who give understanding to faith, grant me that I may understand, as much as You see fit, that You exist as we believe You to exist, and that You are what we believe You to be.

[2] Now we believe that You are something of which nothing greater can be thought.

All that needs to be said about sentence 1 is that it is Anselm's prayer to God, asking for His help.

Sentence 2, however, requires more attention. Anselm presents his definition of God as "something than which nothing greater can be thought." To clarify what Anselm means, let's imagine variations of this definition.

- Mt. Everest is a mountain than which nothing greater can be thought.

- A banana split is a dessert than which nothing greater can be thought.

- Disney World is an entertainment park than which nothing greater can be thought.

Now, you try a few similar sentences.

_____ is a(n) _____ _____ _____

than which nothing greater can be thought.

ontology The branch of metaphysics that deals with the nature of being. Immanuel Kant was the first to identify Anselm's proof as "ontological."

cosmos The universe. A cosmological proof of God's existence, often contrasted with an ontological proof, begins with the universe to show that only God could be the designer of the universe and therefore God must exist.

_____ is a(n) _____

than which nothing greater can be thought.

_____ is a(n) _____

than which nothing greater can be thought.

If we say that Mt. Everest is a mountain than which nothing greater can be thought, we are saying considerably more than that Mt. Everest is the tallest mountain on earth. We are saying that Mt. Everest is taller than *any mountain that can be conceived.* We are claiming that Mt. Everest exceeds every mountain, even mountains in our imagination. In the same way, if we say that Disney World is an entertainment park than which nothing greater can be thought, we are saying that Disney World exceeds not only every actual entertainment park, but also every imaginary, every conceivable, entertainment park.

Now these claims about Mt. Everest and Disney World are obviously false. We can easily conceive of a mountain greater than Mt. Everest—for example, a mountain a thousand miles high. And we can easily conceive of an entertainment park greater than Disney World—for example, an entertainment park exactly like Disney World but which is free. But if we define *God* as "something than which nothing greater can be thought," are we talking about something that exists or doesn't exist? Is there actually a being so great that we can't, *even in imagination,* conceive of a greater being? Anselm, of course, says such a being—God—exists. His strategy is to attack atheism.

What Must Even an Atheist Admit About God?

Here are the next three sentences of Anselm's argument. Underline his answer to the question, "What must even an atheist admit about God?"

> [3] Or can it be that a thing of such a nature does not exist, since "the Fool has said in his heart, there is no God" [Psalm 13]?
> [4] But surely, when this same Fool hears what I am speaking about, namely, "something than which nothing greater can be thought," he understands what he hears, and what he understands is in his mind, even if he does not understand that it actually exists. [5] For it is one thing for an object to exist in the mind, and another thing to understand that an object actually exists.

We'll go through this slowly.

In sentence 3, "Or can it be that a thing of such a nature does not exist, since 'the Fool has said in his heart, there is no God,'" Anselm presents the Fool in Psalms who says there is no God. The Fool, of course, represents atheism.

In sentences 4 and 5 Anselm answers our question, "What must even an atheist admit about God?"

> [4] But surely, when this same Fool hears what I am speaking about, namely, "something than which nothing greater can be thought," he understands what he hears, and what he understands is in his mind, even if he does not understand that it actually exists. [5] For it is one thing for an object to exist in the mind, and another thing to understand that an object actually exists.

Anselm begins his attack on the Fool (and atheism) in sentences 4 and 5 by saying that the definition of God as "something than which nothing greater can be thought" exists at least in the Fool's mind if not in reality. In other words, even though the Fool says there is no God, the Fool must admit that God does exist, if only in a limited sense, as a concept in the Fool's mind.

Putting this another way, to deny that God exists in reality, the Fool must admit that God exists in his mind—so that he knows what he is denying.

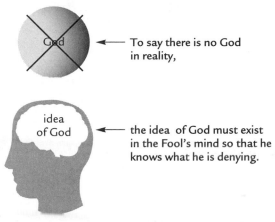

To say there is no God in reality,

the idea of God must exist in the Fool's mind so that he knows what he is denying.

The Fool's Mind

Now, let's go on to sentences 6–8 of the proof. Note how by using the example of a painter, Anselm continues to elaborate his answer to the question, "What must even an atheist admit about God?"

[6] Thus, when a painter plans before hand what he is going to execute, he has [the picture] in his mind, but he does not yet think that it actually exists because he has not yet executed it. [7] However, when he has actually painted it, then he both has it in his mind and understands that it exists because he has now made it. [8] Even the Fool, then, is forced to agree that something than which nothing greater can be thought exists in the mind, since he understands this when it hears it, and whatever is understood is in the mind.

What point is Anselm making about the painter?

_____

_____

_____

_____

By talking about the painter, what point is Anselm making about the Fool?

_____

_____

_____

_____

Now, summarize the major points Anselm has made in sentences 1–8 (you don't have to paraphrase each sentence).

_____

_____

_____

_____

_____

_____

_____

_____.

Next, almost out of nowhere, Anselm makes a surprisingly powerful attack on atheism.

What Is Wrong with an Atheist's Understanding of the Idea of God?

I've requoted sentence 8 so that you can see the context of Anselm's attack on atheism.

> [8] Even the Fool, then, is forced to agree that something than which nothing greater can be thought exists in the mind, since he understands this when he hears it, and whatever is understood is in the mind.
> [9] And surely that than which a greater cannot be thought [God] cannot exist in the mind alone. [10] For if it [God] exists solely in the mind even, it [God] can be thought to exist in reality also, which is greater.

How can Anselm suddenly claim that God exists not only in the Fool's mind, but *also* in reality? It is certainly obvious that the definition of God exists in the Fool's—or anyone's—mind, but how can the leap be made from that definition of God to God's actually existing?

A paraphrase of sentence 9 would be:

God cannot exist only in the mind.

Sentence 10 provides evidence for sentence 9 and could be stated as:

Because if God exists in the mind, then God can be thought to also exist in reality and existing in reality is greater than existing only in the mind.

You probably almost follow Anselm's attack on atheism. Let me state his argument as simply as I can and then use a diagram to show the difference between Anselm's and the Fool's view of God.

Anselm is saying that the Fool is wrong when he says God exists only in the mind. Anselm's reasoning is as follows: *A God who exists both in the mind and in reality is greater than a God who exists only in the mind.*

Anselm is asking us to choose between two versions of God, the Fool's version of God, which exists only in the mind, and Anselm's version of God, which exists in the mind *and* reality. Here is a diagram showing both views:

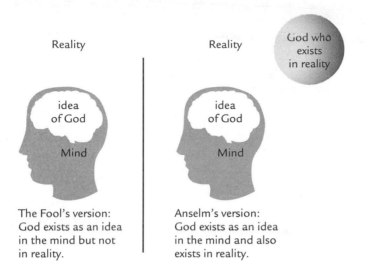

Reality	Reality	God who exists in reality
idea of God	idea of God	
Mind	Mind	

The Fool's version: God exists as an idea in the mind but not in reality.

Anselm's version: God exists as an idea in the mind and also exists in reality.

Now, the question is, How do we decide which of these two pictures is correct? Is it the case, as the Fool believes, that God exists only as an idea in the mind or, as Anselm believes, is it the case that God exists as an idea in the mind *and* also in reality?

Anselm points out, quite logically, that to decide what kind of being God is, we should look at what we mean by the definition, the essence, of God. For example, if I asked you to look at what I was holding and decide if it was a duodecahedron, you would look up duodecahedron in a dictionary, learn its definition, its essence, and then compare the definition to the object.

Recall that Anselm, early in his proof, says that anyone, even the Fool, understands the definition of God. The word "God" refers to a being "than which nothing greater can be thought," that is, a supreme being, a being that can't be exceeded even in our imagination. And so the issue is straightforward. Which of the two pictures above shows God as we use the word "God"? Which shows God as the truly supreme being?

I would say (the Fool's picture, Anselm's picture) because _____

_____

_____ .

Anselm argues that the supreme being who exists in our mind *and* in reality portrays the essence of the supreme being, the being "than which nothing greater can be thought." The Fool's version of the supreme being is a mere idea, hardly a supreme being at all.

Now read carefully. The next section of the proof is the brilliant and difficult core of the ontological argument.

Why Are Atheists Self-Contradictory?

You are now at the heart of Anselm's argument. Read this page, and the next two pages slowly.

A self-contradictory statement is a statement that disproves itself. For example, "the road from here to the corner is a straight curve" is self-contradictory. Curves can't be straight; thus, the statement disproves itself. Anselm wants to show that atheism is self-contradictory, that it disproves itself. According to Anselm, if we analyze what an atheist is saying, we will see that to say God does not exist is the same as saying God is not-God. And just as it is self-contradictory to say a curve is straight or black is not-black, it is obviously self-contradictory to say God is not-God.

But *how* does Anselm show that atheists are self-contradictory?

I've requoted sentences 9 and 10 to give you the context for Anselm's attempt to show that atheists are self-contradictory.

> [9] And surely that than which a greater cannot be thought [God] *cannot exist in the mind alone* [italics added]. [10] For if it [God] exists solely in the mind even, it [God] can be thought to exist in reality also, which is greater.
>
> [11] If then that than which a greater cannot be thought exists in the mind alone, this same that than which a greater cannot be thought is that than which a greater can be thought. [12] But this is obviously impossible.
>
> [13] Therefore, there is absolutely no doubt that something than which a greater cannot be thought exists both in the mind and reality.

Sentence 11 is the most difficult sentence to understand in the entire proof. I'll use three steps to clarify its meaning. First, I'll divide the sentence into two parts and underline key phrases; second, to clarify Anselm's pattern of reasoning, I'll substitute synonyms for the more complex phrases; finally I'll relate the entire sentence to the Fool's and Anselm's pictures of God.

First, let's break sentence 11 into smaller pieces, and highlight key phrases.

1. "If then <u>that than which a greater cannot be thought</u> exists in the mind alone,

2. this same <u>that than which a greater cannot be thought</u> is **that than which a greater *can* be thought.**"

Note that the two underlined sections are identical. Next note that the bold-faced section is the *opposite* of the underlined sections.

(Don't go further until you understand what I just said!)

Now let's take the second step and replace the complex underlined and bold-faced words with synonyms.

"That than which a greater cannot be thought" is, remember, Anselm's definition of God. (God is a being who can't be exceeded even in our imagination.)

"That than which a greater *can* be thought" is, therefore, the opposite of God (for shorthand, we'll call the opposite of God, not-God).

Observe how much clearer Anselm's pattern of reasoning becomes when we use synonyms for his complex phrases.

1. If then God exists in the mind alone,

2. this same God is not-God.

Anselm is accusing the Fool of being self-contradictory.

Just as it is self-contradictory to say a curve is straight or black is not black, it is self-contradictory to say God is not God.

But why does Anselm believe the Fool is being self-contradictory?

Let's take the third step, and look again at the Fool's and Anselm's versions of God.

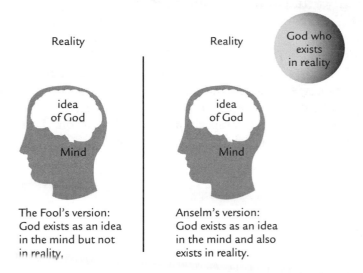

Reality   Reality   God who exists in reality

idea of God   idea of God

Mind   Mind

The Fool's version: God exists as an idea in the mind but not in reality.

Anselm's version: God exists as an idea in the mind and also exists in reality.

Which of these two pictures shows a being "than which none greater can be conceived"?

I would say (the Fool's, Anselm's) because _____

_____

_____.

Look at the Fool's picture of God. He is saying that God, the supreme being, exists only in the mind. This means the Fool is claiming that the greatest being that can be conceived of *exists as a mere idea*. Isn't this clearly wrong? The greatest being that can be conceived of would exist as an idea in the mind *and in external reality*. The Fool's picture of the supreme being is far less supreme than is Anselm's picture. By picturing the supreme being as nonsupreme, the Fool is picturing God as not-God.

One more time.

Let's say the Fool showed you his picture of God and exclaimed, "You can't conceive of a greater being than this!" How would you reply?

I would say _____

_____

_____.

All you would have to do to refute the Fool would be to show him Anselm's picture. A God who exists both in the mind and in reality is clearly greater than one who exists only in the mind. The Fool is claiming that God, an unlimited being, is limited to existing as a mere idea. Thus, he is being self-contradictory. The Fool's picture of God is not God.

After the difficulties involved in understanding Anselm's answer to the earlier questions, you will be happy to know that Anselm's answer to our last question is simple to understand.

How Can a Refutation of Atheism Prove That God Exists?

Self-test: Is Anselm a rationalist or empiricist? (The answer is on page 377.)

Anselm has shown that it is wrong to say that God exists in the mind alone and right to say God exists in the mind *and* in reality. Anselm believes he has shown atheism is wrong in such a way that also proves that theism, belief in God, is right. Just as a light can be either on or off, God can exist or not exist. If it is wrong that the light is off, then it is right that the light is on; if it is wrong that God doesn't exist, then it is right that God does exist.

Well, has Anselm convinced you?

I believe _____

_____

_____.

Now, before looking at some common objections to the ontological argument, test your own understanding by completing the following exercise.

EXERCISE 17.1
What Are the Key Points in the Ontological Argument?

Use your own paper to answer the following questions about key points in the ontological proof:

1. God can be defined as that than which a greater cannot be thought. What does this mean?

2. God, as a concept, exists in the mind of anyone who denies God's existence. What is Anselm's evidence for this?

3. When the Fool says God doesn't exist, he is being self-contradictory and is really saying that God is not-God. How does Anselm show that the Fool is being self-contradictory?

4. The Fool's picture of God existing only in the mind is really a picture of not-God. How does this prove that God exists?

What Are Some Objections That Can Be Offered to the Ontological Argument?

We'll consider three kinds of objections to Anselm's proof: those by students, one by a contemporary of Anselm, and one by Immanuel Kant, an eighteenth-century German philosopher we will explore later on our tour.

Here are some of the most frequent student objections and my best answers.

Question: What on earth is Anselm trying to do? Isn't his proof just a word game?

Answer: Anselm is trying to prove God's existence by examining God's essence, God's defining characteristics. Just as when we think of a triangle, we must think of a figure that has three sides, so when we think of God, we must think of a being who has existence. According to Anselm, the ultimate being of the universe could hardly be defined as the ultimate being of the universe if He existed as nothing but an idea in our heads.

Anselm is not playing a word game. He is trying to show that by investigating a particular word, "God," we can find irrefutable evidence of God's existence.

Question: How can Anselm say that just because someone has an idea of God, that means God actually exists? I have an idea of Superman, but that doesn't mean that Superman actually exists.

Answer: The idea of God is different, according to Anselm, from the idea of anything else. Contrast the idea of God with the idea of Superman.

When we think of Superman we think of a being who can fly, "is able to leap tall buildings at a single bound," who is very rapid, "faster than a speeding bullet," and who is moral, "fights a never ending battle for Truth, Justice, and the American Way." But when we think of Superman we do *not* think of a being than whom none greater can be conceived. It is easy to think of a being greater than Superman—for example, someone who wouldn't be paralyzed by Kryptonite, someone who could read minds, someone who could create matter.

God, however, is very different, not only from Superman but also from everything else in the universe. *We can add nothing to our idea of God to make our idea greater.* We can always improve our idea of anything else. Superman, a dessert, Disney World, are all easy to surpass in our conceptions. *Nothing except God is a being than whom none greater can be thought.*

Thus, while it is true that our idea of Superman does not prove Superman's existence, our idea of God, unlike any other idea we could have, does prove God's existence. To think of God as lacking existence is as impossible as thinking of a square lacking sides.

Question: Isn't there something fishy about defining God as "that than which a greater cannot be thought"?

Answer: "That than which a greater cannot be thought" is an unusual, but accurate, way to define God. To say God is "that than which a greater cannot be thought" is equivalent to saying God is the supreme being.

There are many definitions of God that all amount to the same thing. God is the ultimate being; God is the supreme being in all reality; God has all perfections. But when Anselm carefully and brilliantly chooses the definition of God as "that than which a greater cannot be thought," he most clearly points at the contradiction committed by the Fool or anyone else who says God does not exist. To say God does not exist is really to say, as you have seen, that God exists as a mere idea. However, to say God exists as a mere idea is to say God, the supreme being, is really not-God, the nonsupreme being.

Question: But why can't God "not exist"? A triangle can "not exist."

Answer: You are right that a triangle can "not exist" but God has one very important characteristic that no triangle or anything else has. To make clear God's absolutely unique characteristic, let's think first about triangles.

Let us say you draw a perfect triangle on the board. Your perfect triangle has three absolutely straight lines and its interior angles exactly equal 180 degrees. Your triangle has all the perfections that a triangle can have. But, of course, having absolutely straight sides and interior angles exactly equaling 180 degrees does not guarantee that your triangle will exist forever. You can simply wipe it off the board. Triangles can exist or not exist. Existing is not one of a triangle's, even a perfect triangle's, defining characteristics. Get clear on this. A perfect triangle has only triangle perfections; it doesn't have all perfections—it isn't indestructible.

Now God is a quite different case. God's essence is that He has *all* perfections; God is a being who can't be exceeded even in our imaginations. If God had one less than all perfections, we could think of a being greater than God. And if he has all perfections, according to Anselm, he must have the perfection of existence in reality.

Question: But is something that exists in reality "more perfect" than something that doesn't exist? I can imagine a city that is far more perfect than any actual city.

Answer: Take two perfect cities that are identical, except that one exists and one doesn't exist. Isn't the city that exists infinitely more perfect than the imaginary city?

I believe the city that exists (Is, Isn't) infinitely more perfect than the imaginary

city because _____

_____

_____.

From Anselm's point of view, of two identical beings who are defined as perfect, the one that exists is far more perfect than the one that doesn't. A God who exists in reality is far more perfect than a God who exists only in the Fool's skull.

If you still don't buy this, which would you rather have, a perfect *imaginary* GPA, or a perfect *actual* GPA? Which is truly perfect, the GPA that doesn't exist or the GPA that does exist?

I would say the GPA that (does, does not) exist is truly perfect because

_____

_____

_____.

Question: Can't you just put all this in a nutshell? It's too confusing. What's Anselm saying?

Answer: I can't put the basic idea of the ontological argument more clearly than this: If you subtract three-sidedness from a triangle, you no longer have a triangle, a three-sided geometrical figure. Therefore, triangles must have three sides. If you subtract existence from God, you no longer have God, a perfect being. Therefore, God must exist.

Question: Is Anselm right?

Answer: Though most philosophers think Anselm is wrong, there has been a recent revival of interest in the ontological argument. A group of American philosophers of religion, using the latest techniques of modern logic, have defended the soundness of a version of Anselm's argument. According to one authority, Anselm's position "which twenty years ago was thought as dead as the dodo is now alive and well and living in Indiana and California."[1]

Question: What do philosophers say is wrong with Anselm's argument?

Answer: Answering that question would be doing too much of your thinking for you. However, some of the exercises that follow will give you interesting clues.

EXERCISE 17.2
The Gaunilo Puzzle

After Anselm published his proof of God's existence, he was soon attacked by a fellow monk, Gaunilo. Following is a short but central excerpt from Gaunilo's attempted refutation of Anselm:

"They say that there is in the ocean somewhere an island which, because of the difficulty (or rather the impossibility) of finding that which does not exist some have called the 'Lost Island.' The story goes that it is blessed with all manner of priceless riches and delights in abundance, much more even than the Happy Isles, and having no owner or inhabitant, it is superior everywhere in abundance of riches to all those other lands that men inhabit. Now, if anyone tells me that it is like this, I shall easily understand what is said, since nothing is difficult about it. But if he should then go on to say, as though it were a logical consequence of this: You cannot any more doubt that this island that is more excellent than all other lands truly exists somewhere in reality than you can doubt that it is in your mind; and since it is more excellent to exist not only in the mind alone but also in reality, therefore it must needs be that it exists. For if it did not exist, any other land existing in reality would be more excellent than it, and so this island [the Lost Island], already conceived by you to be more excellent than others, will not be more excellent. If, I say, someone wishes to persuade me that this island really exists beyond all doubt, I should either think that he was joking, or I should find it hard to decide which of us I ought to judge the bigger fool—I, if I agree with him, or he, if he thought that he had proved the existence of this island with any certainty."

Here are two questions to prepare you for a tough puzzle:

1. What is Gaunilo saying about the Lost Island?
2. How would Gaunilo use his example of the Lost Island to attack Anselm's proof of God's existence?

The Gaunilo puzzle: Once you understand Gaunilo's argument, you may believe that he has succeeded in defeating Anselm. Anselm, however, according to all commentators I am aware of, successfully answered him. In fact, Gaunilo is

---

[1] Bryan Magee, *The Great Philosophers*, (New York: Oxford University Press, 1987) p. 71.

Philosophy, Anselm, and the Prison of Language

From Anselm's point of view, existence is a perfection, because if something is perfect, it can lack nothing; and lacking existence means lacking a great deal. If you had a perfect hexagon and it lacked the perfection of existence, then the hexagon, according to Anselm, could hardly be perfect.

Immanuel Kant and other critics of Anselm think he is wrong. They hold that existence is not a perfection. Kant would say that a perfect hexagon is an enclosed geometrical figure with six exactly equal sides joined to each other by 60-degree angles. To say a perfect hexagon exists or does not exist, for Kant, does not make the sides any more equal or the angles any more precise. Saying that the perfect hexagon has the "perfection of existence" adds absolutely nothing to its meaning.

The large and profound question here is "What is language?" Does language point *beyond* itself or only *at* itself? If Anselm is right, then an investigation of the word "God" will point beyond the word to God's actual existence; if Anselm's critics are right, then an investigation of the word "God" points only to the word "God." Is language a prison or a window? Or, as Anselm argues in the case of the word "God," can language be a prison window?

probably remembered only because of how elegantly Anselm destroyed his argument. Therefore, match wits with Anselm. How could Gaunilo's argument be demolished in a way that is consistent with the ontological argument?

For most introductory students, this is a tough puzzle; I hope it inspires you to know that only about one student in twenty can solve it. Of course, any successful solution to the puzzle would begin with thorough answers to questions 1 and 2 above.

EXERCISE 17.3
Kant's Attack on the Ontological Argument

Immanuel Kant made what many believe is the decisive attack on Anselm's ontological argument. Underline key passages and fill in the [_____] with the correct reference words.

A hundred real thalers [units of German currency] do not contain the least coin more than a hundred possible thalers. For as the latter [_____] signify the concept, and the former [_____] the object and the positing of the object, should the former [_____] contain more than the latter [_____], my concept would not, in that case, express the whole object, and would not therefore be an adequate concept of it [_____].

My financial position is, however, affected very differently by a hundred real thalers than it is by the mere concept of them . . . ; yet the conceived hundred thalers are not themselves in the least increased through thus acquiring existence outside my concept.

By whatever and by however many predicates we may think a thing—even if we completely determine it—we do not make the least addition to the thing when we further declare that this thing *is*. Otherwise, it would not be exactly the

VOCABULARY MAP

St. Anselm

Anselm's **metaphysics,** his view of reality, is clearly **dualistic;** all that exists is divided between the realm of God and the physical universe. As a **Christian dualist,** Anselm can be distinguished from a **Platonic dualist** because Anselm holds that God, as described in the Judeo-Christian tradition, occupies the supreme position in reality, as opposed to the Form of the Good.

Anselm's **epistemology,** his view of the knowledge process, is clearly **rationalistic.** In

other words, Anselm believes that the mind can know some truths independently of the senses. As demonstrated in this chapter, Anselm holds that the mind gains knowledge of God's existence by turning inward, away from the sense world, and examining an idea, specifically the idea of God.

In general, one can say that philosophers who hold that the inner way into the mind is the path to truth are **rationalists;** those who hold that the outer way into the physical world is the road to truth are **empiricists.**

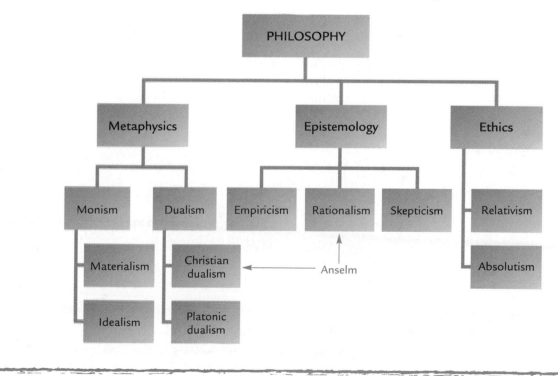

same thing that exists, but something more than we had thought in the concept; and we could not, therefore, say that the exact object of my concept exists.

The attempt to establish the existence of a supreme being by means of the famous ontological argument of Descartes [borrowed from Anselm] is therefore merely so much labour and effort lost; we can no more extend our stock of [theoretical] insight by mere ideas, than a merchant can better his position by adding a few noughts [zeros] to his cash account.

Use your own paper for the following:

1. What point is Kant making about a hundred real thalers and a hundred imaginary thalers?

2. Paraphrase the second sentence of Kant's argument ("For as the latter . . . ").

3. Paraphrase the fourth sentence of Kant's argument ("By whatever and by . . . ").

4. Anselm argues that a being that exists in the mind and in reality is greater than a being that exists only in the mind. How does Kant attack this argument?

5. Who is right, Kant or Anselm?

SUMMARY

Anselm tries to proves God's existence by refuting atheism. He begins by defining God as a being of that none greater can be thought. His next point is that even an atheist (the Fool) must admit that this definition exists in the understanding. This leads Anselm to argue that limiting God to existence as a concept in the understanding is defining God as not-God. To say that God is only an idea is to contradict the definition of God as a being of that none greater can be thought. A being of that none greater can be thought must be more than an idea, must actually exist.

EXERCISE 17.4
Looking Back

Use your own paper to paraphrase the answers to the five questions that guided our analysis of Anselm's argument.

1. What is a definition of God?

2. What must even an atheist admit about God?

3. What is wrong with an atheist's understanding of the idea of God?

4. Why are atheists self-contradictory?

5. How can a refutation of atheism prove that God exists?

EXERCISE 17.5
Looking at the World Through Anselm's Eyes

Answer the following from Anselm's point of view; use evidence from our analysis of the ontological argument.

1. T F There is nothing about God that can be understood by the human mind.

   Evidence: _____
   _____
   _____.

2. T F By analyzing the concept of God, we can absolutely prove that God exists.

   Evidence: _____
   _____
   _____.

3. T F The only way to prove that God exists is to look at the glory of the universe He has created.

   Evidence: _____
   _____
   _____.

4. T F God is to His existence as a triangle is to three-sidedness.

   Evidence: _____
   _____
   _____.

5. T F While a being may not actually exist who is greater than God, it is possible to imagine such a being.

   Evidence: _____
   _____
   _____.

ANALYSIS OF YOUR PHILOSOPHICAL SELF-PORTRAIT

To see how your views about the nature of reality stack up against Anselm's, read my analysis below, rethink your position, and then circle what you believe is the correct answer. I've underlined Anselm's answers.

1. <u>T</u> F *It is possible to prove that God exists.*

    Answering this question True makes you some variety of theist, one who believes in God's existence. However, you could answer this question False and still believe God existed; you simply might hold that the God you believe in cannot be known through proof.

    In regard to proofs of God's existence, there are two major positions. One position holds that understanding leads to faith; in other words, a proof of

God's existence will create the faith necessary to believe in God. A second position holds that faith leads to understanding; in other words, belief in God must come prior to understanding, or even proof of, God's existence.

Which of these two positions do you think is Anselm's?

The (first, second) position is Anselm's because _____

_____

_____ .

2. <u>T</u>   F   *God can be defined.*

Perhaps you answered False because you felt that defining God would mean fully understanding God; you might also believe that since fully understanding God is impossible, defining God is impossible. Defining a thing, however, is different from fully understanding it. We could define the earth as the third planet from the sun, but this would not mean that we had a full understanding of the earth. Knowing the defining characteristics of X is not the same as knowing everything that can be known about X.

3. T   <u>F</u>   *Nothing that exists is perfect.*

Anselm would answer this False because, from his view, everything *but* God is imperfect. He would even go one step further. If God did not exist, he would not be perfect. According to Anselm, existence is a primary feature of God's perfection.

4. T   <u>F</u>   *It is possible to think of God as not existing.*

Anselm would answer this False. Just as it is impossible to think of a triangle as a two-sided figure, because this would mean thinking of a triangle as lacking one of its defining characteristics (three sides), so it is impossible to think of God as a nonexisting being, because this would mean thinking of God as lacking one of his defining characteristics (existence). What is a good argument against this position?

_____

_____

_____

_____ .

5. T   <u>F</u>   *It is possible to imagine a being superior to God.*

Imagine that you are thinking of a being superior to God. What is more supreme than supreme? What is higher than highest? It is precisely the impossibility of conceiving of a being greater than God that Anselm uses to refute the Fool. The Fool's God exists *only* in his mind, and thus it is easy to conceive of a greater being—one who exists in actuality.

6. <u>T</u>   F   *The mind can know truths independently of the senses.*

Anselm holds this is True. By analyzing the idea of God, Anselm takes the inner path to God. As you will see in the next chapter, by analyzing the physical world, Aquinas takes the outer path to God. The inner path is rationalistic; the outer path is empirical.

7. <u>T</u> F *It is greater for a thing to exist in the mind and in external reality than for it to exist only in the mind.*

A True puts you in Anselm's camp.

Isn't a perfect academic transcript that exists only in your mind inferior to one that exists in your mind and actuality?

I say _____

_____

_____.

What would Kant say?

_____

_____

_____.

(This question gets at the same issue as questions 3 and 4; check to see that you held the same position in all cases.)

Evaluation: Number of points in agreement with Anselm = _____ of 7 possible.

A position of Anselm's that you strongly (support, oppose) is _____

_____

because _____.

GOOD BOOKS

Hartshorne, Charles. *Anselm's Discovery.* LaSalle, Ill.: Open Court, 1962. A review of Anselm's position by a contemporary philosopher who argues that a version of Anselm's argument is correct.

Mackie, J. L. *The Miracle of Theism: Arguments For and Against the Existence of God.* Oxford: Clarendon Press, 1982. A good overview.

NEXT STOP

St. Thomas Aquinas argues that there are five ways, far stronger than Anselm's, to prove God's existence.

18
St. Thomas Aquinas
Five Ways to Prove God's Existence

YOUR PHILOSOPHICAL SELF-PORTRAIT

Add more details to your philosophical self-portrait by answering the questions below and offering evidence for your answers.

1. T F Just as one could prove that a whole is larger than one of its parts simply by thinking about the concept of whole, so one could prove that God exists simply by thinking about the concept of God.

    Evidence: _____
    _____.

2. T F Knowledge of God's existence is implanted in us at birth.

    Evidence: _____
    _____.

3. T F If God existed and were truly all-powerful, then evil wouldn't exist in our world.

    Evidence: _____
    _____.

4. T F Because all that exists can be explained as caused by nature or the human will, God is not needed as an explanation of the universe.

    Evidence: _____
    _____.

5. T F There must have been some first cause, which had no preceding cause, that started the universe.

    Evidence: _____
    _____.

6. T F We know God exists because, if God didn't exist, the universe wouldn't exist.

    Evidence: _____.

7. T F Because some things in nature (rocks, plants, animals) are more perfect and others are less perfect, we can deduce that God, the source of all perfection, exists.

    Evidence: _____.

8. T F Everything in nature is guided by a divine intelligence.

    Evidence: _____.

On this section of the tour, we examine St. Thomas Aquinas's attack upon Anselm's ontological argument for God's existence and Aquinas's own proofs of God's existence.

Aquinas attacks Anselm's position by arguing that God's existence is not self-evident.

Key ideas in Aquinas's five proofs may be summarized as follows: (1) God is the First Mover, or initiator of the motion we observe in the universe; (2) God is the First Cause of the effects we observe in the universe; (3) God causes the universe to continue to exist; (4) God is the source of the hierarchy of perfections we observe in the universe; (5) God is the intelligence that guides nature.

Although the following thought experiment may contain an enormous error, almost all of my students find it an excellent proof of God's existence.

THOUGHT EXPERIMENT

You're walking along the beach. Blue sky, big waves, white clouds. You find a pocket watch lying in the sand and pick it up. The watch is keeping perfect time. Opening the back of the case, you observe the precise motion of the tiny parts. Each jeweled gear and coiled spring moves with perfect regularity.

Now which of these two alternatives is most plausible?

1. The workings of the watch fell into the case by accident, and then random motion, over many years, jiggled everything into the perfect order you observe.

2. The perfect order you observe was designed by a watchmaker.

The most plausible alternative is (1, 2) because _____
_____
_____.

If you are like 99 percent of my students, you answered 2. The intelligent design of the watch testifies to the existence of a human intelligence, a watchmaker, as its designer.

But how could this be taken as evidence that God exists?

Everything in the natural world of the beach—the sun, clouds, sky, motion of the tides—is enormously more intricate than the pocket watch. However elaborate the workings of a timepiece, they are nothing compared to the stunning complexity of even the smallest part of nature. A million jeweled gears could not raise the tide an inch or turn a seagull through the air. A sand crab, a bit of seaweed, or a drop of water is infinitely more complex than any human creation. And so, isn't the following obvious?

If the relatively simple design of a pocket watch testifies to the existence of a watchmaker, then the cosmic design of the universe testifies to the existence of a universe maker. Just as it is impossible that a pocket watch could have developed by accident, but must have been designed by a human intelligence, so it is impossible that the universe could have developed by accident, but must have been designed by a cosmic intelligence. Thus a cosmic intelligence, God, exists.

I (agree, disagree) because _____

_____

_____ .

The main points of the proof presented in the thought experiment could be stated as follows:

1. The universe exhibits an exceedingly complex design.
2. Such a design could only have been created by an intelligence.
3. Therefore, the universe was designed by an intelligence.
4. This intelligence is God.
5. Therefore, God exists.

Attack the weakest point in this proof.

The weakest point is (1, 2, 3, 4, 5) because _____

_____

_____ .

The argument from design was presented in the form of the watch argument by William Paley in the nineteenth century and since has been adopted by Christian organizations, including the Campus Crusade for Christ.

The strategy of this argument, called the argument from design, is to reason from the seen, the well-ordered universe, to the unseen, God's existence.

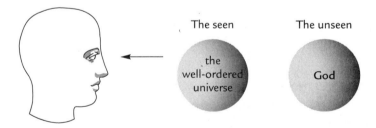

Thus, unlike Anselm's approach, the argument from design is empirical rather than rationalistic. Anselm ignores his senses and turns inward to analyze the idea of God; the argument from design uses sense information and turns outward to analyze the well-ordered universe as evidence for God's existence.

If you found the argument from design convincing, then you're probably going to be a strong supporter of Aquinas's five proofs of God's existence. If you didn't, you have a tough challenge ahead.

St. Thomas Aquinas, a medieval Christian, believed that the greatest philosopher who ever lived was a Greek pagan. And he held that the most famous proof of God's existence, Anselm's, proved nothing.

Aquinas calls Aristotle, with simple magnificence, the Philosopher. In Aquinas's view, no one compares to the Father of Science. Aquinas holds that Aristotle's analysis of the natural world is unrivaled and accepts Aristotle's description of form and matter, actuality and potentiality, and the Four Causes. In addition, Aquinas believes that Aristotle's proof of God's existence as the Unmoved Mover is sound. Thus, it is not surprising that Aquinas rejects Anselm's ontological argument. Following Aristotle, Aquinas is an empiricist. He holds that all knowledge of the universe begins with the senses. Though Aquinas agreed with the premises of Anselm's Christianity, he disagreed with Anselm's inner route to God. For Aquinas, the outer, Aristotelian way is the only way. The visible universe provides the only philosophical evidence for the existence of the invisible Creator.

Aquinas, one of the greatest philosophers of all time, accomplished far more than we will be able to explore on our tour. (For a summary of his achievements, see the box describing his life.) As your introduction to Aquinas's philosophy, we'll try something new—a wisdom midterm.

I'll start by giving you substantial help in understanding Aquinas's method and his first proof of God's existence—and then give you much less help than you've received thus far on our tour in exploring the next three of Aquinas's proofs. This will be your wisdom midterm. In this chapter, your tour guide will, at least for a while, let go of your hand.

I'll start by answering the following two questions:

- How does Aquinas attack Anselm's proof of God's existence?
- What is Aquinas's first proof of God's existence?

After I answer these questions, you'll tackle the next three questions on your own.

- What is Aquinas's second proof of God's existence?
- What is Aquinas's third proof of God's existence?
- What is Aquinas's fourth proof of God's existence?

I'll conclude the chapter by answering the following:

- What is Aquinas's fifth proof of God's existence?
- How does Aquinas answer the two objections?
- What do Aquinas's proofs have in common?

Let's begin with Aquinas's criticism of Anselm.

How Does Aquinas Attack Anselm's Proof of God's Existence?

All of the selections on this part of the tour are from Aquinas's *Summa Theologiae.* The *Summa,* as it is called, is a huge philosophical work made up of 512

Thomas Aquinas (c. 1225–1274)

As a youth Thomas Aquinas was often teased by his fellow students for being "a dim wit" and "dumb as an ox."[1] A heavyset man who was slow in his movements and speech but quick in thought, Aquinas was the outstanding scholar and philosopher of the Middle Ages.

Thomas Aquinas was born into nobility in the castle of Rocca Secca in Italy—the seventh son of Teodora and Landolfo, Count of Aquino

---

[1] Quoted in Henry Thomas, *Understanding the Great Philosophers* (Garden City, N.Y.: Doubleday, 1962), p. 178.

and relative of Frederick II, Holy Roman Emperor. Named after his grandfather, who had been commander of the imperial forces, Thomas came from a long line of aristocratic soldiers. Young Thomas, however, showed little interest in the military, preferring instead to sit quietly at the feet of the friars who visited his father's castle and listen to their stories of the spiritual life.

Aquinas's parents had great dreams for their youngest son. When Thomas was five, they placed him in the Benedictine Abbey of Monte Cassino, where he remained until 1239 when Frederick II, who was at odds with many of the official teachings of the Roman Catholic Church, expelled the monks. A bright student and original thinker, Thomas entered the university at the age of fourteen. After graduating from the University of Naples in 1244, he rejected careers in the military and politics and joined, over his parents' protest, the newly established evangelical Dominican Order.

Distressed by their youngest son's defiance—especially after the zealous Dominican monks refused to let the mother visit her son—his parents arranged to have his brothers kidnap him. They locked Thomas in a tower in the family castle where he remained for a year. Here, in an effort to cure him of his spiritual "madness," his family brought him erotic books and tried to tempt him with a beautiful prostitute. However, even imprisonment by his own parents did not dissuade

"Questions" dealing with a broad range of philosophical and theological issues. Each Question is subdivided into Articles that explore various aspects of the Question. Understanding the way the Articles are organized will greatly simplify your reading.

Each Article begins with a question, followed by several "objections," which

Thomas Aquinas (continued)

Thomas from his calling. According to some accounts, his family gave up trying to convert Thomas back to the ways of the world and let him go. Other accounts claim that he was rescued from the castle tower by friends and whisked away to Paris. In either case, following his release, Aquinas continued his studies in philosophy and theology in Paris. He also studied in Cologne under the Dominican Albertus Magnus, who was one of the leading scholars of the period and came to revere Aquinas as a great and holy man.

In 1256 Aquinas completed his magistrate (doctorate) in theology and was appointed professor of theology at the University of Paris. It was here that he undertook a serious study of the philosophy of Aristotle. Aristotle's works had been rediscovered by the Arabs in the Middle Ages and made their way into western Europe across the Spanish border. When the University of Paris received its charter in 1215, the study of Aristotle's works was forbidden. Although the ban was not officially lifted until 1366, it was gradually ignored. Aquinas readily took to Aristotle's philosophy, reinterpreting it in the light of Christian doctrine and referring to Aristotle in his writings as simply "the Philosopher."

Aquinas returned to Italy in 1272 and taught at the University of Naples for about a year until illness forced him to stop his teaching and writing. In 1274 Pope Gregory X invited Aquinas to come to Lyons to take part in the Second Council of Lyons. However, Aquinas never completed the trip. While on his way to Lyons, he died at the monastery Fossanova, not far from his birthplace.

Aquinas was canonized by the church in 1323 and given the honor of being proclaimed Doctor of the Church in 1567. His authority as the leading philosopher of the Roman Catholic Church was officially established in 1879 by Pope Leo XIII in the encyclical *Aeterni Patris*.

An active teacher and writer throughout his career, Aquinas produced several large treatises on theological and philosophical issues. His most important scholastic works, like the *Summa Theologiae* (1265–73), bring together Christian doctrine and the teachings of Aristotle. His other works include *Scriptum in IV Libros Sententiarum* (1252–57), *De Ente et Essentia* (1253), *De Principiis Naturae* (1253), *Contra Impugnantes Dei Cultum et Religionem* (1256), *Questiones Disputate de Veritate* (1256–59), *In Librum Boethii de Trinitate Expositio* (1257–58), *Summa de Veritate Catholicae Fidei Contra Gentiles* (1259–64), *Quaestiones Disputatae de Potentia Dei* (1265), *Compendium Theologiae* (1265–69), *Questio Disputata de Anima* (1269), *De Unitate Intellectus* (1270), and *De Aeternitate Mundi* (1271).

present answers that Aquinas believes are *false*. Next, a quotation is introduced with the phrase "On the contrary." The quotation supplies evidence from an authoritative source, often the Bible, for the position Aquinas believes is true. Aquinas then presents his own view of the true answer to the question. Finally, Aquinas answers each of the objections.

Thus, the pattern of the Articles (illustrated by the question of God's existence) is as follows:

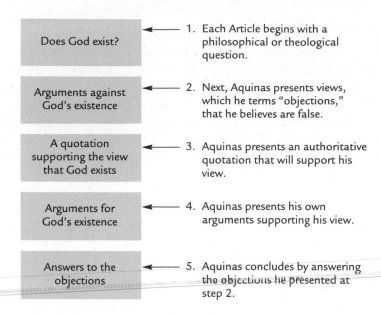

The Organization of Aquinas's Articles

Does God exist?	1. Each Article begins with a philosophical or theological question.
Arguments against God's existence	2. Next, Aquinas presents views, which he terms "objections," that he believes are false.
A quotation supporting the view that God exists	3. Aquinas presents an authoritative quotation that will support his view.
Arguments for God's existence	4. Aquinas presents his own arguments supporting his view.
Answers to the objections	5. Aquinas concludes by answering the objections he presented at step 2.

Part of the pleasure in reading Aquinas is watching him work himself into philosophical difficulties in the objections in each Article and then work himself out of these difficulties by the end. He presents the very useful philosophical lesson that the stronger the arguments that you can raise *against* your own position and then defeat, the stronger your position.

EXERCISE 18.1
Thinking Like Aquinas

To get a feel for the pattern of Aquinas's reasoning, make up your own Article answering the question, "Does God exist?" You can take one of three positions: God exists; God doesn't exist; it is not possible to know whether God exists. Set up your Article as follows.

Question: Does God exist?

Objection 1: Present a strong argument for what you believe is the *false* answer to the question.

Objection 2: Present another strong argument for what you believe is the *false* answer to the question.

Quotation: Find (or invent) a quotation that supports what you believe is the true answer to the question.

Your position: Present your own strongest argument for what you believe is the true answer to the question.

Reply 1: Present an argument that destroys Objection 1.

Reply 2: Present an argument that destroys Objection 2.

In the first selection below, Aquinas examines the question, "Whether the Existence of God Is Self-Evident?" Let me say a few words about self-evidence.

A self-evident truth is so obviously true that it requires no additional proof. To use Aquinas's example, if I say, "The whole is greater than one of its parts," the truth of this statement is self-evident because the truth requires no additional proof. An analysis of the concept of whole and part automatically produces the evidence that wherever I have a whole, I necessarily have something that is greater than one of its parts.

However, if I say, "The triangle is red," the truth of this statement is not self-evident. The statement is not self-evident because it requires additional proof. Analysis of the concepts triangle and red does not automatically produce the evidence that wherever I have a triangle I necessarily have something red. Additional evidence is needed; for example, I must go look.

Thus, when Aquinas asks, "Whether the Existence of God Is Self-Evident?" he is asking, is the relationship between God and His existence like the relationship between whole and part or like the relationship between red and triangle. If the relationship between God and His existence is like the relationship between whole and part, *then merely thinking about God will prove that He exists;* if the relationship is like the relationship between triangle and red, then thinking about God will not prove His existence, and one must go look for other evidence.

Which side would Anselm be on? Would he argue that God's existence is self-evident or not?

Anselm (would, would not) argue that God's existence is self-evident because

_____

_____

_____

EXERCISE 18.2
Do Self-Evident Truths Exist?

On your own paper, decide if each of the following is self-evident or not. Explain your reasoning.

Example: All dogs are cute.

Answer: Not self-evident

Explanation: If you analyze the concept of "dogs," you will discover that dogs are four-legged and that dogs are mammals, but you will not find the concept "cute." Thus, while it may be true that *some* dogs are cute, it is not self-evidently true that all dogs are cute.

1. A bird in the hand is worth two in the bush.
2. The word "Augustine" has nine letters.
3. A straight line is the shortest distance between two points.
4. Carbon dioxide is CO_2.
5. Nonexistence has no existence.

6. Whatever is, is.

7. Something is greater than nothing.

8. Cows are mammals.

9. Bessie is a cow.

10. Water freezes at 32 degrees Fahrenheit.

11. The sun will rise tomorrow.

12. The square root of 4 is 2.

13. Mt. Fuji is beautiful.

14. God is Love.

15. Tables have four legs.

16. Thinking implies the existence of something doing the thinking.

17. *Myst* is the world's greatest computer game.

18. All humans are created equal.

19. A triangle has three sides.

20. God exists.

Each of the paragraphs below from Aquinas's Article contains one or more conclusions and one or more pieces of evidence.[1] Underline each conclusion with a double line and underline each piece of evidence with a single line.

First Article

Whether the Existence of God Is Self-Evident?
We proceed thus to the First Article:

Objection 1. It seems that the existence of God is self-evident. Now those things are said to be self-evident to us the knowledge of which is naturally implanted in us, as we can see in regard to first principles. But as Damascene says, *the knowledge of God is naturally implanted in all.* Therefore, the existence of God is self-evident.

Obj. 2. Further, those things are said to be self-evident which are known as soon as the terms are known, which the Philosopher [Aristotle] says is true of the first principles of demonstration. Thus, when the nature of a whole and of a part is known, it is at once recognized that every whole is greater than its part. But as soon as the signification of the word "God" is understood, it is at once seen that God exists. For by this word is signified that thing than which nothing greater can be conceived. But that which exists actually and mentally is greater than that which exists only mentally. Therefore, since as soon as the word "God" is understood it exists mentally, it also follows that it exists actually. Therefore the proposition "God exists" is self-evident.

Remember, this is Anselm's definition of God.

[1] From St. Thomas Aquinas, *Summa Theologica*, "Treatise on God" Part 1, trans. the Fathers of the Dominican Province (New York: Benziger Books, 1947).

Obj. 3. Further, the existence of truth is self-evident. For whoever denies the existence of truth grants that truth does not exist: and if truth does not exist, then the proposition "Truth does not exist" is true: and if there is anything true, there must be truth. But God is truth itself: *I am the way, the truth and the life.* Therefore "God exists" is self-evident.

On the contrary, No one can mentally admit the opposite of what is self-evident; as the Philosopher states concerning the first principles of demonstration. But the opposite of the proposition "God is" can be mentally admitted: *The Fool said in his heart, There is no God.* Therefore, that God exists is not self-evident.

I answer that, A thing can be self-evident in either of two ways; on the one hand, self-evident in itself, though not to us; on the other, self-evident in itself, and to us.

A proposition is self-evident because the **predicate** is included in the essence of the **subject,** as "Man is an animal," for animal is contained in the essence of man. If, therefore the essence of the predicate and subject be known to all, the proposition will be self-evident to all; as is clear with regard to the first principles of demonstration, the terms of which are common things that no one is ignorant of, such as being and non-being, whole and part, and such like.

If, however, there are some to whom the essence of the predicate and subject is unknown, the proposition will be self-evident in itself, but not to those who do not know the meaning of the predicate and subject of the proposition. Therefore, it happens as Boethius says, "that there are some mental concepts self-evident only to the learned, as that incorporeal substances are not in space."

Therefore I say this proposition, "God exists," of itself is self-evident, for the predicate is the same as the subject; because God is His own existence as will be hereafter shown (Q. 3 A. 4). Now because we do not know the essence of God, the proposition is not self-evident to us; but needs to be demonstrated by things that are more known to us, though less known in their nature—namely, by effects.

Reply Obj. 1. To know that God exists in a general and confused way is implanted in us by nature, inasmuch as God is man's beatitude [supreme happiness]. For man naturally desires happiness, and what is naturally desired by man must be naturally known to him. This, however, is not to know absolutely that God exists; just as to know that someone is approaching is not the same as to know that Peter is approaching, even though it is Peter who is approaching; for many there are who imagine that man's perfect good which is happiness, consists in riches, and others in pleasures, and others in something else.

Subject and predicate: The subject of a sentence is a noun (person, place, or thing) about which something is affirmed or denied. The word or phrase that "does" the affirming or denying is the predicate. For example, in the sentence "Aquinas is wise," "Aquinas" is the subject noun and "is wise" is the predicate, what is affirmed about Aquinas. In the sentence, "Man is an animal," "Man" is the subject noun and "is an animal" is the predicate, what is affirmed about Man. Aquinas's point is that a claim is self-evident if, and only if, an analysis of the subject shows that it contains the predicate.

Reply Obj. 2. Perhaps not everyone who hears this word "God" understands it to signify something than which nothing greater can be thought, seeing that some have believed God to be a body. Yet, granted that everyone understands that by this word "God" is signified something than which nothing greater can be thought, nevertheless, it does not therefore follow that he understands that what the word signifies exists actually, but only that it exists mentally. Nor can it be argued that it actually exists, unless it be admitted there actually exists something than which nothing greater can be thought; and this precisely is not admitted by those who hold that God does not exist.

Reply Obj. 3. The existence of truth in general is self-evident but the existence of a Primal Truth is not self-evident to us.

Now, let's look at each section of the Article in more detail.

First of all, review the concept of self-evidence. State an example of a self-evident truth and then a truth that is not self-evident; then describe the difference between the two.

A self-evident truth is _____

_____.

A truth that is not self-evident is _____

_____.

The difference between the two truths is _____

_____.

Thus, when Aquinas is asking, "Whether the existence of God is self-evident?" what is he asking?

Aquinas is asking _____

_____.

The first objection is an argument *against* the existence of God being self-evident. Paraphrase the evidence and the conclusion.

The evidence is _____

_____

_____.

The conclusion is _____

_____.

The second objection is also an argument *against* the existence of God being self-evident. Paraphrase the evidence and the conclusion.

The evidence is _____

_____

_____.

The conclusion is _____

_____.

The third objection is also an argument *against* the existence of God being self-evident. Paraphrase the evidence and the conclusion.

The evidence is _____

_____

_____.

The conclusion is _____

_____.

Which of these three objections seems to you to be the strongest?

I believe the strongest objection is (1, 2, 3) because _____

_____

_____.

Which of the three objections seems to you to be the weakest?

I believe the weakest objection is (1, 2, 3) because _____

_____

_____.

Now reread the passage beginning *"On the contrary."* This is an argument *against the objections,* supported by a quotation from an authoritative source. Paraphrase the evidence and conclusion; next explain how it attacks the objections; finally, explain the relevance of the quotation about The Fool.

The evidence against the objections presented by "On the contrary" is _____

_____

_____.

The conclusion that Aquinas is trying to prove is _____

_____.

The quotation supports Aquinas's argument because _____
_____
_____.

Now reread the paragraph beginning "*I answer that.*" This section presents what Aquinas believes is the true answer to the question, "Whether the existence of God is self-evident?" What are the two kinds of self-evident statements Aquinas distinguishes between?

One kind of self-evident statement could be defined as _____
_____.

An example would be _____
_____.

A second kind of self-evident statement could be defined as _____
_____

An example would be _____
_____.

Which of the two kinds of self-evident statements, according to Aquinas, is "God exists"?

The kind of self-evident statement "God exists" is _____
_____ because, according to Aquinas,
_____
_____
_____.

Summarize Aquinas's position in the "*I answer that*" section.

Aquinas is saying _____
_____
_____.

Has Aquinas successfully refuted the objections?

I would say (yes, no) because _____
_____
_____.

Paraphrase Aquinas's Reply to Objection 1.

Aquinas is saying _____

_____

_____.

The point he is making about Peter is _____

_____.

How does this attempt to refute Objection 1?

_____

_____.

Is Aquinas successful?

I would say (yes, no) because _____

_____

_____.

Paraphrase Aquinas's Reply to Objection 2.

Aquinas is saying _____

_____

_____.

What is the difference between existing actually and existing mentally?

To exist actually is _____.

To exist mentally is _____.

The difference is _____

_____.

How does Aquinas use this distinction?

Aquinas argues _____

_____

_____.

How does all this attempt to refute Objection 2?

_____

_____

_____.

Is Aquinas successful?

I would say (yes, no) because _____

_____

_____.

Paraphrase Aquinas's Reply to Objection 3.

Aquinas is saying _____

_____

_____.

Why is the "existence of truth in general" self-evident?

Because _____

_____

_____.

What Primal Truth, would you guess, is Aquinas talking about?

The Primal Truth of _____.

What is it about this Primal Truth that makes it *not* self-evident?

_____

_____

_____.

Has Aquinas successfully answered Objection 3?

I would say (yes, no) because _____

_____

_____.

Now, here is the hardest question in this section: How has Aquinas answered St. Anselm's ontological argument?

Aquinas's answer to the ontological argument is _____

_____

_____.

Now let's examine Aquinas's first proof of God's existence.

What Is Aquinas's First Proof of God's Existence?

In the following Article, Aquinas sets out to prove God's existence in five ways. Because this Article is significantly longer than the previous one, we will examine it in shorter sections. (Remember, after stating the question, Aquinas begins with objections that state what he thinks are *false* answers to the question.)

Third Article

Whether God Exists?

We proceed thus to the Third Article:

Objection 1. It seems that God does not exist; because if one of two contraries be infinite, the other would be altogether destroyed. But the word "God" means that He is infinite goodness. If, therefore, God existed there would be no evil discoverable; but there is evil in the world. Therefore God does not exist.

Paraphrase the conclusion and evidence in the first objection.

The conclusion is _____.

The evidence is _____

_____

_____

Objection 2. Further, it is superfluous [beyond what is required] to suppose that what can be accounted for by a few principles has been produced by many. But it seems that everything we see in the world can be accounted for by other principles, supposing God did not exist. For all natural things can be reduced to one principle, which is nature; and all voluntary things can be reduced to one principle, which is human reason, or will. Therefore there is no need to suppose God's existence.

The conclusion is _____.

The evidence is _____

_____

_____

Which of the two objections to God's existence is the strongest?

The strongest objection is the (first, second) because _____

_____

Now read Aquinas's first proof of God's existence. Underline his conclusion and key pieces of evidence. Read the marginal note on actuality and potentiality.

On the contrary, It is said in the person of God: *I am Who am.*

I answer that, The existence of God can be proved in five ways.

The first and more manifest [obvious] way is the argument from motion. It is certain, and evident to our senses, that in the world some things are in motion. Now whatever is in motion is put in motion by another, for nothing can be in motion except it is in potentiality to that towards which it is in motion; whereas a thing moves inasmuch as it is in act. For motion is nothing else than the reduction of something from potentiality to actuality. But nothing can be reduced from potentiality to actuality, except by something in a state of actuality. Thus that which is actually hot, as fire, makes wood, which is potentially hot, to be actually hot, and thereby moves and changes it. Now it is not possible that the same thing should be at once in actuality and potentiality in the same respect, but only in different respects. For what is actually hot cannot simultaneously be potentially hot; but it is simultaneously potentially cold. It is therefore impossible that in the same respect and in the same way a thing should be both mover and moved, i.e., that it should move itself. Therefore, whatever is in motion must be put in motion by another. If that by which it is put in motion be itself put in motion, then this also must needs be put in motion by another, and that by another again. But this cannot go on to infinity, because then there would be no first mover, and, consequently, no other mover; seeing that subsequent movers move only inasmuch as they are put in motion by the first mover; as the staff moves only because it is put in motion by the hand. Therefore it is necessary to arrive at a first mover, put in motion by no other; and this everyone understands to be God.

Aquinas's conclusion is, obviously, that God exists. Paraphrase his evidence.

_____

_____

_____

_____ .

Now think like Aquinas. Assume you are observing a line of dominoes falling into each other. Use this observation to conclude that God exists.

_____

_____

_____

_____ .

Therefore, God exists.

You may recognize that Aquinas borrows the terms *potentiality* and *actuality* from Aristotle. Remember that according to Aristotle, anything can have two states: actuality or potentiality. Actuality describes what a thing currently is; potentiality describes what a thing can become. Thus, my heated coffee, in regard to its warmth, is in a state of actuality; but it has the potentiality to become cold. Actuality and potentiality can be linked together in a chain of alternating states. Clay is in a state of actuality which has the potentiality to become bricks; bricks are in a state of actuality which has the potentiality to become a wall; a wall is in a state of actuality which has the potentiality to become the supporting structure of a house, and so forth. Aquinas argues that in regard to motion, this chain of actuality and potentiality cannot be infinitely long. There must be a beginning which "everyone understands to be God."

How strong is Aquinas's first proof of God's existence?

I believe it is (very strong, strong, weak, very weak) because _____

_____   _____

_____ .

Now, as I promised at the beginning of this chapter, I'll let go of your hand. Read each of the following proofs carefully; underline key passages; look for evidence that supports Aquinas's conclusion that God exists. Practice the skills you've learned on our tour. Think of this as your wisdom midterm.

What Is Aquinas's Second Proof of God's Existence?

Here is Aquinas's second proof of God's existence:

> The second way is from the nature of the efficient cause. In the world of sense [physical world] we find there is an order of efficient causes. There is no case known (neither is it, indeed, possible) in which a thing is found to be the efficient cause of itself; for so it would be prior to itself, which is impossible. Now in efficient causes it is not possible to go on to infinity, because in all efficient causes following in order, the first is the cause of the intermediate cause, and the intermediate is the cause of the ultimate cause, whether the intermediate cause be several, or one only. Now to take away the cause is to take away the effect. Therefore if there be no first cause among efficient causes, there will be no ultimate, nor any intermediate cause. But if in efficient causes it is possible to go on to infinity, there will be no first efficient cause, neither will there be an ultimate effect, nor any intermediate efficient causes; all of which is plainly false. Therefore it is necessary to admit a first efficient cause, to which everyone gives the name of God.

Aquinas borrows another concept from Aristotle—that of efficient cause. Aristotle, as you will recall, held that there are four causes: material, formal, final, and efficient. The material cause is the "stuff," physical or nonphysical, that constitutes an object; the formal cause is the essence of an object; the final cause is the goal or purpose of the object; the efficient cause is the source or origin of the object. Thus, taking a human as an example: our material cause is flesh and bone; our formal cause is reason; our final cause is happiness; our efficient cause is our biological parents.

Summarize the evidence in this second proof that leads to Aquinas's conclusion that God exists.

_____

_____

_____

_____

_____ .

Does his argument convince you?

I must say the argument is (convincing, not convincing) because _____

_____

_____.

What Is Aquinas's Third Proof of God's Existence?

Now look at Aquinas's third proof of God's existence. Observe that his argument is broken up into a set of subarguments, each one ending with "therefore." To aid in your analysis, place a number at the beginning of each new subargument.

With the terms *possibility* and *necessity*, Aquinas distinguishes between two kinds of existing things. A thing that has possible existence can either exist or not exist. For example, this book has possible existence; it can either exist or not exist. However, a thing that has necessary existence *must* exist. God, according to Aquinas, is the only entity that has necessary existence. In other words, unlike this book, God must exist; it is impossible for God not to exist.

Aquinas is saying that everything that has possible existence passes through the cycle of generation and corruption. This book, at some earlier time, was generated and, at some later time, will be corrupted, will pass away.

The third way is taken from possibility and necessity, and runs thus. We find in nature things that are possible to be and not to be, since they are found to be generated, and to corrupt, and consequently, they are possible to be and not to be. But it is impossible for these always to exist, for that which is possible not to be at some time is not. Therefore, if everything is possible not to be, then at one time there could have been nothing in existence. Now if this were true, even now there would be nothing in existence, because that which does not exist only begins to exist by something already existing. Therefore, if at one time nothing was in existence, it would have been impossible for anything to have begun to exist; and thus even now nothing would in existence—which is absurd. Therefore, not all beings are merely possible, but there must exist something the existence of which is necessary. But every necessary thing either has its necessity caused by another, or not. Now it is impossible to go on to infinity in necessary things which have their necessity caused by another, as has been already proved in regard to efficient causes. Therefore we cannot but postulate the existence of some being having of itself its own necessity, and not receiving it from another, but rather causing in others their necessity. This all men speak of as God.

Summarize Aquinas's third proof of God's existence.

_____

_____

_____

_____

_____

_____.

Does his argument convince you?

I must say the argument is (convincing, not convincing) because _____

_____ _____

_____.

What Is Aquinas's Fourth Proof of God's Existence?

Here is Aquinas's fourth proof of God's existence. Read it several times and underline key points.

> The fourth way is taken from the gradation to be found in things. Among beings there are some more and some less good, true, noble, and the like. But "more" and "less" are predicated of different things, according as they resemble in their different ways something which is the maximum, as a thing is said to be hotter according as it more nearly resembles that which is hottest; so that there is something which is truest, something best, something noblest, and, consequently, something which is uttermost being; for those things that are greatest in truth are greatest in being, as it is written in *Metaph.* ii. Now the maximum in any genus is the cause of all in that genus; as fire, which is the maximum of heat, is the cause of all hot things. Therefore there must also be something which is to all beings the cause of their being, goodness, and every other perfection; and this we call God.

Here is a paraphrase of Aquinas' argument arranged as a set of five interlocking subarguments.

1. Because some beings are more or less good, more or less noble, or more or less true, therefore there is a gradation of value in all beings.

2. A gradation of value, however, implies that there is something of highest value. Therefore, if there are beings who are more or less good, more or less noble, and more or less true, there must be a being who has the highest value—that is, who is perfectly good, noble, and true.

3. That which is most true has the most reality (see marginal note). That which is perfectly true has absolute, complete reality. Therefore, a being exists who has absolute, complete reality.

4. And just as the less hot is caused by the more hot, so the less real is caused by the more real. Therefore, beings who have less reality are caused by the being who has absolute reality.

5. The being who causes the reality of all other beings is what everyone calls God.

Therefore, God exists.

Aquinas is referring to concepts found in Aristotle's *Metaphysics*. Aquinas agrees with Aristotle that the more "truth" something has, the greater its "reality." This is a difficult concept for modern readers to grasp because we usually think of something as either true or not true, real or not real.

Think of a photograph in a book of a painting of the Matterhorn. According to the view of Aristotle and Aquinas, the photograph in the book would be "less real" and have "less truth" than the painting of the Matterhorn, and the painting of the Matterhorn would be "less real" and have "less truth" than the Matterhorn itself. You should be able to see that this makes a kind of sense. The reality of the photograph depends upon the reality of the painting, and the reality of the painting depends upon the reality of the Matterhorn. Thus, it could be said that the Matterhorn has the most reality and the most truth.

In biological terms developed by Aristotle, a genus is smaller than a family but larger than a species. Thus, the human species is part of the genus of mammals and the genus of mammals is part of the family of vertebrates (animals with segmented backbones). When Aquinas refers to the "maximum in any genus," he is thinking of the members of a genus as forming a kind of pyramid with "the maximum" in the genus being the cause of everything "beneath" the maximum. For example, salt could be said to be the maximum of the genus of salty things and thus is the cause of the saltiness in all salty things. To use Aquinas's example, fire is the maximum of the genus of all hot things and thus is the cause of heat in all hot things.

Now assume you believe that Aquinas is absolutely wrong. Attack each of the subarguments.

Against subargument 1, it could be argued _____

_____.

Against subargument 2, it could be argued _____

_____.

Against subargument 3, it could be argued _____

_____.

Against subargument 4, it could be argued _____

_____.

Against subargument 5, it could be argued _____

_____.

Here is a very difficult challenge. Think like Aquinas. How would he answer each of your attacks? If you can successfully answer your attacks on Aquinas, then you have made a significant advance in philosophical thinking. One of the best ways to understand a philosopher is to imagine how the philosopher would respond to the strongest attacks that could be made against his or her position.

Very well. I'll accept the challenge. In response to my attack on subargument 1,

Aquinas might answer _____

_____

_____.

In response to my attack on subargument 2, Aquinas might answer _____

_____

_____.

In response to my attack on subargument 3, Aquinas might answer _____

_____

_____.

In response to my attack on subargument 4, Aquinas might answer _____

_____

_____.

In response to my attack on subargument 5, Aquinas might answer _____

_____

_____.

Overall, does Aquinas's argument convince you?

I must say the argument is (convincing, not convincing) because _____

_____

_____.

What grade would you give yourself on your wisdom midterm?

I deserve an (A, B, C, D, F) because _____

_____.

Now, giving you more help, I'll return to my tour guide duties.

What Is Aquinas's Fifth Proof for God's Existence?

Let's explore Aquinas's last proof of God's existence.

> The fifth way is taken from the governance of the world. We see that things which lack intelligence, such as natural bodies, act for an end, and this is evident from their acting always, or nearly always, in the same way, so as to obtain the best result. Hence it is plain that not fortuitously [by mere chance], but designedly, do they achieve their end. Now whatever lacks intelligence cannot move towards an end unless it be directed by some being endowed with knowledge and intelligence; as the arrow is shot to its mark by the archer. Therefore some intelligent being exists by whom all natural things are directed to their end; and this being we call God.

Aquinas's fifth proof for God's existence rests upon his analysis of the behavior of "things which lack intelligence." Using an acorn as an example of a something that lacks intelligence, paraphrase his argument.

The point Aquinas is making about acorns and similar "natural bodies" is _____

_____.

From this he concludes that God exists because _____

_____.

Aquinas, borrowing a concept from Aristotle, argues that all of nature, every "natural body," is unthinking but displays characteristics of something guided by an intelligence. To understand this, imagine three different toy cars. Toy car X has a crooked wheel and is powered by a windup key. When released, it buzzes around the room randomly bumping into things. Because of its crooked wheel,

Aquinas borrows the concept of "act for an end" from Aristotle. Recall that according to Aristotle, every thing that exists has a final cause, acts for an end. When a chicken is pecking corn, it is acting for the end of feeding itself; when people go out dancing on Friday night, they are acting for the end of being entertained. Aristotle and Aquinas also argue that acting for an end occurs with plants and inanimate objects. In their view, when an acorn sprouts into an oak it acts for the end of becoming an tree; when water flows downhill, it acts for the end of reaching lower ground. Of course, acorns and water are not "thinking" about their ends; they are merely, to use another Aristotelian phrase, activating their potential. Acorns have the potential of becoming oaks; water has the potential of flowing downhill.

its action is unpredictable. Toy car Y is powered by remote control. As long as you are carefully guiding it, the car's action is completely predictable; however, if you look away, its course is hardly more predictable than toy car X. Toy car Z, however, has a built-in computer chip that directs it to avoid every obstacle; whether you're watching or not, car Z never bumps into anything. In addition, the chip can be programmed so that the car always performs the same actions. To sum up, the behavior of toy car X is completely unpredictable; toy car Y is much more predictable, because it is guided by human intelligence, but the intelligence is external to the car and must be continuously engaged in guiding the car; toy car Z is entirely predictable because, while it doesn't think itself, its internal design operates automatically and independently of any additional help by an intelligence.

Which of these three cars would Aquinas say exhibits the characteristics of the acorn and all "natural bodies"? (This is a tough question that most students will miss. Think carefully; then read the explanation in the marginal note. No cheating!)

I would say, in Aquinas's view, acorns and all other "natural bodies" are like toy

car (X, Y, Z) because he is saying _____

_____.

At this point, you should understand the key point Aquinas is making about every object in the natural world that lacks intelligence.

Now, look one more time at the proof and then try to put Aquinas's entire argument in your own words.

The fifth way is taken from the governance of the world. We see that things which lack intelligence, such as natural bodies, act for an end, and this is evident from their acting always, or nearly always, in the same way, so as to obtain the best result. Hence it is plain that not fortuitously, but designedly, do they achieve their end. Now whatever lacks intelligence cannot move towards an end unless it be directed by some being endowed with knowledge and intelligence; as the arrow is shot to its mark by the archer. Therefore some intelligent being exists by whom all natural things are directed to their end; and this being we call God.

Aquinas is saying _____

_____

_____

_____.

Therefore, God exists.

Is this proof convincing or unconvincing?

The proof is (convincing, unconvincing) because _____

_____

_____.

Toy car X certainly does not behave, in Aquinas's view, like nature. Toy car X is unpredictable; and nature, according to Aquinas, is predictable. Toy car Z, at least so far as the fourth proof of God's existence is concerned, is not like nature either. Aquinas compares nature to an arrow guided by an archer. Toy car Z is *self-guiding*, though it has a design which testifies to the existence of an intelligent designer. Toy car Y is most like Aquinas's portrait of nature because it is continuously guided by an intelligence. Unthinking nature, according to Aquinas, exhibits characteristics of intelligent guidance; it behaves like an arrow guided to its target by an archer. God, so to speak, shoots acorns at the target of oaks.

How Does Aquinas Answer the Two Objections?

Aquinas concludes his investigation of God's existence by answering the two objections that began the Article. To make his answers clearer, I'll precede each answer with the original objection.

Objection 1. It seems that God does not exist; because if one of two contraries be infinite, the other would be altogether destroyed. But the word "God" means that He is infinite goodness. If, therefore, God existed there would be no evil discoverable; but there is evil in the world. Therefore God does not exist.

Here is Aquinas's answer:

Reply Obj. 1. As Augustine says: Since God is the highest good, He would not allow any evil to exist in His works, unless His omnipotence and goodness were such as to bring good even out of evil. This is part of the infinite goodness of God, that He should allow evil to exist, and out of it produce good.

Put his reply in your own words and evaluate whether it is successful or unsuccessful in answering Objection 1.

Aquinas's reply to the first objection is _____

_____

_____.

I think it is (successful, unsuccessful) because _____

_____.

Here is Objection 2, followed by Aquinas's reply.

Obj. 2. Further, it is superfluous to suppose that what can be accounted for by a few principles has been produced by many. But it seems that everything we see in the world can be accounted for by other principles, supposing God did not exist. For all natural things can be reduced to one principle, which is nature; and all voluntary things can be reduced to one principle, which is human reason, or will. Therefore there is no need to suppose God's existence.

Reply Obj. 2. Since nature works for a determinate end under the direction of a higher agent, whatever is done by nature must needs be traced back to God, as to its first cause. So also whatever is done voluntarily must also be traced back to some higher cause other than human reason or will, since these can change and fail; for all things that are changeable and capable of defect must be traced back to an immovable and self-necessary first principle, as was shown in the body of the Article [the current Article].

Put Aquinas's reply in your own words and evaluate whether it is successful or unsuccessful in answering Objection 2.

Aquinas's reply to the second objection is _____

_____

_____.

Trying to Prove the Existence of an Invisible Aspect of Reality

We can now pause for a moment in our tour to gain a broader perspective.

To understand the problem faced by Aquinas and many other philosophers who try to prove the existence of an invisible aspect of reality, imagine that you are convinced an invisible man lives in your bedroom. Further imagine that you want to prove to a friend that you are not crazy. Consider three versions of your problem.

1. If the invisible man is mute and incapable of affecting anything in the physical world, then you have a very difficult, perhaps impossible, task. You can offer your friend no sense evidence that the invisible man exists. Perhaps you can talk about a feeling you have of the invisible man's presence or an intuition of his being. Because you have no external evidence, you have to rely on internal evidence; and, of course, the reliability of your internal evidence, because it is not your friend's internal evidence, will be very difficult for your friend to assess.

2. Now consider a slightly easier case. Assume that the invisible man, though mute and incapable of affecting anything in the physical world, can send a single telepathic thought—"I am the invisible man and I exist." After considerable introspection, you manage to discover inner proof that the thought is true and cannot have

come from any other source (imagination, memory, the physical world, and so forth). Unlike the first case, your internal evidence is now no longer entirely private. You can ask your friend to examine her ideas and the friend can discover her own message, "I am the invisible man and I exist." You can then use your proof to show that the thought can only have come from an invisible man.

3. Now consider a case that appears still easier. Assume that the invisible man can respond to your requests and also can affect things in the visible world. Proof seems quite simple now. You ask the invisible man to move a book, and the book floats across your bedroom. You ask the invisible man to raise the blinds, and the blinds go up. After your friend convinces herself that you aren't playing tricks, she will probably be convinced, despite her astonishment, that the invisible man exists.

What does all this have to do with philosophical proofs of the existence of an invisible aspect of reality?

Rationalists face the tough case of trying to use internal evidence to prove the existence of the invisible; empiricists face the *apparently* easier case of using external evidence to prove the existence of the invisible.

A rationalist holds that, for one reason or

I think it is (successful, unsuccessful) because _____

_____ .

What Do Aquinas's Proofs Have in Common?

All of Aquinas's proofs are empirical, rather than rationalistic. In other words, Aquinas begins with information that comes to him through his senses rather than information that comes to him independently of his senses. Aquinas rea-

another, the senses cannot be trusted. If the existence of the invisible is to be proven, then the philosopher must turn inward and look for indisputable internal evidence. Perhaps, as in the first case above, the philosopher has an intuition, a bare feeling of the existence of the invisible. But, because such evidence is entirely private, it will convince no one else. The rationalist faces the paradoxical problem of finding public private knowledge. Each of the great rationalists followed a different strategy.

Parmenides tried to show that the invisible unchanging One existed by arguing that all visible change is an illusion, because visible change involves the impossibility of existence becoming nonexistence.

Plato argued that the invisible realm of Forms existed because, among other reasons, our mind has knowledge of perfect and eternal Truths which it remembers from its previous existence in the realm of Forms.

Augustine argued that an invisible and divine God existed because our minds possess universal truths which only God's inner illumination makes possible.

Anselm argued that an invisible God, a being than whom none greater can be conceived, existed because an analysis of the idea of God proves God must exist.

Descartes, as you will soon learn, argued that an invisible and divine God existed because, among other reasons, only God can be the cause of the idea of God.

Proving the existence of an invisible reality is apparently easier for an empiricist. Just as you convince your friend by reasoning from the visible effect (the book floating in the air) to the invisible cause (the invisible man), so the empiricist argues from the visible to the invisible.

Aristotle and Aquinas both begin with visible motion to prove an invisible First Mover. Aquinas continues with visible causes and effects, visible generation and corruption, visible gradations of perfection, and visible goal-directed behavior of inanimate bodies to prove the existence of the invisible God.

Before the end of the tour, however, you will discover that the empirical approach to proving the existence of the invisible can become quite tortured—and finally, perhaps impossible.

The empiricist George Berkeley will begin by trying to convince you that you have no empirical knowledge of matter and will end by trying to convince you that physical reality is an illusion and All is God.

To make matters still more challenging, the empiricist David Hume will try to convince you that not just rationalism, but also empiricism, leads to a dead end. Hume argues that not only can't we prove the existence of the invisible from the visible, but we also can't even prove the existence of the visible!

sons from the visible to the invisible. In the first proof, he reasons from visible motion to the invisible First Mover. In the second proof, he reasons from visible causes and effects to God as the invisible first cause.

Now, what about the other proofs?

In the third proof Aquinas reasons from visible _____

_____ to _____ .

In the fourth proof Aquinas reasons from visible _____

_____ to _____ .

In the fifth proof Aquinas reasons from visible _____

_____ to _____.

Here is a diagram representing the first proof.

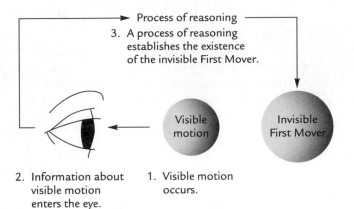

2. Information about   1. Visible motion
visible motion   occurs.
enters the eye.

EXERCISE 18.3

Diagramming Aquinas's Proofs

On your own paper, using the example above, make diagrams of the second through fifth proofs of God's existence.

Note that in each of the proofs Aquinas reasons from a different aspect of the visible to establish *a different aspect of the invisible God*. Thus, by reasoning from visible motion, he can establish that God is the invisible cause of all motion. By reasoning from visible causes and effects, he can establish that God is not just the cause of all motion, but also the first cause of all that exists. What features of God does Aquinas establish in the other three proofs?

In the third proof, Aquinas establishes that God is _____

_____.

In the fourth proof, Aquinas establishes that God is _____

_____.

In the fifth proof, Aquinas establishes that God is _____

_____.

SUMMARY

After arguing against Anselm that God's existence is not self-evident, Aquinas presents his five proofs for God's existence. The first proof begins with the motion we observe in the world and argues that God exists as the First Mover. The second proof begins with the efficient causes we observe in the world and argues that God exists as the First Cause. The third proof begins with the growth and decay we observe in the world and argues that if the universe were the only

VOCABULARY MAP

St. Thomas Aquinas

Aquinas's **metaphysics,** his view of reality, is clearly **dualistic.** Like Anselm and almost all other Christian thinkers, he sharply distinguishes between the realm of God and the physical universe.

Aquinas's **epistemology,** his view of the knowledge process, is **empirical.** As demonstrated in this chapter, Aquinas holds that knowledge of God's existence comes through the senses. For example, by examining the vast and intricate design of the universe, as revealed through our senses, we can deduce that God exists.

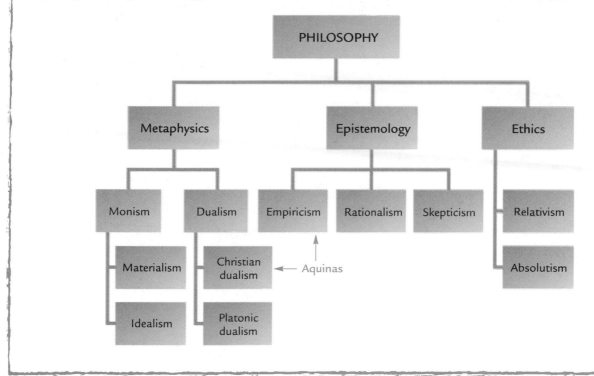

thing that existed, it would have at some time passed out of existence. Therefore, God exists as the necessary cause of the continued existence of the universe. The fourth proof begins with the range of perfections we observe in the world and argues that God exists as the perfect source of these perfections. The fifth proof begins with the "intelligent," goal-directed behavior of unthinking nature and argues that God exists as the intelligent guide of nature.

EXERCISE 18.4
Looking Back

Use your own paper to briefly answer each of the following questions.

1. How does Aquinas attack Anselm's proof of God's existence?

2. What is Aquinas's first proof of God's existence?

3. What is Aquinas's second proof of God's existence?

4. What is Aquinas's third proof of God's existence?

5. What is Aquinas's fourth proof of God's existence?

6. What is Aquinas's fifth proof of God's existence?

7. How does Aquinas answer the two objections?

8. What do Aquinas's proofs have in common?

EXERCISE 18.5

Judging Arguments

Look at your summaries of Aquinas's five proofs in Exercise 18.4. Select the proof that you believe is strongest; augment it with additional evidence. Select the proof that you believe is the weakest, and write an argument that attacks it.

EXERCISE 18.6

Reviewing the Five Proofs

Decide if the following statements are consistent (C) or inconsistent (I) with Aquinas's five proofs of God's existence and his replies to the objections. Use your own paper to explain your answer.

1. C I Knowledge comes through the senses.

2. C I All of reality is divided into two parts.

3. C I God is All.

4. C I By examining the idea of God, one can prove God exists.

5. C I Everything has a cause.

6. C I Evil originates in the human will.

7. C I The Last Days are at hand.

8. C I God created the universe.

9. C I It is possible to reason from the invisible to the visible.

10. C I Inanimate objects are capable of rational thought.

11. C I God has no cause.

12. C I God is the Unmoved Mover.

ANALYSIS OF YOUR PHILOSOPHICAL SELF-PORTRAIT

To see how your views about the nature of reality stack up against Aquinas's, read my analysis below, rethink your position, and then circle what you believe is the correct answer. I've underlined Aquinas's answers.

1. T <u>F</u> *Just as one could prove that a whole is larger than one of its parts simply by thinking about the concept of whole, so one could prove that God exists simply by thinking about the concept of God.*

Aquinas, as you remember from the first Article we examined, holds that God's existence is self-evident, but he makes a distinction between two kinds of self-evidence.

The two kinds of self-evidence were _____

_____.

2. <u>T</u>   F   *Knowledge of God's existence is implanted in us at birth.*

As you learned in this chapter, Aquinas's position on this point is somewhat equivocal. He agrees that everyone is born with knowledge of God, but we possess this knowledge only "in a general and confused way." Our inborn desire for happiness is really a desire for God, but some of us, instead of seeking God, seek wealth and pleasure.

Do you agree? Does everyone have a natural desire for happiness?

I (agree, disagree) because _____

_____

_____.

Is a desire for happiness actually a desire for God?

I (agree, disagree) because _____

_____

_____.

3. T   <u>F</u>   *If God existed and were truly all-powerful, then evil wouldn't exist in our world.*

True puts you on the side of Objection 1 and, of course, against Aquinas. However you answered this question, how do you evaluate Aquinas's Reply to Objection 1?

I think Aquinas's reply is (satisfactory, unsatisfactory) because _____

_____

_____.

Every serious philosophical Christian has had to find some way to answer the question, "If a perfect God created everything, why does evil exist?" Three of the philosophically most popular answers have been Augustine's, Aquinas's, and Descartes's.

Augustine pursued the interesting strategy of arguing that God was not to blame for the existence of evil because evil had no existence. Evil, Augustine held, was the absence of goodness and thus was, strictly speaking, "nothing." An evil act was evil only because it lacked goodness; an evil man was evil only because his soul lacked goodness. Thus, just as an artist, insofar as she is an artist, could be said to be the creator only of things that have existence, so God is the creator only of things that have existence—and is not the creator of the nothingness of evil.

Aquinas, as you can tell from his reply to Objection 1, pursued an approach different from Augustine's. Evil does exist but it has, so to speak, no sting. God's power, Aquinas asserts, produces good from all evil; thus, evil is never triumphant, has no permanently effective place in reality. Aquinas would probably argue that when we view evil and see it only as evil, we are seeing only half the story. Though evil is part of the tale, God finishes it.

Descartes differs from both Augustine and Aquinas by locating the source of evil, which he more innocuously terms "error," in the human will. Descartes believes that we are creations of a perfect God and explains our imperfection by arguing that we are as perfect as God could have made us; we have finite knowledge because we are finite creatures, but we have the very best kind of will, one that is absolutely free. Thus, it is the misuse of the freedom of our free will, our greatest gift from God, that is the source of our errors, our "evil." God could have made us so that we were never mistaken; but he would have had to deny us freedom, and this would have made us less perfect. Consequently, Descartes takes the paradoxical position that we are more perfect because we make mistakes than we would be if we never made mistakes.

Which of these three arguments against evil is the weakest?

I would have to say (Augustine's, Aquinas's, Descartes's) is the weakest because _____

_____

_____ .

Which of these three arguments against evil is the strongest?

I would have to say (Augustine's, Aquinas's, Descartes's) is the weakest because _____

_____

_____ .

4. T _F_ *Because all that exists can be explained as caused by nature or the human will, God is not needed as an explanation of the universe.*

True puts you on the side of Objection 2 and against Aquinas. Thus, you take the view that the universe is a kind of closed system. All activities in the universe can be explained by forces within the universe; there is nothing beyond what we see around us that affects what we see around us. Odds are that you are some variety of empirical materialist; you believe that all that is real is what can be known by the senses.

False, of course, makes you some variety of theist. You hold that the universe is an open system. All that we see cannot be explained by all that we see. If you hold that we have knowledge of what is "beyond" only by reasoning based upon what we see, then you are an empiricist. If you hold that the mind, independently of the senses, has some way of directly accessing information about the "beyond," then you are a rationalist.

However you answered this question, how do you evaluate Aquinas's Reply to Objection 2?

I think Aquinas's reply is (satisfactory, unsatisfactory) because _____

_____

_____ .

Would dualism be incompatible with a True answer to this question?

I believe True would be (compatible, incompatible) with dualism because

_____

_____

_____ .

5. <u>T</u> F *There must have been some first cause, which had no preceding cause, that started the universe.*

A True allies you with Aquinas's first proof of God's existence and with Aristotle, from whom Aquinas borrowed this proof. For students, this is one of the most popular arguments for God's existence.

Many philosophers, however, believe this proof has a glaring weakness. Can you spot it?

The most obvious weakness I can see in Aquinas's first proof is _____
_____.

This could be considered a weakness because _____
_____
_____.

Perhaps Aquinas would try to correct this weakness by arguing _____
_____.

6. <u>T</u> F *We know God exists, because if God didn't exist, the universe wouldn't exist.*

A True means you probably would agree with Aquinas's third proof of God's existence. Would it be possible to agree with this proof and be a monist, one who believes all of reality is basically one kind of thing?

Aquinas's third proof of God's existence would be (consistent, inconsistent) with monism because _____
_____
_____.

7. <u>T</u> F *Because some things in nature (rocks, plants, animals) are more perfect and others are less perfect, we can deduce that God, the source of all perfection, exists.*

If you answered this True, then you probably agree with Aquinas's fourth proof of God's existence. Would it be possible to agree with this proof and be a rationalist?

Aquinas's fourth proof of God's existence would be (consistent, inconsistent) with rationalism because _____
_____
_____.

8. <u>T</u> F *Everything in nature is guided by a divine intelligence.*

Answering this True puts you in accord with Aquinas's fifth proof of God's existence and also with the twentieth-century philosopher Teilhard de Chardin—who held the interesting view that evolution, far from being inconsistent with Christianity, was directed by God's spirit. The entire universe in its development from matter to life to more intelligent life is a kind of vast, God-directed symphony, driving toward what de Chardin called the "Omega point," an ultimate spiritual unity of all existence at the end of time. If de Chardin's position intrigues you, read his *Phenomenon of Man* (New York: Harper & Row, 1965).

Evaluation: Number of points in agreement with Aquinas = _____ of 8 possible.

A position of Aquinas's that you strongly (support, oppose) is _____

_____

because _____

_____

_____ .

GOOD BOOKS

Burrill, Donald R., editor. *The Cosmological Arguments.* Garden City, N.Y.: Anchor Books, 1967. An excellent source for an analysis of empirical arguments, like Aquinas's, for God's existence.

Kenny, Anthony. *Five Ways: St. Thomas Aquinas' Proofs of God's Existence.* London: Routledge & Kegan Paul, 1969. A discussion of the five proofs.

NEXT STOP

By doubting everything, René Descartes arrives at truths that can't be doubted.

19
Descartes
How to Destroy Skepticism

YOUR PHILOSOPHICAL SELF-PORTRAIT

Add more details to your philosophical self-portrait by answering the questions below and offering evidence for your answers.

1. T F   Very little, if anything, can be known for certain.
    Evidence: _____
    _____
    _____.

2. T F   From the fact that you are a thinking being, it is possible to prove that you exist.
    Evidence: _____
    _____
    _____.

3. T F   From the fact that you exist, it is possible to prove that you are a thinking being.
    Evidence: _____
    _____
    _____.

4. T F   It is possible, without using knowledge gained by the senses, to prove that God exists.
    Evidence: _____
    _____
    _____.

5. T F   You could not have the idea of a perfect being (God) unless an actual perfect being (God) existed.
    Evidence: _____
    _____
    _____.

PREVIEW

As preparation for analyzing René Descartes's quest for certainty in his *Meditations on First Philosophy*, you play a wisdom game to determine what, if anything, you know for certain.

Descartes borrows several important ideas from philosophers before him. The Greek philosopher Sextus Empiricus's skeptical arguments provide Descartes with a beginning for his search for unquestionable truths; Descartes endorses many aspects of the medieval Christian image of God; he supports Anselm's ontological argument; as his philosophical foundation, Descartes uses Augustine's proof that doubting our existence proves our existence.

Descartes's analysis of matter, his sharp split between mind and body, his rejection of traditional authorities, and his methodical introspection add several important new elements to the history of philosophy.

Here is a wisdom game.

Your goal is to convince yourself that you know at least one truth for certain. My goal is to convince you that you don't.

And so, from 0 percent certain to 100 percent certain, how confident are you about each of the following?

1. Tomorrow's weather: _____% certain.

2. Next month's weather: _____% certain.

3. Where you will be living ten years from now: _____% certain.

4. God's existence: _____% certain.

5. 2 + 2 = 4: _____% certain.

6. The physical universe exists: _____% certain.

7. Your GPA at the end of this year: _____% certain.

8. The fact that you exist: _____% certain.

9. The next movie to win the Oscar for Best Picture: _____% certain.

10. The distance from Biffle's computer to Biffle's refrigerator: _____% certain.

11. The single truth you know more certainly than any other is _____

    _____. Of this truth, you are _____% certain.

Now, as your next step in this wisdom game, arrange your answers, 1–11, on the following scale. Thus, if you held that you had no certainty about number

10 above, the distance from my computer to my refrigerator, you would place a 10 at the 0 percent certainty end of the scale.

Certainty = 0%   25%   50%   75%   100%

Now, if you are not 100 percent certain of any of the statements, 1–11 above, then you've lost the wisdom game. You have no wisdom, except perhaps the paltry knowledge that you know nothing for certain. But, if you're like most of my students, you have decided that at least one of the following can be known with 100 percent certainty.

- God exists.
- The physical universe exists.
- 2 + 2 = 4
- You exist.

As the next step in the wisdom game, let me explain what it means to be 100 percent certain that any statement is true. *A statement that is 100 percent certain is impossible to doubt.* If you can doubt any of the above, even in the slightest way, then you are not absolutely certain of its truth.

As a demonstration of this principle, let's begin with a simple example. I've never met a student who had 100 percent certainty about next month's weather. Why? Because it is very possible to doubt the nature of next month's weather. Where there is doubt about the weather, obviously there can't be 100 percent certainty about the weather.

Now, look again at the four truths many students believe they can know absolutely for certain. Isn't it obviously possible to doubt each one? Watch me. I'll doubt them for you.

- I doubt that God exists.
- I doubt that the physical universe exists.
- I doubt that 2 + 2 = 4.
- I doubt that I exist.

Isn't it obvious that nothing keeps me from doubting these statements? And where doubt is possible, 100 percent certainty flies out the window.

And so you lose the wisdom game. You can't know anything for certain because any statement you make is possible to doubt.

You might object at this point, "Well, *you* can doubt those statements but I don't."

My answer: *A statement that is 100 percent certain would be impossible for anyone to doubt.* So you still lose the wisdom game. All of the statements above— any statement you wish to make—can be doubted by someone at some time.

And so don't I win? You can't know anything for certain.

René Descartes (1596–1650)

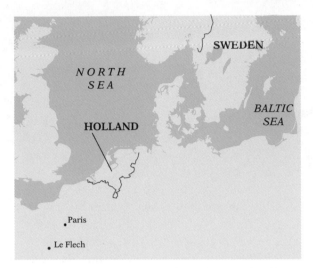

On the night of November 10, 1619, René Descartes, then twenty-three, had three life-changing dreams. In the first dream, ghosts appeared to him in the midst of a fearsome storm. The terrified young scholar tried to beat them back, but they swept him away on a violent wind. Escaping, he staggered to a nearby chapel but was unable to get inside. People passed by—including an evil genius who tried to seduce him. As Descartes fought to exorcise the evil genius, he woke up. Sleep came again and with it a second dream. In the second dream Descartes was looking through a book of poems. In it was a line from Ausonius: "What path in life shall I follow?" In the third and decisive dream, Descartes heard a noise "like a thunderclap," which he thought was the Spirit of Truth descending upon him. The next morning, he was convinced the dreams foretold that he would develop a unifying method for philosophy and would establish the foundation of a "wonderful new science." He intended his new method to place philosophy firmly in the modern world of new sciences and free it from its reliance on ancient authority.

René Descartes was born in 1596 at La Haye in Touraine, France. Having fragile health as a youth, he was allowed to sleep late in the day. Later in life, these long mornings became periods for philosophical reflection. Descartes attended La Flèche, a school run by the Jesuits, and studied philosophy and mathematics. Philosophy, as studied in Descartes's day, included the natural sciences as well as what we would think of as the more normal philosophical topics of logic (the study of the rules of reasoning), metaphysics (the study of the nature of reality), and ethics (the study of the nature of virtue). The young Descartes's intellectual skills were apparent to all.

The philosophical part of the curriculum at La Flèche was based upon the works of Aristotle and his medieval commentators. Even though the revolutionary views of Galileo and Kepler had not penetrated the Jesuit school, Descartes's mathematical studies were up to date. He studied the geometry of the ancients and the algebra of the moderns (from the Arabs). The intellectual contradiction between medieval philosophy, with its unquestioned assumptions about the universe, and the more rigorous "modern" mathematics may have laid the foundation for Descartes's search, later in life, for new, unquestionable certainties.

After his schooling, Descartes began an attempt to learn from, as he put it, "the book of the world." From age twenty-two to age thirty-two, he traveled through the Netherlands, Poland,

You are (right, wrong) because _____

_____

_____

_____

René Descartes (continued)

Bohemia, Austria, and Germany and served in two armies.

In 1622, Descartes sold his estates in France and used the proceeds to finance a new life in pursuit of truth. He moved to Holland, a more philosophically liberal country than was seventeenth-century France, and he wrote *Rules for the Direction of the Mind,* his first sketch of his method of philosophy. Descartes openly rejected the belief that the earth was the center of the cosmos as an ancient and vulgar falsehood. Five years later, Descartes finished *The World,* a discussion of the primary principles of all physics. He assumed a natural rather than a divine order for the celestial bodies. Descartes imagined God starting with matter endowed with nothing but the mathematical qualities of extension (three-dimensionality) and motion. As architect of the universe, God merely lent His aid to matter's proper distribution, organization, and continuation. God, in Descartes's view, became the watchmaker and the universe His divinely balanced watch. The only two spiritual, nonphysical substances were God and the human mind. Like Copernicus, Descartes asserted the movement of the earth. However, learning that the Inquisition had forced Galileo to recant his views supporting the Copernican theory, Descartes, a true son of the Church and a cautious man, decided to withhold publication of *The World.*

In 1637, Descartes published *Discourse on Method,* an introduction to his philosophy and also a preface to his works in other sciences. He also published *La Géométrie,* which made an extremely important contribution to mathematics.

His book linked algebra and geometry by means of a coordinate system that still bears his name: Cartesian. This system made Descartes one of the pioneers in the development of calculus.

At the age of forty-five, Descartes published *Meditations on First Philosophy.* In the *Meditations,* as you will soon learn, Descartes attempted to construct a universe of interrelated truths balanced upon a single, perfect certitude, his own existence as a "thinking thing."

In 1648, upset by local academic bickering and the possibility of physical harm by opponents of his works, Descartes accepted a position as tutor to Queen Christina of Sweden. Though Sweden promised a safe haven, he was not entirely eager to live in the land of "polar bears and ice."

Queen Christina, a remarkable woman, could speak five languages and rode and fenced as well as most men. She hired Descartes to teach her the "new philosophy"—that is, his own thinking. Ironically, teaching philosophy to someone who actually wanted to learn it caused Descartes's death. Christina insisted on meeting with him at five in the morning when her mind was clearest to do rigorous philosophical work. Descartes's lifelong habit had been to linger in bed until late. The demands of rising early each morning and the harsh weather of Stockholm weighed on him. On returning from a teaching session on an especially cold morning, Descartes contracted pneumonia; he died on February 11, 1650, at 54 years of age.

Descartes's major works include *Meditations on First Philosophy* (1641), *Principles of Philosophy* (1644), and *Discourse on Method* (1647).

As you will soon discover, René Descartes will argue that one of the four statements above *is* impossible to doubt, *for anyone.* Descartes believes that there is a single statement of such magical certitude that when anyone attempts to doubt its truth, its truth is automatically proved. Descartes goes on to argue that from the 100 percent certainty of this marvelous truth, the absolute certainty of the other statements above will follow *if they are considered in the right sequence.*

So, as your last step in the wisdom game, match wits with Descartes. Which of the four statements above will he claim is impossible for anyone to doubt, and then in what order can the truth of the other statements be established?

1. _____ (impossible to doubt)

2. _____

3. _____

4. _____

No philosopher before Descartes, and perhaps none after him, ever attempted to accomplish so much in so few pages. His groundbreaking *Meditations on First Philosophy* is about the length of a comic book.

Descartes's strategy was unique. Philosophers before him had constructed large numbers of philosophical arguments to solve large numbers of philosophical problems. Instead of hopscotching from problem to problem, Descartes believed that *if the correct starting place could be found, the great riddles of philosophy could be solved in a single leap*. Begin with a perfect truth, borrow some concepts from the past, line the problems up in the proper order, and the bookshelf of 2,000 years of philosophizing can be replaced by fifty pages. Descartes believed that he had discovered a shortcut to wisdom.

To prepare you for an investigation of the first half of Descartes's *Meditations on First Philosophy*, I'll answer the following questions:

- What does Descartes borrow from the past?

- What is new in Descartes's philosophy?

- What are key ideas in the first three *Meditations*?

- What are some techniques for reading Descartes?

Let's begin with the few key ideas Descartes adopts from his predecessors.

What Does Descartes Borrow from the Past?

Descartes borrows important concepts from Greek and medieval Christian philosophers we've examined on the tour (and two we have not).

If I could have added a few more chapters to this text, I would have certainly included one on Sextus Empiricus, who flourished around 200 A.D. He was a Greek philosopher and physician about whom little is known except his skeptical arguments. According to Sextus, reason should be rigorously used to attack all certainty, even certainty in reason. In a famous metaphor, Sextus compares such a use of reason to a medicine for poison which causes the stomach to relieve itself not only of the poison but also of the medicine itself. In order to discover a truth that can be known 100 percent for certain, Descartes uses Sextus's arguments, which attack the senses as a source of certitude. (In *Meditation I*, we will examine these arguments in detail.) Having used Sextus to show what *can't* be known for certain, Descartes can then develop his own position in succeeding meditations about what *can* be known for certain.

To prove God's existence, Descartes uses Plato's concept of the relationship between the perfect and the imperfect. In dialogues like the *Phaedo, Symposium,* and *Republic,* Plato argued that whenever we make a judgment such as "This is not a perfectly beautiful painting," we imply that we have an idea about Perfect Beauty itself. Just as our idea of a one-foot rule can be traced back to our actual experience of a one-foot rule, our idea of Perfect Beauty can be traced back to our actual experience with Perfect Beauty (in Plato's argument, as you recall, to a time before our birth in the realm of Forms). We can reason that Perfect Beauty exists every time we use knowledge of it to judge that something is not perfectly beautiful.

Descartes adapts Plato's idea to a proof of God's existence. Descartes knows he is an imperfect being. But this implies that he also knows what a perfect being is. The idea of a perfect being could only have come from a real perfect being. Therefore, whereas Plato concludes that Perfect Beauty exists, Descartes concludes that the perfect being, God, exists. (We will talk more about this proof in the pages ahead.)

Descartes also borrows from his philosophical predecessors in the Middle Ages. He continues the tradition of medieval philosophy that God left his stamp on his mind much as a potter leaves his mark on his pot. Echoing many medieval prayers, Descartes contemplates this God in wonder and delight at the end of *Meditation III.* One of Descartes's proofs of God's existence repeats key ideas in Anselm's ontological argument. Descartes's first 100 percent certitude, that his thinking is absolute proof of his own existence, was first stated by Augustine.

Now try summing this up.

Some of the major ideas Descartes borrows from the past are _____

_____

_____   _____

_____ .

What Is New in Descartes's Philosophy?

Several important new aspects of Descartes's philosophy have earned him the title of the "father of modern philosophy."

In *Meditation II,* Descartes analyzes a piece of wax and distinguishes between what is learned about the wax through the senses and what is learned by the mind. In the process, he develops a new definition of the essential characteristics of a substance. Because the color, shape, smell, and solidity of the wax change when it becomes warm, none of those things can be part of its essential character. The wax is still wax whether it is hard or soft, bright or dull, sweet-smelling or scentless. Descartes argues that all these changing characteristics come to us through our senses, and therefore our senses do not tell us about the unchanging, essential characteristics of the wax. Only inspection by our minds reveals that wax and therefore all other substances are, in essence, spatially extended, flexible, and capable of changing form. This nonsensory definition of matter will eventually lead to Newton's mathematical description of matter in the eighteenth century.

Just as "Platonic" is used to
refer to Plato's philosophy
and "Aristotelian" is used to
refer to Aristotle's philosophy,
"Cartesian" is used to refer to
Descartes's philosophy.

Descartes thus argues that what the mind knows for certain did not come from the senses. In fact, all through the *Meditations,* Descartes describes the mind as completely separable from the body. Such a sharp distinction between mind and body has been labeled "Cartesian dualism" and has been an important legacy to the history of psychology. In one sense, Descartes's journey inward into the privacy of his own mind makes possible Freud's psychoanalytic self-examination at the beginning of the twentieth century.

Descartes shares his medieval predecessors' concern with God's existence; but unlike the proofs of philosophers before him, Descartes's proof of God's existence depends on his prior proof of his own existence. This is an important shift. When Anselm demonstrates God's existence in his ontological argument, he does it in the context of a long prayer, the *Proslogium* (not included on the tour). Anselm is dissatisfied with his proof when it doesn't make him feel closer to God. When Descartes uses similar arguments, he does it in the context of a meditation designed to make him feel more sure of his own conclusions. The goal of Anselm's proof is to draw him upward to God; Descartes's proof is subsumed by a larger and more important goal, his own philosophical peace of mind.

Descartes almost never quotes anyone. One medieval proof of the truth of an argument is to show that the Bible, or Aristotle, or someone who lived long ago stated the same thing. Thus, to be true is to be consistent with the wisdom of the past. Descartes is suspicious even of his own past. In *Meditation I,* he deliberately sets himself adrift from all his past beliefs. In *Meditation III,* he questions what he established in *Meditation II.* In *Meditation IV,* he has to review again what he said in *Meditation III.* Not only does he find no comfort in a truth that someone wise held to be true long ago, but also he finds no comfort in a truth he held to be true moments ago. The past, even his own past, is always to be viewed with suspicion.

Augustine, Anselm, and Aquinas, Descartes's three great medieval predecessors, spent a large amount of time explaining the relationship between a perfect God and an imperfect creation. If we place too great an emphasis on God's perfection, an unbridgeable chasm opens between the divine and the created. Thus, the problem for medieval philosophy is simultaneously to demonstrate the absolute chasm between the universe and God and to define some bridge (grace, Christ, reason, faith?) across that chasm. Descartes, a Renaissance philosopher, spends a large amount of time trying to get out of his own head. It is not so much the disorder of the universe that troubles him as the disorder of his own thoughts. The chasm Descartes is worried about is between his thought and its object. He does not think about the universe and God as much as he thinks about his own thinking about the universe and God.

And so what are some of the new aspects of Descartes's philosophy?

The points that are new in Descartes are _____

_____

_____

_____.

Undeceiving the Deceived Senses

Assume Descartes is looking at Escher's picture. First of all, what would he (or anyone else) notice that is strange about the waterfall and the stream that feeds it?

It is strange that _____

_____

_____ .

    Descartes presents arguments in his first mediation that the senses deceive us. Assume he used this picture as evidence for this position. What might he say?

Descartes might say that this picture is evidence that the

senses deceive us because _____

_____

_____ .

    In the sixth of Descartes's meditations (not included on this tour) he concludes that, strictly speaking, the problem is not with our senses, but with our mind's *judgment* about what our senses tell us. The senses provide us with an accurate portrait of what appears to be real; there need be no error until the mind judges that what appears to be real is actually real.
    And so how could Descartes use this picture as evidence that the senses do not deceive us?

This picture could be offered as evidence that the senses do not deceive us because

_____

_____

_____ .

    Which is the correct view: (a) Descartes's initial position that the senses deceive us or (b) his final position that the senses do not deceive us?

The correct position is (a, b) because _____

_____

_____ .

M. C. Escher, *Waterfall,* 1948.

What Are Key Ideas in the First Three *Meditations*?

On this tour we'll closely examine the first three of Descartes's six meditations. At the end of Meditation III, I'll summarize the concluding meditations.

BOX 19.1

Descartes and the Renaissance

One of the easiest ways to understand the Renaissance (1330–1650) is to see that Columbus's voyage to North America in 1492 was a typically Renaissance activity. From the fourteenth to the seventeenth century, exploration of new worlds characterized human activities not only in sea voyages but also in art, architecture, literature, religion, science, and philosophy. Like Columbus, Renaissance explorers left the old world behind, used incomplete maps to find new places, and radically extended the horizons of human knowledge. Descartes's *Meditations,* in the spirit of his age, can be seen as an attempt to plant old values upon new ground.

Near the beginning of the fourteenth century, Giotto, a painter from Florence, Italy, began to explore a new kind of painted world. His figures, unlike those of his predecessors and contemporaries, were three-dimensional, subtly shaded, lifelike. Giotto's Virgin seemed to be sitting on her throne rather than, in the medieval fashion, being awkwardly attached to it. His baby Jesus looked like an infant rather than a miniature adult. Giotto's painfully dead Christ looked as if he had once been vigorously alive; Christ in the Middle Ages looked as ghostly living as dead. Thus, Giotto discovered a new dramatic space. Whereas the medieval artist wanted the viewer to recall the pain of Christ's death, Giotto created a painted space in which the death was reenacted. Under his hand, religious art changed from a collection of holy signs to a window on a religious drama. Giotto's drama on the other side of the window was the new world that other Renaissance artists explored.

At the beginning of the fifteenth century, Filippo Brunelleschi, then an unsuccessful Italian architect, traveled to Rome and began to take measurements of thousand-year-old Roman buildings. Apparently, no one had ever done such a thing. Nearly twenty years later, Brunelleschi created the first piece of Renaissance architecture. On top of the medieval Cathedral of Florence, he erected a dome inspired by his Roman studies. In other words, he erected a pagan space on top of a Christian building. To some eyes, the result looked as odd as it sounds. But Brunelleschi became one of the first Renaissance explorers to establish a solution for other adventurers of the new age: Use an old map, obtained from the Romans (who got theirs from the Greeks), to found a new place.

The development of the theater from the Middle Ages to the seventeenth century is a good example of the Renaissance exploration of new worlds. With the collapse of the western Roman Empire in the fifth century A.D. and the rise of Christianity, theatrically staged plays vanished as a form of entertainment for nearly a thousand years. Instructive religious dramas presented in the church as part of the Mass slowly evolved into medieval mystery plays staged on church grounds. From the churchyard, these religious dramas moved to the marketplace and toured the countryside on wagons. It was not until the sixteenth century that drama broke entirely free of the church and set out on its own, largely be-

In *Meditation I,* Descartes asks his fundamental question: Is there anything of which I can be certain? In his quest for certainty, Descartes vows to doubt all his former opinions. If there are grounds for doubting them, they cannot be completely certain. Descartes is searching for a foundation, for solid rock underneath the shifting soils of his world. He doubts his senses and even has a difficult time distinguishing dreaming from reality. At this point, he finds no reliable method for telling dreams from waking experience. He imagines there

cause of the Renaissance interest in classical Roman and Greek theater. The first permanent indoor theater since the days of the Romans was designed by the Italian architect Palladio in Vincenza, Italy, in 1585. As a new theatrical space emerged from the canopy of the church, so did the characters presented in plays. Shakespeare, who belonged to the generation preceding Descartes's, created characters who occasionally were so familiar with their new fictional world that they realized they were on stage. At the conclusion of *The Tempest*, a character addresses the audience and urges them to applaud the play they have just seen. Shakespeare not only created a new world but also populated it with citizens who sent messages back to the old.

Martin Luther, like his near contemporary Columbus, looked for a new route to an old place. Columbus, of course, wanted to find a shorter route to India. Luther wanted to sail completely around the Catholic Church and arrive, without an encumbering cargo of priests, at God. In 1517, Luther presented ninety-five theses against the church and offered to debate all comers. Following St. Paul, Luther held that salvation could be achieved only by faith in Jesus Christ. Thus, all the sacraments of the church, from baptism to priestly hierarchy, were excess baggage. Because salvation was strictly a matter of individual faith, the believer stood before God in a new land, beyond the controlling influence of Rome. Like Columbus, however, Luther may not have arrived where he intended. His pronouncement of a shorter, simpler route to the divine opened

up centuries of religious warfare (which continue to this day in Northern Ireland) between Protestant and Catholic.

The development of astronomy in the sixteenth and seventeenth centuries is a literal example of the Renaissance exploration of new worlds. Until the advances of Nicolaus Copernicus (1473–1543), Tycho Brahe (1546–1601), Johannes Kepler (1571–1630), and Galileo (1564–1642), few had questioned that the universe was exactly as it appeared, a starry spectacle with the earth at its center. This geocentric view was supported not only by the testimony of the senses and Aristotle but also by the church. An earth-centered cosmology supported a God-centered philosophy and vice versa. So frightening was the new space discovered by the Renaissance astronomers that, so the story goes, when Galileo offered a priest a view through his new telescope, the churchman declined to look. Arrested by the Inquisition in 1633 and shown the instruments of his torture, Galileo decided the new universe wasn't out there and recanted his views.

Thus by Descartes's day, waves of Renaissance explorers had opened up new worlds— literary, artistic, theological, and astronomical. The new intellectual continents discovered by Luther and the astronomers were the most troublesome to the established order, and the church showed itself quite ready to burn rash explorers. Descartes understood his delicate task as dismounting the old views from their crumbling base and erecting them upon a new foundation.

is an evil spirit, a great deceiver, who misleads him on every possible occasion. If he can find a truth that even an all-powerful evil spirit could not deceive him about, he will have found an initial 100 percent certitude. *Meditation I* ends with nothing certain except that nothing appears certain.

Meditation II rescues the project of doubt from absolute skepticism by the famous argument that the only idea that cannot be doubted is that "*I* am doubting." When I doubt, I can doubt everything except that I must exist in order to doubt that I exist. Thus, this truth is impossible for anyone, at any time, to doubt. Doubting our existence proves our existence because we must exist in order to do the doubting. Or, as Descartes puts it, "'I am, I exist' must be true whenever I state it or mentally consider it." But what or who is this "I"? For Descartes, the "I" is a thing that thinks. Descartes has a "clear and distinct" idea of the mind in a way that there is no clear and distinct idea of the body. At the end of *Meditation II*, Descartes states, "For so far I do not admit in myself anything other than the mind." Thus Descartes's process of methodological doubting has led to the certainty that he can doubt everything except the mind, the "I" that doubts.

Meditation III takes as one of its tasks the proof of God's existence. It is important to remember the direction of Descartes's thought here: From the certainty of the self comes the certainty of God. That is new. One of his arguments is that the idea of a supremely perfect being comes from a supremely perfect cause (God). Something that is more perfect (the idea of God) cannot be produced by something that is less perfect (Descartes's mind). Therefore, God exists because He is the only possible cause of Descartes's idea of Him. In the second proof, Descartes argues that God must exist in order to guarantee Descartes's continued existence. Since Descartes cannot be the continuous cause of his own existence, God must be that cause and therefore God must exist.

Now, having summarized some of the key ideas in the first three of the six meditations, let me give you some help in getting started reading Descartes.

What Are Some Techniques for Reading Descartes?

Let's look carefully at the first paragraph of Descartes's *Meditations on First Philosophy*.

Here is the first sentence:

For several years now, I've been aware that I accepted many falsehoods as true in my youth, that what I built on the foundation of those falsehoods was dubious, and accordingly that once in my life I would need to tear down everything and begin anew from the foundations if I wanted to establish any stable and lasting knowledge.

What do you think that means?

Descartes is saying _____

_____.

Let's closely examine this long sentence. One good strategy in analyzing long sentences is to look at the phrases separated by commas. For example:

For several years now, I've been aware that I accepted many falsehoods as true in my youth. . . .

That much, standing alone, is not terribly difficult to understand. What happened in his youth?

He _____.

Now add the next phrase to it.

For several years now, I've been aware that I accepted many falsehoods as true in my youth, **that what I built on the foundation of those falsehoods was dubious** . . .

He is describing a progression. First something happened in his youth, and then something else happened.

He is saying _____.

Now add the rest of the sentence to see what the conclusion of the progression is.

For several years now, I've been aware that I accepted many falsehoods as true in my youth, that what I built on the foundation of those falsehoods was dubious, **and accordingly that once in my life I would need to tear down everything and begin anew from the foundations if I wanted to establish any stable and lasting knowledge.**

The first sentence is crucial because it states Descartes's problem and what he will have to do to solve it. The section in boldface above presents his proposed solution.

His problem is _____

_____.

His solution is _____

_____.

At this point, you probably understand the first sentence better than when you first read it. Here is the rest of the first paragraph. Reread it several times, break sentences into smaller, more understandable pieces, make your own notes in the margin, underline important points.

But the task seemed enormous, and I waited until I was so old that no better time for undertaking it would be likely to follow. I have thus delayed so long that it would be wrong for me to waste in indecision the time left for action. Today, then, having rid myself of worries and having arranged for some peace and quiet, I withdraw alone, free at last earnestly and wholeheartedly to overthrow all my beliefs.

Now try to paraphrase each sentence.

In the first sentence, he is saying _____

_____.

In the second sentence, he is saying _____

_____.

In the third sentence, he is saying _____

_____.

So, what is the first paragraph about?

What he is going to do is _____

_____

because _____

_____

_____.

One fact you have probably discovered on the tour is that the reading pattern for understanding philosophy is different from your normal reading pattern. Usually you read in a straight line. You begin at the beginning and go on to the end. Reading most philosophy in that fashion, as you have probably learned, is simply impossible. You must circle back, stop, reflect, translate ideas into your own words in the margin, underline, go back again, and then move slowly forward. If you are not sure what to write in the margins of the *Meditations* ahead, just try to answer this question over and over: "What is the general idea of this paragraph?" Put question marks in the margins where you are confused.

Besides the occasional complexity of Descartes's sentences, his philosophical method may cause you difficulty. Before I began to read philosophy, I imagined that philosophical thinking was something one did when one couldn't sleep, and it went something like this: "The universe is such a big place. I am so small. Where does the universe end? If I went way out into space and came to the end of the universe, what would be beyond that? Something? Nothing? What am I thinking about?"

By *philosophical* I meant anything that seemed big and confusing. You are about to discover what Descartes means by philosophical thinking. Whereas my questions led me to greater confusion, his led him to greater clarity. Draw a line across the page wherever he seems to begin an important new question. Sometimes he questions his own answers. Read very slowly at these points. Part of his method is to say things he eventually decides are false. There are some excellent examples of this in *Meditation I*. I'll point them out when they occur.

Now think back over what I have said since the beginning of this unit on Descartes, and make whatever notes you need to guide you on your way.

When I think back about what I've learned about Descartes, I want to remember

_____

_____

_____

_____.

The First Meditation:
"On What Can Be Called into Doubt"

Searching for a truth that cannot be doubted, Descartes tears his beliefs down to their foundations. He discovers that nothing certain comes to him through his senses and that he cannot tell dreaming from waking. If Descartes cannot prove that God is no deceiver, then he cannot know even the simplest mathematical truths. To guard against returning to his former misplaced confidence in his beliefs, Descartes concludes *Meditation I* by imagining an evil demon, "supremely powerful and cunning, who works as hard as he can to deceive me."

Note the special way Descartes argues with himself. He believes he cannot know anything for certain unless he argues as strongly as he can against certitude. Label the arguments *Pro* that support certainty; label the arguments *Con* that attack certainty. *Pro* arguments take Descartes closer to his goal of perfect knowledge; *Con* arguments take him farther away.

Meditation I

For several years now, I've been aware that I accepted many falsehoods as true in my youth, that what I built on the foundation of those falsehoods was dubious, and accordingly that once in my life I would need to tear down everything and begin anew from the foundations if I wanted to establish any stable and lasting knowledge. But the task seemed enormous, and I waited until I was so old that no better time for undertaking it would be likely to follow. I have thus delayed so long that it would be wrong for me to waste in indecision the time left for action. Today, then, having rid myself of worries and having arranged for some peace and quiet, I withdraw alone, free at last earnestly and wholeheartedly to overthrow all my beliefs.

To do this, I don't need to show each of them to be false; I may never be able to do that. But, since reason now convinces me that I ought to withhold my assent just as carefully from what isn't obviously certain and indubitable as from what's obviously false, I can justify the rejection of all my beliefs if in each I can find some ground for doubt. And, to do this, I need not run through my beliefs one by one, which would be an endless task. Since a building collapses when its foundation is cut out from under it, I will go straight to the principles on which all my former beliefs rested.

Of course, whatever I have so far accepted as supremely true, I have learned either from the senses or through the senses. But I have occasionally caught the senses deceiving me, and it's prudent never completely to trust those who have cheated us even once.

But, while my senses may deceive me about what is small or far away, there may still be other things that I take in by the senses but that I cannot possibly doubt—like that I am here, sitting before the fire, wearing a dressing gown, touching this paper. And on what grounds might I deny that my hands and the other parts of my body exist?—unless perhaps I liken myself to madmen whose brains are so rattled by the persistent vapors of melancholy that

Some falsehoods, such as the existence of Santa Claus, that you accepted as true in your youth are _____
_____
_____
_____.

Instead of refuting each of his beliefs individually, Descartes decides to _____
_____
_____
_____.

Circle the word "but" whenever it introduces a new *Pro* or *Con* argument.

Descartes had decided that although his senses may be wrong about _____
_____
_____,
they could not be wrong about
_____
_____
_____.

they are sure that they're kings when in fact they are paupers, or that they wear purple robes when in fact they're naked, or that their heads are clay, or that they are gourds, or made of glass. But these people are insane, and I would seem just as crazy if I were to apply what I say about them to myself.

This would be perfectly obvious—if I weren't a man accustomed to sleeping at night whose experiences while asleep are at least as far-fetched as those that madmen have while awake. How often, at night, I've been convinced that I was here, sitting before the fire, wearing my dressing gown, when in fact I was undressed and between the covers of my bed! But now I am looking at this piece of paper with my eyes wide open; the head that I am shaking has not been lulled to sleep; I put my hand out consciously and deliberately and feel. None of this would be as distinct if I were asleep. As if I can't remember having been tricked by similar thoughts while asleep! When I think very carefully about this, I see so plainly that there are no reliable signs by which I can distinguish sleeping from waking that I am stupefied—and my stupor itself suggests that I am asleep!

Suppose, then, that I am dreaming. Suppose, in particular, that my eyes are not open, that my head is not moving, and that I have not put out my hand. Suppose that I do not have hands, or even a body. I must still admit that the things I see in sleep are like painted images which must have been patterned after real things and, hence, that things like eyes, heads, hands, and bodies are real rather than imaginary. For, even when painters try to give bizarre shapes to sirens and satyrs, they are unable to give them completely new natures; they only jumble together the parts of various animals. And, even if they were to come up with something so novel that no one had ever seen anything like it before, something entirely fictitious and unreal, at least there must be real colors from which they composed it. Similarly, while things like eyes, heads, and hands may be imaginary, it must be granted that some simpler and more universal things are real—the "real colors" from which the true and false images in our thoughts are formed.

Things of this sort seem to include general bodily nature and its extension, the shape of extended things, their quantity (that is, their size and number), the place in which they exist, the time through which they endure and so on.

Perhaps we can correctly infer that, while physics, astronomy, medicine, and other disciplines that require the study of composites are dubious, disciplines like arithmetic and geometry, which deal only with completely simple and universal things without regard to whether they exist in the world, are somehow certain and indubitable. For, whether we are awake or asleep, two plus three is always five, and the square never has more than four sides. It seems impossible even to suspect such obvious truths of falsity.

Nevertheless, the traditional view is fixed in my mind that there is a God who can do anything and by whom I have been made to be as I am. How do I know that He hasn't brought it about that, while there is in fact no earth, no sky, no extended thing, no shape, no magnitude, and no place, all of these things seem to me to exist, just as they do now? I think that other people sometimes err in what they believe themselves to know perfectly well. Mightn't I be deceived when I add two and three, or count the sides of a square, or do even

In this paragraph, Descartes changes his mind about

_____

_____

because _____

_____

_____.

Even if he is dreaming, Descartes now decides that he can

be certain about _____

_____

_____.

Reread this and the previous two paragraphs. The stages Descartes has already gone

through are _____

_____

_____

_____

_____

_____.

Geometry is more certain than

astronomy because _____

_____

_____

_____.

"Nevertheless," "Maybe," and "But" are the first words of this paragraph and the next three paragraphs. Throughout the *Meditations*, circle key words like these to show where the argument is moving in a new direction.

simpler things, if we can even suppose that there is anything simpler? Maybe it will be denied that God deceives me, since He is said to be supremely good. But, if God's being good is incompatible with His having created me so that I am deceived always, it seems just as out of line with His being good that He permits me to be deceived sometimes—as he undeniably does.

Maybe some would rather deny that there is an omnipotent God than believe that everything else is uncertain. Rather than arguing with them, I will grant everything I have said about God to be fiction. But, however these people think I came to be as I now am—whether they say it is by fate, or by accident, or by a continuous series of events, or in some other way—it seems that he who errs and is deceived is somehow imperfect. Hence, the less power that is attributed to my original creator, the more likely it is that I am always deceived. To these arguments, I have no reply. I'm forced to admit that nothing that I used to believe is beyond legitimate doubt—not because I have been careless or playful, but because I have valid and well-considered grounds for doubt. Hence, I must withhold my assent from my former beliefs as carefully as from obvious falsehoods if I want to arrive at something certain.

But it's not enough to have noticed this: I must also take care to bear it in mind. For my habitual views constantly return to my mind and take control of what I believe as if our long-standing, intimate relationship has given them the right to do so, even against my will. I'll never break the habit of trusting and giving in to these views while I see them for what they are—things somewhat dubious (as I have just shown) but nonetheless probable, things that I have much more reason to believe than to deny. That's why I think it will be good deliberately to turn my will around, to allow myself to be deceived, and to suppose that all my previous beliefs are false and illusory. Eventually, when I have counterbalanced the weight of my prejudices, my bad habits will no longer distort my grasp of things. I know that there is no danger of error here and that I won't overindulge in skepticism, since I'm now concerned, not with action, but only with gaining knowledge.

I will suppose, then, not that there is a supremely good God who is the source of all truth, but that there is an evil demon, supremely powerful and cunning, who works as hard as he can to deceive me. I will say that sky, air, earth, color, shape, sound, and other external things are just dreamed illusions that the demon uses to ensnare my judgment. I will regard myself as not having hands, eyes, flesh, blood, and senses—but as having the false belief that I have all these things. I will obstinately concentrate on this meditation and will thus ensure by mental resolution that, if I do not really have the ability to know the truth, I will at least withhold assent from what is false and from what a deceiver may try to put over on me, however powerful and cunning he may be. But this plan requires effort, and laziness brings me back to my ordinary life. I am like a prisoner who happens to enjoy the illusion of freedom in his dreams, begins to suspect that he is asleep, fears being awakened, and deliberately lets the enticing illusions skip by unchallenged. Thus, I slide back into my old views, afraid to awaken and to find that after my peaceful rest I must toil, not in the light, but in the confusing darkness of the problems just raised.

"These views" refers to ___

_____

_____

_____.

This is one of the most famous paragraphs in the *Meditations*. The advantage to Descartes of supposing "an evil demon" exists who is deceiving him is

_____

_____

_____.

The main "problems just

raised" are _____

_____

_____

_____.

What Can Be Learned
About Philosophy from Descartes?

The most common question my students ask about the *Meditations* is simply "Why is Descartes doing this?"

Descartes appears to be troubling himself with doubts about issues that don't seem doubtful. Knowledge, despite what Descartes says in *Meditation I*, certainly seems to come through the senses. Therefore, my students ask, why should a philosopher go back and forth through complex arguments wondering about something that is so obvious?

Right now, you might say, you are getting knowledge about Descartes by reading this book. Your eyes scan the page; your brain processes the information. Therefore, you might justifiably wonder, why isn't the way the mind and the senses work just as obvious to Descartes? Why doesn't he just conclude that "all my beliefs rest on data that have come to me through my senses and that my mind organizes; thus, my beliefs have a sturdy foundation"? End of meditation.

By this point on the tour, many students take their objections about Descartes even further and attack philosophy in general. Why on earth do philosophers worry about all the problems they worry about? Philosophers' reasonings are just mind games. Anyone can tell reality from illusion, right from wrong, fact from error. No one needs a difficult-to-understand philosophical manuscript as a guidebook to daily life.

Thus, Descartes seems to be just another egghead making simple things complex. The *Meditations* are fancy talk about the obvious. Philosophers are dogs worrying a meatless bone. The world is the world. Knowledge is knowledge. The true is the true and the false is the false. And that is that.

I hope it surprises you when I say that, with one exception, I agree. I have spent 99 percent of my life not worried in the slightest about Descartes's problems. I sit in chairs and never wonder if I am dreaming that I'm sitting there. These are my hands, and 2 + 3 is certainly 5. God has better things to do than deceive me about such obvious truths. Except on the occasion I will soon describe, I keep my evil demon locked up. Just like you, I trust my senses. It is too much trouble not to. If I had to think about whether or not my fingers were touching the computer keyboard right now and whether or not pushing down each key would put "real" information on the screen and whether or not your senses would work accurately when you read these black squiggles, I'd never write a word. In the same way, I imagine, a physicist doesn't wonder if, because matter is mostly empty space, her cup will fall through the table when she sets it down. Nor does she worry that because there is a discontinuity between quantum theory and celestial mechanics, her dinner might cook improperly.

Our unexamined beliefs about daily life do very well in guiding us through the world we live in. We don't need to understand the nature of truth to use the microwave.

So why bother with Descartes?

As I said earlier, I bother with Descartes only on one kind of occasion. The rest of my hours, I can do without him.

As long as I attend to the small mysteries of life, Descartes is useless. A thousand questions stream at me every day, and I do not appeal to what I know about Descartes for help. Is it cold enough to wear a coat? Should I have hamburger again tonight? Will my darling get angry if I refuse to watch *The Sound of Music*? On these and many other occasions, Descartes is mute and irrelevant.

I turn to Descartes and philosophy for guidance only when I lift my eyes from life's small mysteries to its Great Mysteries. To put this paradoxically, philosophy is rarely important and therefore very important.

Does God exist? Where did the universe come from? Do I have a soul? When I confront these questions, everything I have learned about when to wear a coat, how often to have hamburger, and how to anticipate the moods of my darling becomes irrelevant. Only Descartes and other philosophers show me how to think about the Great Mysteries. In fact, I cannot very usefully confront any of the Great Mysteries on my own. Because I spend 99 percent of my time not thinking about such things, I have no clue to how to think about life's biggest questions. There is the universe. How do I think about it? It's big. It's starry. And? I must turn to philosophy to see how great minds have considered the question. When I want to contemplate the workings of the cosmos, I need those whom the centuries have selected as the wisest guides. On the rare occasions when I get my head above the clouds, I do well to lay against the starry sky templates of genius.

And so why is Descartes doing what he is doing? Is it a fair criticism to argue that he does not address life's daily problems, that his writings are hard to understand, and that he makes the simple complex? What's philosophy about anyway?

It is no good criticizing philosophy because it does not address life's daily problems, just as it would be no good criticizing an astronomical telescope because it does not help you watch TV. Philosophy is a big-view kind of thing. Stay away from it when you're looking for mild entertainment. But don't criticize philosophy for not being a small-view kind of thing. The globe is not useless because it doesn't help you find the shortest route to work.

Nor is it any good criticizing philosophy for being difficult to understand. You and I spend most of our lives among life's small mysteries. We are, by nature and habit, small, unsystematic thinkers. Philosophy requires that we think grandly and carefully. Among other strange mental practices, philosophy asks us to think about thinking. This is rather like putting your toe behind your ear. Of course it hurts. The toe has voyaged into the land of non-ordinary toeness. So your mind will hurt after reading philosophy. Everyone's does. Philosophy cramps the mind into unnatural contortions. But its promise is enlightenment.

This needs to be stressed. Philosophy promises enlightenment. Why do we twist our minds into unnatural philosophical contortions? Because philosophy promises true answers to the Great Mysteries! In the *Meditations*, Descartes will establish all that can be known for certain, prove God's existence three ways, describe the nature of the mind, show a way to avoid all error, destroy every basis for doubt, and construct a world of certitude. That's worth at least stretching your toe in the direction of your ear.

Finally, it is no good criticizing philosophy for making the simple complex. Actually, philosophy shows the complexity of the simple. Think for a second about washing machines. You would certainly say that a washing machine is less complex than all of reality. And yet a washing machine is mystery enough to confound most consumers. There are thick manuals that do nothing but explain the workings of washing machines. Certainly the interactions of the mind and the cosmos are more complex than devices that force soapy water through our clothes. If washing machines are not simple, then certainly neither are the mind and the nature of reality. And if we grant that our home appliances are very complicated and need specialists (such as washing-machine repair people) for their analysis, then we also ought to grant that the workings of reality need specialists (such as philosophers) for their analysis. And just as we would not expect to be able to follow the reasonings in a washing-machine repair manual at first glance, so we should not expect to follow the reasonings of a philosophical meditation at first glance. Where does this leave you? One-third of the way through an exploration of a great philosophical exploration. Take heart. Philosophy is difficult because it is a non-ordinary (perhaps someday you will say an extraordinary) kind of thinking; philosophy is useless for life's small mysteries because it is a tool designed for life's Great Mysteries; and philosophy is hard to comprehend because it is a specialized kind of knowledge you are unfamiliar with.

Philosophy is a toe-behind-the-ear sort of thing that promises enlightenment.

The Second Meditation: "On the Nature of the Human Mind, Which Is Better Known Than the Body"

Descartes discovers his first 100 percent certitude: "I must finally conclude that the statement 'I am, I exist' must be true whenever I state it or mentally consider it." Next, he carefully expands this truth into the definition of himself as a "thinking thing." Finally, Descartes examines a piece of wax to convince himself that he can know the existence of his mind far more clearly than he can know anything through his senses.

Remember that Descartes is arguing with himself. He is seeking new certitudes by carefully exploring arguments against those certitudes. Pay careful attention to any question Descartes asks himself. Does Descartes's answer to his question increase or decrease his confidence in his knowledge? Label answers *Pro* that increase Descartes's confidence in his knowledge; label answers *Con* that decrease his confidence in his knowledge.

Meditation II

The major causes of doubt from "yesterday's meditation" are

_____

_____

_____

_____

_____ .

Yesterday's meditation has hurled me into doubts so great that I can neither ignore them nor think my way out of them. I am in turmoil, as if I have accidently fallen into a whirlpool and can neither touch bottom nor swim to the safety of the surface. I will struggle, however, and try to follow the path that I started on yesterday. I will reject whatever is open to the slightest doubt just as though I have found it to be entirely false, and I will continue until I find something certain—or at least until I know for certain that nothing is certain. Archimedes required only one fixed and immovable point to move the whole earth from its place, and I too can hope for great things if I can find even one small thing that is certain and unshakable.

I will suppose, then, that everything I see is unreal. I will believe that my memory is unreliable and that none of what it presents to me ever happened. I have no senses. Body, shape, extension, motion, and place are fantasies. What then is true? Perhaps just that nothing is certain.

But how do I know that there isn't something different from the things just listed that I do not have the slightest reason to doubt? Isn't there a God, or something like one, who puts my thoughts into me? But why should I say so when I may be the author of those thoughts? Well, isn't it at least the case that I am something? But I now am denying that I have senses and a body. But I stop here. For what follows from these denials? Am I so bound to my body and to my senses that I cannot exist without them? I have convinced myself that there is nothing in the world—no sky, no earth, no minds, no bodies. Doesn't it follow that I don't exist? No, surely I must exist if it's me who is convinced of something. But there is a deceiver, supremely powerful and cunning, whose aim is to see that I am always deceived. But surely I exist, if I am deceived. Let him deceive me all he can, he will never make it the case that I am nothing while I think that I am something. Thus having fully weighed every consideration, I must finally conclude that the statement "I am, I exist" must be true whenever I state it or mentally consider it.

But I do not yet fully understand what this "I" is that must exist. I must guard against inadvertently taking myself to be something other than I am, thereby going wrong even in the knowledge that I put forward as supremely certain and evident. Hence, I will think once again about what I believed myself to be before beginning these meditations. From this conception, I will subtract everything challenged by the reasons for doubt that I produced earlier, until nothing remains except what is certain and indubitable.

What, then, did I formerly take myself to be? A man, of course. But what is a man? Should I say a rational animal? No, because then I would need to ask what an animal is and what it is to be rational. Thus, starting from a single question, I would sink into many that are more difficult, and I do not have the time to waste on such subtleties. Instead, I will look here at the thoughts that occurred to me spontaneously and naturally when I reflected on what I was. The first thought to occur to me was that I have a face, hands, arms, and all other equipment (also found in corpses) which I call a body. The next thought to occur to me was that I take nourishment, move myself around, sense, and think—that I do things which I trace back to my soul. Either I didn't stop to think about what this soul was, or I imagined it to be a rarified air, or fire, or ether permeating the denser parts of my body. But, about physical objects, I didn't have any doubts whatever: I thought that I distinctly knew their nature. If I had tried to describe my conception of this nature, I might have said this: "When I call something a physical object, I mean that it is capable of being bounded by a shape and limited to a place; that it can fill a space as to exclude other objects from it; that it can be perceived by touch, sight, hearing, taste, and smell; that it can be moved in various ways, not by itself, but by something else in contact with it." I judged that the powers of self-movement, of sensing, and of thinking did not belong to the nature of physical objects, and, in fact, I marveled that there were some physical objects in which these powers could be found.

But what should I think now, while supposing that a supremely powerful and "evil" deceiver completely devotes himself to deceiving me? Can I say that I have any of the things that I have attributed to the nature of physical objects?

Margin notes:

Number each of the places in this paragraph where Descartes seems to change his mind.

Underline Descartes's first certitude.

The word "but" introduces important shifts in Descartes's argument. Circle each one on this and the following pages. Paraphrase the idea he is introducing in the margin.

In this paragraph, underline each of the beliefs Descartes was certain about before *Meditation I.*

I concentrate, think, reconsider—but nothing comes to me; I grow tired of the pointless repetition. But what about the things that I have assigned to soul? Nutrition and self-movement? Since I have no body, these are merely illusions. Sensing? But I cannot sense without a body, and in sleep I've seemed to sense many things that I later realized I had not really sensed. Thinking? It comes down to this: Thought and thought alone cannot be taken away from me. I am, I exist. That much is certain. But for how long? As long as I think—for it may be that, if I completely stopped thinking, I would completely cease to exist. I am not now admitting anything unless it must be true, and I am therefore not admitting that I am anything at all other than a thinking thing—that is, a mind, soul, understanding, or reason (terms whose meaning I did not previously know). I know that I am a real, existing thing, but what kind of thing? As I have said, a thing that thinks.

What else? I will draw up mental images. I'm not the collection of organs called a human body. Nor am I some rarified gas permeating these organs, or air, or fire, or vapor, or breath—for I have supposed that none of these things exist. Still, I am something. But couldn't it be that these things, which I do not yet know about and which I am therefore supposing to be nonexistent, really aren't distinct from the "I" that I know to exist? I don't know, and I'm not going to argue about it now. I can only form judgments on what I do know. I know that I exist, and I ask what the "I" is that I know to exist. It's obvious that this conception of myself doesn't depend on anything that I do not yet know to exist and, therefore, that it does not depend on anything of which I can draw up a mental image. And the words "draw up" point to my mistake. I would truly be creative if I were to have a mental image of what I am, since to have a mental image is just to contemplate the shape or image of a physical object. I now know with certainty that I exist and at the same time that all images—and, more generally, all things associated with the nature of physical objects—may just be dreams. When I keep this in mind, it seems just as absurd to say "I use mental images to help me understand what I am" as it would to say "Now, while awake, I see something true—but, since I don't yet see it clearly enough, I'll go to sleep and let my dreams present it to me more clearly and truly." Thus I know that none of the things that I can comprehend with the aid of mental images bear on my knowledge of myself. And I must carefully draw my mind away from such things if it is to see its own nature distinctly.

But what then am I? A thinking thing. And what is that? Something that doubts, understands, affirms, denies, wills, refuses, and also senses and has mental images.

That's quite a lot, if I really do all of these things. But don't I? Isn't it me who now doubts nearly everything, understands one thing, affirms this thing, refuses to affirm other things, wants to know much more, refuses to be deceived, has mental images (sometimes involuntarily), and is aware of many things "through his senses"? Even if I am always dreaming, and even if my creator does what he can to deceive me, isn't it just as true that I do all these things as that I exist? Are any of these things distinct from my thought? Can any be said to be separate from me? That it's me who doubts, understands, and wills is so obvious that I don't see how it could be more evident. And it's also me who has mental images. While it may be, as I am supposing, that absolutely nothing of which I have a mental image really exists, the ability to have mental images really does exist and is a part of my thought. Finally, it's

The single truth Descartes has established thus far is

_____

_____

_____.

He knows this for certain because _____

_____.

The reasons for his conclusion in the last two sentences in this paragraph are _____

_____

_____

_____

_____.

What he is adding to his definition of himself as a "thinking thing" is _____

_____

_____

_____

_____.

me who senses—or who seems to gain awareness of physical objects through the senses. For example, I am now seeing light, hearing a noise, and feeling heat. These things are unreal, since I am dreaming. But it is still certain that I seem to see, to hear, and to feel. This seeming cannot be unreal, and it is what is properly called sensing. Strictly speaking, sensing is just thinking.

From this, I begin to learn a little about what I am. But I still can't stop thinking that I apprehend physical objects, which I picture in mental images and examine with my senses, much more distinctly than I know this unfamiliar "I," of which I cannot form a mental image. I think this, even though it would be astounding if I comprehended things which I've found to be doubtful, unknown, and alien to me more distinctly than the one which I know to be real: my self. But I see what's happening. My mind enjoys wandering, and it won't confine itself to the truth. I will therefore loosen the reins on my mind for now so that later, when the time is right, I will be able to control it more easily.

Let's consider the things commonly taken to be the most distinctly comprehended: physical objects that we see and touch. Let's not consider physical objects in general, since general conceptions are very often confused. Rather, let's consider one, particular object. Take, for example, this piece of wax. It has just been taken from the honeycomb; it hasn't yet completely lost the taste of honey; it still smells of the flowers from which it was gathered; its color, shape, and size are obvious; it is hard, cold, and easy to touch; it makes a sound when rapped. In short, everything seems to be present in the wax that is required for me to know it as distinctly as possible. But, as I speak, I move the wax toward the fire; it loses what was left of its taste; it gives up its smell; it changes color; it loses its shape; it gets bigger; it melts; it heats up; it becomes difficult to touch; it no longer makes a sound when struck. Is it still the same piece of wax? We must say that it is: no one denies it or thinks otherwise. Then what was there in the wax that I comprehended so distinctly? Certainly nothing that I reached with my senses—for, while everything having to do with taste, smell, sight, touch, and hearing has changed, the same piece of wax remains.

Perhaps what I distinctly know was neither the sweetness of honey, nor the fragrance of flowers, nor a sound, but a physical object that once appeared to me one way and now appears differently. But what exactly is it of which I now have a mental image? Let's pay careful attention, remove everything that doesn't belong to the wax, and see what's left. Nothing is left except an extended, flexible, and changeable thing. But what is it for this thing to be flexible and changeable? Is it just that the wax can go from round to square and then to triangular, as I have mentally pictured? Of course not. Since I understand that the wax's shape can change in innumerable ways, and since I can't run through all the changes in my imagination, my comprehension of the wax's flexibility and changeability cannot have been produced by my ability to have mental images. And what about the thing that is extended? Are we also ignorant of its extension? Since the extension of the wax increases when the wax melts, increases again when the wax boils, and increases still more when the wax gets hotter, I will be mistaken about what the wax is unless I believe that it can undergo more changes in extension than I can ever encompass with mental images. I must therefore admit that I do not have an image of what the wax is—that I grasp what it is with only my mind. (While I am saying this about a particular piece of wax, it is even more clearly true about

The previous topic Descartes now returns to is his doubt

about _____

_____.

Descartes is now going to convince himself again that he cannot be certain of even the most obvious facts that come through his senses. Underline the important points he makes in this and the next two paragraphs. Add your own explanatory notes in the margin.

The reason his grasp of the wax "is not visual, tactile, or pictorial" is _____

_____

_____

_____

_____

_____ .

What Descartes learned about his senses by examining the wax

was _____

_____

_____ .

What he learned about his mind

was _____

_____

_____ .

Descartes's main point in this

paragraph is _____

_____

_____

_____

_____ .

wax in general.) What then is this piece of wax that I grasp only with my mind? It is something that I see, feel, and mentally picture—exactly what I believed it to be at the outset. But it must be noted that, despite the appearances, my grasp of the wax is not visual, tactile, or pictorial. Rather, my grasp of the wax is the result of a purely mental inspection, which can be imperfect and confused, as it was once, or clear and distinct, as it is now, depending on how much attention I pay to the things of which the wax consists.

I'm surprised by how prone my mind is to error. Even when I think to myself nonverbally, language stands in my way, and common usage comes close to deceiving me. For, when the wax is present, we say that we see the wax itself, not that we infer its presence from its color and shape. I'm inclined to leap from this fact about language to the conclusion that I learn about the wax by eyesight rather than by purely mental inspection. But, if I happen to look out my window and see men walking in the street, I naturally say that I see the men just as I say that I see the wax. What do I really see, however, but hats and coats that could be covering robots? I *judge* that there are men. Thus I comprehend with my judgment, which is in my mind, objects that I once believed myself to see with my eyes.

One who aspires to wisdom above that of the common man disgraces himself by deriving doubt from common ways of speaking. Let's go on, then, to ask when I most clearly and perfectly grasped what the wax is. Was it when I first looked at the wax and believed my knowledge of it to come from the external senses—or at any rate from the so-called "common sense," the power of having mental images? Or is it now, after I have carefully studied what the wax is and how I come to know it? Doubt would be silly here. For what was distinct in my original conception of the wax? How did that conception differ from that had by animals? When I distinguish the wax from its external forms—when I "undress" it and view it "naked"—there may still be errors in my judgments about it, but I couldn't possibly grasp the wax in this way without a human mind.

What should I say about this mind—or, in other words, about myself? (I am not now admitting that there is anything to me but a mind.) What is this "I" that seems to grasp the wax so distinctly? Don't I know myself much more truly and certainly, and also much more distinctly and plainly, than I know the wax? For, if I base my judgment that the wax exists on the fact that I see it, my seeing it much more obviously implies that I exist. It's possible that what I see is not really wax, and it's even possible that I don't have eyes with which to see—but it clearly is not possible that, when I see (or, what now amounts to the same thing, when I think I see), the "I" that thinks is not a real thing. Similarly, if I base my judgment that the wax exists on the fact that I feel it, the same fact makes it obvious that I exist. If I base my judgment that the wax exists on the fact that I have a mental image of it or on some other fact of this sort, the same thing can obviously be said. And what I've said about the wax applies to everything else that is outside me. Moreover, if I seem to grasp the wax more distinctly when I detect it with several senses than when I detect it with just sight or touch, I must know myself even more distinctly—for every consideration that contributes to my grasp of the piece of wax or to my grasp of any other physical object serves better to reveal the nature of my mind. Besides, the mind has so much in it by which it can make its conception of itself distinct that what comes to it from physical objects hardly seems to matter.

And now I have brought myself back to where I wanted to be. I now know that physical objects are grasped, not by the senses or the power of having mental images, but by understanding alone. And, since I grasp physical objects in virtue of their being understandable rather than in virtue of their being tangible or visible, I know that I can't grasp anything more easily or plainly than my mind. But, since it takes time to break old habits of thought, I should pause here to allow the length of my contemplation to impress the new thoughts more deeply into my memory.

Thinking About *Meditation II*

We'll start each of these sessions in the same way. Tell me in a general way what *Meditation II* was about.

The main points Descartes made were _____

_____

_____

_____.

How would you state the first truth Descartes discovers that not even an all-powerful demon could deceive him about?

On page _____, he says, "_____

_____." This is his first

certitude because _____

_____. An all-powerful

demon (or even Mr. _____) could not deceive him about this because as soon as the attempt to deceive him occurred, Descartes would know

for certain that _____

_____

because _____.

I would say the strengths of what he says are _____

_____.

The major weaknesses I see are _____

_____.

In Latin, as you may know, Descartes's first certitude is *cogito, ergo sum.* "I think; therefore, I am." Though it is not stated in precisely this form in these *Meditations,* it is in his *Discourse on Method.* Sometimes the assertion *cogito, ergo sum* is held to be a circular argument and therefore invalid. For example, it is a circular argument if I say you can trust me because Jack says I never lie, and you can trust Jack because I say he never lies. In this kind of argument, *A* proves *B* and *B* proves *A;* therefore, nothing is proved. Now think about the statement "I think; therefore, I am." Can you see why this might be something like a circular argument?

It might be argued that the *A* part is _____

_____ and the *B* part is _____ .

The way *A* appears to prove *B* is _____

_____ .

The way *B* appears to prove *A* is _____

_____ .

Does this show that Descartes is arguing in a circle and therefore has not found

his 100 percent certitude? I would say _____

_____

_____ .

Now go back to pages 437–438 and read the paragraphs again where he talks about the piece of wax. Try to put yourself in Descartes's place. As you make additional notes in the margin, you will begin to understand that with each rereading, philosophical arguments become slightly clearer.

Very well. Let us say I am holding a piece of wax. I am sitting near a fire in my

dressing gown. As I examine the wax visually, I see _____

_____

_____ . It smells _____ .

It feels _____ .

If I knock it on the arm of my rocking chair, it sounds _____

_____ . Now hold it

close to the fire. Everything changes. It appears _____ .

It smells _____ . It feels _____

_____ . And it sticks to the arm of my rocker!

What can I conclude from all this? I must conclude something about what I know with my senses and something about what I know with my mind. What I have

learned about things I know through my senses is _____

_____ . And what I

have learned about what I know with my mind is _____

_____ . This

relates to the statement *cogito, ergo sum* because _____

_____.

Now read this last paragraph in *Meditation II*. Underline important sections and make your own notes in the margin.

[1] And now I have brought myself back to where I wanted to be. I now know that physical objects are grasped, not by the senses or the power of having mental images, but by understanding alone. [2] And since I grasp physical objects in virtue of their being understandable rather than in virtue of their being tangible or visible, I know that I can't grasp anything more easily or plainly than my mind. [3] But since it takes time to break old habits of thought, I should pause here to allow the length of my contemplation to impress the new thoughts more deeply into my memory.

What, in general, is he saying in each numbered section?

I conclude that in section 1, Descartes is saying _____

_____. In section 2, he is

saying _____

_____. In section 3, he

reminds himself that _____

_____.

Now, let's look at this important paragraph in more detail. He has just finished examining the wax. Why, in section 1, is it obvious to him "that physical objects are grasped, not by the senses or the power of having mental images, but by understanding alone"?

When I imagined I held the wax, I did not really know what it was through my

senses because _____.
And I couldn't be said to know it through my imagination because when I try to

know wax in imagination what happens is _____

_____. Therefore, I know the

wax only by my understanding because _____

_____.

In section 2, Descartes says, "I can't grasp anything more easily or plainly than my mind." How does he get to this point from what you just said?

Because I cannot be said to know the wax through my senses or my imagination,

but only through my intellect, Descartes's point is that _____

_____

_____.

In section 3, he refers to "new thoughts" and says he will take a while to get accustomed to them. What are these new thoughts and why does he need to think more about them?

In short, the new thoughts are _____ _____.

And what is difficult to accept about this is _____

_____. But does Descartes ever discover any other truths he can be 100 percent certain of besides *cogito, ergo sum*?

EXERCISE 19.1
Review I

Decide if the following statements are consistent (C) or inconsistent (I) with ideas Descartes presents in the first two paragraphs of *Meditation II*.

1. C   I   There is a way to defeat the evil demon.

2. C   I   The doubts from *Meditation I* remain.

3. C   I   The only certainty may be that there is no certainty.

4. C   I   Concepts that can be partially doubted should be treated differently from concepts that can be entirely doubted.

5. C   I   Descartes, unlike Archimedes, will need to find more than one indubitable truth.

EXERCISE 19.2
Review II

Label each of the following statements consistent (C) or inconsistent (I) with ideas Descartes presents in paragraph 3 of *Meditation II*.

1. C   I   If Descartes denies that he has senses and a body, then he can't prove that he exists.

2. C   I   Descartes proves that God exists.

3. C   I   The deceiver could not deceive Descartes into believing he, Descartes, does not exist.

4. C   I   Even if there is no physical world, it does not follow that Descartes's mind does not exist.

5. C   I   Descartes proves that he exists.

EXERCISE 19.3
Organizing Ideas

Number the following ideas in the order in which Descartes introduces them in *Meditation II*.

_____ a. He examines the wax with his senses.

_____ b. He knows for certain that he exists.

_____ c. He notes that his mind, rather than his senses, understands the wax clearly.

_____ d. He assumes that he knows nothing for certain.

_____ e. He realizes that his imagination cannot make an accurate mental picture of all the possible shapes that the wax could take.

_____ f. He is a thinking thing.

EXERCISE 19.4
Reasoning More Effectively

One benefit of studying Descartes is learning how to reason more effectively. He often uses examples to make a point. On your own paper, answer the questions that follow each of Descartes's examples.

1. "Archimedes required only one fixed and immovable point to move the whole earth from its place, and I too can hope for great things if I can find even one small thing that is certain and unshakable."

   a. Archimedes is being compared to?

   b. "One fixed and immovable point" is being compared to?

   c. Moving "the whole earth from its place" is being compared to?

   d. The point of this analogy is?

2. "Let's consider the things commonly taken to be the most distinctly comprehended: physical objects that we see and touch. Let's not consider physical objects in general, since general conceptions are very often confused. Rather, let's consider one particular object. Take, for example, this piece of wax."

   a. "Distinctly comprehended" means?

   b. An example of a "general conception" might be?

   c. The goal in examining the wax is to find out about what?

   d. The wax is an example of what?

3. "But, if I happen to look out my window and see men walking in the street, I naturally say that I see the men just as I say that I see the wax. What do I really see, however, but hats and coats that could be covering robots? I _judge_ that there are men. Thus I comprehend with my judgment, which is in my mind, objects that I once believed myself to see with my eyes."

   a. The error Descartes believes he makes when he says he "sees" the men and the wax is?

   b. What is the purpose of mentioning "robots"?

   c. What general point is Descartes making about his senses?

   d. What general point is Descartes making about judgment?

   e. Errors of the type described in this example are caused by?

   f. What does the last sentence conclude?

   g. What evidence is offered for the conclusion in the last sentence?

EXERCISE 19.5
Evidence and Conclusion

All arguments can be divided into two parts: evidence and conclusion. For example:

1. All men are mortal.

2. Socrates is a man.

3. Therefore, Socrates is mortal.

Sentences 1 and 2 are evidence that supports the conclusion in sentence 3.

Think back over *Meditations I* and *II*. What evidence, if any, does Descartes offer for each of the following conclusions?

Meditation I

1. The senses cannot be trusted.
2. He cannot be certain that he is sitting beside the fire in his dressing gown.
3. He is not a madman.
4. His dreams must be copies of something real.
5. He can be certain of simple mathematical truths.
6. He cannot be certain of simple mathematical truths.
7. He cannot be certain that God is not a deceiver.

Meditation II

8. The evil demon cannot deceive him about everything.
9. He exists.
10. He is a thinking thing.
11. He can know his essence as a thinking thing more clearly than he can know a piece of wax.

EXERCISE 19.6

Judging the Evidence

Now grade Descartes's evidence for 1–11 in Exercise 19.5. Use the following scale:

A: An excellent argument, strong, sensible, would certainly convince a thoughtful person.

B: A good argument, certainly more convincing than nonconvincing, but some areas need more development and/or might be open to doubt.

C: A flawed argument, certainly not worthy of a great philosopher. Would need significant improvement to convince a thoughtful person.

D: Any thoughtful person would find it a weak, easy-to-attack argument.

F: A terrible argument that would not convince even someone who desperately wanted to be convinced.

1. Grade each argument.
2. Briefly explain your grade.
3. For each argument you graded "C" or lower, offer evidence that shows why Descartes's argument is weak.

The Third Meditation: "On God's Existence"

Descartes summarizes his progress and then discovers a test for further certitudes. Anything he knows as "clearly and distinctly" as he knows the truth that he exists must be 100 percent certain. Descartes realizes that until he proves that God exists and is no deceiver, he cannot add to his store of perfect knowledge. Because Descartes has only established himself as a "thinking thing," he investigates the nature of his thoughts to see if this will help him prove God's existence.

Continue to circle the word "but" when it introduces a shift in the argument; note Descartes's answers to the question he asks himself.

Meditation III is quite difficult. We will stop halfway through to think about what you read. It probably would be sensible to set aside an hour or two for the second half of the *Meditation*. Follow my margin notes carefully and add your own.

Meditation III

I will now close my eyes, plug my ears, and withdraw all my senses. I will rid my thoughts of the images of physical objects—or, since that's beyond me, I'll write those images off as empty illusions. Talking with myself and looking more deeply into myself, I'll try gradually to come to know myself better. I am a thinking thing—a thing that doubts, affirms, denies, understands a few things, is ignorant of many things, wills, and refuses. I also sense and have mental images. For, as I've noted, even though the things of which I have sensations or mental images may not exist outside me, I'm certain that the modifications of thought called sensations and mental images exist in me insofar as they are just modifications of thought.

That's a summary of all that I really know—or, at any rate, of all that I've so far noticed that I know. I now will examine more carefully whether there are other things in me that I have not yet discovered. I'm certain that I am a thinking thing. Then don't I know what's needed for me to be certain of other things? In this first knowledge, there is nothing but a clear and distinct grasp of what I affirm, and this grasp surely would not suffice to make me certain if it could ever happen that something I grasped so clearly and distinctly was false. Accordingly, I seem to be able to establish the general rule that whatever I clearly and distinctly grasp is true.

But, in the past, I've accepted as completely obvious and certain many thoughts that I later found to be dubious. What were these thoughts about? The earth, the sky, the stars, and other objects of sense. But what did I clearly grasp about these objects? Only that ideas or thoughts of them appeared in my mind. Even now, I don't deny that these ideas occur in me. But there was something else that I used to affirm—something that I used to believe myself to grasp clearly but did not really grasp at all: I affirmed that there were things besides me, that the ideas in me came from these things, and that the ideas perfectly resembled these things. Either I erred here, or I reached a true judgment that wasn't justified by the strength of my understanding.

But what follows? When I considered very simple and easy points of arithmetic or geometry—such as that two and three together make five—didn't I see them clearly enough to affirm their truth? My only reason for judging that I ought to doubt these things was the thought that my God-given nature might deceive me even about what seems most obvious. Whenever I conceive of an all-powerful God, I'm compelled to admit that, if He wants, He can make it the case that I err even about what I take my mind's eye to see most clearly.

List what you believe you know clearly and distinctly. _____
_____
_____
_____
_____.
List what you know less clearly and less distinctly. _____
_____
_____
_____
_____.
What Descartes knows clearly and distinctly is _____
_____
_____.
Assume Descartes is looking up toward the sky. At this point in the argument, he can be certain that _____
_____
_____.
But he can have no certainty that _____
_____
_____

Underline the sentence in which he returns to his first certitude.

Eventually, what he must determine about God is _____

_____

_____

because _____

_____

_____ .

Descartes's point in the last sentence in this paragraph is

_____

_____

_____

_____

because _____

_____

_____

_____ .

An example of an innate idea

might be _____

_____ ;

an example of an acquired idea

might be _____

_____

_____ ;

an example of a created idea

might be _____

_____

_____ .

But, when I turn to the things that I believe myself to grasp very clearly, I'm so convinced by them that I spontaneously burst forth saying, "Whoever may deceive me, he will never bring it about that I am nothing while I think that I am something, or that I have never been when it is now true that I am, or that two plus three is either more or less than five, or that something else in which I recognize an obvious inconsistency is true." And, since I have no reason for thinking that God is a deceiver—indeed, since I don't yet know whether God exists—the grounds for doubt that rest on the supposition that God deceives are very weak and "metaphysical." Still, to rid myself of these grounds, I ought to ask as soon as possible whether there is a God and, if so, whether He can be a deceiver. For it seems that, until I know these two things, I can never be completely certain of anything else.

The structure of my project seems to require, however, that I first categorize my thoughts and ask in which of them truth and falsity really reside. Some of my thoughts are like images of things, and only these can properly be called ideas. I have an idea, for example, when I think of a man, of a chimera, of heaven, of an angel, or of God. But other thoughts have other properties: while I always apprehend something as the object of my thought when I will, fear, affirm, or deny, these thoughts also include a component in addition to the likeness of that thing. Some of these components are called volitions or emotions; others, judgments.

Now, viewed in themselves and without regard to other things, ideas cannot really be false. If I imagine a chimera and a goat, it is just as true that I imagine the chimera as that I imagine the goat. And I needn't worry about falsehood in volitions or emotions. If I have a perverse desire for something, or if I want something that doesn't exist, it's still true that I want that thing. All that remains, then, are my judgments; it's here that I must be careful not to err. And the first and foremost of the errors that I find in my judgments is that of assuming that the ideas in me have a similarity or conformity to things outside me. For, if I were to regard ideas merely as modifications of thought, they could not really provide me with any opportunity for error.

Of my ideas, some seem to me to be innate, others acquired, and others produced by me. The ideas by which I understand reality, truth, and thought seem to have come from my own nature. Those ideas by which I hear a noise, see the sun, or feel the fire I formerly judged to come from things outside me. And the ideas of sirens, hippogriffs, and so on I have formed in myself. Or maybe I can take all of my ideas to be acquired, all innate, or all created by me: I do not yet clearly see where my ideas come from.

For the moment, the central question is about the ideas that I view as derived from objects existing outside me. What reason is there for thinking that these ideas resemble the objects? I seem to have been taught this by nature. Besides, I find that these ideas are independent of my will and hence of me—for they often appear when I do not want them to do so. For example, I now feel heat whether I want to or not, and I therefore take the idea or sensation of heat to come from something distinct from me: the heat of the fire by which I am not sitting. And the obvious thing to think is that a thing sends me its own likeness, not something else.

I will now see whether these reasons are good enough. When I say that nature teaches me something, I mean just that I have a spontaneous impulse to believe it, not that the light of nature reveals the thing's truth to me. There is an important difference. When the light of nature reveals something to me (such as that my thinking implies my existing) that thing is completely beyond doubt, since there is no faculty as reliable as the light of nature by means of which I could learn that the thing is not true. But, as for my natural impulses, I have often judged them to have led me astray in choices about what's good, and I don't see why I should regard them as any more reliable on matters concerning truth and falsehood.

Next, while my sensory ideas may not depend on my will, it doesn't follow that they come from outside me. While the natural impulses of which I just spoke are in me, they seem to conflict with my will. Similarly, I may have in me an as yet undiscovered ability to produce the ideas that seem to come from outside me—in the way that I used to think that ideas came to me in dreams.

Finally, even if some of my ideas do come from things distinct from me, it doesn't follow that they are likenesses of these things. Indeed, it often seems to me that an idea differs greatly from its cause. For example, I find in myself two different ideas of the sun. One, which I "take in" through the senses and which I ought therefore to view as a typical acquired idea, makes the sun look very small to me. The other, which I derive from astronomical reasoning (that is, which I make, perhaps by composing it from innate ideas), pictures the sun as many times larger than the earth. It clearly cannot be that both of these ideas are accurate likenesses of a sun that exists outside me, and reason convinces me that the one least like the sun is the one that seems to arise most directly from it.

All that I've said shows that, until now, my belief that there are things outside me that send their ideas or images to me (perhaps through my senses) has rested on blind impulse rather than certain judgment.

Still, it seems to me that there may be a way of telling whether my ideas come from things that exist outside me. Insofar as the ideas of things are just modifications of thought, I find no inequality among them; all seem to arise from me in the same way. But, insofar as different ideas present different things to me, there obviously are great differences among them. The ideas of substances are unquestionably greater—or have more "subjective reality"—than those of modifications or accidents. Similarly, the idea by which I understand the supreme God—eternal, infinite, omniscient, omnipotent, and creator of all things other than Himself—has more subjective reality in it than the ideas of finite substances.

"Light of nature" is Descartes's phrase for reason.

One idea Descartes has about the sun is _____ _____, and the other idea is _____ _____. The idea that appears least true about the sun is _____ ___ _____ because _____ _____ _____. The main problem Descartes is trying to solve in this meditation is _____ _____ _____ _____ _____ _____ _____.

Thinking About the First Half
of *Meditation III*

Let's halt here for a few moments of reflection. What, in general, has Descartes been thinking about?

The major points I noted were _____ _____

_____

_____

_____.

How can Descartes tell when he has arrived at his goal of finding 100 percent certitudes? How can he tell the difference between a concept that is 99.99 percent certain and one that is perfectly 100 percent certain?

His first 100 percent certitude is, of course, "I think; therefore, I exist." He realizes at the beginning of *Meditation III* that he has discovered not only a perfect certitude in this statement but also a way of measuring the certainty of other statements. He grasps the perfect truth of "I think; therefore, I exist" with "clarity and distinctness." Any other claim that he grasps in this same way will be equally certain. Thus, we might say that Descartes can tell if he has found other 100 percent certitudes when he grasps them with 100 percent clarity and 100 percent distinctness.

Using your list of truths on page 420 and any other concepts you wish, fill in the following scale by making five statements and labeling each for clarity and distinctness. (Instead of focusing on the truth of the statement, focus on how clearly and distinctly you grasp the truth of the statement.)

100 percent clarity and distinctness: _____

_____ percent clarity and distinctness: _____

_____ percent clarity and distinctness: _____

_____ percent clarity and distinctness: _____

_____ percent clarity and distinctness: _____

0 percent clarity and distinctness: _____

Now compare this scale with the statements you made in the wisdom game at the beginning of this chapter. Has reading Descartes produced any differences in the way you think about what you know?

Rereading my responses in the wisdom game, I notice _____

_____

_____.

Comparing this with the clarity and distinctness scale, I realize _____

_____

_____.

Now we are going to reread two sections in which Descartes carefully thinks over the source of mental errors. This is obviously an important topic if he is looking for truths he can be 100 percent certain about. His search will be greatly simplified if he can find some general rules for telling true ideas from false ideas. Add your own underlining to the following. Your margin notes should simply try to put Descartes's ideas into your own language.

> All that remains, then, are my judgments; it's here that I must be careful not to err. And the first and foremost of the error that I find in my judgments is that of assuming that the ideas in me have a similarity or conformity to things outside me. For, if I were to regard ideas merely as modifications of thought, they could not really provide me with any opportunity for error.

You are standing in the desert. Ahead you see a shimmering lake. You thus have the idea in your mind of a lake. What is true and what is false about this idea?

What is true about the idea in my mind is simply _____ _____

_____. What would lead me to error would be

to judge that the idea in my mind is _____. Thus, mental

errors about my senses arise when _____

_____.

What Descartes means when he says, "If I were to regard ideas merely as modifications of thought they could not really provide me with any opportunity for error,"

is _____

_____. And

how this relates to the idea of the lake in my mind is _____

_____.

Now reread the following section, adding your own underlining and margin notes.

[1] . . . it often seems to me that an idea differs greatly from its cause. [2] For example, I find in myself two different ideas of the sun. One, which I "take in" through the senses which I ought therefore to view as a typical acquired idea, makes the sun look very small to me. The other, which I derive from astronomical reasoning (that is, which I make, perhaps by composing it from innate ideas), pictures the sun as many times larger than the earth. It clearly cannot be that both of these ideas are accurate likenesses of a sun that exists outside me, and reason convinces me that the one least like the sun is the one that seems to arise most directly from it.

[3] All that I've said show that, until now, my belief that there are things outside me that send their ideas or images to me (perhaps through my senses) has rested on blind impulse rather than certain judgment.

Start with section 1. Give me two examples of differences you have experienced between "an idea" and "its cause."

Let us say the idea is _____ _____ and

the cause is _____.

The obvious difference is _____

_____. One of the most common

examples of this might be the cause _____ and the

mistaken idea of _____. The difference

is _____.

Fine. Now put yourself in Descartes's place and think about the sun as he does in section 2.

Very well. I am looking at the sun. The idea that I have of the sun that comes

through my eyes is _____.
But I have another idea of the sun, which is perhaps born with me, as he says.

This second idea of the sun is _____.

The difference between these two ideas is _____

_____. Error would arise in

the case of the first idea only if I _____.

Now read section 3 again. Probably for the third or fourth time! It is central to *Meditation III.*

The essential point he is making in section 3 is _____

_____.

EXERCISE 19.7
Organizing Concepts

Number the following concepts in the order in which Descartes presents them in the first half of *Meditation III.*

_____ a. He has discovered no evidence proving that his sensory ideas are accurate copies of objects.

_____ b. He must prove that God exists and that God is no deceiver before he can discover other certitudes.

_____ c. He categorizes his thoughts into volitions, emotions, and judgments.

_____ d. A clear and distinct grasp of something is required to know a thing for certain.

_____ e. The light of nature is different from natural impulse.

_____ f. His ideas are either innate, acquired, or produced by him.

EXERCISE 19.8
Paraphrasing Arguments

1. Paraphrase the first argument in paragraph 8 ("For the moment, the central question . . . "). Because _____

_____,

_____

_____.

2. Paraphrase the first argument in paragraph 9 ("I will now see whether these reasons . . . "). Because _____

_____ ,

_____

_____ .

3. Paraphrase the first argument in paragraph 10 ("Next, while my sensory ideas may not . . . "). Because _____

_____ ,

_____

_____ .

4. Paraphrase the first argument in paragraph 11 ("Finally, even if some of my ideas . . . "). Because _____

_____ ,

_____

_____ .

5. Now look at paragraphs 8, 9, 10, and 11. Paragraph(s) _____ refute arguments in paragraph(s) _____ .

EXERCISE 19.9
Evidence and Conclusion

All arguments can be divided into two parts: evidence and conclusion. The evidence is presented as reason for believing the conclusion. Evidence can be thought of as one or more "because" statements that lead to a conclusion.

(Because) Socrates is a human.

(Because) All humans are mortals.

Socrates is a mortal. (Conclusion)

Underline the conclusion in each of the following arguments:

_____ 1. I think I exist. I can be absolutely certain I exist. I must exist in order to think I exist.

_____ 2. I cannot tell for certain that external objects exist. I cannot tell if my ideas are not accurate copies of external objects. If my ideas are not accurate copies of external objects, then I cannot know for certain that external objects exist.

_____ 3. God could be deceiving me. God is all-powerful.

_____ 4. It is not possible that anything I've grasped clearly and distinctly could be false. In the future, I can use it as a general rule that anything I grasp clearly and distinctly is true.

_____ 5. I need to prove that God is no deceiver. God might be deceiving me. If God is deceiving me, then I can't know anything for certain.

_____ 6. I should be careful when I make judgments about my ideas being copies of external objects. I can make errors when I judge that my ideas are copies of external objects.

EXERCISE 19.10
Organizing Arguments

Omitting argument 1, number the arguments in Exercise 19.9 in the order in which they occur in *Meditation III*, and give the paragraph number of each argument.

Preview of the Second Half of *Meditation III*

In the concluding section of *Meditation III*, Descartes introduces a number of difficult concepts: subjective reality, formal reality, eminent reality, and reality being "transferred" from cause to effect.

Subjective reality is the reality of ideas. Formal reality is, among other things, the reality of the physical world. Eminent reality, it will turn out, is God's reality. For Descartes, subjective reality is "less real" than formal reality and formal reality is "less real" than eminent reality. This is hard for modern readers to grasp because we usually think of something as either "real" or "not real," without "more" or "less" in between. A lake is real; a mirage is not real. A person is real; a dragon is not real.

To get a sense of Descartes's way of thinking, consider three things: the actual Pocahontas, the Disney animated film *Pocahontas,* and a dream about the Disney film. The actual Pocahontas could be said to be more real than the Disney film, and the Disney film could be said to be more real than a dream about the film. If Pocahontas hadn't existed, then the film *Pocahontas* wouldn't exist; if the film *Pocahontas* didn't exist, then the dream about the film wouldn't exist. Similarly for Descartes, God is more real than the physical world, and the physical world is more real than ideas about the physical world. If God didn't exist, then the physical world wouldn't exist; if the physical world didn't exist, then ideas about the physical world wouldn't exist. God's eminent reality makes possible the physical world's formal reality, which, in turn, makes possible the ideas' subjective reality.

Descartes holds that these realities influence each other in a special, one-directional way. Something "more real" can be the cause of something "less real," but not vice versa. God can be the cause of the reality of a physical object, not vice versa. God can be the cause of the reality of a physical object, but not vice versa. A physical object can be the cause of an idea of a physical object, but not vice versa. Descartes's way of stating this one-directional influence is to say that the degree of reality in the cause is always equal to or greater than the degree of reality in the effect.

This concept of reality and cause and effect is important for the proof of God's existence that Descartes develops in the following section from *Meditation III*. God, remember, has eminent reality. Descartes's idea of God is therefore an idea of a being with eminent reality. Descartes himself has merely formal reality. Therefore, Descartes could not be the cause of his idea of God. Descartes has too little reality! Only God could be the cause of Descartes's idea of God. Therefore, God exists.

Meditation III (continued)

Now, the light of nature reveals that there is at least as much in a complete efficient cause as in its effect. For where could an effect get its reality if not from its cause? And how could a cause give something unless it had it? It follows both that something cannot come from nothing and that what is more perfect—that is, has more reality in it—cannot come from what is less perfect or has less reality. This obviously holds, not just for those effects whose reality is actual or formal, but also for ideas, whose reality we regard as merely subjective. For example, it's impossible for a nonexistent stone to come into existence unless it's produced by something containing, either formally or eminently, everything in the stone. Similarly, heat can only be induced in something that's not already hot by something having at least the same degree of perfection as heat. Also, it's impossible for the *idea* of heat or of stone to be in me unless it's been put there by a cause having at least as much reality as I conceive of in the heat or the stone. For, although the cause doesn't transmit any of its actual or formal reality to the idea, we shouldn't infer that it can be less real than the idea; all that we can infer is that by its nature the idea doesn't require any formal reality except what it derives from my thought, of which it is a modification. Yet, as the idea contains one particular subjective reality rather than another, it must get this reality from a cause having at least as much formal reality as the idea has subjective reality. For, if we suppose that an idea has something in it that wasn't in its cause, we must suppose that it got this thing from nothing. However imperfect the existence of something that exists subjectively in the understanding through an idea, it obviously is something, and it therefore cannot come from nothing.

And, although the reality that I'm considering in my ideas is just subjective, I ought not to suspect that it can fail to be in an idea's cause formally—that it's enough for it to be there subjectively. For, just as the subjective existence of my ideas belongs to the ideas in virtue of their nature, the formal existence of the ideas' causes belongs to those causes—or, at least, to the first and foremost of them—in virtue of the causes' nature. Although one idea may arise from another, this can't go back to infinity; we must eventually arrive at a primary idea whose cause is an "archetype" containing formally all the reality that the idea contains subjectively. Hence, the light of nature makes it clear to me that the ideas in me are like images that may well fall short of the things from which they derive, but cannot contain anything greater or more perfect.

The more time and care I take in studying this, the more clearly and distinctly I know it to be true. But what follows from it? If I can be sure that the subjective reality of one of my ideas is so great that it isn't in me either formally or eminently and hence that I cannot be the cause of that idea, I can infer that I am not alone in the world—that there exists something else that is the cause of the idea. But, if I can find no such idea in me, I will have no argument at all for the existence of anything other than me— for, having diligently searched for such an argument, I have yet to find one.

Of my ideas—besides my idea of myself, about which there can be no problem here—one presents God, others inanimate physical objects, others angels, others animals, and still others men like me.

As to my ideas of other men, of animals, and of angels, it's easy to see

---

Underline each important point in this paragraph. Add your own paraphrase in the margin.

An example of a cause would
be _____ ,
and the effect it creates would
be _____
_____ .

Circle each "it" in this paragraph and draw an arrow to the word or phrase referred to.

The last sentence, "Hence, the light . . . " is the conclusion of an argument. Reread this and the preceding paragraph several times. Number each important point that leads to this conclusion. Essentially, Descartes is

arguing _____
_____
_____
_____
because _____
_____
_____
_____ .

Descartes is looking for an idea that could not have originated from himself. Underline this unique idea when you find it.

that—even if the world contained no men but me, no animals, and no angels—I could have composed these ideas from those that I have of myself, of physical objects, and of God.

And, as to my ideas of physical objects, it seems that nothing in them is so great that it couldn't have come from me. For, if I analyze my ideas of physical objects carefully, taking them one by one as I did yesterday when examining my idea of the piece of wax, I notice that there is very little in them that I grasp clearly and distinctly. What I do grasp clearly and distinctly in these ideas is size (which is extension in length, breadth, and depth), shape (which arises from extension's limits), position (which the differently shaped things have relative to one another), and motion (which is just change of position). To these I can add substance, duration, and number. But my thoughts of other things in physical objects (such as light and color, sound, odor, taste, heat and cold, and tactile qualities) are so confused and obscure that I can't say whether they are true or false—whether my ideas of these things are of something or of nothing. Although, as I noted earlier, that which is properly called falsehood—namely, *formal* falsehood—can only be found in judgments, we can still find falsehood of another sort—namely, *material* falsehood—in an idea when it presents what is not a thing as though it were a thing. For example, the ideas that I have of coldness and heat are so unclear and indistinct that I can't tell from them whether coldness is just the absence of heat, or heat just the absence of coldness, or both are real qualities, or neither is. And, since every idea is "of something," the idea that presents coldness to me as something real and positive could justifiably be called false if coldness were just the absence of heat. And the same holds for other ideas of this sort.

"Such ideas" refers back to

_____

_____ .

For such ideas, I need not posit a creator distinct from me. I know by the light of nature that, if one of these ideas is false—that is, if it doesn't present a real thing—it comes from nothing—that is, the only cause of its being in me is a deficiency of my nature, which clearly is imperfect. If one of these ideas is true, however, I still see no reason why I couldn't have produced it myself—for these ideas present so little reality to me that I can't even distinguish it from nothing.

Of the things that are clear and distinct in my ideas of physical objects, it seems that I may have borrowed some—such as substance, duration, and number—from my idea of myself. I think of the stone as a substance—that is, as something that can exist on its own—just as I think of myself as a substance. Although I conceive of myself as a thinking and unextended thing and of the stone as an extended and unthinking thing so that the two conceptions are quite different, they are the same in that they both seem to be of substances. And, when I grasp that I exist now while remembering that I existed in the past, or when I count my various thoughts, I get the idea of duration or number, which I can then apply to other things. The other components of my ideas of physical objects—extension, shape, place, and motion—can't be in me formally, since I'm just a thinking thing. But, as these things are just modes of substance, and as I am a substance, it seems that they may be in me eminently.

The possible origin of his idea of "duration or number" is

_____

_____

_____ .

All that's left is my idea of God. Is there something in this idea of God that couldn't have come from me? By "God" I mean a substance that's infinite, independent, supremely intelligent, and supremely powerful—the thing from which I and everything else that may exist derive our existence. The more I consider these attributes, the less it seems that they could have come from me alone. So I must conclude that God necessarily exists.

While I may have the idea of substance in me by virtue of my being a substance, I who am finite would not have the idea of infinite substance in me unless it came from a substance that really was infinite.

And I shouldn't think that, rather than having a true idea of infinity, I grasp it merely as the absence of limits—in the way that I grasp rest as the absence of motion and darkness as the absence of light. On the contrary, it's clear to me that there is more reality in an infinite than in a finite substance and hence that my grasp of the infinite must somehow be prior to my grasp of the finite—my understanding of God prior to my understanding of myself. For how could I understand that I doubt and desire, that I am deficient and imperfect, if I didn't have the idea of something more perfect to use as a standard of comparison?

And, unlike the ideas of hot and cold which I just discussed, the idea of God cannot be said to be materially false and hence to come from nothing. On the contrary, since the idea of God is completely clear and distinct and contains more subjective reality than any other idea, no idea is truer *per se* and none less open to the suspicion of falsity. The idea of a supremely perfect and infinite entity is, I maintain, completely true. For, while I may be able to suppose that there is no such entity, I can't even suppose (as I did about the idea of coldness) that my idea of God fails to show me something real. This idea is maximally clear and distinct, for it contains everything that I grasp clearly and distinctly, everything real and true, everything with any perfection. It doesn't matter that I can't fully comprehend the infinite—that there are innumerable things in God which I can't comprehend fully or even reach with thought. Because of the nature of the infinite, I who am finite cannot comprehend it. It's enough that I think about the infinite and judge that, if I grasp something clearly and distinctly and know it to have some perfection, it's present either formally or eminently—perhaps along with innumerable other things of which I am ignorant—in God. If I do this, then of all my ideas the idea of God will be most true and most clear and distinct.

But maybe I am greater than I have assumed; maybe all the perfections that I attribute to God are in me potentially, still unreal and unactualized. I have already seen my knowledge gradually increase, and I don't see anything to prevent its becoming greater and greater to infinity. Nor do I see why, by means of such increased knowledge, I couldn't get all the rest of God's perfections. Finally, if the potential for these perfections is in me, I don't see why that potential couldn't account for the production of the ideas of these perfections in me.

None of this is possible. First, while it's true that my knowledge gradually increases and that I have many as yet unactualized potentialities, none of this fits with my idea of God, in whom absolutely nothing is potential; indeed, the gradual increase in my knowledge shows that I am *imperfect*. Besides, I see that, even if my knowledge were continually to become greater and greater, it would never become actually infinite, since it would never become so great as to be unable to increase. But I judge God to be actually infinite so that nothing can be added to his perfection. Finally, I see that an idea's subjective being must be produced, not be mere potentiality (which, strictly speaking, is nothing), but by what is actual or formal.

He concludes that God exists because _____

_____

_____

_____

_____ .

The idea of God is "most true" because _____

_____

_____

_____

_____

_____ .

The doubt he raises concerning his previous view of God is

_____

_____

_____

_____ .

Underline the sentences in which he refutes the doubt in the previous paragraph.

The new question he raises now
is _____

_____.

The reason he raises the new

question is _____

_____

_____.

The four possible sources for
his existence are

1. _____

2. _____

3. _____

4. _____

The source he investigates first

is _____.

When I pay attention to these things, the light of nature makes all of them obvious. But, when I attend less carefully and the images of sensible things blind my mind's eye, it's not easy for me to remember why the idea of an entity more perfect than I am must come from an entity that really is more perfect. That's why I'll go on to ask whether I, who have the idea of a perfect entity, could exist if no such entity existed.

From what might I derive my existence if not from God? Either from myself, or from my parents, or from something else less perfect than God—for nothing more perfect than God, or even as perfect as Him, can be thought of or imagined.

But, if I derived my existence from myself, I wouldn't doubt, or want, or lack anything. I would have given myself every perfection of which I have an idea, and thus I myself would be God. And I shouldn't think that it might be harder to give myself what I lack than what I already have. On the contrary, it would obviously be much harder for me, a thinking thing or substance, to emerge from nothing than for me to give myself knowledge of the many things of which I am ignorant, which is just an attribute of substance. But surely, if I had given myself that which is harder to get, I wouldn't have denied myself complete knowledge, which would have been easier to get. Indeed, I wouldn't have denied myself *any* of the perfections that I grasp in the idea of God. None of these perfections seems harder to get than existence. But, if I had given myself everything that I now have, these perfections would have seemed harder to get than existence if they were harder to get—for in creating myself I would have discovered the limits of my power.

I can't avoid the force of this argument by supposing that, since I've always existed as I do now, there's no point in looking for my creator. Since my lifetime can be divided into innumerable parts each of which is independent of the others, the fact that I existed a little while ago does not entail that I exist now, unless a cause "re-creates" me—or, in other words, preserves me—at this moment. For, when we attend to the nature of time, it's obvious that exactly the same power and action are required to preserve a thing at each moment through which it endures as would be required to create it anew if it had never existed. Hence, one of the things revealed by the light of nature is that preservation and creation differ only in the way we think of them.

I ought to ask myself, then, whether I have the power to ensure that I, who now am, will exist in a little while. Since I am nothing but a thinking thing— or, at any rate, since I am now focusing on the part of me that thinks—I would surely be aware of this power if it were in me. But I find no such power. And from this I clearly see that there is an entity distinct from me on whom I depend.

"This power" refers to _____

_____.

But maybe this entity isn't God. Maybe I am the product of my parents or of some other cause less perfect than God. No. As I've said, there must be at least as much in a cause as in its effect. Hence, since I am a thinking thing with the idea of God in me, my cause, whatever it may be, must be a thinking thing having in it the idea of every perfection that I attribute to God. And we can go on to ask whether this thing gets its existence from itself or from something else. If it gets its existence from itself, it's obvious from what I've said that it must be God—for it would have the power to exist on its own and hence the power actually to give itself every perfection of which it has an idea, including every perfection that I conceive of in God. But, if my cause gets its existence from some other thing, we can go on to ask whether this other thing gets its existence from itself or from something else. Eventually, we will come to the ultimate cause, which will be God.

It's clear enough that there can't be an infinite regress here—especially since I am concerned, not so much with the cause that originally produced me, as with the one that preserves me at the present moment.

And I can't suppose that several partial causes combined to make me or that I get the ideas of the various perfections that I attribute to God from different causes so that, while each of these perfections can be found somewhere in the universe, there is no God in whom they all come together. On the contrary, one of the chief perfections that I understand God to have is unity, simplicity, inseparability from everything in Him. Surely the idea of the unity of all God's perfections can only have been put in me by a cause that gives me the ideas of all the other perfections—for nothing could make me aware of the unbreakable connection of God's perfections unless it made me aware of what those perfections are.

Finally, even if everything that I used to believe about my parents is true, it's clear that they don't preserve me. Insofar as I am a thinking thing, they did not even take part in creating me. They simply formed the matter in which I used to think that I (that is, my mind, which is all I am now taking myself to be) resided. There can therefore be no problem about my parents. And I am driven to this conclusion: The fact that I exist and have an idea in me of a perfect entity—that is, God—conclusively entails that God does in fact exist.

All that's left is to explain how I have gotten my idea of God from Him. I have not taken it in through my senses; it has never come to me unexpectedly as the ideas of sensible things do when those things affect (or seem to affect) my external organs of sense. Nor have I made the idea myself; I can't subtract from it or add to it. The only other possibility is that the idea is innate in me, like my idea of myself.

It's not at all surprising that in creating me God put this idea into me, impressing it on His work like a craftsman's mark (which needn't be distinct from the work itself). The very fact that it was God who created me confirms that I have somehow been made in His image or likeness and that I grasp this likeness, which contains the idea of God, in the same way that I grasp myself. Thus, when I turn my mind's eye on myself, I understand, not just that I am an incomplete and dependent thing which constantly strives for bigger and better things, but also that He on whom I depend has all these things in Himself as infinite reality rather than just as vague potentiality and hence that He must be God. The whole argument comes down to this: I know that I could not exist with my present nature—that is, that I could not exist with the idea of God in me—unless there really were a God. This must be the very God whose idea is in me, the thing having all of the perfections that I can't fully comprehend but can somehow reach with thought, who clearly cannot have any defects. From this, it's obvious that He can't deceive—for, as the natural light reveals, fraud and deception arise from defect.

But before examining this more carefully and investigating its consequences, I want to dwell for a moment in the contemplation of God, to ponder His attributes, to see and admire and adore the beauty of His boundless light, insofar as my clouded insight allows. As I have faith that the supreme happiness of the next life consists wholly of the contemplation of divine greatness,

His problem in the first sentence is _____
_____
_____.

His answer is _____
_____
_____.

Underline the source of his idea of God.

The source of his idea of God cannot be _____

because _____
_____
_____.

Nor can the source be _____
_____
_____

because _____
_____
_____.

The source of his idea of God must be _____
_____

because _____
_____
_____
_____.

The reason God cannot be a deceiver is _____
_____
_____
_____.

Descartes achieves a pinnacle in the last paragraph. It is
_____
_____
_____
_____.

I now find that contemplation of the same sort, though less perfect, affords that greatest joy available in this life.

Thinking About *Meditation III*

Begin as before by thinking back over what you read and summarizing your general impression.

The points that Descartes made that I understand most clearly were _____

_____

_____

_____.

In the second half of *Meditation III*, which you just read, Descartes presents two proofs for God's existence. I will guide you through the first proof and summarize the second.

In the first proof, Descartes begins by looking for some idea in his mind that he could not have caused. In other words, if he can find some idea that did not come from him, the idea must have come from somewhere else. Thus, he can add to the 100 percent certitudes he is seeking that something exists outside himself (and this something else will turn out to be God). Remember that until halfway through *Meditation III*, he has only proved his own existence, defined himself as a thinking thing, and established some general rules for telling true ideas from false ideas. In the section below, which you have already read once, he sets up a general rule for telling if one of his ideas must have originated from something other than himself.

If I can be sure that the subjective reality of one of my ideas is so great that it isn't in me either formally or eminently and hence that I cannot be the cause of that idea, I can infer that I am not alone in the world—that there exists something else that is the cause of the idea. But, if I can find no such idea in me, I will have no argument at all for the existence of anything other than me.

As he sorts through the ideas in his mind, what is he looking for?

Looking carefully at the first sentence in the quotation, I would say he is looking

for _____.

If he finds this, he will know _____.

If he doesn't find this, he will have to conclude _____

_____. Therefore,

it is important that he find what he is looking for!

Sometimes very simple examples help. I'll offer one and you can add your own. My uncle dug a fishpond. He stocked the pond with perch. One day, he caught a large fish that he couldn't identify. If the fish was a perch, then he could conclude that it probably had been produced by the fish in the pond. If the fish wasn't a perch, he could conclude that some outside source (a friendly neighbor?) had put it there. Descartes is looking through the ideas in his head. If he finds one that could not have come from other ideas in his head or that could not have come from him, then he can conclude that it came from somewhere else. And, it seems, he can know this with 100 percent certitude. Now try your example.

My example is _____

_____. This is like Descartes's situation

because _____

_____.

And what is this idea that he believes he could not be the cause of?

I don't think I would be wrong if I said the idea is _____

_____.

Something tells me that if you are not right you soon will be. Read this, another passage from *Meditation III.*

All that's left is my idea of God. Is there anything in this idea of God that couldn't have come from me? By "God" I mean a substance that's infinite, independent, supremely intelligent, and supremely powerful—the thing from which I and everything else that may exist derive our existence. The more I consider these attributes, the less it seems that they could have come from me alone. So I must conclude that God necessarily exists.

While I may have the idea of substance in me by virtue of my being a substance, I who am finite would not have the idea of infinite substance in me unless it came from a substance that really was infinite.

Try to think through this as Descartes would.

An interesting problem. I have looked through all the ideas in my mind, searching to see if there are any that could not have come from my own mind. At last, I come

to the idea of _____.
As I examine this idea, I define it as the idea of a being who is

_____.

Now, why couldn't this idea have come from my own mind? The answer must lie in a description of what I know myself to be and what is peculiarly different about

this idea. I am a being who is _____.

This idea is about a being who is _____.

Therefore, this idea could not have come from me because _____

_____.

Through much of *Meditation III*, Descartes discusses cause and effect and relates these concepts to both his first and his second proof of God's existence. Try to do the same.

An example of a cause is _____. The effect it produces is

_____. The question is, Applying this to Descartes's first proof of God's existence, is the idea of God in my mind the cause or the effect? And, whichever it is, how does this relate to the argument that God, not I, produced the idea? I will say that when I think of God and the idea of God in my

mind, the cause is _____ and the effect is _____, and this

can be used to show that God exists because _____.

Thus, I could not be the cause of the idea because _____.

Now let's move on to Descartes's second proof of God's existence. Here is a key section from that proof. Underline important parts and put your own examples in the margins.

Since my lifetime can be divided into innumerable parts each of which is independent of the others, the fact that I existed a little while ago does not entail that I exist now, unless a cause "re-creates" me—or, in other words, preserves me— at this moment. For, when we attend to the nature of time, it's obvious that exactly the same power and action are required to preserve a thing at each moment through which it endures as would be required to create it anew if it had never existed. Hence, one of the things revealed by the light of nature is that preservation and creation differ only in the way we think of them.

I ought to ask myself, then, whether I have the power to ensure that I, who now am, will exist in a little while. Since I am nothing but a thinking thing— or, at any rate, since I am now focusing on the part of me that thinks—I would surely be aware of this power if it were in me. But I find no such power. And from this I clearly see that there is an entity distinct from me on whom I depend.

The first proof for God's existence starts with the idea of God in Descartes's mind and shows that God must be the cause of this idea. The second proof of God's existence, which you just read, starts with Descartes's and shows that God must exist as the continuous re-creator of Descartes's existence. Because this proof is a bit more subtle than the first, I'm going to do most of the work.

Let us say I tried to refute Descartes by arguing that the pumping of my heart was the cause of my continuing to exist. He would simply point out that he is talking not about my life but about my whole existence. My heart causes my life to continue, but what causes my heart and everything else about me to continue to exist? Our hearts keep us alive, but what causes our hearts to continue in physical existence from one moment to the next? His answer would be that only God could be the cause of our continued existence.

Perhaps I could try to answer Descartes by saying that I myself am the cause of my own continued existence. I am typing this at 9:01 in the morning, and my existing at 9:01 in the morning causes me to continue to exist at 9:02 in the morning. Each moment of my life is an effect created by a previous cause, and that previous cause is the previous moment of my life. Therefore, God is not the cause of my continued existence; I am.

Descartes would probably answer that I really don't understand what it means for one thing to cause another. And perhaps he is right. When I move my fingers on the keyboard and cause the keys to move, my fingers are the cause and the movement of the keys is the effect. But for my fingers to cause the keys to move, my fingers and the keys *must exist at the same moment*. In fact, this is the case with all relations between a cause and an effect. When one thing causes another, the two must exist at the same moment. If *A* is said to cause *B*, they must meet at some particular moment; otherwise, it would be impossible for *A* to be the cause of *B*.

Maybe I understand. Take the simple case of two objects capable of motion. Let

us say a _____ rolls up to a _____ and causes

the second object to move. The two objects must exist at the same moment of

time for one to affect the other, because if they didn't, _____

_____. Descartes's point

seems to be that _____.

But how does this relate to his proof of God's existence?

He is arguing that only God and not we ourselves could be the cause of our continued existence. When I suggest that my existing at 9:01 is the cause of my existing at 9:02, he can refute this by pointing out that for one thing to have any effect on another, the two must exist *at the same time*. Thus, a self existing at 9:01 could not be the cause of the same self existing at 9:02 because the former obviously doesn't exist at the same time as the latter. Therefore, there must be something else that maintains the self in existence from one separate moment to the next, and that something Descartes goes on to define as God.[1]

Thus, in *Meditation III*, Descartes offers two very different proofs of God's existence. In the first proof, Descartes analyzes his idea of God and discovers that this idea could have been caused only by God. In the second proof, Descartes analyzes the continuity of his, Descartes's, existence and discovers that this continuity could have been maintained only by God.

Let's see how far we've come. Think back about what you learned about Descartes at the beginning of the chapter. Then look back through your notes for the first three meditations. What is all this really about?

Very well. I will make it brief, but completely clear. The main concepts at the be-

ginning of the chapter were _____

_____

_____

_____

_____.

---

[1] I am indebted to Ronald Rubin for drawing my attention to and clarifying a key aspect of Descartes's second proof for God's existence.

In *Meditation I,* Descartes went through a long argument questioning his beliefs.

He was seeking _____.
He was even able to question whether he could be certain his body was where it

appeared to be by arguing _____

_____

_____.

Then he imagined an all-powerful evil spirit so that _____

_____.

In *Meditation II,* he established his first truth by showing that _____

_____. In

addition, he carefully examined a piece of wax to demonstrate to himself that

_____

_____.

Meditation III could be divided into two parts. In the first part, his most important

points were _____

_____

_____.

In the second part, his most important points were _____

_____

_____

_____.

Now do one more task, and then I'll summarize the last three meditations
for you. First, summarize Descartes's first proof of God's existence in no more
than four sentences. Then state the general idea of the second proof.

The first fact is _____

_____.

The second fact is _____

_____.

Add to this a third obvious fact that _____

_____.

And my fourth sentence is simply that from the above it is obvious that God must exist. However, learning from Descartes, I would offer this criticism of one of my first three sentences.

And that is that _____ _____

_____

_____.

Finally, what he seems to be arguing in the second proof of God's existence is

_____

_____

_____.

Now, here is a summary of the last three meditations. Note how Descartes is able to significantly increase his list of certitudes.

Meditation IV continues with a description of the characteristics of God and begins to explore questions about truth and error. God, whose existence Descartes just proved, cannot be a deceiver. A God who deceived would not be perfect—that is, would not be God. But if God cannot deceive, where do errors and mistakes come from? Descartes says that error is a function of the incorrect application of will to the objects of the understanding. We can will to do more than we can immediately and correctly understand. Nonetheless, he goes on to assert that those things that we perceive *clearly and distinctly* are true. Descartes's quest for certainty is now a function of finding the clear and distinct.

Meditation V offers an additional proof of the existence of God and begins to consider the reality of the sense world that he has been doubting so vigorously throughout the previous meditations. In his proof, Descartes argues that just as it is impossible to conceive of a mountain range without valleys, he cannot conceive of God except as existing. God is to His existence as a mountain range is to mountain valleys; wherever you have one, you necessarily have the other. God has all perfections; one perfection is existence; therefore, God must exist. (This is a restatement of Anselm's ontological argument.) Having once again demonstrated the existence of God, Descartes can affirm all knowledge of clear and distinct ideas—even knowledge, in principle, of the world. God, who created him, would be a deceiver if Descartes's clear and distinct ideas about the world were false. Once the self is certain, God is certain, and the existence of the world and material objects can be, at least in principle, saved from Descartes's original project of doubt.

Meditation VI deals with the existence of physical things and the distinction between the mind and the body. Since God is not a deceiver and since there must be some cause of the ideas of physical reality, "it follows that physical objects exist." To a twentieth-century philosopher, accustomed to thinking in a different fashion, this assertion might seem obvious. But for Descartes, *Meditation VI* has redeemed the reality of the self, of God, and of the world. Given a single 100 percent certain truth, his own existence, Descartes has saved his world from destruction by doubt.

VOCABULARY MAP
René Descartes

Descartes's **metaphysics,** his view of reality, is strongly **dualistic.** First of all, he, like other Christian thinkers, sharply distinguishes between the realm of God and the physical universe. God is perfect and unchanging; everything in the physical universe (including humans) is imperfect and changing. Thus, reality is dual, has two opposing aspects. Descartes is also considered a metaphysical dualist for another reason. He strongly distinguishes between aspects of reality that are free (God and the human mind) and aspects of reality that are not free, that are mechanistic (the rest of the universe). According to Descartes, God and the human mind are governed by free will; the elements of the rest of the universe, from planets to cats, have no more freedom of choice in their actions than do the gears of a clock.

Descartes's **epistemology,** his view of the knowledge process, is **rationalistic.** Like the rationalists before him, Descartes holds that the mind can gain knowledge independently of the senses. Only by turning inward, away from the senses, does Descartes discover his first truth, the certitude of his own existence testified to by his thinking.

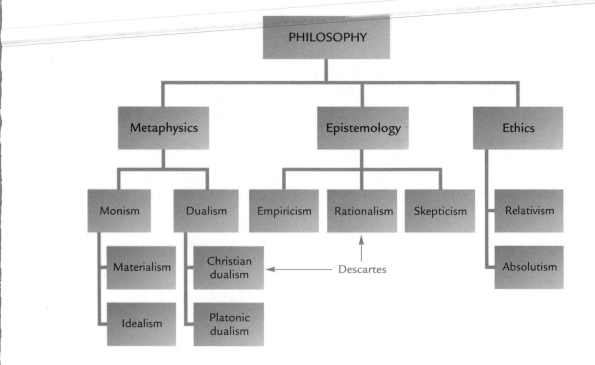

SUMMARY

You played a wisdom game to determine if you could know anything for certain. Descartes will argue that beginning with the certainty that his thinking establishes his existence, a large number of other important truths can be known for certain. He borrows skeptical arguments from Sextus Empiricus, the ontological argument from St. Anselm, and Augustine's assertion that the self cannot successfully doubt its own existence. New elements in Descartes's philosophy include his analysis of matter, his sharp distinction between the mind and body, his rejection of traditional authorities, and his methodical introspection.

In the first meditation, Descartes attempts to doubt everything. In the second meditation, he establishes his own existence as a thinking being as his first 100 percent certainty. In the third meditation, Descartes offers proofs of God's existence.

EXERCISE 19.11
Looking Back

Use your own paper to answer each of the following:

1. What does Descartes borrow from the past?
2. What is new in Descartes's philosophy?
3. What are key ideas in the first three meditations?
4. What are some techniques for reading Descartes?

AN ANALYSIS OF YOUR PHILOSOPHICAL SELF-PORTRAIT

To see how your views stack up against Descartes's, read my analysis below, rethink your position, and then circle what you believe is the correct answer. I've underlined Descartes's answers.

1. T <u>F</u> *Very little, if anything, can be known for certain.*

    As you saw in *Meditation I,* Descartes *begins* by doubting everything. However, by the end of *Meditation VI* he has established a long list of certitudes. If you are a skeptic, then prepare to meet one of your toughest opponents. If you believe skeptics are wrong, then Descartes may be one of your strongest allies.

2. <u>T</u> F *From the fact that you are a thinking being, it is possible to prove that you exist.*

    This concept is at the core of Descartes's philosophy. Even if I can't tell whether I'm awake or asleep or whether the physical universe exists or whether God exists or even whether 2 + 2 = 4, I can certainly know that I am *thinking* about these things. Thus, I can be sure that I am a thinking being. And if I know I am a thinking being, I certainly also know that I exist. How could I be a thinking being, if I, the one doing the thinking, *didn't* exist? Thus, it seems obviously true that from the fact that I am a thinking being, I can prove that I exist.

    Many philosophers, however, argue that Descartes is wrong.
    What error do you see in his reasoning?

    Perhaps his error is _____

    _____

    _____.

3. T <u>F</u> *From the fact that you exist, it is possible to prove that you are a thinking being.*

I don't think Descartes would agree.

Assume you know that you exist. That's all you know. If all you know is that you exist, you could not prove that you are a thinking being. You can't get from you-as-existing to you-as-thinking. In fact, whenever you start pondering the relationship between your thinking and your existence, the first truth you come up with, according to Descartes, is that you are *thinking*. Thus, the certainty of thinking comes before the certainty of existence.

4. <u>T</u> F *It is possible, without using knowledge gained by the senses, to prove that God exists.*

Descartes believes this is true, but many of my students, even those who believe in God, argue that it is false. They believe that one must, at least, *hear* about the concept of God, in order to know that God exists. Thus, knowledge of God comes through the senses (in this case, the ear).

Descartes would argue that no teacher could instruct you in the nature of an all-knowing, all-good, all-powerful being, because nothing remotely resembling such a being could be presented to you. Almost anything *but* God could be explained in words, but words fall infinitely short of God's divine nature. Thus, the only way you can genuinely understand the term "God" is if God Himself planted this understanding in your mind.

Do you agree or disagree?

I (agree, disagree) because _____

_____

_____.

5. <u>T</u> F *You could not have the idea of a perfect being (God) unless an actual perfect being (God) existed.*

Descartes believes both that all our ideas must have some source and that we all have an idea of a perfect being. Where could this idea have come from? It could not have come from an imperfect being. How could something imperfect give us any conception of something perfect? Therefore, our idea of a perfect being could only have come from an *actual* perfect being. Therefore, God, the perfect being exists. Descartes will elaborate this important proof in *Meditation III.*

How strong, at this point, do you think the proof is?

I believe the proof is (very strong, strong, weak, very weak) because _____

_____

_____.

Evaluation: Number of points in agreement with Descartes = _____ of 5 possible.

A position of Descartes's that you strongly (support, oppose) is _____

_____

because _____

_____

_____.

GOOD BOOKS

Frankfurt, Harry G. *Demons, Dreamers, and Madmen: The Defense of Reason in Descartes' Meditations*. Indianapolis: Bobbs-Merrill, 1970. A classic analysis of Descartes's Meditations.

Sesonkske, Alexander, and Fleming, Noel, editors. *Meta-Meditations: Studies in Descartes*. Belmont, Calif.: Wadsworth, 1965. A good sampling of modern analyses of Descartes.

NEXT STOP

John Locke argues that Descartes's philosophy is "metaphysical rubbish."

20

John Locke
Prisoners in the Mind's Vault

YOUR PHILOSOPHICAL SELF-PORTRAIT

Add more details to your philosophical self-portrait by answering the questions below and offering evidence for your answers.

1. T F Everyone is born with an idea of right and wrong.
    Evidence: _____
    _____.

2. T F Everyone is born with an idea of God.
    Evidence: _____
    _____.

3. T F Every society, no matter how primitive, has the idea of God.
    Evidence: _____
    _____.

4. T F The mind at birth is empty of all ideas.
    Evidence: _____
    _____.

5. T F When we know an object, we know only our idea of the object, not the object itself. For example, when we know a table, we know only our idea of the table, not the table itself.
    Evidence: _____.

6. T F Our idea of an object is an accurate copy of the object itself. For example, our idea of a table is an accurate copy of the table itself.
    Evidence: _____.

7. T F Not only do we have sense knowledge of the qualities of an object, but we also have sense knowledge of the matter of an object. For example, not only do we have sense knowledge of the color of a table, but we also have sense knowledge of the matter of the table that contains the color.
    Evidence: _____.

PREVIEW

We'll undertake a thought experiment to clarify the position of the British empiricists who believed that we do not know the world, only our ideas—which we assume are accurate copies of the world. Locke's epistemology holds that (1) there are no **innate ideas;** (2) all our knowledge comes through our senses and is either the result of external experience (Sensation) or internal experience (Reflection); (3) primary qualities of size, shape, weight, texture, and motion exist in the external world, while secondary qualities of color, sound, taste, and scent are produced by our senses and thus do not exist in the external world; (4) though matter exists, we have no sense knowledge of matter—Locke concludes that matter is an "I know not what." Key features of Locke's epistemology are explored in selections from his *Essay Concerning Human Understanding.*

THOUGHT EXPERIMENT

Imagine that you have been locked up in a windowless room all your life. All you know of the outside world comes to you over a TV monitor set into the wall.

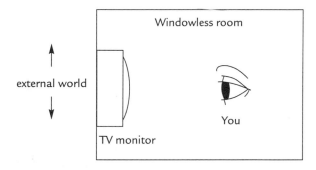

The only program is *My Front Yard.* You watch the screen as neighbors come and go, as one electronic day follows another, as televised seasons pass. You are the Supreme Couch Potato.

One day, you begin to wonder if the images on the screen are accurate. You wonder, in other words, to what degree the TV is like a window. Are the TV's images good or poor copies of the world on the other side of the wall? Do you have a front yard? Neighbors? Are there seasons "out there"?

Perhaps nothing exists except delusory images inside the frame of your monitor. You don't live in a room. You live in all there is of the universe.

Can you think of any way, *merely by looking at the TV screen,* that you could determine whether its images were reliable copies of an external world?

_____

_____

_____.

innate idea an idea that is present in the mind at birth and thus is not learned through the senses. For example, many Christians hold that the idea of God is innate.

Now let us say that some lucky day a door appears beside the TV. You fling the door open and discover the external world.

The first thing you do is compare what you see to the images that have appeared on the monitor. You will know instantly if you have lived a life of delusion because you can compare what the televised images have told you about the world with the world itself.

What does this thought experiment have to do with the current section of the tour?

John Locke (1632–1704)

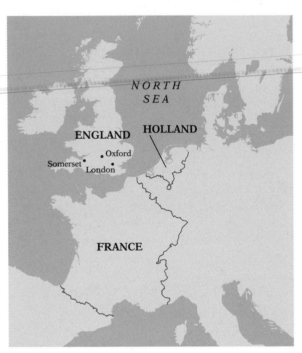

The seventeenth century in England was a time of political oppression and civil strife. When John Locke was seventeen, King Charles I was captured, tried for treason, and beheaded. This event, in which the citizenry triumphed over the monarch, helped to shape Locke's lifelong faith in democracy and the power of the people. An ardent supporter of natural human rights and an outspoken critic of the doctrine of the divine right of kings, Locke was one of the leading players in the shift in Western cultures from monar-chy to democracy. A deeply religious man, Locke argued that these rights, especially the right of individuals to own property, were grounded in the biblical account of God's giving Adam dominion over the earth. Locke's radical democratic ideals served as an inspiration for the American Revolution; many of the ideas for the American Declaration of Independence came directly from Locke's *Two Treatises of Government*.

Born in 1632 in Somerset, England, Locke was raised in a liberal Puritan family. His family was deeply involved in political activism. His father, a lawyer, fought on the parliamentary side in the first rebellion against Charles I.

At fourteen, Locke entered Westminster School, where he studied the classics, Hebrew, and Arabic. In 1652 Locke received a studentship at Christ's Church, Oxford, where he was sent to study Greek and Latin. Although he was considered by his classmates to be the brightest student at the college, he found little pleasure in his studies. Following his graduation, Locke was given a position as instructor of Greek at the college. His father's death in 1661 left him with a small inheritance. Unhappy with Scholastic philosophy (a medieval approach that relied on authority as a source of truth) because he found it too obscure and useless, Locke used the opportunity to change careers. He began the study of medicine but did not complete his course work because of his own poor health.

We are about to examine selections from *An Essay Concerning Human Understanding*, an important work by John Locke, the first of three philosophers collectively known as the British empiricists. Locke, along with George Berkeley and David Hume, held that all that we know of the world is based upon ideas produced by our senses. For example, we do not know a table itself, but only our idea of a table. Thus, between the mind's eye and the world is a screen of ideas. This screen of ideas may or may not give us an accurate picture of the world.

Perhaps you now see the philosophical point of the thought experiment. Just as the images on the TV monitor were the only intermediaries between you and the outside world, so, for Locke and the other British empiricists, the images in our minds are the only intermediaries between us and the outside

---

John Locke (continued)

In 1665 Locke entered the diplomatic service. Two years later, Lord Ashley, the earl of Shaftesbury and Locke's close friend from Oxford, invited Locke to stay with him as the family physician. Although Locke had not yet completed his Doctorate of Medicine—no degree was required at the time to practice medicine—he was, by all accounts, an excellent and respected physician.

A man of the people, Locke dressed in plain English clothes of sober gray cloth and wrote at a level that was understandable to those who weren't scholars. On the other hand, Locke was also very secretive and suspicious; these qualities may have saved his life, given the oppressive political climate in England at the time. In 1675, Locke left England to spend several years in France. When he returned to England, he learned that Lord Ashley had been involved in a plot against King Charles II and had been forced to flee to Holland, a haven of free thought. Because of his close association with the Earl of Shaftesbury and his own democratic ideals, Locke was kept under surveillance by the English government. Fearful for his safety, Locke eventually took refuge in Holland, living there under an assumed name. After King James II took over the throne of England he denounced Locke as a traitor and demanded that the Dutch return him to England. Not much effort was made to comply with the King's order, and Locke remained in Holland.

Locke did not return to England until shortly after the Glorious Revolution of 1688, when James II's daughter Mary and her husband William of Orange were placed on the throne of England. Back in London Locke continued his writing. In 1690 he published his *Two Treatises of Government* in which he attacked the theory of the divine rights of kings.

During the last thirty years of his life, Locke was plagued by a persistent cough that was only made worse by the soot-filled London air. At the invitation of his friends, Lord and Lady Masham, Locke moved to their estate outside of London. Here Locke was able to devote himself completely to his studies, to the extent that his health allowed.

Locke died peacefully in 1704. Lady Ashley was at his bedside reading the Psalms to him. "His death," a friend wrote, "was like his life, truly pious, yet natural, easy and unaffected."[1]

Locke believed that philosophy must be of practical use. His treatises on civil government, education, and religion were very popular among the people. His most important works include *An Essay Concerning Human Understanding* (1689), *Two Treatises of Government* (1690), *Some Thoughts Concerning Education* (1693), and *The Reasonableness of Christianity* (1695).

---

[1] As quoted in Paul Edwards, editor, *The Encyclopedia of Philosophy*, vol. 4 (New York: Macmillan, 1967), p. 488.

world. Our mind is a windowless room within which we view ideas, which we assume are accurate copies of the external world.

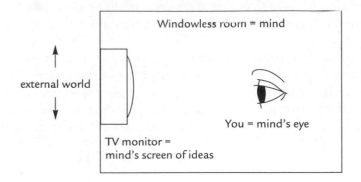

Just as it would be very difficult, perhaps impossible, to judge the accuracy of the televised images, it is very difficult, perhaps impossible, to judge the accuracy of the mind's images. To make matters much worse, whereas the thought experiment allowed you to escape from the room and compare reality with images of reality, the British empiricists argue that there is no way you can step outside your mind to compare reality with your mind's images of reality. We are prisoners in the mind's vault.

BOX 20.1

The British Empiricists Versus the Continental Rationalists

The history of philosophy often opposes two groups of seventeenth- and eighteenth-century philosophers. The British empiricists John Locke, George Berkeley, and David Hume are contrasted with the Continental rationalists René Descartes, Baruch Spinoza, and Gottfried Leibniz. The Continental rationalists are united on at least two points: First, the mind can know truths independently of the senses; second, it is the business of philosophy to build large, all-explaining systems. The British empiricists, opposing the rationalists, are united on at least two points: The mind knows truths only through the senses; it is the business of philosophy to show why large, all-explaining systems are not possible.

The British empiricists, the subject of this and the next two chapters of the tour, looked back to Aristotle and believed that there was nothing in the mind that had not come through the senses. Breaking from Aristotle, however, Locke, Berkeley, and Hume argued that the senses do not give us an entirely reliable portrait of reality. We don't know reality itself, but only our ideas, which we falsely assume are accurate copies of reality. Thus, when we look at a table, we do not know the table, but only our imperfect idea of the table. As you will soon learn, Locke held that some of the ideas which we believe come *through* the senses are produced *by* the senses; Berkeley held that the idea of matter, which we think comes through the senses, is an illusory idea; Hume held that whole categories of ideas which appear to come through the senses, especially those central to science, were illusory. Thus, the British empiricists used empiricism to attack not only rationalism, but also empiricism.

Let that sink in for a moment.

You look at trees, sky, birds. You know these things not directly but only through your ideas of trees, sky, birds. If you didn't have your ideas, obviously, you could have no knowledge of trees, sky, and birds.

You take it on faith that your idea of a tree is an accurate copy of a tree itself. You believe that your idea of the tree in the yard equals the real tree in the real yard. Your idea has bright leaves waving in the wind. You believe the real tree has exactly the same number of bright leaves waving in exactly the same way in the real wind.

But here is the problem.

Holding that your ideas are perfect copies of the world is exactly like holding that the images on the TV screen are perfect copies of the world. But, whereas you could escape from the room to compare the images on the TV with things in the world, you can't escape from your mind to compare your mental image of a tree with a real tree.

Perhaps you want to say that you could touch the tree. This, you believe, would show you that your idea of the tree was exactly like the real tree. But you would be wrong.

Touching the tree would only give you *another idea of the tree*, this idea produced by sensations in your fingers. When you change from looking at the tree to touching the tree, you would only be changing from the eyes' "channel" of ideas to the fingers' "channel" of ideas. First, you have your inner TV tuned to receive images from the eyes and then you tune the inner TV to receive images from the fingers. Unfortunately, no matter where you go or what you do, you cannot step outside your mind to compare your ideas of reality with reality itself.

Summarize the most important points I just made.

You said _____

_____

_____.

EXERCISE 20.1

An Initial Reaction to the British Empiricists

Decide and explain your position on each of the following principles supported by the British empiricists (you can, of course, change your mind later).

1. The mind gains knowledge only through the senses.

I (agree, disagree) because _____

_____.

2. We do not know things themselves, but only our ideas of things.

I (agree, disagree) because _____

_____.

3. It is not possible to compare our idea of a thing, such as our idea of a table, with the thing itself, such as the table itself.

I (agree, disagree) because _____

_____.

Locke, Berkeley, and Hume reacted to our position as viewer of the mind's ideas in progressively more radical ways. According to John Locke, as you will soon see, some of the most obviously "real" images on our inner TV are deceptive. For Locke, the inner TV has startlingly poor reception. According to George Berkeley, our most cherished idea about the world—that matter exists—is completely illusory. The inner TV is so unreliable that it must be philosophically reconstructed. According to David Hume, not only is the inner TV completely out of whack (in ways Berkeley and Locke never dreamed of) but the viewer's existence is also doubtful. When you look for yourself as observer of your ideas, you can't find who's looking.

John Locke often has a strange effect on my classes. His description of the mind and senses is initially so appealing that many of my students are willing to follow wherever he leads. Locke appears to be nothing but a supporter of common sense. Then, out of nowhere, he presents two arguments that our inner TV has remarkably bad reception. Though many students complain, few find any escape from his conclusions.

To prepare you for this (at the very least) challenging section of the tour, I'll first give you an overview of Locke's epistemology and guide you through a model of the way he believes the mind and senses operate; then I'll describe Locke's two arguments, which will make you wonder if your mind is in tune with reality; finally, once I've made you aware of what Locke is up to, you can grapple firsthand with selections from *An Essay Concerning Human Understanding*.

I'll answer the following questions:

- According to Locke, how—and what—do we know?
- What is a model of Locke's epistemology?
- What is Locke's startling argument about the senses?
- What is Locke's startling argument about matter?
- What are some of the main features of Locke's *Essay*?

According to Locke, How— and What—Do We Know?

Locke wants to know how the mind operates. Can the mind know anything for certain? If so, how much can the mind know?

One of the first questions Locke asks is whether innate ideas exist. If innate ideas exist (and if they're accurate), then we are born with a collection of truths. If they don't exist, then we must look elsewhere for certainty.

Locke starts by asking if we are born with basic principles of logic already in our minds.

And so, take this personally. Were you born with basic principles of logic such as: "the whole is equal to the sum of its parts" and "whatever exists, exists"?

I would say I (was, was not) born with these ideas because _____

_____

_____.

According to Locke, if it is true that these ideas are innate, then everyone should have them. But, children and mentally impaired people lack such ideas. Therefore, simple ideas like "the whole is equal to the sum of its parts" and "whatever exists, exists" cannot be innate.

After concluding that logical concepts are not inborn, Locke next considers the idea of God. Can we be certain that God exists because we are born (as Descartes believed) with the idea of God implanted in our minds?

The idea of God (is, is not) innate in me because _____

_____

_____.

Locke argues that many people, even many societies, have no conception of God. If the idea of God were innate, then everyone would have such an idea, but everyone doesn't. Thus, the idea of God cannot be innate.

Having concluded that we have no innate ideas, Locke then investigates the source of our ideas. If they aren't present in our minds at birth, where did they come from? The answer seems obvious to him. All our ideas come from, as Locke puts it, EXPERIENCE. There are two modes of experience. Sensation (use of the senses) acquires ideas from the external world; Reflection (mental activities like willing, believing, and imagining) generates ideas in the internal world. Do you agree that every idea you have in your mind can be traced back to either external or internal experience?

I (agree, disagree) with Locke because _____

_____

_____.

Locke believes that all our ideas can be traced back to experiences we have had since our birth. Ideas like the whole being equal to the sum of its parts, and God's existence can all be derived from something we learned through our senses during our life.

What Is a Model of Locke's Epistemology?

Let's make a simple model of Locke's theory of knowledge and slowly add details until we arrive at the two startling arguments.

Right now I am looking at a mahogany table in my study. All visual knowledge that I have of the table, according to Locke, originates in the table. The information passes through my eye and then arrives as an idea of the table in my brain where, so to speak, it is "viewed" by the mind's eye. Here is a diagram of the process.

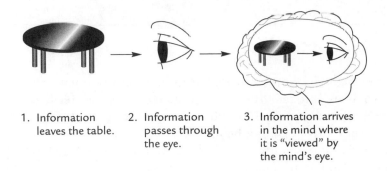

1. Information leaves the table.

2. Information passes through the eye.

3. Information arrives in the mind where it is "viewed" by the mind's eye.

So far, so good. If you are like most of my students, Locke's analysis of the knowledge process makes perfect sense to you. Information begins "out there" in the world, goes through our senses, and produces that which we view in our minds. Simple.

Now, let's add another detail that, chances are, you will also believe is correct. In order to describe how information is transferred from an object to our senses, Locke says there are two "motions."

First, a motion in the object sends information to our senses, and a second motion in our senses receives the information. Allowing for the fact that Locke in the eighteenth century describes this process with different terminology than we would use in the twentieth century, this is the way most people understand the knowledge process. Instead of saying there is a motion in the table and another motion in the senses, we would probably say that the table "gives off" light waves and the nerves in our eyes "process" this information and send it to the brain. Thus, here is our slightly more complex model of Locke's epistemology.

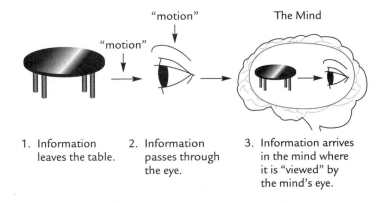

1. Information leaves the table.

2. Information passes through the eye.

3. Information arrives in the mind where it is "viewed" by the mind's eye.

Now, let's pause here for a moment. Do you see that what Locke is saying implies that I have no *direct* knowledge of the mahogany table (or anything else in the sense world)? I don't know the table itself; I only know my idea of the table. I don't view the table; I view my viewing of the table.

Look at the diagram above. I don't know anything about the table at stage one. The table itself is just "out there"—it has produced no knowledge in my mind.

And, obviously, I don't know anything about the table itself at stage two. The information from the table is simply producing a "motion" in my eye. No knowledge of the table itself has arrived in my mind.

At stage three, I finally have an image of the table, *but I can't compare the image with the original.*

To get the force of Locke's point, imagine you are communicating with Madame X over the Internet. Then, a picture of Madame X arrives. You don't really know if the picture looks like the person who has been sending you e-mail until you can compare the picture with the real Madame X. If you never see the real Madame X, you have no way of knowing if the picture looks like her or not. Maybe Madame X is Mr. Z.

In the same way, all the knowledge I have of the table is my idea, my mental image, of the table. I cannot compare the mental image to the actual table. Thus, I don't know if the mental image is accurate or not.

And so, translating all this back into the terms of our initial thought experiment, here is precisely the position that Locke puts us in: We don't look out at the world, we look at our inner TV's image of the world and hope the images are accurate.

You're now ready to face Locke's two arguments that our inner TV, the mind's screen of ideas, gets terrible reception. Our ideas, according to Locke, are not in sync with reality.

What Is Locke's Startling Argument About the Senses?

Locke distinguishes between two kinds of qualities that appear to come to us from the world. Primary qualities are, among others, shape and size. Secondary qualities are, among others, color and sound. Thus, assume I knock my fist on my black mahogany table. The primary qualities are the table's squarish shape and its size; its secondary qualities are its black color and the sound that is produced when I knock on it.

Now, to put Locke's first, startling argument in a nutshell: *Primary qualities come from the world; secondary qualities are produced by the senses.* The color and sound on our inner TV come from the TV, not the external world!

Is Locke right?

Color is just the way my eyes interpret light waves that originate on the surface of the mahogany table. If I had a different combination of rods and cones in my eyes, I would see the table as another color. Color is produced by, in Locke's term, motions in the eye, not in the world. So the world itself must be colorless. And what is sound? Knocking on the table simply produces an effect that vibrates bones in the middle ear. What I hear as sound is really bones wiggling. No wiggling bones, no sound.

It seems that Locke forces us to conclude that our inner TV is out of whack; it gives us such poor reception that it adds its own colorful, noisy signal to the world's silent, colorless signal.

Do you agree or disagree? Are color and sound not in the external world but only produced by our senses? Offer an example that supports your position.

I (agree, disagree) that color and sound are not in the external world but only

produced by our senses because _____

_____

_____.

For example, _____

_____.

When you read Locke's *Essay Concerning Human Understanding*, you'll have an extended opportunity to consider his argument.

What Is Locke's Startling Argument About Matter?

Here is what Locke claims: Because we don't know anything about the world except primary qualities, we have no sense knowledge of matter itself! Every image on our inner TV that we think is an image of matter is an illusory image.

In order to explain Locke's argument, I'll have to first explain the difference between essential and nonessential characteristics. An essential characteristic of an object is central to its nature; a nonessential characteristic of an object is not central to its nature. For example, look at this sentence:

This sentence has five words.

The sentence has two nonessential characteristics, italics and underlining, and one essential characteristic, the group of words that make up the sentence.

Note that I can strip away the nonessential characteristic of the italics, and the sentence still communicates the same meaning:

This sentence has five words.

And I can strip away the nonessential characteristic of the underlining and the sentence still communicates the same meaning:

This sentence has five words.

But if I make the slightest change to the essential characteristic of the group of words themselves, then the meaning, the core, of the sentence changes:

This sentence has   words.

Thus, changing nonessential characteristics changes nothing important; that's why they're *non*essential. Changing essential characteristics changes something very important; that's why they're essential.

Now sum up the points I made about essential and nonessential characteristics using your own example.

Very well, I'll take the example of _____.

Its nonessential characteristics are _____.

Its essential characteristics are _____.

Now we are ready to investigate Locke's startling argument about matter.

Matter, we would certainly want to say, is an essential characteristic of any physical object. Looking at the mahogany table, I *believe* I see not only its shininess and black color but also its matter. Shininess and black color are nonessential characteristics; matter, I want to say, is an essential characteristic.

It seems that just as I could remove italics and underlining from the sentence we investigated and still perceive the essential characteristic of its group of words, I could also remove shininess and black color from the table and still perceive its essential characteristic of matter.

But according to Locke, when I strip away shininess and black color, *I have no remaining sense knowledge of matter.* All I have sense knowledge of are nonessential qualities, not the essential quality of matter.

What?

I've probably lost you.

Let's go over that two more times.

The Vanishing Table

Here is a drawing of a shiny, black table.

First, I'll slowly remove the shine.

Next, I'll slowly remove the blackness.

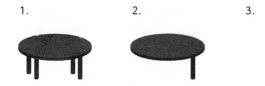

Nothing left over!

It makes no difference that I am merely using a drawing. Anything I look at has only three characteristics: reflectivity, color, and shape. When I remove reflectivity, I have a dull object of a certain color and shape. But when I remove the color, the shape—and thus the matter—vanishes as well. I have no sense knowledge of shape or matter without the color. In other words, when I remove what I think are nonessential characteristics, there is no essential characteristic, certainly no sense knowledge, of matter remaining.

The Invisible Wall

Look across the room at anything you wish—for example, a white wall. You think you see at least two nonessential characteristics: whiteness and (some degree of) reflectivity. You also think you see one essential characteristic: the matter of the wall.

But, in fact, you have no sense knowledge of the matter. Strip away the color and reflectivity and you see nothing. Why? You can't see a colorless object.

At this point you might be slightly tempted to agree with Locke. Matter must be "underneath" qualities, but you just can't see it.

Even if you're still foggy on this or the earlier argument, don't worry. You'll be able to grapple with them again when we examine *An Essay Concerning Human Understanding*

What Are Some of the Main Features of Locke's *Essay*?

An Essay Concerning Human Understanding is Locke's major philosophical work. In his preface, Locke says the philosopher is a mere "underlabourer" who must clear the way by "removing some of the rubbish that lies in the way of our knowledge." Much of the rubbish he is referring to belongs to Descartes and other rationalistic philosophers.

Locke describes the impetus for his investigation.

> Five or six friends meeting at my chamber, and discoursing on a subject very remote from this [God and morality], found themselves quickly at a stand, by the difficulties that rose on every side. After we had a while puzzled ourselves, not coming any nearer solution of those doubts which perplexed us, it came into my thoughts, that we took a wrong course; and that before we set ourselves upon inquiries of that nature, it was necessary to examine our own abilities, and see what objects our understanding were, and were not, fitted to deal with.

To resolve the problems raised by this conversation with his friends took Locke twenty years! The result was a long work divided into four parts.

Book I of Locke's *Essay* is an attack upon the doctrine of innate ideas. Locke argues against the position taken by Descartes and other rationalists that the mind, at birth, contains ideas.

Book II, probably the philosophically most important part of Locke's *Essay*, is an examination of the sources and nature of the mind's ideas. All our ideas come from either the operation of the senses on the world or the operations of the mind (believing, willing, imagining, and so forth). Locke distinguishes between two kinds of ideas: Simple ideas like red, cool, and sweet have no other parts; complex ideas are created from two or more simple ideas, such as a red, cool, sweet apple. In his discussion of material objects, Locke introduces the important concepts of primary and secondary qualities. Primary qualities—size, shape, weight, texture, and motion—are *in* material objects themselves; secondary qualities—color, scent, sound, and taste—are *not in* objects themselves but are produced by our senses. Thus, in Locke's view the world itself is colorless, odorless, silent, and tasteless. In Book II, Locke also examines the difficult concept of substance (physical matter). According to Locke, we have no sense knowledge of matter. Matter exists but is, in Locke's phrase, an "I know not what."

Book III of the *Essay* is an analysis of the role language plays in the knowledge process.

Book IV of the *Essay* presents Locke's view of what can be known for certain. He agrees with Descartes that we can have indubitable knowledge of particular objects, such as a table. He strongly disagrees with Descartes, however, about universal and/or scientific knowledge. In Locke's view, there is no way the mind can know any "laws of nature" for certain. Thus, all-explaining systems like those of Descartes and the other Continental rationalists are "rubbish."

EXERCISE 20.2
Looking Back

Answer the following questions on your own paper.

1. The British empiricists posed what problems about knowledge? (Use the thought experiment at the start of this chapter to answer this question.)

2. According to Locke, how—and what—do we know?

3. What is a model of Locke's epistemology?

4. What is Locke's startling argument about the senses?

5. What is Locke's startling argument about matter?

6. What are some of the main features of Locke's *Essay*?

READING:
EXERPTS FROM *AN ESSAY CONCERNING HUMAN UNDERSTANDING*

Excerpts from Locke's essay follow. After most of the sections, I've included tasks and/or explanations to help you analyze his position. I've made slight changes in Locke's eighteenth-century spelling and grammar to make his essay clearer for modern readers. Fill in all [_____] with the word referred to.

Book I

Chapter 1: Introduction

1. *An inquiry into the understanding, pleasant and useful.*—Since it is the *understanding* that sets man above the rest of sensible beings [all animals, including humans], and gives him all the advantage and dominion which he has over them, it [_____] is certainly a subject, even for its nobleness, worth our labour to enquire into. The understanding, like the eye, whilst it [_____] makes us see and perceive all other things, takes no notice of itself; and it requires art and pains to set it at a distance, and make it its own object. But whatever be the difficulties that lie in the way of this inquiry; whatever it be that keeps us so much in the dark to ourselves; sure I am that all the light we can let in upon our own minds, all the acquaintance we can make with our own understandings, will not only be very pleasant, but bring us great advantage in directing our thoughts in the search of other things.

Locke's goal is to explore the

_____.

Which of the following are consistent (C) or inconsistent (I) with points in the paragraph above?

1. C I   It is easier to investigate the understanding than the eye because the mind need only investigate itself, not something external to it.

2. C I   It is easier to investigate the eye than the understanding because a physical thing like the eye is easier to understand than a nonphysical thing like the mind.

3. C I   It is equally difficult to investigate the eye and the understanding because it is difficult for both the eye and the understanding to observe their own operations.

In the next section, not included on our tour, Locke develops arguments showing that there are no innate ideas. The following excerpt presents his argument that the idea of God is not innate.

Chapter 4: Considerations on Innate Principles

8. *Idea of God not innate.*—If any idea can be imagined innate, the *idea* of God may, of all others, for many reasons, be thought so; since it is hard to conceive how there should be innate moral principles without an innate idea of a Deity: without a notion of a lawmaker, it is impossible to have a notion of a law, and an obligation to observe it. Besides the atheists taken notice of amongst the ancients, and left branded upon the records of history, has not navigation discovered, in these latter ages, whole nations, at the Bay of Soldanis, in Brazil, in Boranday, and the Caribbee Islands, etc., amongst whom there was to be found no notion of a God, no religion? . . . Perhaps, if we should with attention mind the lives and discourses of people not so far off, we should have too much reason to fear that many, in more civilized countries, have no very strong and clear impressions of a Deity upon their minds; and that the complaints of atheism made from the pulpit [made by preachers in church] are not without reason.

How does Locke use the example of recently discovered nations to argue that there is no innate idea of God?

_____

_____

Summarize the idea in the last sentence of section 8.

_____

_____

THOUGHT EXPERIMENT: THE COSMIC POLL

Imagine that at some time in the future we were able to conduct a poll of every intelligent being in the universe. We discover that they *all* have an idea of God. What effect, if any, would this have on the argument that the idea of God is innate?

_____

_____

What effect, if any, would the Cosmic Poll have on the argument that God exists?

_____

_____

9. *The name of God not universal or obscure in meaning.*—But had all mankind everywhere a notion of a God (whereof yet history tells us the contrary), it would not from thence follow that the idea of him was innate, . . . especially if it be such an idea as is agreeable to the common light of reason, and naturally deducible from every part of our knowledge, as that of a God is. For the visible marks of extraordinary wisdom and power appear so plainly in all the work of the creation, that a rational creature who will but seriously reflect on them, cannot miss the discovery of a Deity; and the influence that the discovery of such a Being must necessarily have on the minds of all that have but once heard of it, is so great, and carries such a weight of thought and communication with it, that it seems stranger to me that a whole nation of men should be any where found so brutish as to want the notion of a God, than that they should be without any notion of numbers, or fire.

T or F: Locke believes that everyone has an idea of God.

Underline the following statements that are consistent with points in the paragraph above. (You may choose more than one.)

1. There is no God.
2. Even if everyone had an idea of God, this would not prove that the idea of God was innate.
3. Evidence of God's existence is present in the world of nature.
4. Only nations that have discovered fire and numbers will have discovered the idea of God.
5. God gives humans the idea of numbers and the power to create fire.

What would Locke's reaction be to the findings in the Cosmic Poll (in the Thought Experiment above) that every intelligent being believed in God? Would he have to agree that the idea of God is innate?

_____

_____

_____.

Having attacked the doctrine of innate ideas, Locke now turns, in Book II, to his description of the origin of our ideas.

Book II

Chapter 1: Of Ideas in General and Their Original [Origin]

1. *Idea is the object of thinking.*—Every man being conscious to himself that he thinks, and that which his mind is applied about whilst thinking being the ideas that are there, it is past doubt that men have in their minds several ideas, such as are those expressed by the words "whiteness, hardness, sweetness, thinking, motion, man, elephant, army, drunkenness," and others. It is in the first place then to be inquired, How he comes by them?

I know it is a received doctrine, that men have native [innate] ideas and original characters stamped upon their minds in their very first being. This opinion I have at large examined already; and, I suppose, what I have said in the foregoing Book will be much more easily admitted, when I have shown whence the understanding may get all the ideas it has, and by what ways and degrees they may come into the mind; for which I shall appeal to every one's own observation and experience.

2. *All ideas come from sensation or reflection.*—Let us then suppose the mind to be, as we say, white paper, void of all characters, without any ideas; how comes it to be furnished [with ideas]? Whence comes it by that vast store [of ideas], which the busy and boundless fancy of man has painted on it with an almost endless variety? Whence has it all the materials of reason and knowledge? To this I answer, in one word, from EXPERIENCE; in that all our knowledge is founded, and from that it ultimately derives itself. Our

observation, employed either about external sensible objects, or about the internal operations of our minds, perceived and reflected on by ourselves, is that which supplies our understandings with all the materials of thinking. These two are the fountains of knowledge, from whence all the ideas we have or can naturally have, do spring.

The two "fountains of knowl-

edge" are _____

_____.

According to Locke, all our ideas come from:

_____

_____.

THOUGHT EXPERIMENT: MIND SURGERY

In the section above Locke introduces his famous comparison of the mind to white paper. This is often referred to as the doctrine of the *tabula rasa* (blank tablet). Locke argues that all the contents of our mind come from either external or internal experience. By external experience, Locke means experience that passes through the senses; by internal experience, Locke means inner reflection upon the ideas that came through the senses or inner reflection upon how the mind operates. Assume that you agree with Locke and then imagine you can look inward at the contents of your mind and are able to trace several of your ideas to their origin.

What experience, internal or external, might have been your first encounter with the following ideas?

1. Sharing is good.
2. Every whole is equal to the sum of its parts.
3. Every effect has a cause.
4. God is the supreme being.

A possible origin of idea 1 would be _____

_____.

A possible origin of idea 2 would be _____

_____.

A possible origin of idea 3 would be _____

_____.

A possible origin of idea 4 would be _____

_____.

Now argue against Locke. Pick one of the ideas and try to show that it could *not* have come from your experience and therefore must have been innate.

Idea _____ could not have come from my experience because _____

_____

_____ .

Therefore, it must be innate.

3. *The objects of sensation one source of ideas.*—First, our senses, conversant about particular sensible objects [individual aspects of things we know with our senses], do convey into the mind several distinct perceptions of things, according to those various ways wherein those objects do affect them; and thus we come by those *ideas* we have of yellow, white, heat, cold, soft, hard, bitter, sweet, and all those which we call sensible qualities [such as hot, cold, bitter, known by the senses]; which when I say the senses convey into the mind, I mean, they from external objects convey into the mind what produces there those perceptions. This great source of most of the ideas we have, depending wholly upon our senses, and derived by them to the understanding, I call, SENSATION.

Look around your room. What would be some examples of ideas of sensible qualities produced by sensation? (Be careful to limit yourself to sensible *qualities*—that is, the shininess of a desktop and not the desktop itself; before long you'll see why this is an important limitation on knowledge.)

Some examples of sensible qualities produced by sensation in this room would be

_____

_____ .

4. *The operations of our minds the other source of them.*—Secondly, the other fountain, from which experience furnishes the understanding with ideas, is the perception of the operations of our mind within us, as it is employed about the ideas it has got; which operations, when the soul comes to reflect on and consider, do furnish the understanding with another set of ideas which could not be had from things without [outside the mind]: and such are perception, thinking, doubting, believing, reasoning, knowing, willing, and all the different actings of our own minds; which we being conscious of, and observing in ourselves, do from these receive into our understanding as distinct ideas, as we do from bodies affecting our senses. This source of ideas every man has wholly in himself: and though it be not sense, as having nothing to do with external objects, yet it is very like it, and might properly enough be called internal sense. But as I call the other Sensation, so I call this REFLECTION, the ideas it [_____] affords being such only as the mind gets by reflecting on its own operations within itself. By Reflection,

Soul for Lock, and many other philosophers, is a synonym for mind.

then, in the following part of this discourse, I would be understood to mean that notice which the mind takes of its own operations, and the manner of them, by reason whereof there come to be ideas of these operations, in the understanding. These two, I say, viz. [namely], external material things as the objects of Sensation, and the operations of our own minds within as the objects of Reflection are, to me, the only originals from whence all our ideas take their beginnings. The term *operations* here, I use in a large sense, as comprehending not barely [only] the actions of the mind about its ideas, but some sort of passions arising sometimes from them, such as is the satisfaction or uneasiness arising from any thought.

Thus, Locke argues that all our knowledge has one of two origins: external experience (Sensation) or internal experience (Reflection). How would Locke describe each of the following italicized ideas? Underline the correct term in the parentheses.

1. I *believe* (Sensation, Reflection) I see a *blue ball* (Sensation, Reflection).
2. I have the concept of *my existence* (Sensation, Reflection).
3. This *coin* (Sensation, Reflection) is *shiny* (Sensation, Reflection).
4. I *doubt* (Sensation, Reflection) this coin is shiny.
5. I *believe* (Sensation, Reflection) in *God* (Sensation, Reflection).

In the next section, underline the conclusion.

5. *All our ideas are of the one or the other of these.*—The understanding seems to me not to have the least glimmering of any ideas which it doth not receive from one of these two. External objects furnish the mind with the ideas of sensible qualities, which are all those different perceptions they [_____] produce in us; and the *mind* furnishes the understanding with ideas of its own operations. These, when we have taken a full survey of them, and their several modes, combinations, and relations, we shall find to contain all our whole stock of ideas; and that we have nothing in our minds which did not come in one of these two ways. Let any one examine his own thoughts, and thoroughly search into his understanding, and then let him tell me, whether all the original ideas he has there, are any other than of the objects of his senses, or of the operations of his mind considered as objects of his reflection; and how great a mass of knowledge soever he imagines to be lodged there, he will, upon taking a strict view, see that he has not any idea in his mind but what one of these two have imprinted, though perhaps with infinite variety compounded and enlarged by the understanding, as we shall see hereafter.

What is Locke's argument in this section?

Locke argues that _____

_____

_____.

6. *Observable in children.*—He that attentively considers the state of a child at his first coming into the world, will have little reason to think him stored with plenty of ideas that are to be the matter of his future knowledge. It is by degrees he comes to be furnished with them: and though the ideas of obvious and familiar qualities themselves before the memory begins to keep a register of time and order, yet it is often so late before some unusual qualities come in the way, that there are few men that cannot recollect the beginning of their acquaintance with them; and if it were worth while, no doubt a child might be so ordered as to have but a very few even of the ordinary ideas till he were grown up to a man. But all that are born into the world being surrounded with bodies that perpetually and diversely affect them, variety of ideas, whether care be taken about it or no, are imprinted on the minds of children. Light and colours are busy and at hand everywhere when the eye is but open; sounds and some tangible qualities fail not to solicit their proper senses, and force an entrance to the mind; but yet I think it will be granted easily, that if a child were kept in a place where he never saw any other but black and white till he were a man, he would have no more ideas of scarlet or green, than he that from his childhood never tasted an oyster or a pineapple has of those particular relishes [tastes].

T or F: Locke believes children could be born with the innate ideas of black and white.

Underline the following statements that are consistent with points in the section above. (You may choose more than one.)

1. When children come into the world their minds are filled with numerous ideas that they will use in their future.
2. No idea in a child's mind is innate.
3. If a child saw only the colors black and white, the child would have no idea of the color scarlet.
4. Knowing the taste of an oyster and pineapple is compared to knowing the color of black and white.

How does Locke use the example of a child's mind to support his argument about the source of ideas?

_____

_____

_____.

In the next chapter, Locke distinguishes between simple and complex ideas and then examines simple ideas.

Chapter 2: Of Simple Ideas

1. *Uncompounded appearances.*—The better to understand the nature, manner, and extent of our knowledge, one thing is carefully to be observed concerning the ideas we have; and that is, that some of them are *simple*, and some *complex*.

Though the qualities that affect our senses are, in the things themselves,

Underline key points Locke makes about simple ideas.

so united and blended that there is no separation, no distance between them; yet it is plain the ideas they produce in the mind enter by the senses simple and unmixed. For though the sight and touch often take in from the same object at the same time different ideas; as a man sees at once motion and colour, the hand feels softness and warmth in the same piece of wax; yet the simple ideas thus united in the same subject are as perfectly distinct as those that come in by different senses. The coldness and hardness which a man feels in a piece of ice being as distinct ideas in the mind as the smell and whiteness of a lily, or as the taste of sugar and smell of a rose: and there is nothing can be plainer to a man than the clear and distinct perception he has of those simple ideas; which, being each in itself uncompounded, contains in it nothing but one uniform appearance or conception in the mind, and is not distinguishable into different ideas.

How about an easy question? How many simple ideas would a cold, hard, white snowball produce in your mind?

_____ ideas.

According to Locke, though the qualities of coldness, hardness, and whiteness would be united in the snowball, they would produce clearly distinct, simple ideas in the mind.

What would be another example of qualities united in an object, which would produce distinct, simple ideas in the mind?

A table might have the qualities of _____

and _____

and _____.

In the next section, Locke continues his examination of simple ideas.

2. *The mind can neither make nor destroy them.*—These simple ideas, the materials of all our knowledge, are suggested and furnished to the mind only by those two ways above mentioned, viz., sensation and reflection. When the understanding is once stored with these simple ideas, it has the power to repeat, compare, and unite them, even to an almost infinite variety, and so can make at pleasure new complex ideas. But it is not in the power of the most exalted wit or enlarged understanding, by any quickness or variety of thought, to invent or frame one new simple idea in the mind, not taken in by the ways before mentioned; nor can any force of the understanding destroy those that are there. The dominion of man in this little world of his own understanding, being much-what [about] the same as it is in the great world of visible things, wherein his power, however managed by art and skill, reaches no farther than to compound and divide the materials that are made to his hand, but can do nothing towards the making the least particle of new matter, or destroying one atom of what is already in being. The same inability will every one find in himself, who shall go about to fashion in his understanding any simple

Locke is making a comparison. Just as it is impossible for a blind man to have an idea of colors, so it is impossible for

us to _____

_____.

idea not received in by his senses from external objects, or by reflection from the operations of his own mind about them. I would have any one try to fancy any taste which had never affected his palate, or frame the idea of a scent he had never smelt; and when he can do this, I will also conclude, that a blind man has ideas of colours, and a deaf man [has] true distinct notions of sounds.

Which of the following characteristics of simple ideas does Locke describe? (You may choose more than one.)

1. Simple ideas can be mentally combined to make complex ideas.
2. Complex ideas can be reduced to simple ideas.
3. Simple ideas cannot be created by the mind.
4. All simple ideas come from either external objects or internal reflection.
5. Just as a blind man cannot create the idea of color, the mind cannot create a simple idea.

Irony is saying one thing and meaning another. For example, at the start of the *Euthyphro*, Socrates praises the wisdom of Meletus, his accuser, in such a way that we know Socrates is insincere. In the last sentence of the section above, Locke is ironic. What does Locke say, and what does he mean?

Putting Locke's ideas in my own words, he says _____

_____.

But what he means is _____

_____.

Assume an individual is born with brain damage that incapacitates the sense of touch. Take Locke's view and list some of the simple ideas this individual would lack.

_____

_____

_____

In the next chapter, Locke makes some startling claims about the mind and its knowledge. Before we examine those claims, let's summarize Locke's important points thus far.

1. The understanding will be investigated in order to determine what we can and cannot know.
2. Our minds at birth are as empty of information as a blank slate (the doctrine of the tabula rasa).
3. All the mind's ideas come from experience.
4. The mind's experience is either of external objects (sensation) or internal states (reflection).

5. The mind has two kinds of ideas: simple and complex. Simple ideas, like shininess, hardness, coolness, are "uncompounded"; that is, they have only one part. Complex ideas are made of simple ideas.

6. Because the mind cannot invent an idea that it has no experience of, the mind cannot invent simple ideas. Inventing simple ideas would be as impossible as a blind man inventing colors.

How far are you willing to go with Locke? How many of these points are true? Looking at points 2–6, decide your own philosophical position, but be careful you don't agree to something that will get you into trouble later!

In point 2 Locke is (right, wrong) because _____

_____

_____.

In point 3 Locke is (right, wrong) because _____

_____

_____.

In point 4 Locke is (right, wrong) because _____

_____

_____.

In point 5 Locke is (right, wrong) because _____

_____

_____.

In point 6 Locke is (right, wrong) because _____

_____

_____.

Chapter 8: Some Further Considerations
Concerning Our Simple Ideas

7. *Ideas in the mind, qualities in bodies.*—To discover the nature of our ideas the better, and to discourse of them intelligibly, it will be convenient to distinguish them [_____], as they are ideas or perceptions in our minds, and as they are modifications of matter in the bodies that cause such perceptions in us; that so we may not think (as perhaps usually is done) that they [_____] are exactly the images and resemblances of something inherent in the subject; most of those of sensation being in the mind no more the likeness of something existing without us than the names that stand for them are the likeness of our ideas, which yet upon hearing they [_____] are apt to excite in us.

Here is Locke's point. We must distinguish between our idea of a quality and the quality as it actually exists in an object. For example, our *idea* of coldness, which we get from holding a snowball, is different from the actual coldness *in the snowball*. Our *idea* of coldness has something to do with a tingling sensation in our fingertips. But the actual coldness *in the snowball* is not tingling fingers.

Imagine you put your hand into a fire. Make Locke's distinction between the idea of the heat of the fire produced in your mind and the actual heat in the fire.

Locke is saying the idea of heat in my mind involves _____

_____, but the actual heat of the fire

_____.

In the next section Locke further clarifies the difference between ideas in our minds and qualities in objects.

> 8. *Our ideas and the qualities of bodies.*—Whatsoever the mind perceives in itself, or is the immediate object of perception, thought, or understanding, that I call *idea*; and the power to produce any idea in our mind, I call *quality* of the subject wherein that power is. Thus a snowball having the power to produce in us the ideas of white, cold, and round, the powers to produce those ideas in us as they are in the snowball, I call qualities; and as they are sensations or perceptions in our understandings, I call them ideas; which ideas, if I speak of them sometimes as in the things themselves, I would be understood to mean those qualities in the objects which produce them in us.

Thus, ideas are produced by qualities. The quality of heat produces the idea of heat; the quality of roundness produces the idea of roundness—but remembering the earlier point, the quality *in the object* is very different from the idea of the quality *in our mind*.

In the next section, Locke describes the most basic of all qualities, primary qualities.

> 9. *Primary qualities of bodies.*—Qualities thus considered in bodies are, First, such as are utterly inseparable from the body, in what estate soever it [_____] be; such as, in all the alterations and changes it suffers, all the force can be used upon it, it constantly keeps; and such as senses constantly find in every particle of matter which has bulk enough to be perceived, and the mind finds inseparable from every particle of matter, though less than to make itself singly be perceived by our senses: e.g., take a grain of wheat, divide it into two parts, each part has still solidity, extension, figure, and mobility; divide it again, and it retains still the same qualities: and so divide it on, till the parts become insensible [too small to be sensed]; they must retain still each of them all those qualities. . . . These I call *original* or *primary* qualities of body, which I think we may observe to produce simple ideas in us, viz., solidity, extension, figure, motion or rest, and number.

Primary qualities of any object are the qualities it maintains no matter how we divide it. To use Locke's example, if we take a grain of wheat and divide it into ever smaller parts, its parts will always be solid, three-dimensional, have a shape, and be capable of motion. These permanent qualities of an object Locke calls its primary qualities. Describe the primary qualities of this book.

_____

_____

_____.

The next little section has a bombshell.

> 10. *Secondary qualities of bodies.*—Secondly, such qualities, which in truth are nothing in the objects themselves, but powers to produce various sensations in us by their primary qualities, i.e., by the bulk, figure, texture, and motion of their insensible parts, as colours, sounds, tastes, etc., these I call secondary qualities.

Locke now makes a very important distinction between primary and secondary qualities. Primary qualities are bulk (size), figure (shape), texture, and motion; secondary qualities are color, sound, taste, and so forth. *While making this distinction, Locke sneaks in a startling claim.* Eventually, I'll explain his point, but for now what very upsetting claim do you believe he has just made?

The upsetting claim is _____

_____.

Now, read the next five sections very carefully. Locke begins to build a case for an epistemological position that almost all of my students initially find outrageous. Underline key points.

> 11. *How primary qualities produce their ideas.*—The next thing to be considered is, how bodies produce ideas in us; and that is manifestly [obviously] by impulse, the only way which we can conceive bodies operate in.

How do we get the idea of the snowball into our brain? Locke says by "impulse"—that is, by some kind of motion in the object. A modern rephrasing might be to say that, for example, the snowball "emits" roundness and coldness to our senses.

> 12. *By motions both external and in us.*—If, then, external objects be not united to our minds when they produce ideas in it, and yet we perceive these original qualities in such of them as singly fall under senses, it is evident that some motion must be thence continued by our nerves or animal spirits, by

some parts of our bodies, to the brains or the seat of sensation, there to produce in our minds the particular ideas we have of them. And since the extension, figure, number, and motion of bodies of an observable bigness, may be perceived at a distance by the sight, it is evident some singly imperceptible bodies must come from them to the eyes, and thereby convey to the brain some motion which produces these ideas which we have of them in us.

How, according to Locke, do you get the idea of "bigness" or any other idea?

Let us say you are looking at a mountain. Two kinds of "motions" must be involved, one that begins in the mountain and continues in space and another that begins in your eye and continues to your brain. A modern scientist, adding details of the emission of light rays and the operation of nerves in the eye and brain, would agree. A "motion" in the mountain sends particles of light through space and then various other "motions" in our retina and brain interpret the light particles as "bigness." Locke has, so far, said nothing startling.

Continue to underline key points.

13. *How secondary qualities produce their ideas:*—After the same manner that the ideas of these original qualities are produced in us, we may conceive that the ideas of secondary qualities are also produced, viz., by the operation of insensible particles on our senses. . . . The different motions and figures, bulk and number of such particles, affecting the several organs of our senses, produce in us those different sensations which we have from the colours and smells of bodies; e.g., that a violet, by the impulse of such insensible particle, of matter of peculiar figures and bulks, and in different degrees and modifications of their motions, causes the ideas of the blue colour and sweet scent of that flower to be produced in our minds. It being no more impossible to conceive that God should annex such ideas to such motions with which they have no similitude, than that he should annex the idea of pain to the motion of a piece of steel dividing our flesh, with which that idea has no resemblance.

Locke now begins to develop what I called in the introduction his first startling argument. To put it briefly, Locke claims that while primary qualities like size, shape, and solidity are *in* things, secondary qualities like color, smell, and sound are *only in us*.

In Locke's view, the smell of the violet is only in our nose, not in the violet; the color of the violet is only in our eye, not in the violet. Think about this for a moment.

According to Locke, all the colors, scents, sounds, and tastes you think are in the world are *illusions*. The world itself is colorless, scentless, textureless, noiseless, and tasteless. Secondary qualities of color, scent, sound, and taste are produced by the interaction of our senses with the world.

What is Locke's evidence for arguing that our senses produce the grand and continuous illusion of a colorful, scented, noisy, tasty, world?

Consider his example of a piece of steel slicing your finger. Your finger feels pain. The pain is certainly *not in the steel*. Pain is simply the sensation that steel produces in your finger. And just as it would be ridiculous for you to claim that your finger pain is in steel, so it is ridiculous for you to claim that steel color (or any other secondary quality) is in steel. Just as finger pain is produced by your sense of touch, steel color is produced by your sense of sight.

Locke continues to elaborate his position on secondary qualities in the next two sections.

14. *They [secondary qualities] depend on the primary qualities.*—What I have said concerning colours and smells may be understood also of tastes and sounds, and other the like sensible qualities; which, whatever reality we by mistake attribute to them, are in truth nothing in the objects themselves, but powers to produce various sensations in us, and depend on those primary qualities, viz., bulk, figure, texture, and motion of parts, as I have said.

15. *Ideas of primary qualities are resemblances; of secondary, not.*—From whence I think it is easy to draw this observation, that the ideas of primary qualities of bodies are resemblances of them [_____], and their patterns do really exist in the bodies themselves; but the ideas produced in us by these secondary qualities have no resemblance of them at all. There is nothing like our ideas existing in the bodies themselves. They are, in the bodies we denominate from them, only a power to produce those sensations in us: and what is sweet, blue, or warm in idea, is but the certain bulk, figure, and motion of the insensible parts in the bodies themselves, which we call so [sweet, blue, or warm].

Let's go over this startling argument.

Imagine you are holding Descartes's piece of wax. The wax feels cold and solid in your hand, smells sweet to your nose, tastes honeyish on your tongue. You tap the wax on the arm of your chair and hear a tapping sound. You look at the wax and it is yellowish, three-dimensional, and obviously capable of being moved.

Under Locke's analysis you have two kinds of ideas in your mind: ideas that come from primary qualities and ideas that come from secondary qualities.

The ideas that come from primary qualities are *in the wax;* the ideas that come from secondary qualities are not in the wax but are *produced by your senses.* The primary qualities in the wax are its size, shape, three-dimensionality, and capacity for movement. The secondary qualities produced by your senses are the coldness (produced by your fingertips), the sweet smell (produced by your nose), the tapping sound (produced by your ear), the honey taste (produced by your tongue), and the yellowish color (produced by your eye).

If you walk out of the room and leave the wax behind, the wax in itself has no color, taste, or scent. And, according to Locke, the ideas of color, taste, and scent in the mind are no more like qualities in the wax than the idea of pain is like a quality in a piece of steel.

In the next section, Locke offers examples that support his argument that secondary qualities exist only in the mind.

This is not the manna referred to in the Bible but a vegetable substance used in Locke's day for a laxative.

According to Locke, most people would say that the sweetness of sugar is (pick one):
a. a sensation produced by the tongue
b. in the sugar itself.

16. *Examples.*—Flame is denominated hot and light; snow, white and cold; and manna, white and sweet, from the ideas they produce in us. Which qualities are commonly thought to be the same in those bodies that those ideas are in us, the one the perfect resemblance of the other, as they are in a mirror; and it would by most men be judged very extravagant, if one should say otherwise. And yet he that will consider that the same fire that at one distance produces in us the sensation of warmth, does at a nearer approach produce in us the far different sensation of pain, ought to consider what reason he has to say that his idea of warmth which was produced in him by the fire, is actually in the fire, and his idea of pain which the same fire produced in him the same way is not in the fire. Why is whiteness and coldness in snow, and pain not, when it produces the one and the other idea in us, and can do neither, but by the bulk, figure [shape], number, and motion of its solid parts?

You are standing across the room from a blaze in a fireplace. Looking at the fire, you believe the warmth is "in the fire"—that is, the warmth is part of the fire itself. As you move closer to the fire, the warmth changes to unpleasant heat. The unpleasant heat you also believe is "in the fire." Extending your hand closer to the fireplace, the unpleasant heat changes to intense pain. The intense pain, of course, you do not think is "in the fire" but in your fingertips.

Locke's point is that just as you are certainly *right* in thinking the pain is a sensation produced by the fire in your fingertips, you are certainly *wrong* in thinking the warmth is something that is in the fire. Just as there would be no pain without the nerve endings in the skin that register pain, so there would be no warmth without the same nerve endings in the skin that register warmth. *Warmth is just as much a sensation that is produced by your senses as pain.* And if warmth is *produced* by our senses, then so also are all other secondary qualities like color, scent, taste, and sound. The world itself is a colorless, odorless, tasteless, silent place.

Locke drives his point home in the next two sections. Underline his major conclusions.

17. *The ideas of the primary alone really exist.*—The particular bulk, number, figure [shape], and motion of the parts of fire or snow are really in them, whether any one's senses perceive them or no; and therefore they may be called *real qualities,* because they really exist in those bodies. But light, heat, whiteness, or coldness, are no more really in them than sickness or pain is in manna. Take away the sensation of them; let not the eyes see light or colours, nor the ears hear sounds; let the palate not taste, nor the nose smell; and all colours, tastes, odours, and sounds, as they are such particular ideas, vanish and cease, and are reduced to their causes, i.e., bulk, figure, and motion of parts.

What are the *real* qualities of this book?

According to Locke, the real qualities of this book are _____

_____ .

Thus, what are the *unreal* qualities of this book?

According to Locke, the *unreal* qualities of this book are _____

_____.

18. *Secondary exist only as modes of the primary.*—A piece of manna of a sensible bulk is able to produce in us the idea of a round or square figure; and, by being removed from one place to another, the idea of motion. This idea of motion represents it as it really is in the manna moving; a circle or square are the same, whether in idea or existence, in the mind or in the manna; and this, both motion and figure are really in the manna, whether we take notice of them or no: this everybody is ready to agree to. Besides, manna, by the bulk, figure, texture, and motion of its parts, has a power to produce the sensations of sickness, and sometimes of acute pains or gripings, in us. That these ideas of sickness and pain are not in the manna, but effects of its operations on us, and are nowhere when we feel them not: this also every one readily agrees to. And yet men are hardly to be brought to think that sweetness and whiteness are not really in manna, which are but the effects of the operations of manna by the motion, size, and figure of its particles on the eyes and palate. as the pain and sickness caused by manna are confessedly nothing but the effects of its operations on the stomach. . . . Why the pain and sickness, ideas that are the effects of manna, should be thought to be nowhere when they are not felt; and yet the sweetness and whiteness, effects of the same manna on other parts of the body, by ways equally as unknown, should be thought to exist in the manna, when they are not seen nor tasted, would need some reason to explain.

Locke's point about manna is

_____

_____.

Take the example of a carton of sour milk. Looked at from Locke's point of view, the carton has the primary qualities of size, shape, and moveability. Locke would say he was just as positive as anyone else that these primary qualities are actually a part of the carton of milk. In addition, he would be confident that our ideas of these primary qualities are accurate copies of the primary qualities themselves. There can be no difference, he would argue, between our *idea* of the rectangularity of the carton and the *actual* rectangularity of the carton. A rectangle is a rectangle, whether it is in the external or the internal world.

Now, let us say I open the carton and drink some of its contents. I would describe the milk as a white substance that tastes terrible. In other words, I believe the whiteness is *in* the milk and the terrible taste is what the milk produces on my tongue. But Locke points out that just as the terrible taste is not in the milk, neither is the whiteness.

Just as terrible taste is a quality produced by my tongue, whiteness is a quality produced by my eyes. Independent of our tongues, terrible taste would have no existence; independent of our eyes, whiteness would have no existence. If humans had no tongues, we would never attribute terrible taste to sour milk because the taste is not *in* the milk itself; it is a quality produced by the taste buds on our tongues. If humans were blind we would not attribute whiteness to milk because whiteness is not in the milk itself; it is a quality produced by the rods and cones in our eyes.

What am I saying and do you agree or disagree?

You are saying _____

_____

_____.

I (agree, disagree) because _____

_____

_____.

Now let's consider Locke's second startling argument.

Chapter 23: Of Our Complex Ideas of Substances

1. *Ideas of substances, how made.*—The mind being, as I have declared, furnished with a great number of the simple ideas conveyed in by the senses, as they are found in exterior things, or by reflection on its own operations, takes notice also, that a certain number of these simple ideas go constantly together; which being presumed to belong to one thing, and words being suited to common apprehensions, and made use of for quick dispatch, are called, so united in one subject, by one name; which, by inadvertency, we are apt afterward to talk of and consider as one simple idea, which indeed is a complication of many ideas together: because, as I have said, not imagining how these simple ideas can subsist by themselves, we accustom ourselves to suppose some *substratum* wherein they do subsist, and from which they do result, which therefore we call *substance*.

What important points has Locke just made about substance?

Locke is saying _____

_____

_____.

To understand Locke's second startling argument, let's set aside our carton of sour milk and go back to the black mahogany table. (A table is a much more substantial example of substance than milk.)

How could Locke think it would be wrong to say that the characteristics of blackness and shininess reside in the substance of the table? In Locke's view, though I have sense knowledge of shininess and blackness, I have no sense knowledge of the substance of the table underneath the shininess and blackness.

Think about it.

How could I have sense knowledge of something *underneath* blackness? Let us say the top of the table is covered with a black cloth. The only way I could have sense knowledge of what is under the black cloth would be to strip the cloth away. Before I stripped the black cloth off the table, however, the cloth would block all my sense knowledge of the hidden table top.

In the same way, the only way I could have sense knowledge of what is under the black *color* of the table top would be if I could strip the black color away. The black color blocks all sense knowledge of the substratum of matter. *But unlike the cloth . . . I can't strip the black color off the table to see what it hides.* Thus, I can have no sense knowledge of the table's matter.

Do you agree or disagree?

I think you (can, can't) have sense knowledge of the matter under the black color

because _____

_____

_____.

Assume I *could* strip the black color off the table top, perhaps by applying an acid wash. Nothing would be gained. Another color would take the place of black. I could never get down to sense knowledge of the matter underneath *all* color.

Will you admit that we don't see matter, we see only color and assume the matter is underneath?

I believe _____

_____

_____.

Perhaps you want to say that I could just touch the table. Then, I would have sense knowledge of the table's matter. Pushing down on the top of the table, I would feel the hardness of matter.

Before you read my response, what do you think? Would pushing down on the top of the table allow me to feel the hardness of matter?

I would say _____

_____

_____.

The question is really whether I have two pieces of sense information or one when I press on the table top. If I feel *both* matter and hardness, then I have, obviously, two pieces of sense information: I know matter *and* I know hardness. However, if pressing on the table top I feel *only* hardness, then I have, obviously, only one piece of sense information: I know only hardness.

Are you with me? How many pieces of sense information would Locke believe I have when I press on a table?

Locke would have to say you have (two, one) piece(s) of sense information be-

cause he believes _____

_____.

I press my finger on the table. I feel hardness and what else? Frankly, I feel only hardness. Try as I might to feel two things, matter and hardness, only one thing comes through—hardness and more hardness and more hardness. I can't feel the matter underneath the hardness.

Let me try again. I touch the table and focus all my attention upon the patch of skin on my finger. How many sensations do I feel?

The only way I could possibly say that I have two pieces of sense information is to say that I feel matter *being* hard. So let me try to describe two sensations. Starting with hardness, I say it is something resistant to touch, something spread across my fingertip, something "undentable." That's hardness. But now how do I describe matter?

All I can do to describe matter is use *the same words:* Matter is something resistant to touch, something spread across my fingertip, something "undentable."

Every word I would use to describe matter is simply a word for hardness. I have only one sensation, the sensation of hardness, not two sensations, the sensation of hardness and the separate sensation of matter.

I can no more touch the matter under *the hardness than I can see the matter* under *the blackness. Just as the black color kept me from seeing the hidden matter; so the hardness kept me from feeling the hidden matter.*

Try it for yourself.

I look at the wall across the room. The color is _____.
Now the question is, Do I have two sensations or one? Can I see the color *and* the matter under the color or do I just see the color? I must say I have (two, one)

sensation(s) because _____

_____

_____

But let us say, I touch the table I am sitting at. It feels _____.
Now the question is, Do I have two sensations or one? Do I feel the hardness of the table *and* the matter under the hardness or do I just feel the hardness? I must

say I have (two, one) sensation(s) because _____

_____

_____

In the next section, Locke adds more details to his startling argument. (I've divided the section into four parts.)

2. [A] *Our idea of substance in general.*— So that if anyone will examine himself concerning his notion of pure substance in general, he will find he has no other idea of it at all, but only a supposition of he knows not what support of such qualities which are capable of producing simple ideas in us; which qualities are commonly called **accidents.**

[B] If any one should be asked, what is the subject wherein colour or weight inheres, he would have nothing to say, but the solid extended parts: and if he were demanded, what is it that that solidity and extension inhere in, he would not be in a much better case than the Indian before mentioned, who saying that the world was supported by a great elephant, was asked, what the elephant rested on; to which his answer was, a great tortoise: but being again pressed to know what gave support to the broad-backed tortoise, replied, something, he knew not what.

[C] And thus here, as in all other cases where we use words without having clear and distinct ideas, we talk like children; who being questioned what such a thing is which they know not, readily give this satisfactory answer, that it is *something;* which in truth signifies no more, when so used, either by children or men, but that they know not what; and that the thing they pretend to know, and talk of, is what they have no distinct idea of at all, and so are perfectly ignorant of it, and in the dark.

[D] The idea, then, we have to which we give the general name substance, being nothing but the supposed, but unknown, support of those qualities we find existing, which we imagine cannot subsist *sine re substante,* [meaning] without something to support them, we call that support *substantia;* which, according to the true import of the word, is, in plain English, standing under, or upholding.

What is Locke saying in paragraphs [A], [B], [C], and [D]?

Locke's main points in [A] are _____

_____

_____ .

Locke's main points in [B] are _____

_____

_____ .

Locke's main points in [C] are _____

_____

_____ .

Locke's main points in [D] are _____

_____

_____ .

Here is a model that will sum up some of the major points of Locke's epistemology, his theory of knowledge.

accident In philosophy, a term for the nonessential characteristics of a thing. Locke's point is that all we know of a thing, such as a black table, are its nonessential (accidental) qualities, its blackness, not its essential qualities, its matter.

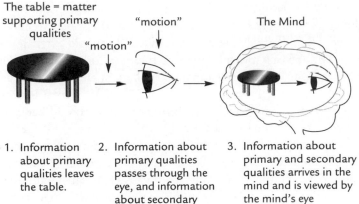

The table = matter supporting primary qualities

"motion"

"motion"

The Mind

1. Information about primary qualities leaves the table.

2. Information about primary qualities passes through the eye, and information about secondary qualities is added by the eye.

3. Information about primary and secondary qualities arrives in the mind and is viewed by the mind's eye (no information, however, about matter is actually viewed).

Now let's go over the model.

1. Beneath the table's primary qualities of size and shape is its matter. This is an important point: Locke believes matter exists. He only argues that we have no sense knowledge of matter.

   A "motion" in the table sends information about primary qualities to the eye.

2. The eye receives information about primary qualities, and, unknown to the naive observer, adds its own sense information about secondary qualities. In the case of the mahogany table, the eye adds sense information about the secondary qualities of shininess and blackness. (Secondary qualities, remember, don't exist in the world.)

3. The mind receives information about the primary and secondary qualities of the table.

   The mind is in danger of believing two falsehoods: the table itself has secondary qualities, and the mind has sense knowledge of matter.

Locke's startling arguments are about these last two issues.

His first startling argument is that the world has no secondary qualities and is, in fact, silent, colorless, odorless, and tasteless. Noise, color, scent, and taste are what our human senses add to the world; these qualities are not in the world itself.

Locke's second startling argument is that we have no sense knowledge of matter. Though matter is underneath primary qualities, these same primary qualities block us from knowledge of matter. We can't see the matter beneath the blackness of the table top; we see only the blackness itself. We cannot feel the matter beneath the hardness of the table top; we feel only the hardness itself.

In the next section, Locke compares matter to spirit (mind) in order to show that it is wrong to believe matter doesn't exist.

As you will see in the next section, Locke believes that simply because we have no sense knowledge of matter, we cannot say that matter doesn't exist. Size and shape are qualities of something (matter) that exists, but exactly what that something is "we know not what."

5. *As clear an idea of spirit as body.*—The same happens concerning the operation of the mind, viz., thinking, reasoning, fearing, which we concluding not to subsist of themselves, nor apprehending how they can belong to body, or be produced by it, we are likely to think these the actions of some other substance, which we call spirit; whereby yet it is evident, that having no other idea or notion of matter, but something wherein those many sensible qualities which affect our senses do subsist; by supposing a substance wherein thinking, knowing, doubting, and a power of moving, do subsist; we have as clear a notion of the substance of spirit as we have of body; the one being supposed to be (without knowing what it is) the *substratum* to those simple ideas we have from without; and the other supposed (with a like ignorance of what it is) to be the *substratum* to those operations which we experiment in ourselves within. It is plain, then, that the idea of corporeal substance in matter is as remote from our conceptions and apprehensions as that of spiritual substance or spirit; and therefore, from our not having any notion of the substance of spirit, we can no more conclude its nonexistence than we can, for the same reason, deny the existence of body: it being as rational to affirm there is no body, because we have no clear and distinct idea of the substance of matter, as to say there is no spirit, because we have no clear and distinct idea of the substance of a spirit.

"Spirit" is Locke's word for mind.

This section is challenging. Read it several times and make notes in the margin.

Summarize Locke's main points about spirit.

Locke is saying _____

_____

_____.

Summarize Locke's main points about matter.

Locke is saying _____

_____

_____.

Now answer several True/False questions about Locke's position in this passage.

1. T F We have no direct knowledge of spirit.
2. T F We have no direct knowledge of matter.
3. T F Spirit does not exist.
4. T F Matter exists.
5. T F Simply because we have no sense knowledge of matter or spirit, it would be wrong to say matter and spirit do not exist.

Now, let's conclude our tour of Locke's *Essay Concerning Human Understanding* with his view of the origin of our knowledge of God.

33. *Idea of God.*—For if we examine the idea we have of the incomprehensible Supreme Being, we shall find, that we come by it the same way; and that the complex ideas we have both of God and separate spirits are made up of the simple ideas we receive from reflection: having, from what we experiment in ourselves, got the ideas of existence and duration, of knowledge and power, of pleasure and happiness, and of several other qualities and powers which it is better to have than to be without; when we would frame an idea the most suitable we can to the Supreme Being, we enlarge every one of these with our idea of infinity; and so, putting them together, make our complex idea of God.

Answer the following True/False questions about Locke's position in this passage.

1. T F We have sense knowledge of God.
2. T F We have an idea of God.
3. T F Our idea of God comes from God.
4. T F We create our idea of God by expanding ideas that come to us from sources other than God.

Now, you are ready to see at what points your epistemology agrees with Locke's. Here is a summary of Locke's position; decide if you agree or disagree and then offer evidence that supports your decision.

1. There are no innate ideas.

I (agree, disagree) because _____

_____

_____.

2. All our knowledge is based on Sensation (knowledge produced by the senses) and Reflection (knowledge produced by the mind's operations).

I (agree, disagree) because _____

_____

_____.

3. Our sense knowledge can be divided into primary qualities (size, shape, weight, texture, motion) and secondary qualities (color, sound, taste, and smell).

I (agree, disagree) because _____

_____

_____.

4. Primary qualities are part of the external world.

I (agree, disagree) because _____

_____

_____.

5. Secondary qualities are produced only by our senses.

I (agree, disagree) because _____

_____

_____.

6. We have no sense knowledge of matter.

I (agree, disagree) because _____

_____

_____.

7. Even if we have no sense knowledge of matter, we can be sure matter exists.

I (agree, disagree) because _____

_____

_____.

8. God exists.

I (agree, disagree) because _____

_____

_____.

9. We produce our idea of God by expanding ideas we get from sources other than God.

I (agree, disagree) because _____

_____

_____.

Locke set out to discover how much the mind can know. What did he conclude? There are at least three consequences of his investigation.

1. Because the mind can have sense knowledge of the primary qualities of objects, then the mind can be somewhat certain of the findings of science.

2. Because secondary qualities are produced by the senses, then the mind cannot be entirely certain of the findings of science.

3. Because the mind has no innate ideas or knowledge of matter, we cannot build grand deductive systems about all of reality like Descartes and the other Continental rationalists.

What is your response to each of these points?

This is a good place to summarize your position on key aspects of Locke's philosophy.

In regard to consequence 1, I (agree, disagree) because _____

_____

_____.

In regard to consequence 2, I (agree, disagree) because _____

_____

_____.

In regard to consequence 3, I (agree, disagree) because _____

_____

_____.

Blunt Questions

My students' blunt questions about Locke usually focus on the two startling arguments. I've found two thought experiments, one about an alien, and another about a powerful video-editing computer, helpful in explaining his position.

Question: Isn't it ridiculous to say that the world has no color? Everything we know with our senses has some kind of color.

Answer: Let's begin by distinguishing between an object's subjective and objective characteristics and then I'll propose a thought experiment.

If you are eating a bag of popcorn, the objective characteristics of the popcorn involve the number of kernels in the bag, the size of each kernel, the amount of butter and salt on each kernel, and so forth. The subjective characteristics of the popcorn involve how "good" the popcorn tastes and smells, whether there is "too much" or "too little" salt and butter, and so forth. The objective characteristics of the popcorn are characteristics everyone can agree upon. The number of kernels can be counted, their size can be measured, and so forth. Objective characteristics are *in the object*. The subjective characteristics of the popcorn are characteristics that vary with individual taste. Some people might find the popcorn too salty; others might find it insufficiently buttery; others might find it just right. Subjective characteristics are *in the subject*.

Now, try this thought experiment: Assume that there is an intelligent alien with senses different from ours. The alien hears different sound frequencies than we do, perceives different light waves than we do, smells scents that we don't. You and the alien (who speaks perfect English) investigate a bag of popcorn.

If you are discussing the popcorn with the alien, the two of you will have no problem agreeing on the number of kernels in the bag. The number of kernels is objective, does not depend upon your senses or the alien's. No matter how unusual the alien's senses, they still won't add or subtract a single kernel from the bag. Nor will you have any difficulty agreeing with the alien on the size of the kernels. If the alien is huge, then it might find the kernels "tiny"; if the alien is minuscule, then it might find the kernels "huge"; but no matter the alien's size or the condition of its senses, the actual dimensions of the *popcorn itself* will not be increased or decreased in the slightest. The size of the kernels is objective, in the object, and does not depend upon the subject's senses. In fact, you will have no difficulty in agreeing with the alien on any objective quality of the popcorn, because all of the popcorn's objective qualities are *in the popcorn*.

However, when you begin to investigate the scent, taste, and color of the popcorn, the alien can legitimately have one view and you can have another. Scent, color, and taste are subjective qualities, produced by the individual's subject's senses. To take just one example, let's say the alien has a cold and its nose-thing is stopped up. You describe the popcorn as having a "buttery scent"; the alien says it is scentless. You are both right. Scent is determined by the subject doing the sensing. However, whether or not either of you has a stopped-up nose-thing, there are still the same number of kernels in the bag. The number of kernels is objective.

What does this have to do with Locke? Translating all this back into his language, primary qualities are objective, in the object. Secondary qualities are subjective, in the subject. Size, shape, weight, texture, and the ability to move are primary qualities, objective, in the object. Color, scent, taste, and sound are secondary qualities, subjective, in the subject. Thus, in Locke's view, whether you're an alien with alien senses or a human with human senses, the *world itself* is colorless, scentless, tasteless, and silent because color, sound, scent, taste, and sound are added to the world by the act of sensing.

Question: How on earth can Locke deny that we have sense knowledge of matter? Matter is everywhere.

Answer: To understand Locke's point, try this thought experiment: Imagine there is a powerful computer that can edit out any aspect of a videotape. Thus, you can program the computer to edit out any particular color, sound, or motion. Now, let's say you make a video of the scene out your window. The tape shows a boy playing basketball. Feeding the tape into the computer, you can edit out the boy, the basketball, the shiny hoop, or any other aspect of the scene.

Let's say you program the computer to edit out only the evidence of matter on the tape. What would you expect to be the result? A blank tape? Nothingness? Blackness? No way. *The images on the tape would remain unchanged*.

Matter is not color, so if the computer edited out matter, all the colors would remain. And matter is not shape. Shape is just a colored location. So all the shapes would remain on the tape. And if all the colors and shapes remain, *then the video would look absolutely unchanged*.

Why?

Because Locke is right. We have no sense knowledge—in this case, no visual knowledge—of matter.

EXERCISE 20.3
Looking at the World Through Locke's Eyes

How would Locke have answered each of the following? Present evidence consistent with Locke's position. Check your answers against the analysis of your philosophical self-portrait on page 510.

1. T   F   Infants are born with knowledge that was not acquired through their senses.

   Evidence: _____

   _____

   _____.

2. T   F   Everyone is born with an idea of right and wrong.

   Evidence: _____

   _____

   _____.

3. T   F   Everyone is born with an idea of God.

   Evidence: _____

   _____

   _____.

4. T   F   Every society, no matter how primitive, has the idea of God.

   Evidence: _____

   _____

   _____.

5. T   F   The mind at birth is empty of all ideas.

   Evidence: _____

   _____

   _____.

6. T   F   When we know an object, such as a table, we know only our idea of the table, not the table itself.

   Evidence: _____

   _____

   _____.

7. T   F   Our idea of an object, such as a table, is an accurate copy of the table itself.

   Evidence: _____

   _____

   _____.

8. T   F   Not only do we have sense knowledge of the qualities of an object, such as the color of a table, but we also have sense knowledge of the matter of an object, such as the matter that contains the color of the table.

   Evidence: _____

   _____

   _____.

VOCABULARY MAP
John Locke

Locke is a **Christian metaphysical dualist.** This means that he holds that all of reality is divided between the realm of the biblical God and the physical universe.

Locke's **epistemology**—his view of the knowledge process—is, as you know by now, **empirical.** The mind at birth is a blank slate that is filled up by information that comes through the senses.

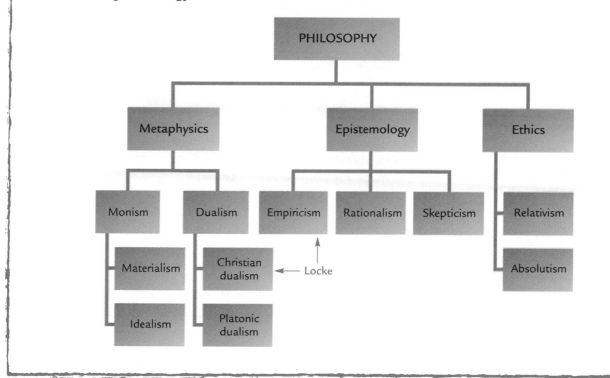

SUMMARY

The British empiricists believe that all knowledge comes through the senses and that we do not know the world, only our ideas about the world. Locke holds that there are no innate ideas. All knowledge comes from external (Sensation) or internal (Reflection) experience. The primary qualities of size, shape, weight, texture, and motion are objective, in the world. The secondary qualities of color, scent, sound, and taste are subjective, produced by the sensing subject. Though matter exists, we have no sense knowledge of matter. God exists; our idea of God is created by expanding ideas we have from sources other than God.

ANALYSIS OF YOUR PHILOSOPHICAL SELF-PORTRAIT

To see how your views stack up against Locke's, read my analysis below, rethink your position, and then circle what you believe is the correct answer. I've underlined Locke's answers.

1. T <u>F</u> *Everyone is born with an idea of right and wrong.*

    In Exercise 20.3, if you personally believe the answer to the first question is False, then philosophical consistency would require that you answer this question False as well. Believing that infants have no innate ideas, you would also believe that people are not born with an idea of right and wrong (or, see number 3 below, with an idea of God).

    If you hold that innate ideas *do* exist, then you are in the camp of Plato and Descartes. Almost whatever you believe in philosophy, geniuses back you up.

2. T <u>F</u> *Everyone is born with an idea of God.*

    Locke probably had René Descartes in his sights when he wrote the opening chapters of *An Essay Concerning Human Understanding*. Descartes, of course, argued that only God's reality is sufficient to cause the idea of God. Thus, we can be assured not only that the idea of God is innate, but also that God exists. Without this argument, the second half of Descartes's *Meditations on First Philosophy* collapses. Beginning with God's existence, Descartes goes on to deduce that we can have legitimate confidence in mathematics, the results of the sciences, and our carefully examined sense reports about the world (because God is no deceiver).

    In Locke's view, Descartes's errors were a major pile of "rubbish" that needed to be cleaned from Philosophy's temple.

3. T <u>F</u> *Every society, no matter how primitive, has the idea of God.*

    Students often claim that every society "believes in God." This is certainly false. Primitive religion, holding that the world is populated by spirits and/or totem animals, has nothing like an idea of a single, all-powerful God; Buddhism, among other religions, has no conception of God. Locke, using neither of these examples, held that societies exist that have no conception of God.

4. <u>T</u> F *The mind at birth is empty of all ideas.*

    Students often argue that infants are born with knowledge because babies have a sucking reflex and other "natural" skills. The question is, of course, whether an instinctual behavior qualifies as knowledge.

    Locke would have said that knowledge is only something one *consciously* knows. For example, he argues that because children and idiots don't consciously know that the whole is equal to the sum of its parts, they do not have an innate idea about the relationship between a whole and its parts. A baby, in the same view, would not have sucking as an innate idea because the baby doesn't consciously know how to suck.

    Modern linguists, like Noam Chomsky, have introduced new evidence supporting the existence of innate ideas by arguing that there is a deep logic "hardwired" into the brain that gives us the capacity to learn language. Thus, Chomsky and others argue that language-acquisition skills are present in every human mind at birth. (See A. Radford, *Transformational Syntax: A Student's Guide to*

Chomsky's Extended Standard Theory, Cambridge University Press, 1988, for an enlightening discussion of Chomsky's position.)

5. <u>T</u> F   *When we know an object, we know only our idea of the object, not the object itself. For example, when we know a table, we know only our idea of the table, not the table itself.*

It's hard to know how to disagree with Locke here. How can we know anything without first having an idea of the thing? This, of course, raises a serious problem. If we know only ideas of things and not things, how do we know our ideas are accurate copies of things? How can we get out of the mind's vault?

6. T <u>F</u>   *Our idea of an object is an accurate copy of the object itself. For example, our idea of a table is an accurate copy of the table itself.*

Locke's exact position on this question is that only our ideas of the primary qualities of the table—its size, shape, and weight—are accurate copies of the table itself. Our ideas of secondary qualities—color, texture, and so forth—are not part of the table but are produced by our senses.

7. T <u>F</u>   *Not only do we have sense knowledge of the qualities of an object, but we also have sense knowledge of the matter of an object. For example, not only do we have sense knowledge of the color of a table, but we also have sense knowledge of the matter of the table that contains the color.*

Locke held that matter existed but was an "I know not what." Many students believe that Locke lacked the nerve to develop his analysis to its logical conclusion. If we have no idea of matter, how can Locke assert that matter exists? Further, if secondary qualities are produced by the senses, then why aren't primary qualities produced by the senses? Isn't everything just an idea?

Berkeley, as you will see in a moment, went eagerly where Locke feared to tread.

Evaluation: Number of points in agreement with Locke = _____ of 7 possible.

A position of Locke's that you strongly (support, oppose) is _____

because _____

_____ .

GOOD BOOKS

Lamprecht, S., editor, *Locke Selections*. New York: Scribners, 1928. A Locke reader that shows the range of Locke's philosophical/political thought.

Priest, Stephen. *The British Empiricists*. London: Penguin, 1990. A helpful overview.

NEXT STOP

George Berkeley out-Lockes Locke.

21

George Berkeley
Inside God's Mind

Two central premises of George Berkeley's philosophy are (1) matter does not exist and (2) what appears to be matter is actually God's ideas. Unlike Locke, who believes that only secondary qualities (color, sound, scent, and taste) are ideas, Berkeley holds that primary qualities (size, shape, motion, and texture) and secondary qualities are ideas. In metaphysics, whereas Locke believes that matter exists as an "I know not what" underneath primary qualities, Berkeley argues that matter is an illusion.

Here is a wisdom game called Refute Berkeley.

Your goal is to show that George Berkeley's philosophy is completely wrong. Destroy his evidence. Smash his conclusions. Reduce his arguments to absurdity. Only by trying your hardest to refute Berkeley will you discover the strength of his cunning proofs.

Of course, to win Refute Berkeley, you'll first have to understand what he's saying. I'll do my best to help you think through his positions and then give you numerous opportunities to destroy his philosophy. Because you might think a competition between you and a famous philosopher would be unfair, at the end of the game you will judge the winner.

Here is the core of Berkeley's philosophy:

- Matter does not exist.

- What appears to be matter is really a collection of God's ideas.

Perhaps after reading these two apparently absurd statements, you feel you'll have no problem winning Refute Berkeley.

How confident are you that you can disprove Berkeley's views?

I feel _____

because _____

_____.

Before you take your first crack at Berkeley, let me amplify his position.

According to Berkeley, matter is an illusion. The matter of this book is an illusion. The matter that you think is your body has no reality. The entire world has no more physical substance than a ghost. In addition, all that appears to be matter is really a collection of God's ideas. The apparent matter of this book is nothing but God's thoughts. God is thinking your body. The entire world is actually inside God's mind. If God stopped thinking, everything would vanish.

What is it like to look at reality through Berkeley's eyes?

I look out my window and see a girl dribbling a basketball, two pigeons on a roof, the snowy slopes of Cherokee Peak.

According to Berkeley, all I know are my *ideas* about external reality, not external reality itself. I do not have direct knowledge of the girl, the pigeons, or

George Berkeley (1685–1753)

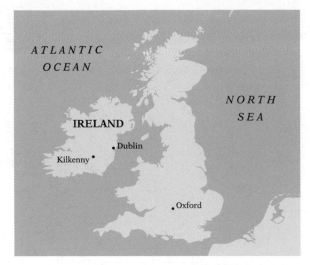

Born in Kilkenny, Ireland, George Berkeley was the eldest of six sons. His parents, who both lived to be almost ninety, were of English descent. While Berkeley was close to his brother Robert, who later had a distinguished career in the church, he greatly disliked his youngest brother, Thomas, who was a scoundrel and a womanizer. When Berkeley learned that some of his money had been used without his knowledge to defend Thomas on charges of bigamy, he was furious. He stated that he would not have spent half the sum "to have saved that villain from the gallows."[1]

---

[1] Quoted in A. A. Luce, *The Life of George Berkeley, Bishop of Cloyne* (New York: Greenwood Press, 1968), pp. 11–12.

At the tender age of fifteen, Berkeley was sent to Trinity College in Dublin, where he studied the philosophies of Locke, Newton, and Descartes as well as mathematics and physics. Although Berkeley was interested in science, he also regarded the scientific revolution, which was in full progress at the time, as the beginning of the decline of philosophical thought.

Berkeley graduated from college at the age of nineteen and a few years later was elected to a fellowship at Trinity. He remained a fellow at Trinity for seventeen years and occupied various positions, including tutor, librarian, junior dean, and lecturer in Greek and Hebrew.

Unlike most philosophers, Berkeley developed his philosophy and did most of his philosophical writing when he was still in his twenties. Berkeley's philosophical writings were not well received, and he soon turned his energies elsewhere. Deciding he wanted to settle in Bermuda, Berkeley and his new wife established a college on the island so that planters' sons and Indians from the mainland could be trained for the Christian ministry.

Apparently Berkeley was very persuasive and managed to convince Parliament to pass a bill allocating funds for the new school. Having also obtained promises of generous donations from members of the aristocracy, Berkeley and his wife set sail for the New World. They took

Cherokee Peak. I only know my ideas of the girl, the pigeons, and Cherokee Peak. Thus, in Berkeley's view, the only real things are ideas. Matter is an illusion.

Having made this startling claim, Berkeley goes one step further. He argues that if God did not exist to think the external world, then all I see would disappear. Everything I am looking at is really a collection of God's ideas. The girl, the pigeons, and Cherokee Peak are not physical, but mental. God thinks all that I see. My ideas are copies of God's ideas.

To aid in tabulating your score in this wisdom game, each opportunity

George Berkeley (continued)

up residence in Newport, Rhode Island, where Berkeley planned to establish farms to provide food for his new college in Bermuda. During his stay in America, Berkeley had a major influence on American intellectual life. He helped found the University of Pennsylvania and also donated land and books to Yale University.

However, his grand dream of a college in Bermuda was not to be. For four years Berkeley waited, in vain, for the money Parliament had promised. Without his presence and enthusiasm, the British government soon lost interest in Berkeley's vision. In 1731 when at last it became apparent that the funds were being diverted by the government to other uses, Berkeley returned to Ireland.

The failure of the Bermuda project left Berkeley disheartened, and an illness that had previously troubled him now became chronic. Although the exact nature of his illness is not clear, it caused him great pain and internal bleeding. He blamed his illness on his lifestyle, lamenting: "Studious persons . . . pent up in narrow holes, breathing bad air, stooping over their books, are much to be pitied. . . . My own sedentary course of life has long since thrown me into an ill habit, attended with many ailments, particularly a nervous colic, which rendered my life a burden."[2]

It was during this time that Berkeley began taking tar water, a mixture of pine tar and water, for his ailments. His gradual recovery convinced him that tar water was the cure for all illness.

Shortly after returning to Ireland, Berkeley was made bishop of Cloyne, where he remained as a cleric for most of the rest of his life. As bishop, he devoted his energy to providing better education, health care (including touting the miraculous healing powers of tar water), and economic opportunities for the poor in his parish. Berkeley was of such popularity that even today, more than 200 years after his death, the people of Cloyne still affectionately refer to him simply as "the Bishop."

In 1753, after moving to Oxford with his wife and family, Berkeley died peacefully on January 14.

Berkeley's first major work, *Essay Towards a New Theory of Vision,* was published in 1709 when he was only twenty-four. His other major philosophical works are *A Treatise Concerning the Principles of Human Knowledge* (1710) and *Three Dialogues Between Hylas and Philonous* (1713).

---

[2] Quoted in A. A. Luce, *The Life of George Berkeley,* p. 25.

to play Refute Berkeley will be numbered in curly brackets. Here is your first chance to play Refute Berkeley. Why is it false to say matter doesn't exist?

Very well. It is false to say matter doesn't exist for the following reason:

_____

_____

_____. {1}

And why is it false for Berkeley to say that what appears to be matter is really a collection of God's ideas?

It is false to say that matter is really God's ideas for the following reasons:

_____

_____

_____. {2}

Now, I'll answer three questions about Berkeley and then guide you through selections from his *Three Dialogues Between Hylas and Philonous*. Along the way, in addition to your usual tasks as a philosophical tourist, you'll get nineteen more chances to play Refute Berkeley.

Here are the three questions:

- What is Berkeley's purpose?
- What is the difference between Berkeley's and Locke's epistemology?
- What is the difference between Berkeley's and Locke's metaphysics?

What Is Berkeley's Purpose?

Bishop George Berkeley was, as you might suppose, a serious Christian. He held that three views current in his day endangered Christian life. The dangerous views were (1) the skeptical belief that nothing could be known for certain, (2) the atheistic belief that all was matter, and (3) the belief that God had no continuous involvement with the universe.

Berkeley, as you'll soon learn in his *Three Dialogues Between Hylas and Philonous,* abhorred skepticism. A good Christian, he held, can be no friend to doubt. Berkeley feared that Locke and others were leading believers in the wrong direction. It seemed a short step from saying that matter is an "I know not what" to saying reality is an "I know not what." Using a unique strategy, Berkeley attempted to counter the skepticism that might spring from the view that matter is unknowable by arguing that matter doesn't exist.

By showing that matter didn't exist, Berkeley would also be able, obviously, to refute the atheists who held that all was matter. Berkeley, as a Christian, had a strong belief in the spiritual, nonphysical world. Followers of Thomas Hobbes, among others, held that matter was the only reality (see Box 21.1). By undercutting arguments for the existence of matter, Berkeley believed he had demolished a stronghold of atheism.

Berkeley also objected to the increasingly popular view of God as architect of an entirely mechanical universe. According to Isaac Newton and many others, God created the universe, set it in motion, and then allowed it to run on its own (see Box 21.2). Such a God would have no continuous involvement in human life. By arguing that the world was a collection of God's ideas, Berkeley changed the image of God from one who designed the universe to one who, by his thinking, continuously kept the universe in existence. In place of a God who stood far off at the beginning of time, Berkeley substituted a God who surrounds and sustains us.

Thomas Hobbes (1588–1679)

Thomas Hobbes was an English political theorist whose philosophy has been briefly characterized as nominalist, materialist, absolutist, and anticlerical.

As a nominalist, Hobbes held that concepts like table, justice, and squareness did not, as philosophers like Plato believed, exist in a realm independent of the physical world, but were merely "names." Most modern people are nominalists; they believe that if there were no tables, there would be no such thing as the independently existing concept of table.

As a materialist, Hobbes held that the proper study of philosophy was limited to physical bodies in motion. In his view, even the human mind was a thing composed of matter and thus operated according to mechanistic laws.

As an absolutist, Hobbes held that because the natural state of human life is "nasty, brutish, and short," individuals must surrender power to an absolute monarch to achieve peace and security.

Finally, Hobbes was anticlerical. He held that the spiritual life of the individual should not be controlled by any church. When Hobbes published his views in *Leviathan,* even his friends were shocked. He quickly gained a reputation as an atheist and heretic.

Now let's get a clearer idea of Berkeley's theory of knowledge by contrasting it with Locke's.

What Is the Difference Between Berkeley's and Locke's Epistemology?

Though they were both empiricists and thus believed all knowledge comes through the senses, Locke and Berkeley strongly disagreed about *how much* knowledge comes through the senses.

Locke, as you remember, distinguished between the secondary qualities of color, sound, taste, and smell and the primary qualities of size, shape, texture, and motion. Secondary qualities are produced by our senses; primary qualities are produced by the world. According to Locke, secondary qualities are merely mental; primary qualities exist in external reality. Berkeley held that secondary *and* primary qualities are mental. Everything we know is an idea. There are no primary, nonmental qualities of size, shape, texture, and motion in the external world. All of Locke's primary qualities, in Berkeley's view, are actually ideas in God's mind.

Note that thus far I have offered a weak presentation of Berkeley's position. I have submitted none of his arguments in support of his view. Why have I presented his position so weakly? To give you a head start in Refute Berkeley.

Keep attacking. Select *one* primary quality (size, shape, texture, or motion) and prove it is correct to say that the primary quality you selected exists in the external world.

One of the greatest scientists of all time, English mathematician and physicist Isaac Newton made important discoveries in mathematics, optics, and physics. He performed groundbreaking researches into the nature of light, invented the reflecting telescope, and was one of the first to discover the central principles of calculus.

In his most important work, *Philosophiae Naturalis Principia Mathematica* ("Mathematical Principles of Natural Philosophy," referred to as the *Principia*), Newton described, among other principles, the law of gravitation. Providing a firm, mathematical foundation for the work of the earlier astronomers Galileo, Copernicus, and Kepler, the *Principia* presented the solution to a wide range of problems from the movement of the tides to the orbits of the planets. Newton remarked, "If I have seen further it is by standing on the shoulders of Giants."

David Hume termed Newton "the greatest and rarest genius that ever arose for the ornament and instruction of the [human] species."

I am looking at an object, _____. If I focus just on its

primary quality of _____, my evidence for its existence in the external

world is _____

_____

_____.

I am positive I know this quality itself and not merely my idea of the quality because

_____

_____

_____. {3}

Now, let's contrast Berkeley's and Locke's theories of reality.

What Is the Difference Between Berkeley's and Locke's Metaphysics?

Locke, as you remember, held that though we have no sense knowledge of matter, matter exists underneath the primary qualities of size, shape, texture, and motion. In Locke's view, we can be certain that matter exists because if matter *didn't* exist as the substratum of the objects we experience in the world, then primary qualities would not exist. If the matter of this book didn't exist, then its primary qualities wouldn't exist.

Berkeley, as you now know, holds that matter is an illusion. He summed up his metaphysics in a short Latin phrase, *esse est percipi,* to be is to be perceived. What does this mean?

Look at these statements:

- To be is to be water.
- To be is to be changing.
- To be is to be unchanging.

You probably recognize these three statements as versions of the metaphysics of Thales, Heraclitus, and Parmenides. These three philosophers tried to describe what it means "to be"—that is, what it means to exist. Thus, when Berkeley says, "to be is to be perceived," he is trying to describe what it means to exist.

Consider Thales. To say "to be is to be water" is to say that water is the essence of all that exists. When Berkeley says "to be is to be perceived," he is saying that "to be perceived" is the essence of all that exists. Thus, just as Thales would assert there is nothing real outside the realm of water, so Berkeley would assert there is nothing real outside the realm of *perception*.

Now let's take a next step in understanding "to be is to be perceived." What does it mean to say that there is nothing real outside the realm of perception? Berkeley would distinguish between two kinds of perception, external (through the senses) and internal (within the mind). While it is not true in the case of external perception that to be is to be perceived, it is true in the case of internal perception that to be is to be perceived.

Consider the difference between my looking at my cocker spaniel Nelly and my thinking about Nelly.

When I look at Nelly, I certainly don't bring her into existence. When I stop looking at Nelly, she certainly doesn't cease to exist. There is nothing about external perception that has anything to do with Nelly's existence. Thus, in the case of external perception, to be is *not* to be perceived.

But what about when I *think* about Nelly? When I internally perceive the idea of Nelly, the idea of Nelly springs into existence. When I stop internally perceiving the idea of Nelly, the idea of Nelly ceases to exist. It is my internal perceiving, then, that makes the idea of Nelly—in fact, any idea—exist. Thus, in the case of internal perception, to be *is* to be perceived.

Now, try your own example. What is the difference between internal and external perception?

> Right now I am looking at an object, _____. If I stop looking at it, then it (does, does not) cease to exist. Thus, in the case of external perception, to be (is, is not) to be perceived. Now I am *thinking* about the same
>
> object. If I stop thinking about the idea of _____, then the idea (does, does not) cease to exist. Thus, in the case of internal perception, to be (is, is not) to be perceived.

Thus, when Berkeley says "to be is to be perceived," he means, to be is to be *mentally* perceived: *To be is to be an idea!*

Do you find that shocking?

All that exists are ideas and minds thinking ideas.

That's precisely Berkeley's view of reality.

At this point you might want to object by saying, "You just said that Nelly, the real Nelly, is not an idea. The real Nelly does not start to exist when you think about her or cease to exist when you stop thinking about her. How can Nelly be an idea?"

According to Berkeley, the real Nelly, the barking, playful Nelly, is not *my* idea. In Berkeley's view, Nelly is *God's* idea. God is thinking Nelly and everything else in the universe.

I look out my window. I see houses, mountains, trees, clouds. All is God's idea. Everything that exists is inside God's mind. To be *is to be mentally perceived by God.*

Here is a diagram that shows Berkeley's picture of reality.

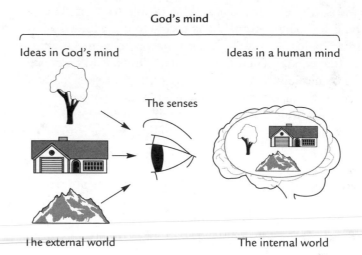

Now, moving from the simpler to the more complex, I'll make several points about Berkeley's picture of reality.

1. All information that we have about reality comes through our senses. Thus, as I pointed out earlier, Berkeley, like Locke, is an empiricist.

2. There are only two kinds of real entities: minds, which Berkeley calls spirits, and ideas. Human minds exist inside God's mind.

3. When a human mind knows things in the external world, it is knowing God's ideas.

4. Just as human minds, by thinking, make internal things (human ideas) exist, God's mind, by thinking, makes external things (God's ideas) exist.

Now play Refute Berkeley again. Pick two of the four points above and present your strongest arguments that each is completely wrong.

First, I'll pick point _____. This is entirely wrong because

_____

_____

_____. {4}

Now, I'll take point _____. This is entirely wrong because

_____

_____

_____. {5}

Here are two limericks by R. Knox. The second one states Berkeley's view of reality.

> There was a young man who said, "God
> Must think it exceedingly odd
> If he finds that this tree
> Continues to be
> When there's no one about in the Quad."

The reply:

> Dear Sir:
> Your astonishment's odd:
> I am always about in the Quad,
> And that's why the tree
> Will continue to be,
> Since observed by
> > *Yours faithfully,*
> > > God

Thus far in my presentation of Berkeley, I have told you only his purpose (to combat skepticism, atheism, and the view of God as uninvolved architect of the universe) and *what* he believes (that matter does not exist and that what appears to be matter is really God's ideas). I have not presented any of Berkeley's arguments supporting his beliefs. At this point in playing Refute Berkeley, you probably believe you have the lead. Get ready for his counterattack. To examine his cunning arguments, we'll turn to his *Three Dialogues Between Hylas and Philonous.*

Berkeley presents a dialogue between two characters, Hylas (whose name comes from the Latin word for matter) and Philonous (whose name means "mind lover"). Hylas argues for materialism; Philonous presents Berkeley's views.

Excerpts from Three Dialogues Between Hylkas and Philonous

HYLAS: It is indeed something unusual; but my thoughts were so taken up with a subject I was discoursing of last night, that finding I could not sleep, I resolved to rise and take a turn in the garden.

PHIL: It happened well, to let you see what innocent and agreeable pleasures you lose every morning. Can there be a pleasanter time of the day, or a more delightful season of the year? That purple sky, those wild but sweet notes of birds, the fragrant bloom upon the trees and flowers, the gentle influence of the rising sun, these and a thousand nameless beauties of nature inspire the soul with secret transports; its faculties too being at this time fresh and lively, are fit for those meditations, which the solitude of a garden and tranquillity of the morning naturally dispose us to. But I am afraid I interrupt your thoughts: for you seemed very intent on something.

HYLAS: It is true, I was, and shall be obliged to you if you will permit me to go on in the same vein; not that I would by any means deprive myself of your company, for my thoughts always flow more easily in conversation with a friend, than when I am alone: but my request is, that you would suffer me to impart my reflexions to you.

PHIL: With all my heart, it is what I should have requested myself if you had not prevented me.

HYLAS: I was considering the odd fate of those men who have in all ages, through an affection of being distinguished from the vulgar, or some unaccountable turn of thought, pretended either to believe nothing at all, or to believe the most extravagant things in the world. This however might be borne, if their paradoxes and skepticism did not draw after them some consequences of general disadvantage to mankind. But the mischief lies here; that when men of less leisure see them who are supposed to have spent their whole time in the pursuits of knowledge professing an entire ignorance of all things, or advancing such notions as are repugnant to plain and commonly received principles, they will be tempted to entertain suspicions concerning the most important truths, which they had hitherto held sacred and unquestionable.

PHIL: I entirely agree with you, as to the ill tendency of the affected doubts of some philosophers, and fantastical conceits of others. I am even so far gone of late in the way of thinking, that I have quitted several of the sublime notions I had got in their schools for vulgar opinions. And I give it you on my word: since this revolt from metaphysical notions to the plain dictates of nature and common sense, I find my understanding strangely enlightened, so that I can now easily comprehend a great many things which before were all mystery and riddle.

In the opening of the dialogue, how does Berkeley set the scene?

The time of day is _____. The weather is _____

_____. The specific location is _____. Hylas has

been thinking about _____.

Though Hylas is not Berkeley's mouthpiece, Hylas does voice Berkeley's concerns about skepticism. Berkeley, as I pointed out earlier, worried about the effect of skepticism on Christian spiritual life. Doubts about important philosophical issues would hardly have a beneficial effect upon a believer's relationship with God.

Philonous, agreeing with Hylas, says he has dropped a number of skeptical and "fantastical" views from his own philosophy in favor of the "plain dictates of nature and common sense."

In the next section, we discover that part of Philonous's common sense is to hold that there is no such thing as matter! (Philonous uses the phrase "material substance" for matter.)

HYLAS: I am glad to find there was nothing in the accounts I heard of you.

PHIL: Pray, what were those?

HYLAS: You were represented, in last night's conversation, as one who maintained the most extravagant opinion that ever entered into the mind of man, to wit, that there is no such thing as *material substance* in the world.

PHIL: That there is no such thing as what philosophers call *material substance*, I am seriously persuaded: but, if I were made to see anything absurd or sceptical in this, I should then have the same reason to renounce this that I imagine I have now to reject the contrary opinion.

HYLAS: What! Can anything be more fantastical, more repugnant to common sense, or a more manifest piece of scepticism, than to believe there is no such thing as *matter*?

PHIL: Softly, good Hylas. What if it should prove that you, who hold there is, are, by virtue of that opinion, a greater *sceptic*, and maintain more paradoxes and repugnances to common sense, than I who believe no such thing?

HYLAS: You may as soon persuade me, the part is greater than the whole, as that, in order to avoid absurdity and scepticism, I should ever be obliged to give up my opinion in this point.

PHIL: Well then, are you content to admit that opinion for true, which upon examination shall appear most agreeable to common sense, and remote from scepticism?

HYLAS: With all my heart. Since you are for raising disputes about the plainest things in nature, I am content for once to hear what you have to say.

Answer these two fairly simple questions about this passage:

1. T F Hylas believes that Philonous's position on matter is consistent with skepticism.

2. T F Both Hylas and Philonous agree that skepticism is to be avoided.

PHIL: Pray, Hylas, what do you mean by a *sceptic*?

HYLAS: I mean what all men mean—one that doubts of everything.

PHIL: He then who entertains no doubts concerning some particular point, with regard to that point cannot be thought a *sceptic*.

HYLAS: I agree with you.

PHIL: Whether does doubting consist in embracing the affirmative or negative side of a question?

HYLAS: In neither; for whoever understands English cannot but know that doubting signifies a suspense between both.

PHIL: He then that denies any point, can no more be said to doubt of it, than he who affirms it with the same degree of assurance.

HYLAS: True.

PHIL: And, consequently, for such his denial is no more to be esteemed a *sceptic* than the other.

HYLAS: I acknowledge it.

PHIL: How comes it to pass then, Hylas, that you pronounce me a *sceptic*, because I deny what you affirm, to wit the existence of matter? Since, for aught you can tell I am as peremptory in my denial, as you in your affirmation.

HYLAS: Hold, Philonous, I have been a little out in my definition; but every false step a man makes in discourse is not to be insisted on. I said indeed that a sceptic was one who doubted of everything; but I should have added, or who denies the reality and truth of things.

PHIL: What things? Do you mean the principles and theorems of sciences? But these you know are universal intellectual notions, and consequently independent of matter. The denial therefore of this does not imply the denying them.

HYLAS: I grant it. But are there no other things? What think you of distrusting the senses, of denying the real existence of sensible things, or pretending to know nothing of them. Is not this sufficient to denominate a man a *sceptic*?

One important difference between Hylas and Philonous is that Hylas believes _____ _____ _____

while Philonous believes _____ _____.

Philonous argues that he is not a skeptic because _____ _____.

PHIL: Shall we therefore examine which of us it is that denies the reality of sensible things, or professes the greatest ignorance of them; since, if I take you rightly, he is to be esteemed the greatest *sceptic*?

HYLAS: That is what I desire.

These questions shouldn't give you too much difficulty.

1. T F Hylas and Philonous agree that a skeptic is one who doubts, as opposed to one who has either positive or negative beliefs.

2. T F Philonous believes there is no evidence to support the laws of science.

Philonous is going to argue, at length, that it is less skeptical and more consistent with common sense to hold that matter *doesn't* exist than to hold that matter does exist.

To prepare for his attack and as your next opportunity to play Refute Berkeley, offer your three strongest pieces of evidence to support the conclusion that matter does exist.

1. _____

_____

_____.

2. _____

_____

_____.

3. _____

_____

_____.

Therefore, matter exists. {6}

Philonous prepares for his assault on the existence of matter by getting Hylas to think about how we know that sensible things (physical objects) exist.

PHIL: What mean you by Sensible Things?

HYLAS: Those things which are perceived by the senses. Can you imagine that I mean anything else?

PHIL: Pardon me, Hylas, if I am desirous clearly to apprehend your notions, since this may much shorten our inquiry. Suffer me then to ask you this farther question. Are those things only perceived by the senses which are perceived immediately? Or, may those things properly be said to be *sensible* which are perceived *mediately* or not without the intervention of others?

HYLAS: I do not sufficiently understand you.

PHIL: In reading a book, what I immediately perceive are the letters; but mediately, or by means of these, are suggested into my mind the notions of God, virtue, truth, etc. Now, that the letters are truly sensible things, or perceived by sense, there is no doubt: but I would know whether you take the things suggested by them to be so too.

HYLAS: No, certainly: it were absurd to think *God* or *virtue* sensible things; though they may be signified and suggested to the mind by sensible marks, with which they have an arbitrary connexion.

PHIL: It seems then, that by *sensible things* you mean those only which can be perceived immediately by sense?

HYLAS: Right.

Which of the following are consistent (C) or inconsistent (I) with Philonous's distinction between "immediate" and "mediate" knowing?

1. C I   You "immediately" read these words but do not have "immediate" knowledge of the information they represent.

2. C I   "Mediate knowledge" of an object comes before "immediate knowledge" of an object.

3. C I   If all we possess is "mediate knowledge," then certainty is not possible.

4. C I   Physical objects are those that are perceived "immediately."

PHIL: Does it not follow from this, that though I see one part of the sky red, and another blue, and that my reason does thence evidently conclude there must be some cause of that diversity of colours, yet that cause cannot be said to be a sensible thing, or perceived by the sense of seeing?

HYLAS: It does.

PHIL: In like manner, though I hear variety of sounds, yet I cannot be said to hear the causes of those sounds?

HYLAS: You cannot.

PHIL: And when by my touch I perceive a thing to be hot and heavy, I cannot say, with any truth or propriety, that I feel the cause of its heat or weight?

HYLAS: To prevent any more questions of this kind, I tell you once for all, that by *sensible things* I mean those only which are perceived by sense; and that in truth the senses perceive nothing which they do not perceive immediately: for they make no inferences. The deducing therefore of causes or occasions from effects and appearances, which alone are perceived by sense, entirely relates to reason.

PHIL: This point then is agreed between us—That *sensible things are those only which are immediately perceived by sense.* You will farther inform me, whether we immediately perceive by sight anything beside light, and colours, and figures; or by hearing, anything but sounds; by the palate, anything beside tastes; by the smell, beside odours; or by the touch, more than tangible qualities.

Philonous's point is _____
_____.

HYLAS: We do not.

This passage, which makes a distinction between "immediate" and "mediate" knowing, is extremely important for Philonous's and Berkeley's entire argument.

What we immediately know is an effect; what we mediately know is the cause. Let's begin by distinguishing between cause and effect and then relate this distinction back to immediate and mediate knowing.

1. I look at the lightbulb in the ceiling. The *effect* that I know through my senses is the light pouring across the ceiling. The *cause* that I have to reason about is the operation of the electricity upon the filament in the bulb,

the power plant that produces the electricity, the water that turns the turbines in the power plant, and so forth.

2. I tap my pencil on the arm of my chair. The *effect* that I have sense knowledge of is a tapping sound. The *cause* that I have to reason about is the weight and density of the pencil, the weight and density of the chair's arm, the force that I used to bring the pencil down on the chair's arm, and so forth.

3. I bite into a piece of chocolate. The *effect* that I have sense knowledge of is the sweet taste. The *cause* that I have to reason about is the collection of ingredients in the chocolate, the way those ingredients operate upon my taste buds, the way the nerves in my taste buds react, and so forth.

These three examples point toward the same concept: I know effects directly through my senses, but I have to reason about causes.

Now I'll translate the distinction between cause and effect back into Berkeley's language.

1. I *immediately* know the effect of the light but only *mediately* know the light's cause.

2. I *immediately* know the effect of the tapping sound but only *mediately* know the tapping sound's cause.

3. I *immediately* know the effect of the chocolate taste but only *mediately* know the chocolate taste's cause.

Immediate knowledge comes to me directly through my senses; mediate knowledge is produced by my reasoning about sense knowledge. Immediate knowledge is knowledge of effects; mediate knowledge is knowledge about causes.

Now offer three examples of immediate knowledge of effects and mediate knowledge of causes. To make your task simpler, focus, as I did, on just one sense (sight, hearing, taste, touch, or smell).

First, I'll take the example of _____. The sense I

am using is _____. The immediate knowledge is _____.

The mediate knowledge is _____.

Second, I'll take the example of _____. The sense I

am using is _____. The immediate knowledge is _____.

The mediate knowledge is _____.

Third, I'll take the example of _____. The sense I

am using is _____. The immediate knowledge is _____.

The mediate knowledge is _____.

Now, let's go back to one of the examples in this passage. I see red and blue in the sky. That's all I see. Just the red and the blue. I *do not* see the causes of red and blue. I do not see all the principles that the sciences of optics, weather, and light refraction would describe as the causes of the colors. My *immediate* sense knowledge is knowledge of red and blue; my *mediate* knowledge is knowledge of the causes of red and blue.

Is it wrong to say, as Berkeley does, that I have immediate sense knowledge of red and blue but only mediate knowledge of the cause of the red and blue?

> It (is, is not) wrong to say you have immediate sense knowledge of red and blue but only mediate knowledge of the cause of red and blue because

_____

_____

_____.

Philonous believes he has established that "sensible things [things known by the senses] are those only which are immediately perceived by sense." In the next section, he continues his exploration of sensible things.

PHIL: It seems, therefore, that if you take away all sensible qualities, there remains nothing sensible?

HYLAS: I grant it.

PHIL: Sensible things therefore are nothing else but so many sensible qualities, or combinations of sensible qualities?

HYLAS: Nothing else.

PHIL: Heat then is a sensible thing?

HYLAS: Certainly.

PHIL: Does the reality of sensible things consist in being perceived? Or, is it something distinct from their being perceived, and that bears no relation to the mind?

HYLAS: To *exist* is one thing, and to be *perceived* is another.

Which of the following are consistent (C) or inconsistent (I) with the passage above?

1. C I If the sensible qualities of a ball are its redness, roundness, and softness, then removing these qualities would leave nothing but the ball's sensible matter.

2. C I This page is nothing but its sensible qualities.

3. C I According to Hylas, if you stop perceiving this page, then this page ceases to exist.

To help you decide if number 3 above is consistent or inconsistent with Hylas's position that "to *exist* is one thing, to be *perceived* is another," consider these two alternatives:

- If the existence of this page *is* identical with the perception of this page, then whenever you look away from the page, the page *ceases* to exist.

- If the existence of this page *is not* identical with the perception of this page, then whenever you look away from this page, the page *continues* to exist.

Decide which of these two is consistent with Hylas's position and you'll not only know the answer to number 3 above but also know which position Philonous argues *against* in the next few sections.

PHIL: I speak with regard to sensible things only. And of these I ask, whether by their real existence you mean a subsistence exterior to the mind, and distinct from their being perceived?

HYLAS: I mean a real absolute being, distinct from, and without any relation to, their being perceived.

PHIL: Heat therefore, if it be allowed a real being, must exist without the mind?

HYLAS: It must.

PHIL: Tell me, Hylas, is this real existence equally compatible to all degrees of heat, which we perceive; or is there any reason why we should attribute it to some, and deny it to others? And if there be, pray let me know that reason.

Hylas's point is _____
_____.

HYLAS: Whatever degree of heat we perceive by sense, we may be sure the same exists in the object that occasions it.

PHIL: What! The greatest as well as the least?

HYLAS: I tell you, the reason is plainly the same in respect of both. They are both perceived by sense; nay, the greater degree of heat is more sensibly perceived, and consequently, if there is any difference, we are more certain of its real existence than we can be of the reality of a lesser degree.

Let us say you are standing in front of a fire. You have the perception of heat. According to Hylas, would the heat be independent of or dependent upon your perception of the heat?

Hylas would hold that the heat is (independent of, dependent upon) my perception of the heat. I would (agree, disagree) with Hylas because

_____

_____

_____.

Philonous next wants to know if the degree of heat changes Hylas's view.

PHIL: But is not the most vehement and intense degree of heat a very great pain?

HYLAS: No one can deny it.

PHIL: And is any unperceiving thing capable of pain or pleasure?

HYLAS: No, certainly.

PHIL: Is your material substance a senseless being, or a being endowed with sense and perception?

HYLAS: It is senseless without doubt.

PHIL: It cannot therefore be the subject of pain?

HYLAS: By no means.

PHIL: Nor consequently of the greatest heat perceived by sense, since you acknowledge this to be no small pain?

HYLAS: I grant it.

PHIL: What shall we say then of your external object; is it a material substance, or no?

HYLAS: It is a material substance with the sensible qualities inhering in it.

PHIL: How then can a great heat exist in it, since you own it cannot in a material substance? I desire you would clear this point.

Philonous argues as follows:

1. An intense heat is an intense pain.
2. The sensible quality of the heat is therefore an intense pain.
3. An intense pain can exist only in the perceiver, not in the fire.
4. Therefore, an intense heat is in the perceiver, not in the fire.
5. Therefore (by extension), sensible qualities are in us, not in things.

Philonous is arguing that a fire isn't hot! And, by extension, he is arguing that all that we think we sense in the world is, in fact, only our ideas. How should Hylas argue against Philonous?

Here is your next chance to play Refute Berkeley. Where is the weakest point (1–5) in Philonous's argument?

The weakest point is _____ because _____

_____

_____. {7}

Note how Hylas attempts to escape from Philonous in the next section by arguing that point 1 above, an intense heat is an intense pain, is wrong.

HYLAS: Hold, Philonous, I fear I was out in yielding intense heat to be a pain. It should seem rather, that pain is something distinct from heat, and the consequence or effect of it.

PHIL: Upon putting your hand near the fire, do you perceive one simple uniform sensation, or two distinct sensations?

HYLAS: But one simple sensation.

PHIL: Is not the heat immediately perceived?

HYLAS: It is.

PHIL: And the pain?

HYLAS: True.

PHIL: Seeing therefore they are both immediately perceived at the same time, and the fire affects you only with one simple or uncompounded idea, it follows that this same simple idea is both the intense heat immediately perceived, and the pain; and, consequently, that the intense heat immediately perceived is nothing distinct from a particular sort of pain.

By "both" Philonous is referring to _____ and _____.

HYLAS: It seems so.

Hylas tries to argue that an intense heat is something different from the pain it causes. Let's go back to the fire and consider the situation from Hylas's point of view and then from Philonous's. You are standing next to a fire. You extend your hand toward the blaze and, before long, feel "a most vehement and intense degree of heat" causing you "a very great pain." From Hylas's point of view, the pain in your hand is one thing, the heat in the fire is another. In other words, you can clearly distinguish between the pain in your fingers and the heat in the fire. The pain is *in* your fingers, whereas the heat is *in* the fire. Despite the pain in your fingers, you believe fire possesses the sensible quality of heat.

Philonous would disagree. When you move your hand toward the fire, you feel only one sensation, finger pain. You do not have two sensations, finger pain *and* heat in the fire. Thus, you cannot say that heat is a sensible quality in the fire. If you know only *x* (finger pain) and not *y* (heat in the fire), then you can make no claims about *y*.

The question comes down to this: When you put your hand near the fire, do you have two sense perceptions or one?

1. Hylas holds that you have a sense perception of heat in the fire *and* pain in your fingers. Thus, you can know that heat is a sensible quality in the fire.

2. Philonous holds that you have only a sense perception of pain in your fingers. Thus, you have no knowledge of heat as a sensible quality in the fire.

Which position is correct?

I believe (1, 2) is correct because _____

_____

_____.

In the next section, Hylas appears to cave in—and then tries to save himself.

PHIL: Again, try in your thoughts, Hylas, if you can conceive a vehement sensation to be without pain or pleasure.

HYLAS: I cannot.

By "vehement" Philonous means intense.

PHIL: Or can you frame to yourself an idea of sensible pain or pleasure in general, abstracted from every particular idea of heat, cold, tastes, smells, etc.?

HYLAS: I do not find that I can.

PHIL: Does it not therefore follow, that sensible pain is nothing distinct from those sensations or ideas, in an intense degree?

HYLAS: It is undeniable; and, to speak the truth, I begin to suspect a very great heat cannot exist but in a mind perceiving it.

PHIL: What! Are you then in that *sceptical* state of suspense, between affirming and denying?

HYLAS: I think I may be positive in the point. A very violent and painful heat cannot exist without the mind.

PHIL: It hath not therefore, according to you, any real being?

HYLAS: I own it.

PHIL: Is it therefore certain, that there is no body in nature really hot?

HYLAS: I have not denied there is any real heat in bodies. I only say, there is no such thing as an intense real heat.

PHIL: But, did you not say before that all degrees of heat were equally real; or, if there was any difference, that the greater were more undoubtedly real than the lesser?

HYLAS: True: but it was because I did not then consider the ground there is for distinguishing between them, which I now plainly see. And it is this: because intense heat is nothing else but a particular kind of painful sensation; and pain cannot exist but in a perceiving being; it follows that no intense heat can really exist in an unperceiving corporeal substance. But this is no reason why we should deny heat in an inferior degree to exist in such a substance.

Before we go further, let's reexamine your position at the end of the last section. Here is a slight revision of the two alternatives with a diagram representing each:

1. Hylas's position: Your hand near a fire has a sense perception of pain in your fingers *and* a sense perception of heat in the fire.

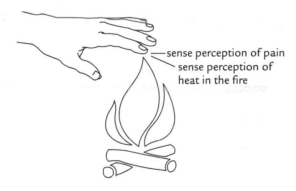

2. Philonous's position: Your hand near a fire has *only* a sense perception of pain in your fingers and *no* sense perception of heat.

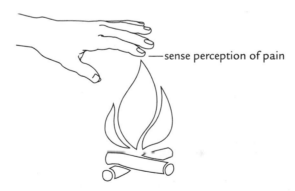

Which picture is correct? Before you answer, note that a very important point is involved in these two alternatives. In the case of position 1, Hylas's position, you know both your immediate reaction to the world (the pain) and the material world itself (the actual heat in the fire). In the case of position 2, Philonous's position, you know only your immediate reaction to the world (the pain)

and nothing about the material world itself (the supposed heat in the fire). Thus, the question is, Do we know any reality but the reality of our ideas? According to the first picture, which Berkeley holds is wrong, we know our ideas and the material world. According to the second picture, which Berkeley holds is correct, we know only our ideas.

Now look carefully at the pictures. Which is correct? (If your opinion hasn't changed, offer new evidence for your position.)

I believe (1, 2) is correct because _____

_____

_____ .

In the preceding passage, Hylas tries to save himself by arguing that he has made only a small error. Hylas holds that Philonous may be right about intense degrees of heat being nothing but intense degrees of pain, but lesser degrees of heat would be different. Lesser degrees of heat would not involve intense pain, and thus one could say that lesser degrees of heat were *in* the fire, not merely in one's sensing of the fire.

Philonous, of course, will not let Hylas escape so easily. Underline the important points in the next section. Note where the argument turns from investigating heat to investigating cold.

> PHIL: But how shall we be able to discern those degrees of heat which exist only in the mind from those which exist without it?
>
> HYLAS: That is no difficult matter. You know the least pain cannot exist unperceived; whatever, therefore, degree of heat is a pain exists only in the mind. But, as for all other degrees of heat, nothing obliges us to think the same of them.
>
> PHIL: I think you granted before that no unperceiving being was capable of pleasure, any more than of pain.
>
> HYLAS: I did.
>
> PHIL: And is not warmth, or a more gentle degree of heat than what causes uneasiness, pleasure?
>
> HYLAS: What then?
>
> PHIL: Consequently, it cannot exist without the mind in an unperceiving substance, or body.
>
> HYLAS: So it seems.
>
> PHIL: Since, therefore, as well those degrees of heat that are not painful, as those that are, can exist only in a thinking substance; may we not conclude that external bodies are absolutely incapable of any degree of heat whatsoever?
>
> HYLAS: On second thoughts, I do not think it so evident that warmth is a pleasure as that a great degree of heat is a pain.
>
> PHIL: I do not pretend that warmth is as great a pleasure as heat is a pain. But, if you grant it to be even a small pleasure, it serves to make good my conclusion.
>
> HYLAS: I could rather call it an *indolence*. It seems to be nothing more than a

By "without the mind" Philonous means "outside the mind."

privation of both pain and pleasure. And that such a quality or state as this may agree to an unthinking substance, I hope you will not deny.

PHIL: If you are resolved to maintain that warmth, or a gentle degree of heat, is no pleasure, I know not how to convince you otherwise than by appealing to your own sense. But what think you of cold?

HYLAS: The same that I do of heat. An intense degree of cold is a pain; for to feel a very great cold, is to perceive a great uneasiness: it cannot therefore exist without the mind; but a lesser degree of cold may, as well as a lesser degree of heat.

PHIL: Those bodies, therefore, upon whose application to our own, we perceive a moderate degree of heat, must be concluded to have a moderate degree of heat or warmth in them—and those, upon whose application we feel a like degree of cold, must be thought to have cold in them.

HYLAS: They must.

Here is where things stand.

Hylas agrees that when we feel the pain of an intense heat or an intense cold, we cannot say that the intense heat or intense cold is *in* an object, because it is absurd to say an object has the feeling of pain. Intense, painful heat and intense, painful cold exist only in a perceiving mind, not in the external world.

However, Hylas holds that lesser degrees of heat and cold do not force him into this position. Less painful degrees of heat and cold can be said to be in the world's objects, since this doesn't involve the absurdity of saying an object in the world feels pain.

Is Hylas right in believing that lesser degrees of cold or heat can be said to exist in an object?

I believe Hylas is (right, wrong) because _____

_____

_____.

In the next section, Philonous mounts an intriguing new argument.

PHIL: Can any doctrine be true that necessarily leads a man into an absurdity?

HYLAS: Without doubt it cannot.

PHIL: Is it not an absurdity to think that the same thing should be at the same time both cold and warm?

HYLAS: It is.

PHIL: Suppose now one of your hands hot, and the other cold, and that they are both at once put into the same vessel of water, in an intermediate state; will not the water seem cold to one hand, and warm to the other?

HYLAS: It will.

For the cold hand, the water will feel _____; for the hot hand, the water will feel

_____.

PHIL: Ought we not therefore, by your principles, to conclude it is really both cold and warm at the same time, that is, according to your own concession, to believe an absurdity?

HYLAS: I confess it seems so.

PHIL: Consequently, the principles themselves are false, since you have granted that no true principle leads to an absurdity.

Summarize the important points in Philonous's argument against Hylas.

_____

_____

_____ .

Philonous's attack on Hylas is based on a classic argument strategy, the *argumentum ad absurdum*. You may recall this technique from our analysis of Gaunilo's attack on Anselm.

The basic idea of the *argumentum ad absurdum* is that if one can show that a belief leads to an obvious absurdity, then the belief is false. Thus, assume someone believed that being outside with wet hair caused sore throats. You could attack this belief by showing that if it were true that being outside with wet hair caused sore throats, then it would also be true that swimming, which involves getting wet hair, caused sore throats. But since it is absurd to say that swimming causes sore throats, it is false to say that being outside with wet hair causes sore throats. You can see the *argumentum ad absurdum* pattern. Someone claims *X* is true. You attack by responding, if *X* is true, then *Y* is true, but since it is absurd to say *Y* is true, then *X* isn't true.

To prepare to understand Philonous's argument, try the *argumentum ad absurdum* technique yourself. Assume someone claims that having a black cat cross your path will give you seven years' bad luck.

Well, if it were true that having a black cat cross your path would give you seven

years' bad luck, then it would also be true that _____

_____ .

But this is absurd because _____

_____

_____ .

Therefore, it can't be true that _____

_____ .

Try it one more time. Assume someone believes the earth is flat.

Well, if it were true that the earth is flat, then it would also be true that

_____

_____ .

But this is absurd because _____

_____

_____ .

Therefore, it can't be true that _____

_____ .

Now, let's look at Philonous's *argumentum ad absurdum*.

Hylas has held that if we have a sensation of warmth or coolness, then there must be an external object that has warmth or coolness. For example, Hylas believes I could reason from the warmth or coolness in my hand to an external object that actually had warmth or coolness in it.

This belief certainly sounds sensible. But then Philonous points out that Hylas's view leads to an absurdity.

Assume that my right hand is hot and my left hand is cold and I thrust both hands into tepid water. Reasoning from the warmth in my right hand, I would believe the tepid water was cold; reasoning from the coldness in my left hand, I would believe the tepid water is warm. But since it is absurd to say that the tepid water is simultaneously hot and cold, it must be false to say that the *sensation* of warmth or coolness is evidence of an *external object's* actually possessing warmth or coolness.

The sensation of warmth or coolness tells us only about the thing *doing the sensing*—the hand—not the thing supposedly being sensed—the water.

Now here is your next chance to play Refute Berkeley. Do your best to show that Philonous is wrong.

Philonous's example of the hot and cold hands is wrong because

_____

_____

_____ . {8}

In the next section, Hylas makes one final attempt to defend his position.

HYLAS: But, after all, can anything be more absurd than to say, *there is no heat in the fire*?

PHIL: To make the point still clearer; tell me whether, in two cases exactly alike, we ought not to make the same judgment?

HYLAS: We ought.

PHIL: When a pin pricks your finger, does it not rend and divide the fibres of your flesh?

HYLAS: It does.

PHIL: And when a coal burns your finger, does it any more?

HYLAS: It does not.

PHIL: Since, therefore, you neither judge sensation itself occasioned by the pin, nor anything like it to be in the pin; you should not, conformably to what you have now granted, judge the sensation occasioned by the fire, or anything like it, to be in the fire.

HYLAS: Well, since it must be so, I am content to yield this point, and acknowledge that heat and cold are only sensations existing in our minds. But there still remain qualities enough to secure the reality of external things.

Let's recapitulate the dialogue thus far.

1. Hylas is arguing that matter exists, and Philonous is arguing that matter does not exist.

2. Philonous, examining only the sense of touch, tries to convince Hylas that touch gives us no sense knowledge of matter. Whenever we have the sensation of hot or cold, we have only the *sensation* of hot or cold and not the additional sensation of a material object *causing* the hot or cold.

3. Thus, our sensation of hot or cold is in us, not in a material object.

4. Therefore, we have no sense knowledge, at least so far as the sense of touch is concerned, of material objects.

Setting aside point 1, which merely states the difference between Hylas and Philonous, play Refute Berkeley and attack either point 2, 3, or 4.

Point _____ is false because _____

_____

_____. {9}

Now, in the passage above, what point does Philonous make about the pin?

_____

_____.

And what point does Philonous make about the coal?

_____

_____.

How do these two points, added together, support the conclusion that we have no sense knowledge of matter through our sense of touch?

_____

_____

_____.

In the next long section, Philonous argues that taste, smell, and hearing give us no evidence of material objects. Make notes in the margin; draw a line across the page wherever Philonous completes an investigation of a sense.

PHIL: But what will you say, Hylas, if it shall appear that the case is the same with regard to all other sensible qualities, and that they can no more be supposed to exist without the mind, than heat and cold?

HYLAS: Then indeed you will have done something to the purpose; but that is what I despair of seeing proved.

PHIL: Let us examine them in order. What think you of tastes—do they exist without the mind, or no?

HYLAS: Can any man in his senses doubt whether sugar is sweet, or wormwood bitter?

PHIL: Inform me, Hylas. Is a sweet taste a particular kind of pleasure or pleasant sensation, or is it not?

HYLAS: It is.

PHIL: And is not bitterness some kind of uneasiness or pain?

HYLAS: I grant it.

PHIL: If therefore sugar and wormwood are unthinking corporeal substances existing without the mind, how can sweetness and bitterness, that is, pleasure and pain, agree to them?

HYLAS: Hold, Philonous, I now see what it was deluded me all this time. You asked whether heat and cold, sweetness and bitterness, were not particular sorts of pleasure and pain; to which I answered simply, that they were. Whereas I should have thus distinguished:—those qualities, as perceived by us, are pleasures or pains; but not as existing in the external objects. We must not therefore conclude absolutely, that there is no heat in the fire, or sweetness in the sugar, but only that heat or sweetness, as perceived by us, are not in the fire or sugar. What say you to this?

PHIL: I say it is nothing to the purpose. Our discourse proceeded altogether concerning sensible things, which you defined to be, the things we *immediately perceive by our senses*. Whatever other qualities, therefore, you speak of as distinct from these, I know nothing of them, neither do they at all belong to the point in dispute. You may, indeed, pretend to have discovered certain qualities which you do not perceive, and assert those insensible qualities exist in fire and sugar. But what use can be made of this to your present purpose, I am at a loss to conceive. Tell me then once more, do you acknowledge that heat and cold, sweetness and bitterness (meaning those qualities which are perceived by the senses), do not exist without the mind?

HYLAS: I see it is to no purpose to hold out, so I give up the cause as to those mentioned qualities. Though I profess it sounds oddly, to say that sugar is not sweet.

PHIL: But, for your farther satisfaction, take this along with you: that which at other times seems sweet, shall, to a distempered palate, appear bitter. And, nothing can be plainer than that [diverse] persons perceive different tastes in the same food; since that which one man delights in, another abhors. And how could this be, if the taste was something really inherent in the food?

HYLAS: I acknowledge I know not how.

PHIL: In the next place, *odours* are to be considered. And, with regard to these, I would fain [gladly] know whether what hath been said of tastes does not exactly agree to them? Are they not so many pleasing or displeasing sensations?

HYLAS: They are.

PHIL: Can you then conceive it possible that they should exist in an unperceiving thing?

HYLAS: I cannot.

PHIL: Or, can you imagine that filth and ordure affect those brute animals that feed on them out of choice, with the same smells which we perceive in them?

HYLAS: By no means.

Philonous is arguing that because the same food can taste differently to different people, therefore, _____

_____

_____

_____

_____.

PHIL: May we not therefore conclude of smells, as of the other forementioned qualities, that they cannot exist in any but a perceiving substance or mind?

HYLAS: I think so.

PHIL: Then as to *sounds*, what must we think of them: are they accidents really inherent in external bodies, or not?

HYLAS: That they inhere not in the sonorous bodies is plain from hence: because a bell struck in the exhausted receiver of an air-pump sends forth no sound. The air, therefore, must be thought the subject of sound.

PHIL: What reason is there for that, Hylas?

HYLAS: Because, when any motion is raised in the air, we perceive a sound greater or lesser, according to the air's motion; but without some motion in the air, we never hear any sound at all.

PHIL: And granting that we never hear a sound but when some motion is produced in the air, yet I do not see how you can infer from thence, that the sound itself is in the air.

HYLAS: It is this very motion in the external air that produces in the mind the sensation of *sound*. For, striking on the drum of the ear, it causes a vibration, which by the auditory nerves being communicated to the brain, the soul is thereupon affected with the sensation called *sound*.

PHIL: What! Is sound then a sensation?

HYLAS: I tell you, as perceived by us, it is a particular sensation in the mind.

PHIL: And can any sensation exist without the mind?

HYLAS: No, certainly.

PHIL: How then can sound, being a sensation, exist in the air, if by the *air* you mean a senseless substance existing without the mind?

HYLAS: You must distinguish, Philonous, between sound as it is perceived by us, and as it is in itself; or (which is the same thing) between the sound we immediately perceive, and that which exists without us. The former, indeed, is a particular kind of sensation, but the latter is merely a vibrative or undulatory [wavelike] motion in the air.

PHIL: I thought I had already obviated that distinction, by the answer I gave when you were applying it in a like case before. But, to say no more of that, are you sure then that sound is really nothing but motion?

HYLAS: I am.

PHIL: Whatever therefore agrees to real sound, may with truth be attributed to motion?

HYLAS: It may.

PHIL: It is then good sense to speak of *motion* as a thing that is *loud, sweet, acute,* or *grave.*

HYLAS: I see you are resolved not to understand me. Is it not evident those accidents or modes belong only to sensible sound, or *sound* in the common acceptation of the word, but not to *sound* in the real and philosophic sense; which, as I just now told you, is nothing but a certain motion of the air?

PHIL: It seems then there are two sorts of sound—the one vulgar, or that which is heard, the other philosophical and real?

HYLAS: Even so.

PHIL: And the latter consists in motion?

HYLAS: I told you so before.

By "former" Hylas refers to

_____ ;

by "latter" Hylas refers to

_____ .

PHIL: Tell me, Hylas, to which of the senses, think you, the idea of motion belongs? To the hearing?

HYLAS: No, certainly; but to the sight and touch.

PHIL: It should follow then, that, according to you, real sounds may possibly be *seen* or *felt,* but never *heard.*

HYLAS: Look you, Philonous, you may, if you please, make a jest of my opinion, but that will not alter the truth of things. I own, indeed, the inferences you draw me into sound something oddly, but common language, you know, is framed by, and for the use of the vulgar: we must not therefore wonder if expressions adapted to exact philosophic notions seem uncouth and out of the way.

Hylas accuses Phil of making the "jest," joke, that _____

_____

_____ .

PHIL: Is it come to that? I assure you, I imagine myself to have gained no small point, since you make so light of departing from common phrases and opinions; it being a main part of our inquiry, to examine whose notions are widest of the common road, and the most repugnant to the general sense of the world. But, can you think it no more than a philosophical paradox, to say that *real sounds are never heard,* and that the idea of them is obtained by some other sense? And is there nothing in this contrary to nature and the truth of things?

HYLAS: To deal ingenuously [openly], I do not like it. And, after the concessions already made, I had as well grant that sounds too have no real being without the mind.

Philonous's attack on the senses of taste and smell is similar to his attack on the sense of touch. Summarize his key points.

Philonous argues that the sense of taste gives us no evidence of matter because

_____

_____

_____ .

Philonous argues that the sense of smell gives us no evidence of matter because

_____

_____

_____ .

Now, let's investigate together some of what Philonous says about the sense of sound.

Hylas wants to distinguish between the sound as we hear it and the sound as it exists in the air. The sound as we hear it is a sensation in our ear; the sound as it exists in the air is a "motion." According to Hylas, the motion in the air is the *actual* sound, the "sound in the real and philosophic sense." Philonous, however, neatly trips him up by pointing out that motion is something that is known by touch or sight. Thus, Hylas is led to the absurdity of holding that the "real" sound is known not by hearing but by sight or touch. This would be as strange as saying that "real" colors are known by smell or that "real" scents are known by hearing.

To get clearer on the difference between the positions of Hylas and Philonous, consider how they would analyze the famous problem of the tree falling in the forest. If there is no one to hear the tree fall, does it make a sound?

Hylas would say the tree (does, does not) make a sound because

_____

_____

_____.

Philonous would say we have no evidence of the tree itself making a sound because

_____

_____

_____.

In the next section, Hylas and Philonous examine the sense of sight.

PHIL: And I hope you will make no difficulty to acknowledge the same of colours.

HYLAS: Pardon me: the case of colours is very different. Can anything be plainer than that we see them on the objects?

PHIL: The objects you speak of are I suppose, corporeal substances existing without the mind?

HYLAS: They are.

PHIL: And have true and real colours inhering in them?

HYLAS: Each visible object hath that colour which we see in it.

PHIL: How! Is there anything visible but what we perceive by sight?

HYLAS: There is not.

PHIL: And, do we perceive anything by sense which we do not perceive immediately?

HYLAS: How often must I be obliged to repeat the same thing? I tell you, we do not.

PHIL: Have patience, good Hylas; and tell me once more, whether there is anything immediately perceived by the senses, except sensible qualities. I know you asserted there was not; but I would now be informed, whether you still persist in the same opinion.

HYLAS: I do.

PHIL: Pray, is your corporeal substance either a sensible quality, or made up of sensible qualities?

HYLAS: What a question that is! Who ever thought it was?

PHIL: My reason for asking was, because in saying, *each visible object hath that colour which we see in it,* you make visible objects to be corporeal substances; which implies either that corporeal substances are sensible qualities, or else that there is something besides sensible qualities perceived by sight: but, as this point was formerly agreed between us, and is still maintained by you, it is a clear consequence, that your corporeal substance is nothing distinct from sensible qualities.

HYLAS: You may draw as many absurd consequences as you please, and endeavour to perplex the plainest things; but you shall never persuade me out of my senses. I clearly understand my own meaning.

PHIL: I wish you would make me understand it too. But, since you are unwilling to have your notion of corporeal substance examined, I shall urge that point no farther. Only be pleased to let me know, whether the same colours which we see exist in external bodies, or some other.

HYLAS: The very same.

PHIL: What! Are then the beautiful red and purple we see on yonder clouds really in them? Or do you imagine, they have in themselves any other form than that of a dark mist or vapor?

HYLAS: I must own, Philonous, those colours are not really in the clouds as they seem to be at this distance. They are only apparent colours.

PHIL: *Apparent* call you them? How shall we distinguish these apparent colours from real?

HYLAS: Very easily. Those are to be thought apparent which, appearing only at a distance, vanish upon a nearer approach.

PHIL: And those, I suppose, are to be thought real which are discovered by the most near and exact survey.

HYLAS: Right.

Answer the following questions about this passage on sight.

1. T F Hylas holds that color is an internal, not an external, phenomenon.
2. T F Hylas agrees with Philonous that there are some sensible qualities that are not immediately perceived by the senses.
3. T F Hylas believes that real colors are actually part of external objects but apparent colors are not.
4. T F Hylas believes that corporeal substance is not made up of sensible qualities.

To help you answer question 4 above, consider the following: By "corporeal substance," Hylas and Philonous mean matter. The question is, of course, does matter have an external existence? Let's, recalling Descartes, look at a cube of wax. When the wax is cold, two of its sensible qualities are its hardness and dark-brown color. If I heat the wax, it becomes soft and light brown. Common sense would say that the sensible qualities change but the wax itself, the corporeal substance of the wax itself, remains the same. To answer question 4 above, decide if Hylas would support or oppose this commonsense view.

In the next section, Philonous asks Hylas to consider color microscopically.

PHIL: Is the nearest and exactest survey made by the help of a microscope, or by the naked eye?

HYLAS: By a microscope, doubtless.

PHIL: But a microscope often discovers colours in an object different from those perceived by the unassisted sight. And, in case we had microscopes magnifying to any assigned degree, it is certain that no object whatsoever, view through them, would appear in the same colour which it exhibits to the naked eye.

HYLAS: And what will you conclude from all this? You cannot argue that there are really and naturally no colours on objects: because by artificial managements they may be altered, or made to vanish.

PHIL: I think it may evidently be concluded from your own concessions, that all the colours we see with our naked eyes are only apparent as those on the clouds, since they vanish upon a more close and accurate inspection which is afforded us by a microscope. Then, as to what you say by way of prevention: I ask you whether the real and natural state of an object is better discovered by a very sharp and piercing sight, or by one which is less sharp?

HYLAS: By the former without doubt.

PHIL: Is it not plain from *Dioptrics* that microscopes make the sight more penetrating, and represent objects as they would appear to the eye in case it were naturally endowed with a most exquisite sharpness?

HYLAS: It is.

PHIL: Consequently the microscopical representation is to be thought that which best sets forth the real nature of the thing, or what it is in itself. The colours, therefore, by it perceived are more genuine and real than those perceived otherwise.

HYLAS: I confess there is something in what you say.

Underline the most important points Philonous makes in this paragraph.

PHIL: Besides, it is not only possible but manifest [obvious], that there actually are animals whose eyes are by nature framed to perceive those things which by reason of their minuteness escape our sight. What think you of those inconceivably small animals perceived by glasses? Must we suppose they are all stark blind? Or, in case they see, can it be imagined their sight hath not the same use in preserving their bodies from injuries, which appears in that of all other animals? And if it hath, is it not evident they must see particles less than their own bodies; which will present them with a far different view in each object from that which strikes our senses? Even our own eyes do not always represent objects to us after the same manner. In the jaundice every one knows that all things seem yellow. Is it not therefore highly probable those animals in whose eyes we discern a very different texture from that of ours, and whose bodies abound with different humors, do not see the same colours in every object that we do? From all which, should it not seem to follow that all colours are equally apparent, and that none of those which we perceive are really inherent in any outward object?

HYLAS: It should.

PHIL: The point will be past all doubt, if you consider that, in case colours were real properties or affections inherent in external bodies, they could admit of no alteration without some change wrought in the very bodies themselves; but, is it not evident from what hath been said that, upon the use of microscopes, upon a change happening in the humors of the eye, or a variation of distance, without any manner of real alteration in the thing itself, the colours of any object are either changed, or totally disappear? Nay, all other circumstances remaining the same, change but the situation of some objects, and they shall present different colours to the eye. The same thing happens upon viewing an object in various degrees of light. And what is more known than that the same bodies appear differently colored by candlelight from what they do in the open day? Add to these the experiment of a prism which, separating the heterogeneous rays of light, alters the colour of any object, and will cause the whitest to appear of a deep blue or red to the naked eye. And now tell me whether you are still of opinion that every body hath its true real colour inhering in it; and, if you think it hath, I would fain know farther from you, what certain distance and position of the object, what peculiar texture and formation of the eye, what degree or kind of light is necessary for ascertaining that true colour, and distinguishing it from apparent ones.

Philonous is arguing that colors are not in external bodies. Which of the following positions are consistent (C) or inconsistent (I) with his views?

1. C   I   According to Philonous, what Hylas terms real colors are no more real than what Hylas terms apparent colors.

2. C   I   According to Philonous, what Hylas terms real colors change at closer inspection.

3. C   I   According to Philonous, if real colors actually existed, a microscopic investigation of them would be less accurate than inspection by the naked eye.

4. C   I   According to Philonous, because "inconceivably small animals" see objects differently than we do, we must assume that the sensible characteristics of objects, including their color, are determined by the observer and are not in the objects themselves.

5. C   I   According to Philonous, if colors were inherent in external bodies, then the colors would remain the same no matter the position or size of the observer.

6. C   I   According to Philonous, the color of an object is independent of the kind of light shining on the object.

What point is Philonous making in the last sentence of the preceding selection?

Philonous is arguing that _____

_____

_____.

In the next section, Hylas tries to escape from Philonous's objections by arguing that light is the source of external color (and not the observer's eye, as Philonous has argued).

HYLAS: I own myself entirely satisfied, that they are all equally apparent, and that there is no such thing as colour really inhering in external bodies, but that it is altogether in the light. And what confirms me in this opinion is, that in proportion to the light colours are still more or less vivid; and if there be no light, then are there no colours perceived. Besides, allowing there are colours on external objects, yet, how is it possible for us to perceive them? For no external body affects the mind, unless it acts first on our organs of sense. But the only action of bodies is motion; and motion cannot be communicated otherwise than by impulse. A distant object therefore cannot act on the eye, nor consequently make itself or its properties perceivable to the soul. Whence it plainly follows that it is immediately some contiguous substance, which, operating on the eye, occasions a perception of colours: and such is light.

Hylas is arguing that _____

_____

_____

_____.

PHIL: How! Is light then a substance?

HYLAS: I tell you, Philonous, external light is nothing but a thin fluid substance, whose minute particles being agitated with a brisk motion, and in various manners reflected from the different surfaces of outward objects to the eyes, communicate different motions to the optic nerves; which, being propagated to the brain, cause therein various impressions; and these are attended with the sensations of red, blue, yellow, etc.

PHIL: It seems then the light does no more than shake the optic nerves.

HYLAS: Nothing else.

PHIL: And consequent to each particular motion of the nerves, the mind is affected with a sensation, which is some particular colour.

HYLAS: Right.

PHIL: And these sensations have no existence without the mind.

HYLAS: They have not.

PHIL: How then do you affirm that colours are in the light; since by light you understand a corporeal substance external to the mind.

HYLAS: Light and colours, as immediately perceived by us, I grant cannot exist without the mind. But in themselves they are only the motions and configurations of certain insensible particles of matter.

PHIL: Colours then, in the vulgar sense, or taken for the immediate objects of sight, cannot agree to any but a perceiving substance.

HYLAS: That is what I say.

PHIL: Well then, since you give up the point as to those sensible qualities which are alone thought colours by all mankind beside, you may hold what you please with regard to those invisible ones of the philosophers. It is not my business to dispute about them; only I would advise you to bethink yourself, whether, considering the inquiry we are upon, it be prudent for you to affirm—*the red and blue which we see are not real colours, but certain unknown motions and figures which no man ever did or can see are truly so.* Are not these shocking notions, and are not they subject to as many ridiculous inferences, as those you were obliged to renounce before in the case of sounds?

At this point it might be useful to recapitulate some of Philonous's arguments about color.

1. If the red and blue tints in clouds are not real colors because these colors change when inspected more closely, then all colors are not real because all colors change when inspected more closely (microscopically).

2. If external objects have colors actually inherent in them, then these colors should be the same for all observers, no matter the size or position of the observer. Microscopic animals, who have a different size and position than we do, must see colors differently than we do; thus, colors are determined by the observer and are not in external objects.

3. If real colors are different from apparent colors, then there should be some "right" quality of light, some "right" condition of the observer's eye, some "right" distance from the object that allows us to distinguish between real and apparent colors. But there is no "right" quality of light, condition of the observer's eye, or distance from the object. Thus, real colors have no more reality than apparent colors.

Note that each of these positions argues that colors are not in external objects. Play Refute Berkeley again and show that Philonous is wrong. Destroy every argument above.

Very well. Argument 1 is wrong because _____ _____

_____

_____. {10}

Argument 2 is wrong because _____

_____

_____. {11}

Argument 3 is wrong because _____

_____

_____. {12}

In the passage above, Hylas tries to escape from Philonous by arguing that while color and light are not external objects themselves, there *are* still external objects, "insensible particles of matter" that create the sensations of light and color by "shaking" the optic nerve. Hylas, of course, is in a difficult position. He is proposing the existence of material entities that are so nebulous and uncertain that, as Philonous points out, "no man ever did or can see" them.

Hylas, under Philonous's attack, has steadily retreated. Hylas first held that the sense of touch gave us evidence of matter but then abandoned this position because the only sensations we feel in touch—like heat, cold, and pain—cannot be said to be *in* matter. To review, Philonous's argument is clearest when considering the sensation of pain.

If I am blindfolded and a pin is stuck in my finger, then I know nothing about the pin itself. My only sense knowledge is pain. Pain is only information about what is happening to my finger, not information about the pin itself; thus, I have no sense knowledge of the pin itself.

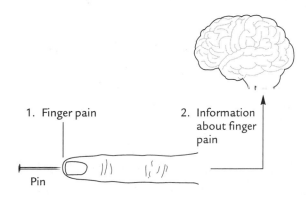

1. Finger pain

2. Information about finger pain

Pin

Note that the only sensation relayed to the brain is information about finger pain, not information about the pin. And since finger pain is not, of course, in the pin, but only in the nerves in the finger, finger pain provides no information about the pin. The only reality we know consists of ideas—in this case, the idea of finger pain. We have no information about matter—in this case, the pin.

Under attack by a similar argument, Hylas abandoned his position on both taste and smell. Philonous pointed out that tastes and smells are conditions produced by our senses and are not in matter. This point is made especially clear by Philonous's example of "brute animals" who feed on things that smell "offensive" to us. If the offensive smell was really *in* the object, then the animals would, like us, be repulsed by it. But what smells awful to us smells scrumptious to some animals. Thus, the smell is determined not by the object but by the one doing the smelling. Smell is not in the smellee but in the smeller.

Hylas next turned his attention to sounds and tried to distinguish between "real" sound and sound in the ear. Real sound, according to Hylas, was a "motion" in the air. But Philonous refuted this position by using an *argumentum ad absurdum*. If it were true that real sound is motion in the air, then it would be true that sound would be visible and not audible. But since it is absurd to say sound is visible and not audible it must be false to say that the real sound is a motion in the air.

Hylas next turned his attention to color, with the results described above. What will be his next move?

In the next section, Hylas runs to Locke.

HYLAS: I frankly own, Philonous, that it is in vain to stand out any longer. Colours, sounds, tastes, in a word all those termed *secondary qualities*, have certainly no existence without the mind. But by this acknowledgment I must not be supposed to derogate anything from the reality of matter, or external objects; seeing it is no more than several philosophers maintain, who nevertheless are the farthest imaginable from denying matter. For the clearer understanding of this, you must know sensible qualities are by philosophers divided into *primary* and *secondary*. The former are extension, figure, solidity, gravity, motion, and rest; and these they hold exist really in bodies. The latter are those above enumerated; or, briefly, all sensible qualities beside the primary; which they assert are only so many sensations or ideas existing nowhere but in the mind. But all this, I doubt not, you are apprised of. For my part, I have been a long time sensible there was such an opinion current among philosophers, but was never thoroughly convinced of its truth until now.

According to Hylas, the primary qualities of this book would be _____ _____ .

The secondary qualities of this book would be _____ _____ .

According to Hylas, (primary, secondary) qualities reside in the book because _____ _____ _____ .

Hylas's position is, of course, Locke's position, which now gives Berkeley, via Philonous, a chance to refute Locke.

PHIL: You are still then of opinion that extension and figures are inherent in external unthinking substances?

By "extension and figures," Phil means "occupying space and having a shape."

HYLAS: I am.

PHIL: But what if the same arguments which are brought against secondary qualities will hold good against these also?

HYLAS: Why then I shall be obliged to think, they too exist only in the mind.

PHIL: Is it your opinion the very figure and extension which you perceive by sense exist in the outward object or material substance?

HYLAS: It is.

PHIL: Have all other animals as good grounds to think the same of the figure and extension which they see and feel?

HYLAS: Without doubt, if they have any thought at all.

PHIL: Answer me, Hylas. Think you the senses were bestowed upon all animals for their preservation and well-being in life? Or were they given to men alone for this end?

HYLAS: I make no question but they have the same use in all other animals.

PHIL: If so, is it not necessary they should be enabled by them to perceive their own limbs, and those bodies which are capable of harming them?

HYLAS: Certainly.

PHIL: A mite therefore must be supposed to see his own foot, and things equal or even less than it, as bodies of some considerable dimension, though at the same time they appear to you scarce discernible, or at best as so many visible points?

HYLAS: I cannot deny it.

PHIL: And to creatures less than the mite they will seem yet larger?

HYLAS: They will.

PHIL: Insomuch that what you can hardly discern will to another extremely minute animal appear as some huge mountain?

HYLAS: All this I grant.

PHIL: Can one and the same thing be at the same time in itself of different dimensions?

HYLAS: That were absurd to imagine.

PHIL: But, from what you have laid down it follows that both the extension by you perceived, and that perceived by the mite itself, as likewise all those perceived by lesser animals, are each of them the true extension of the mite's foot; that is to say, by your own principles you are led into an absurdity.

HYLAS: There seems to be some difficulty in the point.

Summarize Philonous's argument against Hylas.

Philonous argues that _____

_____

_____

_____.

PHIL: Again, have you not acknowledged that no real inherent property of any object can be changed without some change in the thing itself?

HYLAS: I have.

PHIL: But, as we approach to or recede from an object, the visible extension varies, being at one distance ten or a hundred times greater than another. Does it not therefore follow from hence likewise that it is not really inherent in the object?

HYLAS: I own I am at a loss what to think.

PHIL: Your judgment will soon be determined, if you will venture to think as freely concerning this quality as you have done concerning the rest. Was it not admitted as a good argument, that neither heat nor cold was in the water, because it seemed warm to one hand and cold to the other?

HYLAS: It was.

PHIL: Is it not the very same reasoning to conclude, there is no extension or figure in an object, because to one eye it shall seem little, smooth, and round, when at the same time it appears to the other, great, uneven, and regular?

HYLAS: The very same. But does this latter fact ever happen?

PHIL: You may at any time make the experiment, by looking with one eye bare, and with the other through a microscope.

HYLAS: I know not how to maintain it; and yet I am loath to give up *extension*, I see so many odd consequences following upon such a concession.

Philonous is arguing that

_____

_____

_____

_____.

PHIL: Odd, say you? After the concessions already made, I hope you will stick at nothing for its oddness. But, on the other hand, should it not seem very odd, if the general reasoning which includes all other sensible qualities did not also include extension? If it be allowed that no idea, nor anything like an idea, can exist in an unperceiving substance, then surely it follows that no figure, or mode of extension, which we can either perceive, or imagine, or have any idea of, can be really inherent in matter; not to mention the peculiar difficulty there must be in conceiving a material substance, prior to and distinct from extension to be the *substratum* of extension. Be the sensible quality what it will—figure, or sound, or colour, it seems alike impossible it should subsist in that which does not perceive it.

HYLAS: I give up the point for the present, reserving still a right to retract my opinion, in case I shall hereafter discover any false step in my progress to it.

Which of the following are consistent (C) or inconsistent (I) with Philonous's argument?

1. C   I   If visible extension is *in* an object, then visible extension shouldn't depend upon the position of the observer.

2. C   I   The visible extension of an object varies with the observer's position.

3. C   I   Because the ideas we have of an object, like its size, are not *in* the object but are produced by us, we have no accurate idea of the object itself.

Having attacked Hylas's conception of extension, Philonous now moves on to motion.

PHIL: That is a right you cannot be denied. Figures and extension being dispatched, we proceed next to *motion*. Can a real motion in any external body be at the same time very swift and very slow?

HYLAS: It cannot.

PHIL: Is not the motion of a body swift in a reciprocal proportion to the time it takes up in describing any given space? Thus a body that describes a mile in an hour moves three times faster than it would in case it described only a mile in three hours.

HYLAS: I agree with you.

PHIL: And is not time measured by the succession of ideas in our minds?

HYLAS: It is.

PHIL: And is it not possible ideas should succeed one another twice as fast in your mind as they do in mine, or in that of some spirit of another kind?

HYLAS: I own it.

PHIL: Consequently the same body may to another seem to perform its motion over any space in half the time that it does to you. And the same reasoning will hold as to any other proposition: that is to say, according to your principles (since the motions perceived are both really in the object) it is possible one and the same body shall be really moved the same way at once, both very swift and very slow. How is this consistent either with common sense, or with what you just now granted?

HYLAS: I have nothing to say to it.

Philonous is trying to convince Hylas that the sensible quality of motion is not in objects, but in the perceiver. What is his argument?

_____

_____

_____

_____.

In a moment, I'm going to summarize Philonous's argument about the primary qualities of extension and motion, but first let's clarify his position by thinking, as we did with Locke, about the difference between objective and subjective characteristics.

Right now I am thinking of an equilateral triangle. My normal view is that its objective characteristics are, among others, that it is an enclosed geometrical figure having three equal sides. These characteristics of an equilateral triangle are objective because they would be the same for everyone. Here are two minds, yours and mine, thinking of equilateral triangles:

Your mind thinking about an equilateral triangle.

My mind thinking about an equilateral triangle.

Though your triangle is large and mine is small, we are both thinking of an equilateral triangle because we are thinking of a triangle with three equal sides.

Now let us say that, while thinking of the triangle, I feel that it is beautiful and symmetrical. You, however, feel the equilateral triangle is ugly and pointy.

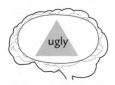 

Your mind thinking about an equilateral triangle and feeling that it is ugly.

My mind thinking about an equilateral triangle and feeling that it is beautiful.

The beauty or ugliness of the equilateral triangle is *subjective* because beauty or ugliness is not *in* the triangle but is determined by the subject's feeling about the triangle. You have one feeling and I have another. The "three-equal-sidedness" of the equilateral triangle is *objective* because it is not determined by the subject but is in the object itself. No matter how we feel about the equilateral triangle, it still has three equal sides. *Subjective characteristics vary because they depend upon the subject; objective characteristics do not vary because they do not depend upon the subject.*

Now make the same points I just made but use a square as an example.

The objective qualities of a square are _____

_____. I might add subjective qualities to the

square like _____. The
difference between objective and subjective qualities is that objective qualities

_____, while subjective qualities

_____.

Remember, objective qualities, such as those of a triangle or square, do not vary because they are determined by object; subjective qualities, such as those we *add* to a triangle or square, do vary because they are determined by subject.

Here is how the distinction between objective and subjective qualities relates to Philonous's argument. Philonous (like Berkeley) holds that the primary qualities of extension and motion (along with secondary qualities of taste, smell, color, and sound) *are not objective but subjective, because they vary, depending upon the observer.*

Now I'll summarize Philonous's (and Berkeley's) arguments about extension and motion.

1. Extension is subjective because it varies among different observers.

Assume a ladybug and I are looking at the same equilateral triangle. I judge the extension of the triangle to be small. The ladybug, however, judges the extension of the triangle to be large. Thus, the extension of the triangle is subjective because *it is not in the triangle but varies among different observers.*

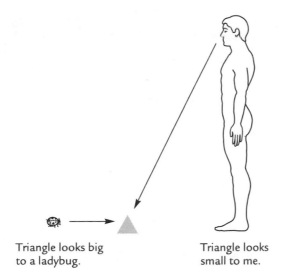

Triangle looks big
to a ladybug.

Triangle looks
small to me.

I see the extension of the triangle as small; the ladybug sees the extension of the triangle as big. Therefore, extension is subjective, determined by the subject, not objective, determined by the object.

2. Extension is subjective because it varies based upon the position of the observer.

I look at an equilateral triangle from across the room, and it appears to have a small extension. When I cross the room and look at the triangle close up, it appears to have a much larger extension. Thus, the extension of the triangle is subjective because *it is not in the triangle* but varies based upon the position of the observer.

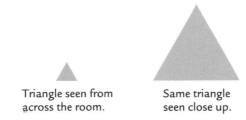

Triangle seen from
across the room.

Same triangle
seen close up.

If the extension of the triangle were genuinely objective, in the object, then extension would not vary with my position. Since extension obviously varies with my position, extension is subjective, in the viewing subject.

3. Motion is subjective because it varies with different observers.

Let us say I have a wooden equilateral triangle and move it across the top of my table. I have the idea that the motion is slow. You, however, have the idea that the motion is fast. Thus, the motion of the wooden triangle is subjective because it is not in the triangle but varies with different observers.

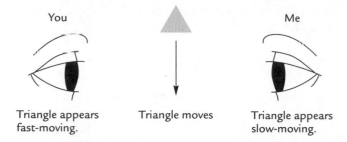

You

Triangle appears
fast-moving.

Triangle moves

Me

Triangle appears
slow-moving.

If motion were objective, then it would be the same for all viewers because it is genuinely in the object—in this case, a triangle, moving. But motion—fastness or slowness—can vary from observer to observer. Thus, motion is subjective, in the subject doing the observing.

To sum up, objective characteristics are observer-independent. Subjective characteristics are observer-dependent. Extension and motion are subjective characteristics because these characteristics are observer-dependent. Extension and motion vary depending upon the size and position of the observer.

Now, playing Refute Berkeley again, do your best to show that Philonous and Berkeley are wrong. Attack each of the arguments (1–3) above. In essence, you must argue that extension and motion are objective, in objects, not subjective, in the observing subject.

Argument 1 is wrong because _____

_____

_____.

Thus, extension is objective. {13}

Argument 2 is wrong because _____

_____

_____.

Thus, extension is objective. {14}

Argument 3 is wrong because _____

_____

_____.

Thus, motion is objective. {15}

Note that in the next section, Philonous uses a slightly different argument to attack the concept of solidity. Underline important points.

Phil: Then as for *solidity,* either you do not mean any sensible quality by that word, and so it is beside our inquiry: or if you do, it must be either hardness or resistance. But both the one and the other are plainly relative to our senses: it being evident that what seems hard to one animal may appear soft to another, who hath greater force and firmness of limbs. Nor is it less plain that the resistance I feel is not in the body.

HYLAS: I own the very sensation of resistance, which is all you immediately perceive, is not in the *body;* but the cause of that sensation is.

PHIL: But the causes of our sensations are not things immediately perceived, and therefore are not sensible. This point I thought had been already determined.

HYLAS: I own it was; but you will pardon me if I seem a little embarrassed: I know not how to quit my old notions.

PHIL: To help you out, do but consider that if extension be once acknowledged to have no existence without the mind, the same must necessarily be granted of motion, solidity, and gravity; since they all evidently suppose extension. It is therefore superfluous to inquire particularly concerning each of them. In denying extension, you have denied them all to have any real existence.

Philonous says that hardness is subjective because it varies from observer to observer. What is hard to one animal (observer) might be soft to another animal (observer). Hardness, and thus solidity, is not a primary quality that is in objects but a secondary quality that is produced by the subject doing the sensing.

Hylas tries to counterattack by saying that while the sensation of hardness is not in the object, the *cause* of the sensation of the hardness *is* in the object. In other words, there is something in objects that produces in us the subjective sensation of hardness.

Philonous points out that all we know is what we immediately perceive. We only immediately perceive hardness. We have no immediate perception of something hidden in objects that causes our perception of hardness.

In the Dialogue, after the passage you've just read, the argument takes a bit of a detour. In a section I have omitted, Philonous and Hylas investigate, among other topics, the concept of abstractions. Philonous convinces Hylas that abstract concepts like extension and motion have no meaning.

In the next passage, the argument returns to the direct investigation of external objects. Hylas continues his attempt to prove to Philonous that matter exists.

HYLAS: I acknowledge, Philonous, that, upon a fair observation of what passes in my mind I can discover nothing else but that I am a thinking being, affected with variety of sensations; neither is it possible to conceive how a sensation should exist in an unperceiving substance. But then, on the other hand, when I look on sensible things in a different view, considering them as so many modes and qualities, I find it necessary to suppose a *material* substratum, without which they cannot be conceived to exist.

PHIL: *Material substratum* call you it? Pray, by which of your senses came you acquainted with that being?

HYLAS: It is not itself sensible; its modes and qualities only being perceived by the senses.

PHIL: I presume then it was by reflexion and reason you obtained the idea of it?

HYLAS: I do not pretend to any proper positive idea of it. However, I conclude it exists, because qualities cannot be conceived to exist without a support.

Hylas, here, takes Locke's position on matter.

PHIL: It seems then you have only a relative notion of it, or that you conceive it not otherwise than by conceiving the relation it bears to sensible qualities?

HYLAS: Right.

PHIL: Be pleased therefore to let me know wherein that relation consists.

HYLAS: Is it not sufficiently expressed in the term *substratum,* or *substance*?

PHIL: If so, the word *substratum* should import that it is spread under the sensible qualities or accidents?

HYLAS: True.

PHIL: And consequently under extension?

HYLAS: I own it.

PHIL: It is therefore somewhat in its own nature entirely distinct from extension?

HYLAS: I tell you, extension is only a mode, and matter is something that supports modes. And is it not evident the thing supported is different from the thing supporting?

PHIL: So that something distinct from, and exclusive of, extension is supposed to be the substratum of extension?

HYLAS: Just so.

PHIL: Answer me, Hylas. Can a thing be spread without extension? or is not the idea of extension distinct from the extension necessarily included in *spreading*?

HYLAS: It is.

PHIL: Whatsoever therefore you suppose spread under anything must have in itself an extension distinct from the extension of that thing under which it is spread?

HYLAS: It must.

PHIL: Consequently, every corporeal substance, being the *substratum* of extension, must have in itself another extension, by which it is qualified to be a *substratum:* and so on to infinity. And I ask whether this be not absurd in itself, and repugnant to what you granted just now, to wit, that the *substratum* was something distinct from and exclusive of extension?

HYLAS: Aye but, Philonous, you take me wrong. I do not mean that matter is *spread* in a gross literal sense under extension. The word *substratum* is used only to express in general the same thing with *substance.*

Hylas clings to the idea that matter exists. However, instead of arguing that we have sense knowledge of matter itself, he argues, as Locke did, that we can deduce that matter exists as a substratum, an entity underneath the qualities we know by our senses.

First, let's clarify the notion of substratum and then see how it applies to Hylas's position. The substratum of a building is the earth it stands upon. The substratum of your knowledge of this book is your knowledge of reading. The substratum of a healthy economy is the high rate of employment of its citizens. If the substratum of X is Y, then X is supported by, or made possible by, Y. Give your own example of substratum.

The substratum of _____ would be _____

because _____ is supported by _____.

Hylas argues that, though matter itself is not known directly by the senses, the sensible qualities of color, sound, extension, and so forth rest upon the substratum of matter. If matter didn't exist, then color, sound, and extension would have no support, would cease to exist. Just as a soap bubble would vanish without its supporting pocket of air, so sensible qualities would vanish without their supporting matter.

This view often strongly appeals to my students. Hylas seems to make sense. For example, let's say I examine a piece of wax. It is cool and hard. Coolness and hardness are the wax's sensible qualities. Hylas would say that if there were no matter underneath these sensible qualities, then coolness and hardness couldn't exist. This certainly *seems* reasonable. While I have sense knowledge only of sensible qualities, it seems I must deduce that matter exists as a substratum supporting these qualities.

Consider your own example.

Some of the sensible qualities of _____ would be

_____ and _____. Matter would seem to be the

substratum of these sensible qualities because _____

_____

_____.

Philonous zeros in on the sensible quality of extension. If matter, according to Hylas, is the substratum of sensible qualities, then matter is the substratum of extension. But this involves what appears to be an insoluble problem.

Let's examine the wax again. Besides the sensible qualities of hardness and coolness, the wax also has the sensible quality of extension. The wax has a certain size and shape. But how is matter a substratum of extension? How does matter stand underneath or give support to extension *and still be different from extension*? There appears to be no way to answer this question. If matter is the substratum of hardness and coolness, then just as the earth is one thing and a building is another, so matter is one thing and hardness and coolness are another. All right. Perhaps there is some way that this can be so. But if matter is the substratum of *extension*, then matter is one thing and extension is another. How can matter, which is not extension, give any support for extension?

Extension is size. Thus, the question is how can that which has no size give support for that which *is* size? Answer me that.

I would have to say _____

_____

_____. {16}

Hylas objects that Philonous is being too literal. It is too literal to say that matter stands under sensible qualities as, say, legs stand under a body. But Hylas is not able to describe any other way in which matter stands underneath, is a substratum of, sensible qualities. Can you? If matter is not physically underneath the sensible qualities of extension, color, and sound, in what sense *is* it underneath these sensible qualities?

My answer is _____

_____

_____.

Philonous would argue that a question like "How can that which has no size support something that is size?" is so difficult to answer because there is no answer. There is no answer, in Philonous's (and Berkeley's) view, because one is looking for something, matter, that does not exist. In the same way, one could not answer the question "What is the fourth side of a triangle?" because one is looking for something that does not exist. Look all you wish for matter, and you will have no more luck finding it than finding a triangle's fourth side.

After Philonous confounds Hylas on a number of other problems related to matter, the first of the Three Dialogues ends as follows. Underline at least three important points.

PHIL: You are therefore, by your principles, forced to deny the reality of sensible things; since you made it to consist in an absolute existence exterior to the mind. That is to say, you are a downright *sceptic*. So I have gained my point, which was to show your principles led to scepticism.

HYLAS: For the present I am, if not entirely convinced, at least silenced.

PHIL: I would fain know what more you would require in order to a perfect conviction. Have you not had the liberty of explaining yourself all manner of ways? Were any little slips in discourse laid hold and insisted on? Or were you not allowed to retract or reinforce anything you had offered, as best served your purpose? Hath not everything you could say been heard and examined with all the fairness imaginable? In a word, have you not in every point been convinced out of your own mouth? And, if you can at present discover any flaw in any of your former concessions, or think of any remaining subterfuge, any new distinction, colour, or comment whatsoever, why do you not produce it?

HYLAS: A little patience, Philonous. I am at present so amazed to see myself ensnared, and as it were imprisoned in the labyrinths you have drawn me into, that on the sudden it cannot be expected I should find my way out. You must give me time to look about me and recollect myself.

PHIL: Hark; is not this the college bell?

HYLAS: It rings for prayers.

PHIL: We will go in then, if you please, and meet here again tomorrow morning. In the meantime, you may employ your thoughts on this morning's discourse, and try if you can find any fallacy in it, or invent any new means to extricate yourself.

HYLAS: Agreed.

Summarize three of the points you underlined.

First, _____

_____

_____.

Second, _____

_____

_____.

Third, _____

_____

_____.

Now look back at your first five attempts to play Refute Berkeley. You had not encountered his arguments yet and were doing your best to refute his two central views: (1) matter does not exist and (2) what appears to be matter is actually God's ideas. Now that you have worked your way through his proofs, how strong do your first attempts to disprove Berkeley look to you?

I would say my arguments were generally _____

because _____

_____

_____.

Thus far, Berkeley has tried to analyze each sense—touch, taste, smell, hearing, and sight—to show that we have no sense knowledge of matter. Now play Refute Berkeley in a slightly different way. The following, 1–3, are typical of the weakest arguments students offer against Berkeley. Note that each answer begins with a conclusion and then presents a weak piece of evidence. Improve the evidence against Berkeley.

1. I know I touch matter because I can feel matter.

This argument can be improved by saying, "I know I touch matter because

_____

_____

_____." {17}

2. I know matter produces sound because nothing else but matter could produce sound.

This argument can be improved by saying, "I know matter produces sound because

_____

_____

_____." {18}

3. I know matter has three dimensions because I can see three dimensions.

This argument can be improved by saying, "I know matter has three dimensions

because _____

_____

_____." {19}

Note that we have only considered Berkeley's arguments for the first of his propositions, that matter does not exist. Here, from the remaining two dialogues, are his arguments that God exists as the thinker of the material world.

It must be owned that I entirely agree with what the holy Scripture says, "That in God we live and move and have our being" [Acts 17:28]. . . . Take here in brief my meaning:—It is evident that the things I perceive are my own ideas, and that no idea can exist unless it be in a mind: nor is it less plain that these ideas or things by me perceived, either themselves or their archetypes, exist independently of my mind, since I know myself not to be their author, it being out of my power to determine at pleasure what particular ideas I shall be affected with upon opening my eyes or ears: they must therefore exist in some other mind, whose will it is they should be exhibited to me. The things, I say immediately perceived are ideas or sensations, call them which you will. But how can any idea or sensation exist in, or be produced by, anything but a mind or spirit? This indeed is inconceivable. And to assert that which is inconceivable is to talk nonsense: is it not?

Paraphrase Berkeley's argument.

Berkeley is saying _____

_____

_____

_____

_____

_____

Now play Refute Berkeley and show that what he is saying is wrong.

Berkeley is wrong because _____

_____

_____

_____

_____. {20}

In the next passage, Berkeley repeats some of his points and goes on to prove the existence of God as an "omnipresent eternal mind."

When I deny sensible things an existence out of the mind, I do not mean my mind in particular, but all minds. Now, it is plain they have an existence exterior to my mind, since I find them by experience to be independent of it. There is therefore some other mind wherein they exist, during the intervals between the times of my perceiving them: as likewise they did before my birth, and would do after my supposed annihilation. And, as the same is true with regard to all other finite created spirits, it necessarily follows there is an *omnipresent eternal mind*, which knows and comprehends all things, and exhibits them to our view in such a manner, and according to such rules, as he himself hath ordained, and are by us termed the *laws of nature*.

Paraphrase Berkeley's argument.

Berkeley is saying _____

_____

_____

_____

_____.

Now play Refute Berkeley one last time and show that what he is saying is wrong.

Berkeley is wrong because _____

_____

_____

_____

_____. {21}

In Exercise 21.3, you'll have a chance to decide who, Berkeley or you, won the game Refute Berkeley.

Here is a blunt question about Berkeley that a student recently asked me.

Question: Berkeley believes matter doesn't exist. Why do philosophers believe such absurd things?

Answer: Reading philosophy requires the faith that an apparently absurd position has genuine merit. This faith, however, is not blind but rather is built upon the simple but important truth that the philosopher has survived what could be called the "be quarreled with or perish" test.

Philosophers survive initially because they breed fruitful discord. Their arguments are both attractive enough to gain intelligent followers and troubling enough to gain intelligent opponents. Once this goes on for more than a generation, a philosopher becomes "historically interesting." This means that, besides acquiring additional intelligent supporters and opponents, the philosopher attracts commentators. Commentators explain what the philosopher "really" said and link the philosopher's work to that of other philosophers. If this process continues for several centuries, the philosopher becomes almost permanently cemented into the edifice of philosophy. It is eventually seen that any clear understanding of the history of philosophy must include this philosopher. Supported or opposed, the philosopher is *impossible to ignore.* Thus, you can be certain that a philosopher like Berkeley has seemed absurd to many generations of earlier readers, and you can also be certain that you wouldn't be reading Berkeley in the twentieth century if his arguments were genuinely absurd. To put this another way, to read Berkeley or any other apparently absurd philosopher in the history of philosophy, you must have the faith that their arguments would never have come into your hands if their arguments were as absurd as they seem at first glance.

We don't know who the truly ridiculous philosophers were. They never survived the first generation of their readers.

SUMMARY

Berkeley is an empiricist who holds that all knowledge comes through the senses. Investigating each of the senses in *Three Dialogues Between Hylas and Philonous,* Berkeley argues that because all we know are ideas, ideas are the only reality. In addition, since it is absurd to suppose that external reality vanishes when we are not thinking about it, God must exist as the thinker of external reality.

EXERCISE 21.1
Looking Back

Use your own paper to answer the following:

1. What is Berkeley's purpose?

2. What is the difference between Berkeley's and Locke's epistemology?

3. What is the difference between Berkeley's and Locke's metaphysics?

VOCABULARY MAP
George Berkeley

Berkeley's **metaphysics,** his view of reality, is **monistic.** He holds that all of reality is one kind of thing, and that one thing is ideas, specifically God's ideas. This makes him a **monistic idealist.** A philosophical *ideal*ist is not to be confused with an *ideal*ist; the latter holds lofty values, the former holds that ideas are the central element of reality.

Berkeley's **epistemology,** his view of the knowledge process, is **empirical.** He holds that all that we know about the ideas that constitute the apparently physical world comes to us through our senses.

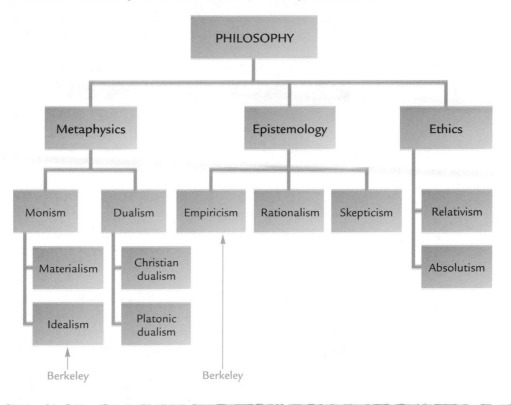

EXERCISE 21.2

Looking at the World Through Berkeley's Eyes

How would Berkeley answer each of the following? Offer evidence from this chapter.

1. T   F   There is no knowledge in our minds that did not come through our senses.

    Evidence: _____

    _____

    _____.

2. T F It is incorrect to believe, as Plato did, that all of reality is divided between the physical world and the realm of Forms.

Evidence: _____

_____

_____.

3. T F It is incorrect to believe, as Aristotle did, that physical substances are composed of matter and form.

Evidence: _____

_____

_____.

4. T F It is incorrect to believe, as Augustine, Anselm, Aquinas, Descartes, and Locke did, that God exists.

Evidence: _____

_____

_____.

5. T F Because to be is to be perceived, if all humans died, all reality would vanish (because reality is no longer perceived by anyone)

Evidence: _____

_____

_____.

EXERCISE 21.3
Who Won Refute Berkeley?

To calculate your score in Refute Berkeley, put yourself in the position of an objective reader who has read Berkeley's arguments on this section of the tour and your attempts to refute him. Go back to each curly bracket and mark points in the margin. Give yourself one point if an objective reader of this section of the tour would find that your answer is clearly superior to Berkeley's view. Give yourself no points if an objective reader of this section of the tour would find your answer neither better nor worse than Berkeley's view. Take away one point if an objective reader of this section of the tour would find that your answer is clearly inferior to Berkeley's view.

EXERCISE 21.4
Metaphysics at the Grand Canyon

This task will help you summarize some of the views of reality you have investigated on the tour. Assume that the philosophers listed below were gathered on the rim of the Grand Canyon. You conduct an interview and ask each the same question: "Looking at the Grand Canyon, what is the difference between appearance and actuality?"

For example, Thales might answer, "The appearance is that there are two kinds of things in this scene: the rocky walls and the river far below. In fact, since All is Water, the rocks are actually another form of water."

How would each of the following answer the question?

1. Heraclitus
2. Parmenides
3. Plato
4. Aristotle
5. Descartes
6. Locke
7. Berkeley

ANALYSIS OF YOUR PHILOSOPHICAL SELF-PORTRAIT

To see how your views stack up against Berkeley's, read my analysis below, rethink your position, and then circle what you believe is the correct answer. I've underlined Berkeley's answers.

1. T <u>F</u> *Matter exists.*

    Most students would answer this True; pride yourself on being an odd bird if you didn't. Berkeley, as you've learned from this section of the tour, holds that matter is an illusion. He wasn't being frivolous. His serious purposes, as I mentioned earlier, were to combat skepticism, atheism, and the view of God as uninvolved architect of the universe. If you are confident that matter exists, then you must believe that you refuted each of Berkeley's many arguments. The English essayist and lexicographer Samuel Johnson unphilosophically dismissed Berkeley's views by saying, "I refute Berkeley thus" and kicked a rock. A stubbed toe, Johnson believed, could not be produced by a collection of ideas. Berkeley would have said that toe pain was no evidence of rock matter. Others have remarked that Berkeley's arguments "produce no conviction, though they cannot be refuted."

2. T <u>F</u> *We have sense knowledge of matter.*

    Berkeley tries to thoroughly examine each sense, to show that all we know are our ideas. And therefore, because ideas aren't matter, we cannot know anything about matter. If you want to reply that just because we don't have sense knowledge about matter, that doesn't prove matter doesn't exist, Berkeley is ready for you. Matter thus falls into the category of all other things we have no sense knowledge about—fairies, trolls, goblins, and so forth. As the philosophical enemy of materialism, Berkeley would be quite content to have turned matter into a fairy tale.

3. <u>T</u> F *All knowledge comes through our senses.*

    If you answered this True, but disagree with Berkeley, you are certainly happy to know that he is only one of several varieties of empiricist. Other empiricists examined on our tour are Aristotle, Aquinas, Locke, and Hume. If you think there is something wrong with *both* empiricism and rationalism, you will be intrigued by Immanuel Kant.

4. <u>T</u> F *All we know about any object are our ideas about the object. For ex-
    ample, all we know about a table are our ideas of the table.*

    If you hold this is False, then you have a very difficult position to defend. How
    do you know the table or any other external thing except through your ideas?
    Is there a nonmental way of knowing? I've said that for almost every belief,
    there is some philosopher who will support you, but on this one, you're on your
    own. However, if you answered this True, then your position is not much bet-
    ter. If all we know are ideas, then how can we be certain that our idea of, for
    example, matter is an accurate copy of matter itself? How do we escape from
    the mind's vault?

5. <u>T</u> F *The physical universe is nothing but God's thoughts.*

    If you answered this True, then you love Berkeley. Actually, holding that the
    universe is nothing but God's thoughts is a remarkably beautiful conception.
    God thinks every leaf in every tree, his thought flies every bird in the air and
    swims every fish through the sea. God thinks each color, sound, shape, and mo-
    tion that surrounds us. Though you may think Berkeley completely wrong, it
    would be hard to conceive of a vision that made God more powerfully present
    in our world.

    Evaluation: Number of points in agreement with Berkeley = _____ of 5 possible.

    A position of Berkeley's that you strongly (support, oppose) is _____

    _____

    because _____

    _____

    _____.

GOOD BOOKS

Berkeley, George. *Principles of Human Knowledge/Three Dialogues.* Edited by Roger Wool-
    house. New York: Penguin, 1988. If you enjoyed the dish of Berkeley you sampled in
    this chapter, here is the feast.
Lavine, T. Z. *Socrates to Sartre.* New York: Bantam, 1984. The chapters on Locke, Berkeley,
    and Hume are exceptional. All in all, a superb and inexpensive introduction to
    philosophy.

NEXT STOP

**Prepare to have your most cherished convictions
smashed. You're about to meet the Emperor of
Doubt, David Hume.**

22

David Hume

How to Destroy Certainty About the World, Self, and Mind

YOUR PHILOSOPHICAL SELF-PORTRAIT

Add more details to your philosophical self-portrait by answering the questions below and offering evidence for your answers.

1.   T   F   Every idea can be traced back to a sense impression.

   Evidence: _____

   _____ ,

2.   T   F   Absolute certainty is possible only in the concepts of math and geometry.

   Evidence: _____

   _____ .

3.   T   F   Our senses can never provide us with absolute certainty.

   Evidence: _____

   _____ .

4.   T   F   The self is our unchanging identity.

   Evidence: _____

   _____ .

5.   T   F   The existence of the self can be proved by the senses.

   Evidence: _____

   _____ .

6.   T   F   The existence of the self can be proved by looking at the internal world of the mind.

   Evidence: _____

   _____ .

7.   T   F   Our thoughts come from our minds.

   Evidence: _____

   _____ .

PREVIEW

Hume's goal is to describe the principles of human nature as accurately as Isaac Newton described the principles of physical nature. According to Hume, knowledge can be divided into sense impressions and ideas based upon sense impressions. Any idea that cannot be traced back to a sense impression is meaningless. All knowledge claims are either a relation of ideas or a matter of fact. Relations of ideas can be certain but provide no information about the world. Matters of fact provide information about the world but are not certain. Hume argues that we have no evidence for the existence of the self or mind.

David Hume's books are full of philosophical bombshells.

Hume will convince you of the following:

- You have no evidence of the existence of your self.
- You have no evidence of the existence of your mind.
- You have no evidence of any cause producing any effect.
- You have no evidence that God exists or doesn't exist.
- You cannot prove mass murder is wrong.

According to many commentators, Hume is the most influential philosopher ever to write in English. Odds are, if we polled all the philosophers in England and America, the majority, maybe even the vast majority, would agree that the central elements of Hume's philosophy have never been refuted. Thus, in this section of the tour, you will be wrestling with a philosopher who many believe is unbeatable.

No philosopher has astounded, aggravated, and finally convinced more of my students than has David Hume. Parmenides astounds and aggravates but rarely convinces. Ditto Berkeley. In many ways, Hume's conclusions are more outrageous than those of any other philosopher we've investigated, but his arguments are so overwhelming that many of my students, almost against their will, become Humeans. And then they wish they weren't.

So be on your guard. The following pages may not merely upset your philosophical applecart, they could blow it to smithereens.

Hume, in a phrase, is a skeptic by way of empiricism. In other words, he begins with the view that all that we know comes through our senses, in order to show how little we know. One way to begin to understand Hume, therefore, is to understand skepticism.

Skepticism is the view that little or nothing can be known for certain. A skeptic is a dedicated doubter. Socrates had a strong skeptical strain. He doubted that the citizens of Athens knew what they thought they knew. Though he failed, he tried to teach Euthyphro and others the virtues of self-doubt. Socrates doubted, with only partial irony, that he had any wisdom. To take another example, agnosticism is the skeptical position that we cannot prove or disprove God's existence. The theological skeptic holds that God may, or may not, exist but that we cannot know either way. Skepticism is philosophical fence-sitting.

Now you may be skeptical about some issues and not skeptical about others. You may believe that there isn't enough information to dispel serious doubts on a particular topic. The stronger your doubts, the stronger your determination to stay on the fence.

EXERCISE 22.1
Evaluating Your Own Skepticism

To begin to understand Hume's skepticism, circle what you believe is the correct statement in each of the following groups. Every "c" presents the skeptical position and means you have strong doubts about *both* of the other alternatives. After each group, explain your answer.

1. Ghosts
   a. Ghosts exist.
   b. Ghosts don't exist.
   c. It isn't possible to know whether or not ghosts exist.
   Explanation: _____
   _____
   _____.

2. Aliens
   a. Aliens exist.
   b. Aliens don't exist.
   c. It isn't possible to know whether or not aliens exist.
   Explanation: _____
   _____
   _____.

3. God
   a. God exists.
   b. God doesn't exist.
   c. It isn't possible to know whether God exists.
   Explanation: _____
   _____
   _____.

4. The laws of science
   a. The laws of science accurately describe the universe.
   b. The laws of science don't accurately describe the universe.
   c. It is not possible to know whether or not the laws of science accurately describe the universe.
   Explanation: _____
   _____
   _____.

David Hume (1711–1776)

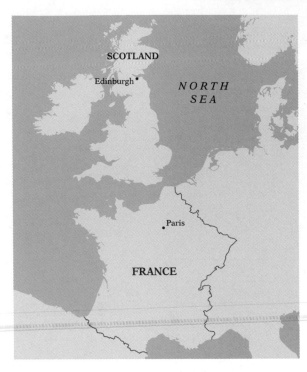

A quick mind trapped in a large clumsy body, Scottish philosopher David Hume was once described by the earl of Charlemont as looking more like "a turtle-eating Alderman than a refined philosopher."[1] Hume was born in Edinburgh, Scotland, in 1711. His father, who died when Hume was a child, was a distant cousin of the earl of Home and owned a small estate called "Ninewells."

Most of Hume's early education was over-

seen by his widowed mother, Katherine Falconer, who described young David as "uncommon wake-minded"—a local expression for very alert. At the age of sixteen, Hume was already engaged in study that would produce the first volume of his greatest philosophical work, *A Treatise of Human Nature*. Hume's mother came from a family of lawyers and hoped her young genius would enter the legal profession. At the age of fifteen, Hume entered the University of Edinburgh to study law. But he soon came to dislike his courses, preferring instead to study philosophy on his own.

Three years after entering the university, Hume decided to give up the study of law, in defiance of his family's wishes, and become a philosopher. This decision, according to his autobiography, made him "infinitely happy"; nonetheless, the following year Hume slipped into a depression that lasted until he was twenty-three. During this time he had spells of despair where he comforted himself by overeating, eventually becoming fat and ungainly. Hume believed that his depression was largely due to the study of philosophers like Cicero, Seneca, and Plutarch, who continually warned about death, shame, and "all other Calamities of Life."[2] It was in reaction to their philosophies that Hume developed his own views. At the age of twenty-three, Hume moved to France, where he spent the next three years (1734–37) writing the draft

[1] Quoted in Frederick Copleston, *A History of Philosophy*, Vol. V (Garden City, N.Y.: Doubleday, 1959), p. 260.

[2] Quoted in Ben-Ami Scharfstein, *The Philosophers: Their Lives and the Nature of Their Thought* (New York: Oxford University Press, 1980), pp. 190–196.

Obviously you can be skeptical on some issues and not skeptical on others. Complete skepticism is probably impossible. If you believe that nothing at all can be known for certain, then you believe at least *one* thing can be known for certain—that nothing is certain.

Hume is a partial skeptic. Though he holds that we can know sense impressions and mathematical truths, he believes we lack key certitudes about the self, the mind, cause and effect, God, and moral values.

To help you understand Hume's philosophy, I'll answer the following questions:

David Hume (continued)

of his major philosophical work, *A Treatise of Human Nature.*

Hume was popular, witty, and a respected man of letters. His great passion, as he admitted, was for "literary fame" and he wrote several essays on moral, political, historical, and economic subjects. His skepticism and opposition to all established religion also gave him the reputation of being an "infidel."

Despite his achievements, Hume did not earn his living as a professional philosopher. Although he applied for a position in philosophy at both the universities of Edinburgh and Glasgow, he never succeeded in getting a job as an academic. Hume instead worked in various government positions and also served a brief stint as a companion to a mad nobleman. In 1752 he became keeper of the Advocates Library in Edinburgh. During this tenure as archivist, Hume gained a reputation as an outstanding historian, publishing several short essays and a very well received six-volume *History of England.*

In 1763 Hume went to Paris as secretary to the British Ambassador to France. During his stay in France, Hume became involved with a group of French philosophers. He became especially close to the great French philosopher Jean-Jacques Rousseau, who returned to England with Hume in 1766. However, Rousseau's suspicious nature soured the relationship and the two eventually parted.

Hume was also close friends with Scottish philosopher and economist Adam Smith, who edited Hume's autobiography. The book, entitled *My Own Life,* came out in 1777—the year after Hume's death. In his autobiography Hume described himself as "a man of mild disposition, of command of temper, of an open, social and cheerful humor, capable of attachment, but little susceptible of enmity, and of great moderation in all my passions."

One of Hume's female acquaintances described him as "one of the sweetest tempered Men and the most Benevolent that was born. . . . There was a simplicity and pleasantness of Manners about him that were delightful in Society."[3] His kindness earned him the nickname "Saint David" in Scotland.

Although Hume was well liked by women and had many close female friends, he never married—his proposals of marriage being rejected. Hume died of cancer in 1776, accepting death with that cheerful philosophical attitude that had so endeared him to his friends and acquaintances.

Hume's extensive writings span the fields of philosophy, history, economics, politics, sociology, and esthetics. His major philosophical works included *A Treatise of Human Nature* (1739–40), *An Enquiry Concerning Human Understanding* (1748), *An Enquiry Concerning the Principles of Morals* (1751), *The Natural History of Religion* (1757), and *Dialogues Concerning Natural Religion* (1778).

---

[3] Quoted in Ben-Ami Scharfstein, *The Philosophers: Their Lives and the Nature of Their Thought,* p. 196.

- What is Hume's goal?
- What is Hume's epistemology?
- What are the limitations of knowledge?
- What are the three laws of the association of ideas?
- Can the existence of the self be proven?
- Can the existence of the mind be proven?

In the next chapter, we'll explore Hume's analysis of cause and effect, his attack upon proofs of God's existence, and his positions on metaphysics and ethics.

What Is Hume's Goal?

Hume's goal is to discover the laws of human nature in the same way that Isaac Newton had discovered the laws of physical nature. In the view of the eighteenth century, Isaac Newton had uncovered the essential features of the cosmos. Newton's discovery of the principle of universal gravitation explained the motion of literally everything, from the orbits of the planets to an apple falling from a tree. Newton's stature and achievement in the eighteenth century were summed up by English poet Alexander Pope:

> Nature and Nature's laws lay hid in night;
> God said, Let Newton be, and all was light.

According to Newton, the universe functioned like a gigantic machine, whose parts were as finely tuned to each other as the parts of a clock. One could predict the movements of the planets as easily and as confidently as one could predict the movement of a watch's hands. And just as the universe was a machine, so were animals, plants, the seas, the human body. The universe seemed to be nothing but smaller machines inside larger machines, all ticking within the small circle of the mathematical formulas Newton had discovered.

Before long, according to some Newtonian enthusiasts, the cosmic machine would be so well understood that science would come to an end. There would be nothing left to learn! In addition, since society was only a machine composed of human machines, the history of the future would be written as confidently as a newspaper article. Just as one could predict the movements of a watch's hands for the next twenty-four hours, one could predict the movements of society for the next twenty-four centuries.

In the Enlightenment view, the machinery of the universe hung from Newton's watch chain.

Hume's goal was to duplicate Newton's feat by moving from the outer world of the universe to the inner world of human nature. Though it might seem as if Hume had set himself a more modest task than Newton, Hume believed that understanding human nature would provide a foundation for understanding all of human knowledge. If knowledge turned out to be as limited as Hume expected, then he would have gone even beyond Newton. As Hume saw it, although Newton believed he was describing the cosmic machinery, in fact, Newton had never escaped from the confines of the mind.

In order to understand how Hume tried to undercut scientific confidence with philosophical skepticism, let's turn to an analysis of Hume's epistemology.

What Is Hume's Epistemology?

According to Hume, all our knowledge can be divided into two categories: impressions and ideas. Impressions are the immediate information that comes to us through our senses. Ideas are produced by thinking about impressions. The central difference between impressions and ideas is that impressions are, according to Hume, "livelier" and enter our minds with more "force and violence."

For example, I look out my window and see various features of Cherokee Peak. In Hume's terminology, I have an impression of the whiteness of the peak, an impression of the greenness of the trees around the base, an impression of the grayness of the rocks, and so forth. If I think about these impressions, I can form ideas based upon whiteness, greenness, and grayness. My impressions are immediate and vivid; my ideas are pale copies.

Look at this book and make your own Humean distinction between impressions and ideas.

The sense impressions I have of this book are _____

_____. The ideas I can form about these impressions are

_____. The difference

between impressions and ideas is _____

_____.

Hume's next step is to break impressions into two groups: simple and complex. Thus, when I looked at Cherokee Peak and had the impression of whiteness, it was a simple impression. All I saw was whiteness and nothing else. But I could also look at Cherokee Peak and see a white peak *together with* green trees and gray rocks. This would be a complex impression. Complex impressions are made of many simple impressions.

Now, using your sense knowledge of this book, make your own distinction between simple and complex impressions.

A few simple impressions of this book would be _____

_____.

A complex impression would be _____.

Hume also distinguishes between simple and complex ideas. Simple ideas, as you might guess, are produced by simple impressions. My simple impression of the whiteness of Cherokee Peak produces the simple idea of whiteness.

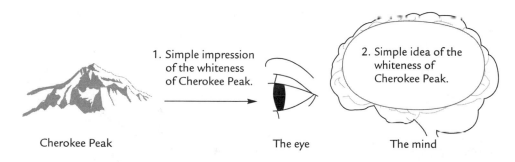

Cherokee Peak   1. Simple impression of the whiteness of Cherokee Peak.   The eye   2. Simple idea of the whiteness of Cherokee Peak.   The mind

Complex ideas can be produced in either of two ways. First, a complex impression can produce a complex idea. Thus, my complex impression of Cherokee Peak's white snow, green trees, and gray rocks can produce my complex idea of Cherokee Peak's white snow, green trees, and gray rocks.

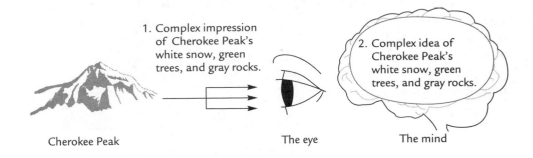

The second way that complex ideas can be produced is by combining simple ideas. Thus, I could take the simple ideas of red, blue, and yellow and create a complex idea of a red, blue, and yellow Cherokee Peak.

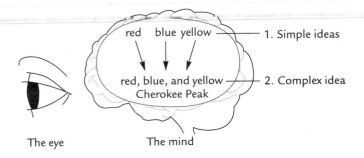

In other words, whenever I imagine something that doesn't exist in the external world, I am combining simple ideas into complex ideas.

Now illustrate your own example of simple ideas and the two kinds of complex ideas:

A simple impression of _____ would produce the simple

idea of _____. A complex impression of _____,

_____, and _____ would produce the complex idea of _____,

_____, and _____. Another kind of complex idea could be formed by

combining the simple ideas of _____, _____, and _____

to produce the complex idea of _____.

I rarely have a student who objects to anything I've said thus far about Hume's epistemology. What could be more obvious? Simple ideas come from simple impressions; complex ideas come from either complex impressions or by combining simple ideas.

But observe what Hume does with his analysis of knowledge. He claims that since all our knowledge can be traced back to simple impressions, *any knowledge not based on a simple impression is meaningless*. Hume will argue that our knowledge of substance, God, mind, and self, as well as cause and effect, is not based on simple impressions, and thus all these terms, so important to philosophers, are meaningless.

> When we entertain, therefore, any suspicion that a philosophical term is employed without any meaning or idea (as is but too frequent), we need but to inquire, from what impression is that supposed idea derived? And if it be impossible to assign any, this will serve to confirm our suspicion [that the idea has no meaning].

Let's say I try to argue that I *can* have ideas that didn't come from simple impressions. For example, I think of a wonderful city with ruby towers, golden walls, and diamond gates. Certainly, I have seen no such city; therefore, my idea of this city does not come from simple impressions.

Hume, however, would quickly reply that everything in my city *did* come from simple impressions. I merely combined those simple impressions into a new complex idea. The complex idea of ruby towers could be traced back to simple impressions that came from rubies and towers; the complex idea of golden walls could be traced back to simple impressions that came from gold and walls; the complex idea of diamond gates could be traced back to simple impressions that came from diamonds and gates.

Explore Hume's way of thinking by imagining a fantastical, complex idea and then trace it back to simple impressions.

Right now I am thinking of _____

_____.

I can trace this complex idea back to the simple impressions of _____

_____

_____.

Thus, Hume holds the classic empiricist position that there is no knowledge in our mind that did not originate in our senses. His powerful addition to this position is that if we do have a concept that *cannot* be traced back to a sense origin, then that concept is meaningless.

Hume solidifies his skeptical position by distinguishing between the only two kinds of knowledge claims we can make and showing that neither provides certainty about the world.

What Are the Limitations of Knowledge?

In Hume's view, all knowledge is limited to two kinds of statements: *relations of ideas* and *matters of fact*.

Mathematics and geometry are the province of relationships of ideas. Thus, when I say that $2 + 2 = 4$ or that a triangle is a three-sided figure, I am relating one idea to another. In the first case, I am relating the idea of $2 + 2$ to the idea of 4; in the second case, I am relating the idea of a triangle to the idea of a three-sided figure.

Now note this important point: *Relations of ideas provide us with absolute certainty but make no statements about the world.* It is absolutely certain that the idea of 2 + 2 equals the idea of 4, but this tells us nothing about the external world. All we have is a relationship of ideas; ideas don't exist in the external world. When you relate the idea of a triangle to the idea of a three-sided figure you *do* have absolute certainty because you have correctly linked two concepts, but you do not have any knowledge of the external world. All you have are two correctly linked concepts. Information about the external world *must be based upon sense impressions.* This brings us to the second kind of statement, matters of fact.

Matters of fact are based upon sense impressions. Thus, when I say "There is a dog on my desk" or "This wooden shape is a triangle," I am making a matter-of-fact statement based upon a sense impression. By "matter of fact," Hume does not mean a statement that is true, but a statement that is based upon a sense impression in the "world of facts." Thus, it could be factually true that there is a dog on my desk or factually false that there is a dog on my desk, but it would still be a matter-of-fact statement to say "there is a dog on my desk." Matters of fact are simply statements, true or false, about the external world.

Now note this important point: *Matters of fact are statements about the world but provide us with no absolute certainty.* This point is often difficult for students to grasp, so please pay close attention. Everything hinges upon grasping the concept of absolute certainty.

If a statement is absolutely certain, it is 100 percent certain. This means there is not the slightest possibility for the statement to be false. Now how do we tell if a statement is 100 percent certain? Descartes suggested the "demon" test. If an all-powerful demon could not deceive Descartes about the certitude of a statement, then that statement would be 100 percent certain. Hume proposes what might be called the "meaningful-contradiction test." If a statement cannot be meaningfully contradicted, then that statement is 100 percent certain.

Here is a statement and its contradiction:

A. There is a dog on my desk.

B. Contradiction: There is no dog on my desk.

Note that statement B is a meaningful contradiction. Thus, statement A is not *absolutely* certain because there is some possibility, no matter how small, that statement B is the case. Statement B could be eliminated only if it had no meaning.

Now, look at this statement and its contradiction:

A. A triangle is a three-sided figure.

B. Contradiction: A triangle is not a three-sided figure.

Note that statement B is *not a meaningful contradiction.* While it does make perfect sense to say "There is no dog on my desk," it makes no sense at all to say "A triangle is not a three-sided figure." Thus, we can be absolutely certain that "A triangle is a three-sided figure" because the statement cannot be meaningfully contradicted.

To sum up: Relations of ideas are absolutely certain, but because they merely relate one idea to another, they provide no information about the world. Matters of fact provide information about the world, but because they can be meaningfully contradicted, they are not absolutely certain.

EXERCISE 22.2
Relations of Ideas, Matters of Fact, and the Meaningful-Contradiction Test

Label each of the following pairs of statements R for relation of idea or M for matter of fact. Explain whether each pair passes the meaningful-contradiction test.

1A. 6 times 6 equals 36.

1B. Contradiction: 6 times 6 does not equal 36.

This (does, does not) pass the meaningful-contradiction test because

_____

_____.

Therefore, statement 1A (is, is not) absolutely certain.

2A. Flipping the light switch causes the light to go off.

2B. Flipping the light switch does not cause the light to go off.

This (does, does not) pass the meaningful-contradiction test because

_____

_____.

Therefore, statement 2A (is, is not) absolutely certain.

3A. A square is a geometrical figure with four equal sides joined by 90-degree angles.

3B. Contradiction: A square is not a geometrical figure with four equal sides joined by 90-degree angles.

This (does, does not) pass the meaningful-contradiction test because

_____

_____.

Therefore, statement 3A (is, is not) absolutely certain.

4A. Arrows are straight.

4B. Contradiction: Arrows are not straight.

This (does, does not) pass the meaningful-contradiction test because

_____

_____.

Therefore, statement 4A (is, is not) absolutely certain.

5A. A straight line is the shortest distance between two points.

5B. Contradiction: A straight line is not the shortest distance between two points.

This (does, does not) pass the meaningful-contradiction test because

_____

_____.

Therefore, statement 5A (is, is not) absolutely certain.

6A. The sun will rise tomorrow.

6B. Contradiction: The sun will not rise tomorrow.

This (does, does not) pass the meaningful-contradiction test because

_____

_____ .

Therefore, statement 6A (is, is not) absolutely certain.

Now, let's investigate the three ways that Hume says we relate our ideas to each other. What are the principles, similar to Newton's principles of physical nature, that operate in human nature?

What Are the Three Laws of the Association of Ideas?

Hume's goal, remember, is to describe the operating principles of human nature in the same way that Newton describes the operating principles of the cosmos. If gravitation is the force that binds objects together, what is the force or principle that binds ideas together? Hume believes there are only three laws of the association of ideas:

- The law of resemblance
- The law of contiguity
- The law of cause and effect

One idea can be linked to another because one idea *resembles* another. For example, as Hume says, "a picture easily leads our thoughts to the original." A picture of the moon easily leads our thoughts to ideas of the moon.

A second way our thoughts are linked together is based on *contiguity*, spatial or temporal. (Contiguity means "the state of being next to or near.") In Hume's example, thinking about one apartment "naturally leads us to think about others" that are nearby. Thinking about the Golden Gate Bridge leads us to think about the bay that the bridge spans.

A final and very important way our thoughts are linked together is through *cause and effect*. Hume's example is "If we think of a wound, we can scarcely keep ourselves from reflecting on the pain which follows it." Thinking of turning a key in a car's ignition will naturally lead us to think of the car starting. As you will see in the next chapter, Hume will make devastating use of this internal principle of cause and effect to attack the concept of cause and effect.

These laws of association of ideas do not operate in the ironclad way of Newton's laws of universal gravitation. Rather, as Hume says, "a gentle force, which commonly prevails" guides us in linking our ideas in one of these three ways. Thus, the "gentle force" could make the spatial link between the Golden Gate Bridge and the bay it spans; but, if we are determined to break this link, we can think of the Golden Gate Bridge and then of anything else we wish—for example, sweet potato pie. The three laws of the association of ideas describe the "normal" flow and linkage of our thoughts.

Now, create your own examples of the three ways ideas can be linked.

An example of linking ideas through resemblance would be the idea of _____

_____, which resembles the idea of _____.

An example of linking ideas through contiguity would be the idea of _____

_____, which brings to mind the idea of _____

_____.

An example of linking ideas through cause and effect would be the idea of the

cause _____, which brings to mind the effect

_____.

EXERCISE 22.3
The Three Laws of Association of Ideas

Consider each of the following pairs of linked ideas. Label the pairs either R (resemblance), CS (contiguity: spatial), CT (contiguity: temporal), CE (cause and effect), or IHDK (I honestly don't know).

_____ 1. The Ace of Hearts: The Ace of Spades

_____ 2. The Mona Lisa: Leonardo da Vinci

_____ 3. A bomb exploding: The sound of the explosion

_____ 4. A carton of milk: The inside of a refrigerator door

_____ 5. The first word of a song: The second word of a song

_____ 6. A blue plum: The blue sky

_____ 7. Desks: Blackboard

_____ 8. Mom: Apple pie

_____ 9. The gravity of the moon: The rising tides

_____ 10. Pressing the keys on a computer keyboard: Letters appearing on a
computer monitor

EXERCISE 22.4
Do You Agree with Hume?

Here's a summary of important points established thus far. Explain why you agree or disagree with each one:

1. All our meaningful ideas can be traced back to a sense impression.

I (agree, disagree) because _____

_____

_____.

2. If an idea cannot be traced back to a sense impression, that idea is meaningless.

I (agree, disagree) because _____

_____

_____.

3. Geometry and mathematics are based upon relations of ideas. Relations of ideas are absolutely certain but tell us nothing about the world.

I (agree, disagree) because _____

_____

_____.

4. Matters of fact are based upon sense impressions. Matters of fact tell us about the world, but are never absolutely certain.

I (agree, disagree) because _____

_____

_____.

5. In the normal course of our thinking, our ideas are linked in only one of three ways: resemblance, contiguity, or cause and effect.

I (agree, disagree) because _____

_____

_____.

Now how does Hume turn these principles into powerful philosophical weapons? Let's begin with his attack upon the concept of the self.

Can the Existence of the Self Be Proven?

In order to understand Hume's attack upon the concept of self, we first need to get clear on what we mean by "self." As a beginning, we can simply say that self is what is referred to when someone uses the word "I." For example:

1. I am happy.
2. I am sad.
3. I am a teacher
4. I am a father.
5. I was an active baby.
6. I was a lazy teenager.

These sentences are descriptions of my self. Self is what *remains the same* as my moods, roles, and age change. I don't have a new self every time I have a new mood. As I change roles from teacher to father, I don't change selves. As I grew from a baby to teenager to adult, my age changed, my body changed, but I still had the same self. It was "I" who was a baby and it is "I" who am an adult. Moods change, roles change, values change, but the self doesn't. Self is the unchanging part of us that *has* changing moods, roles, and values.

Give me your own example.

My mood can change from _____ to _____, but my self

(does, does not) change because _____

_____

_____.

Now what would happen if I tried to find an impression of my unchanging self?

Here is what Hume says:

> . . . from what impression could this idea [of self] be derived? This question is impossible to answer without a manifest contradiction and absurdity; and yet it is a question, which must necessarily be answered, if we would have the idea of self pass for clear and intelligible. It must be some one impression, that gives rise to every real idea. But self or person is not any one impression, but that to which our several impressions and ideas are supposed to have a reference. If any impression gives rise to the idea of self, that impression must continue invariably the same, through the whole course of our lives; since self is supposed to exist after that manner. But there is no impression constant and invariable.[1]

According to Hume, we have no impression of self because an impression of self would have to be an impression of something unchanging and "there is no impression constant and invariable."

Well, let's try to prove Hume wrong. First, I'll look for external and then internal evidence of self.

Here is a group of pictures from my photo album.

Apparently, this seems to give evidence for the existence of my self. The first photo shows me at three months; the second photo shows me at ten; the last photo shows me recently.

---

[1] From David Hume's *A Treatise On Human Nature*, ed. L. A. Selby-Bigge (New York: Oxford University Press, 1888) p. 251.

Aren't these photos an external impression of self? Unfortunately not. Self, as has been pointed out, is what is unchanging. These photos show only the *changing*. Even if you could identify some features in these pictures that are unchanging—for example, the shape of the Biffle nose—this would be no evidence of my unchanging self. I am more than my nose shape. If my nose got broken, I would still be me.

Do you agree? If you looked through your own photo album, would you find an external impression of unchanging self?

I would say _____

_____

_____ .

Well, let me look for an *internal* impression of self. When I look inward at my self, what do I find? As a self, I have

1. Values
2. Emotions
3. Memories
4. Fantasies
5. Goals
6. Needs
7. Abilities
8. Knowledge
9. Faults

And so forth. If I haven't exhausted all the attributes of my self, let me throw in a last catch-all category, personality, to include anything I didn't mention.

The Self

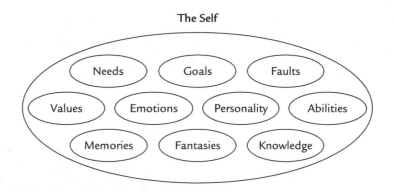

Now, let's look through these one by one to see if I can find my unchanging self:

1. Values: My values changed with each decade, sometimes with each year or month of my life. My values as a child were different from my values

as a teenager, and my values as an adult are different from my values as a teenager. Thus, values couldn't be part of my unchanging self.

2. Emotions: My emotions continuously change. Every time I have a new emotion, I don't have a new self. Thus, emotions can't be part of my unchanging self.

3. Memories: I lose memories and I gain memories. But as the quantity of my memories changes, I don't become more or less me. Thus, memories cannot be part of my unchanging self. Self seems to be what "has" memories. But what is self?

4. Fantasies: My fantasies change all the time. While writing this book, I have the happy fantasy that you'll think philosophy is intriguing and then the unhappy fantasy that you'll think all philosophers are fools. Fantasies change; self doesn't. Thus, fantasies can't be part of my unchanging self.

5. Goals: As I change tasks, my goals change. Right now, my goal is to finish this chapter. After a while, my goal will be to complete a hike. New goals don't bring a new self. Even if all my goals changed completely, I would still have the same self—the same self with a new set of goals.

6. Needs: Every day I live through a blizzard of needs. I need food, excitement, entertainment, rest. Needs come and go too quickly to be part of the unchanging self.

7. Abilities: As my abilities developed from childhood to the present, I still had the same self. Abilities are what my self "possesses" but are not identical to my self.

8. Knowledge: Assume, knock on wood, I was in a car accident and lost half my knowledge. Would I be half a self? No. I would just be poor, half-witted Biffle. Same self, with less knowledge.

9. Faults: What if I turn over a new leaf and lose all my faults? I do not become a different person. I am merely virtuous Biffle. Faults are not identical to my self because even if I somehow, wondrously, lost all of them, I would still be me, faultless me.

10. Personality: Now let's consider the catch-all category. Am I my personality? Assume everything about my personality changes completely. I drop philosophy and take up skydiving. I give up teaching and start bug collecting. I am still the same self. My personality has acquired new attributes, but I am still me. Instead of philosophy-writing, school-teaching Biffle, I'm skydiving, bug-collecting Biffle.

Thus, wherever I look, I find no evidence of unchanging self; all I find are changing attributes. As Hume says,

> For my part, when I enter most intimately into what I call myself, I always stumble on some particular perception or other, of heat or cold, light or shade, love or hatred, pain or pleasure. I never can catch myself at any time without a perception, and never can observe any thing but the perception.

I have tried and could find no impression, internal or external, to correspond to self.

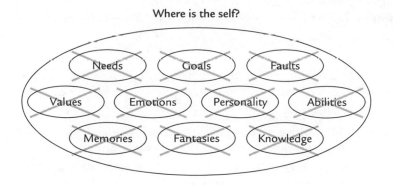

Where is the self?

Help me out. Where is the self? Select two of the aspects of self in the diagram above and argue as forcefully as you can that each gives you information about your *unchanging* self.

First, I'll choose _____. The information this

gives me about my unchanging self is _____

_____

_____.

Next, I'll choose _____. The information this

gives me about my unchanging self is _____

_____

_____.

But perhaps there is one last place to look for self. What if I simply defined self as my mind, the producer of my thoughts. Certainly I can find inner evidence of my mind?

Can the Existence of the Mind Be Proven?

Before reading Hume, I was positive I had a mind. I wasn't quite sure what it was, but it was obvious that I had one. According to Plato, my mind was divided into reason, spirited element, and appetites. According to Aristotle, my mind received all information that came through my senses. I was hardly sure which of these or numerous other descriptions were correct, but I was confident that there was a definite something producing thoughts between my ears.

Reading Hume, however, made me wonder if the word "mind" referred to anything real. In Hume's view, mind is a meaningless concept, a concept lacking a corresponding perception.

Hume says that if I look for my mind, I will find nothing but "a bundle or collection of different perceptions, which succeed each other with an inconceivable rapidity, and are in a perpetual flux and movement." This is Hume's famous doctrine of the mind as a "bundle of perceptions." In other words, when I look for my mind, all I'll find is a group of perceptions, thoughts, but no unchanging mind that is the thinker of the thoughts!

To begin to understand Hume's point, look at this sentence:

My mind is thinking the thought of the color blue.

Hume would agree that the two nouns "thought" and "blue" have meaning. They have meaning because they are tied to real perceptions. We have an inner perception of thoughts, and we have an external perception of the color blue. However, Hume would argue that we have no perception, internal or external, of "mind." Thus, we have the same evidence that mind exists as, say, that the Tooth Fairy exists. The Tooth Fairy and the mind are both concepts that come from no actual perception.

Now take another crack at proving Hume wrong. All you have to do is to describe an inner perception of your mind.

When I look for an inner impression of my mind I find _____

_____.

Let me try to help you. Let us say I look inward and try to have a perception of my mind. What am I looking for? At the very least, I am looking for something that produces my thoughts. The mind may be many things, but it is certainly the origin of ideas. Plato, Aristotle, and others may be right or wrong about mind, but they all would agree that the mind produces thoughts.

Well, let me do some inner looking for my thought producer. I'll perform the following experiment:

1. I will think the thought of an apple.

2. I will observe my mind producing the thought of an orange.

3. I will think the thought of an orange.

If I can catch my mind producing the thought of the orange, then I have defeated Hume. I can say, "Hume, you wanted a perception of my mind and I observed it producing the thought of an orange, so you're wrong. Minds exist."

Very well. Here is my experiment.

1. Right now, I am thinking the thought of an apple. It is red, shiny, smooth, has a small black stem with little green leaves. Now, I'm going to leave the thought of the apple behind, and observe my mind producing the thought of an orange.

2. ———

3. I am thinking the thought of an orange.

Something strange happened. I went immediately from the thought of an apple to the thought of an orange. I couldn't pause at step 2 and observe my mind *producing* the thought of the orange.

I'll try it again, only more slowly and carefully.

1. I am thinking the thought of an apple. I see the apple very clearly. So red, so shiny, so smooth, such green, little leaves. I hold the thought for long seconds. I'm going to think very slowly and just let the apple fade, very

slowly fade, from my consciousness and then intercept the mind as it produces the thought of the orange.

2. ———

3. I am thinking the thought of an orange.

The same thing happened again. The thought of the orange just popped into my mind and *I couldn't observe where it came from.* No matter how hard I try, I cannot perform the second mental act. I cannot observe my mind *producing* thoughts; I simply slip from one thought to another.

You try it.

1. First, I'll think the thought of an apple. It is _____
_____.

2. When I try to observe my mind producing the thought of an orange, what happens is _____
_____.

3. Now I am thinking the thought of an orange.

When I set out to catch an impression of my mind, I had *hoped* something like the following would happen.

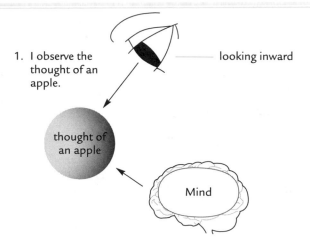

First, I would look inward and observe the thought of an apple.
Next, I *hoped* to observe the mind producing the thought of an orange.

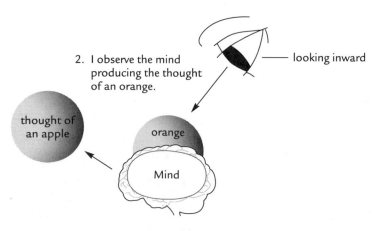

But I failed. I couldn't observe my mind producing the thought of an orange. In fact, what happened was the following:

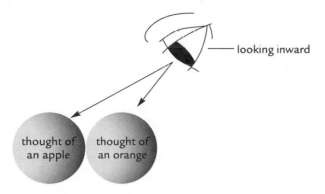

Actually, I could go on thinking about fruit, one thought after another, and *never observe the mind producing any thoughts.*

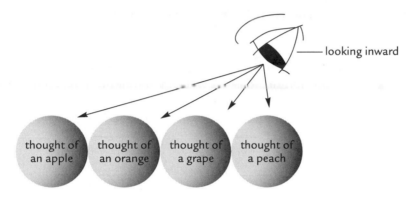

Whenever I look for an inner impression of my mind producing thoughts, *I am blocked by a stream of thoughts.* As Hume puts it, when I look into my mind, all I see are thoughts as they "successively make their appearance; pass, re-pass, glide away, and mingle in an infinite variety of postures and situations." I look inward and observe gliding thoughts but no thinker, no mind producing the thoughts.

I can repeat the experiment as many times as I wish. No matter how often I try to observe the thought of an orange or any other thought arising from my mind, I fail. Thoughts pop into my consciousness one after another. I can find no break in my thought stream, no gap through which I can observe my mind producing thoughts.

Go on. Try it again. Think a string of thoughts about fruit and try to observe your mind producing any of the thoughts.

When I try to observe my mind producing thoughts about fruit, what happens is

_____

_____.

If you are like most students, you have just discovered that you have no impression of the origin of your thoughts. Thoughts just leap into your head *from who knows where.* In Hume's view, you have no more evidence that your mind produces your thoughts than that the chair in the corner produces your thoughts. You just get thoughts with no information about their origin. Thoughts are merely psychic e-mail that flies through your head from regions unknown.

And if you have no impression of the mind, then mind is a meaningless concept. Mind is the Thought Fairy.

If Hume is right, then the consequences of his argument are devastating. Every sentence written about mind is meaningless! All the theories of mind by Plato, Aristotle, Aquinas, Descartes, Locke, Berkeley—poof!

To take a modern example, note what happens to Freud's psychology. According to Freud, the mind can be divided into three regions. The id is the origin of our instinctual desires. The superego is the origin of our sense of society's values. The ego, our consciousness, tries to mediate between id and superego.

Well, if we have no evidence that mind exists, as Hume claims, then we certainly have no evidence that *regions* of the mind—id, superego, and ego—exist.

Freud? Poof! Jung, Adler, Maslow, all psychological research into the nature of mind? Poof! Poof! Poof!

Because we have no impression of mind, thousands of years of investigation of the mind vaporize. Everyone who's been writing about mind could just as well have been trying to figure out how to squeeze sunbeams from cucumbers.

At this point, you might ask, "Well, if our thoughts don't come from our mind, where does Hume say they come from?" Because Hume is a skeptic, his answer is quite simple. *We don't know where our thoughts come from.* Period. Because Hume believes he has proved that we have no evidence of where our thoughts come from, it is hardly fair to ask him to offer evidence of where our thoughts come from. The whole point of skepticism is to demonstrate our lack of knowledge.

Is Hume right or wrong in arguing that we have no evidence for the origin of our thoughts?

Hume is (right, wrong) because _____

_____

_____.

Now, having investigated Hume's arguments about self and mind, in the next chapter you'll be ready for, among other topics, Hume's famous attack upon cause and effect.

SUMMARY

Hume, an empiricist and skeptic, attempted to describe human nature as accurately as Newton described the universe. The knowledge process begins with sense impressions and ends with ideas. Any idea that cannot be traced back to a sense impression is meaningless. All our knowledge claims are either relations of ideas or matters of fact. Mathematics and geometry are relations of ideas. These disciplines provide absolute certainty but no knowledge about the world. Sense impressions are matters of fact. Sense impressions provide information about the world but, because they do not pass the "meaningful contradiction test," are never absolutely certain. Hume argues that we have no evidence for the existence of the self or the mind.

EXERCISE 22.5
Looking Back

Use your own paper to answer the following questions. Paraphrase the information given in this chapter. Use original examples where appropriate.

1. What is a skeptic?
2. What was Newton's significance?
3. What is Hume's goal?
4. What is Hume's epistemology?
5. What are the limitations of knowledge?
6. What are the three laws of the association of ideas?
7. Can the existence of the self be proven?
8. Can the existence of the mind be proven?

EXERCISE 22.6
Looking at the World Through Hume's Eyes

How would Hume respond to the following? Use your own paper to explain your answers.

1. T F Plato was wrong in claiming that the perfect truths known by the mind exist independently of the mind.
2. T F Aristotle was right in saying there is nothing in the mind that did not come through the senses.
3. T F Augustine was wrong in claiming that our certainty is the product of God illuminating our mind.
4. T F Descartes's argument, "I think; therefore, I exist," is invalid.
5. T F Locke was wrong in claiming that the mind at birth is like a blank slate (*tabula rasa*).
6. T F If substance cannot be known by a sense impression, as Locke claims, then we have no evidence of the existence of substance.
7. T F Berkeley was wrong in claiming that ideas are the only reality.
8. T F Nothing can be known for certain.
9. T F It is possible for Einstein's equation, $e = mc^2$ (energy equals mass times the speed of light squared) to correctly express the relation between each of its terms without telling us anything about reality.
10. T F An important goal of philosophy is to show how little can be known.

ANALYSIS OF YOUR PHILOSOPHICAL SELF-PORTRAIT

To see how your views stack up against Hume's, read my analysis below, rethink your position, and then circle what you believe is the correct answer. I've underlined Hume's answers.

1. <u>T</u> F *Every idea can be traced back to a sense impression.*

    True puts you in Hume's camp, but not Locke's or Berkeley's (or that of any other philosopher we've investigated thus far). Locke holds that the idea of substance cannot be traced back to a sense impression, though it is a valid idea nonetheless; Berkeley holds the same for the idea of God.

2. <u>T</u> F *Absolute certainty is possible only in the concepts of math and geometry.*

    Philosophers before Hume, Descartes included, would have agreed that math and geometry provide absolute certainty, but would not have agreed that they are the *only* sources of absolute certainty. If you believe, for example, that you can be absolutely certain that God exists, then you are supported by Aristotle, Anselm, Aquinas, Descartes, Locke, and Berkeley. As in so many cases, siding with Hume puts you up against large numbers of philosophers before him. But, as I pointed out at the start of this section of the tour, you are backed up by thousands of living philosophers.

3. <u>T</u> F *Our senses can never provide us with absolute certainty.*

    Hume would certainly agree with this. No statement based upon the senses will pass the "meaningful-contradiction test." Whenever I say *X* about the world— for example, the sun will rise tomorrow—it is equally meaningful to contradict the statement by saying not-*X* about the world—the sun will *not* rise tomorrow. *As long as a statement has meaning, then there is a possibility it might be true.* Thus, I cannot say that I am absolutely certain that the sun will rise tomorrow, because there is a possibility that it might be true that the sun will not rise tomorrow.

    When we look for absolute certainty, we must look to mathematics and geometry. But the absolute certainty of these two disciplines tells us only about the relationship between ideas, not about the world of sense impressions. If you define the idea of zamboo as identical to the idea of a doodah, then you can be absolutely certain that all zamboos are doodahs. Math and geometry are the realm of zamboos and doodahs, mere ideas that we have defined ourselves and thus endowed with absolute certainty.

4. <u>T</u> <u>F</u> *The self is our unchanging identity.*

    Hume would have answered this True, if the statement were seen as a *definition* of the self. He agreed with the commonsense way of looking at the self as something that does not change. However, he would have answered this False if the statement were seen as asserting that the self exists. As you have learned, Hume argues we have no evidence for the existence of anything in human nature that is unchanging.

    If you answered this question False and believe you have a better, more accurate definition of the self than Hume's, I am sure your teacher will be interested. Under your definition, how many selves do you have and what is their nature? If you hold that self can change absolutely, then how would you respond to the following argument by a murderer? "One of my earlier selves committed the murder. But you can't find me guilty, because I'm a completely different self now. I, the self I am now, didn't commit the crime. I wasn't even there when it happened."

5. T F *The existence of the self can be proved by the senses.*

Hume would argue that the self cannot be anything known by the senses. If you believe you *can* have sense knowledge of your self, then what part of you hasn't changed since your birth and is identical to the person you think you are? If you had plastic surgery and gained or lost an enormous amount of weight, wouldn't you still be the same self—but merely visually different? If you say self is something changing, then would you really become a totally new person with a large weight change and plastic surgery?

6. T F *The existence of the self can be proved by looking at the internal world of the mind.*

It's very tempting to oppose Hume by answering this question True. It certainly seems as if there is something—one student called it a "teensy, tiny, undefinable something"—that exists inside us that is our self. We are sure that we are unique, completely different from all other selves. But our uniqueness would not be proof that we had a self. Uniqueness could be based upon a unique collection of memories, fantasies, goals, and so on unlike anyone else's. But where is the unchanging self, the ongoing identity that *has* the unique collection of memories, fantasies, and goals?

Consider this problem. If I asked you to describe your sense impression of an apple, you could certainly respond by saying, "I have the sense impression of something roundish, shiny, and red." However, if I asked you to describe your self, your unique self unlike anyone else's, that has the sense impression of the apple, what answer could you give that would be different from any answer anyone else could give? Do you really have knowledge of what is unique about your self? And if you don't have this knowledge, *what is the basis for your confidence in the existence of your unique self?*

7. T F *Our thoughts come from our minds.*

Again, it is very tempting to oppose Hume on this. But isn't it true that all we know when we look inward is our thought stream and not the origin of our thoughts? If we try to escape Hume and define mind as the thought stream, then we have as many minds as we have thoughts! If it is any comfort to you, Hume himself was quite upset by many of his own conclusions.

> I dine, I play a game of backgammon, I converse, and am merry with my friends; and when after three or four hours' amusement, I would return to these speculations, they appear so cold, and strained, and ridiculous, that I cannot find in my heart to enter into them farther.

Of course, the fact that a philosophical position is upsetting, even to its author, is no proof that the position is wrong.

Evaluation: Number of points in agreement with Hume = _____ of 7 possible.

A position of Hume's that you strongly (support, oppose) is _____

_____

because _____

_____

_____.

GOOD BOOKS

Flew, Antony. *Hume's Philosophy of Belief.* London: Routledge & Kegan Paul, 1961. A well-regarded introduction to Hume.

Lavine, T. Z. *From Socrates to Sartre.* New York: Bantam, 1984. The chapters on Hume are an excellent introduction to his thought.

NEXT STOP

More Hume. More philosophical bombshells.

23

David Hume

How to Destroy Certainty About Science, God, and Absolute Moral Values

YOUR PHILOSOPHICAL SELF-PORTRAIT

Add more details to your philosophical self-portrait by answering the questions below and offering evidence for your answers.

1. T   F   The principle of cause and effect is an important basis of scientific observation.

    Evidence: _____
    _____.

2. T   F   Our senses teach us that every event has a cause.

    Evidence: _____
    _____.

3. T   F   It is 100 percent certain that the sun will rise tomorrow.

    Evidence: _____
    _____.

4. T   F   Our desires should be guided by our reason, not vice versa.

    Evidence: _____
    _____.

5. T   F   The design of the universe is evidence of God's existence.

    Evidence: _____
    _____.

6. T   F   In the realm of nature, there is a high probability that future events will be like past events.

    Evidence: _____
    _____.

PREVIEW

After analyzing the commonsense concept of cause and effect, we explore Hume's attack upon this concept. Hume argues that all we observe in a cause-and-effect relationship is one event *preceding* another event, not one event *causing* another event. The origin of our concept of the necessary connection between cause and effect is subjective, in the relationship of ideas, not objective, in the physical world. We will also explore Hume's attack upon three proofs of God's existence and the view that reason should guide our desires.

THOUGHT EXPERIMENT

Imagine that a virus affects all human brains and we can no longer reason about the necessary connection between cause and effect. Thus, no one can confidently perform either of the following acts of reasoning:

Cause A produces effect B.

Effect B was produced by cause A.

Science, among many other human activities, would collapse. Though scientists would be able to observe events, they would not be able to link them together.

Thermometers would be of no use because a doctor would not be able to link the effect of an increase in temperature to the cause of a fever.

Stethoscopes would be of no use because the doctor would not be able to link the effect of a thumping sound to the cause of a heart producing the thumping sound.

X-rays would be useless because a doctor would not be able to link the effect of the x-ray portrait to the cause within a patient's body.

In fact, all medical diagnosis would be impossible because doctors would not be able to link any symptom as an effect to any illness as a cause.

Sciences other than medicine would fare no better.

Biologists would not be able to link any biological cause to any biological event—for example, the contraction of a muscle to the movement of a limb.

Astronomers would not be able to link any force to any physical event—for example, the force of gravity to the movement of the planets.

Weather forecasters would not even be able to link dark clouds to rain.

What are some other areas of science, besides the ones I mentioned, that would be impossible if a brain virus wiped out our ability to reason about cause and effect?

_____

_____

_____

Because almost all of science is based on reasoning about cause and effect, the brain virus would wipe out vast regions of science. Events could be observed but not explained.

A large portion of daily life, as well, depends upon reasoning about cause and effect. Affected by our brain virus, people would frequently run out of gas because they couldn't reason from the marker on their gas gauge to the amount of gas in their tank. Nor, would anyone have to worry about watching too much television. Unable to reason about cause and effect, no one would be able to turn on the boob tube.

If a brain virus destroyed your ability to reason from cause to effect, what are some of the normal activities that would vanish from your life?

_____

_____

_____.

Obviously, cause and-effect reasoning is massively important. If we cannot rationally link one event to another, almost every human activity will be drastically altered or cease. But why do we believe in cause and effect? *Because we believe that the cause-and-effect relationship is a key aspect of reality.* External events—a thumping heart, dark clouds, gas in the tank—seem to be nothing but causes for other external events—a sound in a stethoscope, rain, the position of the needle on a gas gauge. Thus, any philosophical attack upon the logical link between cause and effect would strike not only at the core of human thinking but also at the core of our conception of reality.

David Hume, as you may have guessed, makes such an attack.

Though we will deal with several important topics in Hume's philosophy in this section of the tour, our major task will be to analyze his famous criticism of the concept of cause and effect.

I'll answer the following questions:

- What is cause and effect?

- How does Hume attack the cause-and-effect relationship?

- If cause and effect have no real existence, where do we get the idea of cause and effect?

And then, to wrap up our investigation of Hume's philosophy, I'll answer the following:

- Can God's existence be proven?

- What is Hume's position on metaphysics?

- What is Hume's ethics?

After evaluating my answers to all the above, you'll be ready to explore selections from Hume's *An Abstract of a Treatise of Human Nature,* a presentation of the central features of his attack upon cause and effect.

What Is Cause and Effect?

Most commentators on Hume agree with Hume's own estimation that his analysis of cause and effect is the centerpiece of his skeptical position. Thus, we will go very carefully through his argument. Let's begin by clarifying what we mean by a cause-and-effect relationship.

Here are a few more examples, besides those presented in our thought experiment, of cause and effect:

- Billiard ball A strikes billiard ball B, and billiard ball B rolls away. The cause is said to be the movement of billiard ball A; the effect is said to be the movement of billiard ball B.

- Flames from a stove's burner touch the bottom of a pot of water and the water eventually boils. The cause is said to be the heat produced by the flames; the effect is said to be the boiling water.

- A rock breaks a window. The cause is said to be the rock; the effect is said to be the breaking window.

In every case, cause precedes and produces effect.

Think of several more examples of cause and effect.

A cause would be _____,

and an effect would be _____.

A cause would be _____,

and an effect would be _____.

A cause would be _____,

and an effect would be _____.

Note the important difference between two events that are related causally and two events that are simply related sequentially. In a causal relationship, *A* produces *B;* in a sequential relationship *A* simply precedes *B.* For example:

- *Causal relationship:* Pressing the keys on a computer keyboard produces the letters on the screen. One event *causes* another.

- *Sequential relationship:* Pressing one key and then pressing another key. One event *precedes* another.

Now give me your own examples of the difference between a causal relationship and a sequential relationship.

An example of a causal relationship would be _____

_____.

An example of a sequential relationship would be _____

_____.

In a nutshell, Hume is going to argue that every event that we think is causal is only sequential. *We think we observe one event producing another event; all we really observe is one event preceding another event.*

EXERCISE 23.1
Causal Relationships

For each of the following which expresses a causal relationship, identify the cause and effect; where there is no causal relationship, explain why the relationship is *not* causal. For example:

Pushing the doorbell rings the buzzer.

Cause: pushing the doorbell; effect: the buzzer rings.

In the series of positive integers, 8 always comes before 9.

No causal relationship; 8 merely comes before but does not cause 9.

1. When Juan opened the window, light flooded into the room.
2. Light flooded into the room when Juan opened the window.
3. Dr. Kanwackie discovered that cosmetic sample x46 produced lesions on the skin of rabbits.
4. Night follows day.
5. I was thinking about Mary, and then the dog barked.
6. I was thinking about Mary, and then she called on the phone.
7. In direct sunlight, the thermometer on Tang's porch read 106 degrees.
8. When the doctor hit Lulu's knee with his little hammer, her leg jumped.
9. When the doctor hit Paolo's knee with his little hammer, he coughed.
10. The teacher asked, "Are there any questions?" and the air conditioning suddenly stopped.
11. The moon's orbit is controlled by the earth's gravity.
12. The engine merely whirred when Kanika turned the key.
13. In this sentence, "this" came after "In."
14. First there was thunder, and then there was lightning.
15. Tilly popped the balloon with the pin.
16. Before Han died, he prayed and then he went to Heaven.

Hume argues that we cannot logically link any event as cause to any other event as effect. In other words, we have no evidence that any event was produced by any earlier event or will be the cause of any later event. All we observe are sequential—not causal—events.

But how on earth can Hume prove there is no logical link between cause and effect? How will he ever be able to argue that pins don't make balloons pop or that one billiard ball doesn't cause another to move?

How Does Hume Attack
the Cause-and-Effect Relationship?

We'll investigate Hume's argument by taking a very simple case of cause and effect—one billiard ball strikes another. Ball A rolls into ball B, and ball B moves.

The cause is said to be the movement of ball A; the effect is said to be the movement of ball B. What could be more obvious? How can Hume say we cannot logically link the movement of ball A as cause, to the movement of ball B as effect? Aren't our senses giving us all the evidence we need to reason from cause to effect?

To make our billiard ball example very clear, assume we take a movie of the event and clip these three frames.

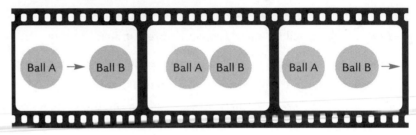

| Frame 1: | Frame 2: | Frame 3: |
| Ball A approaches Ball B. | Ball A contacts Ball B. | Ball B moves away. |

In frame 1, we see ball A, prior to its contact with ball B. In frame 2, we see ball A contacting ball B. In frame 3, we see ball B after its contact with A.

In Hume's view, in order to demonstrate the existence of cause and effect we have to make four observations:

1. Temporal priority
2. Spatial contiguity
3. Constant conjunction
4. Necessary connection

In the case of the billiard balls A and B, the observation of *temporal priority* would be the observation of A moving prior to its contact with B; the observation of *spatial contiguity* would be the observation of A next to B; the observation of *constant conjunction* is the repeated observation of A moving and then B moving; the observation of *necessary connection* is the observation of A producing the effect of B's movement.

Very well. Let's put Hume to the test.

Looking at our three frames of film, see if you can make the observation of temporal priority. Which frame shows the movement of ball A, the supposed cause, existing in time prior to the supposed effect, the movement of ball B?

I would say frame _____ shows temporal priority, A's movement prior to B's movement.

Now, which of the frames shows spatial contiguity? Which frame shows A next to B?

Frame _____ shows ball A next to ball B.

If you are like most students, you have identified frame 1 as an observation of temporal priority and frame 2 as an observation of spatial contiguity. Frame 1 shows the movement of ball A existing in time prior to the movement of ball B; frame 2 shows ball A next to ball B.

Now, let me help you make the observation of constant conjunction. Imagine we play our little film a hundred times. You could observe the constant conjunction of A moving and then B moving.

Thus, you have made three important observations to establish the existence of cause and effect:

1. You have observed temporal priority because you have observed A moving before B's movement.

2. You have observed spatial contiguity because you have observed ball A next to ball B.

3. Finally, playing the film many times allows you to repeatedly observe the constant conjunction of the sequence of events where A moves and then B moves.

Hume would agree that we *can* observe temporal priority, spatial contiguity, and constant conjunction; but he points out that these three observations *do not demonstrate cause and effect*. This is an important point, so before we go on to look for the fourth observation, necessary connection, let's pause for a moment.

Every time we watch a cartoon, a magician performing a trick, or a movie with special effects, we observe temporal priority, spatial contiguity, and—if we repeatedly observe the event—constant conjunction *without observing cause and effect*.

If, over and over, you watch the magician David Copperfield get "cut in half" by a whirling saw, you see:

1. The temporal priority of the saw moving prior to its contact with Copperfield's body.

2. The spatial contiguity of the saw next to Copperfield's body.

3. The constant conjunction of the movement of the saw and the slicing in half of Copperfield's body.

But, of course, you don't see the whirling saw actually causing the effect of a body getting sliced in half because Copperfield's body isn't really sliced in half.

Take another example. When you watch, over and over, the Tyrannosaurus Rex in *Jurassic Park* pluck an actor off the ground and swing his body in the air, you see:

1. The temporal priority of the dinosaur moving prior to its contact with the actor's body.

2. The spatial contiguity of the dinosaur's jaws next to the actor's body.

3. The constant conjunction of the movement of the dinosaur's jaws and the body rising into the air.

But, of course, you don't see the dinosaur *causing the effect* of the actor's body getting plucked off the ground, because the dinosaur is just a computer-generated fiction that has no real effect upon the actor.

Thus, and this is a very important point, just because we observe temporal priority, spatial contiguity, and constant conjunction, we have not observed cause and effect.

Now perhaps you want to say, "I am certain two billiard balls rolling together are a real example of cause and effect. There is no magic trick or special effect involved."

Very well, let's try to make the fourth observation, the observation of necessary connection. You certainly believe that the two events, the movement of ball A and the movement of ball B, are necessarily connected. Which frame shows their necessary connection? In other words, which frame shows the movement of A *producing the effect* of the movement of B?

Frame 1:
Ball A approaches Ball B.

Frame 2:
Ball A contacts Ball B.

Frame 3:
Ball B moves away.

Let's use the process of elimination.

Frame 1 does not show A producing the effect of B. Frame 1 merely shows A moving *before* B.

Frame 2 does not show A producing the effect of B. Frame 2 merely shows A *next* to B.

Do you see that everything comes down to frame 3? Here it is; look at it again.

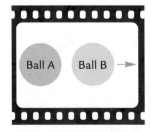

Frame 3:
Ball B moves away.

No matter how closely you investigate frame 3, you will never see ball A producing the effect of the movement of ball B. *All you see is ball B moving away.* The observation of ball B moving away is nothing like the observation of ball A producing the movement of ball B.

Thus, Hume concludes that we have no sense evidence of cause and effect. We can make the observation of temporal priority (frame 1); we can make the observation of spatial contiguity (frame 2); we can make the observation of constant conjunction by playing the frames over and over; but we cannot make the observation, the all-important observation, of necessary connection. No frame shows us the movement of ball A actually producing the movement of ball B!

If we have no sense evidence of necessary connection, we have no evidence of cause and effect. And if we have no evidence of cause and effect, all our logical reasonings about cause and effect are hollow, empty, plain wrong. *We have no more proof that ball A moved ball B than that someone sneezing in China moved ball B.*

I am almost positive that you now believe Hume is loony.

But pause for a moment. Remember the point I mentioned in our tour of Berkeley. If a philosophical position is as foolish as it sounds, then the argument would not have survived the first generation of readers. Thus, your best response is not to reject Hume's argument out of hand but to think through it carefully. Where, specifically, is the weakness in what Hume is arguing?

The weakness in Hume's argument is _____

_____

_____

Here are the most common objections students raise to Hume's analysis. Circle the ones that seem the strongest.

Objection 1: Add more frames. Show all the stages of A approaching B, and then A squashing itself against B, and then B moving away. More frames will show A causing the effect of B.

Objection 2: Though each frame taken individually does not show necessary connection, all three frames taken together will show necessary connection. Look at all three frames and you will see A causing the effect of B.

Objection 3: Frame 2 shows A transferring its momentum to B. Frame 3 shows B moving away after impact. Thus, frames 2 and 3 combined show necessary connection.

Objection 4: You can't see cause and effect. There is an invisible transfer of power from A to B in frame 2. If there were no invisible transfer of power, then you wouldn't see B move away in frame 3.

Now, from Hume's point of view, let me answer each objection.

Objection 1: Add more frames. Show all the stages of A approaching B, and then A squashing itself against B, and then B moving away. More frames will show A causing the effect of B.

Answer: Additional frames will not show any more than our three frames. Additional frames would do no more than add more images like frame 1 or more images like frame 2 or more images like frame 3. *More images will add no new evidence.*

Frame 1 shows temporal priority. One hundred more frames of ball A moving before ball B would not show anything else but ball A moving before ball B. Temporal priority is temporal priority, whether we use a single frame to portray it or a hundred.

Frame 2 shows spatial contiguity. One hundred more frames of the slow-motion impact of A with B would not show anything else but A coming, very slowly, into contact with B. Spatial contiguity is spatial contiguity, whether we use a single frame to portray it or a hundred.

Frame 3 shows B after contact with A. One hundred more frames would do nothing except show B after contact with A. If necessary connection cannot be observed in frame 3, then a hundred more versions of frame 3 will not help.

Thus, adding more frames cannot be the answer, because adding more frames merely adds more of what we already have.

Objection 2: Though each frame taken individually does not show necessary connection, all three frames taken together will show necessary connection. Look at all three frames, and you will see A causing the effect of B.

Answer: If each clue in a murder trial provided no evidence that the defendant was a killer, then adding all the clues together would provide no *additional* evidence that the defendant was a killer. Thus, if each frame taken individually offers no evidence of necessary connection, then adding all three together will provide no additional evidence of necessary connection. Zero plus zero plus zero equals zero.

Showing all the frames together shows only constant conjunction. Constant conjunction is just one event following another, not one event *producing* another. If you watch a merry-go-round, you can observe the constant conjunction of the movement of the red horse following the movement of the blue horse. But all you have observed is a sequence of events, not one event *causing* another. The movement of the red horse does not cause the movement of the blue horse.

Or, to return to our example of the magician: Assume you make a movie in order to understand how a magician performed a trick. Playing the movie at full speed—that is, looking at all the frames together—would be *less helpful* than analyzing each frame individually. Thus, if you cannot locate necessary connection by analyzing each frame above, looking at all of them together will be even less help.

Objection 3: Frame 2 shows A transferring its momentum to B. Frame 3 shows B moving away after impact. Thus, frames 2 and 3 combined show necessary connection.

Answer: Look at frame 2 again.

Frame 2:
Ball A contacts Ball B.

Touch the place in the picture that shows "transferring momentum." *All that frame 2 shows is spatial contiguity.* All that you can *see* is A next to B. You have no observation of the "flow of energy" from A to B or the "transfer of momentum." Thus, you must hold that the "transfer of momentum" is invisible. See objection 4.

Objection 4: You can't see cause and effect. There is an invisible transfer of power from A to B in frame 2. If there were no invisible transfer of power, then you wouldn't see B move away in frame 3.

Answer: Let's consider how Hume would reply to each part of this objection. First, how would he respond to "There is an invisible transfer of power from A to B in frame 2"? As soon as you say that cause and effect is invisible, then you've said, of course, that you can't observe cause and effect. And when you admit you can make no observation of cause and effect, Hume has won! His claim that we have no sense knowledge of cause and effect is precisely what you have admitted to. And since, in his view, all knowledge we have comes through our senses, *we have no knowledge at all of cause and effect.*

The second part of this objection is "If there were no invisible transfer of power, then you wouldn't see B move away in frame 3." If you hold that the movement of B in frame 3 is evidence of an invisible transfer of power from A to B, then you are back where you started. Look at frame 3 all you wish, and you will find no evidence of A producing the movement of B, no evidence of necessary connection.

Now attack the weakest of my answers to the objections.

Your weakest answer was to objection (1, 2, 3, 4) because _____

_____

_____.

Now try to add an objection to Hume's argument that you believe is superior to any of the objections above.

_____

_____

_____.

Some students, despite what I have said, are still convinced that they can observe the "transfer of momentum." Consider this problem.

Let's say I hand you frames from two movies. In the first movie, you see two steel balls come in contact and one ball moves away. In the second movie, you see exactly the same thing. Two steel balls come in contact and the second one moves away. Then I tell you that in one of the movies the movement of the second ball was controlled by a magnet.

If you can really observe cause and effect, how do you tell which movie shows a "transfer of momentum" from Ball A to Ball B?

Movie 1

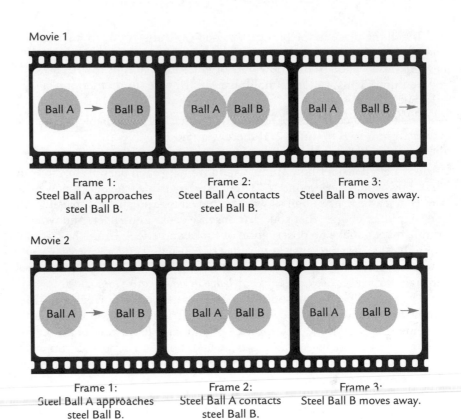

Frame 1:
Steel Ball A approaches
steel Ball B.

Frame 2:
Steel Ball A contacts
steel Ball B.

Frame 3:
Steel Ball B moves away.

Movie 2

Frame 1:
Steel Ball A approaches
steel Ball B.

Frame 2:
Steel Ball A contacts
steel Ball B.

Frame 3:
Steel Ball B moves away.

Here are strips from the two movies. Tell me which one shows the movement of Ball A as the cause of the effect of the movement of Ball B.

My response is _____

_____

_____ .

Obviously, the two strips are identical. In one strip, because of the magnet, there is *no transfer of momentum*. In the other strip, there is a supposed transfer of momentum. *If there is no visible difference between a real transfer of momentum and the illusion of a transfer of momentum, then how can you observe a real transfer of momentum?*
Your answer?

_____

_____

_____ .

Perhaps you want to ask Hume, "If we don't observe cause and effect, where does our idea of cause and effect come from?" Hume is ready for you.

Circular Causation

Escher's drawing could be taken as a portrait of an alternate reality where circular causation occurs. Thus, the left hand is the cause of the effect of the right hand, *and* the right hand is the cause of the effect of the left hand. In the case of circular causation, *X* causes *Y* and *Y* causes *X*.

Now, according to Hume, we must be able to make four different observations before we can verify that any event is the cause of any other event. Which of the following observations (you may choose more than one) would *not* be possible in Escher's alternate reality?

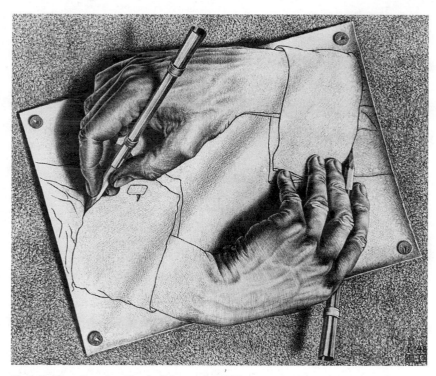

M. C. Escher, *Drawing Hands*, lithograph, 1948.

1. Spatial contiguity: *X* next to *Y*

2. Temporal priority: *X* occurring before *Y*

3. Constant conjunction: *X* and *Y* constantly linked together

4. Necessary connection: *X* producing the effect of *Y*

If this drawing is taken as a portrait of an alternate reality, then we would not be able to observe number(s) _____ because

_____

_____

_____.

Here is an interesting puzzle. Could time exist in an alternate reality in which all events were produced by circular causation?

Time (could, could not) exist in such an alternate reality because _____

_____

_____.

If Cause and Effect Have No Real Existence, Where Do We Get the Idea of Cause and Effect?

Let us imagine a baby who has never seen two billiard balls come together. Billiard ball A rolls slowly toward billiard ball B. The baby has no idea what to expect. Perhaps when A hits B, B will jingle or glow or disappear? Ball A hits ball B, and B moves away. The baby is surprised. The same event happens again and again. Before long, the baby mentally associates the movement of A with the movement of B. As the baby grows, other events are mentally associated with one another. Eventually, the baby develops into an adult, learns to call the mental association of events "cause and effect," and believes that cause and effect are in the world, not in the mind.

Now you can see the importance of one of the three laws of the association of ideas discussed in the previous chapter. Hume stated that we *mentally* link the idea of ball A moving with ball B moving, using the principle of cause and effect. Thus, *cause and effect is not an external phenomena, but merely the way we link ideas together in our minds.*

This is an extremely important point. Hume is saying that cause and effect is a subjective, not an objective, phenomenon. And this makes all the difference in the world. Consider the difference between subjective and objective events:

Objective: God actually exists.
Subjective: You merely *believe* God exists.

Objective: Your mother actually loves you.
Subjective: You merely *believe* your mother loves you.

Objective: You actually passed Introduction to Philosophy.
Subjective: You merely *believe* you passed Introduction to Philosophy.

If something is objectively true, then it is "really" true; if something is subjectively true, then we only believe it is true. In Hume's analysis, the cause and effect we think we see in events is just a projection of our internal association of ideas. We confuse reality with our mental habit. This is almost exactly like the case of an insane person who is not able to tell reality from mental delusions. The cause-and-effect relationship we think we objectively observe in the world is really our deluded projection of ideas we have subjectively linked together in our mind.

Has Hume caused you to doubt that you observe cause and effect?

_____

_____

_____.

Now let's turn from Hume's startling analysis of cause and effect to see what he will say about God.

Can God's Existence Be Proven?

We'll examine Hume's attack on three proofs of God's existence. In the last proof, you'll have an opportunity to do some philosophical exploring on your own.

Let's begin by reviewing two of the proofs of God's existence from earlier on the tour and consider how Hume would criticize each.

Anselm's ontological argument, also used by Descartes, can be summarized as

1. God is a being than whom none greater can be thought.
2. It is greater to exist than not to exist.
3. Therefore, God exists.

In the first statement, Anselm presents a definition of God. When we think of the word "God," we mean the ultimate being, the being who cannot be surpassed in our conceptions, "a being than whom none greater can be thought."

Anselm adds to his definition of God the concept of existence as superior to nonexistence. An entity with the characteristic of existence is "greater" than the same entity lacking the characteristic of existence. To understand Anselm's point, assume that your bank statement shows that you have a million dollars. A million dollars with the characteristic of existence would be greater than a million dollars without the characteristic of existence. In the first case, you actually have a million dollars; in the second case, you have a bank error. Thus, obviously, something with the characteristic of existence would be greater than the same thing lacking the characteristic of existence.

Combining the first two premises, Anselm concludes that God exists: When we think of a being who cannot be surpassed in our conceptions and when we realize that such a being having existence would be greater than such a being not having existence, we must conclude that such a being (God) exists.

To further clarify Anselm's argument, remember that in our analysis of the ontological argument, we contrasted the Fool's picture of God with Anselm's picture of God. The Fool held that God was simply an idea existing only in the mind, whereas Anselm held that God was both an idea in the mind and an actuality, a "real God" existing outside the mind.

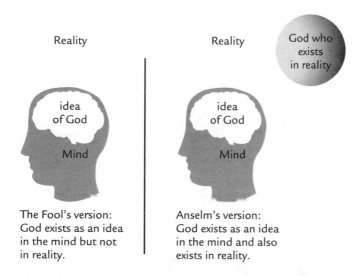

The Fool's version: God exists as an idea in the mind but not in reality.

Anselm's version: God exists as an idea in the mind and also exists in reality.

Anselm is seeking "a being than whom none greater can be conceived." He believes his picture of God fills the bill. A God who exists both as an idea in the mind and as a reality outside the mind is greater than the Fool's picture of God as an idea that exists only in the mind.

Hume would attack Anselm's proof simply by distinguishing between the two kinds of knowledge that he claims are available to us: matters of fact and relations of ideas. Matters of fact, remember, are based upon sense impressions. The God described in the ontological argument obviously cannot be traced back to a sense impression. God is a being who cannot be known by the senses. Thus, Anselm's proof cannot be based on any matter of fact.

Therefore, if the ontological argument has any validity, it must be based upon a relation of ideas. Remember, examples of relations of ideas would be "2 + 2 = 4" or "a triangle is a three-sided figure." The first statement in Anselm's proof *is* a relationship of ideas; the idea of God is related to the idea of God's definition as "a being than whom none greater can be thought." However, recall that in Hume's view, relations of ideas tell us *nothing* about the actual world, only how one idea is linked to another idea. If I relate idea X to idea Y, I certainly don't prove that X or Y actually exists in the world. According to Hume, all Anselm has done in the ontological argument is to link concepts together; he has proven nothing. One idea—the definition of God—plus another idea—existence as superior to nonexistence—only leads to another idea, the idea that God exists. But, just as the idea of your passing a course and your actually passing a course are two different things, the *idea* of God's existing and God's *actually* existing are two different things.

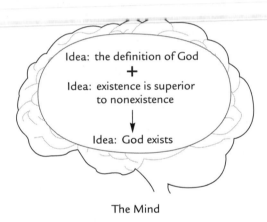

Idea: the definition of God
+
Idea: existence is superior
to nonexistence

Idea: God exists

The Mind

Thus, all Anselm has accomplished is adding ideas together; he has proven nothing about anything outside his mind.

Summarize how Hume would attack the ontological argument.

The ontological argument cannot be based upon knowledge derived from matters

of fact because _____

_____

_____ .

And if the ontological argument is based upon a relationship of ideas, this would

not prove God exists because _____

_____

_____ .

Now let's examine how Hume attacks another proof of God's existence. Here is how one of Descartes's arguments can be summarized:

1. I have an idea of God.

2. Only God has sufficient reality to cause my idea of God.

3. Therefore, God exists.

What concept in this proof do you think Hume will attack?

Hume will attack the concept of _____

_____

_____

because _____.

Descartes begins with an effect, the idea of God. It is obvious, he assumes, that every effect must have a cause. Descartes eliminates himself as the cause of his idea of God because he, Descartes, is an imperfect being. An imperfect being could not cause the idea of a perfect being. Descartes believes that only a perfect being could be the cause of the idea of a perfect being; therefore, God exists as the cause of Descartes's idea of God.

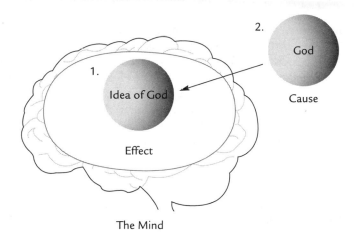

The Mind

Descartes, like Anselm, moves from (1) an idea of God to (2) God's actual existence. In Descartes's proof, however, instead of treating the idea of God as a definition, Descartes treats the idea of God as an effect whose only possible cause is a real God.

As you might have guessed, Hume attacks Descartes's argument because it is based on the concept of cause and effect. In Hume's view, remember, no matter how carefully we think about any two events, we cannot discover their necessary connection. Analyzing the movement of billiard ball B will tell us nothing about its supposed cause in billiard ball A. All we discover in analyzing the movement of B is information about the movement of B.

In the same way, analyzing the *idea* of God will give Descartes no information about this idea's supposed cause in an *actual* God. All Descartes will discover in analyzing his idea of God is information about his idea of God. Examining this idea will reveal no more information about the cause of the idea than examining the movement of billiard ball B will reveal information about the cause of B's movement.

Though Hume attacked the proofs I have just described, he was more concerned—and frankly delighted—to attack the argument from design. This argument can be summarized as follows:

1. The universe exhibits the features of a wondrously perfect design.

2. A wondrously perfect design could only have been created by a divine intelligence.

3. Thus, a divine intelligence (God) exists.

In our investigation of Aquinas, we used the watch on the beach as an illustration of the argument from design. In Hume's day, the argument from design had become, under Newton's influence, the dominant proof of God's existence. Newton, in the view of many, seemed to have discovered God's blueprint. Despite his admiration for Newton, Hume held that there was nothing in Nature that testified to a divine designer.

Before attacking the argument from design, Hume first presents a strong version of its evidence:

> Look around the world: contemplate the whole and every part of it: You will find it to be nothing but one great machine, subdivided into an infinite number of lesser machines. . . . All these various machines, and even their most minute parts, are adjusted to each other with an accuracy, which ravishes into admiration all men, who have ever contemplated them. The curious adapting of means to ends, throughout all nature, resembles exactly, though it much exceeds, the productions of human contrivance; of human design, thought, wisdom, and intelligence. Since therefore the effects resemble each other, we are led to infer, by all the rules of analogy, that the causes also resemble; and that the Author of nature is somewhat similar to the mind of man; though possessed of much larger faculties, proportioned to the grandeur of the work, which he has executed. . . . Whence arise the many conveniences and advantages which men and all animals possess? . . . Any one of them is a sufficient proof of design, and of a benevolent design, which gave rise to the order and arrangement of the universe.[1]

Put Hume's version of the argument from design into your own words:

_____

_____

_____

_____

_____.

Hume attacks the argument from design from a number of angles. I'll present three and let you explore each on your own.

Underline the most important parts of Hume's criticism in the following. (The first sentence states his thesis.)

---

[1] David Hume, *Dialogues Concerning Natural Religion*, ed. Norman Kemp Smith (Edinburgh: Nelson, 1947) Parts II and VIII.

But were this world ever so perfect a production, it must still remain un-certain, whether all the excellences of the work can justly be ascribed to the workman. If we survey a ship, what an exalted idea must we form of the in-genuity of the carpenter, who framed so complicated, useful, and beautiful a machine? And what surprise must we feel, when we find him a stupid mechanic, who imitated others, and copied an art, which through a long suc-cession of ages, after multiplied trials, mistakes, corrections, deliberations, and controversies, had been gradually improving? Many worlds might have been botched and bungled, throughout an eternity, ere this system was struck out: Much labor lost: Many fruitless trials made: And a slow, but continued improvement carried on during infinite ages in the art of world making.[2]

What criticism of the argument from design does Hume offer?

_____

_____

_____

_____

_____.

Here is a second attack on the argument from design:

A great number of men join in building a house or ship, in rearing a city, in framing a commonwealth: Why may not several deities combine in contriv-ing and framing a world? . . . You will find a numerous society of Deities as explicable as one universal Deity, who possesses, within himself, the powers and perfections of the whole society.[3]

Paraphrase Hume's argument and then explain what point he is attacking in the argument from design:

Hume says: _____

_____.

The point in the argument from design that he is attacking is _____

_____

_____.

Here is a third attack by Hume on the argument from design:

Look round this universe. What an immense profusion of beings, animated and organized, sensible and active! You admire this prodigious variety and fecundity. But inspect a little more narrowly these living existences, the only beings worth regarding. How hostile and destructive to each other! How in-sufficient all of them for their own happiness! How contemptible or odious to the spectator! The whole presents nothing but the idea of a blind nature,

---

[2] David Hume, *Dialogues Concerning Natural Religion*, ed. Norman Kemp Smith (Edinburgh: Nelson, 1947) Parts V and VI.
[3] David Hume, *Dialogues Concerning Natural Religion*, ed. Norman Kemp Smith (Edinburgh: Nelson, 1947) Parts V and VI.

impregnated by a great vivifying principle, and pouring forth from her lap, without discernment or parental care, her maimed and abortive children.[4]

Summarize Hume's argument:

The universe is not designed by a divine mind because _____

_____

_____.

Which of Hume's three criticisms do you think is the strongest?

I think the strongest is the (first, second, third) because _____

_____

_____.

Has Hume, in your view, destroyed the argument from design?

Hume (has, has not) destroyed the argument from design because _____

_____

_____.

Now let's consider Hume's general position on the nature of reality.

What Is Hume's Position on Metaphysics?

Metaphysics, as you know, is the study of the nature of reality. Sample metaphysical questions are What is the real? Does God exist? Does the soul exist? What are the characteristics of the physical universe? Does matter exist? In order to place Hume in the context of the metaphysical positions we have studied, complete the following exercise.

EXERCISE 23.2
Metaphysics Review

Link each of the following metaphysical positions to one *or more* of the philosophers we have studied thus far on the tour (Thales, Heraclitus, Parmenides, Plato, Aristotle, Epicurus, Epictetus, Anselm, Aquinas, Descartes, Locke, Berkeley).

1. God exists.
2. All is water.
3. Matter exists.
4. All that is changing has no reality.
5. Only the changing has reality.
6. God is an Unmoved Mover.

---

[4]David Hume, *Dialogues Concerning Natural Religion,* ed. Norman Kemp Smith (Edinburgh: Nelson, 1947) Parts X and XI.

7. Ideas are the only reality.

8. Everything that exists in the physical universe is a combination of matter and form.

9. The gods do not exist.

10. God is the cause of our continued existence.

As you have learned, Hume is a partial skeptic. Thus, he will hold that we don't have much knowledge about reality. There is considerable disagreement among commentators about the degree of Hume's skepticism; however, it is probably safe to say that Hume regards ideas and sense impressions as real. In other words, Hume reduces the vast pretensions of metaphysics to the islands of the human mind and senses. Metaphysical investigations of God, self, matter, the soul, cause, and effect are worthless. In Hume's words:

> Take in hand any volume of divinity or school of metaphysics . . . and let us ask: Does it contains any abstract reasoning concerning quantity or number [relations of ideas]? No. Does it contain any experimental reasoning concerning matter of fact and existence? No. Commit it then to the flames.

Hume's position on metaphysics? If a philosophy or theology book is about anything but the relationship of ideas or sense impressions based upon matters of fact, burn it.

In regard to this text, please ignore his advice.

If Hume places so little value on metaphysics, how could he possibly have an ethics? If we know so little about the nature of reality, how can anything about reality guide our actions?

What Is Hume's Ethics?

In order to understand what is startlingly unique about Hume's ethics, let's contrast his position with Plato's. As you remember, in Plato's view, the human personality is divided into three parts: the reason, the spirited element, and the appetites. The reason is compared to a ruler who must gain the allegiance of the lion of the spirited element in order to master the many-headed beast of the appetites. Ruled by our reason, we experience inner harmony; ruled by our appetites, we experience inner chaos. To be ruled by reason is to be "right side up," guided by the most divine element in our nature. To be ruled by our appetites is to be "upside down," guided by the least rational element in our nature. Thus, Plato presents us with the following pictures of the wise, moral, internally harmonious soul and the foolish, immoral, internally chaotic soul.

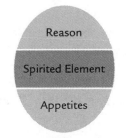

The wise, moral, internally harmonious soul

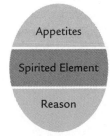

The foolish, immoral, internally chaotic soul

Plato's view of the importance of reason as a ruler of the passions appeals to the common sense of many students. It certainly seems to be the case that we are happiest when we wisely let our reason rule our passions and unhappiest when we unwisely let our passions rule our reason. For example?

An example of my reason wisely ruling my passions would be when _____

_____.

An example of my passions unwisely ruling my reason would be when _____

_____.

Thus, it is startling to read the following claim by Hume:

Reason is, and ought only to be, the slave of the passions, and can never pretend to any other office than to serve and obey them.

How could he say such a thing? How could he say that the proper use of our reason is to be a slave to our passions?

Return to Hume's distinction between our two kinds of knowledge: matters of fact and relations between ideas. If these are the only two kinds of knowledge available to our reason, then neither kind of knowledge could possibly control our passions.

Let's say that you are trying to lose weight and are confronted by a slice of triple chocolate cake. Using the matter-of-fact knowledge available to you, you identify the sense impressions of the chocolate cake. Using the relations-of-ideas knowledge available to you, you link the concept of the cake with the concepts of its ingredients. Neither of these two kinds of knowledge could possibly control your passion for the cake. Your reason knows only that the cake is there and that the cake is defined as being made of certain ingredients. In Hume's view, whether or not you eat the cake, your passion will rule your reason. If you decide to eat the cake, then your passion for the cake will outweigh your passion for weight loss; if you decide not to eat the cake, then your passion for weight loss will outweigh your passion for the cake. In either case, the only function of your reason is to serve your ruling passion. Ruled by cake passion, your reason will do all that is necessary to help you pig out; ruled by weight-loss passion, your reason will do all that is necessary to avoid putting your snout in a chocolate trough.

To get a clearer idea of Hume's unusual view of the function of reason in moral decisions, contrast how he would analyze Socrates' decision to remain in jail with the way Plato analyzes it. In Plato's view, Socrates' divinely inspired reason controls the natural passion of Socrates' body for things of this world. The passions of the body want more earthly life; escaping would guarantee that the bodily passions could continue to be satisfied. Socrates' reason, however, focuses on his implicit contract with Athens. Reason guides Socrates to right action; his body merely wants what is physically pleasurable.

Hume would analyze Socrates' situation differently. Instead of seeing Socrates' reason at odds with his passions, Hume would see Socrates' reason serving his passions. Thus, in Hume's view, Socrates' passion for escaping from this life was greater than his passion for staying alive. All Socrates' reason did was come up with a set of arguments to justify what his passion wanted to do all along.

According to Plato, reason can and must rule the passions; according to Hume the reason can't and shouldn't rule the passions. Which view do you think is more correct?

I think (Plato's, Hume's) view is more correct because _____

_____.

For example, _____

_____;

thus, (Plato, Hume) is right.

Some students try to refute Hume by saying, "If we should let our reason serve our passions, what if I wanted to kill someone? Should my reason serve my passion then?" Hume, as you might guess, has an unsettling answer:

> It is not contrary to reason to prefer the destruction of the whole world to scratching my finger.

Not only is there no way we can prove that murder is wrong, but there is also no way we can even prove that the annihilation of the entire planet is worse than a finger scratch! Go on, match wits with Hume. State an argument that would convince him that, given the choice, he should prefer having his finger scratched to the destruction of all of humanity.

I would say to him _____

_____

_____.

To understand Hume's point, consider the following:

> Take any action allowed to be vicious: Willful murder, for instance. Examine it in all lights, and see if you can find the matter of fact, or real existence, which you call vice. In whichever way you take it, you find only certain passions, motives, volitions and thoughts. There is no other matter of fact in the case. The vice entirely escapes you, as long as you consider the object. You can never find it, till you turn your reflection into your own breast, and find a sentiment of disapprobation, which arise in you, towards this action. Here is a matter of fact: but it is the object of feeling, not of reason. It lies in yourself, not in the object. So that when you pronounce any action or character to be vicious, you mean nothing, but that from the constitution of your nature you have a feeling or sentiment of blame from the contemplation of it. Vice and virtue, therefore, may be compared to sounds, colors, heat and cold, which, according to modern philosophy, are not qualities in objects, but perceptions in the mind.[5]

---

[5] David Hume, *A Treatise of Human Nature*, ed. L. A. Selby-Bigge (New York: Oxford University Press, 1888) pp. 468–469.

Put Hume's argument in your own words:

_____

_____

_____

_____.

Is murder wrong in itself, or do we merely *feel* it is wrong? If murder is wrong in itself, then we can say to Hume, "you should not choose a finger scratch over the destruction of all humanity, because the destruction of humanity would involve millions of wrong actions." However, if murder is merely what we feel is wrong, then Hume can answer us, "I don't share your feeling about murder. Therefore, there is no argument that can prove that everyone's death is worse than a scratch on my finger. You feel one way; I feel another."

What argument can you bring against Hume to show that murder or any wrong action is wrong in itself and not merely a wrong based on human feelings? Observe that if wrong actions are merely based on feelings, then there is no way to say that one feeling is better or worse than another. You feel one way; Hume feels another and that's that.

My response to Hume is _____

_____

_____.

In conclusion, note how Hume's analysis of morality is similar to his analysis of cause and effect. All we know when we observe the movements of billiard ball A and billiard ball B is simply a set of impressions, the events themselves. In the same way, all we know when we observe any human action—for example, a killing—is the event itself. One person's killing another has no more significance than one billiard ball's hitting another. Just as we subjectively project cause and effect upon the two billiard balls, we subjectively project a moral criticism upon the killing. Just as cause and effect are nothing but subjective events that we mistakenly believe are objective events, so moral values are nothing but subjective events that we mistakenly believe are objective events. Morality, just like cause and effect, is nothing but what goes on between our ears.

Thus, if Hume is right, the "moral laws" of every religion and society are no more valid than the "natural laws" of science. Science? Poof. Religious and social morality? Double poof.

Now, let's examine Hume's reasoning at greater length. Following are selections from a summary he published of his first major philosophical work, *A Treatise of Human Nature*. You'll have the opportunity to rethink your position on many of the concepts we've investigated and to consider some new Humean arguments.

READING:
SELECTIONS FROM HUME'S *AN ABSTRACT OF A TREATISE OF HUMAN NATURE*

Our author begins with some definitions. He calls a "perception" whatever can be present to the mind, whether we employ our senses or are actuated with passion, or exercise our thought and reflection. He divides our perceptions into two kinds, viz., "impressions" and "ideas." When we feel a passion or emotion of any kind, or have the images of external objects conveyed by our senses, the perception of the mind is what he calls an "impression"—which is a word that he employs in a new sense. When we reflect on a passion or an object which is not present, this perception is an "idea." "Impressions," therefore, are our lively and strong perceptions; "ideas" are the fainter and weaker. This distinction is evident—as evident as that betwixt feeling and thinking.

When Hume refers to "our author" and "he," he is referring to himself.

To understand Hume's distinction between "perceptions," "impressions," and "ideas," answer the following:

1. T F Perceptions and ideas are types of impressions.
2. T F We have internal and external impressions.
3. T F Ideas are more vivid than impressions.
4. T F When I am angry, I have the inner impression of anger.
5. T F The idea of anger is different from the inner impression of anger.

In the next section, Hume explains the relationship between ideas and impressions.

The first proposition he advances is that all our ideas, or weak perceptions, are derived from our impressions or strong perceptions, and that we can never think of anything which we have not seen without us or felt in our own minds. This proposition seems to be equivalent to that which Mr. Locke has taken such pains to establish, viz. [namely], "that no ideas are innate." Only it may be observed, as an inaccuracy of that famous philosopher, that he comprehends all our perceptions under the term of "idea," in which sense it is false that we have no innate ideas. For it is evident our stronger perceptions or impressions are innate, and that natural affection, love of virtue, resentment, and all the other passions arise immediately from nature. I am persuaded whoever would take the question in this light would be easily able to reconcile all parties. Father Malebranche would find himself at a loss to point out any thought of the mind which did not represent something antecedently felt by it, either internally or by means of the external senses, and must allow that however we may compound and mix and augment and diminish our ideas, that they are all derived from these sources. Mr. Locke, on the other hand, would readily acknowledge that all our passions are a kind of natural instincts, derived from nothing but the original constitution of the human mind.

Our author thinks—

that no discovery could have been made more happily for deciding all controversies concerning ideas than this, that impressions always take the precedence of them, and that every idea with which the imagination is furnished first makes its appearance in a correspondent impression. These latter perceptions are all so clear and evident that they admit of no controversy, though many of our ideas are so obscure that 'tis almost impossible even for the mind which forms them to tell exactly their nature and composition.

Accordingly, wherever any idea is ambiguous he has always recourse to the impression which must render it clear and precise. And when he suspects that any philosophical term has no idea annexed to it (as is too common), he always asks "from what impression that idea is derived?" And if no impression can be produced, he concludes that the term is altogether insignificant. It is after this manner he examines our idea of *substance* and *essence;* and it were to be wished that this rigorous method were more practiced in all philosophical debates.

According to Hume, do ideas produce impressions, or do impressions produce ideas?

Hume says (impressions, ideas) produce (impressions, ideas). For example, when

I am looking at this book, the (impression, idea) of _____

produces the (impression, idea) of _____.

Hume follows Locke and all other strict empiricists in holding that all knowledge comes through the senses. Hume's way of expressing the empiricist principle is to say that all of our ideas can be traced back to our impressions. For example, if I have the *idea* of strawberry ice cream, this can be traced back to the *impression* of strawberry ice cream. But what if I tried to proved that Hume was wrong? Let us say I have the idea of potato ice cream. Couldn't I argue against Hume that I have an idea that does not correspond to an impression? Certainly, I have never seen potato ice cream, so doesn't this show that all me ideas are not linked to impressions?

Hume could answer you by saying that your idea of potato ice cream is linked to

impressions because you have had the impression of _____,

and you have had the impression of _____.
Thus, your idea of potato ice cream was just a combination of ideas produced by separate impressions.

In other writings, Hume elaborates on his distinction between impressions and ideas. Both impressions and ideas are divided into two categories: simple and complex. We investigated the distinction between simple ideas and impressions and complex ideas and impressions in Chapter 22.

Hume's own example is the idea of a gold mountain. He says even though he has never seen a gold mountain, he has had the impression of gold and the impression of mountain. Thus, his idea of a gold mountain is simply the association of ideas produced by separate impressions.

Now try your hardest to refute Hume. Think of an idea that you believe could *not* be traced back to any collection of sense impressions.

I am thinking of _____. I believe this could not be traced back to any collection of sense impressions because

_____

_____ .

In the passage above, Hume argues that understanding that all ideas can be traced back to impressions provides us with a powerful philosophical tool. In short: *If a philosophical idea, which appears to be vague, can be traced back to no impression, then we can be sure that the idea is meaningless.* If we have no impression (as we have seen that Hume argues) of cause and effect, God, self, or mind, then all these terms are meaningless! To give you another sample of Hume's approach, let's undertake a Humean examination of the idea of matter.

When I think of the concept of matter, I think that an apple has matter, my desk has matter, a cloud has matter, and so forth. But what is my idea of matter itself? It certainly seems to be very hazy. When I think of matter itself, I think of "stuff." But what am I thinking about when I think of "stuff"? Frankly, I have an image in my head of a grayish glop that looks a bit like wax. But certainly matter is not gray, gloppish, or waxy. So to clarify my idea of matter, I follow Hume's advice and try to look for the impression that produced it.

I'll use all five of my senses to try to have an impression of the matter of an apple. Using my sense of sight, I see that the apple is red; using my sense of touch, I feel that the apple is smooth; using my sense of smell, I smell the apple's sweet scent; using my sense of taste, I taste the apple's tartness; using my sense of hearing, I hear a crunching sound when I bite into the apple. Which sense gives me an impression of the *matter* of the apple? Any of my senses? All of them? There seem to be only four possible ways that matter could be related to the qualities I sense in the apple.

1. Matter is underneath the sense qualities of the apple.

2. Matter produces the sense qualities of the apple.

3. Matter is identical to the sense qualities of the apple.

4. Matter possesses the sense qualities of the apple and could possess any other sense qualities as well.

To begin, could matter be *underneath* the sense qualities of the apple? This could not be. If matter is underneath the sense qualities of the apple, *then I could have no sense impression of matter itself.* I cannot see what is *underneath* color. I cannot feel what is *underneath* texture. And it doesn't even make sense to say I can smell what is underneath odor, or taste what is underneath taste, or hear what is underneath sound. Thus, matter cannot be what is underneath the sense qualities of the apple.

But perhaps I want to try a slightly different tack and say that matter *produces* the sense qualities of the apple. This would also be wrong. I can only see red; I cannot see what *produces* redness. I can only feel smoothness; I cannot feel what produces smoothness. I can only smell sweetness; I cannot smell what *produces* sweetness. I can only taste tartness; I cannot taste what *produces* tartness. I can only hear the crunching; I cannot hear what *produces* the crunching sound. Thus, I cannot say that matter is what produces the sense qualities of the apple. All I know are the sense qualities themselves, not what produces them.

Perhaps I should say that matter is not underneath these sense impressions and matter does not produce these sense impressions; matter is *identical* to these sense impressions.

If I say matter is identical to the sense qualities of the apple, then I'm no better off than before. If matter is identical to something red, smooth, sweet-scented, tart-tasting, and crunchy-sounding, then everything that doesn't have these sense qualities isn't matter! Thus, matter can't be identical to the sense qualities of the apple because there are many other things that I believe are made of matter that don't have these qualities.

There is one last way out. Maybe I should say that matter is not identical to sense qualities of the apple, but that it merely "has" qualities I sense in the apple and *could have any other qualities as well*. This means matter is a something that could be anything. This definition of matter gets me in the worst trouble of all. Where on earth will I ever get an impression of something that could be anything? I wouldn't even know where to look. Everything I know with my senses—this apple, this desk, this chair—is *a something that is something. I see no somethings that could be anything*. A something that could be anything would, for starters, have:

no color, because it could have any color

no texture, because it could have any texture

no shape, because it could have any shape

Where would I get a sense impression of a colorless, textureless, shapeless matter? Any suggestions?

I believe _____

_____

_____.

So what have I learned from my Humean analysis of matter? I have no knowledge of matter as something *underneath* sense qualities or as something *producing* sense qualities or as something *identical* to sense qualities or as something *capable of having any sense quality*. And with no knowledge of matter itself, my idea of matter is meaningless.

I have discovered that my idea of matter can no more be traced to an actual sense impression than my idea of a square circle could be traced to an actual sense impression. Thus, my idea of matter has no more meaning than my idea of a square circle.

Now, to judge the strength of Hume's position, argue against him. Using your sense of sight as an example, argue as strongly as you can for one of these five options (I've given you an extra, in case you don't like any of mine):

1. Matter is underneath visual sense qualities.

2. Matter produces visual sense qualities.

3. Matter is identical to visual sense qualities.

4. Matter is capable of having any visual sense quality.

5. Matter is _____

_____   _____.

I'll select option _____. My argument is _____

_____

_____

Thus, the idea of matter is a meaningful idea.

In the next section, Hume begins his analysis of cause and effect, an analysis that he and many others after him have regarded as his most important contribution to philosophy. I hope that what I've already said about his analysis earlier in this chapter will make his argument easier for you to follow.

It is evident that all reasonings concerning *matter of fact* are founded on the relation of cause and effect, and that we can never infer the existence of one object from another unless they be connected together, either mediately or immediately. In order, therefore, to understand these reasonings we must be perfectly acquainted with the idea of a cause; and in order to that, must look about us to find something that is the cause of another.

Here is a billiard ball lying on the table, and another ball moving toward it with rapidity. They strike; and the ball which was formerly at rest now acquires a motion. This is as perfect an instance of the relation of cause and effect as any which we know either by sensation or reflection. Let us therefore examine it. It is evident that the two balls touched one another before the motion was communicated, and that there was no interval betwixt the shock and the motion. *Contiguity* in time and place is therefore a requisite circumstance to the operation of all causes. It is evident, likewise, that the motion which was the cause is prior to the motion which was the effect. *Priority* in time is, therefore, another requisite circumstance in every cause. But this is not all. Let us try any other balls of the same kind in a like situation, and we shall always find that the impulse of the one produces motion in the other. Here, therefore, is a *third* circumstance, viz., that of a *constant conjunction* betwixt the cause and effect. Every object like the cause produces always some object like the effect. Beyond these three circumstances of contiguity, priority, and constant conjunction I can discover nothing in this cause. The first ball is in motion, touches the second, immediately the second is in motion—and when I try the experiment with the same or like balls, in the same or like circumstances, I find that upon the motion and touch of the one ball motion always follows in the other. In whatever shape I turn this matter, and however I examine it, I can find nothing further.

This is the case when both the cause and effect are present to the senses. Let us now see upon what our inference is founded when we conclude from the one that the other has existed or will exist. Suppose I see a ball moving in a straight line toward another—I immediately conclude that they will shock, and that the second will be in motion. This is the inference from cause to effect, and of this nature are all our reasonings in the conduct of life; on this is founded all our belief in history, and from hence is derived all philosophy excepting only geometry and arithmetic. If we can explain the inference from the shock of the two balls we shall be able to account for this operation of the mind in all instances.

Before we look at the first stages of Hume's analysis of cause and effect, let's review a very important concept, matters of fact, which Hume uses at the start of the section you just read.

As you recall, Hume distinguishes between two kinds of reasonings: matters of fact and relations between ideas. Matters of fact deal with every kind of reasoning except geometrical and arithmetic. Thus, some examples of matter-of-fact reasoning would be:

1. Because I took an aspirin, my headache vanished.
2. Because I press the keyboard, letters appear on the computer screen.
3. Because of the heat of the flame, the water will boil.

Note that each of these matters of fact are examples of cause-and-effect reasoning.

The cause in example 1 is _____. The effect in example 1 is _____.

The cause in example 2 is _____. The effect in example 2 is _____.

The cause in example 3 is _____. The effect in example 3 is _____.

Because matter-of-fact reasoning describes almost every kind of reasoning, except reasoning about math and geometry, it is obviously very important. Hume, as you already know, will try to show that all matter-of-fact reasoning, especially matter-of-fact reasoning about cause and effect, is inaccurate.

Now let's review examples of reasoning involving relations of ideas.

1. If I combine two units with four units, I will have six units.
2. If I have a straight line, I will have the shortest distance between two points.
3. An infinite series of numbers is a series that will never end.

Offer a few similar examples of your own of reasoning about relations between ideas:

_____

_____

_____.

As you remember, the difference between relations between ideas and matters of fact is that the former are certain but tell us nothing about the world, while the latter are about the world but tell us nothing certain. When I reason that combining two units and four units will give me six units, I can be absolutely certain I am correct if I have correctly related these two ideas. But, of course, since I am only relating ideas, then I have learned nothing about the world. When I reason that pressing the keyboard makes letters appear on the screen, I am obviously reasoning about the world; but why on earth would Hume say I have learned nothing certain?

This question leads us, as you probably have guessed, to his analysis of cause and effect. In the passage you just read, Hume describes three aspects of cause and effect: contiguity, priority, and constant conjunction.

Using his example of billiard balls rolling together, describe each of the three aspects. (For simplicity in identification, assume the "cause" billiard ball is the "first" ball and the "effect" billiard ball is the "second" ball.)

In the case of the first ball hitting the second ball, contiguity would be _____

_____

_____.

In the case of the first ball hitting the second ball, priority would be _____

_____

_____.

In the case of the first ball hitting the second ball, constant conjunction would be

_____

_____.

So far, so good. Now, in the next section, Hume begins his destruction of our cause-and-effect reasoning.

Were a man such as Adam created in the full vigor of understanding, without experience, he would never be able to infer motion in the second ball from the motion and impulse of the first. It is not anything that reason sees in the cause which makes us *infer* the effect. Such an inference, were it possible, would amount to a demonstration, as being founded merely on the comparison of ideas. But no inference from cause to effect amounts to a demonstration. Of which there is this evident proof. The mind can always *conceive* any effect to follow from any cause, and indeed any event to follow upon another; whatever we *conceive* is possible, at least in a metaphysical sense; but wherever a demonstration takes place the contrary is impossible and implies a contradiction. There is no demonstration, therefore, for any conjunction of cause and effect. And this is a principle which is generally allowed by philosophers.

It would have been necessary, therefore, for Adam (if he was not inspired) to have had *experience* of the effect which followed upon the impulse of these

Hume's argument from here to the end of the paragraph is very important to his position. Read it carefully.

two balls. He must have seen in several instances that when the one ball struck upon the other, the second always acquired motion. If he had seen a sufficient number of instances of this kind, whenever he saw the one ball moving toward the other, he would always conclude without hesitation that the second would acquire motion. His understanding would anticipate his sight and form a conclusion suitable to his past experience.

Paraphrase Hume's main points.

_____

_____

_____

_____

_____ .

Assume that Adam, the perfect example of someone with no experience, observed the first ball roll toward the second. He obviously would have no more idea about what would happen next than a baby would. Thinking about the first ball, Adam could not prove that the second ball would move. In other words, he could not reason from the movement of the first ball to the movement of the second ball. *Why is this important?* If Adam could not reason from the movement of the first ball to the movement of the second ball, then neither he, nor anyone, could ever reason from any prior event to any succeeding event. And if no one can reason from prior events to succeeding events, then no one can reason about cause and effect.

Now, *why* can't we reason from cause to effect? (In the following, we'll add to the arguments we've investigated in the first part of this chapter.)

Let's go back to Adam. If God gave Adam the concept of a square, Adam *could* reason from the concept of a square to the concept of a thing having four equal sides. In Hume's terms, Adam could relate the idea of a thing having four sides, because the idea of a square contains within itself the idea of a thing having four sides to the idea of a square. In the same way, Adam *could* reason from the concepts 2 + 4 to the concept of 6, because the concept of combining 2 and 4 leads one automatically to the concept of 6. You can't combine 2 and 4 and not get 6. You can't have a square and not have a four-sided figure. This is what Hume means when he says, "wherever a demonstration takes place the contrary is impossible and implies a contradiction." Demonstrating to himself that squares have four sides and that 2 + 4 = 6, Adam would know it was impossible for squares not to have four sides or for 2 + 4 not to equal 6.

Adam, however, would *not* be capable of such irrefutable reasoning about the movement of the first ball. He could think all he wanted about the movement of the first ball and never discover the movement of the second ball. Whereas a concept of a square necessarily contains the concept of a four-sided figure, the movement of the first ball doesn't include the movement of the second ball.

But perhaps you still want to attack Hume and say, "Let Adam observe the balls coming together a few times. Let him observe constant conjunction. Then, Adam will be able to reason that the movement of the first ball caused the

We'll elaborate on Hume's concept of a "demonstration" in the next section. For now, think of a demonstration as a valid proof.

movement of the second ball. Adam's reasoning will be certain because it is based on repeated experiences."

Hume agrees that our reasoning is based on repeated experiences and then, in the next section, shows the worthlessness of such reasoning. Underline important points.

> It follows, then, that all reasonings concerning cause and effect are founded on experience, and that all reasonings from experience are founded on the supposition that the course of nature will continue uniformly the same. We conclude that like causes, in like circumstances, will always produce like effects. It may now be worth while to consider what determines us to form a conclusion of such infinite consequence.
>
> It is evident that Adam, with all his science, would never have been able to *demonstrate* that the course of nature must continue uniformly the same, and that the future must be conformable to the past. What is possible can never be demonstrated to be false; and it is possible the course of nature may change, since we can conceive such a change. Nay, I will go further and assert that he could not so much as prove by any *probable* arguments that the future must be conformable to the past. All probable arguments are built on the supposition that there is this conformity betwixt the future and the past, and therefore [he] can never prove it. This conformity is a *matter of fact*, and if it must be proved will admit of no proof but from experience. But our experience in the past can be a proof of nothing for the future but upon a supposition that there is a resemblance betwixt them. This, therefore, is a point which can admit of no proof at all, and which we take for granted without any proof.

This paragraph is one of the most challenging and philosophically important on the tour. Read it several times; then try to summarize Hume's main point. Hume is arguing

_____

_____

_____

_____

_____

_____

_____

_____.

Now we have arrived at the heart of Hume's argument. His reasoning is dense, so let's go through it carefully.

Hume says, "It is evident that Adam, with all his science, would never have been able to *demonstrate* that the course of nature must continue uniformly the same, and that the future must be conformable to the past." To understand Hume's point, we must first understand what it means to "demonstrate" something. This will then help us understand why it is that neither Adam nor anyone else can demonstrate that the future will be like the past.

Here is a simplified example of the kind of demonstration Hume is thinking about: Assume we have a circle with a midpoint at A and two points on the circumference, B and C.

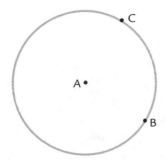

We could certainly demonstrate that B and C were the same distance from A because all points on the circumference of a circle are the same distance from the center. Thus, the demonstration would go like this:

1. All points on the circumference of a circle are the same distance from the center.

2. Therefore, any two points, B and C, on the circumference of a circle must be the same distance from the center of the circle.

Observe that the conclusion above is so certain that it is impossible to imagine a circle with points on its circumference that are *not* the same distance from the center. Go on. Try the impossible.

When I try to imagine a circle with even one point on its circumference farther away from the circle's center than the other points on the circumference, what happens

in my mind is _____

_____

_____ .

Thus, the word "demonstration" for Hume means a proof whose conclusion is so absolutely certain that we cannot even *imagine* the conclusion being false. Once the nature of a circle has been demonstrated, a circle cannot be imagined with points on its circumference that were not equal distances from the center.

Now Hume claims that we *cannot* make a similar demonstration that the "future must be conformable to the past." In other words, reasoning about the relationship between past and future is nothing like reasoning about the relationship between the center of a circle and points on its circumference. Look what happens when we try to make a demonstration about the relationship between past and future.

1. Two billiard balls rolling together in the past produced a given result.

2. Therefore, two billiard balls rolling together in the future will produce the same result.

Is this a demonstration? Remember that a demonstration is a proof whose conclusion is so absolutely certain that we cannot even *imagine* the conclusion being false.

I would say this (is, is not) a demonstration because _____

_____

_____ .

In Hume's view, statements 1 and 2 about the relationship between past and future are no demonstration. We can certainly imagine the conclusion being false; just because two billiard balls produced a result in the past does not mean they will necessarily produce the same result in the future. In the past, the movement of ball A produced the movement of ball B. In the future, the movement of ball A could do absolutely nothing to ball B. Thus, whereas we *can* demonstrate that two points on the circumference of a circle have to be the same distance from the center, we *cannot* demonstrate that an event in the future has to be identical to an event in the past. *And if we can't demonstrate this, then we cannot reason from any cause to any effect!*

Perhaps you are still itching to quarrel with Hume, "Okay. It's not absolutely certain that two billiard balls coming together in the future will behave in a completely identical manner to the way they have behaved in the past—but so what. It is at least *highly probable* they will behave the same. Ninety-nine times out of a hundred, when you roll two balls together, the second ball moves away. Past experience of billiard balls is all the evidence we need to know that there is a high probability that their future behavior will be like their past behavior."

Hume, as you might fear, anticipates this objection. "Nay, I will go further and assert that he [Adam] could not so much as prove by any probable argument that the future must be conformable to the past. All probable arguments are built on the supposition that there is this conformity betwixt the future and the past, and therefore [he] can never prove it."

In brief, Hume is saying that in order to prove there is a high probability that the future will be like the past, we have to *assume* that the future will be like the past. But because there is no way to *prove* that the future will be like the past, we cannot know that there is a high probability that the future will be like the past.

I have probably lost you.

Picture it this way.

A conclusion is supported by evidence.

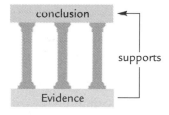

The evidence is what is underneath, what holds up the conclusion.

There are three kinds of relationships between evidence and conclusion. If the evidence is solid, then the conclusion is solid; if the evidence is shaky, then the conclusion is shaky; if the evidence is unknowable, then the conclusion is unknowable.

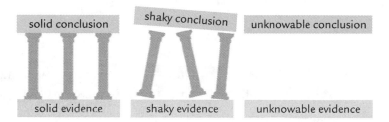

All philosophers are trying to build arguments of the first type and absolutely avoid arguments of the last two types. The crucial ingredient, as you can see, in any argument is the solidity of the evidence. Great evidence = great argument. Terrible evidence = terrible argument.

Now look at this argument. How solid is the evidence?

Conclusion: There is a high probability that the future will be like the past.
Evidence: The future will be like the past.

According to Hume, the evidence is completely unknowable. There is simply no way that we can prove that the future will be like the past. The future hasn't happened yet. It's unknown territory. And since the evidence is unknowable, the conclusion it supports is unknowable. Thus, what may have initially looked like a great argument turns out to be a terrible argument.

> Unknowable conclusion: There is a high probability that the future will be like the past.

[no support]

> Unknowable evidence: The future will be like the past.

Now there are two ways to prove that Hume's analysis is wrong. Try them both.

1. Prove that the future will be like the past.

   I'll try. I know that the future will be like the past because _____

   _____

   _____.

2. Throw out Hume's evidence and find solid evidence to support the conclusion "There is a high probability that the future will be like the past." Fill it in below.

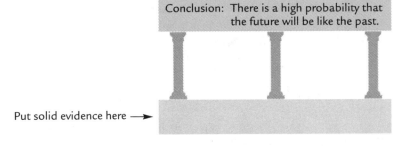

Put solid evidence here →

What is your general response to Hume's argument that we cannot say there is a high probability that any past event will be repeated in the future?

My response is _____

_____

_____.

In the next section, Hume explains the origin of our ideas of cause and effect. (This will be a review of points mentioned in the first half of the chapter.)

> We are determined by *custom* alone to suppose the future conformable to the past. When I see a billiard ball moving toward another, my mind is immediately carried by habit to the usual effect, and anticipates my sight by conceiving the second ball in motion. There is nothing in these objects—abstractly considered, and independent of experience—which leads me to form any such conclusion: and even after I have had experience of many repeated effects of this kind, there is no argument which determines me to suppose that the effect will be conformable to past experience. The powers by which bodies operate are entirely unknown. We perceive only their sensible qualities—and what *reason* have we to think that the same powers will always be conjoined with the same sensible qualities?
>
> It is not, therefore, reason which is the guide of life, but custom. That alone determines the mind in all instances to suppose the future conformable to the past. However easy this step may seem, reason would never, to all eternity, be able to make it.

By "custom" Hume means "mental habit."

In the section above, how does Hume answer the question, "What is the origin of our concept of cause and effect?"

_____

_____

_____

_____.

Hume argues that it is mental "custom," not reason, that makes us think that the future will be like the past. And thus, it is "custom," not reason, that makes us think we observe genuine cause and effect. In short, cause and effect is nothing but a mental habit. Cause and effect is not an event in the world but an event we *add* to the world.

We observe one billiard ball strike another billiard ball, and the ball that is struck moves away. We see this countless times. We mentally associate the idea of the first ball moving with the second ball moving. *And so we confuse what we actually see with what we think we see.* All we *actually* see is the first ball moving and then the second ball moving away; we *think* we see the first ball "transferring its power" to the second ball and "causing" the second ball to move away. All we *actually* observe is one event succeeding another event. We *think* we observe one event causing another event.

Obviously, there is a big difference between one event *following* another and one event *being caused by* another. You turn pages in this book. One event follows another. It would be a mistake to say that turning one page causes you to turn another page. Each page-turning event is entirely separate from the next page-turning event. There is nothing about turning to page 14 that would make you turn to page 15. After turning to page 14, you could throw the book over your shoulder or hum a Beach Boys' tune. Hume argues that events in the world are as separate as turning pages in a book. And so, just as you would be wrong to impose cause and effect on the sequential events of page turning, so you would be wrong to impose cause and effect on any other event in the world. The movement of the first ball transfers no more power to the movement of the second ball than turning one page in a book transfers power to turning the next page in a book.

In the next section, Hume continues his analysis of cause and effect.

> In the considering of motion communicated from one ball to another we could find nothing but contiguity, priority in the cause, and constant conjunction. But, besides these circumstances, it is commonly supposed that there is a necessary connection betwixt the cause and effect, and that the cause possess something which we call a "power," or "force," or "energy." The question is, what idea is annexed to these terms? If all our ideas or thoughts be derived from our impressions, this power must either discover itself to our senses or to our internal feeling. But so little does any *power* discover itself to the senses in the operations of matter that the Cartesians have made no scruple to assert that matter is utterly deprived of energy, and that all its operations are performed merely by the energy of the Supreme Being. But the question still recurs, *What idea have we of energy or power even in the Supreme Being?* All our idea of a deity (according to those who deny innate ideas) is nothing but a composition of those ideas which we acquire from reflecting on the operations of our own minds. Now our own minds afford us no more notion of energy than matter does. When we consider our will or volition *a priori,* abstracting from experience, we should never be able to infer any effect from it. And when we take the assistance of experience it only shows us objects contiguous, successive, and constantly conjoined. Upon the whole, then, either we have no idea at all of force and energy, and these words are altogether insignificant, or they can mean nothing but that determination of the thought, acquired by habit, to pass from the cause to its usual effect.

Paraphrase Hume's point in the last sentence above.

Hume is saying _____

_____

_____.

Hume concludes his analysis of cause and effect by looking at the crucial concept of necessary connection. As you recall from the first half of this chapter, without the observation of the necessary connection between event A and event B, we cannot say that we have observed event A *causing* event B. For example, if we cannot observe the necessary connection between the movement of billiard ball A and the movement of billiard ball B, then we have not observed A causing, producing the movement of, B. All we have observed is a mere sequence of events, A moving followed by B moving.

There is a good chance that you still believe that you can observe a cause producing an effect. Let me clarify Hume's concept of necessary connection and then give you a final chance of proving that you can observe it.

First, I'll distinguish between a connection and a necessary connection. Then, I'll present some genuine examples of necessary connection and distinguish them from what we observe in the case of the two billiard balls. Finally, I'll give you your last chance to prove Hume wrong.

First, let's distinguish between a connection and a *necessary* connection. There is a connection between the top of my table and the table's legs. There would be a necessary connection between the top of my table and its legs if I couldn't have one without the other. Having the top of the table would mean I necessarily had its legs and having the legs would mean I necessarily had the top. Now give your own example of a connection and a necessary connection.

One could say there is a connection between _____ and

_____. There would be a necessary connection between

these two if _____

_____.

Now obviously there is no necessary connection between my table top and its legs. The connection can be broken; I can have the table top without the legs and vice versa. What then would be an example of *genuine* necessary connection?

An example Hume would offer would be a relationship of ideas, the necessary connection between any mathematical or geometrical concept and its definition. For example, there is a necessary connection between the concept of a straight line and its definition, the shortest distance between two points. If you have a straight line, you have the shortest distance between two points. If you have the shortest distance between two points, you have a straight line. If X and Y have a necessary connection, you can't have X without having Y and vice versa.

Give me your own example of the necessary connection between a geometrical concept of a triangle and its definition.

The concept of _____ is necessarily connected to the

definition _____.

When I analyze the concept of a straight line, I find within that concept the idea of the shortest distance between two points. That's why the two concepts are necessarily connected. The analysis of one reveals the presence of the other. It is impossible to think of a straight line that is not the shortest distance between two points, and it is impossible to think of the shortest distance between two points as something other than a straight line.

Investigate necessary connection by analyzing the concept of a square.

When I think of a square, I think of its definition: _____

_____. These two ideas are necessarily connected because I

can't have _____ without also having _____

_____.

Now, let's go back to billiard ball A and billiard ball B. Are these two events *necessarily* connected? Can I think of the movement of billiard ball A without having to think of the movement of billiard ball B? Of course I can. I can think of ball A moving and never give a thought to ball B moving. And I can think of ball B moving and never give a thought to ball A moving. There is no necessary connection between the two events.

Contrast the relationship between the two balls to the relationship between a square and its definition. When I, so to speak, investigate the concept of a square, I discover it contains the concept of four equal sides. That's why square and four equal sides are necessarily connected. However, when I investigate the concept of ball A moving, all I find is ball A moving. I find no information about ball B. Thus, while concepts like square and four-sidedness are necessarily connected, events like the movement of ball A and the movement of ball B are not necessarily connected. And if the movement of the two balls is not necessarily connected, then we cannot reason from one as cause to the other as effect.

Now, take your last crack at Hume. Argue as forcefully as you can that when you observe ball A moving and then ball B moving, you observe the necessary connection between those two events.

_____

_____

_____

_____

_____

_____

_____

_____.

SUMMARY

According to Hume, since all we know comes through our senses and since we have no sense impression of cause and effect, the concept of cause and effect as an external phenomenon is meaningless. The origin of the concept of cause and effect is subjective, in the way we relate ideas together, not objective, in the external world. In addition, since there is no certitude about the external world based upon sense perceptions, then no proof of God's existence can be valid.

According to Hume's ethics, reason does not and should not guide our desires. Every "moral" choice is really a choice guided by the passions of the moment. There is no absolute right or wrong. All moral values are only feelings. Thus, there is no way to prove that one action is morally superior to another.

VOCABULARY MAP

David Hume

Strictly speaking, Hume has no **metaphysics;** he believes metaphysics, descriptions of the nature of all of reality, are not possible.

Hume begins (Chapter 22) as an empiricist, one who holds that all knowledge comes through the senses. But he concludes (Chapter 23) that such little knowledge comes through the senses that skepticism is the correct position. Skepticism is the view that little, if anything, can be known for certain.

Hume's **ethics,** his view of moral values, is **relativistic.** He rejects the view that there is an absolute moral code that applies to everyone at all times and places. In Hume's view, right and wrong actions are determined by, related to, each individual's desires. What is right for one person may be wrong for another.

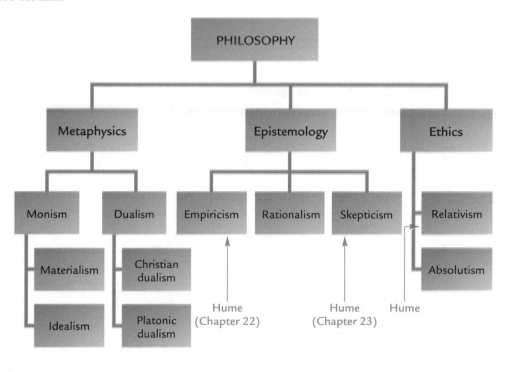

Exercise 23.3
Looking at the World Through Hume's Eyes

How would Hume answer each of the following? Use your own paper to explain your reasoning for your answer.

1. T   F We can know for certain that God does not exist.

2. T   F The Ten Commandments are universal moral truths.

3. T   F There is more truth in the multiplication tables than there is in any science based on observation.

4. T   F Epistemology should replace metaphysics.

5. T   F Insofar as a philosopher is a rationalist, to that degree the philosopher is wrong.

EXERCISE 23.4
Looking Back

Use your own paper to answer the following:

1. What is cause and effect?

2. How does Hume attack the cause-and-effect relationship?

3. If cause and effect have no real existence, where do we get the idea of cause and effect?

4. Can God's existence be proven?

5. What is Hume's position on metaphysics?

6. What is Hume's ethics?

ANALYSIS OF YOUR PHILOSOPHICAL SELF-PORTRAIT

To see how your views stack up against Hume's, read my analysis below, rethink your position, and then circle what you believe is the correct answer. I've underlined Hume's answers.

1. <u>T</u>   F *The principle of cause and effect is an important basis of scientific observation.*

   It's difficult to see how False could be defended for this answer. As argued in the thought experiment at the start of this chapter, the principle of cause and effect is central to scientific inquiry. Even Hume would agree that the principle of cause and effect is an important basis of scientific observation. This, he believed, was what made his argument *against* cause and effect so important.

2. T   <u>F</u> *Our senses teach us that every event has a cause.*

   Most students would answer this True at the beginning of this chapter. Until reading Hume, it certainly seems like a simple and obvious truth that all events have causes. Prior to Hume, no one had ever doubted this apparently obvious principle. Many students, however, after reading Hume's attack on cause and effect are convinced he is right. If you made the switch, you can call yourself a neo-Humean.

3. T   <u>F</u> *It is 100 percent certain that the sun will rise tomorrow.*

   If you still believe this is true, then Hume failed to convince you. In other words, you believe it is just as certain that the sun will rise tomorrow as that $2 + 2 = 4$. Just as there is not even the slightest possibility that $2 + 2$ won't equal 4, there is not even the slightest possibility that the sun won't rise tomorrow. More generally, this probably commits you to the position that truths based upon observation are equal in certainty to the truths of mathematics. If you'd like support for your position, you'll get it, in a very unusual way, from Kant in Chapter 24.

4. T <u>F</u> *Our desires should be guided by our reason, not vice versa.*

If you believe this is True, then you are supported by a noble company of philosophers: Plato, Aristotle, Aquinas, and Descartes, to name a few. Even Epicurus, who held that pleasure was the goal of life, held that we should pursue pleasure rationally.

5. T <u>F</u> *The design of the universe is evidence of God's existence.*

If you answered this True, then you are supported by Aquinas and Newton, to name only two great minds. When Einstein said, "God does not play dice" and rejected the view that the cosmos was governed by chance, he was also supporting the position that the design of the universe is evidence of God's existence. If you side with Hume, then you are supported by many nuclear physicists, like Neils Bohr and Werner Heisenberg, who were Einstein's opponents.

6. T F *In the realm of nature, there is a high probability that future events will be like past events.*

Hume's argument against probability is one of the most difficult arguments for students to accept (or understand)! However, Kant, Hume's great opponent, found Hume's analysis so compelling that it awoke him from philosophical slumbers. Kant found himself forced to agree with Hume that the certainty of the principle of cause and effect could not be located in the world of the senses—and then, in one of the most brilliant feats of modern philosophy, Kant discovered a new origin for the certainty of cause and effect. What was that new origin? Keep touring and find out.

Evaluation: Number of points in agreement with Hume = _____ of 6 possible.

A position of Hume's that you strongly (support, oppose) is

_____

_____

because _____

_____

_____.

NEXT STOP

Immanuel Kant argues that all philosophers before him, including Hume, committed an enormous error.

24

Immanuel Kant
A New Model of the Mind

YOUR PHILOSOPHICAL SELF-PORTRAIT

Because Kant marks an important turning point in the history of philosophy, this questionnaire takes a new form. Decide how strongly you agree or disagree with the statements below. Label your answers SA (strongly agree), A (agree), U (undecided), D (disagree), SD (strongly disagree). In statements 1–5, you will be summing up your position on topics you have spent many hours investigating.

_____ 1. All knowledge in the mind comes through the senses.

Explanation: _____

_____.

_____ 2. The mind can know truths independently of the senses.

Explanation: _____

_____.

_____ 3. Almost nothing can be known for certain.

Explanation: _____

_____.

_____ 4. No human has ever known or ever will know the ultimate nature of reality.

Explanation: _____

_____.

_____ 5. Empiricists, rationalists, and skeptics would have to agree on at least one thing: For knowledge to occur, the mind must receive accurate information about external reality.

Explanation: _____

_____.

_____ 6. The mind actively structures the world it believes it merely passively perceives.

Explanation: _____

_____.

Kant argues that all philosophers before him committed the same massive error about the mind. According to Kant, the mind does not merely receive information, as earlier philosophers had believed, but radically transforms the information it receives. Kant's position is contrasted to earlier views of empiricism and rationalism. A model of Kant's description of the knowledge process is developed. Kant's answer to Humean skepticism supports the certitudes of Newtonian science, but it does not support the view of science as a description of external reality.

It does not matter what your philosophical position is thus far—you're wrong.

You may have been swayed by the long line of empiricists (that began with Aristotle) into believing that all knowledge comes to you through your senses. Or you may have sided with the rationalists who severely criticized the senses and held that the mind has its own window on reality. Or, happily or unhappily, perhaps you have thrown in with Hume and skepticism in general, believing that there is very little that anyone can know for certain. No matter what your philosophical beliefs at this point in the tour, Kant is going to argue that you are absolutely mistaken. In one sense, Kant belongs to no philosophical tradition we have investigated; in another sense, he draws key elements from each.

Kant is going to try to convince you that every philosopher you admire or reject *made the same fundamental error.* Thus, it doesn't matter if you are an empiricist, a rationalist, or a skeptic. You're wrong. To give you a hint of Kant's approach, he argues that every philosopher before him shared a fundamental conception of the way the mind works and that this fundamental conception was false. To say more would spoil the surprises and shocks in store for you.

Kant is commonly regarded, along with Plato and Aristotle (to name only two more), as one of the greatest of all philosophers. One good way to give you a sense of Kant's remarkable intelligence and the new way he looks at philosophy is to give you a chance to match wits with him. On three occasions in this chapter, I will pose questions that Kant brilliantly answered, give you all the background information you need, and then challenge you to match Kant's genius by equaling or even surpassing his answer.

In this chapter, I'll answer the following questions:

- What was Kant's goal?
- What are the differences between empiricists and rationalists?
- What is the similarity between empiricists and rationalists?
- What is Kant's new view of the mind?
- What was Kant's answer to Hume?

After investigating my answer to these questions, you'll be ready to explore a very short selection from Kant's *Critique of Pure Reason.*

Immanuel Kant (1724–1804)

BALTIC SEA

Konigsberg

EAST PRUSSIA

The fourth of nine children and the oldest surviving child, Immanuel Kant was born with a deformed chest; he was plagued with health problems throughout his life. Because of his poor health, Kant watched his diet carefully and maintained a strict regimen. He walked every day, and it was said that he was so regular that people could set their watches by the time he passed their house.

Kant was born in 1724 in Königsberg, a lively commercial center and university town in eastern Prussia. His father was a saddler, and his mother an uneducated German woman and devout Pietist (a Lutheran sect). Kant revered his mother, who was remarkable for her good character, great curiosity, and natural intelligence. She died when he was only twelve, apparently after tasting an ailing friend's medical prescrip-

tion in a goodwill attempt to convince the invalid to take the medicine.

Kant attended both grammar school and college in Koenigsberg. At college, he studied the natural sciences, astronomy, mathematics, and philosophy. Kant's career coincided with the Enlightenment, or Age of Reason. Old social, political, and economic doctrines were being challenged. Scientific breakthroughs in anatomy, physics, astronomy, and chemistry gave rise to an optimistic faith in reason and human progress—a faith shared by Kant.

After completing his studies in 1746, Kant worked as a tutor to the children of various Prussian aristocrats. In 1755 he got a job as privatdozent at the University of Koenigsberg; he was the first major philosopher to be a professional university teacher. As a privatdozent Kant was licensed to give lectures. However, he was paid not by the university, but by the students. He lectured as many as twenty-one hours a week on subjects ranging from fireworks and physical geography to metaphysics. As an instructor, Kant was playful, witty, and entertaining. To his many friends, he was a role model and inspiration. Kant's most notable trait, it was said, was his moral sincerity and his devotion to the idea of duty. One of his students later wrote that Kant's pupils "never left a single lecture in his ethics without having be-

What Was Kant's Goal?

Kant describes the impetus that led him in a new philosophical direction.

> I openly confess that my remembering David Hume was the very thing which many years ago first interrupted my **dogmatic** slumber and gave my investigations in the field of speculative philosophy a quite new direction. I was far from following him in the conclusions at which he arrived.[1]

---

[1] Immanuel Kant, *Prologomena to any Future Metaphysics*, trans. Paul Carus, revised by James W. Ellington (Indianapolis: Hackett Publishing, 1977) p. 5.

Immanuel Kant (continued)

come better men." Despite his popularity as a teacher, Kant remained poor for many years.

Outwardly, Kant lived a very simple existence. Restricted to a quiet life because of his poor health, heavy teaching load, and modest income, he never married or traveled. On two occasions he was near wedlock. However, he waited so long—feeling that he was not yet able to support a wife—that the women finally gave up and found other husbands. Although Kant never traveled or married, he enjoyed socializing. He rarely ate alone, either taking his meals at a nearby hotel or having guests in his own house.

In 1770, after many years of seeking a permanent teaching position at the University of Koenigsberg, Kant was finally appointed professor of Logic and Metaphysics. He remained there as a professor until poor health forced him to retire in 1796.

Kant's first great work in philosophy, *Critique of Pure Reason*, was not published until 1781 when he was in his late fifties. It was followed, however, by other great works in relatively quick succession. Kant's emphasis on individual dignity and autonomy in his philosophical writings was echoed by the political struggle in the Western world for freedom and individual liberty. In 1789 revolution broke out in neighboring France. While Kant passionately defended the French Revolution from afar, he avoided political controversy. His admiration for the French Revolution, nonetheless, earned him the nickname "The Old Jacobin." (The Jacobins were a group of radical middle-class revolutionaries who, under the leadership of Robespierre, seized power in France in 1793.) Unlike the Jacobins, who later advocated terrorism, Kant was a man of peace.

Kant's only brush with political authorities occurred in 1794, following the publication of his book on religion. The Prussian king, who disapproved of Kant's views on religion, asked him not to publish further on the topic; and Kant complied with the king's request.

In his later years, Kant gained considerable fame, and Koenigsberg became a shrine of philosophy. People came from all over to consult Kant on all sorts of issues—including the lawfulness of vaccinations. Kant retired from his teaching position in 1796. He died in 1804, having spent his entire life in Koenigsberg.

Kant's major philosophical works include *Critique of Pure Reason* (1781), *Prolegomena to Any Future Metaphysics* (1783), *Fundamental Principles of the Metaphysics of Morals* (1785), *Metaphysical Foundations of Natural Science* (1786), *Critique of Practical Reason* (1788), *Critique of Judgment* (1790), *On Perpetual Peace* (1795), and *Metaphysics of Morals* (1797).

Kant had been drowsing along with sleepy, unsupported convictions, and Hume snapped him awake:

> . . . since the origin of metaphysics so far as we know its history, nothing has ever happened which could have been more decisive to its fate than the attack made upon it by David Hume.[2]

Kant's goal was to escape the philosophical problems Hume dropped into his lap.

---

[2] Immanuel Kant, *Prologomena to any Future Metaphysics,* trans. Paul Carus, revised by James W. Ellington (Indianapolis: Hackett Publishing, 1977) p. 3.

dogmatic blind belief in unproven principles.

Kant shared Hume's admiration for Newton. However, unlike Hume, Kant believed that the principles of the new science were reliable and absolutely certain. Hume, remember, held that the truths of math and geometry were completely certain but gave no information about the world. Kant believed that the truths of math and geometry and many other categories of truth were absolutely certain and *did* give information about the world. Thus, to take only one crucial principle, Kant believed that the concept of cause and effect was both a necessary and universal characteristic of the world we know with our senses. His problem was to find an answer to Hume's arguments against cause and effect. Kant did not set out to prove that we could have certainty about cause and effect, but to find out what made our certainty about cause and effect *possible*.

Hume, in Kant's view, had successfully destroyed assumptions about the mind's relationship to reality that had been the basis of philosophizing for over 2,000 years. The only way to defeat Hume would be to develop a new and more accurate description of how the mind worked. Because Kant marks such a radical shift in philosophy, especially in understanding the knowledge process, this is a good point in the tour to stop and review. In order to understand what is new in Kant's approach, let's examine the two traditions—empiricism and rationalism—that he radically revised.

What Are the Differences Between Empiricists and Rationalists?

To help you review the history of epistemology, I will look out my window at the apple tree across the street and think like some of the philosophers we've investigated.

I'll start with five empiricists: Aristotle, Aquinas, Locke, Berkeley, and Hume.

I look at the apple tree across the street, green leaves fluttering in a light wind, red apples shining, and think like Aristotle. Everything that comes through my senses falls into one of four categories: matter, essence, origin, or purpose. The wood pulp of the tree is the tree's matter; the botanical definition of the tree is the tree's essence; an apple seed is the tree's origin; producing apples is the tree's purpose. Continuing to think like Aristotle, I understand that these four categories cause the tree to be what it is; thus, they could be described as its "causes." Translating this into Aristotle's terminology, the matter of the tree is its *material cause;* the essence of the tree is its *formal cause;* the origin of the tree is its *efficient cause;* and the purpose of the tree is its *final cause.*

Now, I look at the apple tree and think like Thomas Aquinas. Though I still understand that the tree has the four Aristotelian causes (Aquinas follows Aristotle on many issues), my mind pierces through these causes and understands something deeply marvelous about their design. The apple tree's matter, essence, origin, and purpose fit together into a superbly designed whole and are themselves perfectly joined to the four causes of the earth and the four causes of rain and the four causes of the sun and the four causes of each of the seasons. The perfect design of the apple tree is marvelously linked to the perfect design of the world. I realize that all the superbly crafted wonders I see out my window could only have been created by a supreme Intelligence. Thus, following Aquinas's chain of reasoning, I deduce from the brilliant interlocking design revealed to me through my senses that God exists as the Designer of All.

Next, looking at the apple tree from John Locke's point of view, I understand that all I know about the apple tree are my ideas. I do not see the shape of the apple tree itself, but my idea of the shape of the apple tree; I do not see the color of the apple tree itself, but my idea of the color of the apple tree. I do not know the apple tree directly, but only the way the apple tree is represented in my thoughts. Continuing to think like Locke, I realize that some of my ideas about the apple tree are produced by the apple tree itself and some are produced by my sensing of the apple tree. Thus, my ideas have either an objective or a subjective origin. I look at the apple tree and understand that the size and shape of the tree are objective, in the tree itself. However, the color of the tree is subjective, created by my seeing the tree. Translating this distinction into Locke's terminology, objective features like size, shape, weight, and texture are *primary* qualities because they come first, are in the tree itself; subjective features like color, taste, scent, and sound are *secondary* qualities, because they come second, are added by my senses. But where is Aristotle's matter? I mentally sort through primary qualities and then deduce that though matter is an "I know not what," it must exist; otherwise, primary qualities would not exist. Following Locke's argument, I believe that matter must be the unseen, but supporting, entity hidden by primary qualities.

Now, I think like George Berkeley—and know that Locke did not go far enough. Locke was correct in believing that I do not know the tree itself, that I know only my ideas about the tree. But Locke did not realize that *all* I know are ideas. Ideas are the only reality. The apple tree—and everything else outside my window—is nothing but a collection of ideas. And this means matter has vanished! Ideas of apples hang from ideas of branches, which sprout ideas of leaves. Ideas could not exist without a mind thinking them. Following Berkeley's reasoning, I believe God must exist as the mind that thinks all I see. Thus, my ideas are copies of God's ideas!

Next, I think like David Hume, and everything falls apart. A bird pecks into an apple, and the apple moves. Bird pecking; apple moving: two separate events with no causal connection. The bird leaps off the tree branch, and the branch bounces. Bird leaping, branch bouncing: two separate events with no causal connection. A boy picks up an apple and whacks it with a bat. Bat swinging, apple flying: two separate events with no causal connection. Thinking like Hume, I understand how little I can deduce from what I am seeing. All the impressions that pour into my head are loose and separate, like individual frames of a film. I look inward and observe how I falsely link my ideas of separate impressions into cause-and-effect relationships. I saw the boy swinging the bat and I saw the apple flying, but *I did not see* the bat necessarily connected to the apple flying. The necessary connection was mental, not actual. I imposed the ideas I linked together in my mind upon unlinked events in the world. But now I don't even know, as I continue to think like Hume, who or what is doing the "imposing." I can find no mind producing the thoughts I think I think.

What do all empiricists hold in common? What is it in their view of the knowledge process that makes them empiricists?

The common feature of empiricism is _____

_____   _____

_____ .

EXERCISE 24.1
Thinking Like the Empiricists

Pick an object in your surroundings (not an apple tree!) and write a description of how it would be thought about by Aristotle, Aquinas, Locke, Berkeley, and Hume.

Now, I will look at the apple tree from the point of view of five rationalists: Parmenides, Plato, Augustine, Anselm, and Descartes.

When I think like Parmenides, I see the same tree, of course, as all the empiricists, but I regard my sense knowledge as illusory. Looking at the apple tree, I understand that it has no real existence: The tree is merely reality's mirage. The illusory character of the apple tree becomes especially clear to me when I consider how the apple tree will "change." In order for the tree or anything else to change, something must become nothing. Since it is impossible for something to become nothing, I understand that the changing apple tree—and everything else that appears to change—is an illusion.

Next, I think like Plato and realize that the apple tree is merely a poor copy of the Form of Apple Tree. The apple tree across the street will eventually rot and die, but the Essence of Apple Tree will last forever. Thus, there are really two trees: the changing, imperfect tree I know with my senses and the perfect, eternal Form of Tree I know with my mind. But how do I know about the Form of the Apple Tree? Following Plato's reasoning, I believe the Form of the Apple Tree must be knowledge I recollect from my soul's existence in the realm of Forms prior to my birth.

Next, I think like St. Augustine and certainly believe that Plato was correct. The imperfect tree across the street *is* a mere copy of the Perfect Tree. But, continuing to think like Augustine, Plato was wrong in believing that the knowledge of the Perfect Tree comes from my soul's existence in the realm of Forms prior to my birth. My knowledge of the Form of Apple Tree comes directly from God. God is like a sun illuminating my mind. It is through His light that I see the Essence of Apple Tree. Only He has the power to allow me to see beyond the imperfect, changing tree across the street and perceive the Apple Tree of All Apple Trees. My inadequate senses can know only a few trees; God enlightens my mind and lets me see the perfect, divine universal Tree that exists far above imperfect, earthly, particular trees.

Now, thinking like St. Anselm, I look at the apple tree and compare it with my idea of God. I can think of the apple tree as existing or not existing; therefore, existence is not part of the apple tree's essence. However, when I think of God, an all-perfect being, I *cannot* think of God lacking existence, because that would be the same as thinking of an all-perfect being who lacked a perfection. Thus, when I analyze my idea of God, which is completely unlike my idea of the apple tree or anything else I can know with my senses, I arrive at a proof of God's existence. Whereas even a perfect apple tree would have only a limited number of perfections, God would have to have all perfections. Therefore, I understand that God would have the perfection of existence and thus God *must* exist.

Next, I think like René Descartes and worry about what my senses are telling me. Is that a real tree across the street or only a dream tree? Only if God is no deceiver can I be sure of what I see. And the only way I can prove that God is no deceiver is to turn away from my senses and examine the idea of God in my mind. Looking inward, I realize that only God could cause the idea of God. And if only God could cause the idea of God, then I know that God exists as the cause of my idea of Him. And since God exists, I can, if I carefully use the senses and reason he gave me, be sure that there is a real apple tree across the street.

Now, what do all rationalists hold in common? What is it about their view of the knowledge process that makes them rationalists?

The common feature of rationalism is _____

_____

_____.

EXERCISE 24.2
Thinking Like the Rationalists

Write a description of how an object from your surroundings would be thought about by Parmenides, Plato, Anselm, and Descartes.

EXERCISE 24.3
Open-Book Test!

Using the information you have learned in this chapter and earlier on the tour, match the statements below with one or more of the following philosophers: Aristotle, Aquinas, Locke, Berkeley, Hume, Parmenides, Plato, Anselm, Descartes. Answers to some of the following are debatable. Thus, look forward to convincing your teacher that you scored 100 percent.

1. God exists.
2. The senses should not be trusted.
3. All of reality is divided into two parts.
4. Science accurately describes reality.
5. The mind, at birth, possesses perfect truths.
6. The truths of geometry and mathematics provide no information about the world.
7. There is nothing in the mind that did not come through the senses.
8. The changing, physical world has no reality.

One way to understand the difference between rationalism and empiricism is to see that they have opposing views of the relationship between the mind and the senses. According to all the empiricists we have examined, the senses are the *only* window that the mind has on the world. The entire contents of the mind rest upon five categories of information: ear data, nose data, eye data, tongue data, and skin data. Anything else in the mind— for example, God's existence— rests upon, is deduced from, one of these five kinds of information.

Rationalists take a different view of the relationship between the mind and the senses. They admit that the senses are one window on reality, but hold that the mind has its own window as well. A key feature of rationalism is the conviction that the information that the mind possesses from the senses is vastly inferior to the information that the mind has on its own. Take Augustine, for example. The kind of knowledge the mind has from the senses is of the changing, imperfect world. God's light, however, can shine directly into the mind and reveal the perfect and eternal truths of the Forms. Thus, wisdom begins for Augustine, as it does for all rationalists, in turning away from the window of senses and turning toward the mind's window on the divine.

Now, here is the first of the chances I promised you at the beginning of this chapter to match wits with Kant. The differences between the empiricists and rationalists are obvious. *But what is the similarity?* Kant made what he believed was a startling, world-shaking discovery. All philosophers before him (including the empiricists and rationalists we examined) shared the same incorrect view of the nature of the mind. By recognizing this enormous error, Kant constructed a new epistemology, a new theory of knowledge. Answer the following question correctly and you will have successfully matched wits with one the greatest philosophers of all time:

> What enormous error about the nature of the mind was committed by the empiricists and the rationalists before Kant? (What you have read in this last section gives you all the information you need.)

> Thinking about what I learned from the empiricists and rationalists we just examined, I would have to say that their great error was that they incorrectly viewed
>
> the mind as something that was P ___ ___ ___ ___ ___ ___ rather than
>
> A ___ ___ ___ ___ ___.

What Is the Similarity Between Empiricists and Rationalists?

Kant describes the approach that led him to his new view of the mind:

> . . . hitherto it has been assumed that all our knowledge must conform to objects . . . [but this has] ended in failure. We must, therefore, make trial whether we may not have more success in the tasks of metaphysics, if we suppose that objects must conform to our knowledge.[3]

---

[3] Immanuel Kant, *Critique of Pure Reason,* trans. Norman Kemp Smith (New York: St. Martin's Press, 1956) p. 22.

Kant describes the great error of the past, and then describes his new approach. Try to put what he is saying into your own words.

In the past, _____

_____ .

Kant's new approach will be _____

_____

_____ .

The old, failed way of philosophers was to "assume knowledge must conform to objects"; Kant's new approach will be to see if there is more success by assuming "objects must conform to our knowledge." What exactly does this mean?

Let's look at the old, failed way first.

All the empiricists and rationalists we have examined on our tour did, in fact, assume that "knowledge must conform to objects"; in other words, true information in our minds must be a copy of the external objects of that knowledge. Even philosophers as different as the rationalist Plato and the empiricist Aristotle share this view. In Plato's view, when I have true information in my mind about the Form of Apple Tree, the information must be a copy of the external object of that knowledge, the actual Form of Apple Tree. In Aristotle's view, when I have true information in my mind about the apple tree across the street, the information must be a copy of the external object of that knowledge, the actual apple tree across the street. For both Plato and Aristotle and all the other philosophers we examined, "knowledge must conform to objects"; that is, the true information inside our minds must be a copy of, conform to, an object outside our minds.

Note the similarity between Plato's and Aristotle's picture of the knowledge process. Knowledge begins with (1) an external object and ends with (2) an internal *copy* of that object.

This is not only the view of philosophers before Kant, but it is also the view of most of my students. It seems to be merely common sense to say that when we know something, our knowledge is a copy of an external object of that knowledge. If you have knowledge of this book, then your knowledge must conform to, be a copy of, this book.

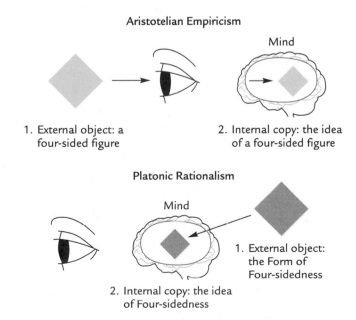

Aristotelian Empiricism

Mind

1. External object: a four-sided figure

2. Internal copy: the idea of a four-sided figure

Platonic Rationalism

Mind

2. Internal copy: the idea of Four-sidedness

1. External object: the Form of Four-sidedness

Let's call the old, failed way the copy model of knowledge. We have knowledge in our mind when that knowledge is a copy of an external object. I have knowledge of the apple tree across the street when my knowledge is a copy of an external object, the apple tree across the street.

Now, here is your second chance to match wits with Kant. Kant will argue that there is something radically wrong with the copy model of knowledge. Think about what happens when you know something. Is the *best* way of understanding this process the way of the empiricists and rationalists we have examined? Answer this question and you will have successfully matched wits with Kant:

What is wrong with the copy model of knowledge? (What you have read thus far and a shrewd analysis of the power of the mind will give you all the information you need.)

The problem with the copy model of knowledge is _____

_____

_____.

In the next section, you'll learn if you have successfully matched wits, thus far, with Kant.

What Is Kant's New View of the Mind?

Thus, "active" and "passive" are the correct answers to your first attempt to match wits with Kant.

In a nutshell, Kant's new view of the mind is that the mind is not passive but *active*. The mind does not passively receive information from the external world, but actively imposes its own order on that information. This activity is what Kant indicates when he says, "Objects must conform to our knowledge." The old view is that the mind passively allows objects to shape its knowledge. Kant's new view is that the mind has a structure that actively shapes the objects it knows. Under the old view, my mind passively allows information about the apple tree across the street to shape my knowledge of the apple tree. Under Kant's new view, my mind has a structure that actively shapes information *into* an apple tree.

In order to begin to understand Kant's new view of the mind, let's start with a simple analogy. The mind is like a pair of red glasses.[4]

Let's say I look at the apple tree across the street through a pair of red glasses. My glasses make the tree look reddish. My glasses, so to speak, actively shape what I know of the tree. The glasses don't merely passively transmit information about the tree, but they also transform that information and color it red. In fact, with my red glasses on, there is no way I can escape the way they transform what I know about the apple tree. The activity of the glasses is automatic and continuous, and it requires no conscious effort.

According to Kant, the mind functions like the red glasses to automatically, continuously, and with no conscious effort shape the information it receives.

---

[4]I owe this comparison to Samuel Enoch Stumpf, *Socrates to Sartre: A History of Philosophy*.

As long as I have the glasses on, I cannot escape or control the way they shaped information about the tree; in the same way, as long as I have a mind, there is no way I can escape or control the way it shapes the information it receives.

Now the question is, "If the glasses add redness to all the data they receive, what does the mind add to all the data it receives?"

Hold on to your philosophical hat.

According to Kant, the mind adds time and space to all its data. In other words, my friend, the mind creates time and space.

What?

Just as the glasses add redness to all information they receive, so the mind adds time and space (and many other characteristics as well) to the information it receives. In the same way that the red glasses automatically, continuously, and without conscious effort shape the information they receive, the mind's concepts of time and space automatically, continuously, and without conscious effort actively shape the information it receives. *Time and space are, so to speak, the internal glasses the mind uses to perceive reality.*

I will say more about this in a moment, but now you can determine how successful you were in your second attempt to match wits with Kant. In Kant's view, the problem with the copy model of knowledge is that, simply put, knowledge is not the result of the mind passively copying information; knowledge is the result of the mind actively *transforming* information. The mind does not passively copy time and space from the information it receives; rather, the mind actively transforms information it receives with its concepts of time and space. Thus, let's call Kant's new view the transformation model of knowledge.

Here is a diagram of Kant's transformation model of knowledge. (The significance of the question mark will be explained in a moment.)

Kant's Transformation Model of the Mind

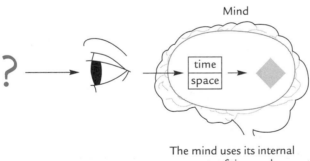

The mind uses its internal concepts of time and space to transform the information it receives into the idea of a four-sided figure.

Using what you've learned thus far, summarize the characteristics of the copy model of knowledge and Kant's transformation model of knowledge.

The characteristics of the copy model are _____

_____

_____ .

The characteristics of the transformation model are _____

_____

_____.

Now let's add a few more details to Kant's transformation model of knowledge.

If I were thinking like Kant, how would I describe what happens when I look at the apple tree across the street?

I stare at the tree. The tree *appears to be* an object that exists in time and space. However, following Kant, I realize the time and space that I believe are "out there" are really my mind's way of structuring the data it receives. Thus, there is a "something" that is not in time and space, which, in some way, transmits information through my senses to my mind. That "something" then is shaped by the mind's concepts of time and space and becomes an apple tree. Kant calls the "something" the thing-in-itself or, more technically, the **noumenon.** What I know after my mind has shaped the noumenon with the concepts of time and space is the **phenomenon,** the apple tree in my mind.

Thus, I can now make a slightly more complex picture of Kant's transformation model of knowing.

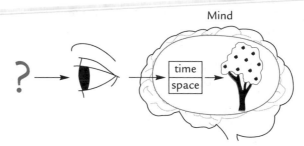

Mind

1. The noumenon, thing-in-itself.

2. The mind uses its internal concepts of time and space to transform the information it receives from the noumenon into the phenomenon of an apple tree.

According to Kant, time and space are not the only concepts that the mind uses to shape noumena into phenomena. Our minds possess twelve categories, the "pure concepts of the understanding," that actively shape all we know. The twelve concepts fall into four groups: quantity, quality, relation, modality.

The pure concepts of the understanding

Quantity: unity, plurality, totality

Quality: affirmation, negation, limitation

Relation: substance-accidents, cause-effect, causal reciprocity

Modality: possibility, actuality, necessity

Let's consider two of these concepts, substance-accidents and cause and effect, in more detail and then increase the complexity of Kant's transformation model of knowledge.

The concepts of substance and accidents is an Aristotelian distinction between the essential and nonessential. Thus, an essential part of the apple tree across the street is that it is a woody plant. A nonessential part of the apple tree is that it now has leaves. Leaves are nonessential to the apple tree because even without leaves (for example, in the winter), it is still an apple tree. The fact that the apple tree is a woody plant is an essential, or we could say a "substantial," part of the tree; leaves and apples are nonessential, or we could say that they are what "accidentally" happens to the tree in certain seasons. Thus, to sum up, the substance of an object is its essential features; the accidents of an object are its nonessential features.

EXERCISE 24.4
Substance-Accidents

Describe the following in terms of substance and accidents.

1. An orange with a leafy stem
2. The Empire State Building
3. This book
4. Elvis Presley in a white, leather jumpsuit
5. A Macintosh computer
6. The moon
7. Your best friend
8. A banana split in a blue bowl

According to Kant, substance-accidents is a mental category that shapes our experience just as time and space are mental categories that shape our experience. When I look across the street and understand the apple tree in terms of what is essential, its substance, and what is nonessential, its accidents, my mind is actively shaping information *into* the apple tree, not passively copying information *from* the apple tree. Translating this back into Kant's terminology, the noumena, the thing-in-itself, is shaped into the phenomenon, the object I know, by the pure concepts of the understanding—in this case, the concept of substance-accidents. Time, space, and substance-accidents are all part of the glasses the mind uses to perceive reality.

Cause and effect is another pure concept of the understanding. Hume, as you'll remember, argued that cause and effect were imposed on the external world by an association of ideas. In Hume's view, the concept of cause and effect is nothing but the mind, through "a gentle force," linking ideas together. In Kant's view, cause and effect are part of the automatic, continuous, nonconscious way the mind organizes all it knows. Cause and effect are, so to speak, hard-wired into the brain. To make this distinction between the two philosophers clearer, let's contrast how Hume and Kant would analyze a single experience.

noumenon/phenomenon
One way to clarify Kant's terms is to think of the difference between a television signal and the image on a television screen. You can't see or hear television signals because they haven't been transformed into three-dimensional images by the circuitry of a television set; you can't see or hear noumena because they haven't been transformed into three-dimensional phenomena by the circuitry of your mind. The mind, however, is far more powerful than any television set. The mind adds time and space to its signal, as well as color, sound, and all other sensory information.

The boy across the street picks up an apple and swats it with his bat. The apple flies into the next yard. Now, according to Hume, all I have observed are the bat swinging and the ball flying, two separate impressions. Through a "gentle force" I link these ideas together in my mind as cause, the bat swinging, and effect, the apple flying. In other words, I mentally create cause and effect. But, according to Hume, nothing forces me to link ideas together this way. If I carefully inspect my inner impressions, I can see that the bat swinging is one thing, that the apple flying is another, and that there is no need to falsely join them together as cause and effect.

Kant takes a radically different view. My mind uses, inescapably uses, the concept of cause and effect to organize its experience. Just as a computer cannot function without the organizing principles of its circuitry, so my mind cannot function without the organizing principles of its understanding. Thus, according to Kant, the concept of cause and effect goes far deeper than Hume realized. Cause and effect are not the result of mental "gentle force" but are absolutely hard-wired into the mind's motherboard. Hume held that without the concept of cause and effect, the mind would function *more* accurately. According to Kant, without the concept of cause and effect (and the other pure concepts of the understanding), *the mind would not function at all.*

Now let's add the twelve pure concepts of the understanding to our Kantian model of the mind.

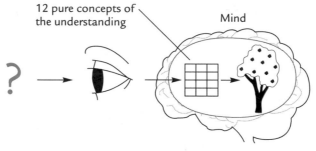

12 pure concepts of
the understanding

Mind

1. The noumenon, thing-in-itself.

2. The mind uses its internal, 12 pure concepts of the understanding to transform the information it receives from the noumenon into the phenomenon of an apple tree.

To sum up what we have said thus far about Kant's model: There are two features of reality that are not revealed by the senses. First, there is a nontime, nonspace something (termed the thing-in-itself or noumenon) that transmits information to the senses. Second, the mind transforms this nontime, nonspace something into a spatial-temporal object through its own twelve concepts of understanding. For example, the concept of substance-accidents shapes information into a combination of essential and nonessential characteristics; the concept of cause and effect shapes information into cause-and-effect relationships. Thus, according to Kant, *the mind actively transforms the reality it believes it merely passively copies.*

Making Sense of the Senseless

According to Kant, the mind automatically and nonconsciously structures a reality which it believes it merely passively receives. Space, for example, is not a feature of the "external" world but a concept the mind uses to create the appearance of an "external" world. If the mind had no built-in concept of "out there," there would be no "out there" there.

Many of Escher's drawings, like this one, can be used to vividly illustrate Kant's point. Trace the figures moving on the staircase. How does your mind use its built-in concept of space to try to make sense of the picture? Pay special attention to what happens as you try to observe the figures "ascending" and "descending."

What my mind tries to do as it traces the figures on the staircase is _____

_____,

but what happens is _____

_____.

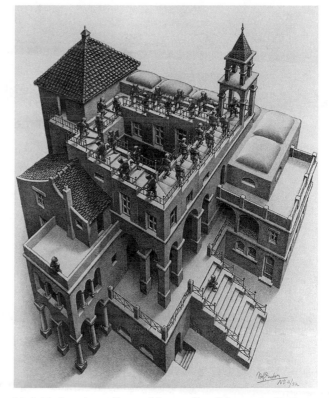

M. C. Escher, *Ascending and Descending*, lithograph, 1960.

Kant would argue that if your mind were not structured to understand space in a predetermined way, Escher's picture could create no mental confusion.

You are now ready to match wits with Kant a third time.

How will Kant answer Hume? Hume took the skeptical position that the mind has no certainty about the world of the senses. He argued that the principle of cause and effect, the cornerstone of science, was only the result of the mind linking ideas together, not a description of events in the sense world. Kant, however, argued that science *did* give accurate information about the sense world. Answer this question, and you will have successfully matched wits with Kant:

How, using Kant's model of the knowledge process, is it possible to have certainty about the sense world?

Certainty about the sense world would be possible because _____

_____

_____

_____

_____.

What Was Kant's Answer to Hume?

Kant's answer to Hume is paradoxical.

Kant argues that we can have absolute certainty about the sense world, but at the price of knowing nothing for certain about ultimate reality. Kant's argument for certainty about the sense world can be stated as follows:

1. The sense world is nothing but the shape given to information by the mind's twelve categories of the understanding.

2. We know the twelve categories of the understanding.

3. Therefore, we can have absolute certainty about the sense world.

Kant's argument for lack of certainty about ultimate reality can be stated as follows:

1. All we can know is what is shaped by the twelve categories of the understanding.

2. Ultimate reality, the realm of things-in-themselves, is not shaped by the twelve categories of the understanding.

3. Therefore, we have no knowledge of ultimate reality, the realm of things-in-themselves.

To understand Kant's paradoxical answer to Hume, think again about the red glasses.

Just as you can be certain that everything you see through the red glasses will have reddish tones, so you can be certain that everything you know will have characteristics of the twelve categories of the understanding. But just as the red glasses keep you from seeing actual colors, colors-in-themselves, the mind's twelve categories keep you from knowing ultimate reality, things-in-themselves.

Neatly sidestepping Hume's arguments, Kant lands in a difficulty of his own. Hume's argument against certainty was based on a view of the mind as a passive copier of information about reality. Because, for example, the sense world transmits no information about cause and effect to the mind, the mind has no knowledge of cause and effect. Kant deftly sidesteps Hume's arguments by substituting a radically new model of the mind. The mind does not passively copy information from the external world, but actively transforms information into what it perceives as an external world. Thus, we can be certain of the principle of cause and effect because cause and effect is one of the categories the understanding uses to organize its information. But this radical new view of the mind left Kant with a major problem. Certainty about the way the mind constructs the sense world blocked all knowledge of ultimate reality, the realm of things-in-themselves. If the mind adds space, time, cause and effect, substance-accidents, and other features of the twelve categories to information, then things-in-themselves exist independently of space, time, cause and effect, substance-accidents, and other features of the twelve categories. So then, what are things-in-themselves? We cannot know. To know ultimate reality is to know things-in-themselves *before* they have been transformed by the mind. This would be as impossible as using red glasses to see colors-in-themselves. Ultimate reality lies just on the other side of the knowable—on the other side of mental lenses we can never remove.

READING:
EXCERPT FROM *CRITIQUE OF PURE REASON*

Because Kant is a difficult writer for even professional philosophers, we are only going to analyze a short (four sentence) selection from one of his most important works, the *Critique of Pure Reason*.[5] Handily enough, these sentences contain an important argument for Kant's view that the mind possesses concepts—in this case, the concept of space, which it uses to organize reality.

Read slowly, and be sure to carefully fill in the blanks.

Space is not an empirical concept which has been derived from outer experiences.

This sentence makes an astounding claim that the rest of the selection will attempt to prove. What is Kant claiming?

Kant's claim is: _____

_____ .

I look out my window at my neighbor Jerry standing next to his old, blue Chevy truck. It certainly seems obvious that I am seeing two things, Jerry and his truck, in space. And it seems more obvious still that all that I know about space itself comes to me from the external world. After all, where else could I get my idea of space except from "out there"? *But Kant is claiming that I am wrong.* My idea of space "is not an empirical concept," is not a concept that comes to me through my senses "from outer experiences," from the external world. What evidence could he find to support this astounding claim?

Read on. (I'll place each new selection from the quotation in boldface.)

Space is not an empirical concept which has been derived from outer experiences. **For in order that certain sensations be referred to something outside me (that is, to something in another region of space from that in which I find myself), and similarly in order that I may be able to represent them as outside and alongside one another, and accordingly as not only different but as in different places, the representation of space must be presupposed.**

Using Jerry and his truck as an example, I'll boil down Kant's statement into a short sentence and emphasize a key word. "For me to know that Jerry and his old blue truck are outside me, the concept of space must be *presupposed*."

---

[5] Immanuel Kant, *Critique of Pure Reason*, trans. Norman Kemp Smith (New York: St. Martin's Press, 1956) p. 23.

If you understand what Kant means by saying that "space must be presupposed," you will grasp the key element in Kant's argument. "To presuppose," in Kant's terms, can be defined as "to require as a prior condition." This may not sound very helpful, so let's begin with a few simple examples. Note how each pair of statements, 1 and 2, means the same thing.

1. In order for a refrigerator to make ice cubes, a temperature of at least 32 degrees must be presupposed.

2. In order for a refrigerator to make ice cubes, a temperature of at least 32 degrees is required as a prior condition.

1. In order for bread to rise, the presence of yeast must be presupposed.

2. In order for bread to rise, the presence of yeast is required as a prior condition.

1. In order for humans to speak, the vibration of the vocal cords is presupposed.

2. In order for humans to speak, the vibration of the vocal cords is required as a prior condition.

Thus, if I say that in order for *X* to happen, *Y* must be presupposed, I mean that in order for *X* to happen, *Y* is required as a prior condition. In order for water to freeze into ice cubes, 32 degrees of cold is required as a prior condition. Now you try it a few times.

1. In order for _____, _____ must be presupposed.

2. In order for _____, _____ is required as a prior condition.

1. In order for _____, _____ must be presupposed.

2. In order for _____, _____ is required as a prior condition.

1. In order for _____, _____ must be presupposed.

2. In order for _____, _____ is required as a prior condition.

Let's return to what Kant is saying about space. Here is the short version of the position I quoted earlier, "For me to know that Jerry and his old blue truck are outside me, the concept of space must be *presupposed*." I can now paraphrase this as "For me to know that Jerry and his old blue truck are outside me, the concept of space is *required as a prior condition*." In other words, if my mind does not first possess the concept of space, then I can have no knowledge of Jerry and his old blue truck outside me. If my mind has no concept of space, there can be no "out there."

Using pictures, here's a summary of what I've said thus far.

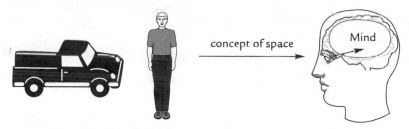

1. I ordinarily believe my concept of space comes to my mind from Jerry and his old blue truck. In other words, I ordinarily believe space is an empirical concept I have learned through my senses.

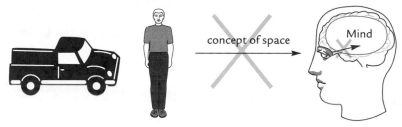

2. According to Kant, my concept of space *does not* come to me from Jerry and his old blue truck. In other words, "space is not an empirical concept which has been derived from external experiences."

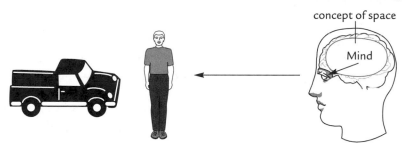

3. According to Kant, it is only because I already have the concept of space in my mind that I can have any knowledge of Jerry and his truck. In other words, it is not the external world that makes possible the concept of space, but the concept of space that makes possible the external world.

Now let's look at the rest of our short quotation from Kant.

Space is not an empirical concept which has been derived from outer experiences. For in order that certain sensations be referred to something outside me (that is, to something in another region of space from that in which I find myself), and similarly in order that I may be able to represent them as outside and alongside one another, and accordingly as not only different but as in different places, the representation of space must be presupposed. . . .

. . . We can never represent to ourselves the absence of space, though we can quite well think it as empty of objects. It [space] must therefore be regarded as the condition of the possibility of appearances, and not as a determination dependent upon them.

Well, let's put Kant to the test. He says, in essence, that we can't imagine the absence of space, but we can imagine the absence of objects in space. All right, I try to imagine the absence of space. What am I imagining? I am imagining emptiness. In other words, I am imagining empty *space.* I continue trying and keep coming up with the same result. Every time I try to imagine the absence of space, I imagine emptiness—empty space. So, Kant is right. I can't imagine the absence of space.

Go on. Try it yourself.

When I try to imagine that space doesn't exist, what I imagine is _____

_____.

Thus, Kant is (right, wrong) when he says we can't imagine the absence of space.

Now I'll go on to Kant's second point. He says that I *can* imagine the absence of objects in space. All right, I try to imagine the absence of objects in space. What am I imagining? I am imagining the same thing I did before, empty space. No objects out there. So Kant seems to be right again. I *can* imagine space without objects.

Prove it to yourself.

When I try to imagine space without objects, what I imagine is _____

_____.

Thus, Kant is (right, wrong) when he says we can imagine space without objects.

But what is Kant's point?

Kant is reinforcing his argument that our concept of space is prior to our concept of objects. If we can think of space without thinking of external objects, then we could not have obtained our concept of space from external objects.

Return to our examples. We can think of yeast without thinking of bread rising. Isn't that right?

That is (right, wrong) because _____.

And we can think of the refrigerator at 32 degrees without thinking of ice cubes. Isn't that right?

That is (right, wrong) because _____

_____.

I've almost never had a student who thought the preceding two positions were wrong. Thus, yeast and the refrigerator at 32 degrees are conceptually prior to bread rising or ice cubes. In the same way, because we can think of space without thinking of objects in space, our concept of space precedes our concept of objects. *And if our concept of space comes before our concept of objects in space, we couldn't have obtained our concept of space from "out there."*

And now let me add a final, very important point that Kant doesn't mention in the quotation discussed here, but which I spent time developing earlier in this chapter. Because we didn't learn our concept of space from the external world, we can be certain that our concept of space is built in, hard-wired into our brain. The concept of space is part of the glasses the mind uses to view reality. Space is not external, but internal.

Well, has Kant convinced you in the argument we just examined?

When Kant claims that space is internal, part of the mind's way of viewing reality,

and not external, I believe he is (right, wrong) because _____

_____   _____

_____.

SUMMARY

Kant describes a radically new knowledge process. Rationalism and empiricism before Kant were based on the view that certainty occurs when the mind passively copies information from external reality. Skepticism, holding the same view of the mind, argued that certainty is not generally possible because the mind has few, if any, accurate copies of external reality. According to Kant, certainty is possible because the world the mind knows has been actively constructed by the mind's own categories. Instead of holding that our "knowledge must conform to objects," Kant developed the view that "objects must conform to our knowledge."

Kant distinguishes between phenomena (the sense world) and noumena (the realm of things-in-themselves). The sense world exists in space and time, operates according to the principle of cause and effect, and has other characteristics endowed by the twelve concepts of the understanding. The realm of things-in-themselves exists outside space and time and lacks the other characteristics of the twelve categories of the understanding.

EXERCISE 24.5
Looking Back

Practice your paraphrasing skills and answer the following:

1. What was Kant's goal?
2. What are the differences between empiricists and rationalists?
3. What is the similarity between empiricists and rationalists?
4. What is Kant's new view of the mind?
5. What was Kant's answer to Hume?

EXERCISE 24.6
Looking at the World Through Kant's Eyes

How would Kant answer each of the following? Use your own paper to explain your answer.

1. T F Knowledge begins with sense experience but is not entirely produced by sense experience.
2. T F We can know for certain that God exists.
3. T F The principles of Newtonian science are absolutely certain.

4. T F Newtonian science is not a description of ultimate reality.

5. T F The mind gives its laws to nature.

6. T F Nature gives its laws to the mind.

7. T F Any future metaphysics will have to be based upon an analysis of the mind's operations.

8. T F The twelve categories of the understanding are innate ideas.

9. T F Space is not a concept learned from sense experience but a concept that makes sense experience possible.

10. T F The world the mind knows cannot exist independently of the mind that knows it.

ANALYSIS OF YOUR PHILOSOPHICAL SELF-PORTRAIT

If reading this chapter has altered your views, enter your new answers below. Label your answers SA (strongly agree), A (agree), U (undecided), D (disagree), SD (strongly disagree). I have put Kant's answers in brackets.

_____ [D] 1. *All knowledge in the mind comes through the senses.*

Kant would probably disagree with this position, but not strongly, because the statement is partly correct. He held that knowledge *does* have a sensory component, but what we know with our senses is organized according to the mind's twelve concepts of the understanding.

_____ [D] 2. *The mind can know truths independently of the senses.*

Just as in the previous answer, Kant would probably disagree with this statement, but not strongly. The twelve categories of the understanding are not known through the senses but can, according to Kant, be known for certain. Kant, of course, would disagree with the standard rationalist view that the truths that come to the mind independently of the senses are copies of an external, nonmental reality (like God or the realm of the Forms).

_____ [SD] 3. *Almost nothing can be known for certain.*

Part of Kant's goal was to refute Hume's skepticism. In his view, all the principles of Newtonian science can be known for certain because they are products of the way the mind organizes the sense world.

_____ [SA] 4. *No human has ever known or ever will know the ultimate nature of reality.*

Kant would categorically agree with this statement. All that humans know is the world constructed by human minds. Thus, we cannot know ultimate reality, the realm that lies beyond the world constructed by our minds.

_____ [SA?] 5. *Empiricists, rationalists, and skeptics would have to agree on at least one thing: For knowledge to occur, the mind must receive accurate information about external reality.*

Kant would agree that earlier philosophers held that knowledge occurs when the mind makes a copy of external reality. However, he hoped to convince adherents of these positions that they held an incorrect model of the mind.

_____ [SA] 6. *The mind structures the world it believes it merely passively perceives.*

This is at the core of Kant's insight. Kant declared that he had achieved a "Copernican Revolution" in philosophy. Just as Copernicus had shifted astronomy from a geocentric, earth-centered, view of the universe to a heliocentric, sun-centered view of the universe, Kant claimed he had shifted metaphysics from an external to an internal orientation, from an examination of ultimate reality to an examination of the mind's operations. This is often termed the "Kantian turn" in philosophy that established the dynamics of the mind as a key new area for philosophical investigation.

Evaluation: Number of points in agreement with Kant = _____ of 6 possible.

A position of Kant's that you strongly (support, oppose) is _____

_____

because _____

_____

_____ .

Nicolaus Copernicus (1473–1543), Polish astronomer. Though Copernicus was influenced by earlier thinkers, he is traditionally, and rightfully, credited with a revolutionary reconception of the solar system. Instead of holding that the sun, planets, and stars revolved about the earth, thus making it the center of the cosmos, Copernicus proposed that the earth and other planets revolved about the sun. His heliocentric (sun-centered) model replaced the geocentric (earth-centered) model of the solar system that dated from the days of Aristotle (fourth century B.C.).

GOOD BOOKS

Kant, Immanuel. *Prolegomena to Any Future Metaphysics.* Translated by P. Carus. Indianapolis: Hackett, 1977. Kant intended this as a simplified introduction to his metaphysics and epistemology. It's readable by a hardy, determined student in an introduction-to-philosophy class. Think of the *Prolegomena* as our tour's Himalayas.

Korner, Stephen. *Kant.* Baltimore: Penguin, 1955. A classic explanation of Kant.

NEXT STOP

You be the judge as two philosophical heavyweights, Immanuel Kant and John Stuart Mill, have an ethical slugfest.

25

Immanuel Kant Versus John Stuart Mill
How to Make Moral Choices

YOUR PHILOSOPHICAL SELF-PORTRAIT

Add more details to your philosophical self-portrait by answering the questions below and offering evidence for your answers.

1. T F The most important thing to consider in making a choice is its consequences.

    Evidence: _____
    _____
    _____.

2. T F We should act as we would want everyone else to act.

    Evidence: _____
    _____
    _____.

3. T F "Do unto others as you would have them do unto you" is the only ethical principle we need to follow in dealing with others.

    Evidence: _____
    _____
    _____.

4. T F All our choices are motivated by the pursuit of pleasure and the avoidance of pain.

    Evidence: _____
    _____
    _____.

5. T F The best choices lead to the greatest happiness for the greatest number of people.

    Evidence: _____
    _____
    _____.

Two opposing ethical positions are considered. According to Immanuel Kant, the consequences of our choices are irrelevant. What we must do is be guided by a good will and make choices that we would want everyone to make. According to John Stuart Mill, the consequences of our choices are all-important. What we must do is make choices that lead to the greatest amount of pleasure for the largest number of people.

THOUGHT EXPERIMENT

You are a computer programmer who wants to save the world. Therefore, you are constructing a Web site, Universal Decision Maker, to teach everyone how to make ethical choices. People will be able to enter any moral problem into your program and learn the difference between a morally good and a morally bad choice. One of your first problems is, obviously, to define for your software the difference between these two choices. This doesn't seem like an easy task. And so, you begin to think,

You could instruct your program so that one characteristic of a morally good choice is

_____

_____.

Perhaps another characteristic of a morally good choice is _____

_____.

Some people might even argue that a characteristic of a morally good choice is

_____

_____.

Before long, you realize that it would be very convenient, *extremely* convenient, if you had a single rule for ethical decision making. You'd call it the Great Ethical Principle.

With the Great Ethical Principle, your program could very easily help people make moral choices. Those choices that followed the principle would be good choices; those that violated the principle would be bad choices. You dream excitedly: In place of the complexity of moral codes, holy books, religious systems, society's laws, one simple rule!

You try out several versions of the Great Ethical Principle.

Perhaps it should be _____

_____.

Or, perhaps it should be _____

_____.

Then you learn that the answer might lie in the works of two philosophers, Immanuel Kant and John Stuart Mill. Each proposed very different versions of a single rule that should guide all ethical decisions.

You realize there are four options:

1. Kant correctly identified the Great Ethical Principle.

2. Mill correctly identified the Great Ethical Principle.

3. Both were wrong, but the Great Ethical Principle can be identified.

4. The Great Ethical Principle cannot be identified (and so, for all practical purposes, it does not exist).

By the end of this chapter, you will make your decision.

To help you, I'll answer the following questions:

- What is the difference between consequentialist and nonconsequentialist ethical theories?

- What is Kant's version of the Great Ethical Principle?

- What are key ideas in Kant's *Foundation for the Metaphysics of Morals*?

- What is Mill's version of the Great Ethical Principle?

- What are key ideas in Mill's *Utilitarianism?*

Let's begin with a description of an important ethical distinction.

What Is the Difference Between Consequentialist and Nonconsequentialist Ethical Theories?

To help you determine if Kant or Mill discovered the Great Ethical Principle that should guide all moral choices, let's pause the tour for a moment and talk about ethics.

As you recall, ethics is the study of the nature of right and wrong human actions. An important ethical distinction is the difference between a morality based upon goals and a morality based on rules. A goal-based morality considers the consequences of a choice; thus, it is consequentialist. A rule-based morality does not consider the consequences of a choice; thus, it is nonconsequentialist.

For example, let us say I am considering cheating on my taxes. From the consequentialist point of view, I must think about the results, the consequences, of my action. Will I be caught? Will I have to pay a fine? Will I have sleepless nights?

However, from the nonconsequentialist point of view, all these future considerations are irrelevant. I must simply determine if cheating on my taxes is right; does cheating violate a moral rule?

To determine if an action is moral or immoral, from the consequentialist point of view, I look forward into the future at the consequences of my choice.

To determine if an action is moral or immoral, from the nonconsequentialist point of view, I ignore the future and simply compare my action with a moral rule.

The key question for the consequentialist is "What are the most important consequences of a choice?"

The key question for a nonconsequentialist is "What is the moral rule that a choice must obey?"

To illustrate the difference between these questions, let me think like the philosophers we have examined. (For convenience, I'll assume that all our philosophers would conclude that I ought not to cheat on my taxes.)

The Consequentialists

According to Plato, Aristotle, Epicurus, and Epictetus the most important consequences of my choices are whether they lead to the goal of happiness. Happiness should be the target, the goal, of all that I choose.

Thinking like Plato, I believe happiness is achieved by having reason rule my bodily desires. Left unchecked, my desires for food, sex, comfort, and possessions would control, even derange, my personality. Thus, I ought not to cheat on my taxes because this would be giving in to bodily desires for the pleasures that additional money would bring.

Thinking like Aristotle, I believe happiness is achieved by choosing the middle path between excess and deficiency. Thus, I should not give too little or too much to the government in taxes. And so, I ought not to cheat on my taxes because this would be paying too little, a deficiency, instead of paying the right amount.

Thinking like Epicurus, I believe happiness is achieved by seeking pleasure and avoiding pain. Many of the most troublesome pains come from unnatural desires. Unnatural desires, such as the desire for costly possessions, are desires that I am not born with and are thus not a genuine part of my personality. Therefore, I ought not to cheat on my taxes because the extra money I would gain would only fuel the pain caused by my unnecessary craving for expensive things.

Thinking like the stoic, Epictetus, I believe that happiness is best achieved when I have peace of mind, *apathia*. I can achieve peace of mind by recognizing that the only thing I can control is my attitude toward the world; I have no control over the world itself. The more worldly possessions I have, the more possessions I have no control over—and thus the greater my worries and the less my peace of mind. Therefore, I ought not to cheat on my taxes because the money I gain could only buy me more troublesome things that I don't really own.

All our consequentialists agree that I should seek happiness, have happiness as my goal. They disagree about the way to achieve it.

The Nonconsequentialists

Every Christian philosopher on our tour is a nonconsequentialist. The only consideration for a Christian is whether an action conforms to God's rules.

Thus, thinking like a Christian philosopher, I see that all the future consequences of cheating on my taxes should be ignored. It does not even matter if cheating on my taxes will lead me to hell. My only consideration must be whether cheating conforms to God's rules. A simple way to determine God's rules is by looking in the Bible. One biblical passage says that I ought to "render unto Caesar what is Caesar's." Thus, according to this passage, I ought to pay my taxes, not cheat on them, because paying would be following God's rules.

What Is Kant's Version of the Great Ethical Principle?

Kant is a nonconsequentialist, one of the most extreme of all philosophers in this category.

As you will see when we examine selections from *Foundation for the Metaphysics of Morals*, Kant reasons as follows:

1. The only purely good thing about humans is a *good will*. Intelligence, bravery, wealth, and other positive features of human life can be thought of as somewhat, but not purely, good. A person could be intelligent, brave, wealthy, and still be evil—imagine, for example, a brilliant, bold, wicked billionaire. Only when intelligence, bravery, wealth, and other features of human life are *guided* by a good will is it guaranteed that these features are good. Thus, it is the good will alone that makes all human attributes good. In Kant's view, if you have a good will, you have all that is required to be good. If you do not have a good will, it does not matter what else you possess; you cannot be good.

2. A good will is good in itself, not because of the results it achieves. If you have a good will and all your efforts fail, your will may be unsuccessful, but it is still good.

3. A good will is independent of any inclination to be good. If you are inclined, have a tendency, to do a good action, then you deserve no moral credit. Only if you deliberately will, deliberately choose, to perform a good action do you deserve moral credit.

4. Kant calls the single rule that should guide all moral decisions the categorical imperative.

One of Kant's three versions of the **categorical imperative** is "Act as though the maxim of your action were by your will to become a universal law." In other words, the single ethical rule is that you should make moral choices based on principles which you would agree that everyone should follow.

For example, if you can't decide between telling a lie or telling the truth, you should make the choice you would want everyone to make. According to Kant, though you might think it is right for you individually to lie, you would never think it is right for *everyone* to lie. Thus, if you act as you would want everyone to act, you would not lie.

Kant's categorical imperative, his version of the Great Ethical Principle, is *choose as you want everyone to choose.* While this sounds simple enough, in a few moments you will see that a more complex understanding of the categorical imperative involves realizing that immoral actions are wrong because they are self-contradictory. Kant will argue that it is as illogical to say that lying is right as to say squares are circles.

Now let's analyze a few key sections from one of the most famous texts in the history of ethics.

What Are Key Ideas in Kant's *Foundation for the Metaphysics of Morals*?

Kant's argument begins as follows:

> Nothing can possibly be conceived in the world, or even out of it, which can be called good without qualification, except a *good will.*

Before I ask you to paraphrase this important sentence, let me clarify what Kant means by "good without qualification" and "a good will."

Start by contrasting these two statements:

1. Juan is good, with the qualification that he doesn't give money to the poor.

2. Persephone is good, without qualification.

To be good *with* a qualification is to be almost, but not entirely, good. Juan is a fabulous person except that he is stingy to the poor.

To be good *without* qualification is to be entirely good. Persephone is an entirely fabulous person; there isn't a single bad thing about her.

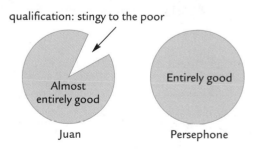

qualification: stingy to the poor

Almost entirely good

Juan

Entirely good

Persephone

Now give me your own example of being good with and without qualification.

It could be said that _____ is good, with the

qualification that _____

_____ .

It could be said that _____ is good without qualification.

Next, in order to understand what Kant means by "a good will," we first have to understand the concept of the will.

Look at these two statements:

1. Despite my inclination to sleepiness, I will that I get out of bed.
2. Despite my inclination to laziness, I will that I run a mile.

My will is the part of my mind that deliberately chooses a course of action. Thus, if I am deliberately choosing, I am willing.

1. Despite my inclination to sleepiness, I *deliberately choose* to get out of bed.
2. Despite my inclination to laziness, I *deliberately choose* to run a mile.

To will to do X is to deliberately choose to do X; to have an inclination to do X is simply to have a leaning, a tendency, to do X. Before long we'll learn more about what Kant means by the will and the difference between the will and an inclination; but for now, try to give me two examples of using your will to make a deliberate choice that is opposed to an inclination.

Though I am inclined to _____, my will makes me

_____ .

Though I am inclined to _____, my will makes me

_____ .

Understanding that willing is equivalent to deliberate choosing, the nature of a *good* will should be clear. The will is good when it deliberately chooses what is good. (Later in Kant's argument we will learn more about the good; that is, that good choices are in accord with the categorical imperative.)

Use what you've learned to paraphrase Kant's first sentence: "Nothing can possibly be conceived in the world, or even out of it, which can be called good without qualification, except a good will."

Kant is saying: _____

_____

_____ .

Let's go on to the second sentence. Note the evidence Kant uses to back up his claim in the first sentence. (As earlier on the tour, whenever I am combining a section we've analyzed with a new section, I'll put the new section in boldface.)

> Nothing can possibly be conceived in the world, or even out of it, which can be called good without qualification, except a *good will*. **Intelligence, wit, judgment, and other talents of the mind, however they may be named, or courage, resolution, perseverance, as qualities of temperament, are undoubtedly good and desirable in many respects; but these gifts of nature may also become extremely bad and mischievous, if the will which is to make use of them, and which, therefore, constitutes what is called character, is not good.**

To understand Kant's point, imagine a talented villain—for example, Superman's antagonist, Lex Luthor. Luthor is intelligent, cunning, brave, and determined. But he uses an evil will to guide these skills. Thus, as Kant would put it, Luthor's good qualities of "temperament," his intelligence, and other positive attributes are guided by a bad "character," his bad will.

And so which is more important, according to Kant—a quality like intelligence or the will that guides intelligence?

Kant says (a quality like intelligence, the will that guides intelligence) is more

important because _____ _____

_____

_____ .

Next, observe how Kant continues to support his opening claim.

> Nothing can possibly be conceived in the world, or even out of it, which can be called good without qualification, except a *good will*. Intelligence, wit, judgment, and other talents of the mind, however they may be named, or courage, resolution, perseverance, as qualities of temperament, are undoubtedly good and desirable in many respects; but these gifts of nature may also become extremely bad and mischievous, if the will which is to make use of them, and which, therefore, constitutes what is called character, is not good. **It is the same with the gifts of fortune. Power, riches, honor, even health, and the general well-being and contentment with one's condition which is called happiness, inspire pride, and often presumption, if there is not a good will to correct the influence of these on the mind, and with this also to rectify the whole principle of acting, and adapt it to its end.**

In all of the above, what general point is Kant making about the difference between a good will and other positive characteristics of human life?

Kant's point is that _____

_____

_____

_____ .

Now read the first paragraph again, paying special attention to its conclusion.

Nothing can possibly be conceived in the world, or even out of it, which can be called good without qualification, except a *good will*. Intelligence, wit, judgment, and other talents of the mind, however they may be named, or courage, resolution, perseverance, as qualities of temperament, are undoubtedly good and desirable in many respects; but these gifts of nature may also become extremely bad and mischievous, if the will which is to make use of them, and which, therefore, constitutes what is called character, is not good. It is the same with the gifts of fortune. Power, riches, honor, even health, and the general well-being and contentment with one's condition which is called happiness, inspire pride, and often presumption, if there is not a good will to correct the influence of these on the mind, and with this also to rectify the whole principle of acting, and adapt it to its end. **The sight of a being who is not adorned with a single feature of a pure and good will, enjoying unbroken prosperity, can never give pleasure to an impartial rational spectator. Thus a good will appears to constitute the indispensable condition even of being worthy of happiness.**

All right. You observe Lex Luthor, a man who does not have "a single feature of a good and pure will," having a wonderfully successful life. What, according to Kant, should you feel and why?

I should feel _____ because

_____

_____

_____.

And so why is a good will "the indispensable condition even of being worthy of happiness"?

Kant argues _____

_____

_____.

Now read the next paragraph, noting especially the last two sentences.

There are even some qualities which are of service to this good will itself, and may facilitate its action, yet which have no intrinsic unconditional value, but always presuppose a good will, and this qualifies the esteem that we justly have for them, and does not permit us to regard them as absolutely good. Moderation in the affections and passions, self-control, and calm deliberation are not only good in many respects, but even seem to constitute part of the intrinsic worth of the person; but they are far from deserving to be called good without qualification, although they have been so unconditionally praised by the ancients. For without the principles of a good will, they may become extremely bad; and the coolness of a villain not only makes him far more dangerous, but also directly makes him more abominable in our eyes than he would have been without it [_____].

Which of the following are consistent (C) or inconsistent (I) with Kant's position?

1. C   I   The ancients believed that moderation was a good without qualification.
2. C   I   The ancients were wrong in believing that moderation was a good without qualification.
3. C   I   Calm deliberation is part of the intrinsic worth of the person.
4. C   I   It is possible for humans to possess moderation in their passions, self-control, and calm deliberation, while still being villains.
5. C   I   A good will is the only thing that guarantees that moderation in the passions will be good.

Pause for a moment.

Kant is claiming something astounding.

Recall how Plato, Aristotle, Epicurus, Epictetus, and other philosophers we've studied have praised moderation in the passions, self-control, and reason (calm deliberation) as absolutely, unconditionally good. The entire goal of Greek ethics and even a segment of Christian ethics could be summed up as living a life of moderation and self-control through reason's control of the passions. And now along comes Kant, who throws this view out the window!

The life of reason is not the highest good; the highest good is the good will that guides the reason.

Kant sees the will's relationship to the personality as similar to a hand's relationship to a tool. Just as a hand could use a hammer to build a fine house or murder someone, so the will can use moderation (or self-control, calm deliberation, or intelligence) for noble or evil purposes. Thus, the intention, the goodness, of the will is *all* important. The value of our other human qualities is entirely determined by the goodness of the will that employs them.

Do you agree?

I (agree, disagree) with Kant that a good will is more important than any other

human quality because _____

_____

_____.

Now read slowly as Kant continues to explore, in the next paragraph, the nature of a good will.

A good will is good not because of what it performs or effects, not by its aptness for the attainment of some proposed end, but simply by virtue of the volition—that is, it is good in itself, and considered by itself is to be esteemed much higher than all that can be brought about by it in favor of any inclination, nay, even of the sum total of all inclinations.

Let's go back to Juan and Persephone. Imagine that Juan is good for two reasons:

1. Juan's will is influenced by good inclinations.
2. He achieves good things.

Persephone, however, is good for one reason:

1. She has a good will (without even considering the goodness of her inclinations and achievements).

According to Kant, Persephone is far more virtuous than Juan.

Juan's will may be influenced by his good inclinations, such as his inclination, to build a home for orphans; and Juan may actually follow through on his good inclinations and build the home, but he is not intrinsically, innately good. He merely has a tendency to be good, and his actions have good consequences.

Persephone, however, is intrinsically good. Her goodness comes prior to any of her actions and is independent of any of her inclinations. Her will doesn't have to be *inclined* to be good; it *is* good. She doesn't have to achieve any good results; her will is good before she achieves anything.

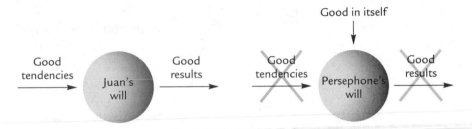

Good tendencies impel Juan's will to achieve good results. Thus, his goodness is outside his will. The good that he achieves is a result of good tendencies prior to his willing and good results that follow of his willing.

Because Persephone's will is good in itself, her good tendencies and good results are irrelevant. Her goodness is within her will.

If I have a good will, then its goodness does not depend upon my inclinations or whether my will ever achieves its goals. What makes my will good is its essential goodness prior to any actions and independent of any positive results.

A good will is good not because of what it performs or effects, not by its aptness for the attainment of some proposed end, but simply by virtue of the volition—that is, it is good in itself, and considered by itself is to be esteemed much higher than all that can be brought about by it in favor of any inclination, nay, even of the sum total of all inclinations. **Even if it should happen that, owing to special disfavor of fortune . . . this will should wholly lack power to accomplish its purpose, if with its greatest efforts it should yet achieve nothing, and there should remain only the good will (not, to be sure, a mere wish, but the summoning of all means in our power), then like a jewel, it would still shine by its own light, as a thing which has its whole value in itself. Its usefulness or fruitlessness can neither add to, nor take away anything from this value.**

Here's a trick question. According to Kant, which of these two people is to be more esteemed?

1. A woman whose good will, "summoning all the means" in her power, leads her to build an orphanage.

2. A woman whose good will, "summoning all the means" in her power, leads her to attempt to build an orphanage, but she fails.

The trick you're trying to play on me is _____

_____

_____ .

I'll tell you what the trick is later. But, for now, read on. Kant introduces the important concept of duty in the next section. As always, underline important phrases.

> We have, then, to develop the concept of a will which is to be esteemed as good in itself without regard to anything else. It dwells already in the natural and sound understanding and does not need so much to be taught as only to be brought to light. In the estimation of the total worth of our actions it always takes first place and is the condition of everything else. In order to show this, we shall take the concept of duty . . .

Let's consider some examples of duty and how it contrasts with inclination before we go on to explore Kant's example.

As a good parent, I have a duty to be loving to my children. As a good driver, I have a duty to obey traffic laws. As a good citizen, I have a duty to vote in elections. My duty, in all cases, is what I ought to do.

Give me a few examples of duties.

As a good student, it is my duty to _____ .

As a good taxpayer, it is my duty to _____ .

As a good friend, it is my duty to _____ .

Now here is Kant's example.

> To be kind where one can is a duty, and there are, moreover, many persons so sympathetically constituted that without any motive of vanity or selfishness they find an inner satisfaction in spreading joy and rejoice in the contentment of others which they have made possible. But I say that, however dutiful and however amiable it may be, that kind of action has no true moral worth. It is on a level with [actions done from] other inclinations. . . . For the maxim lacks the moral import of an action done not from inclination but from duty.

What duty is Kant talking about in the preceding paragraph?

Kant is talking about the duty to be _____ .

Is Kant saying that if someone acts "without any motive of vanity or selfishness" and finds "inner satisfaction in spreading joy," then that person's action is a good action?

Kant (is, is not) saying that because _____

_____

_____ .

Here is a very important point:

Kant contrasts acting from duty with acting from an inclination; only acting from duty, in his view, has moral worth. If you are good simply from an inclination to be good, then your action has no moral value. However, if you are good independently of any inclination to be good, then your action has genuine moral value.

I look out my window at my neighbor Jerry playing catch with his son Scotty. If Jerry is playing catch simply because he has an inclination to play catch, then, in Kant's view, his action has no moral worth. Jerry is only following his tendencies, doing what comes naturally. Jerry's playing catch with his son is no more moral than if he's scratching an itch. He's merely doing what he feels like doing.

However, let us say that Jerry has no inclination at all to play catch. In fact, imagine he is deeply inclined to watch hockey on television. Now, if Jerry resists his inclination and, from a clear conception of his duty as a parent, plays catch with Scotty, then, in Kant's view, he is performing a genuine moral action. Jerry gets all the credit due to a moral person. He is performing a good action, only because the action is good, not because he is following any of his inclinations. In fact, the goodness of his action is all the more clarified, because he is *resisting* his inclinations.

Now present your own distinction between acting from duty and acting from inclination.

One duty of a good Christian would be to _____.

However, this can be opposed by an inclination to _____.

One duty of a good neighbor would be to _____.

However, this can be opposed by an inclination to _____.

In the next section, Kant considers a variation of his example.

But assume that the mind of that friend to mankind was clouded by a sorrow of his own which extinguished all sympathy with the lot of others, and though he still had the power to benefit others in distress their need left him untouched because he was preoccupied with his own [_____]. Now suppose him to tear himself, unsolicited by inclination, out of his dead insensibility and to do this action only from duty and without any inclination—then for the first time his action has genuine moral worth.

What is it about this person's actions that leads Kant to say that "for the first time his action has genuine moral worth"?

What makes this person's actions moral is _____

_____

_____.

EXERCISE 25.1
Kant's Conception of Duty and Moral Value

According to Kant, when we act from a sense of duty, especially when it is opposed to our inclinations, we are acting morally.

Label each of the following actions moral (M) or not moral (N) from Kant's point of view. Several of these, as you may learn from your teacher and classmates, are debatable.

_____ 1. I don't think about my duty to others to be prompt, but I have an inclination to promptness, so I show up for my appointment on time.

_____ 2. I recognize that it is my duty to others to be prompt, and I have an inclination to promptness, so I show up for my appointment on time.

_____ 3. I recognize that it is my duty to others to be prompt, but I have an inclination to be tardy. Nonetheless, I show up for my appointment on time.

_____ 4. I follow my inclination and my duty and serve as a juror.

_____ 5. I want to go to the beach, but decide that what I really ought to do is help my elderly neighbor weed her garden.

_____ 6. I love gardening, and so I help my elderly neighbor weed her garden.

_____ 7. I hate gardening and I hate old people; nonetheless, I deliberately choose to help my elderly neighbor weed her garden.

_____ 8. I do whatever I feel like doing.

_____ 9. I never do what I feel like doing, only what I ought to do.

_____ 10. I hate doing what I should do, but I do it anyway.

EXERCISE 25.2
Who Is the Moral Person?

According to Kant, which of the following would be the most moral person? Use your own paper to explain his position on each.

1. A person who loves children and builds an orphanage because she has had a lifelong urge to help orphans.

2. A person who is indifferent to children and builds an orphanage because she believes it is the right thing to do.

3. A person who is indifferent to children and attempts to build an orphanage because she believes it is the right thing to do, but fails.

4. A person who hates children, attempts to build an orphanage because she believes it is the right thing to do, but fails.

EXERCISE 25.3
Your Conception of Duty and Moral Value

Label 1–10 in Exercise 25.1 moral (M) or not moral (N), from *your* point of view.

Next, Kant provides more detail about what he means by the will.

Everything in nature works according to laws. Only a rational being has the capacity of acting according to the *conception* of laws (i.e. according to principles). This capacity is the will. Since reason is required for the deduction of actions from laws, will is nothing but practical reason.

Let's start with the first sentence, "Everything in nature works according to laws." For example, there are laws in nature that control falling objects, the movement of the planets, the beating of a heart.

And?

There are also laws in nature that control _____

_____.

Now pay careful attention to the concluding three sentences.

Everything in nature works according to laws. **Only a rational being has the capacity of acting according to the *conception* of laws (i.e. according to principles). This capacity is the will. Since reason is required for the deduction of actions from laws, will is nothing but practical reason.**

The tide moves according to laws of nature—specifically, the law of gravity. But if I decide to run along the beach, it isn't gravity that is making up my mind. I am acting according to my *conception* of a law (that is, a principle). In this case, my law or principle is that exercise is good. Now, in order to deduce my action (running on the beach) from my law or principle (exercise is good), I must use my reason. This use of reason—what Kant calls practical reason—is identical to the will.

Let me go over that again with a different example.

Let's say that I begin with the principle that promptness is important. And I take the action of hurrying to an appointment. I use my reason to deduce my action from my principle. Reasoning this way, according to Kant, is the same as willing.

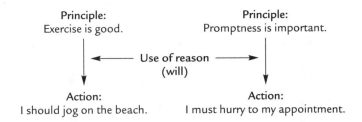

The will is nothing but the use of reason to deduce actions from principles.

Recall that earlier I defined willing as "deliberate choosing." We can now expand that definition; willing is "deliberate choosing of an action deduced from a principle."

EXERCISE 25.4
Principles, Actions, and the Will

Label each statement in the following groups as principle (P), action (A), or practical reasoning (PR). The latter, according to Kant, is the same as willing.

_____ a. Going to the store to buy ice cream for dessert

_____ b. Deciding to go to the store to buy ice cream for dessert

_____ c. Every dinner should have a dessert.

_____ a. Choosing to study hard before a midterm

_____ b. Good grades are important.

_____ c. Studying hard before a midterm

_____ a. We live in an unsafe society.

_____ b. Locking the door at night

_____ c. Reasoning that the door should be locked at night

_____ a. Cheating is okay.

_____ b. Cheating on taxes

_____ c. Deciding to cheat on taxes

Before we conclude our examination of Kant's *Foundation for the Metaphysics of Morals* by examining his famous concept of the categorical imperative, let me summarize what we've learned thus far. Decide your own position on each of the following:

1. While intelligence, moderation, and calm deliberation can be valuable, the only purely good human quality is a good will.

I (agree, disagree) because _____

_____

_____.

2. A good will that does not achieve positive results is just as good as a good will that does achieve positive results. (This is the answer to the trick question.)

I (agree, disagree) because ____   _____

_____

_____.

3. Only when we choose the action that duty commands, independently of our inclinations, does our choice have moral value.

I (agree, disagree) because _____

_____

_____.

4. The will is nothing but the use of reason to deduce actions from principles.

I (agree, disagree) because _____

_____

_____.

Now let's turn to Kant's concept of the categorical imperative.
First let's clarify his terms.
By "categorical" Kant means universal, applying to everyone.
An imperative is a command, something that ought to be obeyed. In this sense, the Ten Commandments could be called the Ten Imperatives. Thus, simply put, the categorical imperative is a command that everyone ought to obey. (We will see in a moment that the force of Kant's command comes not from God, but from reason—making his ethics different from Christian ethics.)
Kant presents several formulations of the categorical imperative; here is one:

> . . . the universal imperative of duty can be expressed as follows: Act as though the maxim of your action were by your will to become a universal law of nature.

Let me interpolate a few explanatory words.

> . . . the universal [applying to everyone] imperative [command] of duty can be expressed as follows: Act as though the maxim [guiding principle] of your action were by your will to become a universal law of nature [a law for everyone].

In other words, the categorical imperative states that it is your duty to act in such a way that the principle that guides your actions should be followed by everyone as a universal law. Understanding this and putting it into practice isn't as complex as you might think.
From the Kantian point of view, determining the morality of an action involves a two-step process:

1. Find the personal principle that guides the action.

2. Attempt to imagine the personal principle as a universal law.

According to Kant, you can no more imagine immoral universal laws than you can imagine round squares. I'll develop this crucial point as I describe several simple examples of the two-step moral decision-making process.
Let's say Mary is thinking of murdering Juana. Is there any way to *prove* that murder is immoral? Can't Mary simply do whatever she wants? Let's apply Kant's two-step process to this problem.

1. *Find the personal principle that guides the action.* Mary's personal principle is simply "I should commit a murder."

2. *Attempt to imagine the personal principle as a universal law.* Mary's personal principle, stated as a universal law, would be "Everyone should commit murder." Now can such a universal law *actually* be imagined? Could there be a society in which everyone murdered everyone? Kant

would argue that the answer is no. A society in which everyone murdered everyone would be a society-less society; this would be as logically impossible as a square-less square.

Here is another example.

Tom is thinking of stealing money from his club treasury. Is there any way to prove that this is immoral? Here is Kant's two-step process.

1. *Find the personal principle that guides the action.* The personal principle that would guide Tom's stealing would be "It is all right for me to steal money instead of earn it."

2. *Attempt to imagine the personal principle as a universal law.* Tom's personal principle stated as a universal law would be: "It is all right for everyone to steal money instead of earn it." Can we imagine such a situation? *No.* A society in which everyone stole money without earning it would be impossible. A society in which no one earned money would be a society without money. Therefore, in a society of thieves, there would be nothing to steal.

To recapitulate each of the examples: We can see what is wrong with Maria's contemplated murder when we try to imagine everyone as a murderer. A society of murderers would be self-extinguishing. It's logically impossible for such a society to exist. Kant's point is quite simple and is appealed to whenever we ask someone, "What if everyone acted that way?" *The categorical imperative simply holds that we should act only in a way that we would be willing for everyone to act.*

For Tom to say it is right for him to steal instead of earn money is the same as saying it is right for anyone to steal instead of earn money. But it is not simply that such a society is wrong, *it is that such a society cannot even be imagined.* A society in which everyone steals is a society in which no one has anything to steal.

Here's a final example.

My neighbor Jerry comes over to borrow ten dollars. I wonder whether it would be ethical to tell him the lie that I don't have the money. And so I use the two-step process.

1. *Find the personal principle that guides the action.* The personal principle that would guide my action is "It is all right for me to tell lies."

2. *Attempt to imagine the personal principle as a universal law.* The personal principle stated as a universal law would be "It is all right for everyone to tell lies." But can I really imagine such a situation? No. What is a lie? A lie is something you tell and expect to be believed. A society of liars would, therefore, be impossible. No one could lie because no one could expect to be believed. A society of liars would be a non-lying society.

Note this very important point: The force behind the categorical imperative is not God but reason. Murder, stealing, and lying are wrong not because they violate God's laws, but because they violate reason's laws. It is no more correct to say lying is right than to say black is white.

Here is one of the harder tasks on the tour. Kant presents several examples, more complex than mine, of acting according to duty. In each, he employs the principles of the categorical imperative that we have examined. After each of his examples, determine what action is being examined, what personal principle (maxim) is involved, and why posing this personal principle as a universal law involves a logical contradiction.

> A man reduced to despair by a series of misfortunes feels wearied of life, but is still so far in possession of his reason that he can ask himself whether it would not be contrary to his duty to himself to take his own life. Now he inquires whether the maxim of his action could become a universal law of nature. His maxim is: From self-love I adopt it as a principle to shorten my life when its longer duration is likely to bring more evil than satisfaction. It is asked then simply whether this principle founded on self-love can become a universal law of nature. Now we see at once that a system of nature of which it should be a law to destroy life by means of the very feeling whose special nature it is to impel to the improvement of life would contradict itself, and therefore could not exist as a system of nature; hence that maxim cannot possibly exist as a universal law of nature, and consequently would be wholly inconsistent with the supreme principle of all duty.

What action is Kant examining?

The action is _____.

Paraphrase the personal principle (maxim) involved.

The personal principle is _____

_____.

When this personal principle is imagined as a universal law, what logical contradiction becomes obvious?

The contradiction is _____

_____

_____.

> Another finds himself forced by necessity to borrow money. He knows that he will not be able to repay it, but sees also that nothing will be lent to him, unless he promises stoutly to repay it in a definite time. He desires to make this promise, but he has still so much conscience as to ask himself: Is it not unlawful and inconsistent with duty to get out of a difficulty in this way? Suppose, however, that he resolves to do so, then the maxim of his action would be expressed thus: When I think myself in want of money, I will borrow money and promise to repay it, although I know that I never can do so. Now this principle of self-love or of one's own advantage may perhaps be consistent with my whole future welfare; but the question now is, Is it right? I change then the suggestion of self-love into a universal law, and state the question thus: How would it be if my maxim were a universal law? Then I see at once that it could never hold as a universal law of nature, but would neces-

sarily contradict itself. For supposing it to be a universal law that everyone when he thinks himself in a difficulty should be able to promise whatever he pleases, with the purpose of not keeping his promise, the promise itself would become impossible, as well as the end that one might have in view in it, since no one would consider that anything was promised to him, but would ridicule all such statements as vain pretences.

What action is Kant examining?

The action is _____.

Paraphrase the personal principle (maxim) involved.

The personal principle is _____

_____.

When this personal principle is imagined as a universal law, what logical contradiction becomes obvious?

The contradiction is _____

_____.

Kant wants to establish an absolutely clear way to tell a moral action from an immoral action. Before Kant, the most popular method would have been to see if the action obeyed God's laws. But after Hume and the attacks by other atheists and agnostics, proof of God's existence involved great philosophical difficulties. And so Kant looks for something far clearer, far more obvious. He believes he has made a bold new discovery. Instead of founding moral principles upon the divine, he will found them upon reason. Under his analysis, the immoral is the self-contradictory, the rationally impossible. When I say it is right to lie (or murder, steal, commit suicide, break promises), I am saying something as illogical as two plus two equals five.

To understand the boldness of what Kant is proposing, think of him as replacing the Ten Commandments and every other command, rule, law, or principle of religion and society with One Commandment.

The One Commandment, which replaces all others, is, *Act as you would want everyone to act.*

Do you agree that this should be the One Commandment (what we have earlier called the Great Ethical Principle)?

I (agree, disagree) because _____

_____

_____.

Next, we examine another great ethical theorist, John Stuart Mill.

What Is Mill's Version
of the Great Ethical Principle?

Mill was an important member of the utilitarians, a group of British thinkers who made significant reforms in England's judicial and legislative systems. Jeremy Bentham, an older colleague of Mill's, provided Mill with several key ethical concepts.

The first paragraph of Bentham's introduction to the *Principles of Morals and Legislation* states one of utilitarianism's central themes:

> Nature has placed mankind under the governance of two sovereign masters, *pain* and *pleasure*. It is from them alone to point out what we ought to do, as well as to determine what we shall do.

In the last sentence, Bentham endorses both *ethical hedonism* and *psychological hedonism*. Ethical hedonism is the view that what we *ought* to do is seek pleasure and avoid pain; psychological hedonism is the view that what we *actually* do is seek pleasure and avoid pain.

This morning I've observed Jerry washing his car, taking his dog Maggie for a walk, and trimming his roses. In Bentham's view, all of Jerry's actions are ruled by the "sovereign masters" of pain and pleasure. His car washing, dog walking, and rose trimming were ruled by his desire to seek pleasure and avoid pain (psychological hedonism), and this is exactly the way Jerry should act (ethical hedonism). In other words, everything Jerry *actually* does is what he *ought* to do.

Now match wits with Bentham's critics who have held there is a contradiction in supporting *both* psychological and ethical hedonism.

Perhaps the contradiction is _____

_____

_____.

Bentham described seven factors that influence an action's pleasure or pain.

1. Intensity (How strong is the pleasure or pain?)

2. Duration (How long will the pleasure or pain last?)

3. Certainty (How certain or uncertain is it that the pleasure or pain will occur?)

4. Nearness or remoteness in time (How soon will the pleasure or pain occur?)

5. Fecundity (Will the pleasure or pain produce other pleasures or pains?)

6. Purity (How likely is it that the pleasure will be followed by other pleasures; how likely is it that the pain will be followed by other pains?)

7. Extent (How many people will be affected by the pleasure or pain?)

Bentham tried to turn these factors into a mathematical system, a "hedonic calculus" that could be used to precisely determine the pleasure or pain—

and therefore, the moral value—of an action. In his spirit, let's say I used a scale from +3 (highly pleasurable) to −3 (highly painful) to determine if I should help Jerry with his yard work.

Thus, I might reason as follows:

1. Intensity of pain: −2 (Yard work is physically difficult.)

    Intensity of pleasure: +1 (I'd feel like a good neighbor.)

2. Duration of pain: −3 (My back will probably hurt tomorrow.)

    Duration of pleasure: +1 (I'll quickly get over my good neighbor feeling.)

3. Certainty of pain: −2 (There's no doubt that yard work will be physically unpleasant.)

    Certainty of pleasure: +1 (The pleasure is somewhat doubtful; if Jerry isn't grateful, I won't feel as happy about helping him.)

4. Nearness or remoteness in time of the pain: −3 (The pain I'm going to feel will be today, not far off in the future.)

    Nearness or remoteness in time of the pleasure: +3 (The pleasure is today's pleasure, not the future's.)

5. Fecundity of pain: −2 (Working in the yard will probably be one pain after another.)

    Fecundity of pleasure: +1 (The pleasure of feeling like a good neighbor is unlikely to produce other pleasures.)

6. Purity of pain: −3 (The pain of working in the yard will likely be a "pure" pain; that is, it won't bring along any pleasures.)

    Purity of pleasure: +1 (The pleasure of being a good neighbor might not be a very "pure" pleasure because it might bring along the pain of aggravation if Jerry isn't grateful.)

7. Extent of pain: −1 (I'll be the only person feeling the pain in my back.)

    Extent of pleasure: +2 (Jerry will be happy for the help; I'll be happy for helping him.)

EXERCISE 25.5
The Pleasure/Pain Balance Sheet

To understand Bentham's approach, use his seven factors, as I have above, to calculate the pleasure and pain of each of the following. Briefly explain each rating.

1. Going to church on Sunday

2. Eating a second helping of a delicious dessert

3. Giving a large sum of money to a charity

Note three things from all this. First, the pleasure and pain of even a simple act, like helping a neighbor, involves a surprisingly complex set of considerations that Bentham's system illuminates. Second, trying to assign number values to pleasures and pains is difficult, even arbitrary. Third, *the entire approach*

John Stuart Mill (1806–1873)

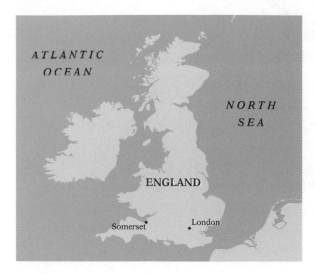

John Stuart Mill never associated with children his own age until he was fourteen. He was educated at home by his father, who started teaching him Greek at the age of three, Latin at age eight, logic at twelve, and political economy at age thirteen. Mill later wrote of his childhood, "I never was a boy; never played at cricket; it is better to let Nature have her way."

Born in London in 1806, John Stuart Mill was the oldest of nine children. His mother was Harriet Burrow Mill, and his father James Mill, a philosopher and journalist. John Stuart Mill was only two years old when his father met Jeremy Bentham, the great utilitarian philosopher and social reformer. The two philosophers struck up a close friendship that lasted a lifetime. The Mill family moved to 1 Queen Square in London to live closer to Bentham and also spent six months of each year with Bentham at Ford Abbey in Somerset. Bentham, who never married or had any children of his own, became absorbed in the education of young John Stuart Mill, preparing him to carry on the utilitarian tradition.

While John Stuart Mill apparently greatly admired Bentham, he was too afraid of his father, a cold, irritable, and arrogant man, to object to his rigid program of education. "Mine," John Stuart Mill later wrote in his *Autobiography*, "was not an education of love but of fear."[1] Mill, on the other hand, was very devoted to his mother, a pretty and good-natured woman, and disliked the way his father treated her. Shortly after their marriage, James Mill fell out of love with his wife and did not bother to hide the fact that he thought her stupid.

At the age of seventeen Mill began working

---

[1] Quoted by Ben-Am Scharfstein, in *The Philosophers: Their Lives and the Nature of Their Thought* (New York: Oxford University Press, 1980), p. 262.

is consequentialist. Whether I should help Jerry has nothing to do with whether I am obeying God's rules, as an orthodox Christian might urge, or whether I can imagine, without contradiction, everyone doing the same thing, as a Kantian might urge. My only consideration as a utilitarian is the pains and pleasures that follow from, that are a consequence of, my act.

To round out our brief discussion of Bentham's utilitarianism, let's consider his famous remark that the goal of human actions is "the greatest good for the greatest number" of people. According to this view, the moral value of my actions is not how much pleasure or pain *I* receive, but how much pleasure or pain *everyone* receives. Thus, if Jerry had a large family who delighted in a well-kept lawn, my singular pains in helping him might be offset by his family's multiple pleasures in viewing the results of my labors. When making a moral choice according to the "greatest happiness" principle, I must look beyond myself to-

John Stuart Mill (continued)

as a clerk for the East India Company, where his father was a high official. Three years later, Mill had an emotional breakdown and sank into a deep depression that lasted for two years. He blamed the depression, in part, on the habit of analyzing everything, which, he said, had a tendency to wear away at his feelings. During this time Mill made a break from the intellectual grip his father had on him and began rethinking his views on utilitarianism.

Like Bentham, Mill was greatly interested in applying utilitarian principles to political matters and social reform. Nineteenth-century England was in the middle of the Industrial Revolution and democratic reform. England was also expanding its empire across the world. A strong supporter of democracy and liberty, Mill advocated free trade, parliamentary reform, secret voting, equality for women, universal suffrage, annual elections, trade unions, and reform of land tenure.

Around 1830 Mill met Harriet Taylor. Although she was married at the time and their relationship become the source of much gossip, they became very close friends. Mill and Taylor married in 1851, after the death of her husband.

A brilliant and highly educated woman, Harriet Taylor—like so many other talented women of the Victorian Age—never published under her own name. However, she had a tremendous influence on Mill's thinking and his radical reformulation of Bentham's utilitarian theory. According to Mill, his great work *On Liberty*, published in 1859, was written by him and his wife.

Both Mill and Taylor, at the time of their marriage, had tuberculosis, and Taylor was an invalid during most of their marriage. Tuberculosis, one of the leading killers in nineteenth-century England, had killed Mill's grandmother, uncle, and one of his brothers as well as his father. Another of Mill's brothers had committed suicide rather than suffer through the final stages of tuberculosis. In 1858, after only seven—albeit happy—years of marriage, Harriet Taylor also fell victim to the disease.

When the East India Company came to an end in 1858, Mill, now a widower, accepted an invitation to run, successfully it turned out, for Parliament. He remained a member of Parliament for ten years. Already in poor health due to tuberculosis, Mill died suddenly in 1873 after contracting a local fever.

Mill's most important philosophical works include *System of Logic* (1834), *Principles of Political Economy* (1848), *On Liberty* (1859), and *The Subjection of Women* (1869).

---

ward other people. What I should do is increase not merely my pleasure, but the pleasure of everyone concerned.

Mill makes at least two important modifications in Bentham's utilitarianism. First, Mill rejects the attempt to assign number values to pleasures and pains. Second, he makes a very important distinction between the *quantity* of a pleasure and its *quality*. In Bentham's view, if the quantity of pleasure produced by scratching a mosquito bite is the same as the quantity of pleasure produced by helping a sick person, then both actions have *equal moral value*. Pleasure is pleasure, and it doesn't matter where it comes from. In Mill's view, as you will see in his essay, physical pleasures are lower, less desirable, than mental pleasures. Therefore, a large amount of the physical pleasure of mosquito-bite scratching could be outweighed by a small amount of the mental satisfaction achieved by helping the sick.

What Are Key Ideas in Mill's Utilitarianism?

With all this in mind, let's now turn to an analysis of a selection from Mill's very influential *Utilitarianism.*

> The creed which accepts [utility] as the foundation of morals, or the Greatest Happiness Principle, holds that actions are right in proportion as they tend to promote happiness, wrong as they tend to produce the reverse of happiness. By happiness is intended pleasure, and the absence of pain; by unhappiness, pain, and the privation of pleasure. To give a clear view of the moral standard set up by the theory, much more requires to be said; in particular, what things it includes in the ideas of pain and pleasure; and to what extent this is left an open question. But these supplementary explanations do not affect the theory of life on which this theory of morality is grounded—namely, that pleasure, and freedom from pain, are the only things desirable as ends; and that all desirable things (which are as numerous in the utilitarian as in any other scheme) are desirable either for the pleasure inherent in themselves, or as means to the promotion of pleasure and the prevention of pain.

Let's play Philosophical Wheel of Fortune.

A morally right action is an action that promotes __ __ __ __ __ __ __ s __.

Therefore, a morally wrong action would be an action that promotes

__ __ __ __ p __ __ __ __ __ __ __.

Happiness is defined as anything that produces __ __ __ __ __ __ r __ and

reduces __ a __ __. Unhappiness, on the other hand, produces __ __ i __

and reduces __ l __ __ __ __ __ __. Therefore, if obeying God's commandments produced more pain than pleasure, a Utilitarian would have to say that action was (moral, immoral).

The "theory of life" that Mill refers to is _____

_____ .

Now, such a theory of life excites in many minds, and among them in some of the most estimable in feeling and purpose, inveterate dislike. To suppose that life has (as they express it) no higher end than pleasure—no better and nobler object of desire and pursuit—they designate as utterly mean and grov-elling; as a doctrine worthy only of swine, to whom the followers of Epicurus were, at a very early period, contemptuously likened; and modern holders of the doctrine are occasionally made the subject of equally polite comparisons by its German, French, and English assailants.

Which of the following are consistent (C) or inconsistent (I) with the pre-ceding paragraph?

1. C I Utilitarianism is opposed to epicureanism.
2. C I Many people reject the view that the goal of life should be seeking pleasure and avoiding pain.
3. C I German, French, and English critics of epicureanism and utilitari-anism believe that both these philosophies are "worthy only of swine."
4. C I Critics of Mill's position believe there is no higher end to life than pleasure.

When thus attacked, the Epicureans have always answered, that it is not they, but their accusers, who represent human nature in a degrading light; since the accusation supposes human beings to be capable of no pleasures except those of which swine are capable. If this supposition were true, the charge could not be gainsaid, but would then be no longer an imputation; for if the sources of pleasure were precisely the same to human beings and to swine, the rule of life which is good enough for the one would be good enough for the other. The comparison of the Epicurean life to that of beasts is felt as degrading, precisely because a beast's pleasures do not satisfy a human being's conceptions of happiness. Human beings have faculties more elevated than the animal appetites, and when once made conscious of them, do not regard anything as happiness which does not include their gratification.

"this supposition" refers to

_____

_____

Mill (believes, does not believe) that humans are capable of pleasures higher than swine.

I do not, indeed, consider the Epicureans to have been by any means faultless in drawing out their scheme of consequences from the utilitarian principle. To do this in any sufficient manner, many Stoic, as well as Christian elements require to be included. But there is no known Epicurean theory of life which does not assign to the pleasures of the intellect, of the feelings and imaginations, and of the moral sentiments, a much higher value as pleasures than to those of mere sensation. It must be admitted, however, that utilitarian writers in general have placed the superiority of mental over bodily pleasures chiefly in the greater permanency, safety, uncostliness, etc., of the former—that is, in their circumstantial advantages rather than in their intrinsic nature. And on all these points utilitarians have fully proved their case; but they might have taken the other, and, as it may be called, higher ground, with entire consistency. It is quite compatible with the principle of utility to recognize the fact, that some *kinds* of pleasure are more desirable than others. It would be absurd that while, in estimating all other things, quality is considered as well as quantity, the estimation of pleasures should be supposed to depend on quantity alone.

Which of the following are consistent (C) or inconsistent (I) with the preceding paragraph?

1. C I Epicureans hold that pleasures involving the higher faculties, such as the pleasure of learning, are superior to those involving only the body, such as the pleasure of eating.

2. C I Other utilitarians, but not necessarily Mill, have held that the pleasures of the higher faculties are intrinsically superior to pleasures involving only the body.

3. C I Mill argues that the quality of a pleasure is more important than the quantity of a pleasure.

Read the next section, and answer the questions. Then, to help you check your understanding and support of utilitarianism, I'll sum up the most important points Mill has made thus far.

If I am asked, what I mean by difference of quality in pleasure, or what makes one pleasure more valuable than another, merely as a pleasure, except its being greater in amount, there is but one possible answer. Of two pleasures, if there be one to which all or almost all who have experience of both give a

Some low-quality pleasures

might be _____

_____

_____

decided preference, irrespective of any feeling of moral obligation to prefer it, that is the more desirable pleasure. If one of the two is, by those who are competently acquainted with both, placed so far above the other that they prefer it, even though knowing it to be attended with a greater amount of discontent, and would not resign it for any quantity of the other pleasure which their nature is capable of, we are justified in ascribing to the preferred enjoyment a superiority in quality, so far outweighing quality as to render it, in comparison, of small account.

Now it is an unquestionable fact that those who are equally acquainted with, and equally capable of appreciating and enjoying, both, do give a most marked preference to the manner of existence which employs their higher faculties. Few human creatures would consent to be changed into any of the lower animals, for a promise of the fullest allowance of a beast's pleasures; no intelligent human being would consent to be a fool, no instructed person would be an ignoramus, no person of feeling and conscience would be selfish and base, even though they should be persuaded that the fool, the dunce, or the rascal is better satisfied with his lot than they are with theirs. They would not resign what they possess more than he for the most complete satisfaction of all the desires which they have in common with him. If they ever fancy they would, it is only in cases of unhappiness so extreme, that to escape from it they would exchange their lot for almost any other, however undesirable in their own eyes.

In the passage above, Mill offers a way to determine the (quality, quantity) of a pleasure.

Assume you are trying to determine whether eating ice cream is a pleasure superior to reading Plato. What, according to Mill, should you consider?

I should consider _____

_____.

Decide your own position on each of the following points presented, thus far, by Mill.

1. The rightness of any action is determined by the happiness it produces.

I (agree, disagree) because _____

_____

_____.

2. The *only* goal of life is pleasure and freedom from pain.

I (agree, disagree) because _____

_____

_____.

3. Pleasures of the higher faculties—that is, "pleasures of the intellect, of the feelings and imagination, and of the moral sentiments"—are clearly superior to pleasures of the senses.

I (agree, disagree) because _____

_____

_____.

4. To determine if one pleasure is superior to another, we need only to determine which of the two pleasures would be chosen by the vast majority of people familiar with both.

I (agree, disagree) because _____

_____

_____.

EXERCISE 25.6
Mill's Pleasure Scale

For each of the two pleasures below, determine which, according to most people who have experienced both, would be rated higher. Use your own paper to explain your reasoning.

1. The pleasure of reading Plato is (superior, inferior) to the pleasure of eating ice cream.

2. The pleasure of watching a Shakespearean play is (superior, inferior) to the pleasure of eating a delicious meal.

3. The pleasure of helping someone in need is (superior, inferior) to the pleasure of receiving a massage.

4. The pleasure of looking at the Mona Lisa is (superior, inferior) to the pleasure of relaxing at the end of a hard day.

5. The pleasure of solving a complex mathematical problem is (superior, inferior) to the pleasure of drinking ice water on a hot afternoon.

EXERCISE 25.7
Your Pleasure Scale

Evaluate 1 through 5 in Exercise 25.6 from *your* point of view. Use your own paper to explain your reasoning.

EXERCISE 25.8
Pleasure Ratings

From your point of view, rate the following activities. Use this scale:

+3 = very highly pleasurable

+2 = highly pleasurable

+1 = pleasurable

0 = neither pleasurable nor painful

−1 = painful

−2 = highly painful

−3 = very highly painful

1. Spending a day at the beach

2. Studying for a midterm

3. Watching the news on television

4. Listening to Mozart

5. Watching *The Sound of Music*

6. Babysitting a two-year-old

7. Eating string beans

8. Paying off your credit card

9. Going for a walk

10. Going into a burning building to save a child's life

11. Praying to God

12. Learning a new software program

13. Gardening

14. Trying new foods

15. Doing this exercise

EXERCISE 25.9

High-Quality Versus Low-Quality Pleasures

According to Mill, high-quality pleasures are associated with the mind; low-quality pleasures are associated with the body. Which of the activities in Exercise 25.8 would he rate as high-quality pleasures? Use your own paper to explain why you agree or disagree.

Let's focus on one of Mill's most famous assertions: "It is better to be a human being dissatisfied than a pig satisfied; better to be Socrates dissatisfied than a fool satisfied."

First, note Mill's point. Because pleasures of the higher faculties are so far superior to the pleasures of the senses, it is better for you to be a dissatisfied human who possesses higher human faculties than to be a satisfied pig who does not possess higher human faculties.

Do you believe this is true?

Assume that, prior to your birth, God asks you to choose one of two lives, that of a dissatisfied genius or that of a satisfied fool. Which would you pick?

I'd pick the life of the (dissatisfied genius, satisfied fool) because _____

_____

_____.

Or let us say you were a dissatisfied Socrates, and a wizard offered to change you into a contented pig. What would you reply?

I would say _____

_____

_____.

It is indisputable that the being whose capacities of enjoyment are low, has the greatest chance of having them fully satisfied; and a highly endowed being will always feel that any happiness which he can look for, as the world is constituted, is imperfect. But he can learn to bear its imperfections, if they are at all bearable; and they will not make him envy the being who is indeed unconscious of the imperfections, but only because he feels not at all the good which those imperfections qualify. It is better to be a human being dissatisfied than a pig satisfied; better to be Socrates dissatisfied than a fool satisfied. And if the fool, or the pig, are of a different opinion, it is because they only know their own side of the question. The other party to the comparison knows both sides.

Mill's point about a pig and

Socrates is _____

_____.

In the next section, Mill answers objections to his position that mental pleasures are qualitatively superior to physical pleasures.

It may be objected, that many who are capable of the higher pleasures, occasionally, under the influence of temptation, postpone them to the lower. But this is quite compatible with a full appreciation of the intrinsic superiority of the higher.

The objection to his position that Mill considers is this: Mental pleasures aren't more preferable than physical pleasures because, in cases of temptation, the satisfaction of the mental pleasure will be set aside for the satisfaction of a physical pleasure. For example, a mathematician might set aside the mental pleasure of solving a math problem for the physical pleasure of a warm bath. If mental pleasures were really so superior, then such choices would never happen.

Match wits with Mill. How will he show that mental pleasures are genuinely superior to physical pleasures?

Perhaps he will say _____

_____

_____.

Now read his answer.

It may be objected, that many who are capable of the higher pleasures, occasionally, under the influence of temptation, postpone them to the lower. But this is quite compatible with a full appreciation of the intrinsic superiority of the higher. **Men often, from infirmity of character, make their election for the nearer good, though they know it to be the less valuable; and this no less when the choice is between two bodily pleasures, than when it is between bodily and mental. They pursue sensual indulgences to the injury of health, though perfectly aware that health is the greater good.**

According to the objection Mill is considering, postponing the satisfaction of a mental pleasure for the satisfaction of the physical pleasure is evidence that mental pleasures aren't superior to physical pleasures. Choosing a warm bath over a hot algebra problem shows that mental pleasures aren't higher than physical pleasures. However, according to Mill, what is the real cause of choosing a lower over a higher pleasure?

Mill says the cause is _____.

His point is _____

_____

_____.

Next, Mill considers a second objection to his position that mental pleasures are superior to physical pleasures. The objection is that because many people, as they age, give up mental pleasures for physical pleasures, mental pleasures are not superior to physical pleasures. For example, many young people have high ideals that, as they age, are sacrificed to "indolence and selfishness."

It may be further objected, that many who begin with youthful enthusiasm for everything noble, as they advance in years sink into indolence and selfishness. But I do not believe that those who undergo this very common change, voluntarily choose the lower description of pleasures in preference to the higher. I believe that before they devote themselves exclusively to the one, they have already become incapable of the other. Capacity for the nobler feelings is in most natures a very tender plant, easily killed, not only by hostile influences, but by mere want of substance; and in the majority of young persons it speedily dies away if the occupations to which their position in life has devoted them, and the society into which it has thrown them, are not favourable to keeping that higher capacity in exercise. Men lose their high aspirations as they lose their intellectual tastes, because they have not time or opportunity for indulging them; and they addict themselves to inferior pleasure, not because they deliberately prefer them, but because they are either the only ones to which they have access, or the only ones which they are any longer capable of enjoying. It may be questioned whether any one who has remained equally susceptible to both classes of pleasures, ever knowingly and calmly preferred the lower; though many, in all ages, have broken down in an ineffectual attempt to combine both.

Based on what you've read, how would Mill answer each of the following?

1. T F Noble feelings are examples of higher pleasures.
2. T F If one has noble feelings as a youth, these feelings will remain in old age.
3. T F People voluntarily give up their youthful, noble feelings.
4. T F People become addicted to lower pleasures because these are the only pleasures available to them.
5. T F People become addicted to lower pleasures because these are the only pleasures they are capable of.
6. T F Trying to satisfy both the higher and the lower pleasures is extremely difficult.

Mill now returns to elaborate upon an earlier point.

From this verdict of the only competent judges, I apprehend there can be no appeal. On a question which is the best worth having of two pleasures, or which of two modes of existence is the most grateful to the feelings, apart from its moral attributes and from its consequences, the judgment of those who are qualified by knowledge of both, or, if they differ, that of the majority among them must be admitted as final.

What is Mill saying?

Mill's point is _____

_____

_____.

In the next section, Mill adds an important point, gained from Bentham, to his argument.

I have dwelt on this point, as being a necessary part of a perfectly just conception of Utility or Happiness, considered as the directive rule of human conduct. But it is by no means an indispensable condition to the acceptance of the utilitarian standard; for that standard is not the agent's own greatest happiness, but the greatest amount of happiness altogether; and if it may possibly be doubted whether a noble character is always happier for its nobleness, there can be no doubt that it makes other people happier, and the world is immensely a gainer by it.

Summarize Mill's point.

Mill is saying _____

_____

_____.

In this chapter you have been trying to determine if Kant or Mill has discovered the Great Ethical Principle, the single rule that should guide all moral choices.

Kant's version of the Great Ethical Principle could be stated: Make choices that you would want everyone to make.

Mill's version of the Great Ethical Principle could be stated: Make choices that lead to the most and highest (that is, mental) pleasure for the greatest number of people.

Which of the following is true?

1. Kant correctly identified the Great Ethical Principle.

2. Mill correctly identified the Great Ethical Principle.

3. Both were wrong, but the Great Ethical Principle can be identified.

4. The Great Ethical Principle cannot be identified (and so, for all practical purposes, it does not exist).

The correct choice is (1, 2, 3, 4) because _____

_____

_____

_____.

Some of the most important ideas I've learned in this chapter are _____

_____

_____

_____

_____

_____.

SUMMARY

In Kant's view, the consequences of a choice have no bearing on the choice's moral value. The morality of a choice is entirely determined by whether we are guided by a good will to obey the categorical imperative. The categorical imperative holds that we choose morally when we would agree that the principle that guides our action could, without logical impossibility, be adopted as a universal law that everyone followed.

In Mill's view, the consequences of a choice absolutely determine a choice's moral value. The morality of a choice is entirely determined by the quality of pleasure it produces and by the "greatest happiness" principle. According to this principle, we should make those choices that will bring the most and highest (that is, mental) happiness to the most people.

EXERCISE 25.10
Looking Back

Use your own paper to answer the following:

1. What is the difference between consequentialist and nonconsequentialist ethical theories?

2. What is Kant's version of the Great Ethical Principle?

3. What are key ideas in Kant's *Foundation for the Metaphysics of Morals*?

4. What is Mill's version of the Great Ethical Principle?

5. What are key ideas in Mill's *Utilitarianism*?

EXERCISE 25.11
Looking at the World Through Kant's Eyes

How would Kant answer each of the following? Using information in this chapter, explain your answer on your own paper.

1. T   F   Only a wise individual can have a truly good will.

2. T   F   Each person has his or her own unique duty.

3. T   F   A person who has a tendency to make good choices is morally superior to a person who has no tendency to make good choices.

4. T   F   What is right for one person is not necessarily right for another.

5. T   F   It is possible to have all our good actions fail and still be a good person.

EXERCISE 25.12
Looking at the World Through Mill's Eyes

How would Mill answer each of the following? Using information in this chapter, explain your answer on your own paper.

1. T   F   It is impossible to make a choice that is not guided by the desire to maximize pleasure and minimize pain.

2. T   F   Utilitarianism is a kind of epicureanism.

3. T   F   All pleasures are equally pleasurable.

4. T   F   Old people, because of their wisdom, are more likely to make moral choices than are young people.

4. T   F   If a gang derives pleasure from beating an individual, then, according to the "greatest happiness" principle, the gang's actions are moral.

EXERCISE 25.13
Kant Versus Mill

Using your own paper, describe how Kant and Mill would analyze each of the following moral problems:

1. A married woman has an affair, gets pregnant, and is considering having an abortion.

2. A woman is given a hundred dollars by her sister, because her sister is a drug addict and cannot resist the temptation of the money. Several days later, the sister demands the money back, saying it is rightfully hers and that she has "bills to pay."

3. A student watches a classmate cheat on a final and considers telling the teacher.

4. A student watches her best friend cheat on a final and considers telling the teacher.

ANALYSIS OF YOUR PHILOSOPHICAL SELF-PORTRAIT

To see how some of your ethical beliefs stack up against Kant's and Mill's, read my analysis below, rethink your position, and then circle what you believe is the correct answer.

1. T (Mill)   F (Kant)   *The most important thing to consider in making a choice is its consequences.*

   Kant, of course, would argue that the results a choice produces have nothing to do with the choice's moral value. A person guided by a good will who accomplishes nothing deserves as much moral credit as a similar person who saves the world.

Mill, on the other hand, would argue that the value of a choice is entirely calculated by the pleasure it produces. Because everything we do is under the sway of the "sovereign masters" of pleasure and pain, those choices that lead to the most pleasure are the best choices. Kant would respond that when the will is guided by *anything* except doing its duty, it is impossible for it to be moral.

2. T (Kant) F *We should act as we would want everyone else to act.*

This, as you now recognize, is a key aspect of the categorical imperative.

3. T (Kant and Mill) F *"Do unto others as you would have them do unto you" is the only ethical principle we need to follow in dealing with others.*

Both Kant and Mill would endorse this biblical position, but for different reasons. The Golden Rule should be followed, from Kant's point of view, because it is a universal rule that produces no logical contradictions. There is nothing self-contradictory about a society in which each person treats others as he or she would want to be treated.

According to Mill, the Golden Rule should be followed because it would produce pleasure for many people.

4. T (Mill) F (Kant) *All our choices are motivated by the pursuit of pleasure and the avoidance of pain.*

Kant holds that we can act independently of any inclination, including inclinations to seek pleasure and/or avoid pain. Mill believes this is impossible.

Your position? (Your answer will make a very important statement about the core of your ethics.)

I believe (Kant, Mill) is right because _____

_____

_____.

5. T (Mill) F (Kant) *The best moral choices lead to the greatest happiness for the greatest number of people.*

Your answer will clarify whether you are a consequentialist (like Mill) or a non-consequentialist (like Kant).

Evaluation: Number of points in agreement with Kant = _____ of 5 possible.

Number of points in agreement with Mill = _____ of 5 possible.

A position of Kant's that you strongly (support, oppose) is _____

_____

because _____

_____

_____.

A position of Mill's that you strongly (support, oppose) is _____

_____

because _____

_____

_____ .

GOOD BOOKS

Bentham, Jeremy. *An Introduction to the Principles of Morals and Legislation.* New York: Methuen, 1982. The key work by a founder of utilitarianism.

Mill, John Stuart. *Autobiography.* New York: Columbia University Press, 1924. One of the all-time great autobiographies.

Paton, H. J. *The Categorical Imperative.* London: Hutchinson, 1946. Useful for understanding Kant's ethical position.

NEXT STOP

Friedrich Nietzsche, the prophet who proclaimed God's death.

26
Friedrich Nietzsche
The Prophet of God's Death

YOUR PHILOSOPHICAL SELF-PORTRAIT

Add more details to your philosophical self-portrait by answering the questions below and offering evidence for your answers.

1. T F God is dead.

    Evidence: _____
    _____
    _____ .

2. T F God does not exist.

    Evidence: _____
    _____
    _____ .

3. T F The greatest people are those who serve God.

    Evidence: _____
    _____
    _____ .

4. T F The greatest philosophers are those who question
           traditional values.

    Evidence: _____
    _____
    _____ .

5. T F The universe had a beginning in time and will have
           an end in time; matter is not eternal.

    Evidence: _____
    _____
    _____ .

6. T F The purpose of each human's life is self-perfection.

    Evidence: _____
    _____
    _____ .

PREVIEW

Friedrich Nietzsche's philosophy is characterized by a frequently aphoristic and/or allegorical style as well as a harsh criticism of earlier philosophers, dualists in general, and Christians in particular. As an atheist, Nietzsche rejects the existence of a higher world, argues that Christian morality is spiritually diseased, and holds that all of life is unified by the will to power. In place of the saint and other esteemed figures of Western culture, Nietzsche advances the overman as the ethical ideal.

THOUGHT EXPERIMENT

Here is a Nietzschean test of your mental health that, according to Nietzsche, you'll almost certainly fail.

Think about the worst experience of your life, such as the day your house burned down, the day you learned that your parents were getting a divorce, or the day when someone close to you died. For shorthand, we'll call it the Nightmare.

Now imagine living through the Nightmare, exactly as it happened, one more time. How do you feel?

I feel _____ because _____
_____.

Take this a step further. Imagine having to live through the Nightmare ten more times. How do you feel now?

I feel _____ because _____
_____.

Finally, raise this psychological test to its highest power. Imagine that you have to live through the Nightmare unendingly, over and over again forever, with no escape. Your feelings?

Now I feel _____ because _____
_____.

Get ready for a shocker.

According to Nietzsche, if you were spiritually healthy, thinking about living any part of your life over again forever, even its worst moments, would cause you joy!

How can he make such a claim?

By the end of the chapter, I'll not only explain Nietzsche's reasoning and why his position is an important part of his philosophy, but also do my best to convince you he's right.

In this chapter I'll answer the following questions:

- What is unusual about Nietzsche's philosophizing?
- What are some of Nietzsche's criticisms of earlier philosophers?
- What is Nietzsche's criticism of Christianity?
- What is Nietzsche's "metaphysics"?
- What is Nietzsche's "ethics"?

After I've answered these questions, we'll examine a selection from Nietzsche's philosophical masterpiece, *Thus Spake Zarathustra*.

What Is Unusual About Nietzsche's Philosophizing?

Thus far on the tour, you have learned that presenting good arguments is a central philosophical task. You have heard arguments from Parmenides that motion is an illusion; from Socrates that he is no corrupter of youth; from Plato that the physical world is a copy of the realm of Forms; from Aristotle that virtue is the middle path between excess and deficiency; from Anselm, Aquinas, and Descartes that God exists; and so forth. You have spent a great deal of time analyzing philosophical arguments, evaluating how strongly their evidence supports their conclusions. Twice, however, you have had a glimpse of alternate ways of doing philosophy.

Heraclitus presents no arguments: "All is Fire"; "The sun is new every day"; "You cannot step into the same river twice." These are not arguments but **aphorisms,** brief, forceful statements meant to represent truths. You are convinced or not convinced by Heraclitus, depending upon whether or not his aphorisms appeal to your sense of the world. Any evidence for or against his position must come from you. Heraclitus's strategy is not to win you over by laboriously leading you through masses of reasons; he simply announces his position in strong, picturesque language and assumes that, if you have wisdom, you will see he is correct. Thus, to do philosophy by aphorism is to assume that the view presented does not need to be proved.

Plato's "Allegory of the Cave" also contains no arguments (though it is preceded and succeeded by arguments). His allegory is simply a beautiful, symbolical story about the nature of reality and the philosopher's path to wisdom. If we find an allegory convincing, it is because, just as in the case of the aphorism, it appeals to our inner sense of things. The allegory that convinces us makes a compelling story out of a philosophical position we already believe or lean toward.

Though Nietzsche uses arguments in his philosophy, he also, as you will soon see, powerfully employs aphorisms and allegories. Let's investigate a few of his aphorisms and describe a method for unraveling them. We will deal with the special problems of his allegories at the end of the chapter when we analyze a selection from *Thus Spake Zarathustra*.

Read and paraphrase each of the following from Nietzsche:

1. "Whatever does not destroy me, makes me stronger."

This means _____

_____

_____.

2. "I mistrust all systematizers and I avoid them. The will to a system is a lack of integrity."

This means _____

_____

_____.

3. "Your love of your neighbors is your bad love of yourselves."

This means _____

_____

_____.

4. "Whoever despises himself still respects himself as one who despises."

This means _____

_____

_____.

A first step in unraveling an aphorism is to think of an example of what it might mean.

Let's look again at the first statement, "Whatever does not destroy me, makes me stronger." All right, let's think of an example of something destructive, such as going through a divorce. Very well, a woman goes through a divorce and is not destroyed. Is there any sense in which she might be stronger? Certainly. Difficult, painful experiences can, for some people, create a stronger spirit, a more resilient character.

You try your own example.

Very well. A destructive experience might be _____

_____.

This could make one stronger because _____

_____

_____.

aphorism A short statement, or saying, which expresses a truth, often in a picturesque or forceful way. Examples: "A bird in the hand is worth two in the bush"; "Don't cry over spilt milk"; "He who lies down with dogs, gets up with fleas."

Before we leave this aphorism, note its paradoxical character. It presents two apparently *opposing* ideas—"being destroyed" and "getting stronger"—and shows how they are closely related. A destructive experience need not, as one would expect, be disastrous, but can be beneficial.

Friedrich Nietzsche (1844–1900)

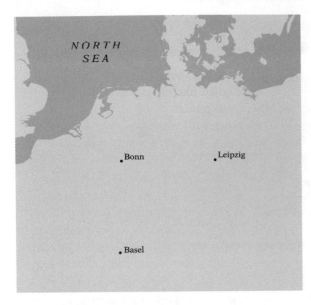

Friedrich Nietzsche is one of Germany's greatest and, until recently, most misunderstood philosophers. During their rise to power, the Nazis used heavily abridged versions of some of Nietzsche's works to justify Aryan superiority. This process was aided, no doubt, by his sister Elizabeth and her husband, Bernhard Forster, an anti-Semite, who had edited some of Nietzsche's notes for publication after Nietzsche's death in 1900. In fact, Nietzsche was highly opposed to all forms of nationalism and certainly would have disapproved of Nazism.

Friedrich Nietzsche was born on October 15,

1844—the birthday of Prussian King Frederick Wilhelm IV, after whom he was named. Nietzsche came from a long line of clergy. His father, a quiet and sensitive man, was a Lutheran minister, and his mother, a high-spirited and resourceful woman, the daughter of a country pastor.

Nietzsche's father spent a great deal of time with his oldest son whom he affectionately called "his little friend" and "Little Fritz." A quiet and very polite child, Nietzsche adored his father and used to sit quietly watching him work. His father was also a gifted musician and whenever "Little Fritz" cried, his father would soothe him by playing the piano.

When Nietzsche was only four, his father died. The death of his father was a terrible blow for young Nietzsche. He later wrote:

Until that time, propriety and joy had always shone on us . . . ; but then black clouds towered up, lightning flashed, and the blows of heaven came down ruinously. In September 1848 my beloved father suddenly became mentally ill. My beloved father had to suffer atrocious pains. His illness continued until July 1849; then the day of deliverance approached. . . . When I woke up in the morning, I heard loud crying, and sobbing all around me. . . . Although I was still very young and inexperienced, I nevertheless had

Let's look at the next aphorism, "I mistrust all systematizers and I avoid them. The will to a system is a lack of integrity." Just as before, let's think of an example of what Nietzsche might be talking about. Let's take Descartes as an example of a systematizer. He certainly tries very hard to make a single coherent system of his views about human nature, the way the mind gains knowledge, the existence of God, and the structure of the universe. He strings many different philosophical problems upon the same long argumentative thread. Nietzsche, however, says he "mistrusts" systematizers and believes they "lack integrity." How could this apply to Descartes? Well, from Nietzsche's point of view, a systematizer like Descartes could be said to lack integrity because he is more interested in wrapping up all loose ends, making a tidy philosophical package, than in facing the genuine confusion, the unsystematical nature of reality.

Friedrich Nietzsche (continued)

an idea of death: the thought of being forever separated from my beloved father struck me and I cried bitterly.[1]

The death left Nietzsche in a household of five women—his mother, his younger sister Elizabeth, his grandmother, and two unmarried aunts. The loss of his father was only the beginning of his troubles. When Nietzsche entered school at the age of six, he was nearsighted like his father and sister. Poor health and headaches caused him to miss long stretches of school. Despite all this, he managed to keep up his studies and gain entrance into college.

During his late teens Nietzsche began having serious doubts about Christianity. After a year of studying theology at the university in Bonn, he decided to transfer to Leipzig to study the classics. When he announced his decision to his family, a great quarrel followed. In the end, however, his mother and sister Elizabeth, who adored him, came around to his side.

During his years at Leipzig, Nietzsche discovered Schopenhauer. Nietzsche's sister Elizabeth later blamed Schopenhauer for turning him against women. Shortly after his graduation from college, Nietzsche received an appoint-

ment as professor of philology (linguistics) at the Swiss University at Basel.

Nietzsche's health grew progressively worse. The violent headaches came more frequently. In 1879, he resigned his post at Basel and turned his attention to philosophy. Nietzsche's despair was further intensified by the breakdown of his friendship with the great composer Richard Wagner, whom he had adopted as a sort of father figure. Nietzsche had a love-hate relationship with women as well. When he proposed to an acquaintance, she turned him down. His female friend Lou Salome, whom he wanted to be his disciple, was apparently unable to deal with his intensity and his family and eventually left him.

During his later years, Nietzsche suffered terribly from pain as well as from isolation. Only in music did he find comfort, spending hour after hour alone in his room playing the piano. It is generally agreed that Nietzsche was suffering from syphilis. It is possible that the syphilis was congenital, since he suffered symptoms associated with syphilis as a child. Nietzsche spent the last ten years of his life hopelessly insane.

Nietzsche's most important philosophical works include *The Birth of Tragedy* (1872), *Human All Too Human* (1878), *The Dawn* (1881), *The Gay Science* (1882), *Thus Spake Zarathustra* (1883), *Beyond Good and Evil* (1886), *Toward a Genealogy of Morals* (1887), and *The Antichrist* (1895).

[1] Quoted by Ben-Am Scharfstein, in *The Philosophers: Their Lives and the Nature of Their Thought* (New York: Oxford University Press, 1980), p. 287.

And note again the paradox of Nietzsche's aphorism. We would expect a philosophical systematizer to be an admirable person; Descartes solves a host of philosophical problems with one lengthy argument. However, in Nietzsche's eyes, such an apparently grand achievement simply represents a lack of honesty. The paradox is that what appears to be a philosophical wonder is really philosophical cowardice.

Now note the three steps in the method I used to analyze Nietzsche's aphorisms. First, I thought of an example that would illustrate the aphorism; next, I related the example back to the aphorism; finally, I tried to see what was paradoxical, apparently contradictory, about the truth represented by the aphorism. (A passion for paradox, as you will soon see, is a central characteristic of Nietzsche's thought.)

Try your hand at unraveling the last two aphorisms.

1. "Your love of your neighbors is your bad love of yourselves."

An example of this might be _____

_____.

The way this example relates to the aphorism might be _____

_____

_____.

What is paradoxical, apparently contradictory, about the aphorism is _____

_____

_____.

2. "Whoever despises himself still respects himself as one who despises."

An example of this might be _____

_____.

The way this example relates to the aphorism might be _____

_____

_____.

What is paradoxical, apparently contradictory, about the aphorism is _____

_____

_____.

Note one final point, very characteristic of Nietzsche's thinking. In all of the aphorisms above and in much of his philosophy, Nietzsche pounds repeatedly on one theme, which might be stated as: *"Reader! What you think is right is wrong; and what you think is wrong is right!"*

Look at the meaning of the four aphorisms again. We think getting destroyed is bad, but it is good; it increases strength. We think making philosophical systems is good, but it is in fact bad; such systems are dishonest. We think loving our neighbor is good, but such love is in fact bad, a product of our own poor self-esteem; we think that when we despise ourselves we feel nothing but self-hatred, but our self-hatred is—well, you fill it in.

Our self-hatred is really a kind of self-respect because _____

_____

_____.

And so, as you read Nietzsche, be prepared to unravel difficult sayings and have some of your dearest convictions about what is right and wrong attacked.

EXERCISE 26.1

Unraveling Nietzsche's Aphorisms

Use the three-step method you practiced above to explain the following on your own paper.

1. "Convictions are prisons."

2. "God is dead."

3. "One must have chaos in one to give birth to a dancing star."

4. "Whoever fights monsters should see to it that in the process he does not become a monster."

What Are Some of Nietzsche's Criticisms of Earlier Philosophers?

Almost all great philosophers take the view that every earlier philosopher made monumental mistakes. (Aquinas, who followed Aristotle as far as possible, is one notable exception.) In fact, it is hardly possible to achieve the status of "great philosopher" without making an important break with the past. But even given this tendency of philosophers to criticize earlier positions, Nietzsche's view of his philosophical predecessors is startlingly harsh. Except for some aspects of pre-Socratic philosophy and some occasional praise of Socrates, Nietzsche has almost nothing good to say about any philosopher before him, certainly none that we have studied on our tour.

In Nietzsche's view, dualism in general and Christianity in particular are the two great ills not only of philosophy, but also of Western culture. Here, for example, is his attack upon a brand of dualism that can be traced back to Plato:

> Every concept originates through our equating what is unequal. No leaf ever wholly equals another, and the concept "leaf" is formed through an arbitrary abstraction from these individual differences, through forgetting the distinctions; and now it gives rise to the idea that in nature there might be something besides the leaves which would be "leaf"—some kind of original form after which all leaves have been woven, marked, copied, colored, curled, and painted, but by unskilled hands, so that no copy turned out to be a correct, reliable and faithful image of the original form.[1]

Nietzsche is saying?

Nietzsche says _____

_____

_____.

In Nietzsche's view, the Form of Leaf is a fiction, a mental error, created by assuming that because leaves have some characteristics in common, these characteristics must have a completely independent existence. For example, I look at an oak leaf and a eucalyptus leaf. I see that they are both green, flat, and

---

[1] From *The Portable Nietzsche*, edited by Walter Kaufmann (New York: Viking Penguin, 1954) p. 46.

longish. I then assume that because they have some characteristics in common that these characteristics must exist *independently* in some third, superior thing, the Form of Leaf. Nietzsche thinks this line of reasoning is absurd. In his view, the only place that green, flat, and longish characteristics exist are in physical things like the leaves I'm looking at. Thus, whereas Plato held that all individual leaves are products of the Form of Leaf, Nietzsche reverses this and says it is from individual leaves that we produce the mental error that the Form of Leaf exists.

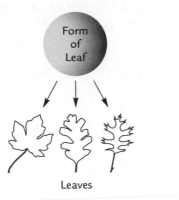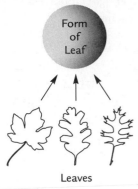

According to Plato, it is from the real Form of Leaf that individual leaves get their existence.

According to Nietzsche, it is from real leaves that humans invent the illusory concept of the Form of Leaf.

Well, do you agree with Nietzsche's criticism of the Realm of Forms?

I think Nietzsche is (right, wrong) because _____

_____

_____

Here is one of his more general indictments of dualism.

The reasons for which "this" world has been characterized as "apparent" are the very reasons which indicate its reality; any other kind of reality is absolutely indemonstrable.[2]

To illustrate Nietzsche's position, I'll look out my window from Plato's point of view and then Nietzsche's.

Looking through Plato's eyes at the people, trees, and houses in my cul-de-sac, I see nothing but changing, temporary, imperfect things. The world that I see has *apparent* reality; it appears real, but of course it isn't, because each thing that I see is a poor copy of an unchanging, eternal, perfect Form. Only things that are unchanging, eternal, and perfect are really real.

Now I look out my window through Nietzsche's eyes. I see the same view as Plato, but interpret it differently. All that I see *is* changing, temporary, and far from perfect; *but that is precisely what makes it real.* The characteristics that Plato would use to degrade the physical, visible world are exactly the charac-

---

[2] From *The Portable Nietzsche*, p. 56.

teristics, the only characteristics, that reality could have. There can't be anything more real than the things I see before me. The "lower" world is the only world.

In Plato's view, the visible world is changing, temporary, and imperfect. These are the characteristics that make it the lower world.

In Nietzsche's view, the visible world is also changing, temporary, and imperfect. These are the characteristics that make it the only real world.

Is Nietzsche's general criticism of dualism right or wrong?

He is (right, wrong) because _____

_____

_____.

EXERCISE 26.2
A Criticism of Dualism

The following is another of Nietzsche's criticisms of dualism. Read it carefully, and then use your own paper to answer questions 1–4.

"**Misunderstanding of the dream.** In the ages of crude primeval culture, man believed that in dreams he got to know another real world; here is the origin of all metaphysics. Without the dream one would have found no occasion for a division of the world. The separation of body and soul, too, is related to the most ancient conception of the dream; also the assumption of a quasi-body of the soul, which is the origin of all belief in spirits; and probably also the belief in gods."[3]

  1. Why is dualism, according to Nietzsche's analysis above, an incorrect view of reality?

  2. What are the strengths of Nietzsche's analysis?

  3. What are the weaknesses of Nietzsche's analysis?

  4. What, in your view, is the origin of dualism?

Let's continue to examine Nietzsche's critique of dualism by exploring his attacks upon Christianity.

---

[3] From *Basic Writings of Nietzsche, Human, All-too-Human,* trans. Walter Kaufmann (New York: Random House, 1968).

What Is Nietzsche's Criticism of Christianity?

Perhaps, before you began this tour, you had heard Nietzsche's most famous, but somewhat puzzling, aphorism, "God is dead." What does it mean?

"God is dead" means _____

_____

_____.

Nietzsche is an atheist, but he does not expend any effort to offer philosophical proof that God does not exist. He assumes that anyone who reads him the way he wants to be read, passionately and seriously, will agree that there is no God. Therefore, "God is dead" doesn't mean God doesn't exist. For Nietzsche, of course there is no God; the important thing to point out is that even *belief* in God is no longer viable, is dead. Writing at the end of the nineteenth century, at the height of the Industrial Revolution, Nietzsche believed that Christianity had received its death blow. The combined forces of capitalism and science had brought society to the brink of *nihilism*. Nihilism is the view that there are no moral values, there is no way to tell right from wrong. (A nihilist would hold, for example, that there is no ethical difference between feeding people and murdering them.)

God is dead; Christianity as a moral force, guiding and controlling people's lives, has passed away; nihilism looms directly ahead. Nietzsche saw himself as not only *a* but also often *the* antireligious prophet who would point a courageous few toward this-worldly salvation.

Now match wits with one of the Christian world's most brilliant opponents. What is the strongest criticism you could make of Christianity?

What is wrong with Christianity is _____

_____

_____.

According to Nietzsche, the Christian is "the domestic animal, the herd animal, the sick human animal." In addition,

> Christianity has sided with all that is weak and base, with all failures; it has made an ideal of whatever contradicts strong life to preserve itself. It has corrupted the reason of even those strongest in spirit by teaching men to consider the supreme values of the spirit as something sinful, as something that leads into error as temptations.[4]

It is often difficult for students to understand the depth of Nietzsche's hatred for Christianity. Because we live in a society based on Judeo-Christian val-

_____

[4]From *The Portable Nietzsche*, p. 571.

ues, it seems inconceivable that anyone would think that pity or humility, for example, could be something diseased. Any value system that helps those in need and that criticizes arrogance seems to us to be unquestionably good. But in Nietzsche's view, *Christian values are extremely deceptive.* What is apparently good is actually rooted in something unquestionably bad.

Christianity developed in the Roman Empire and spread among the poorest classes, the slaves, the outcasts. And what, Nietzsche asks, does it mean to be a member of the poorest classes? It means hatred and envy of those in power. The first Christians were outcasts and thus, in Nietzsche's view, created a value system *solely designed to meet the needs of outcasts.* Pity is a Christian value only because it is what the weak desperately need. Humility is a Christian value only because the weak have—and are—nothing. The early Christians turned being downcast into a virtue. Thus, according to Nietzsche, pity, humility, and all other supposedly noble Christian ideals are simply products of weak, resentful spirits.

Think about that.

Pity is not something intrinsically good. It became a value only because pity was what the masses of the first Christians, the lower classes, required for survival.

I believe Nietzsche is (right, wrong) because _____

_____

_____

Humility is not something intrinsically good. It became a value only because being humble, downcast, was precisely the condition of the first Christians.

I believe Nietzsche is (right, wrong) because _____

_____

_____

Thus, Christian values, which appear to be so positive, are simply the product of resentful slaves who hated the independence, strength, and pride of their rulers.

I believe Nietzsche is (right, wrong) because _____

_____

_____

Here is a key section from *The Antichrist,* Nietzsche's most forceful attack upon Christian metaphysics and ethics. Read slowly, underline important parts, and then we'll analyze it together.

In Christianity neither morality nor religion has even a single point of contact with reality. Nothing but imaginary *causes* ("God," "soul," "ego," "spirit" . . .), nothing but imaginary *effects* ("sin," "redemption," "grace," "punishment," "forgiveness of sins"). Intercourse between imaginary *beings* ("God," "spirits," "souls"); . . . an imaginary *teleology* ("the kingdom of God," "the Last Judgment," "eternal life").

This world of pure fiction is vastly inferior to the world of dreams insofar as the latter *mirrors* reality, whereas the former falsifies, devalues, and negates reality. Once the concept of "nature" had been invented as the opposite of "God," "natural" had to become a synonym of "reprehensible"; this whole world of fiction is rooted in *hatred* of the natural (of reality!); it is the expression of a profound vexation at the sight of reality.

But this explains everything. Who alone has a good reason to lie his way out of reality? He who suffers from it.[5]

What, in general, is Nietzsche saying?

Nietzsche says _____

_____

_____

_____.

Let's start with the first sentence:

In Christianity neither morality nor religion has even a single point of contact with reality.

That is an amazingly large indictment! Let us say I do not have "even a single point of contact with reality." I believe the sun is a spotlight, the earth is a stage, and I am Bob Dylan. In other words, I am utterly mad. In the same way, if Christianity has no contact in any way with reality, then it is equivalent to a mental illness!

Do you agree or disagree?

I (agree, disagree) because _____

_____

_____.

Nietzsche next goes on to list some of the important ways that Christianity is out of contact with reality.

In Christianity, neither morality nor religion has even a single point of contact with reality. **Nothing but imaginary *causes* ("God," "soul," "ego," "spirit" . . .), nothing but imaginary *effects* ("sin," "redemption," "grace," "punishment," "forgiveness of sins"). Intercourse between imaginary *beings* ("God," "spirits," "souls"); . . . an imaginary *teleology* ("the kingdom of God," "the Last Judgment," "eternal life").**

---

[5] From *The Portable Nietzsche*, p. 583.

If I believe that God is the origin of the forgiveness of sins, then I would be thinking of God as the cause and forgiveness of sins as the effect.

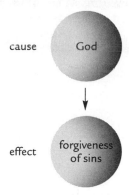

cause — God

effect — forgiveness of sins

Or I could think of God as the cause and grace as the effect, or the soul as the cause and sin as the effect. All these causes and effects, in Nietzsche's view, are imaginary, delusional, not in contact with reality. I am equally deluded if I believe God and souls can communicate or that the world has some goal, a teleology, in the kingdom of God or the Last Judgment. None of these beliefs is any more accurate than the convictions of a madman.

Your response?

To Nietzsche, I would say _____

_____

_____.

In Christianity neither morality nor religion has even a single point of contact with reality. Nothing but imaginary *causes* ("God," "soul," "ego," "spirit" . . .), nothing but imaginary *effects* ("sin," "redemption," "grace," "punishment," "forgiveness of sins"). Intercourse between imaginary *beings* ("God," "spirits," "souls"); . . . an imaginary *teleology* ("the kingdom of God," "the Last Judgment," "eternal life").

    ***This world of pure fiction* is vastly inferior to the world of dreams insofar as the latter *mirrors* reality, whereas the former falsifies, devalues, and negates reality.**

Nietzsche elaborates his position by arguing that the Christian world is worse than a dream world. Let us say that I dream of a blue horse. Because the color blue and horses exist in the waking world, my dream, though false, has some basis in, is a kind of a mirror of, reality. However, if I think of God, then not only is my idea false but, far worse, it "falsifies, devalues . . . negates" the real world. What does this mean? Insofar as I love the illusion of God, I hate the physical world. God is everything; this world, the only real world, is nothing. Thus, Christianity does not simply incorrectly mirror reality, but also degrades it. The Christian image of the world is not just wrong, but also disfiguring.

Nietzsche explains how this came about:

This world of pure fiction is vastly inferior to the world of dreams insofar as the latter *mirrors* reality, whereas the former falsifies, devalues, and negates reality. **Once the concept of "nature" had been invented as the opposite of "God," "natural" had to become a synonym of "reprehensible"; this**

whole world of fiction is rooted in *hatred* of the natural (of reality!); it is the expression of a profound vexation at the sight of reality.

But this explains everything. **Who alone has a good reason to lie his way out of reality? He who suffers from it.**

Nietzsche says?

Nietzsche says _____

_____

_____

_____ .

To sum up, according to Nietzsche, this is how Christianity developed:

1. The lowest elements of society, out of their misery and weakness, developed a value system and an image of God that exactly suited their needs.

2. Nature came to be seen as the opposite of God.

3. Therefore, nature, the only reality, was seen as bad.

4. Christians believed this lie because they hated and suffered from life in the natural world.

Nietzsche's point is subtle. It is not from love of God that Christians developed their hatred of nature. It is because Christians hated nature, the physical world they lived in, that they developed an illusory God that they could love.

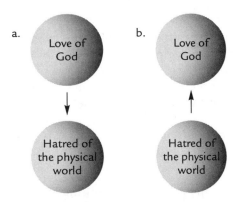

Nietzsche argues that it is not (a) Christian love of an illusory God which produces hatred of the physical world but (b) a hatred of the physical world that produces a love of an illusory God.

Nietzsche makes several indictments against Christianity. Think carefully and decide your position on each. Offer your best evidence.

1. Christianity as a moral force controlling people's lives is dead.

I (agree/disagree) because _____

_____

_____ .

2. All Christian beliefs are out of contact with reality.

I (agree/disagree) because _____

_____

_____.

3. Christian beliefs are rooted in a hatred of reality, the natural world.

I (agree/disagree) because _____

_____

_____.

If the Christian view of reality and way of life are so entirely wrong, what is right?

What Is Nietzsche's "Metaphysics"?

If you keep the following very important points in mind, it is not too difficult to get an overview of Nietzsche's portrait of reality:

1. Because he distrusted philosophical systems, Nietzsche never carefully worked out a view of all that exists. To note Nietzsche's unsystematic approach, I'll refer to his metaphysics as a "metaphysics" (and his ethics as an "ethics").
2. Nietzsche slowly developed his view of the will to power and arrived at the position I describe below only in the last few years of his career.
3. Though it is clearly relevant to his "metaphysics," Nietzsche's account of eternal recurrence is more central to his ethics.

Because Nietzsche believed there was no God, no higher world, we can make the first simple sketch of his "metaphysics" as follows:

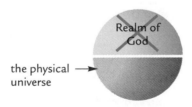

In Nietzsche's view, humans, as well as every other living entity, are driven by the will to power.

> Wherever I found the living, there I found the will to power. . . . Only where there is life, there is also will: not will to life but . . . will to power. There is much that life esteems more highly than life itself: but out of the esteeming itself speaks the will to power."[6]

_____

[6] From *Thus Spake Zarathustra*, "On Self Overcoming," trans. Walter Kaufmann (New York: The Viking Press, 1966).

Very well. I look out my window through Nietzsche's eyes and what do I see? I see, first of all, the living and the nonliving. This is a crucial division, because only the living have a will. My neighbor Jerry, his dog Maggi, even the tree in Jerry's backyard, all have a will and this will wants, desires, power. Now, since Nietzsche never describes how plants and animals can have a will to power, I can only guess. Plants and animals could be seen as being in a kind of competition, a struggle for survival. Perhaps the power they nonrationally want is power over their competitors.

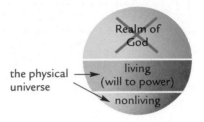

Now let me look closer at my neighbor Jerry. In what sense could he be said to be driven by the will to power? He tells his boy Scotty to clean the yard, take out the trash, do homework. Therefore, Jerry is driven by the will to power over his son. Jerry is a teacher. He is driven, therefore, by a will to power over his students. He also is a sports fan, and by identifying with a team, is driven by a will to power over his team's opponents. All of Jerry's relations with his friends and family, even his loving actions, could be seen as subtle and not so subtle manifestations of his will to power over them.

Do you get Nietzsche's drift?

When I try to see people I know through Nietzsche's eyes, some examples of the

will to power you did not mention would be _____

_____

_____

_____

_____.

Nietzsche makes a very important distinction between two kinds of power, power over others and power over one's self. Nietzsche emphatically rates the first far below the second. The power of the state to make others conform, the power of a tyrant over enslaved masses, the power of a strong person over a weak person, are all manifestations of the will to power, but in its lowest, most despicable form. (It is this belief that makes it impossible to confuse Nietzsche's position with its corruption presented by the Nazis.)

In Nietzsche's view, the highest expression of the will to power is the self's power over itself. Just as an artist takes raw materials and shapes them into a masterpiece, so the greatest example of the will to power is for humans, rare humans, to take the raw material of personality and shape it into human perfection. More will be said about this ideal human type in our next section.

Now let's briefly introduce one last "metaphysical" element to Nietzsche's portrait of reality: the doctrine of eternal recurrence. Prepare for an idea that *always* gets my students' attention.

Eternal recurrence is the view that all events will infinitely repeat themselves. Time is a vast circle. You are here now, and some day you will die. After an enormously long time, everything that can possibly happen in the universe will have happened; and so, since time never ceases, you will be born again and wind up working your way through this textbook, making every mark exactly as you have. Thus, if you are raising your eyebrows now, you've raised them, *in exactly the same way*, an infinite number of times before and will raise them, *in exactly the same way*, an infinite number of times again.

Your reaction?

Right now I'm thinking _____

_____

_____.

Near the very end of his writing career, in an unpublished notebook, Nietzsche sketched out a proof of eternal recurrence (which I've simplified):

1. Space and matter are finite.

2. Time is infinite.

3. Therefore, everything that can happen will happen.

4. Therefore, all events will repeat themselves forever.

Assume that I give you three books and tell you to keep placing them in a new place on the top of a table. I also ask you to never let any of the books occupy the same position. Now, for the first few hours, your task would be fairly easy. But obviously, after a while, because the table top is finite, limited, it would be hard to find new positions for the books. Now, further assume that you had to keep moving the books to new positions *forever*; obviously, you would eventually have to repeat one of the positions, then another, and eventually all of the positions. And since you had to keep moving them eternally, all possible positions would be infinitely repeated.

It really doesn't matter if you had three books or twenty or if you were using a table top or a football field, the key thing, for Nietzsche, is that a limited amount of matter, moving in a limited amount of space, for an infinite amount of time, will produce infinite repetition, eternal recurrence—on table tops, football fields, or in the universe. Everything that can happen will happen—and has happened, over and over, forever.

I (agree, disagree) because _____

_____

_____.

eternal recurrence The view that everything that can happen will happen, over and over again forever. For example, some physicists hold that it is possible that the present expanding universe will eventually contract into an infinitely small point, leading to a new big bang, leading to an expanding universe exactly like ours, leading to another big bang and so forth, eternally. Nietzsche, as you will see, is largely interested in the psychological implications of eternal recurrence. An individual who truly loves life, like the overman, would rejoice at having to reexperience even life's worst moments, repeated forever.

Now let's complete our model of Nietzsche's "metaphysics" and then go on to his views on moral actions.

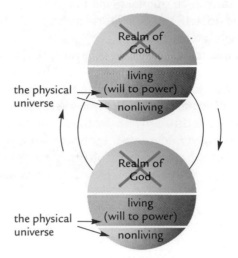

The doctrine of eternal recurrence holds that all possible events in the physical universe will infinitely repeat themselves—time is a circle.

What Is Nietzsche's "Ethics"?

A central ethical question on our tour has been "What is the purpose of human life?" To prepare for an overview of Nietzsche's ethics and his answer to this question, perform the following thought experiment.

THOUGHT EXPERIMENT

All the philosophers whose ethical position we have examined line up. Each, in a phrase, answers the question, "What is the purpose of life?" Whom would you support or oppose?

Heraclitus: Listen to the Logos and understand that all is constant change.

I (support/oppose) Heraclitus's position because _____

_____

_____.

Socrates: Value the soul above bodily and material concerns.

I (support/oppose) Socrates' position because _____

_____

_____.

Plato: Turn your attention from the sense world, attend to the divine Realm of Forms . . . escape from the cave.

I (support/oppose) Plato's position because _____

_____

_____.

Aristotle: Seek the middle path between excess and deficiency.

I (support/oppose) Aristotle's position because _____

_____

_____.

Epicurus: Seek wise pleasure.

I (support/oppose) Epicurus's position because _____

_____

_____.

Epictetus: Seek peace of mind by realizing that you can control only your thoughts, not the world.

I (support/oppose) Epictetus's position because _____

_____

_____.

Augustine: Obey God's will.

I (support/oppose) Augustine's position because _____

_____

_____.

Hume: Let your passions rule your reason.

I (support/oppose) Hume's position because _____

_____

_____.

Kant: Do your duty; make those choices that you would want everyone to make.

I (support/oppose) Kant's position because _____

_____

_____.

Mill: Seek wise pleasure and make choices that will produce the greatest and best happiness for the greatest number of people.

I (support/oppose) Mill's position because _____

_____

_____.

In *Thus Spake Zarathustra*, Nietzsche presents a new ethical ideal for humanity, the overman. "I teach you the overman. Man is something that should be overcome."

Nietzsche's word for the overman, *Ubermensch*, is sometimes translated as superman; but unfortunately for English-speaking readers, this recalls the cartoon hero, rather than a noble, ethical ideal. Superior man, man-who-is-beyond-all-other-men, and—perhaps best of all—*self-perfecting man* are other possible translations for *Ubermensch*.

Let's start our investigation of the overman by briefly contrasting Nietzsche's ethical ideal with an earlier cultural ideal, the saint.

A saint loves God; the overman loves this world. A saint follows past values; an overman creates new values. A saint resists his bodily passions; an overman transforms his bodily passions into something higher, such as a great work of art or, better, a superior version of himself. A saint values humility, service to God, inner peace; an overman values pride, self-perfection, and an inner, self-transforming struggle.

According to Nietzsche, the overman is not achieved by an evolutionary process; he is not "out there" in our future. In fact, some overmen have existed in the past. Nietzsche mentions Goethe, Julius Caesar, and Napoleon as representing aspects of the overman.

> [Goethe] disciplined himself to wholeness, he *created* himself . . . a spirit who has *become free*.[7]
>
> The revolution made possible Napoleon: that is its justification. For a similar prize one should have to desire the anarchical crash of our entire civilization.[8]
>
> Julius Caesar [who] defended himself against sickliness and headaches by tremendous marches, the most frugal way of life, uninterrupted sojourn in the open air, and continuous exertion. . . . The highest type of free man would be sought where the highest resistance is constantly overcome . . . inexorable and fearful instincts that provoke the maximum of authority and discipline against themselves: most beautiful type: Julius Caesar.[9]

---

[7] From *The Portable Nietzsche*, p. 316.
[8] From *The Portable Nietzsche*, p. 317.
[9] From *The Portable Nietzsche*, p. 318.

It is not for their external achievements, works of art or military victories, that Nietzsche values Goethe, Napoleon, and Julius Caesar, but for their hard-won victories over themselves. The overman is a "self-conqueror," a "self-tyrant," and is "perpetually involved in self-overcoming."

In order to transform the self, the overman must possess great inner strength. Overmen do not merely endure emotional and physical hardship, but they also *enjoy* it!

> The most spiritual men, as the *strongest*, find their happiness where others would find their destruction: in hardness against themselves and others. . . . Their joy is self-conquest. . . . Difficult tasks are a privilege to them; to play with burdens that crush others, a *recreation*.[10]

To see to what degree you have characteristics of the overman, recall the thought experiment you performed at the beginning of this chapter. If you had to live the worst part of your life over and over again forever, how would you feel?

I would feel _____,

and I suspect Nietzsche would want me to feel _____.

Here is Nietzsche's version of the test:

> How, if some day or night, a demon were to sneak after you into your loneliest loneliness and say to you: "This life, as you now live it and have lived it, you will have to live once more and innumerable times more; and there will be nothing new in it, but every pain and every joy and every thought and sigh . . . must return to you—all in the same succession and sequence." Would you not throw yourself down and gnash your teeth and curse the demon who spoke thus? Or have you once experienced a tremendous moment when you would have answered him "You are a god, never did I hear anything more godlike!" If this thought were to gain possession of you, it would change you as you are, or perhaps crush you. . . . how well disposed would you have to become to yourself and to life to *crave nothing more fervently* than this ultimate eternal confirmation . . . ?[11]

Here Nietzsche proposes eternal recurrence, the infinite repetition of all your experiences, not as a description of reality, but as a psychological test of the vitality of your spirit. If you had true spiritual strength and truly loved life, then the thought of repeating even the worst parts of your life would cause you *nothing but joy*.

Imagine the reactions of three people who contemplate repeating a painful treatment for cancer.

FIRST PERSON: If I had to go through that again, I'd kill myself.

SECOND PERSON: It would be difficult to go through that again, but life is so important to me, I would.

THIRD PERSON: I love life so intensely that thinking of repeating any part of my life, even its very worst parts, causes me joy.

---

[10] From *The Portable Nietzsche*, p. 57.
[11] From *Basic Writings of Nietzsche, The Gay Science*, p. 341.

Nietzsche, of course, would hold up only the last individual as an ethical ideal. A central characteristic of the overman is life-adoring joy, a joy that is bottomless, that cannot be quenched by any human experience.

> You higher men, do learn this, joy wants eternity. Joy wants the eternity of *all* things, *wants deep, wants deep eternity.*[12]

And so don't you have to agree that Nietzsche's portrait of the overman is powerfully appealing? What could be better than having such strength of spirit, such an intoxication for living, that no matter what happened to you, you felt joy and even the thought of infinitely repeating the worst moments of your life, far from depressing you, made you "crave nothing more fervently"?

Granted, this passion for life is not something you may have ever experienced, but isn't it something that you should aim for, that should be part of your values?

My reaction is _____

_____

_____.

M. C. Escher, *Magic Mirror*, lithograph, 1946.

ILLUSTRATION QUIZ

Escherizing Nietzsche

This is the final illustration quiz, so let's make it simple. What "circular" aspect of Nietzsche's philosophy might Escher's illustration be taken as representing?

The answer is _____

_____

because _____

_____

_____.

Now let's sum up this section by giving Nietzsche's answer to the question, "What is the purpose of human life?" His answer would have two parts.

1. The purpose of human life for the masses is to conform to the values of the past, to love the illusion of God, to use their will to power in its lowest fashion, to have power over others, to hate life in this world.

2. The purpose of human life for a strong, creative few is to create new values, love the goal of the overman, use their will to power in its highest fashion, to have self-perfecting power over themselves, to passionately love every aspect of life in this world.

---

[12] From *Thus Spake Zarathustra*, Book IV.

Your reaction?

I (support/oppose) Nietzsche's view because _____

_____

_____.

Next, we'll examine a selection from *Thus Spake Zarathustra*.

READING:
SELECTIONS FROM *THUS
SPAKE ZARATHUSTRA*

Nietzsche chose Zarathustra as his spokesperson because he believed Zarathustra was the first dualist and thus should be the first to correct dualism's mistakes. (Zarathustra is an alternate spelling for Zoroaster, who was a Persian religious prophet, 628–521 B.C.)

Zarathustra's Prologue

When Zarathustra was thirty years old he left his home and the lake of his home and went into the mountains. Here he enjoyed his spirit and his solitude, and for ten years did not tire of it. But at last a change came over his heart, and one morning he rose with the dawn, stepped before the sun, and spoke to it thus:

"You great star, what would your happiness be had you not those for whom you shine?

"For ten years you have climbed to my cave: you would have tired of your light and of the journey had it not been for me and my eagle and my serpent.

"But we waited for you every morning, took your overflow from you, and blessed you for it.

"Behold, I am weary of my wisdom, like a bee that has gathered too much honey; I need hands outstretched to receive it.

"I would give away and distribute, until the wise among men find joy once again in their folly, and the poor in their riches.

"For that I must descend to the depths, as you do in the evening when you go behind the sea and still bring light to the underworld, you overrich star.

"Like you, I must *go under*—go down, as is said by man, to whom I want to descend.

"So bless me then, you quiet eye that can look even upon an all-too-great happiness without envy!

"Bless the cup that wants to overflow, that the water may flow from it golden and carry everywhere the reflection of your delight.

"Behold, this cup wants to become empty again, and Zarathustra wants to become man again."

Thus Zarathustra began to go under.

You may be a bit baffled already by Nietzsche's Zarathustra. Don't worry. The following four tasks will help reduce your confusion.

1. Begin by making a simple word portrait of Zarathustra. In the following list of opposing terms, circle the single term in each pair that best describes Zarathustra. Explain your reasoning.

   a. happy/sad: Explanation: _____

   _____

   b. egotistical/humble: Explanation: _____

   _____

   c. lonely/self-sufficient: Explanation: _____

   _____

   d. generous/selfish: Explanation: _____

   _____

   e. eager/timid: Explanation: _____

   _____

   f. strong/weak: Explanation: _____

   _____

   g. wise/foolish: Explanation: _____

   _____

2. Nietzsche, as I mentioned in the introduction to this chapter, loves paradoxes, contradictory statements that express truths. Practice your own paradoxical thinking by selecting one of the pairs of opposites above and explain why *each* term in the pair might describe Zarathustra. For example, if you think Zarathustra is both eager and timid, you would explain in what sense he is eager and in what sense he is timid. Simple. Right?

   Zarathustra is both _____ and _____.

   He is _____ because _____

   _____

   and _____ because _____

   _____.

3. What are the similarities Zarathustra sees between himself and the sun?

   Both the sun and Zarathustra are _____

   _____

   _____.

4. Here is a very difficult puzzle that I will solve near the end of this chapter. In the section you have just read, Zarathustra makes a very large mistake. In other words, Zarathustra says or thinks something that Nietzsche will eventually show is incorrect. What do you think is Zarathustra's mistake?

Perhaps Zarathustra's mistake is _____

_____ .

This puzzle is quite important in helping you to understand Nietzsche's style of philosophizing. When I give the answer, I'll explain its importance.

> Zarathustra descended alone from the mountains, encountering no one. But when he came into the forest, all at once there stood before him an old man who had left his holy cottage to look for roots in the woods. And thus spoke the old man to Zarathustra:
>
> "No stranger to me is this wanderer: many years ago he passed this way. Zarathustra he was called, but he has changed. At that time you carried your ashes to the mountains; would you now carry your fire into the valleys? Do you not fear to be punished as an arsonist?
>
> "Yes, I recognize Zarathustra. His eyes are pure, and around his mouth there hides no disgust. Does he not walk like a dancer?
>
> "Zarathustra has changed, Zarathustra has become a child, Zarathustra is an awakened one; what do you now want among the sleepers? You lived in your solitude as in the sea, and the sea carried you. Alas, would you now climb ashore? Alas, would you again drag your own body?"
>
> Zarathustra answered: "I love man."
>
> "Why," asked the saint, "did I go into the forest and the desert? Was it not because I loved man all-too-much? Now I love God; man I love not. Man is for me too imperfect a thing. Love of man would kill me."
>
> Zarathustra answered: "Did I speak of love? I bring men a gift."
>
> "Give them nothing!" said the saint. "Rather, take part of their load and help them to bear it—that will be best for them, if only it does you good! And if you want to give them something, give no more than alms, and let them beg for that!"
>
> "No," answered Zarathustra. "I give no alms. For that I am not poor enough."
>
> The saint laughed at Zarathustra and spoke thus: "Then see to it that they accept your treasures. They are suspicious of hermits and do not believe that we come with gifts. Our steps sound too lonely through the streets. And what if at night, in their beds, they hear a man walk by long before the sun has risen—they probably ask themselves, Where is the thief going?
>
> "Do not go to man. Stay in the forest! Go rather even to the animals! Why do you not want to be as I am—a bear among bears, a bird among birds?"
>
> "And what is the saint doing in the forest?" asked Zarathustra.
>
> The saint answered: "I make songs and sing them and when I make songs, I laugh, cry, and hum: thus I praise God. With singing, crying, laughing, and humming, I praise the god who is my god. But what do you bring us as a gift?"

In the following, underline the differences between the saint and Zarathustra.

When Zarathustra had heard these words he bade the saint farewell and said: "What could I have to give you? But let me go quickly lest I take something from you!" And thus they separated, the old one and the man, laughing as two boys laugh.

But when Zarathustra was alone he spoke thus to his heart: "Could it be possible? This old saint in the forest has not yet heard anything of this, that *God is dead!*"

Part of the trick to understanding *Thus Spake Zarathustra* is to see that Nietzsche is writing a substitute for the Bible. Zarathustra is, thus, a new kind of holy man whose image is meant to contrast with the prophets of the Old Testament, Paul, and especially Jesus. (Therefore, it is no accident that Zarathustra begins his mission at thirty, the same age that Jesus reputedly was when he began preaching.) The Bible contains the old message; Zarathustra brings the new message.

What are some important characteristics of the old message, as represented by the saint whom Zarathustra encounters in the section you have just read?

Some characteristics are _____

_____

_____ .

As contrasted with the saint's views, what are some important characteristics of Zarathustra's new message?

Some characteristics are _____

_____

_____ .

In the next section, Zarathustra presents numerous intriguing details about his new goal for the human race. As you read, mentally contrast Zarathustra's with Jesus's message.

When Zarathustra came into the next town, which lies on the edge of the forest, he found many people gathered together in the market place; for it had been promised that there would be a tightrope walker. And Zarathustra spoke thus to the people:

"*I teach you the overman.* Man is something that shall be overcome. What have you done to overcome him?

"All beings so far have created something beyond themselves; and do you want to be the ebb of this great flood and even go back to the beasts rather than overcome man? What is the ape to man? A laughing stock or a painful embarrassment. And man shall be just that for the overman: a laughingstock or a painful embarrassment. You have made your way from worm to man, and much in you is still worm. Once you were apes, and even now, too, man is more ape than any ape.

"Whoever is the wisest among you is also a mere conflict and cross between plant and ghost. But do I bid you become ghosts or plants?

"Behold, I teach you the overman. The overman is the meaning of the earth. Let your will say: the overman *shall be* the meaning of the earth! I beseech you, my brothers, *remain faithful to the earth,* and do not believe those who speak to you of otherworldly hopes! Poison-mixers are they, whether they know it or not. Despisers of life are they, decaying and poisoned themselves, of whom the earth is weary: so let them go.

"Once the sin against God was the greatest sin; but God died, and these sinners died with him. To sin against the earth is now the most dreadful thing, and to esteem the entrails of the unknowable higher than the meaning of the earth.

"Once the soul looked contemptuously upon the body, and then this contempt was the highest: she wanted the body meager, ghastly, and starved. Thus she hoped to escape it and the earth. Oh, this soul herself was still meager, ghastly, and starved: and cruelty was the lust of this soul. But you, too, my brothers, tell me: what does your body proclaim of your soul? Is not your soul poverty and filth and wretched contentment?

"Verily, a polluted stream is man. Once must be a sea to be able to receive a polluted stream without becoming unclean. Behold, I teach you the overman: he is this sea; in him your great contempt can go under.

"What is the greatest experience you can have? It is the hour of the great contempt. The hour in which your happiness, too, arouses your disgust, and even your reason and your virtue.

"The hour when you say, 'What matters my happiness? It is poverty and filth and wretched contentment. But my happiness ought to justify existence itself.'

"The hour when you say, 'What matters my reason? Does it crave knowledge as the lion his food? It is poverty and filth and wretched contentment.'

"The hour when you say, 'What matters my virtue? As yet it has not made me rage. How weary I am of my good and my evil! All that is poverty and filth and wretched contentment.'

"The hour when you say, 'What matters my justice? I do not see that I am flames and fuel. But the just are flames and fuel.'

"The hour when you say, 'What matters my pity? Is not pity the cross on which he is nailed who loves man? But my pity is no crucifixion.'

"Have you yet spoken thus? Have you yet cried thus? Oh, that I might have heard you cry thus!

"Not your sin but your thrift cries to heaven; your meanness even in your sin cries to heaven.

"Where is the lightning to lick you with its tongue? Where is the frenzy with which you should be inoculated?

"Behold, I teach you the overman: he is this lightning, he is this frenzy."

When Zarathustra had spoken thus, one of the people cried: "Now we have heard enough about the tightrope walker; now let us see him too!" And all the people laughed at Zarathustra. But the tightrope walker, believing that the word concerned him, began his performance.

Some of the values of the overman are _____

_____

_____

_____

_____

_____.

EXERCISE 26.3
Identifying Ethical Principles

The following is a list of ethical principles, statements about proper moral action. Label any principles that are consistent with the old message of the Bible (O), Zarathustra's new message (N), neither the Bible nor Zarathustra (Ne), both the Bible and Zarathustra (B).

Expect debate from your classmates.

_____ 1. Love God.

_____ 2. Love this world.

_____ 3. Love your soul.

_____ 4. Love your body.

_____ 5. Focus upon life after death.

_____ 6. Focus upon this life.

_____ 7. Don't be content with who you are.

_____ 8. What humans can become should be loved; what humans are should be despised.

_____ 9. The goal of life is happiness.

_____ 10. The goal of life is self-perfection.

_____ 11. The goal of life is obedience to the will of God.

_____ 12. Humans should become more-than-human.

_____ 13. The self should completely redesign the self.

Let's look at one of Zarathustra's statements more closely. He is teaching his listeners about the overman, the new goal for humanity.

"What is the greatest experience you can have? It is the hour of the great contempt. The hour in which your happiness, too, arouses your disgust, and even your reason and your virtue."

Begin by trying to paraphrase what Zarathustra is saying.

Zarathustra is saying _____

_____

_____.

To get the radical meaning of Zarathustra's message, let's start by thinking of what one might normally mean by "the greatest experience." For example, falling in love or raising a child or creating a wonderful work of art might be various examples of supreme human experiences.

Other examples might be _____

_____.

Zarathustra, however, says that the very best experience we can have is "the hour of the great contempt." Now, when I have contempt for something, I hate and reject it. If I have contempt for cowardice, then I hate and reject cowardice.

But what does Zarathustra say I should have great contempt for? Cowardice, cruelty, sin? No. I should have great contempt for, feel disgust for, my happiness, my reason, and my virtue!

Why on earth should these apparently very positive things cause me disgust?

Circle any of the following answers that you believe are consistent with Zarathustra's message. (You may, of course, circle more than one.)

1. I should feel disgust for my happiness, reason, and virtue because they keep me who I am, keep me from advancing to the overman.

2. I should feel disgust for my happiness, reason, and virtue because I am a lowly person who could never advance to the overman.

3. I should feel disgust for my happiness, reason, and virtue because they are illusions; there is no such thing as true happiness, correct reasoning, or genuine virtue.

4. I should feel disgust for my happiness, reason, and virtue because if I were truly an overman I would have a very different happiness, reason, and virtue.

5. I should feel disgust for my happiness, reason, and virtue because they make me complacent and I need "frenzy" to become an overman.

6. I should feel disgust for my happiness, reason, and virtue because they keep me from knowing God.

Zarathustra, however, beheld the people and was amazed. Then he spoke thus:

"Man is a rope, tied between beast and overman—a rope over an abyss. A dangerous across, a dangerous on-the-way, a dangerous looking-back, a dangerous shuddering and stopping.

"What is great in man is that he is a bridge and not an end: what can be loved in man is that he is an *overture* and a *going under*.

"I love those who do not know how to live, except by going under, for they are those who cross over.

"I love the great despisers because they are the great reverers and arrows of longing for the other shore.

"I love those who do not first seek behind the stars for a reason to go under and be a sacrifice, but who sacrifice themselves for the earth, that the earth may some day become the overman's.

"I love him who lives to know, and who wants to know so that the overman may live some day. And thus he wants to go under.

"I love him who works and invents to build a house for the overman and to prepare earth, animal, and plant for him: for thus he wants to go under.

"I love him who loves his virtue, for virtue is the will to go under and an arrow of longing.

"I love him who does not hold back one drop of spirit for himself, but wants to be entirely the spirit of his virtue: thus he strides over the bridge as spirit.

"I love him who makes his virtue his addiction and his catastrophe: for his virtue's sake he wants to live on and to live no longer.

Some examples of the kinds of human actions that Zarathustra loves are _____

_____

_____

_____.

"I love him who does not want to have too many virtues. One virtue is more virtue than two, because it is more of a noose on which his catastrophe may hang.

"I love him whose soul squanders itself, who wants no thanks and returns none: for he always gives away and does not want to preserve himself.

"I love him who is abashed when the dice fall to make his fortune, and asks, 'Am I then a crooked gambler?' For he wants to perish.

"I love him who casts golden words before his deeds and always does even more than he promises: for he wants to go under.

"I love him who justifies future and redeems past generations: for he wants to perish of the present.

"I love him who chastens his god because he loves his god: for he must perish of the wrath of his god.

"I love him whose soul is deep, even in being wounded, and who can perish of a small experience: thus he goes gladly over the bridge.

"I love him whose soul is overfull so that he forgets himself, and all things are in him: thus all things spell his going under.

"I love him who has a free spirit and a free heart: thus his head is only the entrails of his heart, but his heart drives him to go under.

"I love all those who are as heavy drops, falling one by one out of the dark cloud that hangs over men: they herald the advent of lightning and, as heralds, they perish.

"Behold, I am a herald of the lightning and a heavy drop from the cloud; but this lightning is called *overman*."

In general, Zarathustra loves

_____

_____

and hates _____

_____.

In this section, Zarathustra presents a long list of the paradoxical characteristics that he loves in a special kind of human being, the one who longs to make the overman possible. Again and again, Zarathustra makes variations on the same point, to prepare for the *over*man, one must be willing to go *under*. An overman is more than man, a beyond-human human. To prepare for such a being, to go under, the individual must leave behind all that keeps one, in Nietzsche's phrase, "merely human." Insofar as you want to keep being who you are, Nietzsche would despise you; insofar as you want to become radically different from who you are (and radically different from any Christian), Nietzsche would love you.

With all this in mind, circle any of the following answers that you believe are consistent with Zarathustra's message. (You may, of course, circle more than one.)

1. The best people are those who seek as much knowledge as they can about the physical universe.

2. The best people are those who "seek behind the stars for a reason to go under."

3. The best people are loyal to the earth, rather than to God.

4. The best people are those who love their virtue, because this will make them powerful role models.

5. The best people are those who love their virtue, because loving virtue means they want to be very different from who they are, and only those who are radically dissatisfied with themselves can prepare for the overman.

6. The best people are those who love their virtue, because loving virtue means that they want to eliminate all that is immoral in them, and this is the only way to become a better person.

7. The best people are those who hate the present.

8. The best people are those who serve the poor.

9. The best people are those who are loyal to their country.

10. The best people are those who want to leave behind who they are.

Now let's look more closely at a key statement by Zarathustra.

What is great in man is that he is a bridge and not an end: what can be loved in man is that he is an *overture* and a *going under*.

Nietzsche loved music. The key to this quotation is simply to understand the nature of a nineteenth-century musical overture. In classical music, the overture of a symphony or opera is a relatively short piece of music at the beginning of the work, which states, in an *undeveloped way*, many of the themes of the music to come. The relationship between an overture and a symphony is approximately the relationship between a movie preview and the movie itself. Thus, what Zarathustra is saying is that what he loves in humanity is that we are a mere preview of what we could become.

Imagine a documentary describing every brilliant philosophical work, every great work of art, every magnificent building, every feat of human genius. Now, contrast two viewers of the documentary. The first viewer applauds enthusiastically because she loves the movie; the second viewer applauds even more enthusiastically because she thinks she's just seen a mere preview of an infinitely greater movie to follow. The second viewer, of course, is the one Zarathustra would love if—*very big if*—Zarathustra's listeners will accept his message. In other words, humanity can be loved as an overture to an exceedingly magnificent symphony—if we are willing to go far beyond what we are. And this will be possible *only if the goal of the overman is accepted*.

Note the reaction of Zarathustra's listeners in the next section.

> When Zarathustra had spoken these words he beheld the people again and was silent. "There they stand," he said to his heart; "there they laugh. They do not understand me; I am not the mouth for these ears. Must one smash their ears before they learn to listen with their eyes? Must one clatter like kettledrums and preachers of repentance? Or do they believe only the stammerer?
>
> "They have something of which they are proud. What do they call that which makes them proud? Education they call it; it distinguishes them from goatherds. That is why they do not like to hear the word 'contempt' applied to them. Let me then address their pride. Let me speak to them of what is most contemptible: but that is the *last man*."

Underline characteristics of the "last man."

And thus spoke Zarathustra to the people: "The time has come for man to set himself a goal. The time has come for man to plant the seed of his highest hope. His soil is still rich enough. But one day this soil will be poor and domesticated, and no tall tree will be able to grow in it. Alas, the time is coming when man will no longer shoot the arrow of his longing beyond man, and the string of his bow will have forgotten how to whir!

"I say unto you: one must still have chaos in oneself to be able to give birth to a dancing star. I say unto you: you still have chaos in yourselves.

"Alas, the time is coming when man will no longer give birth to a star. Alas, the time of the most despicable man is coming, he that is no longer able to despise himself. Behold, I show you the *last man*.

"'What is love? What is creation? What is longing? What is a star?' thus asks the last man, and he blinks.

"The earth has become small, and on it hops the last man, who makes everything small. His race is as ineradicable as the flea-beetle; the last man lives longest.

"'We have invented happiness,' say the last men, and they blink. They have left the regions where it was hard to live, for one needs warmth. One still loves one's neighbor and rubs against him, for one needs warmth.

"Becoming sick and harboring suspicion are sinful to them: one proceeds carefully. A fool, whoever still stumbles over stones or human beings! A little poison now and then: that makes for agreeable dreams. And much poison in the end, for an agreeable death.

"One still works, for work is a form of entertainment. But one is careful lest the entertainment be too harrowing. One no longer becomes poor or rich: both require too much exertion. Who still wants to rule? Who obey? Both require too much exertion.

"No shepherd and one herd! Everybody wants the same, everybody is the same: whoever feels different goes voluntarily into a madhouse.

"'Formerly, all the world was mad,' say the most refined, and they blink.

"One is clever and knows everything that has ever happened: so there is no end of derision. One still quarrels, but one is soon reconciled—else it might spoil the digestion.

"One has one's little pleasure for the day and one's little pleasure for the night: but one has a regard for health.

"'We have invented happiness,' say the last men, and they blink."

And here ended Zarathustra's first speech, which is also called "the Prologue"; for at this point he was interrupted by the clamor and delight of the crowd. "Give us this last man, O Zarathustra," they shouted. "Turn us into these last men! Then we shall make you a gift of the overman!" And all the people jubilated and clucked with their tongues.

But Zarathustra became sad and said to his heart: "They do not understand me: I am not the mouth for these ears. I seem to have lived too long in the mountains; I listened too much to brooks and trees: now I talk to them as to goatherds. My soul is unmoved and bright as the mountains in the morning. But they think I am cold and I jeer and make dreadful jests. And now they look at me and laugh: and as they laugh they even hate me. There is ice in their laughter."

In general, the last man values

_____

_____

_____ .

EXERCISE 26.4
The Last Man

In Zarathustra's view, humanity is at a crossroads. In one direction lies the overman; in the other direction lies the last man. Circle any of the following that are consistent with Zarathustra's description of the last man.

1. The last man could never give birth to the overman.

2. The last man is a conformist.

3. The last man is the last man alive on earth.

4. The last man wants nothing to do with "frenzy" and the creation of "dancing stars."

5. The last man is happy.

6. The last man hates his neighbor.

7. The last man is a risk taker.

8. The last man wants to be the last man.

As a result of being rejected by his listeners, who would be quite happy to be last men, Zarathustra changes his understanding of his goal. In a later section of Zarathustra's Prologue, he says:

> An insight has come to me: companions I need. Living companions I need, who follow me because they want to follow themselves . . . let Zarathustra speak not to the people but to companions. Zarathustra shall not become the shepherd and dog of a herd. To lure many away from the herd, for that I have come. The people and the herd shall be angry with me: Zarathustra wants to be called a robber by the shepherds. . . . Fellow creators, the creator seeks— those who write new values on new tablets. . . . Destroyers they will be called, and despisers of good and evil. . . . Fellow creators, Zarathustra seeks, fellow harvesters and fellow celebrants: what are herds and shepherd . . . to him?

Zarathustra is saying something he has never said before. What is his new insight?

His new insight is _____

_____

_____.

At this point, I can tell you the answer to the difficult puzzle I posed earlier, "What large mistake does Zarathustra make?"

At the beginning of the Prologue, Zarathustra identified with the sun and wanted to "overflow," share his wisdom with everyone. His large mistake is that he completely misjudges humanity's interest in his message. He thought he would be the herd's shepherd, but the masses have no interest in going where he leads. His listeners want the easiest life possible and reject the enormous hardships involved in creating an overman. Zarathustra is shocked to find out that the crowd has no interest in achieving anything greater than the last man's paltry happiness.

In the passage above, Zarathustra understands he is not a sun that will shine upon everyone. His message is for the few, not the many. Instead of being the herd's shepherd, he will be its robber, seeking only those who want to be creators, not conformists.

To recognize that Zarathustra makes mistakes is an important key to understanding Nietzsche's unique method of philosophizing. Zarathustra does not have all the answers; he is learning as he goes. He is always, even to the end of the book, on the way, never fully there. After hundreds of pages, here is how *Thus Spake Zarathustra* concludes:

> Zarathustra has ripened, my hour has come: "this is *my* morning, *my* day is breaking; *rise now, rise, though great noon!*"
>   Thus spoke Zarathustra, and he left his cave, glowing and strong as a morning sun that comes out of dark mountains.

The book ends with Zarathustra setting forth! Nietzsche concludes with his character just getting started. The entire long tale is an overture for an unfinished symphony. Thus, Nietzsche is doing philosophy in a radical new way. Earlier philosophers had tried to convince their readers that they had solved philosophical problems. This can hardly be Nietzsche's goal because he does not want believers; he wants fellow creators. He is not so much trying to solve philosophical problems, as to move the reader to create a new kind of life. Nietzsche, appropriately enough, has a paradoxical goal, to create nonfollowing followers.

If Nietzsche wants us to create new values, he can hardly define those values for us. It would be absurd for him to say, "Create new ethical standards, and, by the way, here they are." Nietzsche can point out the philosophical direction, away from Christianity, away from social conformity, away from the life of ease and paltry happiness, but the exact destination is ours, as creators, to discover. Nietzsche makes this odd problem for his readers easier to solve, by never setting up a finished philosophical system that readers must break out of. We can't follow Nietzsche because we don't know exactly where he is. If we listen to him, we must go beyond what he says.

With all this in mind, let's analyze one final, very challenging and intriguing section from *Thus Spake Zarathustra*. Given that Nietzsche can't tell his best readers, his fellow creators, how to be an overman, he can give details about the *path* toward the overman. In the "Three Metamorphoses," Zarathustra describes three spiritual stages that lead to beginning a new way of life.

What do we know thus far about the overman? He is against Christianity, belief in higher worlds, hatred of the body, conformity, complacent happiness, the life of ease. In addition, he wants to exist "beyond good and evil"—in other words, in a value system completely independent of existing ideas of what is moral and immoral. Finally, the life of the overman is for the very few, the creators, not the many.

One obvious question is, How could one go about, even in the smallest way, heading in the direction of an overman? If being an overman is so wonderful, how do we get started? Well, obviously, leaving behind all accepted values would be extremely difficult. Thus, in the first metamorphosis described below, the spirit engages in activities to build spiritual strength.

Try your hand at being Nietzschean.

If you were going to make your spirit stronger (and didn't believe in God) what would you do?

Perhaps I would _____

_____.

The next step toward the overman, according to Nietzsche, is taken when we turn our back on all previous values. This stage is symbolized by the lion, who defeats the great dragon "Thou shalt." The lion substitutes "I will," self-direction, for "Thou shalt," obedience to existing values.

The final step toward the overman occurs when the spirit becomes a child. As a child, the spirit makes new joyful beginnings.

I've divided the "Three Metamorphoses" into very short sections. Read slowly.

Zarathustra's Speeches on the Three Metamorphoses

Of three metamorphoses of the spirit I tell you: How the spirit becomes a camel; and the camel, a lion; and the lion, finally, a child.

There is much that is difficult for the spirit, the strong reverent spirit that would bear much: but the difficult and the most difficult are what its strength demands.

What is difficult? asks the spirit that would bear much, and kneels down like a camel wanting to be well loaded. What is most difficult, O heroes, asks the spirit that would bear much, that I may take it upon myself and exult in my strength? Is it not humbling oneself to wound one's haughtiness? Letting one's folly shine to mock one's wisdom?

In the first metamorphosis, the spirit becomes a camel and seeks what is most difficult in order to "exult," rejoice, in its strength. Therefore, each of the camel's tasks can be understood as some kind of self-chosen hardship. For example, if you were haughty, then it would be difficult to humble yourself; or, if you were wise, it would be difficult, most difficult, to let your foolishness shine.

Think that through for a moment. Imagine you are extremely proud.

All right, I am extremely proud of my abilities to _____

_____.

If you were this sort of person, a very difficult thing for you to do would be to humble yourself. Right?

I believe _____

_____.

Or let us say you were wise. What would be extremely difficult for you to do?

It would be difficult to _____

_____ .

Slowly read the following. Try to see each statement as a substantial spiritual difficulty. (The numbering is mine, not Nietzsche's.)

> [1] Or is it this: parting from our cause when it triumphs? Climbing high mountains to tempt the tempter?
> [2] Or is it this: feeding on the acorns and grass of knowledge and, for the sake of the truth, suffering hunger in one's soul?
> [3] Or is it this: being sick and sending home the comforters and making friends with the deaf, who never hear what you want?
> [4] Or is it this: stepping into filthy waters when they are the waters of truth and not repulsing cold frogs and hot toads?
> [5] Or is it this: loving those who despise us and offering a hand to the ghost that would frighten us?
> All these most difficult things the spirit that would bear much takes upon itself: like the camel that, burdened, speeds into the desert, thus the spirit speeds into its desert.

The following exercise should help you considerably. I've paraphrased some, but not all, of the numbered sections above. Match my paraphrases with the correct numbers.

_____ It would be difficult to love someone who hated us.

_____ The most difficult time to abandon a campaign we were fighting for would be when it was winning.

_____ It would be very difficult to accept repulsive truths.

_____ It would be very difficult to welcome what we fear the most.

_____ It would be very difficult, when we are in pain, to reject all comfort from others.

Why would anyone do such difficult things? The answer is that "anyone" wouldn't. Only those unique, rare individuals who seek to create new values would want to exult in and build the strength of their spirit.

The next metamorphosis of the spirit is easier to understand.

> In the loneliest desert, however, the second metamorphosis occurs: here the spirit becomes a lion who would conquer his freedom and be master in his own desert. Here he seeks out his last master: he wants to fight him and his last god; for ultimate victory he wants to fight with the great dragon.

Who is the great dragon whom the spirit will no longer call lord and god? "Thou shalt" is the name of the great dragon. But the spirit of the lion says, "I will." "Thou shalt" lies in his way, sparkling like gold, an animal covered with scales; and on every scale shines a golden "thou shalt."

Values, thousands of years old, shine on these scales; and thus speaks the mightiest of all dragons: "All value of all things shines on me. All value has long been created, and I am all created value. Verily, there shall be no more 'I will.'" Thus speaks the dragon.

My brothers, why is there a need in the spirit for the lion? Why is not the beast of burden, which renounces and is reverent, enough?

To create new values—that even the lion cannot do; but the creation of freedom for oneself for new creation—that is within the power of the lion. The creation of freedom for oneself and a sacred "No" even to duty—for that, my brothers, the lion is needed. To assume the right to new values—that is the most terrifying assumption for a reverent spirit that would bear much. Verily, to him it is preying, and a matter for a beast of prey. He once loved "thou shalt" as most sacred: now he must find illusion and caprice even in the most sacred, that freedom from his love may become his prey: the lion is needed for such prey.

Here are some "Thou shalts" which glitter like gold on the dragon whom the lion battles. Thou shalt be a good citizen, obey the golden rule, have pity on the unfortunate, go to church, make a good living, love your neighbor. Add a few more yourself.

Some other Thou shalts are _____

_____

_____.

What is the lion's attitude toward these?

The lion's attitude is _____

_____.

What is the difference, as Zarathustra describes it above, between the lion and the camel?

The camel is _____.

The lion is _____.

Now read about the third metamorphosis of the spirit.

But say, my brothers, what can the child do that even the lion could not do? Why must the preying lion still become a child? The child is innocence and forgetting, a new beginning, a game, a self-propelled wheel, a first movement, a sacred "Yes." For the game of creation, my brothers, a sacred "Yes" is needed: the spirit now wills his own will, and he who had been lost to the world now conquers his own world.

Of three metamorphoses of the spirit I have told you: how the spirit became a camel; and the camel, a lion; and the lion, finally, a child.

What is the difference between the lion and the child?

The lion is _____.

The child is _____.

Think of the camel, the lion, and the child as Zarathustra's description of the bridge between where you are now and the overman you could become. Decide which of the following you support or oppose. Explain your reasoning.

1. Feeling the strength of my spirit, in one of the ways Nietzsche describes.

   I (support/oppose) this approach because _____

   _____.

2. Feeling the strength of my spirit, in many of the ways Nietzsche describes.

   I (support/oppose) this approach because _____

   _____.

3. Rejecting a few of the Thou shalts I have learned.

   I (support/oppose) this approach because _____

   _____.

4. Rejecting all of the Thou shalts I have learned.

   I (support/oppose) this approach because _____

   _____.

5. Creating some of my own values, which are unlike any values that have ever existed.

   I (support/oppose) this approach because _____

   _____.

6. Creating all my own values, which are unlike any values that have ever existed.

   I (support/oppose) this approach because _____

   _____.

EXERCISE 26.5

The Overman Application Form

You might have some fun with this. Assume you are applying to a Nietzschean employer who is only interested in hiring individuals with overman potential. Fill out the following application with the answers your prospective employer is looking for. Use your own paper to explain your reasoning.

1. Yes/No: Do you regularly attend church?

2. Yes/No: Do you own a television?

3. Yes/No: Would you consider yourself a strongly emotional person?

4. Yes/No: Are you good at following directions?

5. How do you like to spend your free time? _____
   _____.

6. What are your personal goals? _____
   _____.

7. What are your career goals? _____
   _____.

8. What is the last year of school you have completed? _____.

9. An immoral person is one who _____
   _____.

10. A moral person is one who _____
    _____.

11. What was your annual salary last year? _____.

12. What are the most positive features of your personality? _____
    _____.

13. What are the most negative features of your personality? _____
    _____.

14. What, in life, is your greatest regret? _____
    _____.

SUMMARY

Nietzsche argues that God is dead, because contemporary society is no longer guided by Christian values. His philosophical style is strongly aphoristic and, in the case of *Thus Spake Zarathustra*, allegorical. Nietzsche harshly criticizes earlier philosophers, especially dualists in general and Christians in particular. Christian metaphysics is not only a false but also a disfiguring description of reality. Christian ethics may appear noble, but, because these values are founded upon a hatred of life and an envy of those in power, they are symptoms of deep spiritual illness. The overman should replace the saint as an ethical ideal. A test of the overman's strength is the depth of joy created by the contemplation of the eternal repetition of every life experience, even the most painful.

EXERCISE 26.6
Looking Back

Practice your paraphrasing skills and answer the following on your own paper.

1. What is unusual about Nietzsche's philosophizing?
2. What are some of Nietzsche's criticisms of earlier philosophers?
3. What is Nietzsche's criticism of Christianity?
4. What is Nietzsche's "metaphysics"?
5. What is Nietzsche's "ethics"?

EXERCISE 26.7
Looking at the World Through Nietzsche's Eyes

How would Nietzsche answer each of the following?

1. T F The old way is the good way.

    Evidence: _____

    _____.

2. T F The greatest metaphysics would completely explain reality.

    Evidence: _____

    _____.

3. T F There is no such thing as Christian sin.

    Evidence: _____

    _____.

4. T F The meek should perish from the earth.

    Evidence: _____

    _____.

5. T F We should strive for peace of mind.

    Evidence: _____

    _____.

6. T F There is no One that unifies the many aspects of life.

    Evidence: _____

    _____.

7. T F Democracy is the best form of government.

    Evidence: _____

    _____.

8. T F A hero like Martin Luther King should be praised more for what he
          made of himself than for what he did for others.

    Evidence: _____

    _____.

ANALYSIS OF YOUR PHILOSOPHICAL SELF-PORTRAIT

To see how your views stack up against Nietzsche's, read my analysis below, re-think your position, and then circle what you believe is the correct answer. I've underlined Nietzsche's answers.

1. <u>T</u> F *God is dead.*

    Perhaps knowing Nietzsche's response to this question will now clarify your own position. Interestingly enough, a group of religious thinkers in the 1960s, men and women who believed in God, were part of a "God is dead" movement.

2. <u>T</u> F *God does not exist.*

    If you answered False, then you are part of a very long line of thinkers: Aristotle, Augustine, Anselm, Aquinas, Descartes, Locke, Berkeley, Kant, and Mill. If you answered True, then so far as this tour is concerned, the line is far shorter: Nietzsche and (still to come) Camus and Sartre. You might also throw in Epicurus, who believed in the gods but held that they had no concern for us. If you're an atheist looking for more company, investigate Hobbes (*Leviathan*) or any of the very interesting atheistic anarchists (Emma Goldman, *Anarchism and Other Essays;* Mikhail Bakunin, *The Political Philosophy of Bakunin;* James Joll, *The Anarchists*).

3. T <u>F</u> *The greatest people are those who serve God.*

    Nietzsche argues that those with the most diseased, life-hating, self-hating spirits are those who see themselves as serving God. If you'd like a brilliant overview of Nietzsche's thought, read Walter Kaufmann's *Nietzsche: Philosopher, Psychologist, and Antichrist.*

4. <u>T</u> F *The greatest philosophers are those who question traditional values.*

    Nietzsche would certainly answer True and, in some moods, would argue that he was the *only* philosopher who had ever properly criticized traditional values.

5. T <u>F</u> *The universe had a beginning in time and will have an end in time; matter is not eternal.*

    Fundamentalist Christians, holding that the Bible is literally true, would have to answer this question True. God created the universe, as described in Genesis, and will bring the universe to an end, as described in Revelations. If this position interests you, there are hundreds of books to choose from, but you might start with *The Late Great Planet Earth,* by Hal Lindsey. If you'd like an overview of the viewpoint of modern physics about the nature of the universe, try Stephen Hawking's slender, challenging, phenomenally best-selling *A Brief History of Time.*

6. <u>T</u> F *The purpose of each human's life is self-perfection.*

    As you may have guessed by now, we have explored only three main answers to this question on the tour. The following have held that self-perfection is the purpose of human life: Plato, Aristotle, Epicurus, Epictetus, and Nietzsche. The main differences between each of these philosophers can be seen in their different conceptions of the perfect self. For example, the perfect self, for Plato, is embodied in the philosopher-king who serves and guides his state selflessly; the perfect self for Nietzsche is the overman who, among other characteristics described in this chapter, wants nothing to do with anyone's state.

Hume represents the second answer to the question. He holds that we cannot know the purpose of human life but counsels us that our reason should serve our passions (and not the other way around as the Greeks argued).

Anselm and other Christian thinkers represent the third answer to this question. They hold that the purpose of human life is obedience to God's will.

Kant represents a special case. He holds that the purpose of human life is to do our duty, simply for the sake of duty itself, regardless of the positive or negative consequences. It is right, for example, to tell the truth simply because this is right, what we would want everyone to do in the same circumstances. The rightness of truth-telling has nothing to do with the obedience to God or the goal of self-perfection.

If you find the question of the purpose of human life fascinating, look into any of the following: Henry David Thoreau, *Walden* (the classic description of the life of simplicity); Leo Tolstoy, *Life and Death of Ivan Ilych* (a story about a man's journey to Christian understanding); Franz Schneider, *Last Letters from Stalingrad* (what soldiers, in this case German, write home when they are convinced they are going to die); David Burns, *Feeling Good: The New Mood Therapy* (a personal favorite, true happiness according to cognitive therapy, which traces its origins back to Epictetus); Mihaly Csikszentmihalyi, *Flow* (a psychological description of the nature of our optimal human state by a widely respected Chicago psychologist); Herman Hesse, *Siddhartha* (a classic tale that introduces many of the main tenets of the Buddhist view of the purpose of life).

If you'd like more by Nietzsche, try *Genealogy of Morals* for Nietzsche's description of the origin of Christian "slave" morality; *The Antichrist* for a violent attack upon Christianity; and *Ecce Homo*, which contains some of the most wonderful chapter titles in the history of philosophy, such as "Why I Am So Clever" and "Why I Am So Wise."

Evaluation: Number of points in agreement with Nietzsche = _____ of 6 possible.

A position of Nietzsche's that you strongly (support, oppose) is _____

_____

because _____

_____.

GOOD BOOKS

Kaufmann, Walter. *Nietzsche*. New York: Meridian, 1956. A good place to start to gain a general understanding of Nietzsche's position and its development.

Nietzsche, Friedrich. *The Portable Nietzsche*. Edited and translated by Walter Kaufmann. New York: Penguin, 1968. Kaufmann is a noted Nietzsche scholar; this is one of the best Nietzsche anthologies.

NEXT STOP

The Modern Reader, a sampler of some of the best of modern philosophy.

A Modern Reader

The following readings are designed to give you a brief sampling of some of the most intriguing thought produced in Europe and America in the last hundred years. This small group of works cannot represent the wide variety of philosophical interests in the twentieth century. As a test of the analytical abilities you have honed on our tour, no annotation tasks or other learning aids are included.

Existentialism Is a Humanism

JEAN-PAUL SARTRE

Jean-Paul Sartre (1905–1980), a leading spokesman of existentialism (which he defines in the following selection), was one of the most influential philosophers of the twentieth century. One of the very few modern thinkers to gain popular recognition, Sartre's gifts were not only philosophical but also literary. Works of fiction, like his novel *Nausea* and his play *No Exit*, popularized views elaborated in his philosophical works like *Being and Nothingness*. In 1964 Sartre declined the Nobel Prize for literature because, committed to a Marxist view of society, he viewed the award as representative of capitalist values.

In the following selection from his essay "Existentialism Is a Humanism," Sartre often uses the phrase "existence precedes essence" to describe human nature. To clarify this phrase, contrast these two statements. The first is non-Sartrean; the second is Sartrean.

1. *In the case of humans, essence precedes existence.* Plato and traditional Christians would agree that this is true. For Plato, the Form of Human, humanity's essence, exists prior to any individual human. For Christians, humanity's essence existed in God's mind prior to any individual human. For both these positions, human essence precedes, comes before, any living person.

2. *In the case of humans, existence precedes essence.* This is Sartre's view and, he claims, the view of all existentialists. First humans exist and then, *by their choices,* create their essence. Human nature is not fixed, pre-established, in the realm of Forms, mind of God, or any other place. Humans are nothing but the freedom to continuously create their defining characteristics. Whereas both the Platonic and the traditional Christian view is that human essence exists in a higher world, Sartre's view is that human essence is created by human choices in this world.

Though this distinction between essence and existence sounds rather technical, Sartre is making a very powerful, even astounding, point. In his view, it is only the case with manufactured objects like books, paper-cutters, and so forth that essence comes before existence. The essence,

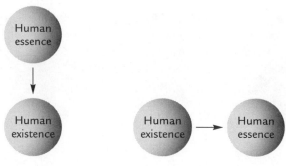

According to Plato and traditional Christians, human essence is prior to human existence. For Plato, human essence exists in the Realm of Forms; for Christians, human essence exists in God's mind. In both cases, human essence is in a higher world.

According to Sartre and other existentialists, human existence is prior to human essence. First we exist in this world, and then by our free choices, create our essence.

idea, of a paper-cutter exists in the manufacturer's mind; and from this essence, a paper-cutter is produced. Because the idea of a paper-cutter comes prior to its existence, the nature of a paper-cutter is forever fixed. However, according to Sartre, this is not true of human beings. We are not things; our nature is not fixed. No one—not God, the Forms, Nature, or any other force—forever determines our essence. We have no defining characteristics because, unlike paper-cutters, we make free choices. Our choices continually invent our essence, our human nature. A paper-cutter can only be a paper-cutter, but I can be a teacher, a jogger, a gardener, or anything else possible in my situation. Thus, in the case of humans, we are in the condition that Sartre terms "nothingness." First we exist, and then, by our free choices, we continually invent ourselves. *There is no such thing as human nature!* We are nothing but our freedom.

. . . What is meant by the term *existentialism*?

Most people who use the word would be rather embarrassed if they had to explain it, since, now that the word is all the rage, even the work of a musician or a painter is being called existentialist. A gossip columnist in *Clartés* signs himself *The Existentialist,* so that by this time the word has been so stretched and has taken on so broad a meaning, that it no longer means anything at all. It seems that for want of an

From Jean-Paul Sartre, *Existentialism* (New York: Philosophical Library, 1967). Reprinted by permission of Philosophical Library Publishers, New York.

advance-guard doctrine analogous to surrealism, the kind of people who are eager for scandal and flurry turn to this philosophy which in other respects does not at all serve their purposes in this sphere.

Actually, it is the least scandalous, the most austere of doctrines. It is intended strictly for specialists and philosophers. Yet it can be defined easily. What complicates matters is that there are two kinds of existentialist; first, those who are Christian, among whom I would include Jaspers and Gabriel Marcel, both Catholic; and on the other hand the atheistic existentialists, among whom I class Heidegger, and then the French existentialists and myself. What they have in common is that they think that existence precedes essence, or, if you prefer, that subjectivity must be the starting point.

Just what does that mean? Let us consider some object that is manufactured, for example, a book or a paper-cutter: here is an object which has been made by an artisan whose inspiration came from a concept. He referred to the concept of what a paper-cutter is and likewise to a known method of production, which is part of the concept, something which is, by and large, a routine. Thus, the paper-cutter is at once an object produced in a certain way and, on the other hand, one having a specific use; and one can not postulate a man who produces a paper-cutter but does not know what it is used for. Therefore, let us say that, for the paper-cutter, essence—that is, the ensemble of both the production routines and the properties which enable it to be both produced and defined—precedes existence. Thus, the presence of the paper-cutter or book in front of me is determined. Therefore, we have here a technical view of the world whereby it can be said that production precedes existence.

When we conceive God as the Creator, He is generally thought of as a superior sort of artisan. Whatever doctrine we may be considering, whether one like that of Descartes or that of Leibnitz, we always grant that will more or less follows understanding or, at the very least, accompanies it, and that when God creates He knows exactly what He is creating. Thus, the concept of man in the mind of God is comparable to the concept of a paper-cutter in the mind of the manufacturer, and, following certain techniques and a conception, God produces man, just as the artisan, following a definition and a technique, makes a paper-cutter. Thus, the individual man is the realization of a certain concept in the divine intelligence.

In the eighteenth century, the atheism of the *philosophers* discarded the idea of God, but not so much for the notion that essence precedes existence. To a certain extent, this idea is found everywhere; we find it in Diderot, in Voltaire, and even in Kant. Man has a human nature; this human nature, which is the concept of the human, is found in all men, which means that each man is a particular example of a universal concept, man. In Kant, the result of this universality is that the wild-man, the natural man, as well as the bourgeois, are circumscribed by the same definition and have the same basic qualities. Thus, here too the essence of man precedes the historical existence that we find in nature.

Atheistic existentialism, which I represent, is more coherent. It states that if God does not exist, there is at least one being in whom existence precedes essence, a being who exists before he can be defined by any concept, and that this being is man, or, as Heidegger says, human reality. What is meant here by saying that existence precedes essence? It means that, first of all, man exists, turns up, appears on the scene, and, only afterwards, defines himself. If man, as the existentialist conceives him, is indefinable, it is because at first he is nothing. Only afterward will he be something, and he himself will have made what he will be. Thus, there is no human nature, since there is no God to conceive it. Not only is man what he conceives himself to be, but he is also only what he wills himself to be after this thrust toward existence.

Man is nothing else but what he makes of himself. Such is the first principle of existentialism. It is also what is called subjectivity, the name we are labeled with when charges are brought against us. But what do we mean by this, if not that man has a greater dignity than a stone or table? For we mean that man first exists, that is, that man first of all is the being who hurls himself toward a future and who is conscious of imagining himself as being in the future. Man is at the start a plan which is aware of itself, rather than a patch of moss, a piece of garbage, or a cauliflower; nothing exists prior to this plan; there is nothing in heaven; man will be what he will have planned to be. Not what he will want to be. Because by the word "will" we generally mean a conscious decision, which is subsequent to what we have already made of ourselves. I may want to belong to a political party, write a book, get married; but all that is only a manifestation of an earlier, more spontaneous choice that is called "will." But if existence really does precede essence, man is responsible for what he is. Thus, existentialism's first move is to make every man aware of what he is and to make the full responsibility of his existence rest on him. And when we say that a man is responsible for himself, we do not only mean that he is responsible for his own individuality, but that he is responsible for all men.

The word subjectivism has two meanings, and our opponents play on the two. Subjectivism means, on the one hand, that an individual chooses and makes himself; and, on the other, that it is impossible for man to transcend human subjectivity. The second of these is the essential meaning of existentialism. When we say that man chooses his own self, we mean that every one of us does likewise; but we also mean by that that in making this choice he also chooses all men. In fact, in creating the man that we want to be, there is not a single one of our acts which does not at the same time create an image of man as we think he ought to be. To choose to be this or that is to affirm at the same time the value of what we choose, because we can never choose evil. We always choose the good, and nothing can be good for us without being good for all.

If, on the other hand, existence precedes essence, and if we grant that we exist and fashion our image at one and the same time, the image is valid for everybody and for our whole age. Thus, our responsibility is much greater than we might have supposed, because it involves all mankind. If I am a workingman and chooses to join a Christian trade-union rather than be a communist, and if by being a member I want to show that the best thing for man is resignation, that the kingdom of man is not of this world, I am not only involving my own case—I want to be resigned for everyone. As a result, my action has involved all humanity. To take a more individual matter, if I want to marry, to have children; even if this marriage depends solely on my own circumstances or passion or wish, I am involving all humanity in monogamy and not merely myself. Therefore, I am responsible for myself and for everyone else. I am creating a certain image of man of my own choosing. In choosing myself, I choose man.

This helps us understand what the actual content is of such rather grandiloquent words as anguish, forlorness, despair. As you will see, it's all quite simple.

First, what is meant by anguish? The existentialists say at once that man is anguish. What that means is this: the man who involves himself and who realizes that he is not only the person he chooses to be, but also a lawmaker who is, at the same time, choosing all mankind as well as himself, can not help escape the feeling of his total and deep responsibility. Of course, there are many people who are not anxious; but we claim that they are hiding their anxiety, that they are fleeing from it. Certainly, many people believe that when they do something, they themselves are the only ones involved, and when someone says to them, "What if everyone acted that way?" they shrug their shoulders and answer, "Everyone doesn't act that way." But really, one should always ask himself, "What would happen if everyone looked at things that way?" There is no escaping this disturbing thought except by a kind of double-dealing. A man who lies and makes excuses for himself by saying "not everybody does that," is someone with an uneasy conscience, because the act of lying implies that a universal value is conferred upon the lie.

Anguish is evident even when it conceals itself. This is the anguish that Kierkegaard called the anguish of Abraham. You know the story: an angel has ordered Abraham to sacrifice his son; if it really were an angel who has come and said, "You are Abraham, you shall sacrifice your son," everything would be all right. But everyone might first wonder, "Is it really an angel, and am I really Abraham? What proof do I have?"

There was a madwoman who had hallucinations; someone used to speak to her on the telephone and give her orders. Her doctor asked her, "Who is it who talks to you?" She answered, "He says it's God." What proof did she really have that it was God? If an angel comes to me, what proof is there that it's an angel? And if I hear voices, what proof is there that they come from heaven and not from hell, or from the subconscious, or a pathological condition? What proves that they are addressed to me? What proof is there that I have been appointed to impose my choice and my conception of man on humanity? I'll never find any proof or sign to convince me of that. If a voice addresses me, it is always for me to decide that this is the angel's voice; if I consider that such an act is a good one, it is I who will choose to say that it is good rather than bad.

Now, I'm not being singled out as an Abraham, and yet at every moment I'm obliged to perform exemplary acts. For every man, everything happens as if all mankind had its eyes fixed on him and were guiding itself by what he does. And every man ought to say to himself, "Am I really the kind of man who has the right to act in such a way that humanity might guide itself by my actions?" And if he does not say that to himself, he is masking his anguish.

There is no question here of the kind of anguish which would lead to quietism, to inaction. It is a matter of a simple sort of anguish that anybody who has had responsibilities is familiar with. For example, when a military officer takes the responsibility for an attack and sends a certain number of men to death, he chooses to do so, and in the main he alone makes the choice. Doubtless, orders come from above, but they are too broad; he interprets them, and on this interpretation depend the lives of ten or fourteen or twenty men. In making a decision he can not help having a certain anguish. All leaders know this anguish. That doesn't keep them from acting; on the contrary, it is the very condition of their action. For it implies that they envisage a number of possibilities, and when they choose one, they realize that it has value only because it is chosen. We shall see that this kind of anguish, which is the kind that existentialism describes, is explained, in addition, by a direct responsibility to the other men whom it involves. It is not a curtain separating us from action, but is part of action itself.

When we speak of forlornness, a term Heidegger was fond of, we mean only that God does not exist and that we have to face all the consequences of this. The existentialist is strongly opposed to a certain kind of secular ethics which would like to abolish God with the least possible expense. About 1880, some French teachers tried to set up a secular ethics which went something like this: God is a useless and costly hypothesis; we are discarding it; but, meanwhile, in order for there to be an ethics, a society, a civilization, it is essential that certain values be taken seriously and that they be considered as having an *a priori* existence. It must be obligatory, *a priori,* to be honest, not to lie, not to beat your wife, to have children, etc., etc. So we're going to try a little device which will make it possible to show that values exist all the same, inscribed in a heaven of ideas, though otherwise God does not exist. In other words—and this, I believe, is the tendency of everything called reformism in France—nothing will be changed if God does not exist. We shall find ourselves with the same norms of honesty, progress, and humanism, and we shall have made of God an outdated hypothesis which will peacefully die off by itself.

The existentialist, on the contrary, thinks it very distressing that God does not exist, because all possibility of finding values in a heaven of ideas disappears along with Him; there can no longer be an *a priori* Good, since there is no infinite and perfect consciousness to think it. Nowhere is it written that the Good exists, that we must be honest, that we must not lie;

because the fact is we are on a plane where there are only men. Dostoievsky said, "If God didn't exist, everything would be possible." That is the very starting point of existentialism. Indeed, everything is permissible if God does not exist, and as a result man is forlorn, because neither within him nor without does he find anything to cling to. He can't start making excuses for himself.

If existence really does precede essence, there is no explaining things away by reference to a fixed and given human nature. In other words, there is no determinism, man is free, man is freedom. On the other hand, if God does not exist, we find no values or commands to turn to which legitimize our conduct. So, in the bright realm of values, we have no excuse behind us, nor justification before us. We are alone, with no excuses.

That is the idea I shall try to convey when I say that man is condemned to be free. Condemned, because he did not create himself, yet, in other respects is free; because, once thrown into the world, he is responsible for everything he does. The existentialist does not believe in the power of passion. He will never agree that a sweeping passion is a ravaging torrent which fatally leads a man to certain acts and is therefore an excuse. He thinks that man is responsible for his passion.

The existentialist does not think that man is going to help himself by finding in the world some omen by which to orient himself. Because he thinks that man will interpret the omen to suit himself. Therefore, he thinks that man, with no support and no aid, is condemned every moment to invent man. Ponge, in a very fine article, has said, "Man is the future of man." That's exactly it. But if it is taken to mean that this future is recorded in heaven, that God sees it, then it is false, because it would really no longer be a future. If it is taken to mean that, whatever a man may be, there is a future to be forged, a virgin future before him, then this remark is sound. But then we are forlorn.

To give you an example which will enable you to understand forlornness better, I shall cite the case of one of my students who came to see me under the following circumstances: his father was on bad terms with his mother, and, moreover, was inclined to be a collaborationist; his older brother had been killed in the German offensive of 1940, and the young man, with somewhat immature but generous feelings, wanted to avenge him. His mother lived alone with him, very much upset by the half-treason of her husband and the death of her older son; the boy was her only consolation.

The boy was faced with the choice of leaving for England and joining the Free French Forces—that is, leaving his mother behind—or remaining with his mother and helping her to carry on. He was fully aware that the woman lived only for him and that his going-off—and perhaps his death—would plunge her into despair. He was also aware that every act that he did for his mother's sake was a sure thing, in the sense that it was helping her to carry on, whereas every effort he made toward going off and fighting was an uncertain move which might run aground and prove completely useless; for example, on his way to England he might, while passing through Spain, be detained indefinitely in a Spanish camp; he might reach England or Algiers and be stuck in an office at a desk job. As a result, he was faced with two very different kinds of action: one, concrete, immediate, but concerning only one individual; the other concerned an incomparably vaster group, a national collectivity, but for that very reason was dubious, and might be interrupted en route. And, at the same time, he was wavering between two kinds of ethics. On the one hand, an ethics of sympathy, of personal devotion; on the other, a broader ethics, but one whose efficacy was more dubious. He had to choose between the two.

Who could help him choose? Christian doctrine? No. Christian doctrine says, "Be charitable, love your neighbor, take the more rugged path, etc., etc." But which is the more rugged path? Whom should he love as a brother? The fighting man or his mother? Which does the greater good, the vague act of fighting in a group, or the concrete one of helping a particular human being to go on living? Who can decide *a priori*? Nobody. No book of ethics can tell him. The Kantian ethics says, "Never treat any person as a means, but as an end." Very well, if I stay with my mother, I'll treat her as an end and not as a means; but by virtue of this very fact, I'm running the risk of treating the people around me who are fighting, as means; and, conversely, if I go to join those who are fighting, I'll be treating them as an end, and, by doing that, I run the risk of treating my mother as a means.

If values are vague, and if they are always too broad for the concrete and specific case that we are considering, the only thing left for us is to trust our instincts. That's what this young man tried to do; and when I saw him, he said, "In the end, feeling is what counts. I ought to choose whichever pushes me in one direction. If I feel that I love my mother enough to sacrifice everything else for her—my desire for vengeance, for action, for adventure—then I'll stay with her. If, on the contrary, I feel that my love for my mother isn't enough, I'll leave."

But how is the value of feeling determined? What gives his feeling for his mother value? Precisely the fact that he remained with her. I may say that I like so-and-so well enough to sacrifice a certain amount of money for him, but I may say so only if I've done it. I may say "I love my mother well enough to remain with her" if I have remained with her. The only way to determine the value of this affection is, precisely, to perform an act which confirms and defines it. But, since I require this affection to justify my act, I find myself caught in a vicious circle.

On the other hand, Gide has well said that a mock feeling and a true feeling are almost indistinguishable; to decide that I love my mother and will remain with her, or to remain with her by putting on an act, amount somewhat to the same thing. In other words, the feeling is formed by the acts one performs; so, I can not refer to it in order to act upon it. Which means that I can neither seek within myself the true condition which will impel me to act, nor apply to a system of ethics for concepts which will permit me to act. You will say, "At least, he did go to a teacher for advice." But if you seek advice from a priest, for example, you have chosen this priest; you already knew, more or less, just about what advice he was going to give you. In other words, choosing your adviser is involving yourself. The proof of this is that if you are a Christian, you will say, "Consult a priest." But some priests are collaborating, some are just marking time, some are resisting. Which to choose? If the young man chooses a priest who is resisting or collaborating, he has already decided on the kind of advice he's going to get. Therefore, in coming to see me he knew the answer I was going to give him, and I had only one answer to give: "You're free, choose, that is, invent." No general ethics can show you what is to be done; there are no omens in the world. The Catholics will reply, "But there are." Granted—but, in any case, I myself choose the meaning they have.

When I was a prisoner, I knew a rather remarkable young man who was a Jesuit. He had entered the Jesuit order in the following way: he had had a number of very bad breaks; in childhood, his father died, leaving him in poverty, and he was a scholarship student at a religious institution where he was constantly made to feel that he was being kept out of charity; then, he failed to get any of the honors and distinctions that children like; later on, at about eighteen, he bungled a love affair; finally, at twenty-two, he failed in military training, a childish enough matter, but it was the last straw.

This young fellow might well have felt that he had botched everything. It was a sign of something, but of what? He might have taken refuge in bitterness or despair. But he very wisely looked upon all this as a sign that he was not made for secular triumphs, and that only the triumphs of religion, holiness, and faith were open to him. He saw the hand of God in all this, and so entered the order. Who can help seeing that he alone decided what the sign meant?

Some other interpretation might have been drawn from this series of setbacks; for example, that he might have done better to turn carpenter or revolutionist. Therefore, he is fully responsible for the interpretation. Forlornness implies that we ourselves choose our being. Forlornness and anguish go together.

As for despair, the term has a very simple meaning. It means that we shall confine ourselves to reckoning only with what depends upon our will, or on the ensemble of probabilities which make our action possible. When we want something, we always have to reckon with probabilities. I may be counting on the arrival of a friend. The friend is coming by rail or street-car; this supposes that the train will arrive on schedule, or that the street-car will not jump the track. I am left in the realm of possibility; but possibilities are to be reckoned with only to the point where my action comports with the ensemble of these possibilities, and no further. The moment the possibilities I am considering are not rigorously involved by my action, I ought to disengage myself from them, because no God, no scheme, can adapt the world and its possibilities to my will. When Descartes said, "Conquer yourself rather than the world," he meant essentially the same thing.

The Myth of Sisyphus
ALBERT CAMUS

Albert Camus (1913–1960), though often associated with existentialism, did not regard himself as an existentialist. Early in his writing career, Camus was a colleague of Sartre's, but the two men broke over Sartre's support of Marxism. In novels like *The Stranger* and *The Plague* and philosophical essays like *The Myth of Sisyphus*, Camus analyzed the human situation in what he believed was a godless universe. We are alienated from ourselves and others and live an "absurd" existence, lacking ultimate meaning or goal. In the face of evil and the certainty of death, we must turn to the simple pleasures of nature and the physical life. Camus received the Nobel Prize for Literature in 1957 and then, three years later, at the height of his powers, died in a car wreck.

From Albert Camus, *The Myth of Sisyphus and Other Essays*, translated by Justin O'Brien (New York: Alfred A. Knopf, 1955). Copyright © 1955 by Alfred A. Knopf, Inc. Reprinted by permission of the publisher.

Read by millions, the following selection from *The Myth of Sisyphus* is one of the few philosophical works of the twentieth century to achieve popular recognition.

The gods had condemned Sisyphus to ceaselessly rolling a rock to the top of a mountain, whence the stone would fall back of its own weight. They had thought with some reason that there is no more dreadful punishment than futile and hopeless labor.

If one believes Homer, Sisyphus was the wisest and most prudent of mortals. According to another tradition, however, he was disposed to practice the profession of highwayman. I see no contradiction in this. Opinions differ as to the reasons why he became the futile laborer of the underworld. To begin with, he is accused of a certain levity in regard to the gods. He stole their secrets. Ægina, the daughter of Æsopus, was carried off by Jupiter. The father was shocked by that disappearance and complained to Sisyphus. He, who knew of the abduction, offered to tell about it on the condition that Æsopus would give water to the citadel of Corinth. To the celestial thunderbolts he preferred the benediction of water. He was punished for this in the underworld. Homer tells us also that Sisyphus had put Death in chains. Pluto could not endure the sight of his deserted, silent empire. He dispatched the god of war, who liberated Death from the hands of her conqueror.

It is said also that Sisyphus, being near to death, rashly wanted to test his wife's love. He ordered her to cast his unburied body into the middle of the public square. Sisyphus woke up in the underworld. And there, annoyed by an obedience so contrary to human love, he obtained from Pluto permission to return to earth in order to chastise his wife. But when he had seen again the face of this world, enjoyed the water and sun, warm stones and the sea, he no longer wanted to go back to the infernal darkness. Recalls, signs of anger, warnings were of no avail. Many years more he lived facing the curve of the gulf, the sparkling sea, and the smiles of earth. A decree of the gods was necessary. Mercury came and seized the impudent man by the collar and, snatching him from his joys, led him forcibly back to the underworld, where his rock was ready for him.

You have already grasped that Sisyphus is the absurd hero. He *is,* as much through his passions as through his torture. His scorn of the gods, his hatred of death, and his passion for life won him that unspeakable penalty in which the whole being is exerted toward accomplishing nothing. This is price that must be paid for the passions of this earth. Nothing is told us about Sisyphus in the underworld. Myths are made for the imagination to breathe life into them. As for this myth, one sees merely the whole effort of a body straining to raise the huge stone, to roll it and push it up a slope a hundred times over; one sees the face screwed up, the cheek tight against the stone, the shoulder bracing the clay-covered mass, the foot wedging it, the fresh start with arms outstretched, the wholly human security of two earth-clotted hands. At the very end of his long effort measured by skyless space and time without depth, the purpose is achieved. Then Sisyphus watches the stone rush down in a few moments toward that lower world whence he will have to push it up again toward the summit. He goes back down to the plain.

It is during that return, that pause, that Sisyphus interests me. A face that toils so close to stones is already stone itself! I see that man going back down with a heavy yet measured step toward the torment of which he will never know the end. That hour like a breathing-space which returns as surely as his suffering, that is the hour of consciousness. At each of those moments when he leaves the heights and gradually sinks toward the lairs of the gods, he is superior to his fate. He is stronger than his rock.

If this myth is tragic, that is because the hero is conscious. Where would his torture be, indeed, if at every step the hope of succeeding upheld him? The workman of today works every day in his life at the same tasks, and this fate is no less absurd. But it is tragic only at the rare moments when it becomes conscious. Sisyphus, proletarian of the gods, powerless and rebellious, knows the whole extent of his wretched condition: it is what he thinks of during his descent. The lucidity that was to constitute his torture at the same time crowns his victory. There is no fate that cannot be surmounted by scorn. . . .

If the descent is thus sometimes performed in sorrow, it can also take place in joy. This word is not too much. Again I fancy Sisyphus returning toward his rock, and the sorrow was in the beginning. When the images of earth cling too tightly to memory, when the call of happiness becomes too insistent, it happens that melancholy rises in man's heart: this is the rock's victory, this is the rock itself. The boundless grief is too heavy to bear. These are our nights of Gethsemane. But crushing truths perish from being acknowledged. Thus, Œdipus at the outset obeys fate without knowing it. But from the moment he knows, his tragedy begins. Yet at the same moment, blind and desperate, he realizes that the only bond linking him to the world is the cool hand of a girl. Then a tremendous remark rings out: "Despite so many ordeals, my advanced age and the nobility of my soul make me conclude that all is well." Sophocles' Œdipus, like Dostoevsky's Kirilov, thus gives the recipe for the absurd victory. Ancient wisdom confirms modern heroism.

One does not discover the absurd without being tempted to write a manual of happiness. "What! by such narrow ways—?" There is but one world, however. Happiness and the absurd are two sons of the same earth. They are inseparable. It would be a mistake to say that happiness necessarily springs from the absurd discovery. It happens as well that the feeling of the absurd springs from happiness. "I conclude that all is well," says Œdipus, and that remark is sacred. It echoes in the wild and limited universe of man. It teaches that all is not, has not been, exhausted. It drives out of this world a god who had come into it with dissatisfaction and a preference for futile sufferings. It makes of fate a human matter, which must be settled among men.

All Sisyphus's silent joy is contained therein. His fate belongs to him. His rock is his thing. Likewise, the absurd man, when he contemplates his torment, silences all the idols. In the universe suddenly restored to its silence, the myriad wondering little voices of the earth rise up. Unconscious, secret calls, invitations from all the faces, they are the necessary reverse and price of victory. There is no sun without shadow, and it is essential to know the night. The absurd man says yes and his effort will henceforth be unceasing. If there is a personal fate, there is no higher destiny, or at least there is but one which he concludes is inevitable and despicable. For the rest, he knows himself to be the master of his days. At that subtle moment when man glances backward over his life, Sisyphus returning toward his rock, in that slight pivoting he contemplates that series of unrelated actions which becomes his fate, created by him, combined under his memory's eye and soon sealed by his death. Thus, convinced of the wholly human origin of all that is human, a blind man eager to see who knows that the night has no end, he is still on the go. The rock is still rolling.

I leave Sisyphus at the foot of the mountain! One always finds one's burden again. But Sisyphus teaches the higher fidelity that negates the gods and raises rocks. He too concludes that all is well. This universe henceforth without a master seems to him neither sterile nor futile. Each atom of that stone, each mineral flake of that night-filled mountain, in itself forms a world. The struggle itself toward the heights is enough to fill a man's heart. One must imagine Sisyphus happy.

The Second Sex
SIMONE DE BEAUVOIR

Simone de Beauvoir (1908–1986), a leading French intellectual, profoundly influenced the feminist movement with her analysis of women's role in society. De Beauvoir met Jean-Paul Sartre while both were students at the Sorbonne in the late 1920s; they became lifelong companions and philosophical allies. While de Beauvoir's thought always maintained a strong existentialist bent, one of her most powerful contributions to modern philosophy lay in her analysis of women not simply as second-class citizens, but also as second-class beings. In works like her autobiographical *Memoirs of a Dutiful Daughter* and the philosophical analysis of *The Second Sex* (a selection follows), de Beauvoir argues that male culture has created an image of women as "Other" and not as fully authentic individuals. From the masculine point of view, women are viewed not as women, but as non-men. The human race is made up of males and other kinds of creatures who, unfortunately, are not males. Thus, in de Beauvoir's analysis, there are not two equal sexes, but a first sex and a second sex. Males are primary; females are secondary. The problem for women is not simply to achieve social equality, difficult enough, but also to achieve something far more profound, metaphysical equality.

For a long time I have hesitated to write a book on woman. The subject is irritating, especially to women; and it is not new. Enough ink has been spilled in the quarreling over feminism, now practically over, and perhaps we should say no more about it. It is still talked about, however, for the voluminous nonsense uttered during the last century seems to have done little to illuminate the problem. After all, is there a problem? And if so, what is it? Are there women, really? Most assuredly the theory of the eternal feminine still has its adherents who will whisper in your

From Simone de Beauvoir, *The Second Sex* (New York: Alfred A. Knopf, 1952). Copyright © 1952 and renewed 1980 by Alfred A. Knopf, Inc. Reprinted by permission of the publisher.

ear: "Even in Russia women still are *women*"; and other erudite persons—sometimes the very same—say with a sigh: "Woman is losing her way, woman is lost." One wonders if women still exist, if they will always exist, whether or not it is desirable that they should, what place they occupy in this world, what their place should be. "What has become of women?" was asked recently in an ephemeral magazine.

But first we must ask: what is a woman? *Tota mulier in utero,* says one, "woman is a womb." But in speaking of certain women, connoisseurs declare that they are not women, although they are equipped with a uterus like the rest. All agree in recognizing the fact that females exist in the human species; today as always they make up about one half of humanity. And yet we are told that femininity is in danger; we are exhorted to be women, remain women, become women. It would appear, then, that every female human being is not necessarily a woman; to be considered she must share in that mysterious and threatened reality known as femininity. Is this attribute something secreted by the ovaries? Or is it a Platonic essence, a product of the philosophic imagination? Is a rustling petticoat enough to bring it down to earth? Although some women try zealously to incarnate this essence, it is hardly patentable. It is frequently described in vague and dazzling terms that seem to have been borrowed from the vocabulary of the seers, and indeed in the times of St. Thomas it was considered an essence as certainly defined as the somniferous virtue of the poppy.

But conceptualism has lost ground. The biological and social sciences no longer admit the existence of unchangeably fixed entities that determine given characteristics, such as those ascribed to woman, the Jew, or the Negro. Science regards any characteristic as a reaction dependent in part upon a *situation*. If today femininity no longer exists, then it never existed. But does the word *woman*, then, have no specific content? This is stoutly affirmed by those who hold to the philosophy of the enlightenment, of rationalism, of nominalism; women, to them, are merely the human beings arbitrarily designated by the word *woman*. Many American women particularly are prepared to think that there is no longer any place for woman as such; if a backward individual still takes herself for a woman, her friends advise her to be psychoanalyzed and thus get rid of this obsession. In regard to a work, *Modern Woman: The Lost Sex*, which in other respects has its irritating features, Dorothy Parker has written:

"I cannot be just to books which treat of woman as woman. . . . My idea is that all of us, men as well as women, should be regarded as human beings." But nominalism is a rather inadequate doctrine, and the antifeminists have had no trouble in showing that women simply *are not* men. Surely woman is, like man, a human being; but such a declaration is abstract. The fact is that every concrete human being is always a singular, separate individual. To decline to accept such notions as the eternal feminine, the black soul, the Jewish character, is not to deny that Jews, Negroes, women exist today—this denial does not represent a liberation for those concerned, but rather a flight from reality. Some years ago a well-known woman writer refused to permit her portrait to appear in a series of photographs especially devoted to women writers; she wished to be counted among the men. But in order to gain this privilege she made use of her husband's influence! Women who assert that they are men lay claim none the less to masculine consideration and respect. I recall also a young Trotskyite standing on a platform at a boisterous meeting and getting ready to use her fists, in spite of her evident fragility. She was denying her feminine weakness; but it was for love of a militant male whose equal she wished to be. The attitude of defiance of many American women proves that they are haunted by a sense of their femininity. In truth, to go for a walk with one's eyes open is enough to demonstrate that humanity is divided into two classes of individuals whose clothes, faces, bodies, smiles, gaits, interests, and occupations are manifestly different. Perhaps these differences are superficial, perhaps they are destined to disappear. What is certain is that right now they do most obviously exist.

If her functioning as a female is not enough to define woman, if we decline also to explain her through "the eternal feminine," and if nevertheless we admit, provisionally, that women do exist, then we must face the question: what is a woman?

To state the question is, to me, to suggest, at once, a preliminary answer. The fact that I ask it is in itself significant. A man would never get the notion of writing a book on the peculiar situation of the human male.[1] But if I wish to define myself, I must first of all say: "I am a woman"; on this truth must be based all further discussion. A man never begins by presenting himself as an individual of a certain sex; it goes without saying that he is a man. The terms *masculine* and *feminine* are used symmetrically only as a matter of form, as on legal papers. In actuality the relation of the two sexes is not quite like that of two electrical poles, for man represents both the positive and the neutral, as is indicated by the common use of *man* to designate human beings in general; whereas woman represents only the negative, defined by limiting criteria, without reciprocity. In the midst of an abstract discussion it is vexing to hear a man say: "You think thus and so because you are a woman"; but I know that my only defense is to reply: "I think thus and so because it is true," thereby removing my subjective self from the argument. It would be out of the question to reply: "And you think the contrary because you are a man," for it is understood that the fact of being a man is no peculiarity. A man is in the right in being a man; it is the woman who is in the wrong. It amounts to this: just as for the ancients there was an absolute vertical with reference to which the oblique was defined, so there is an absolute human type, the masculine. Woman has ovaries, a uterus; these peculiarities imprison her in her subjectivity, circumscribe her within the limits of her own nature. It is often said that she thinks with her glands. Man superbly ignores the fact that his anatomy also includes glands, such as the testicles, and that they secrete hormones. He thinks of his body as a direct and normal connection with the world, which he believes he apprehends objectively, whereas he regards the body of woman as a hindrance, a prison, weighed down by everything peculiar to it. "The female is a female by virtue of a certain *lack* of qualities," said Aristotle; "we should regard the female nature as afflicted with a natural defectiveness." And St. Thomas for his part pronounced woman to be an "imperfect man," an "incidental" being. This is symbolized in Genesis where Eve is depicted as made from what Bossuet called "a supernumerary bone" of Adam.

Thus humanity is male and man defines woman not in herself but as relative to him; she is not regarded as an autonomous being. Michelet writes: "Woman, the relative being. . . ." And Benda is most positive in his *Rapport d'Uriel:* "The body of man makes sense in itself quite apart from that of woman, whereas the latter seems wanting in significance by itself. . . . Man can think of himself without woman. She cannot think of herself without man." And she is simply what man decrees; thus she is called "the sex," by which is meant that she appears essentially to the male as a sexual being. For him she is sex—absolute sex, no less. She is defined and differentiated with reference to man and not with reference to her; she is the incidental, the inessential as opposed to the essential. He is the Subject, he is the Absolute—she is the Other.

NOTE

1. The Kinsey Report [Alfred C. Kinsey and others: *Sexual Behavior in the Human Male* (W. B. Saunders Co., 1948)] is no exception, for it is limited to describing the sexual characteristics of American men, which is quite a different matter.

Do We Survive Death?
BERTRAND RUSSELL

Bertrand Russell (1872–1970), one of the most important English philosophers of the twentieth century, also made important contributions to mathematics, science, education, history, religion, and politics. *Principia Mathematica* (1910–1913), one of his first major works, attempted to prove that all mathematics could be deduced from obviously true principles. He attacked Russian Communism in *The Theory and Practice of Bolshevism* (1920) and set forth his atheistic views in *Why I Am Not a Christian* (1927). Russell's *Human Knowledge, Its Scope and Limits* (1948) links him to the long line of British empiricists that began with Locke. Russell received the Nobel Prize for Literature in 1950.

From Bertrand Russell, "Do We Survive Death?" in *Why I Am Not a Christian,* ed. Paul Edwards (New York: Simon & Schuster, 1957).

A remarkably bold and colorful personality, Russell's pacifistic opposition to World War I cost him his teaching position at Trinity College in 1916 and landed him in jail for six months in 1918; after World War II he engaged in civil disobedience protesting nuclear weapons; in 1967, Russell joined Jean-Paul Sartre in organizing the Vietnam War Crimes Tribunal to investigate U.S. military actions in Vietnam. In the following selection, "Do We Survive Death?"—a chapter from *Why I Am Not a Christian*—Russell makes a strong and typically well-written argument that neither the mind, the soul, nor any other aspect of human personality survives death.

Before we can profitably discuss whether we shall continue to exist after death, it is well to be clear as to the sense in which a man is the same person as he was yesterday. Philosophers used to think that there were definite substances, the soul and the body, that each lasted on from day to day, that a soul, once created, continued to exist throughout all future time, whereas a body ceased temporarily from death till the resurrection of the body.

The part of this doctrine which concerns the present life is pretty certainly false. The matter of the body is continually changing by processes of nutriment and wastage. Even if it were not, atoms in physics are no longer supposed to have continuous existence; there is no sense in saying: this is the same atom as the one that existed a few minutes ago. The continuity of a human body is a matter of appearance and behavior, not of substance.

The same thing applies to the mind. We think and feel and act, but there is not, in addition to thoughts and feelings and actions, a bare entity, the mind or the soul, which does or suffers these occurrences. The mental continuity of a person is a continuity of habit and memory: there was yesterday one person whose feelings I can remember, and that person I regard as myself of yesterday; but, in fact, myself of yesterday was only certain mental occurrences which are now remembered and are regarded as part of the person who now recollects them. All that constitutes a person is a series of experiences connected by memory and by certain similarities of the sort we call habit.

If, therefore, we are to believe that a person survives death, we must believe that the memories and habits which constitute the person will continue to be exhibited in a new set of occurrences.

No one can prove that this will not happen. But it is easy to see that it is very unlikely. Our memories and habits are bound up with the structure of the brain, in much the same way in which a river is connected with the riverbed. The water in the river is always changing, but it keeps to the same course because previous rains have worn a channel. In like manner, previous events have worn a channel in the brain, and our thoughts flow along this channel. This is the cause of memory and mental habits. But the brain, as a structure, is dissolved at death, and memory therefore may be expected to be also dissolved. There is no more reason to think otherwise than to expect a river to persist in its old course after an earthquake has raised a mountain where a valley used to be.

All memory, and therefore (one may say) all minds, depend upon a property which is very noticeable in certain kinds of material structures but exists little if at all in other kinds. This is the property of forming habits as a result of frequent similar occurrences. For example: a bright light makes the pupils of the eyes contract; and if you repeatedly flash a light in a man's eyes and beat a gong at the same time, the gong alone will, in the end, cause his pupils to contract. This is a fact about the brain and nervous system—that is to say, about a certain material structure. It will be found that exactly similar facts explain our response to language and our use of it, our memories and the emotions they arouse, our moral or immoral habits of behavior, and indeed everything that constitutes our mental personality, except the part determined by heredity. The part determined by heredity is handed on to our posterity but cannot, in the individual, survive the disintegration of the body. Thus both the hereditary and the acquired parts of a personality are, so far as our experience goes, bound up with the characteristics of certain bodily structures. We all know that memory may be obliterated by an injury to the brain, that a virtuous person may be rendered vicious by encephalitis lethargica, and that a clever child can be turned into an idiot by lack of iodine. In view of such familiar facts, it seems scarcely probable that the mind survives the total destruction of brain structure which occurs at death.

It is not rational arguments but emotions that cause belief in a future life.

The most important of these emotions is fear of death, which is instinctive and biologically useful. If we genuinely and wholeheartedly believed in the future life, we should cease completely to fear death. The effects would be curious, and probably such as most of us would deplore. But our human and subhuman ancestors have fought and exterminated their enemies throughout many geological ages and have profited by courage; it is therefore an advantage to the victors in the struggle for life to be able, on occasion, to overcome the natural fear of death. Among animals and savages, instinctive pugnacity suffices for this purpose; but at a certain stage of development, as the Mohammedans first proved, belief in Paradise has considerable military value as reinforcing natural pugnacity. We should therefore admit that militarists are wise encouraging the belief in immortality, always supposing that this belief does not become so profound as to produce indifference to the affairs of the world.

Another emotion which encourages the belief in survival is admiration of the excellence of man. As the Bishop of Birmingham says, "His mind is a far finer instrument than anything that had appeared earlier—he knows right and wrong. He can build Westminster Abbey. He can make an airplane. He can calculate the distance of the sun. . . . Shall, then, man at death perish utterly? Does that incomparable instrument, his mind, vanish when life ceases?"

The Bishop proceeds to argue that "the universe has been shaped and is governed by an intelligent purpose," and that it would have been unintelligent, having made man, to let him perish.

To this argument there are many answers. In the first place, it has been found, in the scientific investigation of nature, that the intrusion of moral or aesthetic values has always been an obstacle to discovery. It used to be thought that the heavenly bodies must move in circles because the circle is the most perfect curve, that species must be immutable because God would only create what was perfect and what therefore stood in no need of improvement, that it was useless to combat epidemics except by repentance because they were sent as a punishment for sin, and so on. It has been found, however, that, so far as we can discover, nature is indifferent to our values and can only be understood by ignoring our notions of good and bad. The Universe may have a purpose, but nothing that we know suggests that, if so, this purpose has any similarity to ours.

Nor is there in this anything surprising. Dr. Barnes tells us that man "knows right and wrong." But, in fact, as anthropology shows, men's views of right and wrong have varied to such an extent that no single item has been permanent. We cannot say, therefore, that man knows right and wrong, but only that some men do. Which men? Nietzsche argued in favor of an ethic profoundly different from Christ's, and some powerful governments have accepted his teaching. If knowledge of right and wrong is to be an argument for immortality, we must first settle where to believe Christ or Nietzsche, and then argue that Christians are immoral, but Hitler and Mussolini are not, or vice versa. The decision will obviously be made on the battlefield, not in the study. Those who have the best poison gas will have the ethic of the future and will therefore be the immortal ones.

Our feelings and beliefs on the subject of good and evil are, like everything else about us, natural facts, developed in the struggle for existence and not having any divine or supernatural origin. In one of Aesop's fables, a lion is shown pictures of huntsmen catching lions and remarks that, if he had painted them, they would have shown lions catching huntsmen. Man, says Dr Barnes, is a fine fellow because he can make airplanes. A little while ago there was a popular song about the cleverness of flies in walking upside down on the ceiling, with the chorus: "Could Lloyd George do it? Could Mr. Baldwin do it? Could Ramsay Mac do it? Why, *no*." On this basis a very telling argument could be constructed by a theologically-minded fly, which no doubt the other flies would find most convincing.

Moreover, it is only when we think abstractly that we have such a high opinion of man. Of men in the concrete, most of us think the vast majority very bad. Civilized states spend more than half their revenue on killing each other's citizens. Consider the long history of the activities inspired by moral fervor: human sacrifices, persecutions of heretics, witch-hunts, pogroms leading up to wholesale extermination by poison gases, which one at least of Barnes's episcopal colleagues must be supposed to favor, since he holds pacifism to be un-Christian. Are these abominations, and the ethical doctrines by which they are prompted, really evidence of an intelligent Creator? And can we really wish that the men who practiced them should live forever? The world in which we live can be understood as a result of muddle and accident; but if it is the outcome of deliberate purpose, the purpose must have been that of a fiend. For my part, I find accident a less painful and more plausible hypothesis.

A Dialogue on Wittgenstein's Work
BRYAN MAGEE AND JOHN SEARLE

Ludwig Wittgenstein (1889–1951) attempted to solve all the traditional problems of philosophy by exploring the nature of language. Born into a wealthy Austrian family, Wittgenstein attended Cambridge University, where he was a student of Bertrand Russell's. Wittgenstein's first major work, *Tractatus Logico-Philosophicus*, only seventy-five pages long, argued that the problems of philosophy arose from a misunderstanding of the nature of language. Language "pictures" reality, and anything that cannot be pictured is nonsense. In Wittgenstein's view, philosophical questions like "Does God exist?" or "What is the purpose of life?" are not genuine questions because they stretch language beyond what can be meaningfully asked. Thus, Wittgenstein held that the problems of philosophy, under his approach, are not solved but "dissolved."

In 1919, Wittgenstein gave away his inheritance to work as an elementary school teacher. In 1929 he returned to Cambridge, where he accepted a position as lecturer in philosophy. There Wittgenstein completed *Philosophical Investigations*, which presented an analysis of language radically different from his earlier work. Briefly put, in *Philosophical Investigations*, Wittgenstein abandons his picture theory of language and holds that meaning is determined by how a concept participates in a particular "language game." Instead of a general theory of the limitations of language that dissolves the problems of philosophy, Wittgenstein presents an analysis of the ways language games determine the meaning and limits of philosophical concepts.

Wittgenstein's thought is dense and, even for professional philosophers, difficult to unravel. The following dialogue, first broadcast on the BBC in 1987, between two well-known philosophers, presents key aspects of Wittgenstein's thought. Bryan Magee, the host, is Honorary Senior Research Fellow in the History of Ideas at King's College, University of London; John Searle is a philosophy professor at the University of California, Berkeley.

SEARLE: I think the key to understanding the *Tractatus* is the picture theory of meaning. Wittgenstein

From *The Great Philosophers* by Bryan Magee with the permission of BBC Worldwide Limited. Copyright © Bryan Magee.

believed that if language is to represent reality, if sentences are to represent states of affairs, then there has to be something in common between the sentence and the state of affairs. Since the sentence and the state of affairs it represents have to have a common structure, in that sense the sentence is like a picture of a possible fact. Just as the elements in a picture correspond to objects in the world, and the arrangement of elements in a picture corresponds to a possible arrangement of objects in reality, so sentences contain names which correspond to objects in the world; and the arrangement of names in the sentence corresponds to a possible arrangement of objects in the world.

Now, this idea that sentences are really a disguised form of a picture gives him a remarkable kind of metaphysical lever. *It enables him to read off the structure of reality from the structure of language.* And the reason is that the structure of reality has to determine the structure of language. Unless language mirrors reality in some way, it would be impossible for sentences to mean.

MAGEE: So the crucial point here is that we are able to talk about reality not just because names denote but also because sentences picture. For discourse to mirror the world it is not enough for there to be words that stand for things. For us to be able to say how things are we need also to be able to put words in a particular relation to one another which pictures the relation in which things in the world stand to one another. Thus it is the mirroring of one *structure* by another which is the real key to the possibility of meaningful discourse about the world in language. But now this same fact can be read in the other direction, so to speak. Since we know that for meaningful discourse to be possible the structure of language must mirror the structure of the world, and since we know that meaningful discourse is possible, we are in a position to find out about the structure of the world by analysing the structure of language.

SEARLE: Right. Every meaningful sentence corresponds to a possible fact; and every true sentence corresponds to an actual fact. So we can learn about the *structure* of reality from sentences, independently of whether the sentence is true or false, because the mere meaningfulness of the sentence determines that it must correspond to a possible state of affairs in the world.

But it is important to emphasise that Wittgenstein was not talking about the surface features of sentences in ordinary language. He was not talking about the visible or audible structure of the sentences that you and I are now using to talk to each other. He thought that these surface, visible or audible, features of ordinary language sentences actually concealed the underlying logical structure of the sentence. If we took ordinary sentences and did a logical analysis of how they mean, we could then get down to the ground-floor sentences which constitute the underlying meaningful structures hidden by the ordinary sentences. We would get down to what he calls "the elementary sentences," and in the elementary sentences we would find the strict picturing relationship between the structure of the sentence and the structure of the fact.

He inherits from Frege the idea that the fundamental unit of meaning isn't the word, but rather the sentence. The word only functions, the word only has a meaning, in the context of a sentence. And, as you suggested earlier, it's because the concatenation of words in the sentence itself constitutes a fact that the sentence is able to picture the structure of facts in the world.

MAGEE: I think people will have little immediate difficulty in seeing how a sentence may mirror a fact when the fact exists. But what when I am asserting that a fact does not exist? If I say, "There is a cat on the mat"—okay, people will see that this sentence may picture a state (or possible state) of affairs. But what if I say, "There is not a cat on the mat"? We all know what the sentence means, but what state of affairs can be said to picture—*picture*, mind you? What would a real picture of the absence of a cat on a mat be like? Would it be different from a picture of the absence of a dog?

SEARLE: Wittgenstein thought that words like "not" and "and" and "or" and "if," the so-called logical constants, were not actually part of the picture relationship. He says: "My fundamental thought is that the logical constants do not represent." He thought of these logical words as just ways we have of stringing pictures together, but they aren't them-

selves part of any picture. And that's not so unrealistic if you think about it. For example, across the street from my house in Berkeley is a small park, and posted in the park is a picture of a dog with a red line drawn through it. Now notice that we quite effortlessly understand the red line in a different way from the way we understand the picture of the dog. We know that the picture is not supposed to depict dogs that have a red stripe painted on them. Rather, the line is the negation sign. The whole sign means "No Dogs." So the sign in the park is really a Wittgensteinian sort of picture, at least in the sense that the "not" symbol is used to operate on the picture but is not itself part of the picture.

MAGEE: So we can expand our first formulation by saying that, in the view of the young Wittgenstein, meaningful discourse about the world can be analysed into elementary statements which picture possible states of affairs, and that these elementary statements are either linked together, or postulated as stating possibilities, or set off against each other as stating alternatives, or negated, or whatever it may be, by the so-called logical constants, which are not themselves pictorial.

SEARLE: Yes. Right.

MAGEE: In my introduction to our discussion I said that Wittgenstein was concerned throughout his career to demarcate talk that made sense from talk that did not make sense. How did he draw this line of demarcation in his earlier philosophy?

SEARLE: In his earlier philosophy, in the *Tractatus*, Wittgenstein thought that the only language which strictly speaking makes any sense is fact-stating language. Now, unlike the logical positivists, he didn't relish this conclusion. He didn't think it was such a wonderful result. On the contrary, he thought that it had the consequence that the really important things in life were unsayable, were unstatable. He thought that ethics, religion and aesthetics, for example, were all in the realm of the unsayable. And he once said about the *Tractatus* that the really important part of the book is the part that is left out, the part that is not there at all. But according to the account of meaning given in the *Tractatus* there is a strict demarcation between meaningful or fact-stating language and the other parts of language which are not used to state actual or possible facts in the world and which are therefore, strictly speaking, nonsense. These parts of language try to say something about the important questions of life, but they fail, because what they are trying to say is unsayable.

MAGEE: This is in keeping with the ordinary view commonly held by people who are not philosophers that although ethics, religion and the arts are of fundamental significance in life, language is completely inadequate to say what it is they convey, or are about, or even are.

SEARLE: They are fundamental; but our efforts to discuss them are meaningless, at least as far as the theory of meaning in the *Tractatus* is concerned. And it isn't simply that we can't do them justice; rather, our attempt to do them justice is itself meaningless; we can't say anything meaningful about them at all.

MAGEE: You've said that the key to understanding the early Wittgenstein is the picture theory of meaning. In what way does the later Wittgenstein depart from it?

SEARLE: Though Wittgenstein's ideas are very complex, there is actually a rather simple answer to that question. In his later work, he abandoned the picture theory of meaning in favour of a use or tool conception of meaning. He urges us to think of words as tools, think of sentences as instruments. To get a correct conception of language we need simply to look at how it functions in real life, we need to look at what people do with words. He says, "For a *large* class of cases—though not for all—in which we employ the word 'meaning' it can be defined thus: the meaning of a word is its use in the language."

His early view had the consequence that the structure of the real world determines the structure of language. But in his later work, it is, in a sense, the other way round. In the *Philosophical Investigations*, the structure of our language determines the way we think of the real world. It determines what we count as one object or two objects or the same object; it determines what we count as an object at all. We can't discuss the world and we can't even think of the world independently of some conceptual apparatus that we can use for that purpose. And, of course, the apparatus is provided by language.

Now this gives him a completely different conception of the role of language in our lives. In the early work, fact-stating discourse is really all the meaningful discourse there is. But in the later work,

it turns out that fact-stating discourse is just one type of discourse among many other types, just one type of "language game" along with, strictly speaking, an indefinite number of other types of language game. In his later work, as a consequence of emphasising the use of language, Wittgenstein is constantly calling our attention to the multiplicity, the variety, that we find in uses of language.

MAGEE: It's very striking, this shift of the master-metaphor from language as a picture to language as a tool. Now it's in the nature of a picture that it pictures one particular state of affairs, but it's in the nature of a tool that it can be *used for a number of different tasks*. This aspect of the difference was of great importance to Wittgenstein, wasn't it?

SEARLE: Yes. Wittgenstein is always anxious to insist in the *Investigations* that language is indefinitely extendable, and there isn't any single essence that binds all uses of language together. There isn't any single feature that runs through all of language that constitutes the essence of language. And indeed, for particular words, there needn't even be any particular essence that constitutes the definition of that word. He thinks of many words as having only a "family resemblance" among their various uses. He gives as an example the word "game." And he asks us, what, if anything, do all games have in common? And here, as always, he keeps insisting: Don't just think that they must all have some one thing in common, but rather, look and see what you can find. And then he says that, if you consider the enormous variety of different kinds of games—board games, Olympic games, gambling games, ball games, and so on—what you find is that there isn't any single essence of gamehood, there isn't any single thing that all games have in common, but rather there are a series of crisscrossing and overlapping similarities. It is this phenomenon which he calls "family resemblance."

MAGEE: This point about "don't just take it for granted, but *think*" is always very important with Wittgenstein. Taking your example, one's first reaction is to say, "Oh but it's obvious, all games are diversions of one sort or another." But then one reflects that American football, in which players suffer appalling injuries for huge sums of money, is not a diversion. If you say, "Well it's a diversion for the spectators," that won't do, because most of the various games that are actually played in the world probably never have spectators. And would American football be played without spectators not be a game? If you say, "Well, all games are competitive," that isn't true, because there are games for one person, such as patience and solitaire. And if you say, "Well at least all games are leisure activities, a change from work," that isn't true either, because there are thousands of professionals who play games for a living. And so on and so forth—Wittgenstein's method requires one to work one's way painstakingly through all the examples one can think of; and although the work is, of its nature, detailed, it also calls for imagination, the ability to think of the un-obvious. Wittgenstein himself showed such ingenuity in his use of examples that many of them have become part of the common currency of philosophy. A prolonged analysis of the concept of a game, which we haven't time actually to carry out in this discussion, would show, perhaps surprisingly, that there is no one thing that all games have in common *by virtue of which they are games.* They have certain features in common with innumerable other human activities—for instance, that they are characteristically learnt from others, and characteristically rule-governed—but of course *these* features are not enough to make something a game. And that means that there is no one thing that the word "game" stands for.

SEARLE: Right. Now it might seem as if Wittgenstein is just reminding us of certain obvious points here, that what he is saying is all rather commonsensical. And to a certain extent, that's right. But it is also important to remember that he is militating against a very powerful philosophical tradition. He is militating against a tradition that goes back as far as Plato and Aristotle. He is fighting, first, against his earlier theory that words get their meanings by standing for objects, and secondly, he is fighting against an even older tradition that says that words get their meanings by being associated with ideas in the mind. And third, he is also fighting against a tradition according to which in order for a word to have a meaning, there must be some essence which that word expresses. According to that view, if we can call a whole lot of different things games, it can only be because they have some essential feature of gamehood in common. So, the interest of his remarks about language derives from the radical attack he is making on the philosophical tradition.

Language, Truth and Logic

A. J. AYER

A. J. Ayer (1910–1989), a prominent modern English philosopher, followed Berkeley, Russell, Wittgenstein, and other British empiricists in holding that all knowledge is sense-based. In Ayer's view, metaphysical and ethical statements cannot be statements of fact, but only of emotion. Thus, a remark like "God exists" is meaningful only when rephrased as "I believe God exists" or "I have the feeling that God exists." Ayer comes to this position by a careful analysis of language and what it can and cannot achieve. The follow-

ing selection from *Language, Truth and Logic,* one of his most influential works, elaborates his analysis of the relationship between language and some of the traditional problems of metaphysics.

The Elimination of Metaphysics

The traditional disputes of philosophers are, for the most part, as unwarranted as they are unfruitful. The surest way to end them is to establish beyond question what should be the purpose and method of a philosophical enquiry. And this is by no means so difficult

From A. J. Ayer, *Language, Truth and Logic* (New York: Dover Publications, 1952). Reprinted by permission of Dover Publications, Inc.

a task as the history of philosophy would lead one to suppose. For if there are any questions which science leaves it to philosophy to answer, a straighforward process of elimination must lead to their discovery.

We may begin by criticising the metaphysical thesis that philosophy affords us knowledge of a reality transcending the world of science and common sense. . . .

One way of attacking a metaphysician who claimed to have knowledge of a reality which transcended the phenomenal world would be to enquire from what premises his propositions were deduced. Must he not begin, as other men do, with the evidence of his senses? And if so, what valid process of reasoning can possibly lead him to the conception of a transcendent reality? Surely from empirical premises nothing whatsoever concerning the properties, or even the existence, of anything super-empirical can legitimately be inferred. But this objection would be met by a denial on the part of the metaphysician that his assertions were ultimately based on the evidence of his senses. He would say that he was endowed with a faculty of intellectual intuition which enabled him to know facts that could not be known through a sense-experience. And even if it could be shown that he was relying on empirical premises, and that his venture into a non-empirical world was therefore logically unjustified, it would not follow that the assertions which he made concerning this non-empirical world could not be true. For the fact that a conclusion does not follow from its putative premise is not sufficient to show that it is false. Consequently one cannot overthrow a system of transcendent metaphysics merely by criticising the way in which it comes into being. What is required is rather a criticism of the nature of the actual statements which comprise it. And this is the line of argument which we shall, in fact, pursue. For we shall maintain that no statement which refers to a "reality" transcending the limits of all possible sense-experience can possibly have any literal significance; from which it must follow that the labours of those who have striven to describe such a reality have all been devoted to the production of nonsense.

It may be suggested that this is a proposition which has already been proved by Kant. But although Kant also condemned transcendent metaphysics, he did so on different grounds. For he said that the human understanding was so constituted that it lost itself in contradictions when it ventured out beyond the limits of possible experience and attempted to deal with things in themselves. And thus he made the impossibility of a transcendent metaphysic not, as we do, a matter of logic, but a matter of fact. He asserted, not that our minds could not conceivably have had the power of penetrating beyond the phenomenal world, but merely that they were in fact devoid of it. And this leads the critic to ask how, if it is possible to know only what lies within the bounds of sense-experience, the author can be justified in asserting that real things do exist beyond, and how he can tell what are the boundaries beyond which the human understanding may not venture, unless he succeeds in passing them himself. As Wittgenstein says, "in order to draw a limit to thinking, we should have to think both sides of this limit,"[1] a truth to which Bradley gives a special twist in maintaining that the man who is ready to prove that metaphysics is impossible is a brother metaphysician with a rival theory of his own.[2]

Whatever force these objections may have against the Kantian doctrine, they have none whatsoever against the thesis that I am about to set forth. It cannot here be said that the author is himself overstepping the barrier he maintains to be impassable. For the fruitlessness of attempting to transcend the limits of possible sense-experience will be deduced, not from a psychological hypothesis concerning the actual constitution of the human mind, but from the rule which determines the literal significance of language. Our charge against the metaphysician is not that he attempts to employ the understanding in a field where it cannot profitably venture, but that he produces sentences which fail to conform to the conditions under which alone a sentence can be literally significant. Nor are we ourselves obliged to talk nonsense in order to show that all sentences of a certain type are necessarily devoid of literal significance. We need only formulate the criterion which enables us to test whether a sentence expresses a genuine proposition about a matter of fact, and then point out that the sentences under consideration fail to satisfy it. And this we shall now proceed to do. We shall first of all formulate the criterion in somewhat vague terms, and then give the explanations which are necessary to render it precise.

The criterion which we use to test the genuineness of apparent statements of fact is the criterion of verifiability. We say that a sentence is factually significant to any given person, if, and only if, he knows how to verify the proposition which it purports to express—that is, if he knows what observations would lead him, under certain conditions, to accept the proposition as being true, or reject it as being false. If, on the other hand, the putative proposition is of such a character that the assumption of its truth, or falsehood, is consistent with any assumption whatsoever concerning the nature of his future experience, then, as far as he is concerned, it is, if not a tautology, a mere pseudo-proposition. The sentence expressing it may be emotionally significant to him; but it is not literally significant. And with regard to questions the procedure is the same. We enquire in every case what observations would lead us to answer the question, one way or the other; and, if none can be discovered, we must conclude that the sentence under consideration does not, as far as we are concerned, express a genuine question, however strongly its grammatical appearance may suggest that it does.

As the adoption of this procedure is an essential factor in the argument of this book, it needs to be examined in detail.

In the first place, it is necessary to draw a distinction between practical verifiability, and verifiability in principle. Plainly we all understand, in many cases believe, propositions which we have not in fact taken steps to verify. Many of these are propositions which we could verify if we took enough trouble. But there remain a number of significant propositions, concerning matters of fact, which we could not verify even if we chose; simply because we lack the practical means of placing ourselves in the situation where the relevant observations could be made. A simple and familiar example of such a proposition is the proposition that there are mountains on the farther side of the moon.[3] No rocket has yet been invented which would enable me to go and look at the farther side of the moon, so that I am unable to decide the matter by actual observation. But I do know what observations would decide it for me, if, as is theoretically conceivable, I were once in a position to make them. And therefore I say that the proposition is verifiable in principle, if not in practice, and is accordingly significant. On the other hand, such a metaphysical pseudo-proposition as "the Absolute enters into, but is itself incapable of, evolution and progress,"[4] is not even in principle verifiable. For one cannot conceive of an observation which would enable one to determine whether the Absolute did, or did not, enter into evolution and progress. Of course it is possible that the author of such a remark is using English words in a way in which they are not commonly used by English-speaking people, and that he does, in fact, intend to assert something which could be empirically verified. But until he makes us understand how the proposition that he wishes to express would be verified, he fails to communicate anything to us. And if he admits, as I think the author of the remark in question would have admitted, that his words were not intended to express either a tautology or a proposition which was capable, at least in principle, of being verified, then it follows that he has made an utterance which has no literal significance even for himself.

A further distinction which we must make is the distinction between the "strong" and the "weak" sense of the term "verifiable." A proposition is said to be verifiable, in the strong sense of the term, if, and only if, its truth could be conclusively established in experience. But it is verifiable, in the weak sense, if it is possible for experience to render it probable. In which sense are we using the term when we say that a putative proposition is genuine only if it is verifiable?

It seems to me that if we adopt conclusive verifiability as our criterion of significance, as some positivists have proposed,[5] our argument will prove too much. Consider, for example, the case of general propositions of law—such propositions, namely, as "arsenic is poisonous"; "all men are mortal"; "a body tends to expand when it is heated." It is of the very nature of these propositions that their truth cannot be established with certainty by any finite series of observations. But if it is recognised that such general propositions of law are designed to cover an infinite number of cases, then it must be admitted that they cannot, even in principle, be verified conclusively. And then, if we adopt conclusive verifiability as our criterion of significance, we are logically obliged to treat these general propositions of law in the same fashion as we treat the statements of the metaphysician.

In face of this difficulty, some positivists[6] have adopted the heroic course of saying that these general propositions are indeed pieces of nonsense, albeit an essentially important type of nonsense. But here the introduction of the term "important" is simply an attempt to hedge. It serves only to mark the authors' recognition that their view is somewhat too paradoxical, without in any way removing the paradox. Besides, the difficulty is not confined to the case of general propositions of law, though it is there revealed most plainly. It is hardly less obvious in the case of propositions about the remote past. For it must surely be admitted that, however strong the evidence in favour of historical statements may be, their truth can never become more than highly probable. And to maintain that they also constituted an important, or unimportant, type of nonsense would be unplausible, to say the very least. Indeed, it will be our contention that no proposition, other than a tautology, can possibly be anything more than a probable hypothesis. And if this is correct, the principle that a sentence can be factually significant only if it expresses what is conclusively verifiable is self-stultifying as a criterion of significance. For it leads to the conclusion that it is impossible to make a significant statement of fact at all.

Nor can we accept the suggestion that a sentence should be allowed to be factually significant if, and only if, it expresses something which is definitely confutable by experience.[7] Those who adopt this course assume that, although no finite series of observations is ever sufficient to establish the truth of a hypothesis beyond all possibility of doubt, there are crucial cases in which a single observation, or series of observations, can definitely confute it. But, as we shall show later on, this assumption is false. A hypothesis cannot be conclusively confuted any more than it can be conclusively verified. For when we take the occurrence of certain observations as proof that a given hypothesis is false, we presuppose the existence of certain conditions. And though, in any given case, it may be extremely improbable that this assumption is false, it is not logically impossible. We shall see that there need be no self-contradiction in holding that some of the relevant circumstances are other than we have taken them to be, and consequently that the hypothesis has not really broken down. And if it is not the case that any hypothesis can be definitely confuted, we cannot hold that the genuineness of a proposition depends on the possibility of its definite confutation.

Accordingly, we fall back on the weaker sense of verification. We say that the question that must be asked about any putative statement of fact is not, Would any observations make its truth or falsehood logically certain? but simply, Would any observations be relevant to the determination of its truth or falsehood? And it is only if a negative answer is given to this second question that we conclude that the statement under consideration is nonsensical. . . .

This criterion seems liberal enough. In contrast to the principle of conclusive verifiability, it clearly does not deny significance to general propositions or to propositions about the past. Let us see what kinds of assertion it rules out.

A good example of this kind of utterance that is condemned by our criterion as being not even false but nonsensical would be the assertion that the world of sense-experience was altogether unreal. It must, of course, be admitted that our senses do sometimes deceive us. We may, as the result of having certain sensations, expect certain other sensations to be obtainable which are, in fact, not obtainable. But, in all such cases, it is further sense-experience that informs us of the mistakes that arise out of sense-experience. We say that the senses sometimes deceive us, just because the expectations to which our sense-experiences give rise do not always accord with what we subsequently experience. That is, we rely on our senses to substantiate or confute the judgements which are based on our sensations. And therefore the fact that our perceptual judgements are sometimes found to be erroneous has not the slightest tendency to show that the world of sense-expectation is unreal. And, indeed, it is plain that no conceivable observation, or series of observations, could have any tendency to show that the world revealed to us by sense-experience was unreal. Consequently, anyone who condemns the sensible world as a world of mere appearance, as opposed to reality, is saying something which, according to our criterion of significance, is literally nonsensical.

An example of a controversy which the application of our criterion obliges us to condemn as fictitious is provided by those who dispute concerning the number of substances that there are in the world. For it is admitted both by monists, who maintain that reality is one substance, and by pluralists, who maintain that reality is many, that it is impossible to imagine any empirical situation which would be relevant to the solution of their dispute. But if we are told that no possible observation could give any probability either to the assertion that reality was one substance or to the assertion that it was many, then we must conclude that neither assertion is significant. . . .

A similar treatment must be accorded to the controversy between realists and idealists, in its metaphysical aspect. A simple illustration, which I have made use of in a similar argument elsewhere,[8] will help to demonstrate this. Let us suppose that a picture is discovered and the suggestion made that it was painted by Goya. There is a definite procedure for dealing with such a question. The experts examine the picture to see in what way it resembles the accredited works of Goya, and to see if it bears any marks which are characteristic of a forgery; they look up contemporary records for evidence of the existence of such a picture, and so on. In the end, they may still disagree, but each one knows what empirical evidence would go to confirm or discredit his opinion. Suppose, now, that these men have studied philosophy, and some of them proceed to maintain that this picture is a set of ideas in the perceiver's mind, or in God's mind, others that it is objectively real. What possible experience could any of them have which would be relevant to the solution of this dispute one way or the other? In the ordinary sense of the term "real," in which it is opposed to "illusory," the reality of the picture is not in doubt. The disputants have satisfied themselves that the picture is real, in this sense, by obtaining a correlated series of sensations of sight and sensations of touch. Is there any similar process by which they could discover whether the picture was real, in the sense in which the term "real" is opposed to "ideal"? Clearly there is none. But, if that is so, the problem is fictitious according to our criterion.

NOTES

1. *Tractatus Logico-Philosophicus*, Preface.
2. Bradley, *Appearance and Reality*, 2nd ed., p. 1.
3. This example has been used by Professor Schlick to illustrate the same point.
4. A remark taken at random from *Appearance and Reality*, by F. H. Bradley.
5. e.g. M. Schlick, "Positivismus und Realismus," *Erkenntnis*, Vol. I, 1930. F. Waismann, "Logische Analyse des Warscheinlichkeitsbegriffs," *Erkenntnis*, Vol. I, 1930.
6. e.g. M. Schlick, "Die Kausalität in der gegenwärtigen Physik," *Naturwissenschaft*, Vol. 19, 1931.
7. This has been proposed by Karl Popper in his *Logik der Forschung*.
8. Vide, "Demonstration of the Impossibility of Metaphysics," *Mind*, 1934, p. 339.

What Is Pragmatism?

WILLIAM JAMES

William James (1842–1910), American philosopher and psychologist, was one of the founders of pragmatism, a philosophical movement based upon empirical principles. James, the brother of novelist Henry James, received a medical degree from Harvard in 1869, but did not practice as a doctor. In 1872, he accepted a teaching position at Harvard in physiology, but went on, several years later, to teach psychology and philosophy. His work *The Principles of Psychology* (1890) achieved wide critical and popular success. In James's opinion, emotions are produced by bodily actions, not vice versa. Thus, we feel sadness because we cry; we feel happy because we laugh. In *Pragmatism* (1907) James developed the view that the value of a philosophical theory lay in its "cash value," its usefulness in human actions. Truths are not absolute, but are only helpful guidelines that may change as the universe and human knowledge evolves. In the following selection from *What Is Pragmatism?* James sketches out the main features of pragmatism and then employs the pragmatic method in an analysis of substance (matter).

From William James, *Pragmatism and other Essays* (New York: Washington Square Press, 1963).

The Meaning of Pragmatism

A glance at the history of the idea will show you still better what pragmatism means. The term is derived from the Greek word . . . meaning action, from which our words "practice" and "practical" come. It was first introduced into philosophy by Mr. Charles Peirce in 1878. In an article entitled "How to Make Our Ideas Clear," in the "Popular Science Monthly" for January of that year Mr. Peirce, after pointing out that our beliefs are really rules for action, said that, to develop a thought's meaning, we need only determine what conduct it is fitted to produce: that conduct is for us its sole significance. And the tangible fact at the root of all our thought-distinctions, however subtle, is that there is no one of them so fine as to consist in anything but a possible difference of practice. To attain perfect clearness in our thought of an object, then, we need only consider what conceivable effects of a practical kind the object may involve—what sensations we are to expect from it, and what reactions we must prepare. Our conception of these effects, whether immediate or remote, is then for us the whole of our conception of the object, so far as that conception has positive significance at all.

This is the principle of Peirce, the principle of pragmatism. It lay entirely unnoticed by any one for twenty years, until I, in an address before Professor Howison's philosophical union at the University of California, brought it forward again and made a special application of it to religion. By that date (1898) the times seemed ripe for its reception. The word "pragmatism" spread, and at present it fairly spots the pages of the philosophical journals. On all hands we find the "pragmatic movement" spoken of, sometimes with respect, sometimes with contumely, seldom with clear understanding. It is evident that the term applies itself conveniently to a number of tendencies that hitherto have lacked a collective name, and that it has "come to stay."

To take in the importance of Peirce's principle, one must get accustomed to applying it to concrete cases. I found a few years ago that Ostwald, the illustrious Leipzig chemist, had been making perfectly distinct use of the principle of pragmatism in his lectures on the philosophy of science, though he had not called it by that name.

"All realities influence our practice," he wrote me, "and that influence is their meaning for us. I am accustomed to put questions to my classes in this way: In what respects would the world be different if this alternative or that were true? If I can find nothing that would become different, then the alternative has no sense."

That is, the rival views mean practically the same thing, and meaning, other than practical, there is for us none. Ostwald in a published lecture gives this example of what he means. Chemists have long wrangled over the inner constitution of certain bodies called "tautomerous." Their properties seemed equally consistent with the option that an instable hydrogen atom oscillates inside of them, or that they are instable mixtures of two bodies. Controversy raged, but never was decided. "It would never have begun," says Ostwald, "if the combatants had asked themselves what particular experimental fact could have been made different by one or the other view being correct. For it would then have appeared that no difference of fact could possibly ensue; and the quarrel was as unreal as if, theorizing in primitive times about the raising of dough by yeast, one party should have invoked a 'brownie,' while another insisted on an 'elf' as the true cause of the phenomenon."

It is astonishing to see how many philosophical disputes collapse into insignificance the moment you subject them to this simple test of tracing a concrete consequence. There can be no difference anywhere that doesn't make a difference elsewhere—no difference in abstract truth that doesn't express itself in a difference in concrete fact and in conduct consequent upon that fact, imposed on somebody, somehow, somewhere, and somewhen. The whole function of philosophy ought to be to find out what definite difference it will make to you and me, at definite instants of our life, if this world-formula or that world-formula be the true one.

There is absolutely nothing new in the pragmatic method. Socrates was an adept at it. Aristotle used it methodically. Locke, Berkeley, and Hume made momentous contributions to truth by its means. Shadworth Hodgson keeps insisting that realities are only what they are "known as." But these forerunners of pragmatism used it in fragments: they were precluders only. Not until in our time has it generalized itself, become conscious of a universal mission, pretended to a conquering destiny. I believe in that destiny, and I hope I may end by inspiring you with my belief.

Pragmatism represents a perfectly familiar attitude in philosophy, the empiricist attitude, but it represents it, as it seems to me, both in a more radical and in a less objectionable form than it has ever yet assumed. A pragmatist turns his back resolutely and once for all upon a lot of inveterate habits dear to professional philosophers. He turns away from abstraction and insufficiency, from verbal solutions, from bad *a priori* reasons, from fixed principles, closed systems, and pretended absolutes and origins. He turns towards concreteness and adequacy, towards facts, towards action and towards power. That means the empiricist temper regnant and the rationalist temper sincerely given up. It means the open air and possibilities of nature, as against dogma, artificiality, and the pretence of finality in truth.

At the same time it does not stand for any special results. It is a method only. But the general triumph of the method would mean an enormous change in what I called in my last lecture the "temperament" of philosophy. Teachers of the ultra-rationalistic type would be frozen out, much as the courtier type is frozen out in republics, as the ultra-montane type of priest is frozen out in protestant lands. Science and metaphysics would come much nearer together, would in fact work absolutely hand in hand.

The Pragmatic Method Applied to the Problem of Substance

I am now to make the pragmatic method more familiar by giving you some illustrations of its application to particular problems. I will begin with what is driest, and the first thing I shall take will be the problem of *Substance*. Every one uses the old distinction between substance and attribute, enshrined as it is in the very structure of human language, in the difference between grammatical subject and predicate. Here is a bit of blackboard crayon. Its modes, attributes, properties, accidents, or affects—use which term you will—are whiteness, friability, cylindrical shape, insolubility in water, etc., etc. But the bearer of these attributes is so much *chalk,* which thereupon is called the substance in which they inhere. So the attributes of this desk inhere in the substance "wood," those of my coat in the substance "wool," and so forth. Chalk, wood and wool, show again, in spite of their differences, common properties, and in so far forth they are themselves counted as modes of a still more primal substance, *matter,* the attributes of which are space-occupancy and impenetrability. Similarly our thoughts and feelings are affections or properties of our several *souls,* which are substances, but again not wholly in their own right, for they are modes of the still deeper substance "spirit."

Now it was very early seen that all *we know* of the chalk is the whiteness, friability, etc., all *we know* of the wood is the combustibility and fibrous structure.

A group of attributes is what each substance here is known-as, they form its sole cash-value for our actual experience. The substance is in every case revealed through *them;* if we were cut off from *them* we should never suspect its existence; and if God should keep sending them to us in an unchanged order, miraculously annihilating at a certain moment the substance that supported them, we never could detect the moment, for our experiences themselves would be unaltered. Nominalists accordingly adopt the opinion that substance is a spurious idea due to our inveterate human trick of turning names into things. Phenomena come in groups—the chalk-group, the wood-group, etc.—and each group gets its name. The name we then treat as in a way supporting the group of phenomena. The low thermometer today, for instance, is supposed to come from something called the "climate." Climate is really only the name for a certain group of days, but it is treated as if it lay *behind* the day, and in general we place the name, as if it were a being, behind the facts it is the name of. But the phenomenal properties of things, nominalists say, surely do not really inhere in names, and if not in names then they do not inhere in anything. They *ad*here, or *co*here, rather, *with each other,* and the notion of a substance inaccessible to us, which we think accounts for such cohesion by supporting it, as cement might support pieces of mosaic, must be abandoned. The fact of the bare cohesion itself is all that the notion of the substance signifies. Behind that fact is nothing.

The Leap Beyond Patriarchal Religion

MARY DALY

Mary Daly, a noted radical feminist thinker, teaches at Boston College. In the following selection, she presents a superbly succinct analysis of modern society, Christianity, and the women's movement.

From Mary Daly, "The Leap Beyond Patriarchal Religion," *Quest,* vol. 1, no. 4 (Spring 1975). Reprinted by permission of the author.

Among her influential books are *Beyond God the Father: Toward a Philosophy of Women's Liberation* and *Gyn/Ecology.*

Prolegomena

1. There exists a planetary sexual caste system, essentially the same in Saudi Arabia and in New York, differing only in degree.

2. This system is masked by sex role segregation, by the dual identity of women, by ideologies and myths.

3. Among the primary loci of sexist conditioning is grammar.

4. The "methods" of the various "fields" are not adequate to express feminist thought. Methodolatry requires that women perform Methodicide, an act of intellectual bravery.

5. All the major world religions function to legitimate patriarchy. This is true also of the popular cults such as the Krishna movement and the Jesus Freaks.

6. The myths and symbols of Christianity are essentially sexist. Since "God" is male, the male is God. God the Father legitimates all earthly God-fathers, including Vito Corleone, Pope Paul, President Gerald Ford, the God-fathers of medicine (e.g. the American Medical Association), of science (e.g. NASA), of the media, of psychiatry, of education, and of all the -ologies.

7. The myth of feminine evil, expressed in the story of the Fall, is reinforced by the myth of salvation/ redemption by a single human being of the male sex. The idea of a unique divine incarnation in a male, the God-man of the "hypostatic union," is inherently sexist and oppressive. Christolatry is idolatry.

8. A significant and growing cognitive minority of women, radical feminists, are breaking out from under the sacred shelter of patriarchal religious myths.

9. This breaking out, facing anomy when the meaning structures of patriarchy are seen through and rejected, is a communal, political event. It is a revelatory event, a creative, political ontophany.

10. The bonding of the growing cognitive minority of women who are racial feminists, commonly called *sisterhood*, involves a process of new naming, in which words are wrenched out of their old semantic context. For example, the "sisterhoods" of patriarchy, such as religious congregations of women, were really mini-brotherhoods. *Sisterhood* heard with new ears is bonding for women's own liberation.

11. There is an inherent dynamic in the women's revolution in Judeo-Christian society which is Anti-church, whether or not feminists specifically concern ourselves with churches. This is so because the Judeo-Christian tradition legitimates patriarchy—the prevailing power structure and prevailing world view—which the women's revolution leaves behind.

12. The women's revolution is not only Antichurch. It is a postchristian spiritual revolution.

13. The ethos of Judeo-Christian culture is dominated by The Most Unholy Trinity: Rape, Genocide, and War. It is rapism which spawns racism. It is gynocide which spawns genocide, for sexism (rapism) is fundamental socialization to objectify "the other."

14. The women's revolution is concerned with transvaluation of values, beyond the ethics dominated by The Most Unholy Trinity.

15. The women's revolution is not merely about equality within a patriarchal society (a contradiction in terms). It is about *power* and redefining power.

16. Since Christian myths are inherently sexist, and since the women's revolution is not about "equality" but about power, there is an intrinsic dynamic in the feminist movement which goes beyond efforts to reform Christian churches. Such efforts eventually come to be recognized as comparable to a Black person's trying to reform the Ku Klux Klan.

17. Within patriarchy, power is generally understood as power *over* people, the environment, things. In the rising consciousness of women, power is experienced as *power of presence* to ourselves and to each other, as we affirm our own being against and beyond the alienated identity (non-being) bestowed upon us within patriarchy. This is experienced as *power of absence* by those who would objectify women as "the other," as magnifying mirrors.

18. The presence of women to ourselves which is *absence* to the oppressor is the essential dynamic opening up the women's revolution to human liberation. It is an invitation to men to confront non-being and hence affirm their be-ing.

19. It is unlikely that many men will accept this invitation willingly, or even be able to hear it, since they have profound vested (though self-destructive) interest in the present social arrangements.

Appendix: Wisdom Skills

PRETEST

Circle the correct answer.

1. T F   A paraphrase of a quotation means approximately but not always exactly the same as the original quotation.

2. T F   Some statements are so complex that they are impossible to paraphrase.

3. T F   The best paraphrase of a quotation has the same sentence structure but not the same words as the quotation.

4. T F   In an argument, evidence comes before conclusion, but not vice versa.

5. T F   All arguments must have both evidence and at least one conclusion.

6. T F   A strong argument has more evidence than does a weak argument.

PREVIEW

Paraphrasing philosophical statements and analyzing arguments are two wisdom skills useful to studying philosophy.

Paraphrasing involves dividing the text to be paraphrased into short sections, finding synonyms for key words, and rereading numerous times.

Argument analysis involves identifying evidence and conclusion and distinguishing strong arguments from weak arguments.

In this special section of the tour, I'm going to show you how to accurately translate what a philosopher says into your own language. Then I'm going to give you the tools you need to tell if what is being said is well-supported truth or airy foolishness. I'll answer the following questions:

- What is a method for paraphrasing philosophical statements?
- How can longer philosophical selections be paraphrased?
- How can arguments be analyzed?
- How can the strength of an argument be evaluated?

And so, let's begin with the first question.

What Is a Method for Paraphrasing Philosophical Statements?

You will be happy to know that you can go a long way in philosophy with only two related skills: the ability to paraphrase and the ability to dissect arguments.

Philosophers often use complex language. Translating a philosopher's ideas into your own language is the only way to determine if what they are saying has value. To learn how to paraphrase, we'll use two philosophical statements that are probably simple enough that they don't require paraphrasing and then examine a more complex statement that does require paraphrasing. Let's begin with the following from Aristotle:

All men by nature desire to know.

I recommend that you use a four-step approach to paraphrasing. First, break the philosopher's statement into several smaller parts. Thus,

[1] All men [2] by nature [3] desire to know.

Second, wherever possible, find synonyms or phrases that mean approximately the same thing for each of the parts. Thus,

[1] Every human [2] is born with [3] the desire to have knowledge.

We'll correct Aristotle's sexist language and substitute "humans" for "men." Whether or not Aristotle would have agreed with this correction is open to debate. Note that I have found synonyms for everything except "desire." This is all right. Your paraphrases can contain a few words found in the original quotation.

Third, check to be sure that each part of your paraphrase is the same as the original:

[1] All men = All humans

[2] by nature = are born with

[3] desire to know = the desire to acquire knowledge

I'm a bit troubled by [2]. Aristotle doesn't mean only that we are *born* with the desire to have knowledge but also, more generally, that the desire to have knowledge is part of our unique human makeup. So, I'll make a change:

[1] All men = All humans

[2] by nature = *have as part of their essence*

[3] the desire to know = the desire to acquire knowledge

Thus far, I have changed Aristotle's words into my own but maintained his sentence structure. My [1], [2], and [3] fall in the same order as his [1], [2], and [3]. However, to demonstrate that I really understand what Aristotle is saying, in the fourth step I should be able to invent my own sentence structure and not copy his. I may have to change some of my phrases to do that. Thus, my final paraphrase could be

The desire to acquire knowledge is part of the essence of all humans.

Or,

Acquiring knowledge is a desire that is central to human nature.

By completing steps 1–3, I divided Aristotle's statement into simpler parts and got an idea of their meaning. The completed paraphrase, step 4, was then considerably easier than if I'd omitted the first three steps.

Let's go through this same process again with a simple statement from Immanuel Kant.

Everything in **nature** works according to laws.

Step 1: Divide the quotation into smaller parts.

[1] Everything in nature [2] works according to laws.

Step 2: Find synonyms wherever possible.

[1] All that is in the universe [2] operates according to general principles.

I'm a bit troubled by "general principles" as a synonym for "laws." "General" is a vague word that only weakly modifies "principles." I think I can do better with [2].

[2] operates according to *regulating* principles

Step 3: Check to see that the parts of the paraphrase are the same as the quotation.

[1] Everything in nature = All that is in the universe

[2] works according to laws = operates according to regulating principles

nature Both the living and the non-living—that is, everything in the physical universe.

Step 4: Rearrange the paraphrase to construct a new sentence pattern. Make changes in the original paraphrase as necessary. Thus:

Regulating principles guide each part of the universe.

As you read philosophy you will find that you have three main problems in paraphrasing:

Philosophers use words that you are not familiar with (or they use words you are familiar with in ways you are unfamiliar with).

Philosophers use long, complexly constructed sentences.

You do not understand what a reference word like "it" or "that" refers to.

Here are solutions to these problems.

To solve the problem of unfamiliar vocabulary, you need to find a definition. You may have already noticed that in this book every word or phrase that you may be unfamiliar with is defined in the margins or in context.

To solve the problem of paraphrasing complicated sentences, break the sentence into parts in the way you've just learned. Understanding short sections of a complicated sentence is always easier than understanding the sentence as a whole.

To solve the problem of understanding what words like "it" or "that" refer to, you've just got to stop, go back, and find the word or phrase that is referred to.

Here is a more complex paraphrasing task from David Hume that demonstrates the solution to each of the three problems:

Everyone will readily allow, that there is a considerable difference between the perceptions of the mind, when a man feels the pain of excessive heat, or the pleasure of moderate warmth, and when he afterwards recalls to his memory this sensation, or anticipates it by his imagination.

Before beginning step 1, you must identify what the reference words "this sensation" and "it" refer to. Conveniently enough, both words refer back to the same phrase. Note the brackets below.

Everyone will readily allow, that there is a considerable difference between the perceptions of the mind, when a man feels the pain of excessive heat, or the pleasure of moderate warmth, and when he afterwards recalls to his memory this sensation [the pain of excessive heat or the pleasure of moderate warmth], or anticipates it [the pain of excessive heat or the pleasure of moderate warmth] by his imagination.

In the text, where there is a key reference word or phrase, I signal it by including [_____] after the word or phrase. Stop at that point and identify the reference.

Now that we have identified the references, we can begin.

Step 1: Divide the quotation into smaller parts.

[1] Everyone will readily allow, that there is a considerable difference between the perceptions of the mind, when a man feels the pain of excessive heat, or the pleasure of moderate warmth, [2] and when he afterwards recalls to his memory this sensation, [3] or anticipates it by his imagination.

Step 2: Find synonyms wherever possible. (I've underlined the synonyms.)

[1] Everyone <u>will agree</u> that there is a considerable difference between <u>what the mind knows</u> when <u>we</u> feel pain from excessive heat or pleasure from moderate warmth [2] and when <u>we remember these feelings of pain and pleasure</u> [3] or <u>look forward to these pains or pleasures with our imagination</u>.

Step 3: Check to see that the parts of the paraphrase are the same as the quotation.

[1] Everyone will readily allow, that there is a considerable difference between the perceptions of the mind, when a man feels the pain of excessive heat, or the pleasure of moderate warmth =

[1] Everyone will agree that there is a considerable difference between what the mind knows when we feel pain from excessive heat or pleasure from moderate warmth

[2] and when he afterwards recalls to his memory this sensation =

[2] and when we remember these feelings of pain and pleasure

[3] or anticipates it by his imagination. =

[3] or look forward to these pains or pleasures with our imagination.

Step 4: Use the paraphrase to construct a new sentence pattern. Rephrase sections of the paraphrase if necessary. Here is my completed paraphrase:

The pain or pleasure we imagine from the future or recall from the past is very different from the mind's perception of pain or pleasure in the present.

EXERCISE A.1
Paraphrasing Philosophical Quotations

On your own paper, use the four-step method on the quotations below. The quotations are arranged from the simpler to the more complex.

1. "No one does wrong willingly."—Plato
2. "One ought not to return a wrong or an injury to any person, whatever the provocation."—Plato
3. "What we cannot speak about we must pass over in silence."—Ludwig Wittgenstein
4. "I say that justice is nothing other than the interest of the stronger."—Thrasymachus
5. ". . . your love of your neighbor is your bad love of yourselves."—Friedrich Nietzsche
6. "To abolish religion as the illusory happiness of the people is to demand their real happiness."—Karl Marx
7. "'Tis not, therefore, reason, which is the guide of life, but custom."—David Hume
8. "Men are good in one way, but bad in many."—Aristotle
9. "The weaker are always anxious for justice and equality. The strong pay no heed to either."—Aristotle

10. "There is nothing so absurd but some philosopher has said it."—Cicero

11. "Do not seek to have everything that happens happen as you wish, but wish for everything to happen as it actually does happen, and your life will be serene."—Epictetus

12. "To prefer evil to good is not in human nature: and when a man is compelled to choose one of two evils, no one will choose the greater when he may have the less."   Plato

13. "In so far as the statements of geometry speak about reality, they are not certain, and in so far as they are certain, they do not speak about reality."—Albert Einstein

14. "I do not seek to understand so that I may believe, but I believe so that I may understand; and what is more, I believe that 'unless I do believe I shall not understand' (Isaiah 7:9)."—St. Anselm

15. "There are few circumstances among those which make up the present condition of human knowledge, more unlike what might have been expected, or more significant of the backward state in which speculation on the most important subjects still lingers, than the little progress which has been made in the decision of the controversy respecting the **criterion** of right and wrong."—John Stuart Mill

How Can Longer Philosophical Selections Be Paraphrased?

While it is useful to be able to paraphrase a passage in philosophy sentence by sentence, you will often be asked to summarize the general idea or ideas of a selection too long for such analysis.

I suggest a five-step method for longer selections.

On your first reading simply get a general idea of what the philosopher is talking about. As part of the first reading, underline key phrases and sentences. Use underlining to distinguish important from less important ideas. Try my suggestions with the first paragraph of René Descartes, *Meditations on First Philosophy*.

For several years now, I've been aware that I accepted many falsehoods as true in my youth, that what I built on the foundation of those falsehoods was **dubious,** and accordingly that once in my life I would need to tear down everything and begin anew from the foundations if I wanted to establish any stable and lasting knowledge. But the task seemed enormous, and I waited until I was so old that no better time for undertaking it would be likely to follow. I have thus delayed so long that it would be wrong for me to waste in indecision the time left for action. Today, then, having rid myself of worries and having arranged for some peace and quiet, I withdraw alone, free at last earnestly and wholeheartedly to overthrow all my beliefs.

Don't try to accomplish too much in the first reading; just get the general idea.

What Descartes seems to be talking about is _____

_____.

As your second step in paraphrasing long selections, break up the passage into smaller units and fill in the [_____] references. (I'll do the former and you do the latter.)

[1] For several years now, I've been aware that I accepted many falsehoods as true in my youth, [2] that what I built on the foundation of those falsehoods was dubious, [3] and accordingly that once in my life I would need to tear down everything and begin anew from the foundations if I wanted to establish any stable and lasting knowledge. [4] But the task [_____] seemed enormous, and I waited until I was so old that no better time for undertaking it [_____] would be likely to follow. [5] I have thus delayed so long that it would be wrong for me to waste in indecision the time left for action. [6] Today, then, having rid myself of worries and having arranged for some peace and quiet, I withdraw alone, free at last earnestly and wholeheartedly to overthrow all my beliefs.

Now, what should go in each bracket?

"But the task" refers back to _____;

"undertaking it" refers back to _____.

Obviously, you could not understand what Descartes or any other writer was saying unless you knew what reference words referred to. On the tour, always take the time to fill in the [_____] by writing the word or phrase referred to in the margin.

When making a detailed paraphrase, you'll find it useful to divide all sentences into phrases. However, when making a looser paraphrase, like the one we are working on now, divide only the most complex sentences into phrases; the largest unit should not exceed several sentences.

As your third step, try to summarize each numbered unit. In order to do this, of course, you'll have to read the passage a few more times.

In [1] he is saying _____

_____.

In [2] he is saying _____

_____.

In [3] he is saying _____

_____.

criterion A standard for judgment.

dubious Doubtful.

In [4] he is saying _____

_____.

In [5] he is saying _____

_____.

In [6] he is saying _____

_____.

As your fourth step in understanding a long philosophical passage, insert, wherever you can, your own examples of what the philosopher is talking about. This step is extremely useful. If you can think of your own examples, then you have a fairly good grasp of the points being made.

What examples could you offer for [1]?

[1] For several years now, I've been aware that I accepted many falsehoods as true in my youth

Possible examples of "falsehoods" that one might accept as true in youth would

be _____

_____

_____

_____.

What examples could you offer for the following?

[1] For several years now, I've been aware that I accepted many falsehoods as true in my youth, [2] <u>that what I built on the foundation of those falsehoods was dubious</u>

Examples of the doubtful things that could built on a foundation of falsehoods

would be _____

_____.

What could you offer as an example of the third section of Descartes's complex sentence?

[1] For several years now, I've been aware that I accepted many falsehoods as true in my youth, [2] that what I built on the foundation of those falsehoods was dubious, [3] <u>and accordingly that once in my life I would need to tear down everything and begin anew from the foundations if I wanted to establish any stable and a lasting knowledge.</u>

An example of what Descartes is talking about would be _____

_____

_____.

The fifth step is the most difficult. Go back over steps 1–4 until you have a clear idea what the philosopher is talking about. Reading philosophy is re-reading philosophy. On the tour, you make progress by going backward.

For now, simply retrace steps 1–4 and then try to summarize what Descartes is saying.

Descartes is saying _____

_____

_____

_____

_____.

Your summary at this point should be superior to your brief statement after step 1.

CHECKPOINT: Paraphrasing Long Philosophical Selections

1. Read the selection slowly. Use underlining to sort important from less important ideas. Don't try to accomplish too much at the first reading, simply identify the main concepts.

2. Break complex sentences into phrases; other units should be no longer than several sentences. Use the margin to fill in the reference [_____] words.

3. Reread each unit and get a general idea of what it is saying.

4. Think of examples, where appropriate, for the points the philosopher in making.

5. Go back over steps 1–4 until you can summarize the section as a whole.

EXERCISE A.2
Paraphrasing Longer Passages

Here are several passages you can use to practice the five-step method for paraphrasing longer philosophical selections. The first selection follows the paragraph from Descartes we analyzed. Thus, fill in the [_____] by referring back to Descartes's paragraph. (Incidentally, all the selections below are from the opening of important philosophical works investigated on the tour.)

1. "To do this [_____], I don't need to show each of them [_____] to be false; I may never be able to do that. But, since reason now convinces me that I ought to withhold my assent just as carefully from what isn't obviously certain and indubitable as from what's obviously false, I can justify the rejection of all my beliefs if in each [_____] I can find some ground for doubt. And, to do this [_____], I need not run through my beliefs one

by one, which would be an endless task. Since a building collapses when its foundation is cut out from under it, I will go straight to the principles on which all my former beliefs rested."—René Descartes, *Meditations on First Philosophy*

2. "Every art and every kind of scientific inquiry and also every action and choice, seem to aim at some good. Thus, it has been well said that the good is that at which everything aims.

   "There is a difference, however, among these [_____] aims. What is aimed at is sometimes an activity and sometimes a result or product of an activity. In this latter case [_____] where the aim is some product of an activity, the product is naturally superior to the activity itself."—Aristotle, *Nicomachean Ethics*

3. "Some things are under our control, while others are not under our control. Under our control are conception [having ideas], choice, desire, aversion [intense dislike], and in a word, everything that is our own doing; not under our control are our body, our property, reputation, office [occupation], and, in a word, everything that is not our own doing. Furthermore, the things under our control are by nature free, unhindered, and unimpeded; while the things not under our control are weak, servile [very submissive], subject to hindrance, and not our own. Remember, therefore, that if what is naturally slavish you think to be free, and what is not your own to be your own, you will be hampered, will grieve, will be in turmoil, and will blame both gods and men."—Epictetus, *Encheiridion*

4. "Let no one when young delay to study philosophy, nor when he is old grow weary of his study. For no one can come too early or too late to secure the health of his soul. And the man who says that the age for philosophy has either not yet come or has gone by is like the man who says that the age for happiness is not yet come to him, or has passed away. Wherefore both when young and old a man must study philosophy, that as he grows old he may be young in blessings through the grateful recollection of what has been, and that in youth he may be old as well, since he will know no fear of what is to come."—Epicurus, "Letter to Menoeceus"

5. "Since it is the understanding that sets man above the rest of **sensible beings,** and gives him all the advantage and dominion which he has over them, it [_____] is certainly a subject, even for its nobleness, worth our labour to inquire into. The understanding, like the eye, while it [_____] makes us see and perceive all other things, takes no notice of itself; and it requires art and pains to set it [_____] at a distance, and make it its own object. But whatever be the difficulties that lie in the way of this inquiry; whatever it be that keeps us so much in the dark to ourselves; sure I am that all the light

we can let in upon our own minds, all the acquaintance we can make with our own understandings, will not only be very pleasant, but bring us great advantage in directing our thoughts in the search of other things."—John Locke, *An Essay Concerning Human Understanding*

How Can Arguments Be Analyzed?

Now, let's go on to the second wisdom skill, analyzing arguments. In metaphysics, philosophers argue, among other things, that God exists or doesn't exist; in ethics, philosophers argue, among other things, that virtue is selflessness or selfishness; in epistemology, philosophers argue, among other things, that knowledge comes only through our senses or independently of our senses. Arguments are to philosophy what mortar and bricks are to a bricklayer.

Therefore, you need to learn how to analyze arguments. What is an argument, and how do you take one apart?

Think of an argument as something you are trying to divide into two parts, evidence and conclusion. Evidence is information that supports the conclusion. The conclusion is what needs to be proved.

Before we look at a philosophical argument, let's examine a simpler argument. Consider the following from an imaginary trial:

Evidence: A size 11 shoeprint was found in the victim's blood.

Evidence: Nelly wears a size 11 shoe.

Conclusion: Nelly is the killer.

The question in an argument is always whether the evidence will support the conclusion. Nelly wears size 11 shoes, and so did the killer. Therefore, can we conclude that Nelly did the foul deed? Not on the basis of the evidence presented. The argument establishes only one connection between Nelly and the killer. They both wear the same size shoe.

Let's make the argument somewhat stronger by adding evidence that supplies a second connection between Nelly and the killer:

Evidence: A size 11 shoeprint was found in the victim's blood.

Evidence: Nelly wears a size 11 shoe.

Evidence: Nelly was seen in the neighborhood at the time of the killing.

Conclusion: Nelly is the killer.

Note that as we add more evidence, the argument becomes somewhat stronger. Now Nelly has two connections to the killing. First, she has the shoe size of the killer and, second, she was in the area at the time of the murder. Let's add another piece of evidence:

Evidence: A size 11 shoeprint was found in the victim's blood.

Evidence: Nelly wears a size 11 shoe.

Evidence: Nelly was seen in the neighborhood at the time of the killing.

Evidence: Nelly's diary contained a plan to murder the victim.

Conclusion: Nelly is the killer.

sensible beings Beings that use their senses; that is, humans, animals, and insects.

Things are getting tighter for Nelly. As the argument against her gets stronger, the evidence supports the conclusion more and more. Now there are three connections between Nelly and the killer: shoe size, location, and plan.

In stronger arguments, evidence captures the conclusion; in weaker arguments (like the first Nelly argument), evidence and conclusion fall apart. Your goal in dissecting an argument into evidence pieces and conclusion pieces is to be able to tell if the argument is strong or weak.

Here is a one-sentence argument by René Descartes, from the first selection in Exercise A.1.

> Since a building collapses when its foundation is cut out from under it, I will go straight to the principles on which all my former beliefs rested.

Think of evidence as a "because" statement and a conclusion as a "therefore" statement. Thus, a simple argument would have one "because" statement (one piece of evidence), supporting one "therefore" statement (one conclusion). Using this guideline, an easy way to carve arguments into evidence pieces and conclusion pieces is to insert "because" before what you think might be the evidence and "therefore" before what you think might be the conclusion. After making the insertions, reread the argument. If it doesn't sound right, switch the positions of "because" and "therefore."

For example, which makes the most sense?

1. [because] a building collapses when its foundation is cut out from under it, [therefore] I will go straight to the principles on which all my former beliefs rested.

Does that make sense? We'll try switching the "because" and "therefore" (and keep the because statement first).

2. [because] I will go straight to the principles on which all my former beliefs rested, [therefore] a building collapses when its foundation is cut out from under it.

You can see that the first argument makes more sense than the second argument. Using the evidence of what happens to a building when its foundation is removed, Descartes moves to the conclusion that he should attack the foundational principles of his former beliefs.

When you think you have successfully carved an argument into evidence and conclusion, apply one more test. Ask yourself if the evidence is more obvious than the conclusion. Almost all arguments move from evidence that is more obvious toward a conclusion that is less obvious.

In the simple argument above, Descartes makes one statement about what happens to a building when its foundation is removed and a second statement about how he should proceed to attack the edifice of his beliefs. The behavior of a building without a foundation is more obvious than anything to do with the architectural weaknesses of belief structures. Because it is obvious what buildings do when they have no foundation, the statement about buildings must be the evidence. Thus, we have correctly dissected the argument. We have shown how Descartes reasons from evidence (the more obvious) to conclusion (the less obvious).

How Can the Strength
of an Argument Be Evaluated?

Now, how do you tell if an argument is strong or weak—how do you tell if the evidence has captured the conclusion or allowed it to go free?

Let's look at a sample of the strongest kind of argument, something called a valid syllogism:

1. Socrates is a human.

2. All humans are mortal.

3. Therefore, Socrates is a mortal.

The evidence of 1 and 2 completely captures 3. The evidence is a perfect noose for the conclusion. As a matter of fact, if you look closely, the evidence is merely a longer version of the conclusion. The evidence, as evidence, has already captured the conclusion. If every single human is a mortal and if Socrates is one of those humans, then these two statements entirely contain the conclusion that Socrates is a mortal. In a perfectly strong argument like a valid syllogism, having the evidence means you automatically have the conclusion.

Now look again at the first Nelly argument.

1. A size 11 shoeprint was found in the victim's blood.

2. Nelly wears a size 11 shoe.

3. Nelly is the killer.

The evidence, as we noted earlier, does not capture the conclusion. In a weak argument, having the evidence is nothing like having the conclusion.

You can judge the strength and weakness of any philosopher's argument by deciding which of the arguments above it resembles. Each Nelly argument was stronger than the last; the Socrates syllogism was perfectly strong. The closer an argument is to the syllogism end of the scale, the stronger the argument. When an argument presents evidence that ensnares the conclusion, the philosopher is doing what philosophers ought to do. When an argument's evidence doesn't ensnare the conclusion, then you have caught the philosopher in a serious error.

Now, let's conclude this section by looking at two finer points that will help you dissect philosophical arguments.

First, as you read philosophy, pay close attention to words that point you toward evidence and conclusions. "Since" and "for" are often synonyms for "because" and point to evidence. "Hence," "so," "thus," and "consequently" are synonyms for "therefore" and point to conclusions.

Second, and most unfortunately for you, philosophers often leave out evidence or a conclusion. You perform your surgery and find a missing organ. On these occasions, *you must state the unstated.*

For example, here is another argument from Descartes:

But, I have occasionally caught the senses deceiving me, and it's prudent never completely to trust those who have cheated us even once.

If you try the because/therefore test, you will find the following:

1. [because] I have occasionally caught the senses deceiving me,
2. [therefore], it's prudent never completely to trust those who have cheated us even once.

But Descartes isn't trying to prove something to us about cheaters. He's trying to prove something to us about the senses. Thus, we have to state the unstated conclusion:

1. [because] I have occasionally caught the senses deceiving me, and
2. [because] it's prudent never completely to trust those who have cheated us even once
3. [therefore, I should not entirely trust my senses.]

You can tell if a philosopher has not stated a *conclusion* when the because-therefore test, as it did above, leads to an irrelevant point. You can suspect that a philosopher has not stated *evidence* if the because-therefore test presents an argument that looks too weak. Check to see if the evidence presented implies unstated evidence. Then do the philosophically decent thing. State the unstated.

SUMMARY

You can make considerable progress in philosophy with only two skills: paraphrasing and argument analysis.

Paraphrasing short philosophical selections involves dividing the selection into smaller units, finding synonyms for key words, checking the correctness of the paraphrase, and making a final paraphrase with a sentence structure different from that of the original text.

Paraphrasing longer philosophical selections involves numerous rereadings, breaking the selection into smaller units, identifying reference words, and finding examples for the points the philosopher makes.

Argument analysis involves the following:

1. When the philosopher appears to be trying to prove a point, use the because-therefore test to see if there is a conclusion and evidence.

2. If a conclusion and evidence are present, double-check by seeing if the evidence is less obvious than the conclusion.

3. If a conclusion and evidence are not obviously present, see if it is necessary to state the unstated.

4. Judge the strength of the argument by comparing it to a scale ranging from the weakest Nelly arguments up to the valid syllogism.

5. Look for "since" and "for" as synonyms for "because"; look for "hence," "so," "thus," and "consequently" as synonyms for "therefore."

EXERCISE A.3
Looking Back

Use your own paper and practice your paraphrasing skills by answering the following questions:

1. What is a method for paraphrasing philosophical statements? (Explain each of the four steps.)

2. How can longer philosophical selections be paraphrased? (Explain each of the five steps.)

3. How can arguments be analyzed? (Describe the main features of the method presented.)

4. How can the strength of an argument be evaluated? (What are the distinguishing features of strong and weak arguments?)

EXERCISE A.4
Argument Analysis

Underline the conclusion in each of the following:

1. The mind contains perfect and eternal truths. These truths could not have been learned through the senses. Thus, this knowledge came from some realm other than the sense realm. (a paraphrase of an argument by Plato)

2. God exists. The universe testifies to the existence of a divine creator.

3. Evil exists. God does not exist. If a perfect creator existed, then a perfect creator would not have created a world with evil.

4. God is a being than whom none greater can be conceived. God exists. Only a God who existed would be a being than whom none greater could be conceived. (a paraphrase of an argument by St. Anselm)

5. All knowledge comes through the senses. The senses have no knowledge of substance. Substance does not exist. (a paraphrase of an argument by George Berkeley)

6. Love is what makes the world go round. Therefore, keep the world spinning and love me.

7. "I think; therefore, I exist."—René Descartes

8. If the senses were reliable, they would never deceive us. But the senses do deceive us. The senses are not reliable.

9. "Since the happiness of all angels consists in union with God, it follows that their unhappiness must be found in the very contrary, that is, in not adhering to God."—St. Augustine

10. "Neither can I approve the opinion of some **scholastics** who maintain boldly that what God has done is not absolutely perfect, and that he could have done much better. For it seems to me that the consequences of this opinion are altogether contrary to the glory of God."—Gottfried Leibniz

11. "There are no ideas, which occur in metaphysics, more obscure and uncertain, than those of *power, force, energy* or *necessary connection,* of which it is every moment necessary for us to treat in all our **disquisitions.** We shall, therefore, endeavor, in this section, to fix, if possible, the precise meaning of these terms, and thereby remove some part of that obscurity, which is so much complained of in this species of philosophy."—David Hume

12. ". . . it is possible to fail in many ways (for evil belongs to the class of the unlimited, as the **Pythagoreans** conjectured, and good to that of the limited), while to succeed is possible only in one way (for which reason one is easy and the other difficult—to miss the mark easy, to hit it difficult); for these reasons also, then, excess and defect are characteristic of vice, and **the mean of excellence.** For men are good in but one way, but bad in many."
—Aristotle

13. There is nothing that an omnipotent God could not do. But God cannot do evil. Thus, evil is nothing because that is what God cannot do. (a paraphrase of an argument by Boethius)

14. "Experience, it is said, makes a man wise. That is very silly talk. If there were nothing beyond experience it would simply drive him mad."—Soren Kierkegaard

15. "It seems that the existence of God cannot be demonstrated. For it is an article of faith that God exists. But what is of faith cannot be demonstrated, because a demonstration produces scientific knowledge; whereas faith is of the unseen. Therefore, it cannot be demonstrated that God exists."
—Thomas Aquinas (Aquinas presents this argument in order to disprove it with the following argument.)

16. "The existence of God and other like truths about God, which can be known by natural reason, are not articles of faith, but are preambles [introductory statements] to the articles; for faith presupposes natural knowledge, even as grace presupposes nature, and perfection supposes something that can be perfected.[1] Nevertheless, there is nothing to prevent a man, who cannot

---

[1]". . . faith presupposes natural knowledge, even as grace presupposes nature" means that if X presupposes Y, then the existence of X assumes the existence of Y. Your knowledge of mathematical truths presupposes, or assumes the existence of, mathematics. Grace presupposes nature because the existence of grace assumes the existence of nature. You couldn't have grace, something that transforms nature, unless you also had nature.

grasp a proof, accepting, as a matter of faith, something which in itself is capable of being scientifically known and demonstrated."—Thomas Aquinas

ANALYSIS OF PRETEST

1. T **F** *A paraphrase of a quotation means approximately but not always exactly the same as the original quotation.*

   As you now know, this is False. A paraphrase of any text must have the same meaning as the original text. If you are paraphrasing Kant, you are saying, in effect, "this is exactly what Kant says, but in my words."

      Why are paraphrases important? All clear understanding of language involves paraphrasing. If you give me directions for operating a computer and I have to keep repeating your exact words in order to operate the computer, then the understanding I have is yours, not mine. When I can translate your directions into my own language, my own way of putting things, then I clearly understand what you have told me. I have gone beyond the *words* you used to the *meaning* they conveyed. To put this another way, I genuinely understand Kant only when I can accurately translate from Kant's language into my own.

2. T **F** *Some statements are so complex that they are impossible to paraphrase.*

   False (almost always). This would probably be True only if the complexity of the statement comes from the poor or obscure quality of the writing. It is certainly possible for something to be written so poorly that we can't tell what it means. Philosophers have made many statements whose meaning has been debated for centuries.[2] But if the statement is clearly written, it can always be paraphrased. Why? Any statement can be translated into the meanings of its words. Such a translation will give us the basis of a paraphrase. Even in the case where a phrase like "square meal" doesn't translate into the meanings of its words—a square meal is not a meal with four corners—the phrase itself can be translated into equivalent words, such as "a good or complete meal." So, when trying to paraphrase, take heart. Everything can be said another way.

3. T **F** *The best paraphrase of a quotation has the same sentence structure but not the same words as the quotation.*

   As I tried to point out in this section of the tour, I believe this is False. The best paraphrase of a quotation, the one that demonstrates the most understanding, uses different words *and* a different sentence structure than the quotation does. Consider the following two student paraphrases of: "To be or not to be, that is the question."

      Sarah: "To live or to die, that is the most important issue one can consider."

      Bob: "The most important question one can ask oneself is whether one should live or commit suicide."

---

[2] Let's look at a brief example from a philosopher you have studied. Parmenides held that reality was, among other things, (a) not known by the senses and (b) *round*. Some commentators have believed that he meant that since reality was not known by the senses, then it must be nonphysical (and they have been confused by how something round could be nonphysical); other commentators have believed that since Parmenides stated reality was round, he must have meant reality was physical (and they have been confused by how a physical thing could be not known by the senses). Because we don't know what Parmenides meant, a paraphrase of his position, a restatement in equivalent words, may not be possible.

scholastic (scholasticism) A philosophy, stressing reason's role as a supporter of religious faith, formed in the Middle Ages (A.D. 500–1300). Scholasticism was largely developed by members of religious orders of the Catholic Church.

disquisition A formal investigation of a subject.

Pythagoreans Followers of Pythagoras (c. 582–c. 507 B.C.), a pre-Socratic philosopher about whom little is known. Pythagoreans made important advances in mathematics (the Pythagorean theorem) and music theory.

the mean of excellence Human excellence, according to Aristotle, occurs at the midpoint, the "mean," between the vices of "too much" and "too little." Thus, an excellent appetite avoids an excessive or deficient quantity of food. A sundae which strikes the Aristotelian mean has neither too few nor too many cherries.

Granted, both of these are unpoetic, but Bob demonstrates a slightly higher understanding of Shakespeare than does Sarah. Sarah's meaning is presented within Shakespeare's sentence structure; Bob's meaning is presented within his own sentence structure. Thus, Bob's restatement is more complete. While Sarah paraphrases Shakespeare's content, Bob paraphrases Shakespeare's content and form.

Once you have freed yourself from an author's sentence structure, you can often find many ways to paraphrase his or her thought. If you can present the same philosophical idea in a variety of ways, then you have a richer understanding of the idea than if you can present it in only one way.

4. T _F_ *In an argument, evidence comes before conclusion, but not vice versa.*

False. A conclusion may come at any point—beginning, middle, or end—of an argument. For example, in the *Apology*, Socrates presents a long argument attempting to convince the jurors that he is innocent of the charges brought against him. He states his conclusion that he is innocent near the beginning of his address *before* presenting his evidence.

5. _T_ F *All arguments must have both evidence and at least one conclusion.*

True. Occasionally you will encounter an argument that has an unstated conclusion or unstated evidence, but this means only that the missing parts are not there in such a way that they are there—kind of visibly invisible.

6. T _F_ *A strong argument has more evidence than does a weak argument.*

False. An argument may have an enormous amount of evidence and still be a very weak argument if the evidence is irrelevant to the conclusion. Every lawyer knows the tactic of claiming that all the evidence presented by the other side has nothing to do with the opposition's conclusion.

A strong argument, on the other hand, has evidence that strongly implies the conclusion. In a perfect argument, as I pointed out in this chapter, the evidence so strongly implies the conclusion that the evidence is merely another way of stating the conclusion. For example, here is a very short—but nonetheless perfect—argument.

Evidence: Mona has an apple.

Evidence: Apples are fruit.

Conclusion: Mona has a fruit.

Index

Abraham, R-4
absolutism, 517. *See also* Hobbes
abstraction, 253
absurdity, Camus and, R-7, R-7–R-9
Academy, 183, 250, 252, 316
accidents, 500, 501
  See also nonessential vs. essential characteristics
Achilles, 91–93, 146, 165
actions, goals of, 292–295
actuality, 266–267, 275, 398
Adeimantus, 228
Advocates Library, 569
Aegina, R-7–R-8
Aeschylus, 104
Aesopus, R-8
Aeterni Patris (Leo XIII), 387
aging
  Aristotle and successful life, 290, 309
  Epictetus (stoics) and, 349
  Epicurus on, 318–319
agnosticism, 24, 109
  Hume and, 31
  purpose of human life and, 283–284
  skepticism and, 566
  See also God; reality; skepticism
Albertus Magnus, 387
Alexander the Great, 250, 251, 316
All, 13–14, 38–39
  See also physical universe; reality
allegory, 696
"Allegory of the Cave" (Plato), 184, 194–197, 238
analogy, argument by, 319
Anaxagoras, 145
anguish, R-4–R-5, R-7
animals, Aristotle and, 270, 271, 275, 287, 289, 304, 309
animism, 47
  See also mythic thinking
Annotation Tasks, explanation of, 111
Anselm, Saint
  and God, existence of. *See* ontological argument
  life of, 364
  purpose of life, 736
  works
    Cur Deus homo?, 364
    Monologium, 364
    Proslogium, 364, 422
anthropology, 285
Antichrist, The (Nietzsche), 699, 705–708, 736

antisemitism, R-10, R-13
Anytus, 136, 143, 147, 148, 151
apathia, 340–341, 661–662
  See also stoicism
aphorisms, 696, 697
  of Nietsche, 696–700, 704
Apollodorus, 150, 152
Apology (Plato), 108, 136–154, A-18
appearance as hiding actuality, 77
appearances, the. *See* physical universe
Aquinas. *See* Thomas Aquinas, Saint
Archimedes, 434
architecture, of the Renaissance, 424
argument
  by analogy, 319
  from design, 383–384, 608–610, 638–639
arguments
  allegory vs., 696
  analysis of, methods for, A-2, A-11–A-14, A-18
  aphorisms vs., 696
  circular, 439–440
  See also proofs
argumentum ad absurdum, 534–535
  of Berkeley, 533, 535, 546
Aristophanes, 104, 105, 106, 136, 140
Aristotle
  Aquinas and, 385, 387, 391, 398, 399, 638
  as "common sense" philosopher, 54
  as dualist, 274
  epistemology of, as empiricist, 22, 275–276, 279, 407, 472, 638–639
  ethics of
    humans defined, 286–287
    purpose of human life, 287–291, 292–309, 661
  as Father of Science, 247–248, 251, 255, 257, 268
  God of, 222, 272–273, 275
  Heraclitus and, 59
  impiety charges against, 251
  life of, 250–251
  literary criticism and, 8
  metaphysics of, 249, 252, 269–275, 279–280
    Being, ten categories of, 258–260
    change, 253, 264–269, 271–273
    four causes, 261–263, 267–268, 272–273, 275, 287–288, 638–639
    Plato rejected by, 252–255
    substance, 254–258

paraphrasing of, A-2–A-3
  and Parmenides, 265, 269
  on philosophy, 9
  pragmatic method and, R-22
  on Thales, 46
  on women, R-11
  works
    banning of, 387
    Generation of Animals, 273, 286
    lists of, 251, 273
    Metaphysics, 251, 273, 401
    Nicomachean Ethics, 251, 289–309
Arrian, 341
Artemis, temple of, 58
artisans, Socrates and, 142
artists, Plato's ideas and, 201–202
arts
  goals of, 292, 294–295
  of Renaissance, 424–425
asceticism, 133
Ashley, Lord and Lady, 471
astronomy
  Descartes and, 419
  Newton and, 517
  Renaissance development of, 425
  See also celestial bodies
ataraxia, 317, 329–330, 661
atheism
  Anselm's attack on, 366–372
  Berkeley's attack on, 516
  Camus and, R-7–R-9
  existentialism and, R-3, R-5–R-7
  innate ideas and, 482
  Nietzsche and, 704, 735
  purpose of human life and, 283–284
  Russell and, R-11–R-13
  See also God; reality
Athena (statue, Phidias), 104
Athens, 102–104, 105, 138, 182, 183, 316
atoms, 316–318
attractiveness, Aristotle and, 290
Augustine, Saint, 17, 23, 202, 640, 642
axial age, 251
Ayer, A. J., R-17–R-21

Babylonians, 47, 51
Barnes, Ernest William, R-13
beatitude. *See* happiness
Beauvoir, Simone de, R-9–R-11
"because," A-12, A-13
because-therefore test of arguments, A-12, A-13, A-14

Becket, Saint Thomas, 364
Becoming, 19
Being, 19
   Parmenides. *See* Mysterious X Stuff
   ten categories of, Aristotle, 258–260
   See also existence
Being and Nothingness (Sartre), R-2
belief, Plato's levels of thought, 219–220
Benda, Julien, R-11
Benedictine monks, 386
Bentham, Jeremy, 317, 678–681
Berkeley, George
   empiricism of, 407, 471–474, 517–518,
      521, 561, 563, 639
   life of, 514–515
   Locke compared with, 517–521, 546–
      547, 553–556, 639
   matter as nonexistent
      existence as perception, 519–520,
         527–534, 535–536
      God's ideas and, 514, 518–521, 558–
         559, 564, 639
      immediate vs. mediate perception
         and, 524–527
      primary vs. secondary qualities and,
         518, 546–556
      reality as idea, 513–514
      sense knowledge and, 528–534, 535–
         558, 563–564
      skepticism and, 516, 521–524, 530,
         556
   monism of, 518–521, 561
   as philosopher, 560
   pragmatic method and, R-22
   purpose of, 516–517
   refutations of, attempts at, 563
   works
      Essay Towards a New Theory of
         Vision, 515
      list of, 515
      Three Dialogues Between Hylas and
         Philonous, 515, 521–549, 552–
         559
      Treatise Concerning the Principles of
         Human Knowledge, A, 515
Beyond God the Father: Toward a Philoso-
   phy of Women's Liberation (Daly),
   R-23
Beyond Good and Evil (Nietzsche), 699
bias, against women. *See* women
Bible, 38, 51, 470, 662, 736, R-4, R-11
Biffle, Persephone, 663
Biffle, Saskia, 288
Birmingham, Bishop of (E. W. Barnes),
   R-13
Birth of Tragedy, The (Nietzsche), 699
blame
   Epictetus (stoics) and, 347
   See also duty; responsibility

blank slate (tabula rasa), 484–485, 490
body
   change as constant in, R-12
   mind-brain controversy. *See* mind-brain
      controversy
   soul compared to. *See* soul
   women's inequality and, R-11
   See also mind
Boethius, Anicius Manlius Severinus, 391
Bradley, Frances Herbert, R-18
Brahe, Tycho, 425
brain. *See* body; mind
Britain
   Berkeley and, 514–515
   of nineteenth century, 681
   See also England
British empiricism
   mind, 471–474
   pragmatic method and, R-22
   Russell and, R-11
   vs. Continental Rationalism, 472
   See also Berkeley, George; Hume,
      David; Locke, John
Brunelleschi, Filippo, 424
Buddhism
   pain, soul as shielded from, 238
   purpose of human life, 283
Burns, David, 736

Caaius Musonius Rufus, 340
Caesar, Julius, 714, 715
Cagn, 47
Callias, 140
Callicrates, 104
Camus, Albert, R-7–R-9
Cartesian coordinate system, 419
Cartesian dualism, 422
categorical imperative, 662–663, 674–
   677, 692
Cathedral of Florence, 424
causal relationship, defined, 594
cause and effect
   Berkeley and, 524–527
   Christianity and, Nietzsche on, 706–
      707
   defined, 592–594
   degrees of reality and, Descartes,
      452–457, 460–461
   distinguished, 525–526
   four causes, Aristotle, 261–263,
      267–268, 272–273, 275, 287–288,
      638–639
   Hume and, 576, 595–604, 619–630,
      639, 647–648
   Kant and, 638, 646, 647–648, 650–651
   See also future; God; matter; past
"Cave, Allegory of the" (Plato), 184, 194–
   197, 238
Cebes, 166

celestial bodies
   Aristotle's levels of reality and, 270–271
   Thales and, 45
   See also astronomy
censorship, 387
Cephalus, 228
certainty
   Descartes on. *See* Descartes, René
   Hume and, 570, 573–575, 588
   impossibility of, 416–417
   Kant and, 638, 650–651
   Sextus and destruction of, 420
   tests for, 424–425, 574
   See also nonsense; truth
Chaerephon, 136, 141
change
   as All, Heraclitus, 59–61, 63, 265, 269
   Aristotle and, 253, 264–269, 271–273
   and God, existence of, 400, 405
   as illusion, Parmenides, 74, 77–80, 86–
      87, 265, 269, 640
   monotheism and, 86
   Plato and, 265, 269, 640
   of self, Hume and, 578–582, 588–589
   Thales and, 265
characteristics
   fixed, as nonexistent, R-10
   of matter. *See* matter
   primary. *See* primary vs. secondary
      qualities
Charles I (king of England), 470
Charles II (king of England), 471
children
   Aristotle and, 290, 309
   Epictetus and, 341
   ideas and, Locke, 488, 510
Chomsky, Noam, 510–511
Christian, 35
Christianity
   Berkeley and, 516
   Bible, 38, 51, 470, 662, 736, R-4, R-11
   censorship and, 387
   dualism of, 35, 38, 409, 464, 509
   eternity and, 87
   ethics of
      dualism and, 38
      Kantian ethics distinguished from,
         674
      moral absolutism and, 30, 38
      Nietzsche on, 704–706
      as nonconsequentialist, 662
   existentialism and, R-6
   God
      Anselm's ontological argument for.
         See ontological argument
      circular arguments for, 38
      eternity and, 87
      governments vs., 364, 386
      investiture controversy, 364

logos, 59, 62
  Nietzsche's commentary on, 706–707, 708, 714, 719–721
  persecution by, Inquisition, 419, 425
  persecution of, 340, 341
  Plato's ideas and, 202
  Protestant break in, 425
  purpose of human life, 283, 736
  redemption, 364, R-24
  sexism of, R-24
  stoicism and, 341
Christina (queen of Sweden), 419
circular arguments, 439, 440
class
  Aristotle and, 290
  Epicurus and, 316, 317
  in the Republic, 229
Claucon, 228
Cleanthes, 357
clear thinking, 3
Cleisthenes, 102
Cleon, 106
Clouds, The (Aristophanes), 105, 106
Cloyne, Ireland, 515
cogito, ergo sum. See "I think; therefore, I am"
Coleridge, Samuel Taylor, 247
color
  Berkeley and, 540–545
  Locke and, 477–480, 498–499
Columbus, Christopher, 424, 425
compassion, Epicturus (stoics) and, 356
conclusions, A-11–A-14, A-18
conformity, Nietzsche against, 727–738
conjecture, 219
connection, necessary, 596–602, 628
"consequently," A-13
constant conjunctions, 596–602, 619, 621, 628
contiguity, law of, 576, 619, 621, 628
Continental Rationalists, vs. British empiricists, 472, 481
  See also Descartes, René
contradiction, meaningful, 574, 588
controllable vs. the uncontrollable, stoicism, 341, 342–358, 360, 661–662
Copernicus, Nicolaus, 419, 425, 517, 657
copy model of knowledge, defined, 644
Corinth, 102
corporeal thing, 19
cosmological proof, 365
cosmos, 365
  geocentric vs. heliocentric view of, 419, 425, 657
Courage, Form of, 199, 200, 229
Crito, 106, 149, 152
criterion, A-6, A-7
Critique of Judgment (Kant), 637

Critique of Practical Reason (Kant), 637
Critique of Pure Reason (Kant), 637, 651, 653
Crito (Plato), 108, 164–173
Critobulus, 149, 152
Cronos, 114, 116
Cur Deus homo? (Anselm), 364

Daedalus, 119, 123
Dawn, The (Nietzsche), 699
death
  Aristotle on, 286
  Epictetus (stoics) and, 345, 347, 349, 351, 354–355, 358
  Epicurus on, 320–322, 335
  Plato on, 286
  Russell on, R-11–R-13
  of Socrates, 104, 105, 106
  Socrates on, 137–138, 146–149, 150, 151–154, 178
definitions, examples as improper, 109–110
Delphi, oracle of, 104, 106, 136, 141, 142
democracy
  of Athens, 102–103, 138, 182
  monarchy's transition to, 470
  Plato and, 133–134, 182, 243
  See also government
Democritus, 316–318
demonstration, 623
Descartes, René
  argument analysis of, A-12, A-13–A-14
  and certainty, 424–426, 428
    doubt, 424–426, 429–431
    dreams, 418, 424, 430, 436, 447, 641
    God, 421, 422, 430–431, 444–447, 452–463, 466, 475, 607–608
    "I think; therefore, I am," 435–440, 448, 466
    influences on, 420–421
    method, 419–420
    senses, 421–422, 423, 429, 434–440, 454, 457, 463, 466
  as dualist, 422, 464
  innate ideas and, 475, 510
  Inquisition and, 425
  life of, 418–419
  Locke and, 480, 481, 510
  paraphrasing of, A-6–A-10
  and Plato, 421
  as rationalist, 407, 436–439, 464, 641
  reading of, techniques for, 426–428
  reality, degrees of, 447, 452–457
  as Renaissance philosopher, 422, 424, 425
  Sartre and, R-7
  works, 419
    Discourse on Method, 419
    La Géométrie, 419

Meditations on First Philosophy, 419, 422, 423, 424–426, 429–432, 434–439, 444–450, 452–462, 510, A-6
Principles of Philosophy, 419
Rules for the Direction of the Mind, 419
The World, 419
design, argument from, 383–384, 608–610, 638–639
desire
  Epictetus (stoics) and, 345, 354–355
  Epicurus and, 315, 324–326
  See also emotions; happiness
despair, R-4, R-7
determinism
  Berkeley's attack on, 516
  of Democritus, 318
  of Descartes, 464
  of Epicurus, 318
  existentialism and, R-5
  See also free will
dialectic
  definitions of, 220, 221
  moral Forms and, 199
  Plato's levels of thought and, 219, 220
  Zeno and, 94
Dialogues Concerning Natural Religion (Hume), 569
dialogues of Plato. See Plato
Dionysus, 183
Discourse on Method (Descartes), 419
disease, Epictetus (stoics) and, 350
disquisition, A-16, A-17
"Divided Line" (Plato), 199–200, 219–220
divine right of kings, 470, 471
"Do We Survive Death" (Russell), R-11
dogmatism, 636, 637
doing something, as category of being, Aristotle, 259
Dominican Order, 386, 387
Domitian, 340
Dostoyevsky, Fyodor Mikhaylovich, R-5, R-8
doubt
  Descartes and, 424–426, 429–431
  Socrates and, 566
  See also certainty; skepticism
Draco, 102
dreams
  body-mind split and, Nietzsche, 703
  Christianity and, Nietzsche, 706, 707
  Descartes and, 418, 424, 430, 436, 447, 641
  irrational desires and, Plato, 236
dualism, 16–17
  Anselm, 377
  Aquinas, 409
  Aristotle, 274
  Augustine, 17, 202

dualism *(continued)*
    Christianity, 35, 51, 470, 662, 736, R-4, R-11
    defined, 15
    Descartes, 422, 464
    epistemology and, 38
    ethics and, 38
    Locke, 509
    Plato, 17, 202, 238, 239
    Platonism, 35
    significance of statements and, R-20–R-21
    See also metaphysics
dubious, A-6, A-7
duty, inclination vs., 669–670, 675–677
    See also ethics; responsibility

earth- vs. sun-centered cosmology, 419, 425, 657
Ecce Homo (Nietzsche), 736
education
    Epictetus (stoics) and, 347–348, 353
    Plato and, 183, 229, 233
efficient cause (origin), 261–263, 267–268, 288, 638
    Aquinas's proof of God and, 399
    greater reality of, Descartes, 453
    See also cause and effect
ego, 586
Elea, 94
Eleatic school of philosophy, 76
elements
    Aristotle and, 270–271
    Democritus and, 317
eminent reality, 452
emotions
    changing self and, 581
    death and, R-12–R-13
    desire. *See* desire
    existentialism and, R-5, R-6
    pragmatism and, R-23
    as property of thought, 446
    reason ruled by, 612–614
    youth as swayed by, 297
    See also happiness; pain; pleasure; reason
empiricism, 20, 21–22
    of Aquinas, 385, 406–407, 409, 638–639
    of Aristotle, 22, 275–276, 279, 407, 472, 638–639
    of Berkeley, 407, 471–474, 517–518, 521, 561, 563, 639
    brief history of, 638–639, 642
    British. *See* British empiricism
    defined, 21, 377
    dualism and, 38
    and God, existence of, 21–22, 222, 407
    of Hume, 471–474, 570–575, 616, 631, 639

invisible realities and, 406, 407
of Locke, 471–477, 509, 517–518, 639
pragmatism and, R-21, R-22
rationalism compared to, 247, 642–644
of Russell, R-11
skepticism and, 40
three-step model of, 22
    See also epistemology; rationalism; skepticism
Encheiridion (Epictetus), 341, 342–357
ends vs. means
    Aquinas, 403–404
    Aristotle, 299, 302, 403
    Sartre, R-6
England, 364, 470, 471
    See also Britain
enlightenment
    philosophy as promising, 433–434
    Plato on, 195–197
Enlightenment, the, 636
Enquiry Concerning Human Understanding, An (Hume), 569
Enuma Elish, 47
Epaphroditus, 340
Ephesus, 58
Epictetus
    cognitive therapy and, 736
    on the controllable vs. the uncontrollable, 341, 342–358, 360
    Encheiridion, 341, 342–357
    as ethicist, 341, 661–662
    life of, 340–341
    and Socrates, 347, 360
    See also stoicism
Epicureans. *See* Epicurus
Epicurus
    death and, 320–322, 335
    on desire, 315, 324–326
    as ethicist, 316–317, 661
    on future, 322–323
    on God, 320, 336
    on happiness (ataraxia), 317, 329–330, 661
    life of, 315, 316–317
    metaphysics of, 318
    Mill and, 317, 682–683
    on philosophical study, 318–319
    on pleasure, 317, 324–331, 336
    on wisdom, 330
    works, 317
        "Letter to Herodotus," 317
        "Letter to Menoeceus," 317, 318–319, 320–322, 324–326, 328, 329–330
        "Letter to Pythocles," 317
epistemology, 19–20
    branches of. *See* empiricism; rationalism; skepticism
    brief history of, 638–644
    defined, 8, 9

dualism and, 38
ethics compared to, 27, 38–40
as field of investigation, 12
idealism and, 39–40
Kantian revolution in, 638, 642–648
metaphysics compared to, 19, 38–40, 207, 209
monism and, 39
questions of, 119
See also ethics; metaphysics
equality
    Plato's epistemology and, 210–215
    of women. *See* women
errors, Descartes and, 438, 445–446, 463
Escher, M. C., 18, 26, 52, 202, 268, 603, 649, 716
Essay Concerning Human Understanding, An (Locke), 471, 480–506
Essay Towards a New Theory of Vision (Berkeley), 515
essence
    Aristotle and, 254–257
    defined, 255
    existentialism and, 293, R-2, R-3, R-5
    lack of, in language, R-16–R-17
    Plato and, 254–255
    women and, R-9–R-11
    See also existence
essential vs. nonessential characteristics, 478–480, 500, 647
    See also matter
esthetics, defined, 12
eternal recurrence, 711–712
ethical hedonism, 678
ethics, 27–28
    of Aristotle. *See* Aristotle
    branches of. *See* moral absolutism; moral relativism
    brief summary of, 712–714, 716
    of Christianity. *See* Christianity
    consequentialists, 660–662, 679–680
    defined, 9
    dualism and, 38
    of Epictetus. *See* Epictetus
    of Epicurus, 341, 661–662
    epistemology compared to, 27, 38–40
    existentialism, R-3–R-9
    free will and. *See* free will
    Great Ethical Principle, defined, 659–660
    history of inquiry, 12
    of Hume, 611–615
    idealism and, 40
    of Kant. *See* Kant
    materialism and, 39
    metaphysics compared to, 27, 38–40
    monism and, 39
    Nietzsche and, 704, 709, 712, 714–716, 717–732
    nihilism, 704

nonconsequentialists, 662–677
    of Plato, 29–30, 202, 225–238, 239, 241,
        283, 611–612, 661
    questions of, 27, 108
    relativistic, 631
    rise of, 54, 108
    skepticism and, 40
    Socrates and, 54, 107–108, 209
    utilitarianism and. *See* utilitarianism
    See also epistemology; metaphysics; val-
        ues; virtues
eudaimonia, 288–290, 289, 298–299,
    302–303, 304–309, 661
Eudemian Ethics (Aristotle), 251
Euripides, 104, 106
Euthyphro, 109–111, 162
Euthyphro (Plato), 108–123, 162
Evenus the Parian, 140
Everything, 13–14, 38–39
    See also physical universe; reality
evidence, 4, A-11–A-14, A-18
evil
    as proof against existence of God, 405
    as proof for existence of God, 405
    See also Good; good
excellence, Epictetus (stoics) and, 348
existence
    continuity of, 456–457, 460–461, 516
    essence preceded by, 293, R-2, R-3, R-5
    of God. *See* God
    of invisible realities, 406–407
    of mind, Hume's attack on, 582–586,
        589
    perception as determining, 518–520
    as perfection, 368–369, 374, 376, 640–
        641
    possibility vs. necessity of, 400
    proofs of. *See* proofs
    responsibility and, Sartre, R-3–R-7
    of self. *See* self: existence of
    of truth, as self-evident, 391
    of women, R-9–R-11
    See also Being; essence; reality
existentialism, 292, 293, R-2–R-7
"Existentialism Is a Humanism" (Sartre),
    R-2
extension. *See* space: occupation of
external objects. *See* matter; physical
    universe
external vs. internal experiences
    Kant, 654–655
    Locke, 485–487, 489–490
external, vs. the controllable, stoicism,
    341, 342–358, 360, 661–662

factual significance, R-18–R-21
Falconer, Katherine, 568
falsehoods
    Descartes and, 446, 454
    See also certainty; truth

fame, Aristotle and, 290
fantasy, changing self and, 581
Fate, 51
Fate. *See* determinism; free will
faults, changing self and, 581
Feeling God: The New Mood Therapy
    (Burns), 736
femininity, R-9–R-11
feminism, R-9–R-11, R-23–R-24, A-2
figure. *See* shape (figure)
final cause (purpose), 261–263, 267–268,
    272–273, 275, 288, 399, 638
    Aquinas and, 403
    See also cause and effect; good: Aris-
        totle and
Fire, as the One, 67–68
First Mover. *See* Unmoved Mover
Flavius Arrianus, 341
Fool, ontological argument and, 366–367,
    368–369, 370–371, 605
"for," A-13
forlornness, R-4, R-5–R-7
formal cause (form), 261–263, 288, 399,
    638
    See also cause and effect
formal falsehood, 454
formal reality, 452, 453
forms (Aristotelian), 254–258, 255, 265–
    267
Forms (Platonic). *See* Plato
Forster, Bernhard, 698
Foundation for the Metaphysics of Morals
    (Kant), 663–677
Frederick II (king of Italy), 386
free will
    Aquinas on, 405
    Descartes and, 464
    Epicurus and, 318
    ethics as dependent on, 39, 318
    existentialism and, R-2, R-5–R-7
    God's existence excluded by, 405
    materialism and, 39
    skepticism and, 40
    stoicism and, 340–341, 357
    See also determinism
Frege, Gottlob, R-15
French Revolution, 637
Freud, Sigmund, 422, 586
friendship
    Aristotle and, 292
    Epicurus and, 316–317
*Fundamental Principles of the Metaphysics
    of Morals* (Kant), 637
future
    Epicurus on, 322–323
    Hume and, 623–625, 632, 633
    See also cause and effect; past

Galileo, 418, 419, 425, 517
games, R-16–R-17

Garden, 315, 316, 317
Gaunilo, 375–376
Gay Science, The (Nietzsche), 699
Genealogy of Morals (Nietzsche), 736
Generation of Animals (Aristotle), 273,
    286
Genesis, 51
genus, 401
geocentric vs. heliocentric view of cos-
    mology, 419, 425, 657
geometric figures, Forms of, 184–192
Gide, André, R-6
Gilgamesh, 51
Giotto, 424
goals
    of Aristotle. *See* good: Aristotle and
    changing self and, 581
God
    agnosticism. *See* agnosticism
    animism, 47
    Aquinas and proofs of, 222, 389–394,
        397–404, 638–639
    of Aristotle, 222, 272–273, 275
    atheism. *See* atheism
    Berkeley and, 514, 518–521, 558–559,
        564, 639
    change and, 86
    Christianity and. *See* Christianity
    contemplation of, 457–458
    cosmological proof of, 365
    definitions of, 365–366, 373, 380
    Descartes and, 421, 422, 430–431, 444–
        447, 452–463, 466, 475, 607–608
    dualism and, 38
    empiricism and, 21–22, 222, 407
    Epicurus and, 320, 336
    existentialism and, R-3, R-4
    feminism and, R-24
    "God is dead," Nietzsche, 704, 735
    good vs. evil and existence of, 405
    Hume and existence of, 604–610
    idealism and, 39–40
    as innate idea, 475, 510
    as intelligence of nature, 403–404, 559
    Locke and, 475, 482–484, 504
    monotheism, 86, 273
    ontological proof of. *See* ontological
        argument
    pantheism, 357
    proof(s) for, possibility of, 379–380
    purpose of human life and, 283
    rationalism and, 23, 38, 406–407
    Russell on, R-13
    self-evident existence of, Aquinas, 389–
        394
    skepticism and, 24
    stoicism and, 340–341, 351, 357
    truth as illuminated by, 407
    See also cause and effect; reality;
        religion

gods, holiness and, 115–123
Goethe, Johann Wolfgang von, 714, 715
Golden Rule, 692
   See also categorical imperative
good
   Aristotle and, 292–309
   Descartes and, 431
   Epicurus and, 324, 326, 328
   evil producing, and existence of God, 405
   existentialism and, R-4–R-5
   humans, vs. bad, 232–236
   Russell on, R-13
   without qualification, 663
Good, Form of the
   Aristotle refuting, 300–301
   Plato, 196–197, 199, 200
good fortune, Aristotle and, 289–290
good will. *See* Kant: ethics of; will
Gorgias of Leontium, 140
government
   democracy. *See* democracy
   Hobbes's absolutism and, 517
   laws. *See* laws
   monarchy, transition to democracy of, 470
   in the Republic, 228–229, 243
   vs. religions, 364, 386
Great Ethical Principle, defined, 659–660
Great Pyramid, height of, 46
Greatest Happiness Principle, 682
Gregory X, 387
grief
   process of, 358
   stoicism and, 358
   See also death
Guardians, 229, 243
Gyges' Ring, 228, 241
Gyn/Ecology (Daly), R-23–R-24

happiness
   absurdity and, Camus, R-8–R-9
   Aquinas and God as, 391
   Aristotle and eudaimonia, 288–290,
      289, 298–299, 302–303, 304–309,
      661
   consequentialist ethics and goal of,
      661–662
   Epicurus and ataraxia, 317, 329–330,
      661
   masses defining, 298, 299
   Plato and, 226–238, 242–243, 661
   stoicism and, 340–341
   utilitarianism and, 682, 687
   See also human life, purpose of; pain;
      pleasure
hardness. *See* solidity
Hated Philosopher vs. Loved Tyrant,
   226–238
Hawking, Stephen, 247

hearing, sense of
   Berkeley and, 538–540, 546
   Locke and, 477
heavenly bodies. *See* astronomy
Hector, 146
hedonic calculus, 678–679, 681
hedonism, 133, 327, 678
Hegel, G. W. F., 220
Heidegger, Martin, R-3, R-5
Hellenistic Age, 316
"hence," A-13
Henry I (king of England), 364
Hephaestus, 116
Hera, 116, 209
Heraclitus
   aphorisms of, 696
   Aristotle compared to, 265, 269
   life of, 58–59
   Logos of, 57, 59, 61–64, 67
   the One and the Many and, 59–68, 81
heredity, R-12
Hermias, 250
Hermodorus, 59
Herodotus, 103, 104
Hesiod, 47–48, 65
Hesse, Herman, 736
Hinduism, 222
Hippias of Elis, 140
Hippocrates, 104
History of Animals (Aristotle), 273
History of England (Hume), 569
Hobbes, Thomas, 517
Hodgson, Shadworth, R-22
holiness, 109–111, 133
   in Euthyphro, 109–123
   See also Socrates: trial of
Homer, 51, 65, 196, R-7–R-8
honor, as goal, Aristotle, 299
"How to Make Our Ideas Clear" (Peirce),
   R-21–R-22
Human All Too Human (Nietzsche), 699
human freedom. *See* free will
Human Knowledge, Its Scope and Limits
   (Russell), R-11
human life, purpose of, 282–284
   Aristotle, 287–291, 292–309, 661
   Buddhism and, 283
   duty, 736
   happiness and. *See* happiness
   as nonexistent, 284
   obedience to God's will, 736
   outside world, 283
   reason ruling passions, 736
   as self-perfection, 736
   suggested readings, 736
   within world, 283–284
   See also existence; responsibility
humans
   Aristotle and definition/nature of, 270,
      275–276, 285–287

   definition of, 285–286
   and determinism. *See* determinism
   as duality vs. unity, 286
   free will of. *See* free will
   language of. *See* language
   life, purpose of. *See* human life, pur-
      pose of
   masses of. *See* masses
   Plato and definition/nature of,
      217–218, 227, 230–238, 286
   Sartre and nature of, R-3
   soul of. *See* soul
   See also mind; physical universe; self
Hume, David
   and cause and effect, 576, 595–604,
      619–630, 639, 647–648
   empiricism of, 471–474, 570–575, 616,
      631, 639
   ethics of, 31, 611–615, 631
   goal of, 570
   on God, existence of, 604–610
   ideas
      as category of knowledge, 570–573,
         615–618
      laws governing association of, 576,
         604
      and mind, existence of, 582–586,
         639
      relations of, as statement of knowl-
         edge, 573–576
      simple vs. complex, 571–572
   impressions
      as category of knowledge, 570–573,
         615–618
      matters of fact based on, 574
      and self, existence of, 579–580,
         589–590
      simple vs. complex, 571
   and invisible, existence of, 406
   Kant and, 636–638, 647–648, 650–651
   life of, 568–569
   life, purpose of, 736
   and Locke, 615–616
   matter, analysis of, 616–618
   matters of fact
      in cause and effect, 619–620, 623
      as statement of knowledge, 573, 574–
         575, 620–621
   meaningful contradiction, 574, 588
   on metaphysics, 12, 610–611
   on Newton, 517
   paraphrasing of, A-4–A-5
   as philosopher, 566
   Plato, compared with, 611–613
   pragmatic method and, R-22
   on scientific laws, 21
   as skeptic, 24, 31, 566, 568, 586, 611
   works
      A Treatise of Human Nature, 568–569,
         615–628

History of England, 569
list of, 569
My Own Life, 569
humility, 705
humor, of Socrates, 105, 112, 114, 137
Huxley, Aldous, 40
hypotheses, verifiability, R-18–R-21

"I think; therefore, I am," Descartes, 435–440, 448, 466
Ictinus, 104
id, 586
idealism
    of Berkeley, 407, 471–474, 517–518, 521, 561, 563, 639
    defined, 35, 88
    empiricism and, 39
    ethics and, 40
    of Parmenides, 88
    rationalism and, 39–40
    significance of statements and, Ayer, R-20–R-21
    of Zeno, 99
    See also materialism; monism
ideas
    Berkeley and. *See* Berkeley, George: matter as nonexistent
    Descartes, 446–447, 448–449, 452–460
    Hume and. *See* Hume, David
    innate. *See* innate ideas
    as intermediaries, British empiricism, 471, 475–477, 564
    Locke and. *See* Locke, John
    See also mind; reason; thought
Ideas. *See* Forms
Iliad (Homer), 51, 65
illusion
    change as, Parmenides, 74, 77–80, 86–87, 265, 269, 640
    defined, 75, 77
    matter as
        Berkeley on. *See* Berkeley
        scientific view of, 74
    motion as, 91–96
    senses as, 74, 77–78, 83
    See also change; reality
impiety, charges of. *See* religion; persecution based on
impossibilities, logical vs. physical, 97
inclination, duty vs., 669–670, 675–677
incorporeal thing, 19
individualism, 637
individuals, state as superior to, Aristotle, 296
Industrial Revolution, 681
inference, Hume on, 621
infinity
    Descartes and, 455
    Zeno and, 93, 96, 98

innate ideas, 469
    language as innate, 510–511
    Locke's attack on, 474–475, 480, 482–484, 488, 510
    See also ideas
inorganic level, of Aristotle, 269
Inquisition, 419, 425
insects, Aristotle and, 287
intellectual abstraction, Aristotle's criticism of Platonists and, 253
internal experiences. *See* external vs. internal experiences
investiture controversy, 364
invisible, proof of, 406–407
irony
    defined, 490
    of Locke, 490
    of Socrates, 105, 112, 114, 137
irrational soul, 230–238
Islam, 38, 283, R-13

James II (king of England), 471
James, William, R-21–R-23
Jaspers, Karl Theodor, R-3
Jocobins, 637
Johnson, Samuel, 563
joy of life, Nietzsche and, 715–716
Judaism, 38, 283
    See also antisemitism
judgment
    of mind, Descartes, 423, 438, 445, 446, 454
    of self, stoicism, 347
juries, 138
justice
    Plato and, 30, 234
    Socrates and, 169–173, 178, 228–229
Justice, Form of, 196–197, 199, 200

Kant, Immanuel
    categorical imperative, 662–663, 674–677
    and cause and effect, 638, 646, 647–648, 650–651
    and certainty, 638, 650–651
    epistemological revolution of, 638, 642–648
    ethics of
        Christian ethics distinguished from, 674
        duty vs. inclination, 669–670
        good will, 662–668
        will, defined, 664, 672
    goal of, 636–638
    and Hume, 636–638, 647–648, 650–651
    life of, 636–637
    metaphysics and, 657, R-18
    mind as active vs. passive, 642–648, 651–654, 656, 657

ontological argument and, 365, 376–378
    paraphrasing of, A-3–A-4
    as philosopher, 635, 651
    religion and, R-3
    Sartre and, R-6
    and science, 638, 656
    works
        Critique of Pure Reason, 637, 651, 653
        Foundation for the Metaphysics of Morals, 663–677
        list of, 637
katastematic pleasures, 328–329
Kepler, Johannes, 418, 425, 517
Kierkegaard, Søren Aabye, R-4
kinematic pleasures, 328–329
king archon, 111
knowledge
    changing self and, 581
    nature of. *See* epistemology
Koenigsberg, 636, 637

La Flèche, 418
La Géométrie (Descartes), 419
language
    as deceiving, 438
    as innate skill, 510–511
    logical constants, R-15
    and metaphysics, Ayer, R-17–R-21
    nominalism, 517, R-10, R-23
    nonsense. *See* nonsense
    paraphrasing, methods for, A-2–A-9, A-17–A-18
    philosophy structuring/structured by, R-14–R-17
    as prison vs. window, 376
    sexist, R-24, A-2
Language, Truth, and Logic (Ayer), R-17–R-21
Last Letters from Stalingrad (Schneider), 736
last man, 725–726
laws
    Plato and, 241
    Socrates on, 170–173, 178
    written vs. oral, 102
    See also government
"Leap Beyond Patriarchal Religion, The" (Daly), R-23–R-24
Leibniz, Gottfried, 472
Leo XIII, 387
Leon of Salamis, 149
"Letter to Herodotus" (Epicurus), 317
"Letter to Menoeceus" (Epicurus), 317, 318–319, 320–322, 324–326, 328, 329–330
"Letter to Pythocles" (Epicurus), 317
Leucippus, 316
Leviathan (Hobbes), 517
Life and Death of Ivan Ilych (Tolstoy), 736

light of nature. *See* reason

location, as category of being, Aristotle, 259

Locke, John, 470–471
  Berkeley compared with, 517–521, 546–547, 553–556, 639
  and Descartes, 480, 481, 510
  as dualist, 509
  as empiricist, 471–477, 509, 517–518, 639
  and God, 475, 482–484, 504
  Hume and, 615–616
  ideas
    complex, 481, 488, 489, 491, 498–501
    innate, attack on, 474–475, 480, 482–484, 488, 510
    internal vs. external origin of, 481, 484–488
    simple, 481, 488–498
    vs. qualities, 491–492, 495
  matter
    existence of, 498–503, 507, 511, 639
    qualities of
      essential vs. nonessential characteristics and, 478–480, 500
      ideas producing, 486, 488–489, 491–493, 493–495, 495
      primary vs. secondary, 477–478, 481, 492–495, 502, 504, 506–507, 639
      real vs. unreal, 496–497
  and the mind, 482, 484–485, 486–487, 503, 505–506
  pragmatic method and, R-22
  and sense knowledge, 476–480, 498–503, 507
  works
    An Essay Concerning Human Understanding, 471, 480–506
    list of, 471
    Two Treatises of Government, 470, 471

logic
  arguments, analysis of, A-2, A-11–A-14
  Aristotle as inventor of, 251
  defined, 12
  as innate idea, 474–475
  proofs. *See* proofs
  of self-evident truth, 391
  of sentences, R-15
  verifiability of language and, R-17–R-21

logical constants, R-15

logical impossibility, 97

Logos, 57, 59, 61–64, 67

love
  Epictetus (stoics) and, 345, 360
  God of Aristotle and, 272–273, 279–280

Loved Tyrant vs. Hated Philosopher, 226–238

Luther, Martin, 425

Lyceum, 111, 250–251, 316

Lycon, 136, 143, 151

Magee, Bryan, R-14–R-17

Magna Moralia (Aristotle), 251

majority rule. *See* democracy; masses

Many. *See* One Behind the Many, question of

Marcel, Gabriel, R-3

Marcus Aurelius, 340, 341

Marduk, 47

Marx, Karl, 16, 220

Mary II (queen of England, Scotland, and Ireland), 471

masculinity, R-10–R-11

Masham, Lord and Lady, 471

masses
  Aristotle and, 306
  and death, 321–322
  Epicurus and, 320, 321
  and God, 320
  happiness defined by, 298, 299
  morality of, 169
  Nietzsche and, 725–728
  opinions of, 165–166, 167–168, 306
  philosophers as critics of values of, 54, 108, 133–134, 196–197, 705, 735
  Plato and, 133–134, 182, 243, 306
  See also democracy

material cause (matter), 261–263, 275, 287, 399, 638
  See also cause and effect

material falsehood, 454

material substance. *See* matter

materialism
  defined, 35, 88
  empiricism and, 39
  ethics and, 39
  Hobbes, 517
  and mind-brain controversy, 38–39
  significance of statements and, Ayer, R-20–R-21
  See also idealism; monism

mathematics
  Descartes and, 418, 419
  Hume and, 573–574, 588
  Kant and, 638
  Newton and, 517
  Plato's ideas and, 201
  See also science

matter
  as All, 38–39
  characteristics of
    essential vs. nonessential, 478–480, 500, 647
    objective vs. subjective, 506–507, 549–550, 552, 639

primary vs. secondary qualities. *See* primary vs. secondary qualities
  as component of substance, Aristotle, 254–255, 257, 265–267
  Descartes' definition of, 421
  existence of
    Berkeley. *See* Berkeley, George
    Locke. *See* Locke, John
    God and, Descartes, 419
    Hume's analysis of, 616–618
    Newton's description of, 421
    pragmatism and, James, R-23
    scientific view of, 74
    significance of statements and, Ayer, R-20–R-21
    See also physical universe; reality

maximum, 401

Mbuti Pygmies, 47

mean of excellence, A-16, A-17
  See also middle path

meaning, R-15, R-16–R-17

meaningful contradiction, 574, 588

mechanistic universe. *See* determinism

Meditations on First Philosophy (Descartes), 419, 422, 423, 424–426, 429–432, 434–439, 444–450, 452–462, 510, A-6

Meditations (Marcus Aurelius), 340

Meletus, 112, 113–114, 136, 139–140, 143–146, 147, 150, 151

Memoirs of a Dutiful Daughter (de Beauvoir), R-9

Memorabilia (Xenophon), 106

memory, 581, R-12

men
  feminism and, R-24
  and male as norm, de Beauvoir, R-10–R-11
  See also women

Metaphysical Foundations of Natural Science (Kant), 637

metaphysics
  of Aristotle. *See* Aristotle: metaphysics of
  Ayer's attack on, R-17–R-21
  branches of. *See* dualism; monism
  defined, 8, 9
  epistemology compared to, 19, 38–40, 207, 209
  essence. *See* essence
  ethics compared to, 27, 38–40
  as field of investigation, 12
  Kantian turn in, 657, R-18
  ontology, 365
  of Plato. *See* Plato: Forms
  pragmatism and, R-22
  of pre-Socratics. *See* One behind the Many, question of
  questions of, 12–14
  as term, origin of, 12

of Wittgenstein, R-14, R-16
women's equality in, R-9–R-11
See also epistemology; ethics
Metaphysics (Aristotle), 251, 273, 401
Metaphysics of Morals (Kant), 637
Michelet, Jules, R-11
middle path, Aristotle, 289, 305, 661, A-16, A-17
Miletus, 45
Mill, Harriet Burrow, 680
Mill, James, 680
Mill, John Stuart, 317, 680–687
mind
  as active vs. passive, Kant, 642–648, 651–654, 656, 657
  vs. body. *See* mind-brain controversy
  errors of, Descartes, 438, 445–446, 463
  existence of, Hume's attack on, 582–586, 589
  as intermediary, British empiricists, 471, 475–477, 564
  Locke and, 482, 484–485, 486–487, 503, 505–506
  mortality of, Russell, R-12–R-13
  rationalism and, 22–23
  skepticism and, 24
  stoicism and, 340
  as tabula rasa, 484–485
  will vs., Kant, 665
  See also ideas; reason; soul; thought
mind-brain controversy, 38–39
  Descartes and, 422
  materialism and, 38, 39
  Russell and, R-12–R-13
monarchy, transition to democracy from, 470, 471
monastic life, of Anselm, 364
monism, 15–16
  Berkeley, 518–521, 561
  defined, 15
  Democritus, 316–318
  Epicurus, 318
  epistemology and, 39
  ethics and, 39
  Hobbes, 517
  idealist. *See* idealism
  Marx, 16
  materialist. *See* materialism
  pre-Socratic. *See* One behind the Many, question of
  significance of statements and, R-20–R-21
  See also metaphysics
monistic idealism, 88, 561
Monologium (Anselm), 364
monotheism, 86, 273
moral absolutism, 27–28, 29–30
  dualism and, 38
  idealism and, 40

materialism and, 39
of Plato, 29–30, 202, 239
See also ethics
moral Forms, 199–200, 202, 219, 220
moral relativism, 28, 30–31, 239
  dualism and, 38
  effects of, 133
  of Hume, 31, 631
  materialism and, 39
  Protagoras on, 109
  skepticism and, 40
  See also ethics
motion
  as illusion, 91–96
  as primary quality, Locke, 492–492
  as secondary quality, Berkeley, 548–549, 551–552
  Unmoved Mover and, Aristotle, 272–273, 279–280
murder, Hume on, 613–614
My Own Life (Hume), 569
Mysterious X Stuff, 74, 78, 81–83
mysticism
  idealism and, 40
  The Perennial Philosophy (Huxley), 40
Myth of Sisyphus and Other Essays, The (Camus), R-7–R-9
mythic thinking, 47–48, 49, 54

Napoleon I (emperor of France), 714, 715
Natural History of Religion, The (Hume), 569
nature, A-3
  God as intelligence of, 403–404, 559
  hatred of, 706, 707–708
  See also humans; physical universe
Nausea (Sartre), R-2
Nazis, appropriation of Nietzsche's works by, 698, 710, R-13
necessary connection, 596–602, 628
needs, changing self and, 581
Nero, 339, 340
Newton, Isaac, 516, 517
Nicomachean Ethics (Aristotle), 251, 289–309
Nicomachus, 250
Nietzsche, Friedrich
  aphorisms, understanding, 697–700, 719, 720, 728
  Christianity, criticisms of, 704–709
  on dualism, 701–703
  "ethics" of, 709, 712, 714–716, 717–732
  fascism, appropriation of works by, 698, 710, R-13
  life of, 698–699
  "metaphysics" of, 709–712
  on Thales, 50
  works
    Ecce Homo, 736

    list of, 699
    The Antichrist, 699, 705–708, 736
    Thus Spake Zarathustra, 699, 714, 717–732
    Toward a Genealogy of Morals, 699, 736
nihilism, 704
No Exit (Sartre), 292, R-2
Nobel Prize, R-2, R-7, R-11
nominalism, 517, R-10, R-23
nonessential vs. essential characteristics, 478–480, 500, 647
  See also matter
nonsense
  fact-stating language vs., R-14, R-15–R-16
  verifiability of language and, R-17–R-21
noumena, 646–648, 647, 650
numbers, Forms of, 192–194

objective vs. subjective characteristics, 506–507, 549–550, 552, 639
  Berkeley and. *See* primary vs. secondary qualities: Berkeley
  Locke and. *See* primary vs. secondary qualities: Locke
objective vs. subjective events, Hume and, 604
Odyssey (Homer), 51, 65
Oedipus, R-8–R-9
On Liberty (Mill), 681
On Nature (Heraclitus), 59
On Perpetual Peace (Kant), 637
On the Soul (Aristotle), 273
One, All is. *See* monism
One behind the Many, question of, 43–44, 57–58
  Heraclitus's solution to, 59–68, 81
  Parmenides's solution to, 74–83, 88
  as pre-Socratic question, 106–108
  Thales's solution to, 16, 45, 46–47, 49–50, 51
  Zeno's solution to, 99
  See also reality
One Commandment. *See* categorical imperative
ontological argument, 364, 365–377, 422, 605, 640–641
  Descartes's use of, 422, 463
  of Hume, 606
  objections to, 372–375
    of Aquinas, 385–394
    of Guanilo, 375–376
    of Kant, 376–377
  See also God; proofs
ontology, 365
opposites, identity of, 63–65
oracle at Delphi, 104, 106, 136, 141, 142
original qualities. *See* primary vs. secondary qualities

Ostwald, Friedrich Wilhelm, R-22
Other, women as, R-9–R-11, R-24
overman, 714–716, 717–732

pacifism, R-12, R-13
pain
    Berkeley and, 528–536, 545–546
    Buddhism and, 238
    Epictetus and, 341
    Epicurus and, 324, 336, 661
    Plato and, 238, 242
    utilitarianism and, 678–680
    See also happiness; pleasure
painting, of the Renaissance, 424
Palladio, 425
Panathenaea, 114
pantheism, 357
    See also God; religion
paradox, 71, 697, 718
    of Zeno, 91–96
paraphrasing, methods for, A-2–A-9,
    A-17–A-18
Parker, Dorothy, R-10
Parmenides, 74–83, 86–88, 94, 162, 209,
    407
    Aristotle compared to, 265, 269
Parmenides (Plato), 76, 94, 162
Parthenon, 104
Parts of Animals (Aristotle), 273
passion. See desire; emotions
the past
    Descartes's suspicion of, 422
    Hume and, 623–626, 632, 633
    verifiability of statements regarding,
    R-19–R-20
Patroclus, 146
Paul (apostle), 58
Peirce, Charles, R-21–R-22
Peloponnesian war, 182
perception
    Berkeley and being as. See Berkeley:
    matter as nonexistent
    See also knowledge; senses
Perennial Philosophy, The, 40
perfection vs. imperfection
    Descartes and proof of God's existence,
    421, 422, 453, 455–457, 463, 466
    existence as, 368–369, 374, 376,
    640–641
    medieval philosophers' problem of, 422
    Plato's Forms. See Plato: Forms
    purpose of life and, 736
    See also existence; ontological
    argument
Pericles, 94, 102–103, 104
peripatetic philosophy, 251
persecution. See religion: censorship; reli-
    gion: persecution based on
Persia, 103

personality, 581, R-12
    See also psychology; self
persons. See humans
Phaedo (Plato), 181, 210–212, 242
Phaenarete, 104
phenomena
    defined, 646–648, 647
    See also physical universe; senses
Phidias, 104
Philip of Macedonia, 250
philosopher-king, 229, 250
philosophers
    apparent absurdity of, 560
    happiness and, Aristotle, 290
    methods and activities of, 33–34, 560,
    701
    persecution of. See religion: persecu-
    tion based on
    role of, Locke on, 480
    in society, 54, 108, 133–134, 196–197,
    705, 735
    teaching by, 636–637
    See also individual philosophers
Philosophiae Naturalis Principia Mathe-
    matica (Newton), 517
Philosophical Investigations (Wittgen-
    stein), R-14, R-16, R-17
philosophical self-portrait, creation of,
    3–4
philosophical thought, nature of, 428
philosophical vs. unphilosophical ques-
    tions, 8–11
philosophy
    axial age and, 251
    branches of, 12
    defined, 8, 10–12
    effects of, 8–9
    See epistemology
    See ethics
    first evidence of, 9
    See logic
    See metaphysics
    as public vs. private activity, 220
    reading of. See reading philosophy
    Scholasticism, 422, 470, A-16, A-17
    of sixteenth century, education in, 418
    systems of, arguments against, 481,
    698–699
    unanswered self-refutation in, 76
    use of, 432–434
    See also reality
the Philosopher. See Aristotle
Phthia, 165
physical impossibility, 97
physical universe
    defined, 9
    existence and. See existence
    as illusion, 39–40
    as imperfect copy. See Plato: Forms

    See matter
    as only reality. See materialism
    as shared reality. See dualism
    See also nature; reality
pity, 705
Plague, The (Camus), R-7
plants, Aristotle and, 269, 273, 287, 289,
    304
Plato
    Aristotle and, 183, 252–255
    change and, 265, 269, 640
    Descartes and, 421
    dialogues of, 181–182, 183
        "Allegory of the Cave" in, 184, 194–
        197, 238
        Apology, 108, 136–154, A-18
        Crito, 164–173
        Euthyphro, 108–123, 162
        list of, 183
        Parmenides, 76, 94, 162
        Phaedo, 181, 210–212, 242
        Republic, 181, 194–197, 199, 228–
        229, 230, 232–238, 241, 242, 243
        Symposium, 181
    "Divided Line," 199–200, 219–220
    as dualist, 17, 202, 238, 239
    ethics of, 29–30, 202, 225–238, 239,
        241, 283, 611–612, 661
    as first great philosopher, 54
    Forms, 182–184, 407, 421, 640
        "Allegory of the Cave" and, 196–197
        Aristotle's criticism of, 253, 254–255,
        300–301
        characteristics of, 187–191
        Descartes and, 421
        divided line and, 199–200, 219–220
        education on, 233
        epistemology of, 210–220
        existence of, 184–186, 191–194
        as independent of human mind, 200–
        201
        moral, 199–200, 202, 219, 220
        soul and, 215–218
        as utilized in society, 201–202
    four levels of existence, 199–201, 219–
        220
    Heraclitus and, 59
    Hume compared to, 611–613
    life of, 8, 105, 150, 152, 182–183
    logos of, 62
    masses, opinion of, 306
    metaphysics of. See Plato: Forms
    Nietzsche and, 701–703
    person, definition of, 217–218, 227,
        230–238, 286
    politics and, 182–183
    as rationalist, 23, 209–220, 238, 239,
        640
    and religion, 205

as Socrates' biographer, 104, 105, 106, 181
on Thales, 46
See also Aristotle; Socrates
Platonist, 35
pleasure
Aristotle and, 290, 306–307
Epicurus and, 317, 324–331, 336
hedonism, 133, 327, 678
Plato and, 229, 242
utilitarianism and, 678–681, 682–687
See also happiness; pain
Poetics (Aristotle), 251
poets, Socrates and, 141–142
polemarchus, 228
polis, 102
political philosophy, defined, 12
political science, 285
politics
Aristotle and, 292, 295–297, 298
Kant and, 637
Locke and, 470, 471
Mill and, 681
Plato and, 182–183
Socrates and, 141, 148-1149
See also government
Politics (Aristotle), 251
possessions
Aristotle and happiness and, 306–307
Epictetus (stoics) and, 345, 349–350, 355, 360
Epicurus and, 336
See also wealth
posture, as category of being, Aristotle, 259
potentiality, 266–267, 275, 398, 403
power
feminism and, R-24
will to, 709–711
practical reason, will as, 672
pragmatism, R-21–R-23
Pragmatism (James), R-21–R-23
Praxiteles, 104
predicate, 391
presuppose, as term, 651–652
price to be paid
stoicism and, 353
See also pleasure
Primal Truth, 392
primary vs. secondary qualities
Berkeley and, 518, 546–556
Locke and, 477–478, 481, 492–495, 502, 504, 506–507, 639
objective vs. subjective characteristics and, 506–507, 549–550, 552, 639
See also matter
Principia Mathematica (Russell), R-11
Principles of Morals and Legislation (Bentham), 678

Principles of Philosophy (Descartes), 419
Principles of Political Economy (Mill), 681
Principles of Psychology (James), R-21
Prodicus of Ceos, 140
Prolegomena to Any Future Metaphysics (Kant), 637
proofs
demonstration, 624–625
of God's existence. *See* God
of the invisible, existence of, 406–407
the past as basis of, 422
successful, defined, 363
See also arguments
property rights, 470
Proslogium (Anselm), 364, 422
prostitutes, Epicurus's school and, 316
Protagoras, 108, 109
Protestant Reformation, 425
prudence, Epicurus, 330
Prytaneum, 151
psyche
Aristotle, 286, 287
See also soul
psychological hedonism, 678
psychology, 285, 422, 586, 736
pure concepts of the understanding, 646–648, 656
purpose
final cause. *See* final cause
of life. *See* human life, purpose of
Pythagoras, 58, 201, A-17
Pythagorean theorem, 201
Pythagoreans, A-16, A-17
Pythias, 250

qualities, of matter. *See* under matter
quality
as category of being, 259
of pleasure, vs. quantity. *See* utilitarianism
quantity, as category of being, 259
questions, philosophical vs. unphilosophical, 8–11
quintessence, Aristotle, 270–271

racism, R-10, R-24
Rapport d'Uriel (Benda), R-11
rational soul, 230–238
rationalism, 22–24
of Anselm, 377
of Augustine, 23, 640, 642
de Beauvoir and, R-10
brief history of, 640–642
Continental, 472, 481
defined, 23, 377
of Descartes, 407, 436–439, 464, 641
dualism and, 38
empiricism compared to, 247, 642–644
God, existence of, 23, 38, 406–407

and invisible realities, 406–407
model of, 23
of Parmenides, 86, 88, 640
of Plato, 23, 209–220, 238, 239, 640
pragmatism and, R-22
senses and, 22–23, 86, 642
skepticism and, 40
of Zeno, 99
See also empiricism; epistemology; skepticism
reading philosophy, 292, 294, 426–428, 560
analyzing arguments, A-2, A-11–A-14, A-18
paraphrasing, A-2–A-9, A-17–A-18
reality
analysis of views of, 38–40
defined, 13
greater, greater truth and, 401
humans and. *See* humans
knowledge of. *See* epistemology
levels of, and cause and effect, Descartes, 447, 452–457
nature of. *See* metaphysics
See also nature; physical universe
reason
Aristotle and, 270, 287, 289, 290, 304–305
cause and effect, and, 622–624
Descartes and, 446–447
emotions ruling, 612–614
ethical actions guided by, 662–663, 674–677
Hume and, 611–614
Plato and, 611–612
practical, will as, 672
See also emotions; ideas; mind; thought
Reasonableness of Christianity, The (Locke), 471
redemption, 364, R-24
reflection. *See* external vs. internal experiences
reflectivity, 479–480
reformism, R-5, R-24
reincarnation, 217, 222–223
relationship
as category of being, Aristotle, 259
relativistic ethics, 631
relativity, 71
religion
feminism and, R-23–R-24
God. *See* God
government vs., 364, 386
Hobbes's attack on, 517
Hume and, 569
Kant and, R-3
Marx's views of, 16
Nietzsche and, 704–709
pantheism, 357

religion *(continued)*
  persecution based on
    of Aristotle, 251
    censorship, 387
    Christian Inquisition, 419, 425
    of Socrates. *See* Socrates: trial of
  persecution of, 340, 341
  Plato and, 205
  Socrates and, 142, 144–146, 147, 151, 152
  See also Buddhism; Christianity; Hinduism; Islam; Judaism
Renaissance, 424–425
Republic (Plato), 181, 194–197, 199, 228–229, 230, 232–238, 241, 242, 243
resemblance, law of, 576
responsibility of existence, Sartre, R-3–R-7
  See also duty; ethics
Rhetoric (Aristotle), 251
river, stepping in, 59–60
Roman Catholic Church. *See* Christianity
Roman Empire, 339, 340
Rousseau, Jean-Jacques, 317, 569
Rules for the Direction of the Mind (Descartes), 419
Russell, Bertrand, R-11–R-13, R-14

saints, Nietzsche on, 714, 719–720
Salome, Lou, 699
Samos, 316
San bushmen, 47
Sartre, Jean-Paul, 292, 293, R-2–R-7, R-9, R-12
satisfaction theory of redemption, 364
Schneider, Franz, 736
Scholastic philosophy, 422, 470, A-16, A-17
Schopenhauer, Arthur, 699
science
  Aristotle and, 22
  Berkeley and, 514, 516
  cause and effect, effects of, 632
  context as governing characteristics, R-10
  Descartes and, 430
  Enlightenment and, 636
  goals of, 293, 294–295
  Kant and, 638, 656
  Locke and, 481, 505–506
  moral values and, Russell, R-13
  Newton and, 516, 517
  pragmatism and, R-22
  Renaissance and, 425
  verifiability of statements of, R-19
  See also mathematics
scientific method, empiricism and, 21
Searle, John, R-14–R-17
Second of Council of Lyons, 387

Second Sex, The (de Beauvoir), R-9–R-11
secondary qualities. *See* primary vs. secondary qualities
self
  defined, 578–579, 588
  existence of
    Descartes. *See* Descartes: certainty
    Hume's attack on, 578, 578–582, 588–589
  perfection of, as purpose in life, 736
  power over, Nietzsche, 710–711
  responsibility of, R-3–R-7
  See also humans; mind
self-contradictory statements, defined, 370
self-evident truth, 389–394
self-examination, stoicism and, 341
sensation. *See* external vs. internal experiences
senses
  Descartes and limitations of, 421–422, 423, 429, 434–440, 454, 457, 463, 466
  Heraclitus on, 59
  as idea source, 486, 487
  as illusion, 74, 77–78, 83
    See also rationalism
  impressions of. *See* Hume
  knowledge through. *See* empiricism
  Locke and, 478–480
  rationalism and, 22–23, 86, 642
  skepticism and, 24–25
  See also reason
sensible beings, A-10, A-11
  See also physical universe
sequential relationship, defined, 594
serenity
  stoicism and, 341, 353
  See also happiness
sexism, R-9–R-11, R-23–R-24, A-2
Sextus Empiricus, 420
Shaftesbury, Earl of, 471
shape, 258
shape (figure)
  as primary quality, Locke, 477, 481, 492–495, 496, 502
  as secondary quality, Berkeley, 547–548
Siddhartha (Hesse), 736
sight, sense of, 477, 479–480, 497, 540–545
significance
  concrete consequences and, R-22–R-23
  of propositions, R-17–R-21
Simmias the Theban, 166, 210–212
"since," A-13
sisterhood, R-24
Sisyphus, R-7–R-9
size. *See* space: occupation of

skepticism, 24–25, 566–568, 586
  Berkeley refutation of. *See* Berkeley, George
  defined, 25
  dualism as excluding, 38
  epistemology and, 40
  ethics and, 40
  of Hume, 24, 31, 566, 568, 586, 611
  model of, 25
  of Sextus, 420
  See also empiricism; epistemology; rationalism
slaves and slavery
  Epictetus and, 340, 341, 355, 360
  in Epicurus's school, 316
smell, sense of, Berkeley and, 537–538, 546
Smith, Adam, 569
"so," A-13
society
  moral action as requiring, Aristotle, 292
  philosophers and views of, 54, 108, 133–134, 196–197, 705, 735
sociology, 285
Socrates
  biographer of, Plato as, 104, 105, 106, 181
  change and, 265
  on death, 137–138, 146–149, 150, 151–154, 178
  and equality (*Phaedo*), 210–212
  as ethicist, 54, 107–108, 209
  and holiness (*Euthyphro*), 109–123
  imprisonment of, and refusal to escape (*Crito*), 164–173
  irony and humor of, 105, 112, 114, 137
  and justice, 169–173, 178, 228–229
  on laws, 170–173, 178
  life and death of, 102, 104–106
  Nietzsche and, 701
  and Parmenides, 76
  and politics, 182–183
  pragmatic method and, R-22
  pre-Socratics vs., 106–108
  and religion, 142, 144–146, 147, 151, 152
  trial of, 105, 106, 182
    in the *Apology*, 136–154
    in the *Euthyphro*, 112, 113–114
  and wealth, 133, 147, 154, 162
  and wisdom, 104, 106, 136, 140–143, 149, 152, 162
  See also Plato
solidity
  Berkeley and, 552–553
  Locke and, 499–500
Solon, 102

Some Thoughts Concerning Education
(Locke), 471
sophists, 108, 109
Sophocles, 104, R-8
Sophroniscus, 104
soul
  Aristotle and, 286–287, 304–305
  Epicurus and, 335
  as immortal, 286
  as mortal, 286, 335
  Plato and, 215–218, 227, 229, 230–238,
    242–243, 286
  pragmatism and, R-23
  as reason, Democritus, 317
  reincarnation, 217, 222–223
  Russell on, R-12
  Socrates and right actions for. *See*
    Socrates
  threefold structure of, 232–238
  as universal, 287
  See also mind; self; will
sound. *See* hearing, sense of
space
  mind as creating, Kant, 645–646, 647,
    649, 650–654
  occupation of (extension)
    as primary quality, Locke, 477, 481,
      492–495, 496, 502
    as secondary quality, Berkeley, 547–
      548, 550–551, 555–556
  See also pure concepts of the under-
    standing; time
Sparta, 102, 182
spatial contiguity, 596–602
Spinoza, Baruch, 472
spirit
  Nietzsche's metamorphosis of, 729–
    732
  See also mind
spirited element of soul, 231–238
spirituality
  feminism and, R-24
  See also God; pantheism; religion
standards, judging by, 326
Stasinus, 120
state, as category of being, Aristotle, 259
stoicism, 339–341, 339
  Christianity and, 341
  death and, 345, 347, 349, 351, 354–355,
    358
  desire and, 345, 354–355
  education and, 347–348, 352
  on God, 340–341, 351, 357
  happiness (apathia) and, 340–341,
    661–662
  logos of, 62
  pain and, 341
  virtue and, 341, 350–351

wealth/possessions and, 345, 349–350,
    355, 360
  wisdom and, 341, 351, 360
  See also Epictetus
Stranger, The (Camus), R-7
strength of arguments, evaluating, A-2,
    A-11–A-14, A-18
strife, 65–66, 67
subject, 391
Subjection of Women, The (Mill), 681
subjective reality, Descartes, 447,
    452–457
subjective vs. objective characteristics,
    506–507, 549–550, 552, 639
subjectivity, existentialism and, R-3–R-4,
    R-11
substance
  Aristotle, 254, 255, 258–260
  matter. *See* matter
substance-accidents, 646, 647
  See also space; time
Summa Theologiae (Aquinas), 385–392,
    387, 397–405
superconscious, 586
superman. *See* overman
syllogism, A-13
Symposium (Plato), 181
Symposium (Xenophon), 105
System of Logic, 681

tabula rasa, 484–485, 490
Tantalus, 119
taste, sense of, 497, 536–537, 546
Taylor, Harriet, 681
teleology, 262, 263
temperament, will vs., Kant, 665
Temperance, Form of, 199, 200, 229, 235
temporal priority, 596–602, 619, 621, 628
Thales, 16, 45–47, 49–51, 54, 81, 209,
    265
theater, of the Renaissance, 424–425
Thebes, 102
Theory and Practice of Bolshevism, The
    (Russell), R-11
"therefore," A-12, A-13
thing-in-itself. *See* noumena
Thirty Tyrants, 149, 182
"thisness," 257
Thomas Aquinas, Saint
  and Aristotle, 385, 387, 391, 398, 399,
    638
  dualism of, 409
  as empiricist, 385, 406–407, 409, 638–
    639
  God, existence of, 222, 389–394, 397–
    404, 638–639
  life of, 386–387
  on women, R-11

works
  list of, 387
  Summa Theologiae, 387
Thoreau, Henry David, 736
thought
  Descartes and, 421, 422, 435–440,
    446–447, 448–449, 466
  Hume. *See* Hume: ideas
  Locke and. *See* Locke: ideas
  mind not originator of, 582–586, 589
  philosophical, nature of, 428
  Plato's levels of, 219–220
  pragmatism and, R-23
  See also ideas; mind; reason
Thrasymachus, 228
*Three Dialogues Between Hylas and Phi-
    lonous* (Berkeley), 515, 521–549,
    552–559
Thucydides, 104
Thus Spake Zarathustra (Nietzsche), 699,
    714, 717–732
Tiamat, 47
time
  as category of being, Aristotle, 259
  eternal recurrence, 711–712
  mind as creating, Kant, 645–646, 647
  See also future; past; pure concepts of
    the understanding; space
Tolstoy, Leo, 736
touch, sense of, Berkeley and, 528–536
Toward a Genealogy of Morals (Nietzsche),
    699
Tractatus Logico-Philosophicus (Wittgen-
    stein), R-14–R-16
transformation model of knowledge, de-
    fined, 645
  See also Kant: mind as active vs. passive
*Treatise Concerning the Principles of Hu-
    man Knowledge, A* (Berkeley), 515
Treatise of Human Nature (Hume),
    568–569, 615–628
tree falling in the forest, 540
Triangle, Form of, 184–191, 200–201,
    208–209
truth
  aphorisms as expression of, 696, 697
  Aristotle, 300, 401
  certainty of. *See* certainty
  Descartes's questioning of, 422
  determination of. *See* epistemology
  God as illuminating inner, 407
  greater, and greater reality, 401
  pragmatism and, R-21, R-22
  rationalism vs. empiricism and, 377,
    406–407
  self-evident, 389–394
  of thought, Descartes, 446–447,
    448–449

truth (continued)
verifiability of language and, R-18–R-21
See also certainty; nonsense
tuberculosis, 681
twelve concepts of mind, 646–648, 650–654, 656
Two, All is. *See* dualism
Two Treatises of Government (Locke), 470

Ubermensch. *See* overman
uncompounded appearances, 488–489
undergoing something, as category of being, Aristotle, 259
understanding
Platonic Forms and, 219, 220
See also ideas; mind; reason
universal questions, 10, 11, 12
universe, physical. *See* physical universe
universities, concept of, 183
University of Paris, 387
University of Pennsylvania, 515
Unmoved Mover, 272, 407
unnatural desires, 315, 325, 661
unnecessary desires, 315, 325
unstated conclusions or evidence, A-13–A-14
Uranus (god), 114, 116
utilitarianism
of Bentham, 678–681
of Mill, 680–687

valid syllogism, A-13
values
changing self and, Hume, 580–581
Christian, Nietzsche on, 704–706
Descartes as positing new, 424
existentialism and, R-5–R-7
feminism and, R-24
nature as indifferent to, R-13
Nietzsche and, 704–706, 714, 727, 728–729, 730–732
philosophers as questioning those of majority, 54, 108, 133–134, 196–197, 705, 735

of pleasure, Mill, 681, 683–684, 686–687
See also ethics; virtue
verifiability, R-18–R-21
Vietnam War, 238, R-12
violence, Logos of Heraclitus and, 66
virtues
as goal, Aristotle, 299, 305, 306
Plato and, 234–235, 238
of stoicism (apathia), 341, 350–351
See also ethics; values
visionaries, Plato's ideas and, 202
volition
good will and, Kant, 662–668
See also Kant: ethics of
Voltaire, 317
vortex, 317

Wagner, Richard, 699
Walden (Thoreau), 736
warfare, and belief in immortality, R-13
Water, as the One, 47–48, 49–51
Watson, James, 247
wealth
Aristotle and, 289–290, 299, 306–307
Epictetus (stoics) and, 355
Epicurus and, 329, 330, 336
Plato and, 229, 243
Socrates and, 133, 147, 154, 162
See also possessions
What Is. *See* Mysterious X Stuff
"whatness," 257
Whitehead, Alfred North, on Plato, 182
Why I Am Not a Christian (Russell), R-11–R-13
Wilhelm IV (king of Prussia), 698
will
defined, 664, 672
existence and, R-3–R-7
free. *See* free will
good. *See* Kant: ethics of
mind as. *See* mind
See also mind; reason; self

will to power, 709–711
William I (king of England), 364
William II (king of England), 364
William III (king of England), 471
wisdom
Aristotle and, 289, 290
defined, 8, 10, 11
dialectic and, 220
Epicurus and, 330
as inborn, Plato, 215–217
rationalists and, 642
Socrates and, 104, 106, 136, 140–143, 149, 152, 162
stoicism and, 341, 351, 360
as virtue, 234, 235, 243
Wisdom, Form of, 199
Wittgenstein, Ludwig, R-14–R-17, R-18
women
as contributors to philosophy, 11, 681
Epicurus's school and, 316, 317
inequality of, R-9–R-11, R-23–R-24
Plato and rights of, 229
sexist language, R-24, A-2
as unpublished in own names, 681
Works and Days (Hesiod), 48
World, The (Descartes), 419

Xanthippe, 104
Xenophanes, 58
Xenophon, 105, 106

Yale University, 515
youth
Aristotle on, 297
Epicurus on, 318–319
Socrates and, 137, 140, 142–144, 149–150, 152, 154

Zeno of Citium, 339, 340
Zeno of Elea, 76, 91–95, 98–99, 209
Aristotle compared to, 265, 269
Zeus, 48, 51, 114, 116, 119
Zoroaster, 717